Eshkol

Eshkol:
The Man and the Nation

Terence Prittie

PITMAN PUBLISHING CORPORATION
New York   Toronto   London   Tel Aviv

Copyright © 1969 by Terence Prittie

All rights reserved. No part of this book may be reproduced in any form without permission in writing from the publisher.

Library of Congress Catalog Card Number: 70-79051

Manufactured in the United States of America

Designed by Ben Kann

1. 9 8 7 6 5 4 3 2 1

CROSSROADS TO ISRAEL by Christopher Sykes Reprinted by permission of The World Publishing Company from CROSSROADS TO ISRAEL by Christopher Sykes. Copyright © 1965 by Christopher Sykes

Contents.

Illustrations	*following page 178*
The Land of Israel	*vii*
1	3
2	16
3	28
4	44
5	57
6	75
7	88
8	105
9	121
10	138
11	154
12	172
13	190
14	206
15	223
16	241
17	262
18	280
19	299
20	321
21	339
Bibliography	351
Index	355

The Land of Israel.

The history of any nation is largely written by its most outstanding sons. Such a son of the infant State of Israel was Levi Eshkol, the late Prime Minister. His life and work spanned the formative era of his country's evolution. He was a member of that Second Aliyah, or immigration, whose members arrived in Palestine before 1914 and helped to form first a cohesive Jewish community and then a small but intensely self-reliant and self-aware Jewish state.

This book has been written both as a tribute to the achievements of a man who would have become a leader in any country, and as a history of his life and times. It may help to show why Israel exists as a state today and will continue to do so. If there is a single thread that runs through Eshkol's story, it is that of a personal faith which matches the unshakable, undying faith of the entire Jewish people.

The State of Israel is no more than a speck on any map of the world, one of those countries which are so small that on maps their names have to be abbreviated or written outside their borders. Today it has less than three million inhabitants, well under half the population of New York or London. Less than two and a half million of them are Jews. Yet this tiny country, which has an independent existence of barely 20 years, has more problems than states 20 times her size. Here are just a few of them.

Israel has had to build a community out of incredibly diverse elements over a period of some 20 years. She has taken in immigrants from a hundred countries and has never refused one who was Jewish. There were farmers and shopkeepers from Iraq, peddlers from Morocco, herdsmen from the Yemen, Jews of every kind and description from Europe, most of them destitute and pathetic survivors of Nazi persecution. Only the immigrants from Europe had an obvious affinity with one another, a common cultural heritage and, generally, a common language in Yiddish.

Israel has given all these people homes, jobs, and the Hebrew language. But in building a true community she has been left with two problems which will still take decades to solve. Today, after more than twenty years, the proportion of native-born Israeli "sabras"* has hardly grown at all. The number of European-born and "oriental" Asiatic and North African Jews is now about equal, whereas in 1948 there were six times as many immigrants born in Europe. The "orientals" differ widely among themselves. They arrived in Israel with a far lower standard of living and education. How long will it take for more than a half-million people, and their children, to catch up with more fortunate sabras and former

---

* The sabra is a prickly pear. The term implies a comparison to cactus which, though spiky and tough, bears sweet and tender fruit.

Europeans? Or will they tend to become second-class citizens, an underprivileged majority of the population?

Israel has to pay her way. She has few natural resources, and ever since she became a state in 1948 she has been cut off from her natural markets in the Arab hinterland to the North, South, and East. Her four Arab neighbors—Egypt, Jordan, Syria, and Lebanon—closed their frontiers to her and imposed an economic blockade. Israeli ships were prevented from sailing through the Suez Canal. The Arab countries proclaimed a boycott of all Israeli goods and tried to extend it to the whole of the outside world by threatening firms which did business with Israel.

Part of the business of paying her way entails feeding her population. Israel now produces 85 percent of the food she consumes and has handsome surpluses of fruit, flowers, and vegetables for export. This means she has quadrupled her agricultural output in 20 years. In addition, Israel has built up totally new industries, showing, incidentally, what could be achieved with imagination and hard work throughout the whole Middle East. Economic self-sufficiency is still some way off, and the generous financial help of world Jewry is still needed. But Israel's exports now pay for over 60 percent of her imports, whereas 15 years ago they paid for less than 20. All this has been done while the country had to absorb a million and a quarter immigrants, equal to half of its present population. The immigrants who came from Europe appeared to be broken in body and spirit, while the "orientals" were usually unskilled laborers or had no trade at all.

Israel has had to maintain her security. She is the only country in the world with sworn enemies on all her land frontiers. Those frontiers, moreover, are 600 miles long and next to impossible to defend against a resolute foe. For 20 years Syrian batteries in the Golan Mountains looked down two thousand feet upon the settlements of Galilee and were able to shell them at will. For 20 years Jordanian troops stood only 15 miles from Tel Aviv and in the center of Jerusalem, whose Jewish half was the capital of Israel. Her Arab neighbors have a 20 times larger population and far greater natural resources. In addition, they have been supplied with Russian and Czech arms free of charge, whereas Israel has had to buy her arms at the full market price.

Israel has had to try to maintain something approaching military parity with her immediate Arab neighbors. But in an era of increasingly sophisticated weapons this means that she has, in relation to her size and resources, by far the biggest defense budget in the world. In 1968 defense costs amounted to over three quarters of the total revenue from taxation. During the last months of 1968 the Eshkol government was pleading desperately with the United States for the delivery of 50 Phantom jets. Wryly, Levi Eshkol said to me, "If we get the Phantoms, we can sleep a lot sounder in our beds—that is, if we're not kept awake trying to work out how we can pay for them!"

Linked with the problem of defense is that of population. With its tiny population Israel has to provide the sinews of a sovereign state with a Parliament, a civil service, staffs to run embassies and consulates all over the world, a commercial airline, a merchant navy. Military experts were of the opinion that lack of manpower might make it impossible for Israel to wage war for more than two or three weeks. Certainly, after the June 1967 war, the government made haste to get the country back to a peacetime footing. Only a thin protective screen of troops was left along the Suez Canal and the river Jordan, and a few detachments in the Golan Mountains facing Syria. Israel's defensive strategy continues to depend on quick movement of regular army units and quick mobilization of reserves. With the total manpower available for active military service about 250,000, Israel has almost enough for her needs. But only for the present; the Arab states still seem determined to prepare for a fourth round of the battle and this time they are bent on building up their armed strength more than ever before.

Israel's ability to survive a war lasting months instead of weeks will depend to some extent on increasing her population. But the natural increase, the excess of births over deaths, is running at only around 40,000 a year for the Jewish section of the population, while the annual increase of the Arab minority is nearly 80,000. Members of the Arab minority do not serve in the armed forces. At the same time, the sources of Jewish immigration into Israel have been showing signs of drying up. The Soviet Union, with perhaps three million Jews, has forbidden all emigration. So have some Arab countries which, admittedly, contain only tragic remnants of their once flourishing Jewish communities. The Jews in the countries like the United States and Britain have become acclimatized there and in many cases assimilated with the local population. For them, emigration to Israel involves big sacrifices of position and scope for advancement, of living standards and friends. Israel needs at least 40 thousand immigrants a year, as well as a substantially higher birth rate, if she is to reach her target of five million people before the end of this century.

Finally, Israel needs a lasting peace. How is she to secure it? At the 1967 Khartoum Summit of the Arab states three operative decisions were taken. The first was that there should be no recognition of Israel; the second that there should be no peace negotiations with Israel; the last that there should be no peace settlement. In spite of all the verbiage produced at the time and since the Khartoum Summit, the Arab leaders have made it perfectly plain that the most they can envisage is a return to the uneasy armed truce which lasted, with one break in 1956, from 1948 to 1967. Israel is to be denied all the fruits of her sensational military victory, and the Arab states will do no more than accept a state of "nonbelligerency," which they regard as purely tactical and temporary.

Israel's victory in 1967 was the fourth major shock to Arab pride. The others were the victories in the Sinai campaign of 1956, the War of Independence of 1948, and the creation of the State of Israel, which directly preceded the latter. But for one factor, the fourth major shock might have been too great for the Arab states, and especially their regimes, to sustain. That factor was the virtually unlimited backing given to them in their struggle with Israel by the Soviet Union. This backing was military, moral, political, and economic. It stopped short only of direct Soviet military involvement in the 1967 war.

The reasons for Soviet backing of the Arab cause are so important for the future that they will be dealt with at some length later in this book. Here they can be listed only briefly.

Everlastingly hungry for more power, the Soviet Union has preached East-West détente in Europe primarily for tactical reasons. It did not suit the Soviet theory to have a state of high tension in Europe when there were profitable fields for expansion elsewhere, as well as a growing need to ward off the Chinese challenge for leadership of the Communist world. The Soviet conception of East-West détente was one of minor and superficial improvements in relations between the countries of Western Europe and those of the Warsaw Pact bloc. There could be a few more cultural exchanges or meetings on the football field. There could be slightly increased trade, although the terms of such trade would always be rigorously controlled and weighted in the Soviet interest. But there would be no meeting of minds. For, to the Soviet rulers, the West is still the enemy. The war against capitalism must go on. Indeed, the chief crime committed by the Czechs, when they set out to liberalize conditions in their country in 1968, was that they sought a synthesis of the best elements of Communism and capitalism. The Soviet Union is not interested in an ideal society; it is interested only in its own.

The Soviet Union's family quarrel with China has nothing to do with this book. But the most profitable area for Soviet expansion has, for it is the Middle East.

The Middle East links Asia with Africa and the Mediterranean with the Indian Ocean. It is one of the world's major crossroads. From every point of view the Soviet Union wishes to have a powerful, possibly controlling, interest in the region. This could give Communism a bridge to the socially as well as economically underdeveloped countries of Black Africa. It could bar the western powers from what is still an immensely important trade route.

Predominant Soviet influence in the area would make it possible for the Soviet Union to deny the West the access to its most important source of oil. The Soviet Union would not necessarily make use of such a powerful weapon; but it would certainly threaten such use and levy diplomatic blackmail. In addition, the Soviet Union will want in due course to tap Middle East oil resources for its own needs. So far the Soviet Union has had a surplus of oil of its own. This will not always be the case; indeed, the Soviet Union could become an oil-importing country in the next 15 to 20 years. The Middle East is its obvious source of supply.

There is a sentimental as well as a military and economic reason for the Soviet thrust to the South. For centuries the Russians have dreamed of warm-water ports on the Aegean, the Mediterranean, or the Indian Ocean. The dream may have faded at times but it has never been forgotten. Had Russia fought on until the end of World War I, she might well have secured Constantinople as her share of the spoils. The Bolshevik revolution saved the Allies from the consequences of one of the most disastrous of their promises. For by taking Russia out of the war, the Bolsheviks forfeited their country's claims to territorial annexations.

No blueprint has been published of the Soviet plan to become the dominant power in the Middle East. But the means by which this can be done have been very clearly illustrated. The Soviet Union has extended political and economic as well as a measure of military protection to Egypt, Syria, and Iraq. Even King Hussein of Jordan, who has never ceased to proclaim his acute dislike of Communism, has been induced to visit Moscow. The Soviet Union has fostered friendships with the Sudan, the Yemen, and the newly created South Yemen Federation. New trade agreements have been signed with Iran, and its Shah, too, has visited Moscow.

No longer do the Soviet leaders relish the idea of keeping the Suez Canal closed to all shipping, thus cutting off the western world from the oil it needs. The building of jumbo-sized tankers has made it cheaper and more convenient to carry oil to Western Europe and the United States around the Cape of Good Hope. The canal is too small for vessels of even 30 thousand tons, which is one-tenth the size of the largest new tankers. The economic importance of the canal to the West is declining, but its tactical importance to the Soviet Union is not. Soviet policy is to secure the naval facilities and the use of the airfields on the Red Sea, in the Gulf of Aden, and beyond. They will be the staging posts of the long Soviet "right hook" around to the Persian Gulf. At the same time the Soviet Union will seek to extend its influence into the Persian Gulf by two shorter routes—through Syria and Iraq to the head of the gulf and directly southward through Iran itself.

The Soviet Union has built up a threateningly large fleet in the Eastern Mediterranean.* Its vessels are now a normal part of the scene

* In 1969 it was estimated that the Soviet Union had, on regular call, 10 to 12 submarines; 2 cruisers, one with guided missiles; 7 destroyers; 5 destroyer escorts; 3 minesweepers; 4 amphibious craft; one helicopter carrier with about 20 helicopters; and 20 auxiliary craft. (*Red Fleet*, British Conservative Political Center Publication No. 428, January 1969.)

in the harbors of Egypt and Syria. Soviet warships have sailed into the Persian Gulf. There is no need to establish full-scale Soviet bases in the area; all that is needed is readily and permanently available facilities. The importance of these will become even more apparent when the British military presence in the Persian Gulf ends next year. The Labor government's undertaking to withdraw from the purely "token" bases in Bahrein. Quatar, and Sharjah by 1970, was ill judged and premature. All of the smaller states of the Gulf have depended on British military protection and two of them, Oman and Kuweit, have benefited from actual British military intervention on their behalf. Whatever patchwork alliances are made between the oil-rich smaller states on the one hand and Iran, Saudi Arabia, and Iraq on the other, the British withdrawal will leave a vacuum. It may well be filled by the Nasserite brand of Arab "socialism" and by the Soviet fleet.

The future of Israel is bound up with the future of the whole Middle East. The involvement of the Soviet Union in this area is a relatively new and most dangerous factor. For it means that it is in the Soviet interest to hinder a solution of the Israeli–Arab conflict, by offering friendship and protection to the Arabs, breathing life into the bogey of western "imperialism," and labeling Israel as the West's agent and satellite, thus keeping the Arabs dependent on Soviet tutelage. It would follow rationally that the Middle East pot should be kept boiling, preferably without boiling over, until the Soviet Union has completely consolidated its position in the Middle East and has begun to tap its oil resources.

Thus a new "eastern question" that can have terribly damaging consequences for the West is emerging. Against her will Israel has become enmeshed in this question. It may be trite, but it is still true, to say that Israel therefore stands at the new crossroads in its short history. But again the problems of the future must be dealt with later in this book. Here is a word on the problems of the past.

Since my primary purpose is to trace the story of Levi Eshkol, I must go back in time some 60 years. Eshkol came to what was then Palestine, a part of the Ottoman Empire, in 1914. His reasons for doing so were linked to what was happening in the most important area of Jewish settlement in the world, Southern Russia, even earlier. The 55 years he spent in what has become the State of Israel span a period covering the development of a Jewish national consciousness, the creation of a Jewish national state, and the consolidation of that state as a permanent part of the Middle East.

This is one of the most dramatic events of the twentieth century. But its drama has blinded the eyes of many people to its most essential features. Here I shall mention only three of them.

The children of Israel have never ceased to belong to the land of Israel. It is often and mistakenly supposed that the Jews were divorced from their homeland for nearly two thousand years and have only forced their way back into it as a result of such fortuitous circumstances as the collapse of the Ottoman Empire, the sponsorship of the idea of a Jewish "national home" by Britain, and the atrocious persecution of European Jewry by Hitler. The Jews of Israel are depicted as parvenus and usurpers, and their state as a foreign body in the heart of the Arab world. In the same way, the driving force of the Zionist movement is regarded as an alien philosophy of Central European Jews preaching the "return" to the Holy Land of people who had forfeited whatever right they might have had to live there by reason of their 2000-year absence.

The first point to be made about the reestablishment of the State of Israel is that it did not bridge a gap of 2000 years. Instead, it represented a continuity of Jewish settlement which had never been broken; Jewish communities have never ceased to exist in what today is the State of Israel. Through all periods of history Jews from the outside world sought to augment these communities and in many cases succeeded in doing so. With one interval only, when they were massacred by the so-called "Christian" Crusaders, the Jews have maintained a presence in their holy city of Jerusalem. In 1844, half a century before the Zionist movement came into existence, there were 7120 Jews in Jerusalem against some 5000 Moslems and 3390 Christians. By 1896 there were over 28,000 Jews, as compared to 17,000 Moslems and Christians combined. And in 1948, on the eve of the Israeli War of Independence, Jerusalem had 100,000 Jews, 40,000 Moslems, and 25,000 Christians.

Historian James Parkes* points out that the Zionists were sometimes their own worst propagandists. They ignored their strongest argument, the continuous presence in their own land of the Jews. One reason for this may have been the fact that many of these Jews were deeply religious people completely uninterested in political ideas, who merely wanted to live and die in Palestine. Another reason lay in Zionist insistence on legal rather than moral rights, in regarding the Balfour Declaration of 1917, which pledged Britain to aid in establishing a Jewish national home, as a legal title deed. Far more relevant than those arguments were such facts as the creation of the small but enduring community of Jabne, south-east of Jaffa, centuries ago; the creation of a principal cultural center of Judaism at Safed; and the persistent rebuilding of Tiberias by the Jews each time that city was destroyed by raiding Arab Bedouin.

The second point is that it represented the fulfillment of a faith which had never died, the faith that the children of Israel would one day come into their own. For nearly 2000 years Jews all over the world had prayed for the restoration of Jerusalem—Zion. "And to Jerusalem, thy city, return in mercy and dwell therein; as thou hast

---

* James Parkes, a clergyman of the Church of England, in his *Arabs and Jews in the Middle East*, Gollancz, 1967, and other works.

spoken, rebuild it soon in our days as an everlasting building" was the prayer offered by orthodox religious Jews three times a day. A conventional blessing said by Jews after meals ran: "Have mercy, O Lord, upon Israel thy people, upon Jerusalem thy city." Jews promised never to forget Jerusalem-Zion, and repeated that promise at Passover celebrations, saying, "Next year, in Jerusalem."

The third consideration is that there was never any intention of doing it by force. For 2000 years Jews lived quietly and peacefully in their four holy cities of Jerusalem, Tiberias, Safed, and Hebron and in their scattered settlements elsewhere. The Jewish settlers, who began to arrive in increasingly large numbers after the beginning of the twentieth century, were no less peaceable. Most of them arrived penniless, with no other wish than to till the soil and earn enough to settle on it. The Palestine of the first half of this century was ludicrously underpopulated and underdeveloped. Jewish immigrants wished to establish healthy, balanced communities in what they regarded as their own land, but in the course of doing so they had no intention of dispossessing a single indigenous Arab by force or trickery.

These Jews came singly or in groups, mainly from the Jewish Pale of Settlement in southern and western Russia and Poland. Levi Eshkol was one of them. From the moment he set foot on the shore of Palestine in 1914 his life was intimately linked with the building of a Jewish national home which became the first Jewish state since Roman times. His own story began 19 years earlier in the little town of Oratowo in Southern Russia.

Eshkol

1.

Levi Eshkol was born in 1895 and grew up in the little town of Oratowo, near Kiev in the southern Russian province of the Ukraine. At that time his family name was Shkolnik. Eshkol changed it to its nearest Hebrew equivalent in 1949, after the creation of the State of Israel ("Eshkol," incidentally, means "a bunch" in Hebrew). It was a big family; and his father and mother, Joseph and Deborah or Dvora, had ten children in all. It was also, for a Jewish family in Tsarist Russia, unusually well-to-do. Their big brick house was on the outskirts of the overgrown village or *shtetl*. Joseph sold flour, timber, cattle, and horses. He dealt in real estate, water rights, and fisheries. What was more unusual for a Russian Jew, he leased land, which no Russian Jew could own.

"We were a kind of primitive collective," was Eshkol's memory of his home. "Two uncles living in the place with their families, and a whole horde of children. I remember the yard best, with dozens of cows and whole tribes of chickens. I liked the yard too; it had the feel of the countryside."

Eshkol's early memories were of a full life and a bustling home in Oratowo. Three generations lived in the place. Presiding over the whole family was his grandmother; "very pretty and very clever" was how Eshkol remembered her. She had considerable drive and took the lead in proposing new business ideas. It was her suggestion that Joseph Shkolnik should lease land and raise livestock on it. Not that Joseph needed much encouragement. "My father was a peasant at heart, and the best days of his life were those he spent in the fields."[1]

Love of the soil was something that Eshkol inherited from his father. From his mother he acquired a quick grasp of figures. She was the astonishingly efficient accountant of the family business. Both his father and mother were deeply, although not fanatically, religious, and he was set to work learning the Scriptures at the age of four. "I belonged to that generation," Eshkol recalled, "which really did read the Bible from cover to cover, as well as the 70 learned commentaries. I was sent to a kindergarten at the age of four and when I came home I stayed up at night learning."[2] What he learned then stayed with him; Eshkol quoted the Scriptures liberally and accurately. But he did not inherit his parents' extreme piety; Joseph, for instance, believed implicitly in the eventual coming of the Messiah. Of a more practical turn of mind, Eshkol himself regarded religion as a valuable part of the life of the family and the community, a bond between Jew and Jew.

Possibly, he owed this practical view toward religion to his upbringing. His father wore the long smock-like garment of the traditionalist Jew, but, as Eshkol put it, "allowed himself latitude." His children, as long as they were children, did not have to wear a hat or skullcap, as he did. Nor did they have long side curls. Either Joseph was "liberal" in

3

such matters, or he did not want to overemphasize the Jewishness of his children. The first explanation is the more probable; for a Jewish family like the Shkolniks lived totally apart from the non-Jewish world. "Our only awareness of it," according to Eshkol, "was expressed in the use of the Russian and Ukrainian languages. We learned to speak them perfectly, for we knew that we Jews did business in them. But we had no social contact with Gentiles at all; typically, we celebrated only our Jewish holidays."

In general, his memories of early boyhood were as uncoordinated as those of an average adult. He could remember one or two rabbis, teachers and spiritual leaders of the village, who were considered so important that they were sometimes given a share in any family business they blessed. He could remember the cottages of the shtetl, its orchards and the tall grass of the Ukrainian plains. He could remember, more vividly, the long and earnest discussions about the future that went on in the family circle. Some of them had a particular relevance.

In 1905, for instance, there was an atmosphere of grave alarm. In some towns of the Ukraine there had been vicious, anti-Semitic pogroms, with Jews beaten up and sometimes killed, Jewish property pillaged, and Jewish homes set on fire. Oratowo was spared, probably because it was a small and remote place. But Eshkol recalled that the atmosphere of pogroms "hung over our heads all the time, although the storm passed our district by. For weeks we sat at home with doors barred and boards nailed over the windows, expecting an attack that never came."

And "Although I was scarcely into my teens, I realized in my own immature way that striking back never entered our heads. There was a sense of shame, unexpressed. I wished in a desperate kind of way that I would know what to do when I was older."

Moshe Lilienblum wrote more graphically of the terror which haunted Russian Jews: "We are virtually under siege. The courtyards are barred up, and we keep peering through the grillwork of the court gates to see if the mob is coming to swoop down on us. All the furniture is stored in cellars, we all sleep in our clothes, so if we are attacked we will immediately be able to take the small children and flee. But will they let us flee? Will they have mercy on the youngsters—who don't even know yet that they are Jews, that they are wretches?"

A year earlier Theodor Herzl, the first active protagonist of the idea of a Jewish state, had died. Joseph Shkolnik did not believe that the creation of a Jewish state was practical; he thought that Zion, and Zionism, were spiritual concepts and that salvation had to be sought in the hearts of the Jewish people. But Herzl's death left a sense of loss in the family circle. And almost immediately afterward a Palestine Jew came to the Shkolnik home. Eshkol's recollection was that he had brought fruit from Palestine with him, perhaps something hard-skinned like a pomegranate or cactus fruit. Anyway, it made a big impression on the 9-year-old boy, who jumped up and recited the Song of Deborah for the visitor.

About this time, too, he became aware of the social injustice that afflicted the Jews of Russia. Because they were usually poor and often persecuted, Russian Jews generally believed in the need for social reform. Under Tsarism reform, in the sense of organic progress, was unobtainable. There was only a short jump from the idea of social reform to that of social revolution. Eshkol could remember conversations in the family circle about the need for progress and periodic repetition of the phrase, "Revolution in Russia must be greased with Jewish blood." Joseph Shkolnik, as it happened, was in no sense a revolutionary. His son was never to regard Jewish involvement in the van of a Russian revolutionary movement as a real alternative to the Jews' working out their own salvation in their own way.

Why this should be done and how it should be done were the questions young Eshkol would work out for himself in due course. But something about the historical and social background of a community like Oratowo and a family like the Shkolniks must be explained at this point. For Russian Jewry probably made the major contribution to the creation of the State of Israel.

After the destruction of Jewish Jerusalem by the Romans in the first, and the gallant but doomed revolt of Bar Kochba in the second centuries A.D., a Jewish patriarchate survived in Palestine until the year 429. But Alexandria and Babylon became the most important centers of Judaism, and from there the Jews spread out into Arabia and southern Europe and along the South Mediterranean littoral. From A.D. 800 onward the Jews, under benevolent Islamic rule, prospered in Spain. Islam indeed was immensely more tolerant than primitive Christendom.

Under Charlemagne the Jews began to lose the full rights of citizenship and to be provided with a form of passport which accorded them "protection." In 1096 the First Crusade brought on massacres of the Jews, in both Europe and the Holy Land, and for the next 100 years the Crusaders continued periodically to put the Jews to the sword. The myth of Jewish "ritual murder" of Christians was fostered in England, where in 1144 William of Norwich was said to have had his blood drained off as a religious libation for the Jews. In 1290 England expelled the Jews, who were banished from the realm until Cromwell allowed them back more than 350 years later. The Jews were expelled from France and from a number of German states in the fourteenth century, from Spain and Portugal in 1492 and 1496. In addition to the charge of ritual murder, the Jews were blamed for causing wars, pestilence, and the black death of 1348.

Some Jews returned to Palestine. Others drifted eastward across Europe. In the middle of the fourteenth century Casimir III of Poland gave them generous charters and the Jews began to flock in large numbers to the powerful Polish state, which stretched almost from the Baltic to the Black Sea. They took with them their Yiddish language, a Franconian German dialect they began to write in Hebrew characters. In Poland there was hardly any middle class, and the Jews dropped easily into the positions of middlemen, shopkeepers, traders, settling down almost entirely in towns.

Those growing Jewish communities became separated by language, custom, and sheer distance from the older surviving Jewish settlements along the shores of the Mediterranean. The split between *Ashkenazi,* or Middle European, and *Sephardi,* or Mediterranean, Jewry became virtually complete. But in the long run the Jews of Central and Eastern Europe were to be no better off than before. The three partitions of Poland at the end of the eighteenth century placed most of them under Tsarist tyranny. Here they were confined to the so-called Pale of Settlement, an area which included most of what today is Poland and the two Soviet Socialist Republics of the Ukraine and Byelorussia.

Treatment of the Jews by the tsars was a mixture of the brutal and the slipshod. Catherine the Great excluded them from the general edict on freedom of movement within her dominions. Alexander I considered scattering them over remote parts of Russia. During his reign, in 1816, came an alleged case of ritual murder at Grodno, the first in modern times. There was another in Saratov in the 1850s. Meanwhile, Nicholas I made a determined attempt to "assimilate" the Jews by drafting them for military service and by taking Jewish children over 12 years of age away from their parents in order to indoctrinate them first and conscript them for 25 years in the army afterward.

His successor, Alexander II, abolished this organized theft of Jewish children and reduced all compulsory military service from 25 to 6 years. But he did little else for the Jews. A few were allowed to settle in big cities, where they clustered in the Jewish quarter or ghetto. The bulk of them remained in their shtetls, barred from owning land or enjoying full civil rights, politically completely unemancipated, in a material sense usually very poor. Of the Russian Jews in the late 1860s James Parkes wrote: "The Jewish population had trebled since the beginning of the century, but openings for a fruitful and stable livelihood had scarcely increased. The number of *Luftmenschen,* that is, men of no certain occupation or abode, increased steadily; the thousands registered as peddlers increased in numbers and declined in means."[3]

Anti-Semitism was becoming a menace outside Russia as well as in it. In France the Comte de Gobineau in his *Inégalité des Races Humaines* foreshadowed the "master-race" theories of the Nazis. In England Houston Stewart Chamberlain was proclaiming the splendor of the Aryan race, and in Germany Heinrich von Treitschke coined the phrase *"Die Juden sind unser Unglueck"* (the Jews are our misfortune). Vicious, indeed insane, anti-Semitic ideas were being propagated by men like Karl Lueger in Vienna and August Rohling in Prague. In Austria a defrocked priest, Adolf Lanz, who annexed the name von Liebenstein to which he had no right, was shortly to begin publishing a scurrilous broadsheet *Ostara* which caricatured the Jews in exactly the same way as the *Stuermer* of Adolf Hitler's lieutenant, Julius Streicher. Later still, there was to come the *Protocols of the Elders of Zion,* an obscene forgery which purported to give the details of the "Jewish plot against world civilization."

In 1895 the Dreyfus Affair resulted in the victimization of a totally loyal and innocent Jewish officer in the French Army. In 1898 the procurator of the Russian Holy Synod, Constantine Pobyedonostzev, announced that he would like to drive one-third of the Jews out of Russia, destroy one-third more, and convert the remainder to Christianity. But long before this, hatred of the Jews had exploded into organized violence. In 1871 there were anti-Jewish riots in Odessa. There were fresh and even bloodier riots in 1881, when the assassination of Alexander II was blamed on a "Jewish plot." Jews were forbidden to build new settlements, even in the Pale of Settlement; their attendance at schools was restricted; in Moscow thousands of Jews were evicted from their homes in the middle of Passover.

In 1903 there was a particularly murderous pogrom in Kishinev, when 49 Jews were killed, 92 badly injured, hundreds more beaten and raped, and 10,000 left homeless and destitute. The Russian minister of the interior, Wenceslas von Plehve, commended the periodic pogroms to Tsar Nicholas II as a useful diversionary stratagem to take peoples' minds off such embarrassing subjects as parliamentary reform. When he became prime minister, Stolypin organized pogroms as regular events. He formed the racist Union of the Russian People, which drilled its storm troopers in their so-called Black Hundreds. These anti-Semitic vigilantes were solemnly blessed by Archbishop Vladimir, the metropolitan of the Greek Orthodox Church. The Tsar wore the badge of the Union and thus openly signified his approval of the terror levied on his Jewish subjects.

A single account of a pogrom gives a good idea of what it was like. The pogrom in question took place on the evening of March 3, 1910, in Odessa, and one of the bystanders was Colonel Richard Meinertzhagen, a British Army officer. He was visiting the British Consulate, and the growing tumult outside brought him from the building.

> We watched. The streets were well lit and we could see well in both directions; there was also a small square in front of the house. Russians, many with bludgeons, knives or axes, were rushing all over the place, breaking open barricaded doors and chasing the wretched Jews into the streets where they were hunted down, beaten, and often killed. One old man was axed on the head quite close to us. . . .
> A young woman chased by a Russian rushed frantically into the

Consulate and collapsed on the door-mat. . . . Another Jewish youth was chased, beaten into the gutter, viciously kicked, robbed and left unconscious. . . . The climax arrived when a Russian passed the Consulate dragging a Jewish girl of about twelve years old by her hair along the gutter; she was screaming and the man was shouting. I have no doubt she would have been outraged and then murdered.

The gallant Colonel "dashed out, kicked the Russian violently in the stomach with my heavy Russian boots and landed him a good blow on the jaw; he went down like a log and I carried the child into the Consulate." There the Consul told him how 400 Jews had been killed in a previous pogrom in Odessa: "On the first day of the pogrom all the police were withdrawn from Odessa, and remained away for three days. After that time, an order went forth that the military must stop the massacres; this was effected in a few hours. Some of the rioters, on being shot at in the streets, bitterly complained that they had not had their full three days promised by the authorities."[4]

Colonel Meinertzhagen, in spite of his name and his subsequent keen interest in Zionism, was not a Jew. He took a risk when he assaulted the Russian bully. But he could always have retreated into the British Consulate. The desperate plight of the Jews of Russia was that they could not fight back and could not possibly escape their tormentors. They learned to run for their lives, because it was the only sensible thing to do. Their only hope of revenge was to corner a single pursuer in a dark alleyway.*

Perhaps the most frightening thing about pogroms was their total unpredictability. When a riot started, it was usually without a plan or purpose. And so, in place of a nonexistent enemy, a scapegoat had to be found. The Jews were available; they made by far the most convenient scapegoat. But the Black Hundreds, who often provoked a riot in order to let off steam, sometimes attacked workers too, and in the Caucasus, the Armenians.†

Malamud painted a picture of the terror and indignity of Jewish existence in the Pale of Settlement in *The Fixer*.[5] Any Jew was a "filthy Yid." At any moment he might hear the scream of "Christ-killer" and realize that he was going to be beaten up for no reason at all. He knew that he was, in some undefined way, "different," an object of suspicion

---

* The nightmarish nature of the cruelties inflicted on the Jews is well illustrated by a passage in Bernard Malamud's *The Fixer*, describing a pogrom in Kiev: "When the houses were still smouldering and he was led, with half a dozen other children, out of a cellar where they had been hiding, he saw a black-bearded Jew with a white sausage stuffed into his mouth, lying in the road on a pile of bloody feathers, a peasant's pig devouring his arm" (*The Fixer*, pp. 10–11).

† The pogroms directed against Armenians were not directly connected with those against the Jews. The Armenians were picked on, however, for the same reason as the Jews: both groups were minorities and unable to fight back.

and hatred. If some crime had been committed anywhere in his neighborhood, suspicion might fall on him. The usual view taken by non-Jewish Russians was that a Jew should prove himself innocent before it could be assumed that he was not guilty.

The Jew in the Pale of Settlement was often aware of the absurd superstitions about his people held by Christians. Jews were believed to crucify Christians in secret and use their blood for horrible rituals, to heal women in childbirth, to stop hemorrhages, to cure blindness in infants. Jewish ritual murder was supposed to be the reenactment of Christ's crucifixion. The deliberately slow bleeding of a Christian infant was the repetition of Christ's martyrdom. Then the child's blood would usually be mixed with the Passover bread, or matzos, and so Christ's body would be consumed.

This mad superstition reached its climax in the trial of a Jew, Mendel Beiliss, in Kiev, in 1911, for the alleged ritual murder of a 13-year-old boy, Andrei Yushchinsky, who had been found dead with 47 knife wounds on his body. The child had in fact been murdered by a prostitute, but the account of Beiliss' trial reads like a nightmare. He was a wretchedly poor man, "whose life was taken up with tugging at ends that could barely be made to meet." A Russian journalist at the trial described him as quiet, defenseless, and frightened, hardly more coherent than a trapped animal. Beiliss was accused not only of murdering the boy, but of regarding the extermination of Gentiles as a religious act which would hasten the coming of the Messiah. Beiliss, amazingly, was acquitted; but he must have died many times over during this disgraceful, trumped-up trial.

In the comparative backwater of Oratowo, Eshkol was not, like some of his contemporaries, continually brought face to face with persecution of this gross and horrible kind. One contemporary of his, for instance, is Golda Meir, his successor as Prime Minister. Her family lived in Pinsk, a town of 30,000 inhabitants, and she can remember all too well the howls of drunken, rioting mobs echoing down their street. She recalls one particular incident, when a peasant came up to her and another small girl, banged their heads violently together, and said to them, "That's what we'll do to the Jews! Knock their heads together, and we'll be through with them!"[6] But it became clear to Eshkol that life in the Pale of Settlement was, as he puts it, "of very little use to the Jewish people." He was a big, strong, and intelligent boy and he was disgusted with the way in which the Jews were subjected to indignity and "thrust, like insects, into the cracks in the economy."[7] When he was only 13 or 14, he began to think seriously of emigrating. As it happened, it was roughly at this time that mass emigration of Russian Jews began. In five years, from 1903 to 1907, half a million of them left. Nine out of ten headed for the United States, the land of opportunity and freedom, and about three-quarters of these were destined to go to New York, where they would in time build up the biggest Jewish community in the world.

Still, life in a Jewish shtetl, even in the ghetto of a large town, was not all bad. The inhabitants maintained a real sense of identity.

> Their imprisonment, for all the economic, cultural and social injustice and poverty that it entailed, brought with it one immense advantage—namely that the spirit of the inmates remained unbroken, and that they were not as powerfully tempted to seek escape by adopting false positions as their socially more exposed and precariously established brethren without. The majority of the Jews of Russia and Poland lived in conditions of squalor and oppression; their relations with the outside world suffered from no systematic ambivalence. They were what they were. . . .[8]

The Jews of Russia, in fact, remained a community, at least partly because they were treated as second-class citizens and could not assimilate with the rest of the Russian population.

In the ghetto the Jew was at home. Speaking at the First Zionist Congress in Basle in 1897, Max Nordau put it this way:

> It is plain historical truth to state that only the ghetto gave the Jews a chance of surviving the terrible persecutions of the Middle Ages. In the ghetto the Jew had his own world; it was his sure refuge and it provided the spiritual and moral equivalent of a motherland. . . . In the ghetto all specifically Jewish qualities were esteemed. . . . In the moral sense, the Jews of the ghetto lived a full life.

Inevitably, they were drawn much closer together than members of other communities. Every Jew regarded every other Jew first and foremost as a potential friend and ally. This feeling of comradeship is something Eshkol, for instance, remembered with gratitude. It was one of many reasons why he still spoke of the shtetl with nostalgic emotion. The vast majority of Jews remained peculiarly devoted to family life and to the family hearth, where they were safe from the prying eye of the "superior" Russian townsman or of the brutish Russian peasant. Religion was immensely important to the family and the community, for it was a real solace and encouragement. But Russian Jews maintained, too, an astonishing degree of optimism and gaiety, improbable though this must sound. David Horowitz, governor of the Bank of Israel, called it "the smile within the tears." Yiddish humor was abundant. "Yiddish became a perfect medium for the laughter and tears of a world which was bound to pass, for Jews could scarcely be expected to have three mother-tongues—Hebrew as the language of the national renaissance, Yiddish as that of national memories, together with that which they need to communicate with their Gentile environment."[9] Were three languages too many? Perhaps. But the Jews, even in the State of Israel today, have clung to Yiddish, because of its satire, its mingled elegance and earthiness of humor, its wry and mocking touches, and its aching sentiment.

Russian Jews often found consolation in their predicament. One of the characters, Yahov, in Malamud's *The Fixer* says, "In this shtetl everything is falling apart—but who bothers with leaks in his roof if he's peeking through the cracks to spy on God?"[10] And there is the subtle story of Rabbi Zalman Posner, one of those rare cases of a Jew becoming rich in Russia. When he drove through the streets of Warsaw in his coach, it was stoned by anti-Semitic hooligans. His servant remarked sadly: "Truly we are in exile, when worthless urchins throw stones at an important person like yourself." Rabbi Zalman replied, "Don't worry about it. When the Messiah comes and we have our own State, *they* will drive in luxurious carriages but *we* shall throw stones."

There were many Jews who gloried in their distinctiveness and even sought to increase it by "raising the walls of the ghetto." Indeed, one wonders if someone like Eshkol, had he stayed exclusively in Oratowo, might not have decided that his loyalty lay with its small community and that he should "stick it out" and settle for life there. But, as it happened, he was already at the age of 13 or 14 longing for change. From 13 onward he was mainly privately taught, by the rabbi, for he was showing numerous signs of intellectual promise, an avid desire to read, a retentive memory, a grasp of figures, and a ready application to problems which involved logic. There were very few places available to Jewish students at secondary schools, but Eshkol wanted to go to Odessa, which was becoming one of the major intellectual centers, for East-European Jewry. It was, incidentally, the principal gateway to Palestine for Jewish emigrants who were almost bound to travel there by sea.

There was no room for him in Odessa, but he was determined to enter a secondary school. "Never raise your hands in defeat, but never beat your head against a wall," became one of his favorite sayings. In 1911 a place was found for him at the gymnasium, or secondary school, at Vilna, Lithuania. The next two years there were not just to be intellectually formative; they helped him to make up his mind to go to Palestine.

First, he read voraciously. Vilna was called the "Jerusalem of Lithuania" because of its scholars, poets and Hebraists. Its Jews were noted for their independence of mind and increasing interest in Zionism. There was already a growing literature of Zionism. In 1862 Moses Hess published his *Rome and Jerusalem,* expressing the view that the Jews had a considerable contribution to make to the whole of mankind, but could make it most effectively if they controlled their own destiny, in a land of their own. In 1882 Leo Pinsker wrote *Auto-Emancipation,* in German, and published the book in Berlin. His thesis was that the Jews would be subjected to abuse and contempt as long as they remained homeless waifs scattered all over the world. Pinsker prophetically pointed out that the liberal ideas which were beginning to permeate European society could, paradoxically, turn to the disadvantage of the Jews. For European liberals preached humanitarian ideals, and their realization could result in Jews' being more easily assimilated into European society, thus losing their national and religious identity.

Another exponent of the demand for a "national home" for the Jews was Asher Ginzberg, who began to write towards the end of the century under the Hebrew pseudonym of Ahad Ha'am ("one of the people"). Then Theodor Herzl, a Viennese journalist, published his *Jewish State* in 1896 and a year later organized the First Zionist Congress at Basle. To Herzl, Palestine did not at first seem to be necessarily the only place where a Jewish state could be established; indeed, he did not mention Palestine by name in his book and took no interest in the renaissance of the Hebrew language. By 1903, however, he visited Russia in order to plead for ending the pogroms and transfering the Jews to Palestine with the minister of the interior, von Plehve. In the meantime, his Zionist colleagues had in 1901 created *Keren Kayemeth,* the Jewish National Fund, with the express purpose of buying land in Palestine.

In Vilna young Eshkol was caught up in the ferment of thought about the creation of a Jewish state, a ferment which grew more intense from 1897 onward. But he was brought into close touch with another Russian-Jewish development which to some extent ran counter to Zionism. This was Jewish socialism. Back in 1860 and 1871 the foundations had been laid for some sort of Jewish political activity by the formation of the Alliance Israélite Universelle in France and the Anglo-Jewish Association in England. But these were essentially "self-help" organizations. Of vastly greater significance was the formation of the Jewish Bund in Vilna in 1897.

The Bund was the Socialist League of Jewish Workers of Russia, Poland and Lithuania. It was reformist and Marxist. Its members, like French revolutionaries, demanded bread and liberty. They claimed to be severely practical, in contrast to Zionists whose dreams of a Jewish state seemed as illusory as the prayers of the faithful for the restoration of Zion and the coming of the Messiah. The Bund urged maximum cooperation with all Russian liberals, and it favored the creation of a free Poland which might emancipate its Jewish subjects. The Bund's ideals were political equality and social justice, to be achieved by social revolution. Significantly, it favored retention of Yiddish as a symbol of Jewish identity, and opposed the teaching of Hebrew: it preferred, in fact, the *lingua franca* of the Jews in exile to a national language. In spite of the efforts of Lenin, Trotsky, Plekhanov, and others to capture the Bund as an ally, it aligned itself with the Mensheviks, or socialist moderates, and it was to be swept away with them in the bloody flux of the Bolshevik Revolution.

Eshkol was interested in socialist ideas during his stay in Vilna. Indeed, he had a highly inquisitive and acquisitive mind. Hebrew literature was his first love, but he also read Russian and some Scandinavian classics, Gogol, Pushkin, Tolstoy, Turgenev, Dostoevsky, Ibsen and Bjørnson. He began studying ideological socialist literature. Yet he was a great deal more interested in Zionism. Later in life, he insisted that he was not really a "political animal" at all, that he believed in socialist principles and ideals but had little interest in ideology. Eshkol was undoubtedly restless at that period, and he had no sympathy with the Bund's preaching of *Da-igkeit,* staying where you were. He joined the radical Zionist youth group, *Zeire Zion,* which later became affiliated with the *Hapoel Hatzair* or Working Youth movement for promoting resettlement in Palestine.

An encounter with Joseph Sprinzak, at that time already a settler in Palestine and later speaker of the first *Knesset,* or Parliament, of Israel was a vital one for Eshkol. Sprinzak came on a visit to Vilna, to mobilize young Russian Jews for pioneering work in Palestine. Two decades earlier the Lovers of Zion movement (*Hibbat Zion* or *Hovevei Zion*) had been founded in Odessa, and ever since had been engaged in organizing small groups of pioneers who went by sea to Palestine. Sprinzak represented the practical achievement of settlement as well as the Zionist ideal. Both concepts were immensely attractive to Eshkol. When he had been younger he had thought of becoming a metallurgical engineer (his family traded in coal and metal scrap) or perhaps a geologist. But the land, and that in Palestine meant *working* on the land, was a more intelligible ambition. He believed ever after that this meeting with Sprinzak had removed all doubts from his mind. Sprinzak gave him practical encouragement by providing him with a personal letter of recommendation to use in Palestine should he go there. From then on, his goal was Palestine. The question was how, and, more important, when.

The Jews, ever poking fun at themselves, have coined a saying about a typical Zionist. He is "a Jew who takes money from another Jew, in order to send yet another Jew to Israel." More precisely, an early Zionist had to be highly idealistic as well as resolute and courageous. To settle in Palestine was one thing; if life there did not work out, one could always pack up and go home. But a true Zionist believed it was his duty to help build up the Jewish community in Palestine and help found the Jewish state. He believed it to be the only path open to him that led to true freedom and fulfillment. In the Gentile world the Jew was despised and persecuted; and even if he were treated fairly, he was not of that world. He was in *galut,* in a temporary state of exile which appeared to be never-ending. At the time of the First Zionist Congress, Herzl wrote prophetically, of his concept of a Jewish state: "In five years, in 50 at the most, nobody will laugh at me any more." But up to 1914 the foundation of a Jewish state seemed a very remote prospect indeed. And to leave Russia and go to Palestine meant cutting oneself adrift, from home, family, the Russian-Jewish community, and a whole way of life.

It was while trying to make up his mind when to set out for Palestine that Eshkol came across the writings of Aaron David Gordon. Already in his forties, Gordon had left for Palestine a few years earlier. He had a theory, almost an obsession, that the Jewish people could recapture its "wholeness" only by work on the land. He wrote of the Jewish people as having been "completely cut off from nature and imprisoned within city walls for 2000 years." Gordon had a deep contempt for the petty trading of the *galut* or dispersion; he believed that a balanced Jewish society could be restored only by manual labor in the fields. The soil would be the healer of Jewish sorrows.

"We wanted to build Israel with our own hands," Eshkol told me. "We believed at that time that the community which we would help to create would be 80 percent farmers. Our whole philosophy was contained in the phrase 'back to the soil.' "[11] Eshkol acquired a tenuous personal link with Palestine when one member out of his circle of acquaintances in Vilna packed up to go there. Of greater importance was the arrival of news that two Jewish settlers at Degania, the first collective agricultural settlement established by the Jews in Palestine, had been murdered by marauding Bedouin Arabs. One of them was called Barsky. A short time later Barsky's father sent a letter of condolence to the Degania settlers. In it, he promised that his son's younger brothers would come to Degania to take his place as soon as they reached manhood.

This event may well have played a big part in helping to make up Eshkol's mind for him. Shortly after returning home from Vilna he told his parents that he was going: "Actually, they asked me if I was crazy, but they came around to the idea."[12] One can imagine the anxious discussions that took place. Another settler of the same era, Joseph Baratz, described how his decision led to bitter arguments with his father, while his mother wept and called after him as he was leaving: "Joseph, be a good Jew!" And then Baratz recounts, "I too was crying and I wished I were staying with my father and my mother."[13]

Possibly the Eshkol family was less temperamental and less sentimental. Levi was a tough, strapping young man of 19, handsome with his small dark moustache, confident, well able to look after himself. The family discussions quickly shifted from his decision to the question of what he should take with him. On that subject he was adamant. He was going to take with him enough money only to pay for his passage on some leaky and decaying old freighter that would take him from whatever port he could reach across the Black Sea, or the Aegean and eastern Mediterranean to the port of Jaffa. It was a point of honor with him not to take one cent more than he needed. He set out from home for the mountains of southern Galicia, crossing the Austro-Hungarian frontier at night, fording a small river and making his way across the rolling country of Slovakia to Vienna. From there he travelled to Trieste, and joined the steerage passengers on the ship "Heluan" bound for Jaffa. He carried only a small bag into which he had thrown a few necessities, a spare shirt, a pair of work trousers and a red sweater. Only after he had left Oratowo did he discover that his mother had stuffed in a small colored pillow, perhaps to remind him of home. That affected him more than his leave-taking.

Eshkol was the only person leaving Oratowo. In theory, he was only making a short trip to Palestine; for like every other young Russian he was bound in due course to be called up for compulsory military service. In theory, too, he would be unable to stay in Palestine legally; the Turkish authorities would, he knew, issue him a red card entitling him to stay one month in this province of the Ottoman Empire ostensibly as a pilgrim. After that he would be liable to deportation. It would hardly be possible to visualize tougher terms of emigration.

In Trieste Eshkol joined with nine other youngsters. Like him, they were connected with *Hapoel Hatzair,* which, along with *Poalei Zion,* constituted the only groups in Russia which actively promoted settlement in Palestine and were able to give some practical advice. Even these two groups did not cooperate with each other, and in Jaffa each had a small hostel where new arrivals could put up free for the night and from which they would be sent on their way to find work. *Hapoel Hatzair* concentrated on the practical tasks of settling the land; Poalei Zion had much more political flavor and indoctrinated its members with socialist theories.

On that long and desperately uncomfortable voyage it was encouraging to have the company of young people like himself, imbued with the same ideas and apparently with the same determination. As it happened, by the time World War I was over, less than five years later, not a single one of his companions was still in Palestine. And after a year or so Eshkol himself proposed half-heartedly to return to Russia to serve his time in the army so that no reprisals against his family would be taken on his account. As a matter of fact, he was to return to Russia only once in the course of the next 50-odd years, and then for a few days only. When in January 1914 he took the train from Oratowo, whose sole claim to importance was its being a railway junction, he burned his bridges well and truly.

1. In personal conversation with the author.
2. In personal conversation with the author.
3. James Parkes, *A History of the Jewish People,* Penguin ed., p. 153.
4. Col. Richard Meinertzhagen, *Middle East Diary,* p. 5.
5. Bernard Malamud, *The Fixer,* pp. 10–11.
6. Marie Syrkin, *Golda Meir, Woman with a Cause,* p. 19.
7. In personal conversation with the author.
8. Isaiah Berlin, *Chaim Weizmann,* p. 14.
9. Parkes, *op. cit.,* p. 180.
10. Malamud, *op. cit.,* p. 13.
11. In personal conversation with the author.
12. In personal conversation with the author.
13. Joseph Baratz, *A Village by the Jordan,* p. 10.

2. When 19-year-old Eshkol arrived in Palestine in February 1914 it had a population of about 700,000 spread over what today is Israel and the more populous, or western part, of the present Kingdom of Jordan. There were roughly 100,000 Jews in the country. Nearly 12,000 of them were living in agricultural settlements, and almost all the others in five towns. In Jerusalem there were 50,000, or well over half of its total population. There were relatively small but well-knit Jewish communities in the three other holy cities of Safed, Tiberias, and Hebron; and there was a small colony of Jews in the port of Jaffa and its Jewish suburb founded only five years earlier at Tel Aviv.

There is a widely held belief that the Jews were totally excluded from their native land, from the time of Christ until the very recent past. This belief rests on the supposition that the Balfour Declaration of 1917, which pledged British support for the establishment of a Jewish national home in Palestine, was the real starting point of the Jewish return, and that before that date Palestine had been exclusively occupied by Arabs who were subsequently forcibly dispossessed of their 2000-year inheritance. Indeed, this theory of forcible Jewish occupation of what is today the State of Israel is one of the basic reasons for the refusal of Arab countries to recognize Israel or to make peace with her.

In his *History of Palestine*[1] James Parkes emphasizes the fact that there have always been Jews in what today is the State of Israel, that Jews have patiently and persistently sought to return there from other countries, and that most Jews have never ceased to regard it as their own land. The Jews have, in fact, maintained a stake in their country in the face of every hardship and periodic persecution, and they have cherished the right of any and every Jew to make his home there.

Parkes illustrates the continuity of the Jewish claim to their own country by a number of maps showing the extent of Jewish settlements at various stages of history. Thus, the Jews remained spread over the central, Judaean portion of Palestine for well over 100 years after Christ's death. In the south, the Jewish settlement stretched to Beersheba and well beyond; in the east across the Jordan and as far as the empty Arabian desert. In the north, Galilee was predominantly Jewish.

The Romans destroyed Jerusalem in A.D. 70 and sold many of its Jewish inhabitants as slaves. In A.D. 135, after Bar Kochba's revolt, there was an even more systematic Roman effort to uproot the Jews and disperse them over the empire. But, wherever they could, they hung on. By the seventh century Galilee had become the main Jewish center, but there were enclaves of Jewish settlements along the mountain range of Carmel and to the south of the Dead Sea, in Jerusalem, Hebron, Gaza, Nablus, Jaffa, and Jericho. Four hundred years later the Crusaders found Galilee still the main Jewish center. Most of the other Jewish settlements had shrunk in size but still survived and small groups of Jewish merchants had established themselves on the trade routes east of the river Jordan and on the road from Galilee to Damascus.

In the fourteenth century there was still a solid block of Jewish population in Galilee, but other settlements had dwindled to mere outposts as a result of oppression and uncertainty. Two hundred years went by and brought a slight but significant change. Trade between Europe and the East was growing, especially in spices. The Jews were leaving the land in Galilee. Too many armies had marched through it, killing and ravaging. Once again there were more Jews living in Gaza, Jaffa, and Nablus, all of them trade centers.

The nadir of Jewish settlement in Palestine was reached at the beginning of the nineteenth century. The Jewish population in Galilee had shrunk most and was now scattered among a few small towns. A few Jews, virtually all of them deeply religious people who wanted to end their days there, had crept back to Jerusalem and Hebron. The tiny trading communities in Gaza, Jaffa, and elsewhere survived, but only barely so. And Palestine was becoming steadily poorer under Turkish rule, which had begun in 1515. The Turks had conquered rich areas like Egypt, Syria, and Mesopotamia; they neglected Palestine badly, letting good land relapse into desert, denuding the country of trees, making no effort to find sources of water.

Yet the drift of the Jews back into Palestine began in the first half of the nineteenth century and never ceased. At first the emphasis was on settling deeply religious and strictly orthodox Jews in Jerusalem and the other holy cities. Those people returned to pray, study, and die in their own land. Generally speaking, they were not prepared to work and lived on charitable offerings of Jewish societies in Europe. These chalukah kept to themselves, but their self-chosen indigence excited hostility. In 1883 an English traveler, Laurence Oliphant, wrote of them: "The practical result of this system is to maintain in idleness and mendicancy a set of useless bigots, who combine superstitious observance with immoral practice and who, as a rule, are opposed to every project which has for its object the real progress of the Jewish nation."[2]

In the 1840s a rich London Jew of Sephardic origin. Sir Moses Montefiore, became interested in the prospects of Jewish settlement in Palestine. Sir Moses, born in 1784, had made a fortune on the stock exchange. He paid seven visits to Palestine, building synagogues and hospitals there and, in 1860, the first modern Jewish residential quarter in Jerusalem outside the dank walls of the overcrowded and unsanitary Old City. This residential quarter was the forerunner of present day Jewish Jerusalem, with a population of close to 200,000 inhabitants in 1969.

Even more important, in 1856 Sir Moses bought for Jewish settlers their first orange grove on the outskirts of Jaffa. Four years later, the Alliance Israélite Universelle was founded in Paris; in 1869 it opened the first Jewish agricultural school of Mikveh Yisrael in Palestine. Nine years later Yoel Moshe Salomon, with a group of Hungarian–Jewish and Rumanian–Jewish *halutzim,* or pioneers, built the first large new Jewish village of Petach Tikva, meaning "gateway of hope," about ten miles from Jaffa. From Jerusalem another smaller group, of Rumanian Jews, adventured a few miles into the wild Judaean highlands and founded the village of Motza. The Jewish "return to land" was under way.

In his *Haifa, or Life in Modern Palestine,* Laurence Oliphant gives some revealing glimpses of these early beginnings. In 1882 he paid a visit to the budding Jewish colony on the slopes of Mount Carmel.

> The experiment of associating Jews and Moslem fellahin in field labor will be an interesting one to watch, and the preliminary discussions on the subject were more picturesque than satisfactory. The meeting took place in the storehouse, where Jews and Arabs squatted promiscuously amid the heaps of grain, and chaffered over the terms of their mutual partnership. It would be difficult to imagine anything more utterly incongruous than the spectacle thus presented—the stalwart fellahin, with their wild, shaggy, black beards, the brass hilts of their pistols projecting from their waistbands, their tasselled "kufeihahs" drawn tightly over their heads and girdled with coarse black cords, their loose, flowing "abbas," and sturdy bare legs and feet; and the ringleted, effeminate-looking Jews, in caftans reaching almost to their ankles, as oily as their red or sandy locks, or the expression of their countenance—the former inured to hard labor on the burning hillsides of Palestine, the latter fresh from the Ghetto of some Rumanian town, unaccustomed to any other description of exercise than that of their wits, full of suspicion of all advice tendered to them, and animated by a pleasing self-confidence which I fear the first practical experience will rudely belie.[3]

Oliphant goes on to describe the preliminary discussions between these improbable partners: ". . . the native peasants screaming in Arabic, the Rumanian Israelites endeavoring to outtalk them in German jargon," presumably Yiddish, up to the final breakdown in the early hours of the morning. He noted that the fellahin "had no aversion to the proprietorship by Israelites of their land, on religious grounds. The only difference lay in the division of labor and profit."

Like many other Englishmen who came subsequently to Palestine, Oliphant at first took a low view of both peoples. He found the Arabs amazingly feckless, mostly because they were always digging for treasures and then smashing the valuable Roman shards they unearthed since they "were so very old that they are not worth anything." He did not think the Jews would really work with their hands, but a year later he was considerably impressed by their courage, common sense and adaptability, saying, "Under favorable auspices, colonies of this nature cannot but succeed."[4] Indeed, he writes, "There are three prejudices which have operated against the colonization of Palestine by Jews, and which are all completely unsound; and these are, first, that the Jew cannot become an agriculturalist; secondly, that the country is barren; and, thirdly, that it is unsafe."⁵

Oliphant later visited Petach Tikva, and became confirmed in his opinion that the Jews were learning quickly. "So far as energy, industry, and aptitude for agricultural pursuits are concerned, the absence of which has always been alleged as the reason why no Jewish colony could succeed, the experience of more than two years has now proved that such apprehensions are groundless, and that with a fair chance the Jews make very good colonists." Jewish initiative contrasted with "the helpless ignorance and ingrained indolence of the native fellahin."*

In the 1880s Baron Edmond de Rothschild took up the mantle of Sir Moses Montefiore. He rescued failing Jewish settlements at Zichron in the Carmel mountains, Rishon-le-Zion south of Jaffa, and other places, invested money in them, and introduced overseers with a view to establishing more systematic and profitable farming. At a number of these places vines were planted and wine-making became their chief activity; it still is, and the flourishing Israel wine-making industry is the result of his practical help. But his methods defeated the original purpose of Jewish settlement of the land, which was the "redemption" of Jewish settlers by manual labor in the fields. On the Rothschild estates the settlers tended to turn into a planter class, hiring cheap Arab labor and taking on fellow Jews only when they had to. This was not the way to prepare for the mass immigration of Jews which the Zionists were only a little later to envisage.

The early settlers, moreover, found work on the land very tough going. The land which they bought, or which the Baron and other benefactors bought for them, was meant to be good but often turned out to be swamp or desert. The soil had been neglected for centuries. Often, the early settlers lived in mud huts and tents. The huts actually melted in summer heat, and the tents leaked when it rained. The settlers went down like ninepins with malaria; many of them contracted trachoma. They dressed in rags and lived on a diet of lentils and bean soup. Frequently, they had to beat off Arab marauders, and when the Petach Tikva colonists took their first harvest to Jerusalem, they were stoned by fellow Jews for desecrating the Sabbath.

Within a year or two of its foundation, Petach Tikva was in such difficulties that two colonists were sent all the way to Bialystok in Poland to seek reinforcements. One of them, Abraham Koppelman, was an ec-

---

* Oliphant certainly did not dislike the Palestinian Arabs and he tells many amusing stories about them. One tells of a Bedoun sheik whom Oliphant asked if he could trace his descent back to Abraham. The sheik answered that he could trace it much farther back and that in his understanding Abraham had not been a sheik of a very good family.

centric who recounted that he had come from a veritable Garden of Eden, with a lemon tree outside his window from which he could pluck the fruit for making Russian tea![6] In 1881 nearly half of the colony at Petach Tikva, then 500 strong, died during a malaria epidemic. The survivors sought refuge in the hills and the place was abandoned for two years. Only in 1891 did the settlers plant citrus trees there for the first time, and not until 1896 did they gather their first crop.

Eshkol was to get his first job in Palestine at Petach Tikva, following in the footsteps of Israel's first prime minister, David Ben-Gurion. The latter had arrived in 1906 at a truly critical time for Jewish resettlement. By then all notions of Palestine as a land of milk and honey were dead and buried; too many settlers had returned to Europe sick, suffering, and defeated. Nearly all hard manual labor on Jewish farms was done by Arabs, and the newly arrived Jewish immigrants were told that there was nothing for them to do. In 1904 a leading Zionist, Yosef Vitkin, had issued an appeal that sounded desperate:

> Come to the aid of your people. Rush to their side. Band together; discipline yourselves for life or death; forget all precious bonds of your childhood; leave them behind forever without a shadow of regret, and answer the call of your people. . . . Be prepared to struggle with nature, with disease, and hunger; with people, foes and friends, strangers and brothers, haters of Zion and Zionism. . . . Prepare for the worst![7]

On his arrival Ben-Gurion complained that "the air smelt of charity and baksheesh."[8] At Jaffa, he was appalled by the combination of dirt and dole, and in the afternoon on the day of his arrival, hastened to Petach Tikva on foot. Yet he was filled with exaltation, and with an indefinable feeling that he had returned home. There were for him, as his biographer Maurice Edelman puts it, new stars in a new heaven. Ben-Gurion put something of his feelings into letters which he wrote home: "The howling of jackals in the vineyard, the braying of donkeys in the stables, the croaking of frogs in the ponds, the scent of blossoming acacia, the murmur of the distant sea, the darkening shadows of the groves, the enchantment of the stars in the deep blue . . . everything intoxicated me." And again: "Beautiful are the days in our land, days flushed with light and full of luster, rich in vistas of sea and hill. . . . But infinitely more splendid are the nights; nights deep with secrets and wrapt in mystery. The drops of burning gold, twinkling in the soft blue dome of the sky, the dim-lit purity of the mountains, the lurid crystal of the transparent mountain air—all is steeped in yearning, in half-felt longings, in secret undertones. You are moved by urgings not of this world."[9]

At that time there were about a thousand Arabs working on the Jewish-run farms at Petach Tikva, and only a handful of Jews. According to Ben-Gurion, only 25 Jews did manual jobs there. His first employer, Abraham Poyachevsky, was a hard-headed businessman who saw farming from one angle only—it had to pay. Arab farm laborers were readily available, docile, and ready to accept low wages. Jewish employers had no hesitation in hiring them. Disgusted, Ben-Gurion drifted away to Galilee. There he found things more to his taste.

> No shopkeepers or speculators, no non-Jewish hirelings or idlers living on the labor of others. The men plowed and harrowed their fields and planted their seeds; the women weeded the gardens and milked the cows; the children herded geese on the threshing floor and rode on horseback to meet their fathers in the fields. These were villagers, smelling wholesomely of midden and ripening ear, and burnt by the sun.[10]

The few settlements in Galilee were exceptional, and a cry of woe came at about this time from Arthur Ruppin, an economist and agronomist, who set up the first Zionist office in the country at Jaffa in 1908: "It appears doubtful whether we shall find, anywhere in the world, Jews whose abilities and training would fit them to become successful farmers in Palestine."[11] Ruppin wanted the farmers to begin feeding themselves properly by producing their own milk, poultry, and vegetables. This he believed was an alternative to the "Rothschild system" of having only a single crop grown on a farm that might have two or three different types of soil on it. But he also wanted to see light industries built up that could export a part of their output, and he wanted the liquidation of the chalukah practice of living on charity. Above all, Jews would have to work their own land. As it was, Jewish youth was drifting away from the land and "some of the colonies actually gave the impression of homes for the aged."[12] Ruppin coined the phrase: "We want not dividends, but men."

Ruppin was probably the most formative influence on Jewish settlement in the decade before the outbreak of World War I. He encouraged the formation of purchasing companies for land and urban development and of farm cooperatives for selling products to the Jewish community. The Jews, he pointed out, could not compete at this stage in history with Arab marketing methods; the Arab farmer sent his wife off to sit all day in the market, with a couple of chickens, a big basket of vegetables, and all the time in the world. The cooperative principle, Ruppin believed, could be systematically applied in farming. He advocated concentration on a few areas, rather than the haphazard buying of scattered plots of land all over the country. And he firmly supported the idea of collectivized farming. That was tried out at Sejera in 1908. The idea at Sejera was that a small group of young pioneers should do the actual spade work in clearing land for farming, then move on to another piece of unreclaimed land and do the same thing over again.

The Sejera experiment was not exactly a failure, but in 1910 a permanent collectivized farm was established close to where the river Jordan runs out of the Sea of Galilee. It is an idyllic setting:

> Our village lies in the valley close to where the Jordan flows out of the Sea of Galilee. The hills of Galilee are on one side of us and the mountains of Syria and Transjordan are on the other; and in the distance we see the snow cap of Mount Hermon. In winter the fields are green, then yellow with corn and barley, and in spring there are wild cyclamen everywhere and poppies and cornflowers and many other wild flowers. Degania, the name we gave the village, means cornflower.[13]

In 1911 the working team at Degania consisted of ten men and two women. Six men did the plowing, two were watchmen, one was a secretary-accountant, and one was in reserve. The two women kept house, while the men swapped jobs. It was the women, growing bored with the sameness of life, who insisted on raising the living standards, on keeping chickens and goats, and on buying a stove instead of doing all the cooking on open wood fires. It was a woman, too, who ended all talk of a self-denying ordinance, with no marriages and no children in the kibbutz for its first five years. A young girl arrived from Russia, fell in love, and married one of the kibbutznikim. Another followed her example, and the third child from this second marriage was Moshe Dayan, later to be commander in chief of the Israeli Army and Israel's minister of defense at the time of writing.

Degania began as a cluster of shacks and barns surrounded by open fields. There was not a single tree on the kibbutz, for most of the trees planted earlier had died, since the settlers stuck them into deep pits filled with water. Eshkol was himself to settle within a mile of this first kibbutz; therefore Baratz's description of it, many years later, has some relevance:

> Today we have the most beautiful garden in Galilee. As you come in from the side of the lake the great avenue of cypresses runs from the gate to the water tower; on the left is the oldest part of the garden, very shadowy under the low, silvery branches of the pepper trees, within sound of the beehives and with a lily pond in the middle of it. On the right is the garden we have planted since the war; the trees are still young, but there are bright, tropical shrubs and flowers; on a brilliant stretch of lawn facing the lake we have put up a monument—a piece of rock with the names of the fallen on it. The houses are scattered and half-hidden among the trees, and everywhere there are flowers—yellow and gold and fiery pink, crimson and scarlet. On a hot spring day, when the sky has drained the color from the hills all round, the massed flowers look like suns fallen and blazing against the black cypresses.[14]

Degania became the model for hundreds of collectivized farms, and there are new ones still springing up in Israel. Here, only a word need be said about the way in which it worked. Its members received their land from the Jewish National Fund. They took no wages for their work but sold whatever produce and food grown on the farm they could spare and lived off the proceeds. The money was spent mainly on farm implements, building materials, clothes, and some additional foodstuffs. They built their own water tower and piped water from the Jordan. As their children grew up they taught them in their own school in the kibbutz. Degania was a miniature but self-sufficient community, in its way an epic of human companionship and cooperation. It was proof of the fact that Jews could settle on the land and live off it.

This was the Palestine which Eshkol was to find when he landed at Jaffa in 1914. Under slipshod Turkish administration, it was thinly settled by Jewish pioneers, who lived mainly in Galilee, the coastal plain of Sharon to the north and south of Jaffa, the Carmel mountain range, Jerusalem, and other holy cities. Jewish Palestine had hardly developed the sinews of a national enterprise, but it had a number of institutions which already gave the Jewish community a character totally different from that of the far more numerous Arab population. The Jewish community had two labor movements, Poalei Zion and Hapoel Hatzair, already mentioned. It had several labor unions, although some of them had been dissolved after a year or two and then reformed. From 1907 onward it had its own watchmen's organization, the *Hashomer,* which set out to protect settlements from Arab raiders and thieves and which possessed a very limited number of rifles and blunderbuses for this purpose. It had its own rabbinate, which furnished religious courts of jurisdiction whose authority was readily accepted by the settlers. And it had its own investment fund, launched by Poalei Zion, which also opened offices for employment and information.

Supporting the community in the most practical way possible was the Jewish National Fund, financed by money collected from the Diaspora. The funds thus amassed were used for purchasing land in Palestine wherever it became available. And behind the Jewish National Fund stood the Zionist movement, which believed in steadily increasing Jewish settlement in Palestine. But by 1914 the Zionist movement had hardly made as much progress as might have been expected. In 1899 it had numbered 114,000 members; now it numbered perhaps 140,000. Only 8000 of them lived in Britain, which had a Jewish population of 300,000; and only 12,000 in the United States, where there were 3,000,000 Jews.[15]

One acute observer, Norman Bentwich, told me that on his pre-1914 visits, he found little of the Jewish-state idea in Palestine. The Jews are better than most people at concentrating single-mindedly on one objective at a time; and their pre-1914 objective was to expand Jewish settlement and make it work. The 19-year-old Eshkol considered himself a Zionist when he set out from Oratowo but he probably looked no farther than most of his contemporaries.

As with most other Jewish immigrants, his arrival at Jaffa was inauspicious. Wearing his Russian student's blue suit with brass buttons and clutching his small suitcase, he was carried ashore from the boat on the back of an Arab porter through the pounding surf.* Yet one fellow Jew remembers that Eshkol contrived somehow to look elegant, possibly only by comparison with earlier immigrants who had for the most part worn their only suit of clothes to tatters.[16] It was a rough, windy day. On shore he was given a red ticket by a Turkish customs official, entitling him to one month's stay as a pilgrim. Then he made his way to the Hapoel Hatzair hostel where he was at once surrounded by a group of inquisitive Jews. They asked him why he had come to Palestine, the standard question for new arrivals. But he had been told in Vilna to expect this and answered quite simply that he had come to work. There was a chorus of discouraging comment; there was no work to be had, the living conditions were miserable, he would do much better to take the first ship back to Odessa. Eshkol was a phlegmatic young man and he refused to be depressed. Like others before him, he had a curious feeling that he had come home. He himself said, "In Jaffa I was born a second time." He spent his first night at the house of a friendly settler, Chaim Baruch. In the morning he set out on foot for Petach Tikva to look for work.

He could never forget that first 9-mile tramp.

> There was a stage coach or diligence which could have carried me from Jaffa to Petach Tikva. But it would have cost money; and anyway, I had none. And it was "not done" for a mere settler to take the diligence; that was something for Arab effendis and Jewish overseers only. I couldn't have paid for a donkey ride. I walked behind the diligence in order not to lose my way.[17]

He walked through the purely Jewish settlement of Tel Aviv. Today it is a sprawling city of half a million inhabitants; he remembered it as consisting of a few dozen one-story houses. Then the road led over sand dunes and into the dusty plain of Sharon. At Petach Tikva there were the first signs of cultivation, orange groves and fields of corn and barley. Eshkol reported to a man called Lofban, the editor of the Hapoel Hatzair newspaper, to whom he had a letter of introduction from Joseph Sprinzak. From him he learned about the considerable difficulties of growing citrus fruits, of the tough conditions of work, and of the malaria epidemics. He learned that the settlers called Palestine "the land that devours its own," and that the Arabs called the settlers the "children of death," possibly because some of them committed suicide, possibly because so many of them looked very unhealthy. Two years earlier Jews

---

* Sometimes Jews were turned back by Turkish customs officials. Then, according to one account, they were rowed back to their ships, where the captain would not accept them. And so back and forth, until they bribed the Turkish official—perhaps literally with their jacket or shirt. See Bertha Vester's *Our Jerusalem*, p. 85.

had died in great numbers in the cholera epidemic which swept the whole of Palestine.

It needed persistence to find a job and keep it. Eshkol had plenty of persistence. Photographs of him taken at this time show a tall, erect young man, wearing a striped smock for work in the fields and shouldering a *turifa,* an outsized hoe. He had a small, neatly clipped moustache and a mop of hair which he brushed back from the forehead. He was undoubtedly handsome, and it looked as if he throve on the meager diet of lentils and salted herring. He was first assigned to building a pumphouse, then to weeding. He quickly became a strong, efficient worker, and a popular one too, perhaps because of his habit of singing songs and telling stories as he and his fellows planted or harvested.

Life was undeniably hard. He shared a rented room at Petach Tikva with another young man. All the money they earned was spent on rent and food. On his day off Eshkol used to carry letters to Jaffa and pick up the mail there, walking 18 miles in the day. Soon enough he came down with malaria and was brought back from the fields on a donkey, weak and shaking. He could remember people shouting "Look at Shkolnik riding a donkey! He thinks he's an overseer already!"

He could remember, too, the arguments with Jewish farmers and overseers, who referred to the young pioneers as shmendriks, or ragamuffins, and often preferred to hire Arabs who were more experienced and cost less. He could remember how those Arabs loafed about when the overseer was out of sight but made a great show of industriousness when he made his rounds. He could remember the amazement of the Arabs at the early attempts of the Jewish settlers at irrigation, and the particular occasion when he worked too hard at welding two water pipes together on a swelteringly hot day. He was wielding a heavy hammer on the molten lead used to join the pipes when blood gushed out of his nose. He also studied hard to improve his Hebrew during these early days. The chief pioneer in the spreading of Hebrew was Eliezer Ben Yehuda, who claimed that he had created a Hebrew-speaking community in Jerusalem from the ten families who spoke the language in 1904. Eshkol remembered how on one occasion Ben Yehuda was walking with him behind a wine cart. The tap on its biggest barrel was leaking and the wine was running out onto the road. Ben Yehuda, who had vowed to speak only Hebrew and no other language, shouted to the driver. The fellow did not understand and only shrugged his shoulders, whereupon Ben Yehuda said to Eshkol: "If he can't speak his own language, there's nothing I can do to help him."

Eshkol became a trusted member of the local labor exchange, which drew up rosters of available jobs and allocated them on an equitable basis to applicants. He was elected a member of the Workers' Agricultural Council. For a time he was in charge of the Petach Tikva communal kitchen, a thankless task. "Levi, the son of Deborah," as he was known in the kitchen, was as big a success indoors as out, thanks to his fund of Yiddish jokes and aphorisms. For a time he helped to cook and sell meatballs as an extra to supplement their simple diet. That was recalled years afterward, when he was named an honorary citizen of Petach Tikva. He was a frequent and able speaker at the workers' meetings and conferences and a leader in folksinging and dancing in the open after the day's work was done.

Eshkol was one of the last settlers to arrive before World War I. That made him one of the last of the Second Aliyah, second immigration, which took place in the prewar decade. Later on people joked about Eshkol's having just made the bandwagon of the Second Aliyah of settlers who came out to Palestine to work with their hands. This was a distinction; for those settlers were probably the most idealistic ones of all who ever came to Palestine. They had the true pioneering spirit, and it was not long before Eshkol and some of his fellows decided that the time had come to move from Petach Tikva. "What we needed," Eshkol told me, "was a hinterland for the Jewish population on the coastal belt. True, there was Galilee. But elsewhere settlers had an uphill task; at Hadera, for instance, it was said at the time that every second settler who came there was now sleeping in the cemetery."

A hinterland was needed, too, for Jewish Jerusalem. About that Eshkol talked with an older settler, Mayer Rothberg, known as the "king of the shovel." In August 1914 Rothberg invited him and 16 other young men to join in founding a new agricultural settlement at Atarot, five miles north of Jerusalem on the road to Ramallah (where now Jerusalem's Kalandia airfield is located). The settlement was to be a collective; the group would share everything, food, agricultural implements, even working clothes. And jobs would be allotted on the basis of ability and fitness.

The land around Atarot seemed to grow stones, and at first the settlers lived under the most primitive conditions. A woman settler, Rachel Ben Zvi, remembers Eshkol living "in a shack put together of boughs and trees. An early autumn moon lit the scene, the air was mountain-clean and fresh." This was the first settlement on the uplands north of Jerusalem.[18] Later, the settlers of Atarot built themselves small huts, with three walls only, tin roofs, straw mats on the floors, and a straw mat hung across the doorway. There was some trouble with the local Arab population, which was not as friendly as at Petach Tikva. But there were Arabs who remained lifelong friends too; in 1929 one of them came all the way to Tel Aviv to warn Eshkol of impending trouble, just before the Arab riots which resulted in the slaughter of the Jewish community in Hebron.

Another Arab, who may have been less than friendly, told the settlers that there was a disused well close to where they were living, which could easily be put into working order. Their settlement was on top of a hill, and Eshkol and the others had to make maddening treks up the slope, trying to imitate Arab women by carrying buckets of water on their shoulders, and spilling most of it on the way. They took a look at the "disused well," a huge pit which was filled to the brim with rocks, old tin cans and broken glass, and every sort of rubbish. "We worked away like the devil to empty that pit," Eshkol told me. "After a time we could see water gleaming on the bottom of it. We worked even harder than before. But when we reached the bottom, we found that the water was no more than a residue of rain in a basin of rock."

There were plenty of disappointments of this and other kinds. The Atarot project, indeed, was to end in failure, but not through the fault or lack of effort of the small band of settlers. Turkey had entered the war in October 1914. The Jewish Agency advised the settlers to leave all outlying farms and to withdraw to the main centers of Jewish population where they would be in less danger. Late in the spring of 1915 Eshkol and his companions traveled to Rishon-le-Zion where they undertook a new kind of collective operation, contracting to run one of the old Rothschild farms for a stipulated monthly amount which was paid to the group as a whole. At Rishon Eshkol was to meet and marry his first wife Rivka Marshak, a former student of the secondary school at Herzliya, who had found work in the vineyards. Their marriage was not destined to last; they separated by mutual consent in 1924. One daughter, Noa, was born from this marriage, in 1923. The formal separation took place in 1927, and Rivka died in 1951. But in the meantime Eshkol found himself personally involved in the war, something which he could not have dreamed of when he had set out for Palestine from Russia such a short time before.

1. James Parkes, *History of Palestine*, pp. 180–181.
2. Laurence Oliphant, *Haifa, or Life in Modern Palestine*, p. 69.
3. *Ibid.*, pp. 11–13.
4. *Ibid.*, p. 50.
5. *Ibid.*, p. 62.
6. Howard Sachar, *Aliyah, The People of Israel*, p. 82.
7. *Ibid.*, p. 127.
8. Maurice Edelman, *Ben-Gurion*, p. 36.
9. *Ibid.*, p. 37.
10. *Ibid.*, p. 41.
11. Arthur Ruppin, *Three Decades of Palestine*, p. 7.
12. *Ibid.*, p. 36.
13. Joseph Baratz, *A Village by the Jordan*, p. 47.
14. *Ibid.*, p. 59.
15. Leonard Stein, *The Balfour Declaration*, p. 75 .
16. Elhanan Nitzan's account in the evening paper *Yehiod Ahronot*.
17. In personal conversation with the author.
18. Rachel Ben Zvi, *Coming Home*, p. 308.

3.

With Turkey engaged in the war and the whole country in a state of growing turmoil, Eshkol and his fellow settlers realized that they might be in for a difficult time. Actually, things went reasonably well for a time at Rishon-le-Zion. In a military sense Palestine was a backwater as long as Turkey was not ready to mount a full-scale attack on Egypt and as long as the British garrison there was too weak to do more than sit along the Suez Canal. In an area where there were practically no roads and where the fastest form of travel was on horseback, nothing was likely to happen for some time.

Eshkol and his friends found plenty of work, planting vines at Rishon. According to his own story, he earned two to three francs a day, enough to pay for his lodging and at least one square meal a day, and he planted an average of 80 vines a day and sometimes up to 120. His work in the vineyards was abruptly interrupted early one morning, when he was awakened by wild ringing of the village bells. He dashed out armed with an old Turkish musket he kept at his bedside. Outside, he found everybody heading for the vineyards. He ran with them.

Somewhere above the vineyards was a gray, billowing cloud. There was a hum in the air, then a noise like the clashing of innumerable small sets of cymbals as the locusts dropped down on the vineyards, settling on every twig and leaf, eating everything in sight. The settlers struck out at them with poles and brooms, swatted them with sacks, lit fires in the hope of smoking them off. Their efforts were useless; all the vineyards were lost.

Rishon was a fairly prosperous corner of Palestine. Under Turkish rule Palestine itself was a miserably poor and neglected corner of the crumbling empire. Turkey had lost Tunisia to France in 1881. In 1882 England occupied Egypt and then the Sudan. Italy seized Libya in 1912. In Europe, Turkey lost Macedonia, Rumelia, and northern Greece in 1913. The "Sick Man of Europe" was very sick indeed, although the Turkish soldier was to show once again, in Gallipoli, the Caucasus, and Mesopotamia, that he would fight like a lion.

Palestine had no proper port and, until the last decade of the nineteenth century, no road on which a wheeled vehicle could move. It had virtually no hospitals or schools, other than those of religious foundations or those established by the Jewish settlers during the decade before the outbreak of the war. The Turkish tax system weighed heavily on small farmers, while the rich effendi class made its own terms with the administration. The Turks governed on a shoestring, with the result that there was maladministration and corruption. The Jewish settlers lived frugally and worked hard but were still barely able to maintain themselves. According to one Jewish settler, "The Arabs were even worse off than we were, scratching a pittance out of the neglected soil on the estates of absentee landlords, or wandering from place to place with their few goats, frightened both of robbers and of the police."[1] Arab farmers were practically never out of debt, and the system of land tenure in much of Palestine involved biennial changes of ownership. The cultivator had no incentive to improve his land; on the contrary, he had every reason to milk it dry. Apart from his other troubles, he had to cope with Bedouin raids and the damage done by innumerable flocks of goats whose owners simply sent them off to forage for food.

The war made things much worse. The Turkish overlord in Palestine was the commander of the Fourth Army, Ahmed Djemal Pasha. He was ruthless and capable, able to exert great personal charm on occasions, but deeply suspicious of anyone who was not a Turk. He reserved his darkest suspicions for the Jews, possibly because they had their own settlements, schools, and rabbinical courts, their armed watchmen's service, their Zionist bank, even their stamps and currency tokens issued by the Jewish National Fund. But he treated Jews and Arabs with much the same undiscriminating roughness, regarding the lot of them only as potential cannon fodder or potential troublemakers.

Food and livestock were commandeered, leading to a mass flight from the land. Most of the trees that remained in Palestine were cut down for firewood to run the strategically important railway from Syria to the Hedjaz. Arabs were impressed into the Turkish Army, and these unwilling recruits were usually marched off handcuffed in pairs. Others were forced to work without pay for the Turkish armed forces, building roads and moving supplies along them. Turkish contempt for the Palestinian Arabs was deep-rooted. These were people who were incapable of organizing themselves, of mutual cooperation or mutual trust. During the whole of World War I the Palestinian Arabs showed not the slightest sign of being able to help themselves.

Amazingly enough, the Jewish settlers managed to found four new settlements in Galilee during the war, and to organize a new buying and selling cooperative, the *Mashbir.* as well as the Palestine Workers' Fund.[2] But on the whole they suffered bitterly. Djemal Pasha sent several thousand of them to build roads in Armenia, where they suffered terribly from cold and near-starvation. Hundreds died or were beaten to death when they collapsed on the job. Hundreds more fled to Egypt, and most of those who stayed applied for Turkish citizenship in order to become Ottomanized and cease drawing attention to themselves. This did not stop Turkish soldiers from descending on Jewish settlements, where they rounded up the men, beat them, and sometimes tortured them as well. Even in relatively "settled" communities like Rishon, the situation became grim. Food supplies grew short; unemployment was rife; and starving, destitute Jews flooded in from outlying settlements. Jews began to go into hiding, especially in Galilee, where they were hunted like wild animals in the hills. Eshkol, too, spent much of the time hiding in the vineyards. Sometimes Turkish detachments simply "dug in" and waited for the Jewish settlers to come out, driven from their hiding places by hunger and thirst. On such occasions, their only recourse was to bribe the commander of the detachment, a procedure which, in Eshkol's own case, never failed.

Those who were able to do so continued in their agricultural settlements. In her book *Coming Home* Rachel Ben Zvi gave an account of a settlement near Metullah in the far north of Palestine: "Now they all seemed different. Their faces were thin and tense, but something new and bold was expressed in them. Unkempt hair, calloused hands, ragged sandals or boots. . . . When one of the men relieved another on the watch, he took not only the rifle but the one pair of boots. Yet, for all this austerity, they were wide awake and alive, working by day and guarding by night and full of their vision."[3]

Eshkol remembered the war years as a time of growing deprivation. At one period he had a steady job in the orange groves of Rishon, but this ended when it became impossible to market the citrus crop any longer. He got work at Petach Tikva, where his fellow settlers still found time to engage in a heated controversy over the organization of their own home guard. It was during that period that Eshkol introduced shorts for work in the fields. His precariously patched trousers tore once too often, and he decided to cut off the legs from the knee down and so do a proper job of patching the remainder.

"We were literally starving at times," Eshkol told me. "We saw no meat for months on end, and there came a time when we didn't have a scrap of bread left. I went down to Tel Aviv with some of my friends and we collected flour and lugged it back to Petach Tikva. There, believe it or not, we were nearly lynched by religious Jews for doing our baking after sundown on the Sabbath!"

Once again, Eshkol was in charge of the communal kitchen at Petach Tikva, a dull task and more difficult than before. As food became ever more scarce, there were anxious discussions among the settlers as to what they should do. Most of them were for sticking it out, and waiting for the war to end. Eshkol himself had no doubt as to what that end would be. "It stood to reason that the British would win. But they were so slow about it! First they were advancing on Jerusalem, then they had retreated again. And they kept most of their men back in Egypt, eating their excellent bully-beef."[4]

One of his fellow settlers who changed his mind more than once was David Ben-Gurion. Before the war Ben-Gurion had enrolled as a law student in Constantinople. There, he came in touch with some of the more liberal members of the Young Turk movement of Enver Pasha. The Young Turks were preaching an essentially nationalist movement of regeneration, but Ben-Gurion thought that they might be progressive enough to allow some degree of Jewish emancipation in Palestine. In

1913, during the Balkan War, he volunteered for service in the Turkish army, but his application was turned down.

When World War I broke out, Ben-Gurion had another idea, namely, that the Jews should form their own battalion of the Turkish army and join in the defense of Palestine. But there is no evidence that the Turkish authorities ever considered anything of this kind; they probably thought it much safer to draft members of national minorities into mixed units and send them to serve as far away from their homes as possible. Ben-Gurion was politically active, and the Turks believed that his activities were subversive. Although he had made a declaration of loyalty to the Ottoman Empire, he was arrested and then expelled from the country, and put on a boat sailing for Alexandria. From there he made his way to New York, where he and the future Israeli president Ben Zvi founded the Jewish Palestine Legion Committee. Their purpose now was to enroll American Jews for service in Palestine on the Allied side, but this was to prove a slow business. The majority of American Jews were refugees from Tsarist tyranny. To them Russia was the principal enemy, but Russia was fighting on the Allied side. Palestine was a remote concept to them, and they knew next to nothing about conditions there. On the whole, the feeling among the American Jews, at least until the Bolshevik Revolution overthrew the Tsarist regime and the United States came into the war on the Allied side, was overwhelmingly in favor of neutrality.

Two Jews other than Ben-Gurion were to play the main part in enlisting Jewish support, outside Palestine, for the Allied cause. These were Vladimir Jabotinsky and Joseph Trumpeldor. Both men had served in the Russian army, and Trumpeldor had become an officer, a rare thing for a Russian Jew, and had lost an arm in the Russo-Japanese War of 1905. By early 1915 there were nearly 30,000 Jewish refugees interned at the Gabbari quarantine buildings outside Alexandria. Jabotinsky and Trumpeldor thought that a Jewish corps, or legion, should be raised from among them to fight for the Allies. They argued that the sooner the Turks were defeated, the better for Palestinian Jewry, that a Jewish army could be created which would help to found a Jewish state, and that Allied cooperation could be secured in return for a Jewish war effort on the Allied side.

Jabotinsky, an Odessa Jew who spoke six languages, has been described as the "Jewish d'Annunzio."[5] In 1915, when the Allies landed in Gallipoli, Trumpeldor was put in charge of the Jewish volunteers who comprised the Gallipoli Mule Corps. The British were chary of forming a fighting Jewish unit, and the Mule Corps was used only for transporting supplies and munitions. Jabotinsky, already aged 35, enlisted as a private soldier in the British Army, where his name was altogether too much for his comrades. They called him "Private Jug-o-Whisky" instead.

Jabotinsky had true Jewish persistence as well as friends in high quarters among British Jewry. The complex and often confused discussions which went on over the formation of specifically Jewish units have no part in this book. Suffice it to say that the First Jewish Battalion was eventually formed in February 1917, and marched at its inauguration ceremony from the barracks in the Tower to Whitechapel in the East End with fixed bayonets. The privilege of fixing bayonets was conferred on it by the Lord Mayor of the City of London and the battalion was placed under the command of Lt. Col. Patterson, described as "a big-game hunter and an experienced soldier, a polished diplomat, a good Zionist, and a complete adventurer—in the best sense of the term."[6]

Jabotinsky wrote a lyric account of the inaugural march:

> Tens of thousands of Jews were on the streets, in the windows, and on the roofs. . . . Women wept with joy, old Jews shook their gray beards and murmured prayers. High on his horse, with a rose in his hand thrown to him by a girl from an upper window, was Colonel Patterson, Commander of the Legion, smiling and sending greetings. Hail to you, and you, tailor from Whitechapel and Soho, from Manchester and Leeds! You were good tailors. You found in the dust the tattered rags of Jewish honor, and out of it you made a holy flag![7]

Alas, the high hopes entertained at this inaugural march were scarcely realized. The British government somewhat weakly decided that the battalion should not, after all, be called "Jewish," however Jewish it might be. It was renamed the 38th Royal Fusiliers and it was given the subtitle of "The Judaeans." There was controversy as to whether it should be allowed to carry a Jewish flag—most of the officers and NCO's were non-Jewish and had been drafted into the battalion in order to stiffen up its most unwarlike-looking Jewish privates, and some of these Gentiles objected to any but a British flag. A compromise was reached and the 38th carried a Royal Fusiliers standard and a second flag of blue with a Star of David on it.

The British government was dubious about sending the battalion to Palestine. It seemed an odd collection of people. The non-Jews were hard-bitten and very English veterans. Some of the Jewish rank and file were Zionists, but others were deeply anti-Zionist and had joined largely because they did not want to be drafted in ordinary British regiments where nothing would be done about kosher food and other Jewish observances. There were others who had been transferred from other units simply because they happened to be Jews.

Of the men, one observer said that "with a certain number of exceptions, it would be fair to say that their spiritual home was Whitechapel rather than Palestine."[8] Jabotinsky referred to the battalion as being "not merely a regiment, but a political performing company." And when the 38th did, at last, set out for Palestine, it was an inauspicious departure. "We were bundled into a train under circumstances of such confusion, that the richly swaddled Scroll of the Jewish Law had to be nursed like some romantic foundling in the adoptive arms of an extremely Gentile adjutant." At all events, the 38th did reach its destination, Egypt, and it was in due course to take some part in the war.

The journey to Egypt in the company of the volatile, intensely vocal East-End Jews was almost too much for the tough, fire-eating Jabotinsky. He was heard on more than one occasion muttering savagely that he "would like to kill a *schneider* (tailor)."

But in Palestine the majority of the cruelly suffering Jewish community was still against taking any sort of action which could bring down violent Turkish retribution and which would in addition be totally ineffective. Both political labor groups, Poalei Zion and Hapoel Hatzair, were against Jewish participation in the war. The American branch of Poalei Zion was to go on maintaining this view, even after the United States joined the Allies. Hapoel Hatzair, to which Eshkol belonged, argued that the war in the Middle East could end in stalemate and that an impoverished Turkey would find itself obliged to make concessions to the Jews of Palestine. There was a vague idea, according to Eshkol,[9] that Jewish capital could be used to give Zionism a preponderant financial stake in Palestine. In both Poalei Zion and Hapoel Hatzair, moreover, there were a number of influential pacifists. The Jews, they argued, had come to Palestine to get away from strife which did not concern them. The European war could never be their concern. Therefore, they should stay out of it.

Eshkol's career proved him to be a patient and reflective person. Believing as he did in the near-certainty of an Allied victory, he was bound to take some personal action sooner or later. But in 1917 something happened which undoubtedly helped to make up his mind for him. This was the Balfour Declaration, in favor of the creation of a Jewish national home in Palestine.

To understand the reasons for the Balfour Declaration one must delve back in history.

The idea of a Jewish national home had been canvassed for the best part of a century by non-Jews, before Lord Balfour, British foreign secretary at that time, made his historic declaration. In 1840 Lord Palmerston showed a keen interest in securing a return of the Jews to their native land. Disraeli toyed with the idea but did nothing about it. Another person interested in it was the Emperor Napoleon III of France, whose volatile mind leaped across oceans to explore possibilities of expanding French power. In 1860 a French force landed in Lebanon to lend support to the Christian Maronites against their persecutors, the Druses. Both France and Britain were aware of the geographical importance of the Middle East, and the arguments in favor of installing the Jews as the guardians of this strategically vital area were advanced to Napoleon III by his private secretary, Ernest Laharanne. In his book, *The New Eastern Question*, published in 1860, Laharanne wrote:

> What European power would today oppose the plan that the Jews, united through a Congress, should buy back their ancient fatherland? Who would object if the Jews flung a handful of gold to decrepit old Turkey and said to her: "Give me back my home and use this money to consolidate the other parts of your tottering empire"?

Laharanne went on:

> A great calling is reserved for the Jews: to be a living channel of communication between three continents. You shall be the bearers of civilization to peoples who are still inexperienced, and their teachers in the European sciences. . . . You shall be the mediators between Europe and far Asia. You will come to the land of your fathers decorated with the crown of age-long martyrdom, and there, finally, you will be completely healed of all your ills! Your capital will again bring the wide stretches of barren land under cultivation; your labor and industry will once more turn the ancient soil into fruitful valleys, reclaiming it from the encroaching sands of the desert, and the world will again pay its homage to the oldest of peoples.

Napoleon III was diverted into adventures in other parts of the globe. But France, and Britain, never lost sight of the possibilities of extending their influence in the Middle East. The two countries joined in financing the by then virtually independent khedive of Egypt in 1876, at first competing and finally cooperating in the financing and control of the Suez Canal. They were primarily responsible for the signature of the Constantinople Convention of 1888 on the free navigation of the canal. Meanwhile Britain occupied Cyprus and began to establish treaty relations with some of the hereditary rulers of the Persian Gulf sheikdoms. By the beginning of this century France and Britain had been well and truly drawn into the vortex of the Middle East, and their governments were anxiously speculating about what would happen when the Ottoman Empire collapsed and how Russia could be denied a predominant influence in the area when that took place.

By the beginning of this century, too, Theodor Herzl, the first active protagonist of a Jewish state, had begun putting out diplomatic feelers in the hope of getting something concrete done. With what must seem astonishing courage (he was, after all, only a Viennese journalist), Herzl called on Kaiser Wilhelm II of Germany, Britain's dynamic colonial secretary, Joseph Chamberlain, and even on the sultan of Turkey, Abdul Hamid. Privately, he expressed the opinion that Palestine could be bought from the Sultan in return for Jewish management of Turkey's finances. At the First Zionist Congress of 1897 in Basle he argued, more prosaically, in favor of land purchase in Palestine, the granting of a Jewish loan to the sultan, discreet planning of Jewish immigration, and Jewish development of the soil of Palestine.

With Chamberlain, Herzl discussed alternative projects for a Jewish national home, which might be only temporary but which would serve for what he called a *nacht-asyl,* an overnight refuge. In October 1902, they discussed the possibility of making El Arish, in the Sinai peninsula and only 40 miles from the present Israeli border, the center of Jewish settlement. Chamberlain had no idea where El Arish was, the sort of crass ignorance which would amaze a present-day diplomat, and had to look up the place in an atlas. Only then, Herzl subsequently recounted, did Chamberlain get the drift of what was needed—unoccupied land in the only area of the world which really mattered to Zionist Jews. But the El Arish project never got off the ground. The area was short of water and the proposal was to pump water from the Nile, probably through pipes laid underneath the Suez Canal. Lord Cromer, Britain's proconsul in Egypt, came out against this, on the dubious ground that Nile water could not be spared.

Herzl greeted this decision by buying himself vault number 28 at the Doeblinger cemetery outside Vienna as his family burial place. This may have been a histrionic gesture, for in no time he was busy again, discussing other alternatives for the Jewish national home. He talked to Portugal about founding a colony in Mozambique, to Belgium about leasing land in the Congo, and to Italy about possible Jewish settlements in Libya, upon which the Italians were already casting their eyes.

There was further discussion with Chamberlain, this time about Uganda. The Sixth Zionist Congress in August 1903 rejected the Uganda project, mainly because the Russian delegates insisted that a Jewish national home should be in Palestine and nowhere else. Some of them sat down in the congress hall and broke into open lamentations at the thought of a man like Herzl "traducing" the Zionist mission. It was useless for Herzl to explain patiently that a Jewish base in Uganda would be only auxiliary to the eventual Jewish state in Palestine.[10] Subsequently Herzl made the apposite comment that "the rope was around the necks" of the Russian delegates, who still could not understand. His own efforts to get something done were almost over. Early in 1904 he saw the Pope and King Victor Emmanuel of Italy. The Pope told him that the Catholic Church could not countenance the occupation of holy places by the Jews. Herzl died in August 1904.

The mantle of Herzl was to fall on the shoulders of another, equally prescient Jew. Chaim Weizmann was a Russian Jew, born in the town of Motol in the Pale of Settlement in 1874. He became interested in Zionism as a very young man, at a time when most "reasonable" Jews thought that Herzl's idea of a Jewish state was "insane."[11] Weizmann himself admitted that "to be a Zionist it is not perhaps necessary to be slightly mad; but it helps."[12]

Weizmann decided to come to England in 1904 and to make England his base for the foreseeable future. He had noted how Herzl, a Viennese by birth but virtually stateless and homeless by choice, had flitted between Berlin and Constantinople, between London and Paris, and had failed to build up a cohesive body of opinion anywhere in the Gentile world in support of Zionist aims. Weizmann might well have made his base of operations in Berlin, for German Jewry was rich, influential, and intellectually alive. Paris was an alternative, although Weizmann probably distrusted the pervasiveness of French culture, which France was trying to infiltrate into the Middle East. He admitted himself that his reasons for coming to England were "chiefly intuitive."[13]

But there were, in fact, other, more solid reasons for his choice. As the greatest maritime country in the world, Britain had a vested interest in the Middle East. The Ottoman Empire was ripe for dissolution and Britain was the obvious power to move into a position of dominance in the Middle East. Britain was already established in Egypt and the Sudan, in Aden and on the Persian Gulf. Moreover, Weizmann had a tremendous, almost touching, belief in British institutions and the British way of life. With his uncanny perceptiveness of human character, he may have understood, too, the curious mixture of puritanism and romanticism in the British character which offers the only explanation for the way in which the most improbable Englishmen espoused Zionism. Britain, to put it crudely, was still a Bible country, and to many Britons the Jews were still the "chosen people" with a right to the country which God helped them choose for themselves.

In 1906 Weizmann had an hour's talk with Arthur Balfour in Manchester, a meeting which has, even in retrospect, attracted curiously little attention, since Balfour had been made Prime Minister only a year before. Weizmann himself recalled that he had told Balfour that their religion made Palestine the only place where the Jewish people could make their true home and that "we had Jerusalem when London was a marsh."[14] Weizmann also met, and befriended, the editor of the *Manchester Guardian*, C. P. Scott. At least one historian of Zionism, Isaiah Berlin, regarded this as a turning point in the history of the Zionist movement.[15] Scott became converted to Zionism and put Weizmann in touch with David Lloyd George, Winston Churchill, and others. Weizmann moved to Manchester. In his *The Unromantics. The Great Powers and the Balfour Declaration,* Jon Kimche regards Weizmann's move as providential. It was "the appearance of a man of destiny at the critical point of time. . . . Weizmann worked out his strategy in Manchester. Britain held the key to the gate of Jewish independence."[16] And again, "Manchester became the center of Zionist thought, destined to spread its influence and to leave its imprint upon Zionism and history."[17]

Weizmann's key meetings with British statesmen were those which took place with two successive foreign secretaries, Sir Edward Grey and Lord Balfour, during World War I. He convinced both men of the justice of the Zionist claim to Palestine. Speaking some years later in New York Weizmann said: "I went to Balfour alone; but behind me there stood 80 generations of Jews. The forces accumulated during thousands of years spoke through me, not money, but the voices of our sages, fighters, and heroes who rest in the holy soil of Eretz Israel. Eminent statesmen listened to these voices. It was the voice of history that spoke through my mouth."[18]

In his book, Jon Kimche advanced more solid, sober reasons for the Balfour Declaration. Britain needed to incorporate Palestine in her system of imperial defense. German Zionism was strong and the Kaiser was quite likely, with his usual unpredictability, to emerge as the "protector" of the Zionist cause. The American Jewish vote was of prime importance and could have a considerable influence on the American decision whether to enter in the war. Something also had to be done to break down the over-all, ingrained Jewish pacifism. And Britain owed a debt of gratitude to Weizmann, for his work as a chemist for the British armaments industry. All this was true, but still Balfour's sudden vision may have been the most important factor of all.

The Declaration was made in the form of a letter to Baron Lionel Walter de Rothschild on November 2, 1917. The text was published in the *Times* and other newspapers on November 9. After a short preamble, it read as follows:

> His Majesty's Government view with favor the establishment in Palestine of a national home for the Jewish people, and will use their best endeavors to facilitate the achievement of this object, it being clearly understood that nothing shall be done which may prejudice the civil and religious rights of existing non-Jewish communities in Palestine, or the rights and political status enjoyed by Jews in any other country. . . . I should be grateful if you would bring this declaration to the knowledge of the Zionist Federation.

According to Weizmann, the Declaration was somewhat weaker than originally intended. He believed that both the prime minister and foreign secretary favored a text which would have referred to Palestine as *the* national home.[19] Be that as it may, the Declaration had an effect on world Jewry that was truly electric. For the first time, a great power, and one which was acutely and intimately interested in the Middle East, had come out openly in support of the Jewish claim to set up some organic form of community in Palestine. Of course, it could be held that the Declaration did not totally bind any British government, which only "viewed with favor" a step which was much more dramatic than it might have supposed. The Declaration might have been held, too, to be equivocal, in that it offered something to both the Jews and the indigenous population of Palestine. But it is worth noting that the Declaration referred only to the "civil and religious" rights of the latter; there was no mention of their political or economic rights or interests. Balfour may have thought more deeply than his wise-after-the-event critics have supposed.

Whether or not Balfour envisaged with real clarity the creation of a Jewish state in Palestine is a question which may never be resolved. But the Declaration carried a very obvious implication. This was not missed by C. P. Scott, writing in the *Manchester Guardian* on November 9, 1917:

> We speak of it as a country, but it is not a country; it is at present little more than a small district of the vast Ottoman tyranny. But it will be a country; it will be the country of the Jews. . . . For 50 years the Jews have been slowly and painfully returning to their ancestral home, and even under the Ottoman yoke and amid the disorder of that effete and crumbling dominion they have succeeded in establishing the beginnings of a real civilization. . . . On the conclusion of peace our deliberate policy will be to encourage in every way in our power Jewish immigration, to give full security, and no doubt a large measure of autonomy, to Jewish immigrants, with a view to the ultimate establishment of a Jewish state.

There it was, the vital phrase, "a Jewish state"! Coming from the pen of a distinguished and indeed exceptional British newspaper editor, with a reputation for fair dealing and right thinking, it carried a weight which was beyond the scope of the most brilliant utterances of the most enlightened Jew. The *Manchester Guardian* was, relatively speaking, a newspaper small in readers and financial means. But it was the quality of its readers and its views that counted.

One independent observer, Colonel Richard Meinertzhagen, had this to say: "The Jew, or rather the Zionist, regards us frankly as the instrument sent by God to fulfill the Promise and restore the Holy Land to Israel." He added: "One thing is sure. The Jew, however small his voice, however mild his manner, will in the end be heard and he will succeed. The Arab will trumpet and bluster, others in Europe and America will sing his praises if the local orchestra breaks down, but he will remain where he is, and has forever been, an inhabitant of the East, nurturing stagnant ideas and seeing no further than the narrow doctrines of Mohammed."[20]

On December 2, 1917, Meinertzhagen wrote from Rishon-le-Zion, having arrived there in the van of General Allenby's now steadily advancing British Army. But the Balfour Declaration had already had its effect on the Jewish community in Palestine, and on Eshkol in particular. It ended the period of doubt about taking part in the war, with discretion having so far tilted the balance in favor of inactivity. Eshkol welcomed the Declaration without reservation; it seemed to him to presage an era of hope and progress, in which the Jewish community in Palestine, so poor and isolated in the past, would have a strong protector and patron. He reduced the issue to its simplest form: "My view was that Britain was now going to fight for Israel, and that we should therefore be ready to fight for Britain."[21]

Both Paolei Zion and Hapoel Hatzair were continuing to preach a policy of patience and passive neutrality, at least until the British armies had finally routed the Turks. Eshkol disagreed; he was all for action, arguing for the need to win the gratitude of the Allies by serving on their side. According to one of his contemporaries, "In spite of opposition . . . Levi Shkolnik volunteered. He had been struggling with himself. He recoiled from militarism, even in the form of a Jewish Battalion. But he saw that our volunteering would give new strength to our historic bond and was convinced of the rightness of our fighting."[22] He volunteered to establish contact with the advancing British, by slipping through the Turkish lines and making his way southward from Petach Tikva.

His own memory of this exploit was as follows:

> We say that the Lord preserves the simple, and I certainly had need of his protection. I hadn't much idea where I was going, and the first thing that happened was that I blundered straight into a line of Turkish trenches. I was challenged and I mumbled an answer that I was going on to Rishon for work. They waved me on, as they could see I was unarmed. Then came another set of trenches, and again I was allowed through.
>
> The next thing I knew was that I had bumped into an Australian cavalry patrol. They took me along for questioning, and let me go when some of the Jews of Rishon identified me as a fellow settler. The next day there was a battle, somewhere on the outskirts of Rishon. When it was over, I saw its consequences—the dead lying here and there. I helped to bury them. I remember an Australian kneeling at his comrade's grave and praying.[23]

Eshkol volunteered for service in the British Army. About 50 other settlers from Rishon and the immediate neighborhood did likewise. They went into camp, were fitted out with British uniforms, and began their training. Most of them spoke scarcely a word of English. This led to altercations with their ultra-British NCO's, and Horace Samuel recalls one of the latter continually shouting: "Don't talk that 'orrible cannibal language, speak English!"[24] The British NCO's, indeed, tended to regard all Jews as "bloody," and two of them refused to share a tent with Alexandrian Jews on the obscure grounds that they had been "with natives" before and had found that they disturbed them "at their devotions."[25]

British officers attached to the newly formed Palestinian units had their complaints, too. One was heard to remark that "we have more trouble with one Jewish company than we do with ten Irish regiments"; while another produced a curious theory that Jews were "niggers" because they were "heathens," whereas Christian Arabs were "white men."*

One British officer had a surprising confrontation when he paid a visit to a Palestinian-Jewish barracks late one evening. The sentry on duty was a small, dark Yemenite Jew who had not been able to speak a word of English when he joined up. Since then, he had been busily trying to master the wording of routine orders as well as whatever extra words of English he thought might be useful to him. Quite properly, he challenged the visiting British officer with a wild shout of "Halt! Who goes there?"

"Friend," the officer answered and he could see the Yemenite's small face peering at him in the twilight as he desperately searched his mind for the next phrase he had to use. Then, "Advance friend, and be circumsized!" he cried at the amazed subaltern.[26]

Most of the Palestinians were sent to the training camps first in the area of El Arish in the Sinai peninsula, and later in Egypt near Tel-el-Kebir. Eshkol was drafted as Private L. Shkolnik, No. J.4696, in the 39th battalion of the Royal Fusiliers which was being formed. Sturdy Palestinian Jews were mixed in together with the often stunted, sallow-faced recruits from the East End of London, who were manifestly lost in the deserts of the Middle East. Former sergeant Jacob Halevy asked one of them, named Goldberg, if he was not excited to be in "the land of milk and honey." Goldberg's answer was to scoop up some sandy soil, and say, "Land of *what?* This is muck, bloody muck!" The Palestinians for their part were regarded as highly eccentric when, after firing one of their Lewis guns on a practice shoot, they carefully collected the empty cartridge cases so that they should not be wasted.[27] The Palestinians, again, were scandalized by what Samuel described as a "drunken brigadier" who announced that the venerated Wailing Wall in Jerusalem was "the place where the Jews wagged their bottoms," and the London Jews complained about the lugubrious whine of the Zionist anthem, the "Hatikvah."

The 39th was certainly unlike any other unit of the British Army. Twenty of its soldiers, who were assigned to guarding an ammunition dump, bought 250 books with their pay, in order to spend their off-duty hours improving their minds. Instead of regimental singing, there were

---

* In his *Middle East Diary*, Colonel Richard Meinertzhagen tells a fantastic story of the inspection of the first Jewish battalion by an anti-Semitic brigadier. He found one man with dirty buttons and called him a "dirty little Jew." The commanding officer, Colonel J. H. Patterson, ordered the battalion to fix bayonets and form a square around the brigadier, not letting him out until he apologized! The brigadier reported the incident but for his pains was returned to duty in India from where he had been seconded (*Middle East Diary*, p. 48).

discussion groups where there was much political and philosophical talk which must have made hardened British NCO's want to pinch themselves to see if they were dreaming. Soon after the end of the war there was a mutiny, when the 39th was ordered to Cyprus, and the men's spokesman offered "to clean all the latrines of the whole British army if we are allowed to stay in our own country."[28]

There was a sense of destiny and fulfillment about these Jewish soldiers, too. Here is a description of a New Year's Day service in 1918 near Gaza:

> The number and variety of Jews who gathered were remarkable—over 300 officers and men, some from England, Scotland, and Wales, others from France, still others of Russian origin; some from the Overseas Dominions and from the Orient. The hut of the YMCA was not big enough, and we held the service in an open field under the blue sky, overlooking the blue sea and the blue hills. The reading of the Bible for the day tells of the sojourn of Abraham in this land of the Philistines; and we had to bear witness to the faith of the Jews in the fields over which the Patriarch ruled as a Sheik. The Hebrew scroll from which we read the story had accompanied the Zion Mule Corps to Gallipoli, and come back to Alexandria unscathed. It seemed to us as the Ark of the Covenant to our ancestors in the days of Samuel.

A third Jewish batallion, the 40th Royal Fusiliers, was formed, but none of the three battalions saw actual combat service. This was not the fault of their keen and efficient volunteers, who suspected the British authorities of keeping them on guard duties and transport service so as not to be too much beholden to them. Eshkol himself had a checkered military career before being demobilized more than a year after the end of the war. His own story was that he "had lost three stripes" since he was first demoted from the rank of acting lance-corporal (allegedly because he refused promotion, fearing that it would separate him from his fellow soldiers), then demoted a second time from corporal to private soldier. Eshkol's account of this second incident was that he "had overstayed his leave" when he was allowed to attend the ceremony of the laying of the foundation stone of the Hebrew University in Jerusalem by Lord Balfour. He was put in the stockade for having been absent without leave, court-martialed, and duly "broken."[29] It would have been very hard to explain to a British military court just what the symbolic ceremony on Mount Scopus meant to a young, intensely idealistic Jew.

For Eshkol it was a memorable day. The symbolism of the occasion was matched by the grandeur of the natural scenery.

> Around me a vast half bowl, carved out of the mountain side and ringed with stone benches, was alive from base to rim with the

motley Jewish nation. Beneath me dropped an abyss, a ten-mile plunge of white rock and grey sand to the ribbon of the Jordan and the blue mirror of the Dead Sea—four thousand feet below as a stone falls. Across the chasm, as a backdrop for the speaker's platform, the cliffs of Moab burned 30 miles away in purple and bronze.[30]

Eshkol continued as a plain private soldier until the end of his military service. Later, his military service in what was, after all, a foreign army, must have seemed pure waste of time. He had learned something about the use of arms, and about the value of military discipline. He was described by his contemporaries as a good soldier, who did his duty willingly and well. His drill, his marksmanship, his acquired knowledge of elementary infantry tactics, would all stand him in good stead in the years ahead, when the Jewish community would have to organize an army of its own. And Eshkol liked to recall that he had achieved at least a higher rank than his later mentor and political leader, David Ben-Gurion. The latter ended only as a lance-corporal, possibly because he was better at giving orders than receiving or transmitting them. The British army was perhaps not the best place for individualists in the ranks. But he dearly wanted to get on with the business of living, which entailed in particular the building up of the Jewish community in Palestine and the translation of the thought implicit in the Balfour Declaration into solid achievement.

1. Joseph Baratz, *A Village by the Jordan*, p. 86.
2. Walter Preuss, *The Labour Movement in Israel*, p. 35.
3. Rachel Ben Zvi, *Coming Home*, p. 308.
4. Eshkol, in personal conversation with the author.
5. Horace Samuel, *Unholy Memories of the Holy Land*, p. 2.
6. *Ibid.*, p. 11.
7. Maurice Edelman, *Ben Gurion*, p. 69.
8. Samuel, *op. cit.*, p. 12.
9. Eshkol, in personal conversation with the author.
10. Marvin Lowenthal, *The Diaries of Theodor Herzl*, p. 177.
11. Isaiah Berlin, *Chaim Weizmann*, p. 4.
12. *Ibid.*, p. 11.
13. Chaim Weizmann, *Trial and Error*, p. 123.
14. Meyer Weisgal, ed., *Chaim Weizmann*, p. 132.
15. Berlin, *op. cit.*, p. 31.
16. Jon Kimche, *The Unromantics. The Great Powers and the Balfour Declaration*, introduction, p. ix.
17. *Ibid.*, p. x.
18. Blanche Drysdale's chapter in *Chaim Weizmann*, edited by Meyer Weisgal, p. 145.
19. Weizmann, *op. cit.*, p. 260.
20. Col. Richard Meinertzhagen, *Middle East Diary*, p. 6.
21. Eshkol, in personal conversation with the author.

22. Ben Zvi, *op. cit.*, p. 342.
23. Eshkol, in personal conversation with the author.
24. Samuel, *op. cit.*, p. 15.
25. *Ibid.*, p. 22.
26. Told to the author by Jacob Halevy, a former sergeant in the Palestinian unit in question.
27. Samuel, *op. cit.*, p. 19.
28. Told to the author by Jacob Halevy.
29. Eshkol, in personal conversation with the author.
30. Lowenthal, *op. cit.*, p. 151.

4.

For Eshkol, demobilization from the British Army meant the possibility of returning immediately to the land. During the last, purposeless months in the 39th Royal Fusiliers he had thought of nothing else.

A golden opportunity presented itself at Degania, on the southern shore of the Sea of Galilee.

The pioneer collectivized farm, or *kibbutz,* of Degania had survived the war, but only with the utmost difficulty. It remained in Turkish-occupied territory almost to the end. Communications were disrupted; famine stalked the land. In order to feed themselves, the settlers switched from mixed farming back to growing grain; they had little else besides some plots of vegetables and a few scraggy chickens. With approximately 20 families in the settlement, it meant hiring Arab labor for the harvesting—something that the Degania settlers loathed doing. Their life was a grim struggle most of the time, and during the war years the only exciting events, apart from the repelling of an occasional foray by hungry Bedouin, were births of their children. Joseph Baratz described the wild excitement over the birth of the very first child at Degania; everybody wanted to play with him and he was "shared" among settlers for visits to their huts. By the time there were four children, a nursery was organized, so that three of the four mothers could go on working in the fields. According to Baratz, "Our fears that the children would suffer from the life or the climate proved wrong. The children are fine. The swamps have been dried, the climate has changed. It is hot but the children like it. They run barefoot in summer when the earth is like fire; and it doesn't worry them, because this is where they were born and bred."[1]

However arduous their life became, the settlers remained supremely confident. They had developed a deep-rooted sense of community. One pioneer, arriving at the end of the war in Palestine, described this sense of community in these terms: "Fraternalism between Jew and Jew in those days was so thick you could almost taste it. Perfect strangers were ready to accept each other as brothers; they literally gave each other the shirts off their backs."[2]

The settlers at Degania were still imbued with the enthusiasm of Aaron David Gordon's personal example. Baratz described this quiet, saintly man as looking "like one of those rabbis Rembrandt used to paint." Already middle-aged when he arrived at Degania, so frail that he did not look fit to wield a heavy pick, Gordon preached love for the soil and its ability to turn despair into happiness. "He thought that every nation must have in it people who work on the land and who have a living relationship with the soil and with nature: people who truly know the joy of a good harvest, and the grief of a poor crop, and the changing of the seasons."[3] To Gordon, this relationship to the soil was to be the salvation of the Jewish people who in his opinion had become, through no fault of their own, parasitic and rootless.

In 1920 the Degania settlers, anxious to keep their community reasonably small, found that they had too much land on their hands. They had returned to mixed farming after the war, and their farming was becoming more intensive. Their grant (it became the usual procedure for the Jewish National Fund, the *Keren Kayemet,* to buy land for settlers and lease it to them for 99 years) was of 3000 dunams (4 dunams = 1 acre). Degania decided to hand over 1000 dunams to each of two other kibbutzim. The first of these was to be named Degania B or Bet, while the "mother of the kibbutzim" called itself Degania A or Aleph. The second was later named Beit Zera. The three settlements were to become the kernel of the biggest single area of collectivized farming in Palestine, the so-called "republic of the kibbutzim," with settlements on three sides of the Sea of Galilee and along the banks of the river Jordan to the north and south of it.

Degania B began, according to Eshkol, with 18 young men and two girls. Most of them were already his personal friends, but Eshkol was now the only surviving member, in Palestine, of the party of ten young men who had started out from Trieste seven years before. The nucleus of this group of founder-members at Degania B had been formed by Eshkol during the war years, in Petach Tikva, Atarot, and Rishon, before he joined the British army. He seems to have been very much the accepted leader in the new venture, a born committeeman, a careful but determined planner, with a special gift of being able to get on with people, chiefly because he liked them. Eshkol himself remembered being inhibited by only one circumstance in those early days at Degania: "We could laugh and joke with the girls, but we had a holy horror of marriage. We were literally scared of having families, for we didn't know how the children would be looked after. We led the lives of monks."[4]

The Degania B settlers belonged to the labor group of Kvutzat Avodah. They shared common political and ethical beliefs, in practical socialism and in humanitarian ideals. They also wanted to keep a homogeneity of political and social thinking in their settlement and they did not want to overexpand by accepting new members who might not fit in. However, they quickly found that they needed new recruits and within a few months they had doubled their number to 40. Whereas the first 20 were, like Eshkol, all settlers of the pre-1914 Second Aliyah, the newcomers belonged to the post-1919 Third Aliyah, or third wave of pioneers. Most of this third wave was from Poland; and most of the group which joined Degania B were from the town and neighborhood of Bobruisk. They had begun working not far from Degania, on the Tiberias-Zemach road.

The first task of the settlers was, obviously, to feed themselves and to sell enough of their produce to buy farm implements, seed, and livestock. So at first they grew mainly wheat and barley as "cash crops"; and they began operations with two mules and a small cart. Part of the day the mules and the cart were used to bring water from the Jordan, a few hundred yards from where the first huts were built. The mules got to know the way so well that when a settler who was doing this for the first time went with them, they dragged him on to the usual filling point at the water's edge. After some months the Palestine Settlement Office gave the settlers some old pipes from abandoned Turkish or British army dumps. The settlers were in the process of putting up more permanent buildings in place of their huts, and there were just enough pipes to bring water from the Jordan to a water tower which they had built on the edge of the settlement.

The settlement was a modest one. There were a couple of two-story buildings where most of the settlers slept. Some of the younger men lived above the single long cowshed, which at first housed only farm implements and the mules. Ground was cleared to plant a small orchard, and two more houses were built beyond it. The orchard was destined, long afterward, to be turned into lawns and gardens in the middle of the settlement. There was a tiny communal dining room, next to a primitive kitchen. Sanitation consisted of earth privies, and washing facilities of a single showerbath. The latter was a makeshift affair, which involved careful balancing and tilting of a five-gallon can filled with warm water.

The standard of living was low but was cheerfully accepted. Only very few of those hardy early settlers found conditions too hard and drifted away to towns. They threshed their wheat like the Arabs, with flails, and baked their own bread. To begin with, their staple food was lentil soup, three times a day. Even two years after Degania B had been founded, its settlers did not expect to see more than a morsel of meat once in ten days. But by then, they had their own cows and were eating butter and sour-milk cheese.

The first water faucets were not installed until 1924, and even then hand pumps had to be worked to bring water to the upper stories of their living quarters. Photographs taken in 1921 and 1922 show a half-dozen buildings standing in isolation among bare fields. There was not a tree in sight. For the first three years there were droughts, hampering the early efforts at introducing irrigation by means of narrow open irrigation ditches through the fields. The settlers had very little practical knowledge of farming; they sometimes went to their neighbors at Degania A for advice, sometimes to Arab farmers. A major event was the installation of a small motor pump for bringing water from the Jordan; another was the birth of Degania B's first baby. It was a very hard life, but they throve on it.

Eshkol organized the settlement's first budget. It was his idea that settlers should do odd jobs in the neighborhood, on the roads, and on other farms, so that a little more money could be earned for communal needs. He was responsible for vegetables being grown on a big scale, which led to the planting of citrus and banana groves. A chicken hatchery was built, and the first flowers were planted. And Eshkol took the lead in organizing the defense of the settlement. The local Arabs were friendly enough, but there was a tradition of thieving, which was looked upon more as an occupational hazard than a crime. Bedouin tribesmen occasionally raided Arab as well as Jewish farms, and opposite Degania B in the hills was the notorious Wadi Fijas transit route from the Jordan valley to lower Galilee, where bands of Arab robbers frequently attacked travelers. The Degania settlers mounted guards at night and took rifles out to the fields when they went plowing.

According to his fellow settlers, Eshkol was a natural leader in these early days. He had a hand in everything, was interested in everything. He showed tremendous persistence and patience, and was a perfectionist in everything he did. His human qualities were immensely valuable; he was always ready to give and to take advice. He was a practical man who came to grips with material problems in a practical way, who had a real interest in his fellow settlers, and who loved hard work and the soil.

"Eshkol," according to one contemporary, "was a rock. We had a lot to compete with in those days. The work often became humdrum. There were always the same faces around. We were very isolated, and sometimes we felt very lonely. Here was a man who planned, worked, explained, and laughed a lot." And another view of Eshkol was:

> He was just about the best that the "shtetl" and its way of life produced. The two qualities I would pick out were huge enthusiasm and absolute loyalty to his fellow Jews. Sometimes in the "shtetl" enthusiasm lapsed into fanaticism, but there was nothing of that about Eshkol. He was always a liberal in making allowances for others while expecting the maximum of himself. Where his own work was concerned, he was a camel who could carry almost any load.

Eshkol introduced tugs of war to build up physical strength and competitions in carrying 50-pound sacks. A fellow settler, Kadish Luz, recounted how he and Eshkol had had an all-day competition in loading carts with manure and taking them on their rounds of the fields. At the close of the day both men were utterly exhausted, their faces streaked with sweat and dirt, their shirts limp as wet blotting paper. The tally of their day's work was checked, and it was found that Eshkol had won, by a cartload of manure. His only comment was, "I was lucky." He never was a man to praise himself.

Degania B ranked in every way as a fairly typical kibbutz at this point, and it might be appropriate to say something about the kibbutz movement as a whole, what it stood for and what it still stands for. In his book *Kibbutz: Venture in Utopia* Melford Spiro describes the kibbutz as "a fellowship of those who share a common faith and who have banded together to implement that faith."[5] Or in more concrete terms, the kibbutz movement was an essay in practical communism. Once accepted, all members were equal. They undertook to carry out any work assigned to them by the management of the kibbutz, and they shared equally in the product of that work. All members of the kibbutz were, in theory, "self-employed," for the management was nothing more than a committee which they themselves appointed. "The principle of self-employment," according to one authority on the kibbutz movement, "has its roots in the beginnings of Jewish settlement in Palestine. It stems from the desire of the settlers to foster the productivity of the Jewish nation and to turn its creative energy towards occupations based on manual labor."[6]

The members of the kibbutz did not merely believe in the principles of social justice; they implemented those principles in everyday life. The motto of the kibbutz movement as a whole is "From each according to his ability, to each according to his needs." A member would give of his best, and in return he would be looked after completely, from birth, if he were the son of a kibbutznik, until death. The kibbutz provided education for its young and medical attention for its sick. It provided food, clothes, and lodging for every member. Its members were members for life, although they could leave at any time if they wished, and they were looked after in their old age. There was no "retiring age," for members even in their 80s might be asked to lend a hand with small and light jobs. If a member left the kibbutz, he could take only a few small personal belongings with him, although he would be given a sum of money to tide him over the period during which he would be seeking employment outside the kibbutz. Money, generally speaking, played a small part in the life of the kibbutz; members were given small sums for pocket money only, for the earnings of the kibbutz were mainly used for buying food, seed, farm equipment, and everything else which the settlement needed.

These general conditions were common to every kibbutz. There were variations in some phases of their existence. In some, for instance, all clothing was shared, at least during the initial period of their existence. Often, this became unpopular with the women of the kibbutz, who set store on their personal appearance and had a natural desire to make themselves as attractive as possible. The practice of sharing clothes was dropped gradually in almost all kibbutzim.

Again, there were and still are differences over the upbringing of children. In most kibbutzim children were put into nurseries as soon as their mothers ceased to breast-feed them, and were in due course transferred from the nursery to the children's house. This meant that normally they would see their parents only during the "family hour" in the late afternoon or early evening. But some kibbutzim allowed children to sleep in the family apartment, usually a three-or-more-room bungalow. Degania B was one of these.

The practice of hiring outside labor was frowned upon and usually forbidden. But some kibbutzim expanded their fields of activity faster than their membership. When it was obviously profitable to do so, they hired outside labor. It was, of course, Jewish, so that the general principle of helping to build a "balanced" Jewish community was not traduced.

Melford Spiro picked out a number of thoughts underlying the kibbutz movement. Thus, the moral value of labor was an implicit belief and labor was an end in itself. In the shtetl of the Jewish Pale of Settlement, the *proste,* or vulgar, were those who worked with their hands; the kibbutz, in direct contrast, dignified manual labor. Indeed some kibbutzim experienced a certain revulsion against the life of the shtetl, which they came to regard as being one of *pilpul,* or casuistry.

Spartan ideals were readily adopted by the early settlers. They wanted to set high standards of personal behavior, and there was a reaction against all emblems of comfort, such as smart clothes, strong drink, tobacco, and even the ownership of personal possessions. There was a reaction, too, against sexual license. The feeling that "frontiersmen should live hard" was often somewhat overdone; in some kibbutzim there was active opposition to quite modest improvements in living standards, expressed in the fear that life might become too soft. Sometimes, members objected to hot food as being a luxury.

There was a much-vaunted belief in comradeship. The fellow member was a comrade or *chaver,* whom one treated as a brother. Spiro pointed out that the cult of comradeship sometimes broke down, for brotherly love was not always easy to practice among poeple who lived in so great a contiguity and who were liable to get on each other's nerves. Furious arguments were apt to break out, especially in communal meeting places, such as the dining hall and the shower room, and men sometimes "became blue with rage."[7]

The kibbutz members were generally keen to pursue strictly intellectual interests, and in most kibbutzim there was a lively cultural life, with discussion groups, books, artistic pursuits, music, and later on, films and plays. "The chaver is more than a farmer. He is a farmer with intellectual interests, which is to say that he is not a farmer at all."[8]

Finally, in some kibbutzim there was a veneration for the Soviet Union and the Soviet system. That was natural. The kibbutz movement, after all, practiced pure communism, and its members could hardly be aware of the impurities of the communist system in the Soviet Union.

For a long time there was even a belief in the wisdom and goodness of Josef Stalin, and Spiro suggests that the destruction of their faith in the Soviet Union could shake the faith of the kibbutznikim in their own, unique experiment.[9] This, as it happens, has not occurred.

Eshkol's own view on matters of this sort was pragmatic and practical. He certainly subscribed fully to the belief in manual labor, which he considered made a real man out of the most sedentary Jew. He did not for a moment lose his affection for the shtetl, even gratitude to it for having sheltered him as far as it could. Eshkol was always ready to work until he dropped, but did not venerate Spartan ideals for their own sake. His own sense of comradeship was easy and unaffected, and he did not, like some of his fellows, regard the kibbutz as a refuge from the world and all its evils but as a practical experiment of tremendous value to the whole Jewish community in Palestine.

Without any false sentiment, Eshkol told me of his love for Degania B, where he found friendship and happiness and where he achieved what he set out to do. His fellow members tried to persuade him to stay on, when the time arrived for him to leave. He was made an "honorary" member for life, with the right to retain his own small, neatly but sparsely furnished bungalow. He repaid this gift by giving talks on the political scene and advice on practical problems whenever he returned to Degania. He told me, obviously in all sincerity, that he would like to leave his bones there when he died.

The sense of achievement of Eshkol and his chaverim was undoubtedly heightened by the toughness of their struggle during the early years. One of the chaverim was Yehudah Almog, and Howard Sachar had this to say of him in his book *The People of Israel:* "The land appeared hopelessly barren, and the opportunities for productive settlement seemed almost negligible. But Yehudah and his companions grimly dug in. For several months their only regular article of diet was dried greens. Several of the men came down with malaria, others with typhoid. Yehudah himself lost 20 pounds in the first 60 days—and exulted in the work."[10]

It is still a matter of doubt whether the kibbutz movement would have succeeded but for the financial help which came from the Jewish National Fund. There were a dozen kibbutzim in existence toward the end of World War I, and their number grew rapidly after it had ended. But so did their debts. They amounted to $235,000 in 1921. Three years later they had climbed to $610,000. This represented a loss of 20 percent on a capital investment of $2,610,000.[11] Some kibbutzim folded up. Even by 1931 the total population of the kibbutzim was only 4400, or 2.5 percent of the Jewish community in Palestine. The kibbutz movement was probably saved by the big influx of Jewish immigrants in the 1930s, which gave them a sufficient market for their farm produce. And after World War II the movement expanded even faster. Its population reached 70,000 by 1952, and stabilized at close to 100,000 in the 1960s.

Long before then the kibbutz movement could have been said to have succeeded in the broad sense. It had restored a section of the Jewish community to the soil, and prepared the way for other forms of settlement on the land, in particular for the *moshavim* or farming cooperatives. It had shown the way to the establishment of a "balanced" Jewish community, and had banished the prospect of its becoming a nation of middlemen, living sedentary lives and trading comfortably and profitably at this crossroads of Europe, Africa, and Asia. The kibbutz movement, too, had embodied in itself the virtues and the idealism of pioneering; it was an adventure, which prompted other sections of the community to be appropriately adventurous, to experiment, probe, and progress. Finally, the kibbutz movement had a potential military value which was to be exploited in the 1948 War of Independence. For defense, as well as for all other purposes, the kibbutz was a self-contained unit. During the war the kibbutzim became strong points of particular strategic value because so many of them were in frontier areas.

Of course, kibbutz life has its flaws too. There is a hint of claustrophobia about it. Naturally, there are big advantages in living only a few minutes' walk from one's work and in the pooling of labor. But human beings generally desire and need an element of change in their lives. To live and work in the same place can be mentally debilitating. Again, young people are usually ambitious and usually look for some sort of glamor in their lives. Ambition does drive some of the younger members of the kibbutzim into the outside world, especially after they have lived in it during their period of compulsory military service. The expanding world of commerce and industry is to some extent a magnet. The only glamor which the kibbutz can offer is the ideal of service to the community and, in most cases, scenic beauty. One acute observer wrote that "the ideal of the kibbutzim has been fulfilled, and now they have little to look forward to. . . . There is always a great deal of frustration in the fulfillment of dreams."[12]

Degania B, at all events, had, by 1969, come a long way since its foundation half a century earlier. Although this is chronologically out of place, some account of its progress can best be given here if only to illustrate the contrast between the Degania B of the 1920s and of the 1960s. By 1969 the kibbutz had 310 members, and some 150 children under 18 and therefore not yet qualified for membership. Its total annual turnover was approximately 6 million Israeli pounds, or $1.7 million. It grew grain, vegetables, citrus fruits, grapes, bananas, of the latter alone 2000 tons a year. The farm had 800 head of cattle, 250 of them dairy cows, a chicken farm and an industrial enterprise producing spraying machines and employing 40 workers. Productivity per capita, according to the management, was at least 15 percent above the national average.

More apartments were being built, some with three bedrooms as well as a living room. The dining hall at Degania B is probably one of the best in any kibbutz. There are a swimming pool and a football field. The place is beautiful too, with well kept lawns and flower beds, gay little bungalows with their own gardens, and fine views of the Sea of Galilee, snow-capped Mount Hermon, and the highlands of Syria.

Eshkol was intensely proud of Degania B; to him its foundation represented the first stage in the realization of the high hopes with which he had sailed for Palestine in 1914. He was fond of quoting Psalm 126, "When the Lord turned the captivity of Zion, we were like them that dream." The episode of Degania B was to have a special significance in his life, for the settlement of the whole land was later to become his principal preoccupation. These early postwar years were formative for him in other ways too. They saw the beginning of his active career both in politics and in the Jewish trade union movement in Palestine.

There were no political parties in the strict meaning of the word before 1914. The nearest approach to a party was the *Agudat Israel,* a religious grouping which called for the strict observance of the precepts and practices established under the Torah, for the maintenance of rabbinical jurisdiction and promotion of Jewish education based on religion. In 1919 the founding congress was held at Petach Tikva of *Achdut Ha'avoda,* or Unity of Labor. Its purpose was to unite Jewish labor in Palestine under a political banner. Eshkol was entirely in favor of its principal aim, but he did not attend the congress as a member or delegate. The reason was the attitude of his own pioneering group, Hapoel Hatzair. Eshkol explained the position as follows:

> That wonderful group of men and thinkers in Hapoel Hatzair who were my guides and mentors, and who developed important elements in the ideology of the Jewish workers—the principle of labor, labor settlement, Hebrew culture, a working nation, and a new society—that wonderful group was wrong on one point, namely the question of unity. In its devotion to its principles and the integrity of its ideals, it did not venture to join the union after World War I, so that the unification of the parties was delayed by a decade or more, in fact until 1930.

Hapoel Hatzair wanted to remain outside formal politics, for its leaders had not forgotten their traditional rivalry with Poalei Zion, which now became the nucleus of the new Achdut Ha'avoda.

Some Hapoel Hatzair leaders, like Joseph Sprinzak, were ready to contemplate a step by step union with the new party. Sprinzak's view was that "life itself will unite us." Others were adamant. Somewhat ironically, Eshkol—the chief protagonist of unity—was given the unwelcome duty of informing the Congress of Hapoel Hatzair's negative decision. "I presented the negative reply with a heavy heart and despite my conviction that immediate unity was possible."[13] His own view remained that there was no contradiction between the aims of the congress and the aims of his own group. There was only a difference of emphasis. The congress wanted a political formulation for the labor movement and for the assertion of socialist principles, while Hapoel Hatzair wanted the Jewish worker to become an entrenched and dominant element in all branches of the Jewish economy. Eshkol never altered his views; he was to assert them successfully later on, when he became the principal architect of labor unity.

For a very obvious reason, party politics did not play a major role in Palestine until after World War II. Palestine had been under British rule since the Turkish army was forced out of the country, and General Allenby, with marked tact and good taste, insisted on entering Jerusalem on foot at the head of his victorious forces. In July 1922 the League of Nations confirmed the British mandate over Palestine, which in effect made Britain the trustee power in the area. The League, at the same time, recognized the Balfour Declaration and, with it, the historical connection of the Jewish people with Palestine and their right to reestablish their national home in that country. British rule made the formation of political parties, whether Jewish or Arab, somewhat superfluous, for the single early effort to introduce some sort of representative government under the aegis of the British high commissioner failed completely. More of this later. Yet Jewish interest in political ideas was able to find some expression. The Israel Labor Party, *Mapai*, was founded in 1930 and later became the single most important party in the field. A second religious political group, *Poalei Agudat Israel*, was formed, with virtually exactly the same program as its rival, *Agudat Israel*. An old witticism insists that a Jew on a desert island would first found a synagogue, then found another, in order to have a chance of resigning from the first. An embryonic Communist Party existed from 1919 onward.

Jewish political power resided mainly outside the borders of Palestine. The World Zionist Organization had bases primarily in the United States and Britain, and Chaim Weizmann became its president in 1920. The organization decided that the Jewish National Fund should be the sole instrument of Jewish land policy in Palestine, and the Fund's resources were applied through *Keren Hayesod,* Foundation Fund, for buying land and leasing it to Jewish settlers. The JNF had its own immigration office and agricultural settlement department in Palestine.

In 1921 the Twelfth Zionist Congress held in Carlsbad elected a 13-man executive for Palestine which became the Jewish Agency. This organization was recognized by the League of Nations as the representative organ of Zionism most concerned with the social, political, cultural, and economic interests of the Jewish community in Palestine. The Jewish Agency had two executive branches, in London and Jerusalem. London had been chosen because Britain administered the Palestine Mandate. The Jewish Agency contained the embryo of a Jewish government, for it dealt with every field of activity of the Jewish community and was essentially a policy-making institution. Nothing more need be written here about the World Zionist Organization and the Jewish Agency, but their importance to the building of the Jewish national home cannot be exaggerated. These two bodies produced spokesmen of Jewish aims as well as practical planners to realize them.

One other Jewish organization deserves to be mentioned rather particularly because Eshkol played some part in its foundation. This was the *Histadrut,* or General Federation of Labor. It was formed in December 1920, with a mere 5000 members out of a total Jewish population of over 100,000. It was something more than a trade union, for among its principal aims there were the stimulation of large-scale immigration, employment service for immigrants, and the actual creation of a broadly based working class, in a country where formerly there had been only scattered agricultural settlements and rudiments of industry. Because of these additional aims and responsibilities, the Histadrut became one of the pillars of the Jewish community. Its rapid growth was assured as soon as large-scale immigration began. For the new immigrants were found gainful employment as fast as they arrived and were forced to look beyond the small shops, stands, and pushcarts of the typical Jewish small trader.

Jokingly, Eshkol told me that the Palestine of the early 1920s was the most mixed-up country in the world. "It was a land without water, which had a majority of Arab inhabitants, laws handed down by Turkey, a British administration and an Egyptian currency." This suggests a chaotic picture, and it has become conventional to denigrate the British mandate because of its political confusions and failures. In reality, the British were excellent administrators. In Palestine they built schools and hospitals, roads and railways, and helped to create conditions under which the country made giant strides economically after centuries of neglect and stagnation. The British, and they have been much blamed for this by Arab critics, allowed Jewish institutions to grow and become steadily more representative and more lasting. The result was progress which was often dynamic. Professor Norman Bentwich, a Jew who served under the British mandate, put it in a nutshell—"Before 1914 you wondered how anything ever got done. After 1919 you expected the most grandiose plans to be carried out in a night and a day."[14]

There was one curious episode in Eshkol's life during these early postwar years. Self-defense was, obviously, a vital problem for the Jewish community. One would have expected a great deal of military equipment to have fallen into the hands of the settlers at the end of the war while the Turkish Army was retreating out of the country. But it would appear that the Arabs at that stage were more adept than the

Jews in laying their hands on whatever was to be had. By 1921 Arab raidings of Jewish settlements were becoming endemic, and Eshkol together with Eliahu Golomb was sent to Vienna to procure arms. They were joined by a third "gunrunner," David Hacohen, but all three were caught one day packing rifles in a warehouse in a suburb of the city. By a curious dispensation, Golomb and Eshkol were set free, while Hacohen, who had only been coopted by them when he arrived in Vienna, was sent to jail for a month.

For some reason, Eshkol was reticent about that affair and never himself gave either the place or date of it. He preferred to speak of it as having happened "somewhere in Central Europe."

> It was like something out of a thriller. We were staying in a quiet, dingy hotel on one of the side streets. First we established contact with a Mr. X, who introduced us to a Mr. Y. Then we had a rendezvous with a Mr. Z, who arranged to have a consignment of pistols, rifles, and ammunition delivered to us.
>
> So far, so good! But the next step looked a lot more difficult —getting the arms back to Palestine. We decided that the best way would be to smuggle them inside crates of agricultural machinery. What we couldn't know was that the porter in the building was an informer, working for the local secret service. Just when everything seemed nicely wrapped up and ready for dispatch, the police walked in and put us out of business. That meant an expulsion order for me, with a special clause banning me from ever entering the country again.
>
> This was all in a day's work. But the trouble was that the whole business slipped my mind until I was sent years later as a delegate to a congress in that same Central European capital. I had the pleasure of attending the opening session, but that was all. The following morning two burly plainclothes policemen walked into my hotel and asked to see my passport.

Eshkol was sent on another trip to Europe during that same period. He had had recurrent bouts of malaria at Degania B, like many of the other settlers. He had a powerful physique and plenty of that quality which the Germans call *Ausdauer,* the ability to stick it out, to keep going, to last. An old cure for malaria is a change of air, and his friends in Hapoel Hatzair decided to send him to Lithuania. There, he could kill two birds with one stone—get well, and talk to the members of Zionist youth movements about the need for new settlers in Palestine. Eshkol had the right personality for this; he was tireless in discussion, immensely patient in explaining things, and genuinely in love with the soil and the task of cultivating it. His work in Lithuania, where he lived very simply in a rented bed-sittingroom and read voraciously in his spare time, was thoroughly successful. There were around 170,000 Jews in Lithuania, mostly keenly Zionist, well educated, and independent-minded. Some of the best of the immigrants into Palestine came from there, and one group settled at the Beit Zera kibbutz, next door to Degania B.

He also paid a fleeting visit to Moscow, to attend a Cooperative Congress in Moscow. When called upon to speak, he addressed the meeting in Hebrew. This was regarded as a "Zionist demonstration" and he was advised to leave Moscow at once. He was disappointed in the place. He had imagined Moscow to be the center of social progress and social justice, and expected to find this reflected in the happiness and well-being of its people. He was not prepared for its drabness and lack of laughter. He had another reason for disappointment; he had hoped to visit his family in the Ukraine, but his premature departure made this impossible. His father, as it happened, was already dead. He had been killed in 1917 at a time when bands of armed ragamuffins of all kinds, Bolsheviks, White Guard reactionaries, or just plain bandits, roamed the land. Eshkol's father sent the rest of the family into a nearby town for safety, but himself refused to leave Oratowo. A party of bandits came upon him while he was in the fields and struck him down with an axe. Eshkol's brother Benjamin heard the news, carried the corpse away, and gave it a decent burial.

1. Joseph Baratz, *A Village by the Jordan*, p. 70.
2. Howard Sachar, *Aliya, The People of Israel*, p. 171.
3. Baratz, *op. cit.*, p. 83.
4. Eshkol, in personal conversation with the author.
5. Melford E. Spiro, *Kibbutz. Venture in Utopia*, p. 10.
6. H. Darin-Drabkin, *The Other Society*, p. 93.
7. Spiro, *op. cit.*, p. 105.
8. *Ibid.*, p. 163.
9. *Ibid.*, p. 185.
10. Sachar, *op. cit.*, p. 173.
11. Darin-Drabkin, *op. cit.*, pp. 71 ff.
12. George Mikes, *Milk and Honey: Israel Explored*, p. 26.
13. Eshkol, in personal conversation with the author.
14. In personal conversation with the author.

5.

This book is concerned, in the first instance, with the life and times of Eshkol and with his major part in the building and consolidation of the State of Israel. But at some point something has to be said about the relationship between Jew and Arab, first in Mandatory Palestine and, later on, when the newly founded State of Israel confronted hostile Arab neighbors. For this confrontation, which has continued until the present day, is perhaps the most important single factor in the existence of Israel, just as it is the biggest single issue in the entire Middle East.

One truism, often repeated, about the tragedy of the Middle East situation today is that, in the course of the last three-quarters of a century, Jewish and Arab nationalism have grown at almost exactly the same time, if manifestly not at the same pace. Jewish nationalism has had, as its primary aim, the consolidation of the Jewish community in Palestine; and as its longer-term objective, the creation of a Jewish state, free, independent, unique in its social ideals. Arab nationalism has had more complex aims—to gain independence from Turkish, British, or other yokes, to restore something of the Arab greatness of the past, to work if possible towards Arab unity, and to produce movement towards political and social emancipation as well as economic progress into the twentieth century. It can at once be seen that the Jews had the advantage of having limited, definable objectives, for all their energies became focused on the task of setting up a Jewish state in one particular part of the world. There is still nothing like a unity of purpose in the Arab world. The statement made by T. E. Lawrence appears to be as true as ever, that "Arab unity is a madman's dream."

Much, possibly too much, has been made of the fact that until Jewish and Arab nationalism collided with one another, Jews and Arabs had coexisted during the last two thousand years, for the most part on reasonable terms. Naturally, there was often friction, and there is an old Jewish saying that the reason why Jacob put a stone under his head for a pillow was that he needed something to throw at the Arabs if they attacked him. But the historian James Parkes has often written of the "Arab-Jewish symbiosis," and his firm belief is that the Arabs and the Jews not only were able to live peacefully together but did so to their mutual benefit. To the Moslem Arabs, the Jews were the "people of the Book," and their beliefs and traditions were venerated as, in effect, the foreword to the Moslem faith. In the days of Islamic greatness, until the fifteenth century, Jews often held responsible posts in Arab countries, especially in Spain and North Africa, and played an important part in cultural life.

But the Jews, with a very few personal exceptions, were regarded as second-class citizens in the Arab world. Their existence in its *mellahs* had much in common with that in the European ghetto. In Arab countries they were often forbidden to own land or horses, or to dress in white clothes. They were subject to periodic persecution, although not as violent or prolonged as in Christian countries. The Arab-Jewish symbiosis lost its aura of romance, and the lot of the Jew in the Arab world suffered all the more because of its social, political, and intellectual stagnation. Writing in 1944 on the subject of "Arabia Felix," Hayim Greenberg had this to say.

> A Yemenite Jew may not live together with non-Jews in a fortified town . . . ride a horse or mule on the street . . . build a house more than two stories high . . . wear white clothes . . . carry weapons. Jews must pay a special impost over and above the general taxes for the right to appeal to courts if they are robbed. But, in addition, the law requires a Jew who has been robbed to catch the thief and bring him to court, failing which the Jew is jailed for "concealing a thief." Jews are not qualified witnesses in court, and their oaths are not accepted. When a Jew meets a Moslem he must salute him and inquire about his "exalted" health. A Jew may not enter a public bath, except to stoke the fires of Arabs' bathhouses.[1]

Arab nationalism may not at first have seemed a potential danger to the Jews of the Middle East and North Africa. As James Parkes has pointed out, it was of relatively recent growth when World War I broke out, and was concentrated on the single aim of securing freedom from the persecution, inefficiency, and corruption of Turkish rule[2] (which could even have given it a common purpose with the Jewish communities of the Ottoman Empire). Its beginnings can be traced back to the 1870s, when the first placards and pamphlets appeared calling for the overthrow of the Ottoman Empire. Their writers probably owed more than they would have cared to admit to quite extraneous factors, like the foundation of American Protestant and Jesuit, as well as other Roman Catholic, missions in the Levant. These missions played a big part in creating a small intellectual élite, whose members imbibed western social ideas as well as the knowledge needed to print and publish their views. Christian Arabs played the major part in creating a body of up-to-date grammar, literature, and history for the Middle East.

The early pamphlets directed against Turkish rule were not part of a concerted campaign. Indeed, so vague was Arab interest in them that the only texts which survived were discovered in the dispatches of a conscientious British consul general in Beirut.[3] Their main themes were the garrisoning of Arab areas by locally raised Arab units instead of Turkish troops, recognition of Arabic as an official language, and steps to create an independent Syrian state. In *The Arab Awakening,* George Antonius remarks that these efforts to awaken an Arab consciousness were premature and adds, "It is in the nature of the Arab temperament to conceive action in spasms rather than on a plan of sustained effort."[4] Up to 1914 Arab nationalism did not touch the masses at all, and Antonius notes that one of the most prominent of the nationalist societies of that era, Al Fatat, achieved a maximum membership of 200.[5]

The Moslem world became automatically involved in World War I when Turkey joined the Central Powers. But it was not clear on which side Moslem peoples, for there were virtually no Moslem governments, would align themselves. Turkey's overlordship in the Middle East was resented, but British rule in Moslem Egypt, Sudan, and Northern India was not exactly popular either. Nor was French rule in North Africa. There were attempts on the part of the Central Powers to stir up a *jehad,* or holy war, against the Western Allies. The latter had something more specific to offer, which was freedom from Turkish rule. There may have been an element of immorality in this, for the Western Allies plainly had no definite plans for the Middle East. They thought and negotiated on a pragmatic basis. This led them into half-promises which were often misleading.

It is easy for Arab writers and sympathizers with the Arab cause to wax angry over what they regard as a deceitful British policy. But it must be remembered that almost all Arabs under Turkish rule took no part in the war whatever and those that did played only a very small part in the Middle East theater. During the whole course of the war there was not one spontaneous Arab uprising in Turkish-occupied territory, apart from the Arab revolt in the south-western Arabian province of the Hejaz. Even this single uprising against the Turks would probably have petered out but for British arms and money, and for the individualistic T. E. Lawrence, better known as "Lawrence of Arabia." Richard Aldington put it in these words:

> If the Arabs had risen and had continued guerilla warfare over all the area claimed by Faisal at the Peace Conference, they would indeed have been a valuable aid to their British Allies. But the revolt was limited to the Hejaz (which was too far off and too worthless, except for sentimental religious reasons, to be worth the Turkish effort of recovery) and to desert areas close to the British Army, from which small raids could be made with comparative impunity. Beyond those areas, where there was real danger to be faced and real damage to be done, the Arabs did nothing but talk and conspire.[6]

In his only partially successful effort to debunk Lawrence, Aldington was less than fair about the Hejaz revolt led by Faisal, son of Sherif Hussein of Mecca. Admittedly, the Arab tribesmen only mounted occasional raids on the Hejaz railway that ran from Damascus to Medina. They fought only two real military engagements, capturing the port of Aqaba in the first. The impression given by Lawrence in *Seven*

Pillars of Wisdom and other writings, of a brilliant, decisive campaign fought largely under his command, is misleading. Thanks to considerable British aid, however, the Arabs did achieve three things. They discouraged the use of the Hejaz railway by the Turks for mounting an attack on British Aden, an attack which, if successful, could have closed the Red Sea to British and other Allied shipping. They discouraged any Turkish outflanking operation to the east of the British armies advancing from Egypt into Palestine. And their participation in the war on the Allied side did most to prevent the launching of the jehad by the Turks. Sherif Hussein was, after all, a direct descendant of the Prophet and custodian of the holy places. Turkey's eventual proclamation of a holy war fell flat.

Britain did, however, make overtures to the Arabs which looked suspiciously like firm promises. The first important one was contained in a cable from Field Marshal Lord Kitchener to Sherif Hussein: "If the Arab nation assist England in this war, England will guarantee that no intervention takes place in Arabia." Aldington, rightly, points out that no Arab nation existed at the time, and that the term "Arabia," which appeared in English schoolboys' atlases, could have meant almost anything to the Arabs.[7] Kitchener's ill-worded message may have been intended to forestall Arab military cooperation with Turkey, for it was known that Faisal favored this and was suspicious of the Middle East designs of every one of the chief Allied powers, Britain, France, Russia, and Italy.[8]

But between July 1915 and January 1916 a detailed correspondence took place between Sir Henry McMahon, the first British High Commissioner in Egypt, and Sherif Hussein, which Arab historians have since held to have committed Britain fully to supporting Arab claims to territory in the Middle East. There is just enough room here to give a brief résumé of this correspondence.

On July 14, 1915, Hussein wrote asking for the frontiers of a future Arab state to be defined. He proposed that it should include all of what is today Iraq, Jordan, Syria, and Israel as well as the whole Arabian Peninsula with the exception of Aden.

On August 30, 1915, McMahon answered that discussion of frontiers was premature, since the Turks were in control of "the greater part of those regions." On September 9, 1915, Hussein reiterated his claim to the territories already mentioned: "For our aim, O respected Minister, is to ensure that the conditions which are essential to our future shall be secured on a foundation of reality, and not on highly-decorated phrases and titles."

McMahon allowed nearly seven weeks to elapse before sending his answer of October 24, 1915. There was as much or as little need as before to define frontiers; for the Turks remained in effective control of the Middle East. But McMahon's letter expressly excluded from the area of a future Arab state "the districts of Mersina and Alexandretta and portions of Syria lying to the west of the districts of Damascus. Homs, Hama, and Aleppo cannot be said to be purely Arab and should be excluded from the limits demanded."[9] Britain would also set up "special administrative arrangements" for Bagdad and Basra.

Hussein wrote back almost at once, on November 5, 1915. He did not readily accept the special arrangements for Bagdad and Basra, but agreed that the areas under British military occupation should remain so, pending negotiations. He agreed to the exclusion of Mersina and Alexandretta from a future Arab state but considered that other places mentioned by McMahon were Arab in character. McMahon's third letter was on December 13, 1915; it reiterated Britain's interest in Bagdad and France's in the Syrian littoral. Each man wrote a fourth letter, neither of which added anything to what had been said before, other than to agree to prosecute the war to a victorious conclusion.

The McMahon-Hussein correspondence, it will be seen, made no mention of Palestine or any place in Palestine. Arab spokesmen have, ever since, maintained that this meant that the whole of Palestine was intended to be included in an Arab state. Sir Henry McMahon himself thought otherwise; in a letter to the London *Times* on July 23, 1937, he said that Palestine was not included in his pledge to Sherif Hussein. On sober reflection, it seems impossible that Palestine could have qualified for inclusion. Places like Homs and Hama were excluded because they were not "purely Arab." How much less "purely Arab" were the principal centers of population in Palestine! Jerusalem actually had a large Jewish majority of inhabitants.

There is another point about the McMahon-Hussein correspondence which Arab critics, and even unbiased historians, have missed. How could a British High Commissioner in Cairo pledge great areas of the Middle East to a hereditary ruler in Mecca? At the very most, he could only indicate British intentions in the Middle East. Certainly, he had no authority to negotiate a peace settlement, years in advance of the end of the war, with the ruler of a single, comparatively small and remote province in the Arabian Peninsula. In European terms, the equivalent would have been to map out the future territorial settlement of the whole of the Balkans, plus other Slavonic areas in Central Europe, with the King of Serbia.

At the peace conference, Arab claims were urged by Colonel Lawrence. He made no secret of his own wish, which was that three Arab states should be created, in Lower Mesopotamia, Upper Mesopotamia, and Syria, which should be ruled by the three sons of Sherif Hussein of Mecca.[10] Lawrence also suggested that he had personally "promised" these parts of the Middle East to the Sherif's Hashemite family, and he prophesied that King Ibn Saud of Nejd, which comprised most of inner Arabia, would have to accept the Hashemite dynasty as overlord if he were to survive as a ruler. Lawrence was never in a position to promise parts of the Middle East to anyone. His plans for Hashemite overlordship ended, in the long run, in almost total failure. One son of Hussein, Faisal, became King of Iraq, but his dynasty was to be ousted in 1958. Another son, Abdullah, became King of Jordan. The third son got nothing. Syria went to France, and Ibn Saud of Nejd, far from accepting Hashemite suzerainty, conquered the Hejaz and consolidated his position as ruler of most of the Arabian Peninsula. By 1958 the last surviving remnant of Lawrence's dream was the small and struggling Kingdom of Jordan. By a coincidence, it was the last surviving remnant of Britain's terribly muddled efforts at empire-building in the storm center of the Middle East.*

Long before the peace conference and, indeed, during the actual course of the McMahon-Hussein correspondence, the British Government entered into a completely different set of negotiations, with France. From October 1915 to February 1916 these negotiations were conducted by Sir Mark Sykes on the British side and M. Charles François Georges-Picot on the French. Sykes and Picot actually reached agreement in

* In spite of the number of books written about Lawrence of Arabia, there is still much obscurity about his views on what should have been done about the Middle East. Apart from installing the Hashemites as Britain's allies, he was obviously in favor of a major British commitment in the area. This is illustrated by the letter which he wrote to the poet Robert Graves after World War I: "The Cabinet was half persuaded to make a clean cut of our Middle East responsibilities; to evacuate Mesopotamia, 'Milnerize' Egypt, and perhaps give Palestine to a third party. Mr. Churchill was determined to find ways and means of avoiding so complete a reversal of the traditional British attitude. I was at one with him in this attitude: indeed I fancy I went beyond him in my desire to see as many 'brown' dominions in the British Empire as there are 'white.' It will be a sorry day when our estate stops growing." (*Lawrence and the Arabs*, by Robert Graves, p. 285.) Lawrence was fairly explicit on the subject of Iraq which he wanted given "a liberal measure of self-government" but "controlled by a Treaty with Britain." (Graves, p. 286.)

Another statement quoted by Graves (Graves, p. 288) is, "Arabia will always, I hope, stand out of the movements of the settled parts [Syria and Iraq], as will Palestine too if the Zionists make good. Their problem is the problem of the third generation. Zionist success would enormously reinforce the material development of Arab Syria and Iraq." This statement has a close resemblance to one which he made, allegedly to the historian Sir Lewis Namier: "The problem of Zionism is the problem of the third generation. It is the grandsons of your immigrants who will make it succeed or fail, but the odds are so much in its favor that the experiment is worth backing; and I back it not because of the Jews, but because a regenerated Palestine is going to raise the whole moral and material status of its Middle East neighbors." (*T. E. Lawrence by his Friends*, p. 190.) Weizmann, also, quoted Lawrence as saying that "he thought that the Jews acted as a ferment and were likely to be instrumental in bringing out the latent energies of the Arab people. He thought that Arab redemption was likely to come about through Jewish redemption." (*T. E. Lawrence by his Friends*, p. 184.) On balance, it seems that Lawrence favored Zionism and visualized it as a useful element in a Middle East which might gradually emancipate itself under British protection.

principle by February 1916, although terms continued to be discussed by the British and French governments for another three months. Britain and France were fighting in the war as allies and both had an interest in the Middle East. The agreement which Sykes and Picot reached was clearly binding on the governments of their two countries and its terms have to be set out in brief.

A large part of the Middle East was divided on the Sykes-Picot map into red, blue, and brown zones. The red was to go to Britain, the blue to France; the brown zone was to be given an international regime.

The red, or British, zone would include most of Mesopotamia and a corridor of land running to Palestine which, with the ports of Haifa and Acre, would be partly British. France would get Syria, a corner of purely Turkish Anatolia, and northern Mesopotamia. The brown, international, zone would comprise part of Palestine, including Jerusalem.

Obviously, the McMahon-Hussein correspondence and the Sykes-Picot discussions led to understandings which did not accord with each other and were conducted with very different ends in view. The British Government laid itself open to the charge of double dealing. Admittedly, the McMahon-Hussein correspondence led to no formal agreement. The Foreign Secretary, Lord Curzon, tried to suggest the same thing for the Sykes-Picot agreement, by calling it "a sort of fancy sketch to suit a situation which had not then arisen, and which it was thought extremely unlikely would ever arise."[11] But an undertaking of this kind, entered into during a war by allies, is binding. Sir Mark Sykes himself said that there were people who "do not understand that we have been great not because of liberalism, but because of our extraordinary geographical position which has permitted of our playing the fool."[12] Sir Mark was himself a serious and honorable man, who negotiated what he believed to be a secret agreement in good faith. Later he was to suggest long-term aims for Britain, assumption of the Mandate in Palestine, extension of British control over Mosul and northern Mesopotamia, the maintenance of a good working relationship with France in the Middle East, and the winning of Arab confidence.[13] This was in October 1917 in a letter to Lord Robert Cecil. Since Sykes had by then become a convinced supporter of Zionism into the bargain, it may be that he was far too optimistic and that his advice to the British government erred in that direction.

Antonius calls the Sykes-Picot agreement "a shocking document . . . the product of greed at its worst, that is to say, of greed allied to suspicion and so leading to stupidity, it also stands out as a startling piece of double dealing."[14] Antonius condemned the agreement on four grounds which are worth examining.

He regarded the splitting up of this part of the Middle East into zones as injurious, because its population was homogenous. As to that, since he wrote his book in 1938, there has been ceaseless strife between

Iraquis and Kurds, Christian and Moslem Lebanese, Palestinian and Bedouin Jordanians, Syrians and their Druse minority. There has been no sign of homogeneity.

Antonius considered that by the end of the war the Arab awakening had proved itself and nationalism was the main force in the area. In reality all that the Arab national movement had produced was some secret societies and small-scale military operations on the flank of the Turkish army.

He considered, further, that logic was reversed by giving "backward" inland regions of the Middle East self-government, while the more "mature" Syria and Iraq were put under foreign rule. Since Syria and Iraq gained their independence, they have had revolutions without number, while the "backward" inland regions have had relatively stable government.

Finally, Antonius condemned Britain's role as being one of "total duplicity." He could hardly be blamed for taking this view, but the probability was that Britain simply blundered into a false position.

Hussein first heard of the Sykes-Picot agreement at the end of 1917. Britain and France had promised Tsarist Russia territory in Turkish Armenia, as a codicil to the agreement. The Bolshevik regime renounced this territorial claim and denounced the Sykes-Picot agreement at the same time. It was undoubtedly a shock to Hussein, who afterward used to refer to the British Prime Minister, Lloyd George, as an "acrobat and fox." Only a short time before, Hussein had learned of the Balfour Declaration as well but had been reassured by a special emissary sent to him by the British government, Commander D. G. Hogarth of the Arab Bureau in Cairo. He assured Hussein that no one people would be subjected to another in Palestine, that the holy places would be placed under a special administration, and that the Mosque of Omar in the Old City of Jerusalem would remain under Moslem control.

These points were part of a message which ended: "Since the Jewish opinion of the world is in favor of a return to Palestine and inasmuch as this opinion must remain a constant factor, and further as H. M. Government view with favor the realization of this aspiration, H. M. Government are determined that in so far as is compatible with the freedom of the existing population both economic and political, no obstacle shall be placed in the way of the realization of this ideal." Hogarth reported Hussein to have been satisfied with this badly worded assurance. Indeed, there was no indication that he was in any way opposed to the establishment of the Jewish national home in Palestine. Nor is there any justification for the statement of one authority, Edward Atiyah, that on the announcement of the Balfour Declaration, "the Arabs sensed immediately the real danger to them of this British move."[15]

Indeed, the aspirations of the Jews seemed of far less importance to the Arab leaders than the French seizure of Syria and Lebanon.

The Jews, as the Arabs seemed at first prepared to see it, came to Palestine as members of a scattered and oppressed community. And while the British could to some extent be regarded as deliverers from Turkish tyranny, the French secured a foothold in the Arab Middle East as a colonial power which was already entrenched in Arab North Africa and determined to stay there. However vague Arab nationalist hopes had been, they certainly did not include the prospect of Syria and the Lebanon being turned into provinces of metropolitan France.

It should be remembered, too, that at the outset of the British Mandate, its prospects of enabling successful progress to be made toward a long-term political solution in Palestine were by no means as dim as historians, with the advantage of hindsight, have subsequently made them out to be. It has become a convention to accuse the British governments of the day of having embraced three different and incompatible policies in the Middle East, by making far-reaching promises to both the Arabs and the Jews and at the same time seeking an accommodation with France. One should take a closer look at what Palestine really *was* at that time, through the eyes of the historian James Parkes:

> The failure [of the Mandate] has *not* been due to the criminal character of the basic enterprise. The British were not "giving away a country which did not belong to them," nor forcing upon its proper "owners" an alien immigration of people who had no right to be there. Even apart from the Jewish question, Palestine for nearly two thousand years had not "belonged" exclusively to those who dwell in it. Christians have rights in it which successive Muslim rulers have recognized, and Muslims of other countries have rights in it which the lawlessness of local sheiks and fellaheen do not override. But in addition Jews have rights in it, which Muslim rulers have likewise recognized, and which they have never ceased to exercise up to the shrinking limits of the country's absorptive capacity. The Balfour Declaration "gave" them nothing. It recognized rights which already existed.[16]

This sort of reasoning would not have been foreign to Hussein and his son, the Emir Faisal. The latter had already met Chaim Weizmann, by now the acknowledged spokesman of the Zionist cause, and had been favorably impressed by him. Representing his father at the Paris Peace Conference in January 1919, Faisal had this to say of Palestine in the memorandum of the Arab case:

> The enormous majority of the people are Arabs. The Jews are very close to the Arabs in blood, and there is no conflict of character between the two races. In principles we are absolutely at one. Nevertheless, the Arabs cannot risk assuming the responsibility of holding level the scales in the clash of races and religions that have,

in this one province, so often involved the world in difficulties. They would wish for the effective superposition of a great trustee, so long as a representative local administration commended itself by actively promoting the material prosperity of the country.[17]

Later in the same month Faisal signed an agreement with Weizmann which laid down measures for promoting Jewish immigration into Palestine on a large scale. Under its terms the World Zionist Organization was to send a commission to Palestine to examine the possibilities of economic development there and to forward its views to the Arab states. Several weeks later Faisal confirmed his intention of securing the fullest cooperation between Arabs and Jews in a letter sent to Felix Frankfurter, an American jurist and a leading member of the Zionist delegation in Paris. In his letter Faisal expressed "deepest sympathy" with the Zionist movement and gave an assurance that no differences "in principle" should arise between Jews and Arabs.

One historian, Christopher Sykes, considers that the Faisal-Weizmann agreement and Faisal's memorandum to the peace conference "effectively dispose of the idea that the Balfour Declaration was utterly unacceptable to the gallant leaders of the Arab revolt, and was a cruel repudiation of a solemn pledge."[18] Sykes adds that Faisal would not have been able to push through his agreement, as he would have been denounced by much of the Arab world as a "foreign Bedouin chief." Here he raises an interesting point. The Arabs have regarded the half-promises of Sir Henry McMahon to Hussein, the father, as binding, but have unhesitatingly repudiated the agreement made with the Zionists by Faisal, the son. Neither Hussein nor Faisal was entitled to speak for the Arabs of the Middle East as a whole, and so the Arabs could applaud any advantage obtained by the one from the British, while rejecting any concession made by the other to the Zionists.

The Hussein-McMahon correspondence, the Sykes-Picot agreement, the Balfour Declaration, and the Faisal-Weizmann agreement are four threads in a skein of Middle East diplomacy which was to become increasingly tangled. There has been no space in this book to deal with them in detail. But some account of them is necessary if one is to understand how the British Mandate came into existence and why it failed in the political sense. Some account is necessary, too, of the course which British administration followed in the first postwar period.

It got off to a reasonably quiet start. There was a limited Jewish response to the proclamation of a national home and only 1800 immigrants arrived in 1919. During the next four years arrivals numbered about eight thousand a year. Not even the most rabid Arab nationalist could have maintained that Palestine was being flooded with Jewish immigrants.

But trouble between Arabs and Jews had already started. In April

1920 there were Arab riots in Jerusalem during the course of which 160 Jews were injured. The British authorities took action only after two days, when the rioting had already ended, and one observer remarked: "Looking back now at those hectic days after an interval of ten years, I feel bound coldly and definitely to state that the whole tone of the British officers of those days was unquestionably hostile to the Jews."[19] In May 1921 there were far worse Arab riots at Jaffa. This time the casualties were appalling; 47 Jews and 48 Arabs were killed, 146 Jews and 73 Arabs were wounded. In the Poalei Zion immigrants' hostel 13 Jews were butchered. The Arabs were throughout the aggressors and inflicted all the casualties suffered by the Jews; the Arab losses were mainly at the hands of the British troops and police. In May 1921 too, four Jewish colonies outside Jaffa in the plain of Sharon were attacked. Four Jews were killed at Petach Tikva, where the attack was led by a Bedouin chieftain.

The first British High Commissioner, Sir Herbert (later Lord) Samuel, reacted strangely to the 1921 riots. Although the Arabs had been the aggressors, he clamped down a temporary ban on Jewish immigration. Samuel had already alarmed the Jewish community by appointing as the new Grand Mufti of Jerusalem Haj Amin el Husseini, a violent anti-Zionist who had played a leading part in the 1920 rioting. Samuel, himself a Jew, was anxious to do everything possible to be fair to the Arabs.

The accusation against the British authorities of a bias in favor of the Arabs was probably true, at least in part. Horace Samuel's explanation was:

> The Arabs exhibited invariably far better manners than did the Jews. Nor was this particularly surprising. For good manners are of the essence alike of hospitality and intrigue, in both of which arts the Arabs are past masters. Undoubtedly, during these delicate and crucial days, the Arabs nearly always made the more favorable impression on the majority of officials. . . . For whether they whined, or threatened, or cajoled, or protested, they were nearly always picturesque, ingratiating, sympathetic. The Jews, on the other hand, even when they were in the right, were clumsy, fussy, and aggressive.[20]

There were certainly anti-Semitic undertones among the officials who served the British administration. One of them was forced to resign after howling at some Jews outside a British courtroom, "Don't make so much noise! This isn't a synagogue!" And the comment of another when Samuel was installed as High Commissioner was: "And there I was at Government House, and there was the Union Jack flying as large as life, and a bloody Jew sitting underneath it!"[21] The Jews were often short on social graces too, and Horace Samuel has a wonderful story of the naïve Zionist, Menahem Ussishkin, inviting the suave, cultured, and witty governor of Jerusalem, Sir Ronald Storrs, to dinner. Ussishkin had taken the trouble of inquiring beforehand what the national drink of England was, and Sir Ronald, to his horror, found himself confronted with a bubbling glass of Eno's Fruit Salts when he sat down to dinner.[22]

Anti-Semitism, however, is not an especially British characteristic, and there are other explanations for the British bias in favor of the Arabs—a bias which Zionists, even 50 years later, are apt to regard as some kind of a sinister plot against Jewry.

In the first place, the British administrators who came to Palestine had usually served in some corner or other of the British Empire. They were used to dealing with Indians, Africans, Malays. All such peoples were recognizably different from Europeans; a technique had to be developed for dealing with them, taking account of their history and habits of life. Palestinian Arabs could be treated in much the same way; Jews could not. Jews, mainly of European origin, simply did not fit into the British colonial pattern.

More important, the Palestinian Arabs *behaved* in a manner conducive to colonial administration. They were helpless and, although complaining, they often asked for help. During the period of the Mandate, the Jews of Palestine were building up their own institutions, admittedly needing much help from the Diaspora, and felt correspondingly proud and independent. Sometimes they might *demand* something from the British administration; it was seldom that they asked for help in the manner of people genuinely in need of it. In British colonial experience, you looked on people as your "own," when they depended on you. In this instance, the Arabs did; the Jews didn't. It was as simple as that.

I have deliberately italicized the word "demand" since the third reason for British bias in favor of the Arabs was that the Jews, even when their demands were met, were never satisfied. They invariably had something more to demand; their quivers were filled with an inexhaustible supply of arrows of desire. "The Arabs," one British Mandate official told me, "were sometimes suppliants. At other times they complained bitterly. The Jews put themselves in the position of being formidable adversaries." Who could blame them? The Jews, from being a small, poor, and struggling minority in Palestine, were in the process of building themselves up into a state. To do this they had to keep the pressure on the British Mandatory power.

Apart from the Rabbinical Council and the Histadrut, they had begun to create new representative institutions. The *Asiphat Nivcharim,* or Assembly of Deputies, was a sort of electoral college, numbering 250 and electing members to the *Vaad Leumi,* or General Council. This latter body undertook to represent the interests of the Jewish community to the British authorities, or even to the League of Nations and foreign governments. Its readiness to appeal to opinion outside Palestine was another source of irritation to the officials of the Mandate. Inevitably, too, they resented the Jewish tendency to create a "state within the state," which they felt undermined their own authority. By contrast, the Arabs of Palestine remained almost totally unorganized.

In 1921 Palestine was transferred from the jurisdiction of the Foreign Office, under the anti-Zionist Lord Curzon, to the Colonial Office, under the pro-Zionist Churchill. The Zionism of Winston Churchill, like the Zionism of Arthur Balfour, was a mystery. Probably it owed most to his schooling in the Bible as child and young man, and to a semimystical attachment to Biblical tradition and story. In 1903 Churchill supported the offer of Uganda to the Jews (by Balfour). In 1908 he declared his support of a Jewish national home in Palestine before a Zionist meeting in Manchester. In 1920 he addressed himself to the problem of Zionism in a slightly erratic article in the *Illustrated Sunday Herald*.* Churchill became Colonial Secretary only in 1921. He made the Middle East the target of his immediate attention.

He sent advisers to look at the situation in Palestine, and studied their findings. Next, he offered a legislative council to both the Jews and the Arabs, heavily weighted in favor of the latter. Paradoxically, it was the Arabs who rejected the offer, by insisting on the preconditions that the Balfour Declaration should be annulled and all Jewish immigration suspended.[23] From then on, the Arabs were to turn down a great many British proposals, often to their own detriment.

Churchill next detached Transjordan, that is, parts of Palestine east of the river Jordan, from Mandatory Palestine itself, and allowed it to become an embryonic state under the Emir Abdullah, one of Sherif Hussein's sons. Churchill has sometimes been blamed for a step which may have made the creation of a binational Arab-Jewish state more difficult and which indirectly made the eventual formation of a Jewish state more feasible. Curiously, it was the Jews who objected to this step, since it detached the old territories of the tribes of Reuben, Gad, and half of Manasseh. The Arabs were politically too uninformed and unaware to take much notice; they may even have thought that the creation of the semi-independent Transjordan could be the first step in the achievement of independent Arab statehood for the whole area.

The truth was that Churchill did no more than recognize a *fait accompli*. As one of the most reliable historians of the Arab world, Sir John Glubb, has pointed out in *Syria, Lebanon, Jordan*,[24] the area east of the river Jordan and bordering on the Arabian deserts had simply been left unoccupied by the British authorities. In March 1921 the Emir Abdullah seized the town of Amman with a force of Bedouin tribesmen,

* Churchill wrote that Zionism was the answer to international communism, and Zionism must therefore win "the soul of the Jewish people"—a slight oversimplification!

while at the same time announcing his intention of driving the French out of Syria. Having failed to secure Syria for his brother Faisal, the British Government was perfectly ready to leave Abdullah in undisturbed possession of the largely uninhabited and almost totally landlocked (it had the single Red Sea port of Aqaba) area of Transjordan—of course, under British "protection." Churchill may well have been influenced in this policy of laissez faire by T. E. Lawrence, who was now advising him on Middle East affairs and who later claimed that his work for Churchill was "the best I ever did."[25]

Churchill next produced a White Paper on Palestine, making public his policy statement on July 1, 1922. In it he denied that Palestine had been included within the terms of the McMahon-Hussein correspondence and he asserted that the Jewish community "should know that it is in Palestine as of right and not on sufferance. That is the reason why it is necessary that the existence of a Jewish National Home in Palestine should be internationally guaranteed, and that it should be formally recognized to rest upon ancient historic connections."[26] He also painted a promising picture of the Jewish community.

> During the last two or three generations the Jews have re-created in Palestine a community, now numbering 80,000, of whom about one fourth are farmers or workers upon the land. The community has its own political organs; an elected assembly for the direction of its domestic concerns; elected councils in the towns; and an organization for the control of its schools. It has its elected Chief Rabbinate and Rabbinical Council for the direction of its religious affairs. Its business is conducted in Hebrew, and a Hebrew press serves its needs. It has its distinctive intellectual life and displays considerable economic activity. This community, then, with its town and country population, its political, religious and social organizations, its own language, its own customs, its own life, has in fact "national" characteristics.[27]

Only one passage in Churchill's statement caused concern to the Jewish community. This read as follows:

> Unauthorized statements have been made to the effect that the purpose in view is to create a wholly Jewish Palestine. Phrases have been used such as that Palestine is to become "as Jewish as England is English." His Majesty's Government regard any such expectation as impracticable and have no such aim in view. Nor have they at any time contemplated, as appears to be feared by the Arab Delegation, the disappearance or the subordination of the Arabic population, language, or culture in Palestine. They would draw attention to the fact that the terms of the Declaration referred to [the Balfour Declaration of 1917] do not contemplate that Palestine as a whole

should be converted into a Jewish National Home, but that such a Home should be founded in Palestine.

Churchill's prose always has a resounding ring, even in a state document. But his White Paper discloses some of the anomalies of British policy in Palestine. On July 22, 1921, both Lloyd George and Balfour had assured Weizmann that their interpretation of the Balfour Declaration was that it should lead to the eventual establishment of a Jewish state.[28] Churchill's White Paper seems to reject this interpretation. But while the White Paper worried the Jews, it did not reassure the Arabs. One curious reason for this lies in the phrase, "a National Home," chosen by the Balfour Declaration.

Sir Harold MacMichael, who was British High Commissioner in Palestine during World War II, has pointed out to me that the word "home" is more or less untranslatable into Arabic (for that matter, it exists in very few languages in the world). One of MacMichael's first actions on taking up his post was to ask for the Arabic copy of the Balfour Declaration. In it the word "home" was translated by the Arabic *watan*, which is the equivalent to the Latin *patria*, or "country." This single word may have done much to foster Arab suspicion of Britain's Palestine policy.

Churchill's White Paper has been regarded as a turning point for the Jewish community, followed as it was at a short interval by the promulgation of the British Mandate and its formal confirmation by the League of Nations. Palestine, as it happened, was to enjoy a period of relative calm for the next six years. The reasons for this are clear. Money was being poured into the country by the Jewish Agency, trade was expanding, steady but not spectacular Jewish immigration was easily absorbed, and British administration, at least in the economic sense, was sound and successful. There was, moreover, an exceptional High Commissioner in the person of Field-Marshal Lord Plumer. Firm, upright, courtly of manner, and with a keen wit, he had qualities which appealed to both Arabs and Jews (the latter still insist on mispronouncing his name "Plummer").

Twice at least Plumer dealt with Arab deputations in the manner of a political Gamaliel. One deputation demanded the cancelation of a parade to be held for the folding of the flag of the Jewish battalions of the Royal Fusiliers in the Grand Synagogue of Jerusalem. Plumer gently reminded his visitors that this was no more than the entitlement of any regiment which had served in a good cause. The other deputation complained that Lord Plumer had stood at attention at a Jewish sports meeting in Tel Aviv when the Jewish national anthem, the "Hatikvah," had been played. Plumer's answer was that every Arab knew that a guest could not abuse his host's hospitality, and that he would do just the same at an Arab occasion if the Arabs would introduce an anthem of their own.[29] Sykes humorously remarked that it was said that Plumer's presence in Palestine was worth a battalion, but no battalion was sent out when he retired in July 1928.[30]

Plumer had no sooner gone than fresh trouble began. It took a somewhat ludicrous form. The Wailing Wall near the eastern side of the Old City of Jerusalem is believed to be the only surviving fragment of Herod's Temple and has always been a place of worship for Jews. For Yom Kippur, the Day of Atonement, in September 1928, the Jews of the Old City set up a wooden screen to separate men from women, in accordance with their own religious custom. The Arabs protested to the British authorities that the screen was an obstruction and the British police removed it.* This led to scuffles and then to periodic Arab acts of provocation. Dung carts were driven to and fro past the Wall on Jewish religious festivals, troops of dancing dervishes put on displays in sight of it, and there were Arab threats of building a new highway directly past it.

The controversy over the Wailing Wall festered for nearly a year. Then, in August 1929, real trouble broke out. Two explanations have been given. One is that the old warrior, Jabotinsky, staged a provocative demonstration on August 15, when his followers assembled in front of the Wall and loudly demanded that it should become exclusively Jewish property. The other is that a small Jewish boy had been stabbed to death in the garden of an Arab house, after climbing into it to retrieve his football. This murder, it was asserted, caused the Jewish demonstrations.

One can take one's choice of these explanations. Much more operative is what happened afterwards. Incited by the bellicose and vindictive Mufti Haj Amin Husseini, large numbers of Arabs came into Jerusalem on August 22 and 23, 1929. The best account of what then happened has been given by Christopher Sykes in his *Cross Roads to Israel*.[31] The British Chief of Police made a futile effort to disarm these Arab intruders. He then asked the Mufti for an explanation, and the Mufti answered that the Arabs had armed themselves because they were afraid of being attacked. The Zionist authorities offered 500 volunteers as special constables to reinforce the inadequate British police force of 300 in Jerusalem. The offer was turned down.

On August 24 an Arab mob swept down the Jaffa Road in Jerusalem, looting, burning, and beating up Jews wherever they found them. This was nothing compared to what happened in the holy city of Hebron, where 64 Jews were slaughtered while Arab police stood passively by. Twenty-three of the Jews were stabbed to death in an inn and their bodies dismembered. The Jewish colony in Hebron ceased to exist, for all survivors fled. One explanation for the peculiar brutality in Hebron was that a surprising number of Arab peasants owed money to the Jews

---

* Like the Jews, the Arabs segregate women from men in places of religious worship. They should have been able to understand the Jews' action at the Wailing Wall.

there. There were smaller massacres in Jaffa, Safed, Haifa, and Tel Aviv. The total Jewish death toll was 133 and 339 more were wounded. The Jews killed 6 Arabs, but the British police, intervening too late in the day, killed 110 and wounded 232.

Perhaps the most dreadful commentary on the massacres was that of Lady Passfield, better known as Beatrice Webb, the wife of the Labor Government's Colonial Secretary. She told Weizmann: "I can't understand why the Jews make such a fuss over a few dozen of their people being killed in Palestine. As many are killed every week in London in traffic accidents, and no one pays any attention."[32] Her words are a reminder that professing humanitarians can be among the most callous people in the world.

Her husband's reaction to this terrible atrocity was to produce a White Paper, discouraging Jewish immigration and the import of Jewish capital and limiting Jewish land purchase. It was words like his wife's, and actions like his, that made men like Eshkol, quietly reflective, common-sensible, the reverse of fanatic, despair of British policies in Palestine. Eshkol told me that until the 1929 massacres he had still been inclined to hope for greater clarity and strength of purpose on the part of the British. Churchill's endorsement of the Balfour Declaration had never been repudiated, although it had hardly been implemented. But the Jews of Palestine were prepared, after their ancestors had watched and waited for two thousand years, to be patient a little longer.

Particularly galling for a man like Eshkol, himself a humanitarian socialist, was the fact that a British Labor government could be both spineless and stupid, and that Fabians like the Webbs could wash their hands of mass murders. Eshkol and his friends were not to guess that other Labor politicians would traduce them even more damagingly. The time certainly had not yet come when the leaders of the Jewish community in Palestine would deliberately set out to seek statehood and independence in direct opposition to Britain; 1929 was only a warning signal for both.

1. From *Jewish Frontier*, an anthology.
2. James Parkes, *Arabs and Jews in the Middle East*, p. 10.
3. George Antonius, *The Arab Awakening*, pp. 82–83.
4. *Ibid.*, p. 89.
5. *Ibid.*, p. 112.
6. Richard Aldington, *Lawrence of Arabia*, p. 210.
7. *Ibid.*, p. 145.
8. Antonius, *op. cit.*, p. 152.
9. J. C. Hurewitz, *Diplomacy in the Middle East*, Vol. II, p. 15.
10. Aldington, *op. cit.*, p. 253.
11. *Ibid.*, p. 214.
12. Shane Leslie, ed., *Sir Mark Sykes, His Life and Letters*. p. 259.
13. *Ibid.*, p. 274.

14. Antonius, *op. cit.*, p. 248.
15. Edward Atiyah, *The Arabs,* p. 103.
16. James Parkes, *A History of the Jewish People,* pp. 197–198.
17. Hurewitz, *op. cit.*, p. 38.
18. Christopher Sykes, *Cross Roads to Israel,* p. 48.
19. Horace B. Samuel, *Unholy Memories of the Holy Land,* p. 59.
20. *Ibid.,* p. 35.
21. *Ibid.,* p. 59.
22. *Ibid.,* p. 125.
23. Sykes, *op. cit.*, p. 83.
24. Sir John Bagot Glubb, *Syria, Lebanon, Jordan,* p. 128.
25. Robert Graves, *Lawrence and the Arabs,* p. 286.
26. Hurewitz, *op. cit.*, p. 105.
27. *Ibid.,* pp. 104–105.
28. Sykes, *op. cit.*, p. 79.
29. *Ibid.,* pp. 108–109.
30. *Ibid.,* p. 123.
31. *Ibid.,* pp. 137–140.
32. *Ibid.,* p. 141.

6.

The characteristic which was perhaps needed more than any other by Jewish settlers in Palestine was adaptability, and this characteristic remains highly prized in the State of Israel, which is too small to rely on specialists. In the period of the British Mandate a Palestinian Jew might be asked to turn his hand to anything. He was expected to be able to work with his hands as well as his brain and to take on any work, additional to his normal job, in the interests of the Jewish community.

Levi Eshkol developed a degree of adaptability unusual even for the Jewish settlers of his generation. By working at Degania B he had become an efficient practical farmer. His service in the Royal Fusiliers had taught him the use of arms. He had taught himself accountancy, as a mere sideline, had studied economics, and was learning how to marry theory to practice. He had begun to play a part in politics and in labor organization as soon as he was demobilized from the British army. He was very quickly involved in the problems of the self-defense of the Jewish community. And, as at all times during his working life, he was ready to work around the clock. This was taken for granted by the pioneers of the Second Aliyah.

It was hardly surprising, then, that Eshkol undertook a dozen different jobs, many of them at the same time, during the period of the British Mandate. He was still a member of Degania B and remained acutely interested in the land. He was beginning to make a special study of the problem of water supply. He was co-opted by the Federation of Labor, the *Histadrut,* to help in the management of some of its many industrial and agricultural concerns. He was busy working for the political union of the Labor movement. And for three years, from 1933 to 1936, he was engaged in trying to salvage the persons and belongings of members of the Jewish community in Nazi Germany.

Perhaps the Histadrut offers as good a starting point as any for some account of these multifarious activities. Since its foundation in 1920, it had developed into what one historian called a "labor commonwealth."[1] From its original task of organizing trade unions and working out a policy of labor relations, the Histadrut had moved into many fields. It had become a large-scale owner of cooperative and industrial enterprises and, consequently, a large-scale employer. It acted as a welfare organization for the bulk of the Jewish community. It was a colonizing agency, with a close interest in the utilization of soil and water. It had its own educational programs, and played a big part in encouraging immigration. Continuously, as has already been mentioned, it was working out long-term plans for the creation of an agricultural and industrial proletariat which was to be the dominant element in Jewish society in Palestine. One of its founder members, Berl Katznelson, said with justice that the Histadrut's over-all task was to organize the national rebirth of the Jewish people. In the 1920s and 1930s it was the hub of the Jewish community.

In the field of labor relations its only rival was the small independent union movement built up by Jabotinsky and the right-wing revisionist political group. The Histadrut quickly absorbed the bulk of the Jewish working class (much later, after the foundation of the State of Israel, it was to accept Arab members too), who, with their families, comprised around 30 percent of the Jewish community. The Histadrut looked after wage demands and much besides. In 1926 it persuaded the Mandatory authorities to introduce compulsory accident compensation. In 1927 it secured woman and child welfare regulations, with conditions for the employment of minors. At various stages, notably during the depressions of the early 1920s and the early 1930s, the Histadrut induced workers to share their work, going over to working part-time in order to reduce the number of totally unemployed. It had inherited the *Kupat Cholim,* the sick fund established in 1911 for the malaria-ridden agricultural settlers. This was expanded into an all-embracing welfare organization.

Jewish workers had immense pride in their work and were determined to work creatively. This has made the Histadrut into a unique trade union movement, which is confident of the loyalty of its members and which has the interests of the whole community at heart. Class struggle played a major part in its outlook only in the early stages of its existence, for it commanded the support of the best brains in the Jewish community, from David Ben-Gurion down. It was the place for the most constructive ideas and the most practical achievements.

Inevitably the Histadrut propagated the thoughts that one should "buy Jewish" and employ only Jews. The Jewish community was bound to be poor, since there was a continual influx of more or less destitute immigrants. In the early 1930s strikes and picketing discouraged the hiring of Arab labor by Jewish enterprises. Jewish planters, especially in the citrus trade, were boycotted if they did not conform. The pickets came into conflict with Arab workers and British police. 1935 was a year of chaos, but planters and workers banded together after the wave of Arab terrorism in 1936.[2]

The Histadrut established its own contracting company, *Solel Boneh* (Pave and Build) in 1923. It went temporarily bankrupt but was reformed and prospered. *T'nuva,* the selling cooperative for the collective farms, was run by the Histadrut; so was the general cooperative society of *Hamashbir Hamorkazi.* Later on, the Histadrut was to organize the Egged bus company, the Mekorot water corporation, the Zim shipping line, and the El Al airline, to mention a few. In 1969 the Histadrut had a share of about 70 percent of Israeli agriculture, 40 percent of its building, and over 20 percent of its industry as a whole. Its principal achievements have been to pioneer land reclamation, drainage, construction; to procure tens of thousands of jobs for its members; to protect Jewish labor from exploitation and cut-rate Arab competition; and, most important of all, to help create a climate of labor relations conducive to the benefit of the whole community.

Eshkol played a useful part in the general policy-making of the Histadrut but he was of special use in two areas, agriculture and water. He had had practical experience farming in various parts of the country, and in the late 1920s and 1930s he traveled a great deal on the Histadrut's behalf. In land settlement, there were two particular problems to which he applied himself, the foundation of new settlements for immigrants and the consolidation and improvement of those that already existed.

New settlements were a necessity. Between 1919 and 1929 the population of the Jewish community doubled to 165,000. But in the next five years another 160,000 immigrants arrived. Eshkol, like most of those of the Second Aliyah, believed fervently in the need to create a balanced community, with a fair proportion of it working on the land. Up to 1930, at least, it was possible periodically to buy relatively large parcels of land from the large landowners. These men, of the effendi class, were very often absentees. Normally, they sublet to Arab farmers on a year-to-year basis, giving them no security. Legal titles to property were, indeed, virtually unknown in the Ottoman Empire, and when they were introduced farmers refused to register, probably in order to avoid taxation, and there were no land surveys. "If you were an Ottoman subject you hid from the Government."[3] The British Mandatory authorities tried to safeguard Arab farmers by urging them, even when they were selling land, to keep enough for their families. But the Arabs went to great lengths to avoid British advice and British ordinances; they handed over their land to Jewish buyers and accepted payment at a later date by private agreement.

Thus one Christian Arab family in the Emek, or valley, of Jezreel, disposed of over 40,000 acres to the purchasing commission of the Jewish Agency for $2,900,000 and retired to live a life of luxury and no responsibilities in Beirut. The Emek had been a target for Jewish settlement since the 1890s, although various attempts to purchase land there were stopped by successive Turkish governors of Acre. In the 1920s over 60,000 acres of land were bought there, much of it mosquito-infested swamp. One immediate result was that between 1919 and 1929 the Jewish population of the nearby port of Haifa rose from 3000 to 16,000.

Purchases on such a scale alarmed the Arabs and representations were made to the British authorities. The result was the sending of a commission under Sir John Hope-Simpson to Palestine to report on the effects of Jewish immigration on Arab rural life.

His report was to have a baneful influence on British governmental policy. It was slipshod and inaccurate, and was probably so in part because of Sir John's pioneering use of aerial photography, a surveying technique then in its infancy. It sought to show that Palestine was already being farmed almost to the limit of its capacity and that there was only room for another 100,000 people. Since this 1930 report, the population of the area which Sir John surveyed has increased by 1,800,000 persons; his estimate has already been proved 18 times too low. The report wrote off the whole Beersheba area, simply because it was not being farmed at the time. It made allowance neither for the vast amount of land left fallow as a result of wasteful Arab farming methods, nor for the possibility of planting trees. The Colonial Office drew obvious conclusions from the report, and, as a result, the Passfield White Paper sought to limit Jewish immigration. Passfield himself remarked to Weizmann that there "wasn't room to swing a cat in Palestine."[4]

At that stage of history the Jews had acquired about 375,000 acres in Palestine, slowly, painstakingly, often expensively. Weizmann pointed out to Passfield that in the United States, and even in Britain, there were private estates that were larger. The Hope-Simpson report suggested that the landlessness of 30 percent, or about 25,000 families, of the Arab population outside the towns was caused by their land being bought up by the Jews. The truth was that there had always been plenty of landless Arabs; the effendi class grew rich from their cut-rate labor. As eminently fair a historian as Sir John Glubb arrived at a figure of 8000 dispossessed Arabs.[5] The Jewish Agency estimated that a total Arab population of 5900 was affected by Jewish land purchase. And when the land was sold over the head of an Arab tenant farmer by an absentee landlord, the Jewish Agency paid an indemnity of $200, more than the average annual income of an Arab family on the land.[6]

The picture of Arabs, poor, friendless, and helpless, being *robbed* of their land by rapacious Jews is unreal. The Palestinian Jews acquired land peacefully and with no desire to inflict injury. Their basic concern was to reclaim the soil, to farm it intensively but to live frugally off it. "The Arabs had plenty of land to play with," Eshkol told me. "As a result, we had some cockeyed ideas at first. We thought in terms of two or three hundred dunams [50 to 75 acres] for a family. We learned to think very differently, and to lower our sights. Thirty dunams [seven and a half acres] was enough for a family to live on."

Eshkol found himself concentrating on finding new corners in which to settle the immigrants. He was not a bit impressed by the Hope-Simpson report. His belief at the time was that at least another half-million people could live on the land, and that whole new areas could be opened up for settlement. He traveled a great deal at this time and his advice was invaluable when it came to finding new, often virgin, soil for settlers. New settlements were established, especially in Galilee and the plain of Sharon, which runs from Gaza to the Carmel mountain range south of Haifa. Eshkol was convinced that each new settlement should be carefully planned, and should not try to start its life on a shoestring. In particular, it should be of an economic size.

One of the settlers of the 1920s, Dr. Yosef Weitz, has described to me how blindly enthusiastic immigrant settlers could be. "They started out to farm in the rocks of Galilee, sometimes in groups of only half a dozen, working themselves to the bone in clearing the ground and living off a diet of bread and salted herrings."[7] The era of unplanned, uneconomic settlement had to be ended. The vast enthusiasm of the new settlers was not, in itself, enough to insure success. Eshkol set out to consolidate and rationalize settlement on the land. He worked out the details of a plan to settle a thousand young Jewish families on the soil of Palestine. The essence of the plan was to distribute them among the kibbutzim and moshavim which were already functioning.

There is no accurate gauge of Eshkol's work in the field of land settlement during this period, but it is clear that his policy paid off. The kibbutz movement, which was already a going concern, doubled in size in a decade. The cooperative farms of the moshavim really did take root. They were in due course to become the biggest single form of Jewish settlement on the land.

Eshkol had an inventive mind as well. The first efforts at irrigating the land at Degania B had stuck in his mind. He had an *idée fixe,* rooted in the Scriptures, that irrigation would produce a big breakthrough in farming. In Genesis 2:10 there is the passage: "And a river went out of Eden to water the garden; and from thence it was parted, and became into four heads." And then, in Kings 3:16: "And he said, Thus saith the Lord, Make this valley full of ditches: For thus saith the Lord, Ye shall not see wind, neither shall ye see rain; yet that valley shall be filled with water, that ye may drink, both ye, and your cattle, and your beasts."

There had never been a time in the history of the Middle East when there had not been a desperate need for water over most of the area. Great civilizations were built in the lands of great rivers like the Nile and Euphrates. Small streams dried up in summer and their waters had to be used carefully and stored whenever possible. The arts of irrigation had been practiced by the Egyptians three thousand years before Christ, and at least as early as 1500 B.C. by the Phoenicians in Palestine. The Nabateans built up their civilization in the southern desert of the Negev and in the Biblical Land of Edom, in what is now the southern part of the Kingdom of Jordan, on a basis of wonderfully well-organized water storage. Living mainly in the Judaean and Samarian hills, the children of Israel may have been luckier than many inhabitants of the Middle East. But the Bible abounds with references to the need for water and to the sense of near-luxury when there was water in abundance.

"For us, the first stage was to turn ourselves into simple farmers like the Arabs," Eshkol told me. "Soon enough, we could work harder than Arabs and more efficiently. But the first big breakthrough had to wait until we introduced irrigation. And for that we had to produce the water."

The ceaseless search for water occupied much of Eshkol's time but until the mid-1930s he met with only limited success. A well was found here and there, and in Galilee the settlers began to use more irrigation ditches for growing their vegetables. In 1936 Eshkol met an engineer, Simha Blas, traveling on the narrow-gauge line from Haifa to Degania. Blas had been a kibbutznik in Degania, and he told Eshkol how he had been thinking over the problems of large-scale irrigation and had come to the conclusion that an aqueduct should be built from the river Jordan across Galilee, now the most promising area of Jewish settlement. Blas had plenty of other ideas, and his inventive mind ranged over the length and breadth of Palestine. Eshkol pinned him down to something specific and not too grandiose—the utilization of the Naaman river inland from the port of Acre. This was a modest scheme, involving digging out and banking a section of the river and channeling some of its waters to the farms on both banks of the river. But the waters of the Naaman turned out to be too salty. The project had to be dropped.

That convinced Blas that there had to be a major program to discover new sources of water underground. As Eshkol put it, "There were two Palestines, the one of rocks and soil on which we stood, and the Palestine far below of wells of water. The second was just as important as the first."[8] But a drilling program would cost a lot of money. Blas believed that one of the best prospects was east of Haifa, where the discovery of water would enable a new center of Jewish settlement to be established close to the Emek of Jezreel. His estimate was that at least $20,000 would be needed for initial drillings.

The Jewish community had to count every penny spent on development, and Blas, although an expert on Palestine's geological structure, could give no guarantee that he would strike water. Eshkol argued the case to the Zionist Council, but received, as he remembered it, only the discouraging reply that "he who holds his soul dear should keep away from such things." To the Zionist Council and the Jewish Agency, drilling where there was no record of water having ever been found savored of midsummer madness.

Eshkol solved the financial problem. He had recently returned from Germany, where he had been working out plans for resettling German Jews in Palestine while saving at least some of their capital and property. The transfer of capital abroad was extremely difficult, since the Nazi regime had introduced numerous currency regulations. Eshkol hit on the idea of raising a Reichsmark loan, in Germany, from the German-Jewish community and using the money to purchase all the equipment which would be needed for a large-scale effort to utilize water resources in Palestine.

He first approached leading members of the German-Jewish community personally and secured promises of about $100,000. He next arranged a 20-year loan at 4 percent interest. About $8 million was subscribed; a single family invested 250,000 marks, equivalent to about $100,000. With this money Eshkol began to buy drills, pumps, and pipes in Germany. The company which he and Blas formed to use the loan was named *Mir,* or furrow, and Blas supplied a prospectus with a single pilot project for $200 in it.

The very first drilling, at Kfar Hassidim, six miles east of Haifa, produced excellent results. The subsoil, Eshkol recalled, was "Ukrainian-type black clay, desperate stuff to drill through," and when they struck water he remembered saying, "Now I believe in Blas as I believe in God." In fact, Blas had proved an immensely important point that careful study of existing geological surveys could lead to the discovery of considerable untapped sources of water. The drilling went on, but without publicity. The Arabs were likely to be highly suspicious of any improvement of the land carried out by the Jews. Eshkol had some difficulty sidetracking the demand for celebrations at Kfar Hassidim when the new springs there had produced their first 100,000 cubic metres of piped water.

There were setbacks, too, like the collapse of part of the wall of a small reservoir at Kfar Hassidim. More than 26,100 cubic yards of precious water were lost. Blas gave him the news at Afula, intercepting him as he was on his way from the Histadrut headquarters in Tel Aviv to spend a day or two at Degania B. It was late on a Friday evening, but Eshkol simply turned around and headed back to Kfar Hassidim, where he found that the pipeline at the outlet to the reservoir had not been sufficiently reinforced.

"We had asked the Jewish Agency and, more important, our German shareholders, to buy an idea," Eshkol told me. "Really, faith was most important of all in the business of finding water. Moses had simply struck the rock and water had gushed forth. But we had to have money to make a start." On one point Eshkol was absolutely determined: the water resources of the country should be the property of the community, so that every man should have a right to use them and every man should have water at the same price. For this reason, the Mekorot Water Company was established in 1937, as a nonprofit corporation controlled by the Jewish Agency and the Histadrut's offshoot of the Hevrat Ovdim. Mekorot began work in a shabby office with a staff of 12. In its first year of operation only a few acres along the Naaman river were being systematically irrigated. Thirty years later the company had grown in staff to 1730, and irrigated over 300,000 acres of land. The Kfar Hassidim drillings had launched a program which resulted in a network of pipes and conduits being spread over the whole of Western Galilee.

Land and water were Eshkol's first loves, and he always returned to them gladly. Photographs of him on the land show him at his happiest —shouldering a pick, down on one knee planting a sapling, standing deeply preoccupied, with other settlers around him in the fields. By the late 1930s his face had become lined, his hair had receded, and he had begun wearing glasses. He had put on some weight but he was still physically powerful. He retained his easy genial manner and his ready smile and laugh. This was a man to work for and with. One of his contemporaries[9] told me that Eshkol had a reputation as the best kind of *chaver*, or comrade. He had time for everyone, and sympathy too. Very well read himself, he had a great respect for people of intellect. (At a much later date he organized a fund for writers in the Hebrew language and, with typical humor, told the first beneficiaries from the fund, "Here's the cash; you deserve it. Now you can get down to work criticizing the Establishment!") Down-to-earth in all practical matters, he had an instinctive appreciation of solid worth in an individual. He liked choosing those who were to work with him and he had a special sympathy for black sheep. He was fond of quoting the saying that no society can exist without at least ten *baklanin* or good-for-nothings; he wanted the baklanin on his side.

Eshkol was now closely connected with the work of the Jewish "Home Guard," the Haganah. The 1929 Arab riots had shown that, as time went by, there was even less chance of the Jews' being allowed to settle down in peace with their neighbors. Arab opinion was hardening. In 1933 there were riots directed against the British authorities for allowing increased Jewish immigration (the persecutions of the Jews by Hitler were just beginning). In 1935 the embryonic Arab political groupings for once united in order to present the British with demands for a stop to all immigration, the prohibition of sales of land to Jews, and the institution of an Arab-dominated Parliament. In April, 1936, the Arabs declared a general strike, which lasted for the best part of five months, although badly coordinated and never total. The Mufti was organizing an illegal guerilla army, which was especially active in the Judaean and Samarian hills around Jenin, Nablus, and Latrun. There was a whole rash of attacks on Jews, and during the course of the year at least 80 were killed. In broad daylight the Arab Higher Committee organized the murder of the British District Commissioner of Galilee, L. Y. Andrews, in 1937, and the dynamiting of part of the Jewish quarter in Jaffa.

In the past, the Jewish community had adopted a policy of *Havlagah*, or self-restraint, in the face of Arab attack and provocation. This was in the tradition of the ghetto, where armed resistance was doomed to failure and where Jews had habitually done no more than barricade themselves in their homes. Some Palestinian Jews, of course, struck back when physically assaulted, and the self-defense of agricultural settlements from marauders had become accepted practice. But the thought behind Havlagah was that the Mandatory authorities had a duty to keep the peace and would surely do so to the best of their ability. The Jews could hope to keep the Mandatory authorities to some extent on their side only if they remained orderly and disciplined in face of provocation.

David Ben-Gurion argued that Jewish self-restraint and Arab provocativeness sometimes combined to favor the Jewish community. He told one interviewer that Arab hostility had not proved an unrelieved curse. Persistent Arab antagonism before the establishment of the State of Israel led to a more cohesive Jewish community, to the strengthening of its resolve, and to the development of ingenuity and resources to combat aggression. Arab actions often boomeranged. Thus, the massacre of the Jews of Jaffa helped speed the building of Jewish Tel Aviv. Attacks on Jews in the Old City of Jerusalem drove Jews to the higher ground of West Jerusalem, which they were able to defend in the 1948 War of Independence. The strike of the Arab dock laborers in 1936 forced the Jews to build the port of Tel Aviv.

The Hebron massacre in 1929 was a turning point in Jewish thinking on the subject of defense. Haganah established a regular headquarters and a management committee. Typically, this led to a division of the Jewish defense effort. Jabotinsky and his right-wing revisionists wanted to revive the wartime idea of a Jewish Legion. Jabotinsky argued that it could be put under British command and become in effect a force of vigilantes for the preservation of law and order; the Arabs, he correctly supposed, would be incapable of doing anything along the same lines. Jabotinsky next proposed that a Judaean Regiment should be set up. When nothing came of this, he took his followers out of the Haganah and formed an offshoot, Irgun Haganah Bet, which later developed into the Irgun Zvai Leumi, an organization which turned increasingly to acts of terrorism against both British and Arabs. Part of the tragedy of the split was that Jabotinsky took with him many of the most efficient and dedicated settlers.

Eshkol advised the Haganah, as he advised the Histadrut, on practical problems. He became its chief financial administrator and one of its experts on arms procurement. By 1934 he was running the organization's budget and collecting its funds. He became a member of its Central Committee, first of six, and then of ten members. He was sharply opposed to the split with Irgun, and his attitude was described to me by Alouf Avidar, one of his colleagues in Haganah. "A small group, even if it feels rather differently from the majority, should have put itself at the disposal of a properly constituted and representative defense force like the Haganah. Why should a small group, with arms of its own, have the right to decide on an independent policy which can affect the whole nation? Possession of arms should not be an entitlement to independent action."[10] The trouble was that Irgun, more activist in its approach, was more efficient in collecting arms.

Working often five or six hours in the evening for Haganah in addition to his other tasks, Eshkol gradually organized a valuable central pool of arms. He helped to build up a regular staff where there had previously been only one full-time, paid Haganah man before. And he played a big part in organizing Haganah units in the towns, where the Jews had hitherto been most prone to attack and most helpless.

It was sometime in 1936 that the Haganah leadership began to discuss the possibility of counter-offensive tactics to discourage Arab terrorism. But it was a difficult subject; the Jews did not want to indulge in terrorist acts themselves. They had no clear plan. It seemed for a moment as if the British authorities might step into the breach. The High Commissioner, Sir Arthur Wauchope, was becoming alarmed by increasing Arab lawlessness. He enrolled about 500 Jews as supernumerary police, or *Notrim,* and he offered to put them on a permanent footing and arm them effectively, if Haganah handed in its arms and disbanded.

Haganah refused for two reasons. It was afraid that the Notrim would become an instrument of the Mandatory authorities, and it knew that a more serious struggle with the Arabs lay ahead. Some of the Notrim were drafted into the Jewish Settlement Police. But Haganah had to turn elsewhere for help and inspiration. It found both in a most surprising quarter.

In September 1936, a young British officer, Captain Charles Orde Wingate, arrived in Palestine. According to one of his biographers, he was, in addition to being a zealous Christian and an admirer of Oliver Cromwell, a convinced Zionist who believed that he had a mission in the Middle East. "Long before I reached Palestine I knew what the Jews were seeking, understood what they needed, sympathized with their aims, and knew they were right."[11] Wingate was only a junior officer but he had a magnetic personality which impressed his seniors, however little they liked him. He was much given to bitter sarcasm, called his brother officers "military apes," and made a habit of flouting regulations. He was totally unconventional, ruthless, inspired, and, in the eyes of many of his fellows, plainly crazy. Weizmann called him "my favorite madman."[12]

Plainly, Wingate intended to help the Jews of Palestine in any way possible. He quickly found a pretext for doing so. British tactics in combating the Mufti's Arab guerillas were badly out of date and unimaginative. British army commanders had become convinced that air support would solve their problems. Their habit was to send patrols along the roads, to call up air support when the patrols were fired on, and then undertake a laborious chase long after the guerillas had melted away into the hills. This did not, admittedly, cause heavy British casualties—Arab proficiency with firearms was limited—but it meant that raiders could operate with impunity.

Wingate set out to change this. He applied to General Sir Archibald (later Lord) Wavell for permission to organize Jewish fighting patrols to track down raiders and saboteurs. Wavell's somewhat inscrutable exterior concealed a keen and imaginative brain. Like Wingate, he was unconventional, but only in thought. Wingate's curious habits, of forgetting to shave or salute, dispensing with badges of rank, and treating the officers' mess as if it were simply the worst restaurant in the world, must have horrified a man as shyly polite as Wavell.* But the General instinctively recognized resourcefulness and resolution when he saw them. After sending Wingate to Nazareth as local intelligence officer, he gave him permission to go ahead with his plans.

Wingate had already worked out his tactics. He laid down his *Soldiers' Ten Commandments*. Caring not at all for the regulations of the parade ground, he demanded total dedication in the field. He stressed four precepts for fighting the Arab guerillas: speed of movement, offensive spirit, the use of the vital element of surprise, and ability to fight at night. These four precepts have become part of the standard training of every citizen soldier of the State of Israel.

Wingate set up his headquarters at the Jewish agricultural settlement of Ein Harod, in the shadow of the Gilboan Hills where Saul had been slain in the battle with the Philistines. There he organized his special night squads, ostensibly in order to protect the Haifa oil pipeline but in reality to hunt down Arab raiding parties and destroy them. Wingate taught his Jewish volunteers another valuable lesson. He "led from the front" and set an example of dash, determination, and eye for terrain which the Palestinian Jews never forgot. In the winter of 1937–1938, his patrols were already active. Six months later, when Wavell had already handed over his command to General Haining, Wingate was ordered to disband his special night squads. His commanding officer's confidential report had said that he put Jewish interests before those of his own country, that he was a security risk, and that he should never be allowed to serve in Palestine again.

Wingate himself believed fervently that he would return one day to the Holy Land and would lead a Jewish army to victory. Although that particular dream never came true, he had already done his job in Palestine. The men whom he had trained were to become leaders in the 1948 War of Independence and the founders of the Israeli army. Before he left, Wingate wrote a paper on "The Jewish State, Security and Defense, Interim Period" which was of considerable value to Haganah. Yet another of his precepts, explained in this paper, became an article of faith to the Jews. It was to explain to soldiers just what they were doing and why. As Yakov Dori, who worked directly under Wingate, said afterwards: "They should at least know what they were dying for."

In *Utopians at Bay*, Horace Kallen wrote: "Orde Wingate transformed Haganah from a high-grade sheriff's posse into a passionately disciplined commando, in ideal a body of soldiers whose capacities for individual initiative, resourcefulness, skill, and invention can come into

---

* The author once listened to a lecture by Wavell and met him "in the mess" afterward. The subject matter of the lecture was obviously first-class, but its delivery dry and apologetic.

the most intimate team play with one another."[13] There is also the tribute of General Moshe Dayan: "I never knew him to lose an engagement. He was never worried about odds. . . . There were many men who served with him from Ein Harod who later became officers in the Israeli Army which fought and defeated the Arabs, but they were not the only ones who benefited from his training. In some sense, every leader in the Israeli Army, even today, is a disciple of Wingate. He gave us our technique, he was the inspiration of our tactics."[14]

Wingate's departure coincided with an upsurge of Haganah activity in the fields of organization and of arms procurement. In towns Haganah began to base itself on the cadre principle. The possibility of world war was becoming more obvious daily. The Haganah leaders were prepared for a Jewish contribution if world war came, but they intended to be ready for civil war too. The organization of small, tightly bound groups of men in every local headquarters, with standing orders which could be put instantly into effect, was a necessity. The Arabs were to learn in 1948 how far Haganah had come since the loosely knit home guard of the early 1930s. Late in 1938 Haganah arms-procurement officers were sent to Poland, where they bought about 300 rifles, over 200 machineguns, 10,000 hand grenades and 700 tons of ammunition. Most of these arms were to remain stored for the next ten years, many of them in Jewish-owned factories that established small, secret caches.

In Haganah and, to a minor extent, Irgun, the Jewish community had, by 1939, the necessary means to defend itself. It had also taken one big step toward greater political unity. This was the union of Achdut Ha'avoda and Hapoel Hatzair in 1930. David Ben-Gurion has generally been given the prime credit for this. But the stumbling block in the previous efforts to unite these two socialist parties had been the reluctance of Hapoel Hatzair to give up its unique character of a sort of Order of Labor, a free-and-easy freemasonry, untrammeled by ideology and dedicated to practical achievement. Eshkol, it should be remembered, had been the apostle of labor unity in the past, and Eshkol played the leading part in overcoming the doubts of his friends. The new, unified party was named Mapai, the initials standing for "the Israel labor party." Its basic aims were the continued ingathering of the Jewish people, the reclamation of the land of Israel, and the establishment of a society based on humanitarian principles and social justice.

An even more significant union seemed to have taken place in 1934, when a truce was patched up between the Labor movement and Jabotinsky's revisionists. Jabotinsky and Ben-Gurion agreed that there should be a unified, all-out effort to support Zionist aims in Palestine. Plans were worked out for a union of the Histadrut with Jabotinsky's National Labor Organization (the latter had a mere 7000 members against the 65,000 of the Histadrut). Machinery was to be set up for compulsory arbitration between employers and workers in the event of there being a threat of a strike which could damage the Jewish community. The agreement was reached by the two men in London, but when the news of it leaked prematurely the Histadrut denounced any clause which tied the hands of organized labor. Jabotinsky, an impulsive man, was furious, and the agreement was never ratified. One of the consequences of this was the later formation of Irgun, and the splitting of the Jewish defense effort.

Eshkol, it may be noted at this point, had married for the second time in 1928. His first marriage ended a year earlier, but he had drifted apart from his wife, Rivka Marshak, long before then. It was a clear case of incompatibility, heightened by the problems of the burgeoning Jewish community in Palestine. Rivka failed to identify herself with her husband's work. Married couples can often manage very well without having the same interests; but this was not easy in the Palestine of the 1920s. A daughter, Noa, was born to this first marriage in 1924, but Rivka went off to the United States for a prolonged visit. Absence, in this case, did not make the heart grow fonder.

His second wife, Elisheva Kaplan, came, like Eshkol, from Russia and was the daughter of a pioneer. She was born in 1900 and by 1928 had already developed a consuming interest in the building up of the Jewish community. She was a person of charm, forcefulness, and individuality and she became a leader of the Women's Wing of the Histadrut. Three daughters were born of her marriage to Levi Eshkol; the first, Dvora, in 1930. Their marriage was to last 31 years. It was ideally happy; not just because they remained in love, but because they shared every ideal worth having, the betterment of their own people, their consolidation as a community in the fickle Middle Eastern kaleidoscope, and the eventual betterment of humanity as a whole.

1. Marie Syrkin in *Golda Meir, Woman With a Cause*, p. 99.
2. Howard Sachar in *The People of Israel* gives the best account of this.
3. Christopher Sykes, *Cross Roads to Israel*, p. 117.
4. Meyer Weisgal, ed., *Chaim Weizmann*, p. 125.
5. Sir John Glubb, *Britain and the Arabs*, p. 149.
6. Arthur Ruppin, *Three Decades of Palestine*, p. 213.
7. Dr. Yosef Weitz, in personal conversation with the author.
8. Eshkol, in conversation with the author.
9. Israel Cohen, in personal conversation with the author.
10. Avidar, in conversation with the author.
11. Leonard Mosley, *Gideon Goes to War*, p. 34.
12. *Ibid.*, p. 36.
13. Horace M. Kallen, *Utopians at Bay*, p. 215.
14. Mosley, *op. cit.*, p. 63.

7.

Early in 1933 one of the most outstanding younger members of *Mapai,* the Israel labor party, Chaim Arlosoroff, was sent to Germany to find out as much as he could about the true situation of the 550,000 German Jews. He was to examine two questions in particular: how serious Nazi persecution of the Jews was likely to become, and whether avoidance of Nazi persecution could not be coordinated with the need to increase the immigration of German Jews into Palestine.

Arlosoroff returned to Tel Aviv after only preliminary discussions, although it was already clear to him that Nazi persecution was likely to increase but that the tendency of German Jews would be to "stay put" and hope for better days. Just after his return, while walking contemplatively along the beach at Tel Aviv, he was approached by a man who asked him for a light. He shot Arlosoroff dead, at point-blank range, while the latter was fumbling for a box of matches.

Arlosoroff's fault, in the eyes of Jewish activists, was that he was too much of a moderate, a disciple of Chaim Weizmann, who advocated the maintenance of good relations with the British Mandatory authorities and the use of careful and rational persuasion in order to achieve Zionist aims. Nobody was indicted for this needless and shocking crime, but suspicion remained fastened on one of Jabotinsky's Revisionists followers, Abraham Stavsky. The crime was particularly shocking because, in their struggle to build their community in Palestine, Jews had not hitherto turned against Jews. To be a Jew was in itself sufficient qualification for full membership in their community and for protection by it. By a curious coincidence two parallel main streets in Tel Aviv are today named after Arlosoroff, the victim, and Jabotinsky.

One upshot of the murder was that Levi Eshkol was sent soon afterwards to Germany to carry on Arlosoroff's work. But before describing how he did this, it is well to give some account of the German Jewish community there and what was happening to it.

The Jewish community in the Germany of 1933 was prosperous and contented. Its members had reasons to believe that they were, gradually, becoming accepted as something better than second-class citizens. Kaiser Wilhelm II had helped to make them "respectable" by his friendship with the Hamburg Jew and shipowner, Albert Ballin. Thousands of Jews had served in World War I, and some Jews became prominent in politics during the 1919–1933 era of the Weimar Republic. Eight Jews and four half-Jews were among the first 40 Germans who won Nobel Prizes. Of the 550,000 Jews in Germany, about 100,000 were engaged in commerce, 100,000 were white collar employees, 40,000 were industrial workers, and 25,000 belonged to professions. The Jews of Germany made a contribution to the arts, legal and medical professions, and to science, altogether out of proportion to their numbers.

The Jews of Germany were still very far from being fully assimilated, but they had become acclimatized over the centuries. They did not emigrate readily to Palestine, where they tended to be laughed at because they were often very punctilious, punctual, and Prussian. Other Jews called them "Yecke," the name apparently derived from *Jacke,* or jacket, and from the fact that German immigrants were highly genteel and clung to this garment (in Palestine's warm climate Jews usually wore not jackets but open-necked shirts). A standard gibe at the newly arrived and supposedly self-important German immigrant was to say, *"Nur Sie, Herr Doktor, haben wir erwartet"* ("We have been waiting just for *you,* Herr Doktor"). The German Jews tended to form cliques, stuck to speaking German—they still do in Tel Aviv and Haifa—and found difficulty in learning Hebrew.[1]

Howard Sachar quotes one German Jewish employer as saying: "The fact is that if you want to make money, you just don't come to Israel. It's that simple."[2] Up to 1932, over 70 percent of the relatively few German Jews who did come were industrial or white collar workers. After Nazi persecution began, the percentage dropped to 45, as more and more well-to-do middle-class German Jews came to the conclusion that they must leave a life which had been comfortable and rewarding. They were slow to do so; it was only human to go on hoping that things would improve and that the Nazi storm would blow itself out. And many of them felt like Professor Willstaetter of Munich University, who told Weizmann: "I know that Germany has gone mad, but if a mother falls ill it is not a reason for her children to desert her."

So often in the past the Jews had simply stuck it out when they were persecuted. And, as so often in the past, the Gentile world was not much interested in their lot. The infamous *Protocols of the Elders of Zion*—purporting to prove the existence of a Jewish plot against world civilization—were widely circulated both inside and outside Germany, and there was the usual tendency among anti-Semites to say that the Jews had brought their troubles on themselves, by disloyalty, profiteering, and just being different. Well-informed observers of the German scene regarded Nazi racial persecution as a temporary aberration. Thus, Douglas Reed, in *Insanity Fair:* "The anti-Jewish racket in Germany is a pricked balloon, a hollow bluff, a shop-window exhibit. . . . The Jews know it in their hearts. They may hate National Socialism as much as ever, but they no longer fear it. hey know that they have but to bide their time."[3] Reed maintained that even the Nuremberg racial laws of 1936 merely "meant the end of the bluff. Of what practical importance is a law forbidding German maidservants under the age of 45 to serve in Jewish households? It is a rare insult. It will not drive one Jew from Germany or lessen by one pfennig the turnover of a Jewish trader."[4]

Long before 1936 it should have been obvious that the situation of the Jewish community in Germany was a good deal more serious than regulations about employing an Aryan housemaid might have suggested. Already in 1933, the Nazi regime excluded Jews from public office, civil service, theater, radio, journalism. In 1934 they were barred from the stock exchange, and later from practicing as lawyers or doctors. Jewish shops were boycotted and the books by Jewish authors—Freud, Einstein, Arnold, Rathenau, and Stefan Zweig—were among those flung on the bonfires organized by Hitler's Minister of Propaganda, Josef Goebbels. Even playing music by Jewish composers was banned. Clumsy German wit was sometimes employed against the Jews, and one writer tells of a road sign at a sharp bend in a road near Ludwigshafen: "Drive carefully! Sharp turn! Jews, 75 miles an hour!"[5]

Nazi propaganda against the Jews was singularly disgusting, and it was with never-failing astonishment that one saw at this period decently dressed, outwardly respectable, and often middle-aged Germans staring impassively at the crude cartoons in the *Stuermer*, Julius Streicher's anti-Semitic weekly, displayed at street corners in small glass-framed boxes. One of Streicher's favorite themes was evil Jewish doctors ravishing lovely blonde Aryan girls. Another was the Jews drinking Christian blood. This propaganda, which included the demand for castration of all male Jews, reached its climax in 1938, when during the "Crystal Night" of November 9 to 10 dozens of synagogues were burned to the ground, thousands of Jews were beaten up, and a nation-wide pogrom took place that put even those of Tsarist Russia in the shade.

For Zionist organizations, the problem of helping the Jews who were being persecuted involved deciding on priorities. In the Soviet Union Jewish exclusiveness was being discouraged. Both religious observance and the use of Hebrew were frowned on, and the Soviet rulers made efforts to forestall the Jewish search for a sense of identity by providing the Jews with special areas for "colonization" in the Crimea and Birobidjan. The Soviet desire was to assimilate the Russian Jews, and assimilation was, to the Zionists, almost as great an enemy as persecution.

In Poland there was some discrimination against the Jews, and one Polish politician, Colonel Beck, openly stated that there were "one million Jews too many" in his country. Of the three and a half million in Poland at least one third lived in oppressive poverty. Up to 1919 Polish Jews had traded with the Russian hinterland, for Poland had been a province of Russia. The Jewish middle class in the Pale of Settlement had a genuine *raison d'être*. This was lost when the Poles began to establish their own middle class, for Polish-Jewish trade could not be diverted westward into the more highly developed German market.

Both Russian and Polish Jewry attracted a great deal of Zionist attention at this time. But there was ready understanding for the plight of the German Jews. As early as August 1933 Arthur Ruppin was declaring that "this hostility to the Jews on the part of the German government has definitely become an integral part of its program, and almost an article of faith."[6] Ruppin drew the conclusion that "the best protest against the Jewish policy of the German government is the work of rescue" and that "there is no other escape but by an organized emigration." Ruppin believed that at least 200,000 German Jews would be forced to leave their homes, and that Palestine could take in a third or even half of them. For, as Ruppin saw it, "Palestine is something more than the largest center or refuge for the Jews . . . it is, even for many who do not come to Palestine, the only ray of light left in their lives."[7]

When Eshkol first arrived in Nazi Germany early in 1934, efforts to help the Jewish community there had already begun. The German Jews had, with Zionist backing, formed two organizations of their own. The *Reichsvertretung der deutschen Juden* (The Reich Association of German Jews) was entrusted with representing Jewish interests and needs to the Nazi government, a thankless task. The *Kulturbund* (Cultural Association) tried to maintain the Jewishness of closely knit communities either living in ghettoes or concentrated in less exactly defined sections of German cities. More obviously constructive was the work of the *Aliyat Hanoar*, the youth immigration movement founded by Recha Freier. Working with great circumspection, it managed to send just over 5000 German Jewish children to Palestine between 1934 and 1939.[8] Committees were being formed in several countries to provide help for German Jewry, but it was going to take another three years for a Council for German Jewry to be established in London, aiming at the coordination of the planning of Jewish emigration from Germany.

Eshkol had two paramount objectives. Immigration into Palestine was already rising steeply (it reached 30,000 in 1933, 42,000 in 1934, and 62,000 in 1933). The Jewish community in Palestine needed reinforcements for the struggle which undoubtedly lay ahead. German Jewry could offer the immigrants money, ideas, cultural background. It was therefore doubly necessary to secure as many German Jewish immigrants as possible.

Eshkol's second objective was equally clear cut. German Jewry, compared with Jewish communities elsewhere in the Diaspora, was wealthy. The Nazis intended keeping its wealth in the country. Eshkol had to find means of getting at least some of it out. "In fact," he told me,

> this was meant to be the main purpose of my mission. But I regarded it as even more important to bring the sad, abandoned German Jews home. It was not at all easy. I had to explain what the land of Israel had to offer them, and why they should go there. The older people did not always believe me; so I made a point of going to the young and telling them what Zionism was in practice. There I had more success, for it was a time, surprisingly enough, of

Jewish revival. Young people were coming back to the Jewish faith, sometimes after their parents had left it.[9]

Jabotinsky's Revisionists claimed that Eshkol's mission amounted to "trading with the enemy" and demanded his recall. With his usual phlegmatic calm Eshkol simply got down to work. He found a complex situation to deal with.

After seizing power in March 1933, the Nazis had levied a 10 percent tax on money transferred abroad as blocked marks by emigrants, but the first 1000 Palestine pounds' worth could be transferred at the official rate of exchange by the head of a family or a single person. Rather surprisingly the Jews, as one authority pointed out, regarded this 10 percent tax as a severe burden.[10] They still had little idea of what was in store for them in Nazi Germany. Efforts were quickly made to avoid payment of the tax by organizing trading companies which collected money from Jews wishing to emigrate, purchased German goods with it, exported these goods to Palestine, and reimbursed the emigrants in Palestine pounds. The first company of this kind was called Hanote'a. Its transfers were assisted by organizations in Palestine and Germany— in Palestine, the so-called *Paltreu* (Palestine Trustee Office for the advising of German Jews) and in Germany, Jewish-owned banks, Messrs. Warburg in Hamburg and Wassermann in Berlin. These operations of Hanote'a marked the beginning of the *Ha'avara* (transfer) project for moving Jewish assets from Germany to Palestine.

Jewish property in Germany in 1933 was estimated to have a total value of 12 billion marks ($5 billion). Transfers in the first 15 months of the Nazi regime, up to July 1934, amounted to about 6 million marks.[11] Eshkol and Zwi Schreiber, who was sent with him to Berlin, worked out plans for ordering increased quantities of German goods. They had to speed up the transfer of Jewish funds which had been slowed down by the vast amount of paper work, bureaucratic accounting methods, and lack of sympathy on the part of the German authorities. By mid-1934 applicants were being informed that they would have to wait at least one year for the money paid over to Hanote'a to be available to them and their families in Palestine.

Eshkol and Schneider made an early breakthrough by securing the cooperation of several Jewish companies in Palestine in placing orders for German goods. It was at this time that Eshkol devised his plan for buying steel pipes and pumping equipment for the still embryonic Mekorot water board. In August 1934 these efforts resulted in arrangements for the transfer of five million marks, an immense improvement on previous performance. Eshkol, with commendable common sense, argued that Palestine was justified in importing any German goods if they in fact constituted Jewish "property in kind."

New obstacles appeared. The boycott of German goods by world

Jewry was scarcely an encouragement to the Nazi regime to cooperate in the transfer of exchange to Palestine. At the same time, Germany was interested in building up her export markets. Eshkol and Schreiber played on this interest as well as on the active desire of German steel and engineering firms to retain and fulfill the export quotas allowed them by the Reich Ministry of Economics. In 1935 transfers increased from 9 to 13 million marks (the figures for the other years up to the war were 20 million marks in 1936, 31 million in 1937, 19 million in 1938, and 8 million in 1939).[12] Transfers were helped markedly by a clearing agreement for shipment of Palestine citrus fruits in return for German goods.

But the transfers were being carried out at rates which were increasingly unfavorable to German Jews. This was due partly to German monetary legislation, partly to rising administrative costs, and partly to the need for Jewish export agencies in Germany to grant large bonuses in order to compete with those already given to German exporters by the Nazi Government. The reason for these bonuses was Nazi Germany's desperate need of foreign exchange. New taxes were clamped on exported exchange, including the *Reichsfluchtsteuer,* or flight-from-Germany tax, and the *Exportfoerderungsabgabe,* export incentive contribution. In 1936 it cost a German Jew 12,500 marks to secure 1000 Palestine pounds. In 1937 the cost was 17,500 marks, in 1938 25,000, and in 1939 40,000 marks.[13] These unfavorable exchange rates were a factor in discouraging German Jews from emigrating. Another was the withdrawal of the "privilege" of being allowed to transfer $5700 worth of marks at the official rate of exchange when actually leaving the country. In 1939 German Jews could only buy their tickets with marks and carry $90 worth of foreign currency per person with them.

In retrospect it may seem surprising that the Nazis allowed the monetary transfers to go on at all, considering the increasing violence of their persecution of the Jews. There was a profusion of anti-Jewish legislation after the *Anschluss,* or union with Austria, in March 1938. For Eshkol, his stay in Germany must have been a grim episode. He could not fail to be aware of the humiliation and fear of the Jewish community. Yet so many Jews were unable to make up their minds to leave. About 52,000 came to Palestine between 1933 and 1939; 230,000 stayed in Germany and almost all of them were liquidated by the Nazis. The 52,000 transferred enough marks to buy just over five million Palestine pounds. In one way and another, a further three million Palestine pounds were bought with marks during the same period. These eight million Palestine pounds were of considerable value to Palestine's economy—especially after the outbreak of the Italian-Abyssinian war in 1935 and the subsequent economic depression in much of the Middle East.

In human terms, Eshkol's mission had been tremendously valuable.

He encouraged Jews to leave Germany for other countries as well as Palestine. In the two years up to September 1935, an estimated 60,000 Jews left Germany, and in the following two years another 100,000. Between September 1937 and the outbreak of World War II, although it became more difficult to leave legally and openly, 115,000 more escaped. Thus, in all, roughly half the German-Jewish community was saved. Thanks to Eshkol and others, they fared better than the Jewish communities in Poland, Hungary, Czechoslovakia, and the Soviet Union.

The word "better" can of course be used only relatively. The Jews who remained in Germany and German-occupied Austria were spared none of the torments inflicted on their fellows elsewhere in Europe. Less than 30,000 of the estimated 240,000 German Jews who stayed on survived the Nazi era. Even before the war broke out, life had been made a misery for them. About 30,000 were already in concentration camps. In Vienna alone there were 3000 suicides in 18 months.[14] For a Jew to enter a public park or garden, to visit a swimming pool or a theater was to commit an offence. Jewish libraries and schools were shut down. The Jews could no longer register for any normal form of employment.

In March 1941 the Nazi leadership decided to embark on the total extermination of European Jewry, the "Final Solution," as the Nazi program was called. That program was carried out with a thoroughness exceeded only by the Christian Crusaders in the Holy Land and with a ruthlessness and brutality which are literally without parallel. It is not the purpose of this book to go into the details of this appalling holocaust, but a few facts have to be mentioned. The Nazis slaughtered about six million European Jews in all. Of the pre-1933 German Jewish community of 550,000 less than 30,000 were left after the war; of 200,000 Austrian Jews, only a few hundred. Polish Jewry's loss was more terrible; only 30,000 remained out of three and a half million.

Shortly after the war Weizmann was to write about an aspect of that tragedy beyond human comprehension:

> Now these great places of Jewish learning in Vilna, Warsaw, Kovno, Breslau, Vienna, Pressburg, have been wiped off the face of the earth; the great Jewish archives have been plundered or destroyed, and we have to reconstruct them fragmentarily page by page. We have suffered not only physically; we have been murdered intellectually, and the world scarcely realizes the extent of our affliction. It sounds like a cruel irony when British or American statesmen reproach the remnants of Jewry, when they wish to leave the graves in Germany and Austria and Holland and move to Palestine, where they hope to build a new life. . . .[15]

To Eshkol it was the physical and mental suffering of millions of tortured, trampled-down, and brutally murdered Jews which counted most. There was never more than a trickle of news coming out of Nazi-occupied Europe, but that trickle never ceased. When the news of the destruction of the ghettoes in Poland and Western Russia first reached Palestine, Eshkol joined the thousands of Jews who fasted, in order to show their sense of community with their suffering brethren in Europe. To fast was only an outward sign of the inward bitterness and horror over what was happening. As the terrible stories of Nazi cruelty piled up, Jewish grief knew no bounds; to the Jew in Palestine in particular, it was as if a part of himself was being ripped out.

Could the Western powers have done something to reduce the scale of the Jewish tragedy? Certainly they could have tried harder, as some of their critics have made very plain. One of the most searing indictments of British policy came from Harry Sacher, himself a British Jew and a former editorial writer of the *Manchester Guardian*. In *Israel: The Establishment of a State,* he pointed out that Britain was committed to allow the Jews free entry into Palestine under the terms of the Mandate. Article Six laid down that "the Administration of Palestine, while ensuring that the rights and position of other sections of the population are not prejudiced, shall facilitate Jewish immigration under suitable conditions and shall encourage, in cooperation with the Jewish Agency, close settlement by the Jews on the land, including State lands and waste lands not required for public purposes."[16]

Sacher considers that the British Government contravened this clause of the Mandate in the following ways:

It refused speedy entry of 20,000 Jewish children from Poland, and 10,000 more from the Balkans into Palestine. "They died in the gas chambers."

It recommended that entry permits be "saved up" to be used after the war for other German Jews, supposedly "of a better type" than those from the Balkans—in fact, the Jews against whom the British authorities could not advance the argument that they were unsuitable material as immigrants.

It established that the Jews arriving from Europe without permits would be interned in Cyprus and elsewhere and, presumably because of the trouble caused the British authorities in wartime, would never be allowed into Palestine even after the war.

Finally, it delayed the admission of Jews' coming via Istanbul, the last escape route by land from Nazi-occupied Europe, until mid-July 1943. Then, by an alleged "oversight," the Turkish government was not informed until April 1944 that immigrants using this route would at least be dealt with in British-occupied territory (in this case, former French Syria) instead of being turned back at the Turkish frontier.

One or two figures may indicate what not sealing off the land route might have meant. Of Greece's 70,000 Jews only 10,000 survived. The main center of the Greek Jews was Salonika, within reasonable reach of the Turkish frontier. Likewise, only 10,000 of Yugoslavia's 60,000 Jews survived; many of those who perished might have reached Turkish territory if it had been the logical end of an escape route. Some of the hundreds of thousands of Hungarian and Rumanian Jews who were carted off to the gas chambers might have done the same.

In his book *While Six Million Died* Arthur Morse has other, more damaging accusations to make against Britain, the United States, and other Western countries. These are based on the thought that many more German and Austrian Jews could have been helped to leave their countries before the war, when the Nazis were still ready to let them go. The United States government of President Franklin D. Roosevelt refused to open its doors to Jewish refugees, and accepted only 11,000 between 1933 and 1936. Yet its immigration quotas could have allowed 450,000 people in, since half of the quota was unfilled.

The March 1938 Evian Conference, held for the purpose of facilitating the emigration of German and Austrian Jews, did nothing of the kind. The British representative declared that Britain's colonial empire contained no territory suitable for large-scale settlement of refugees—and this at a time when Britons still gloried in an Empire "on which the sun never set!" The only states ready to accept refugees without putting any destructive argument in the way were Holland and the Scandinavian countries. The United States, France, and Britain were particularly obsessed with the security risks involved.

In April 1943, neutral Sweden offered to accept 20,000 Jewish children for the duration of the war. Sweden asked only for a guarantee that the belligerent Western Powers would accept them after the war. No guarantee was forthcoming. The so-called Riegner Plan of the same period, proposing the rescue of Jewish children from Vichy France, could not be implemented because the United States would not produce money and visas. A Rumanian offer to transfer the bulk of the 185,000 Jews held in concentration camps by early 1942 was blocked for a year by the British and United States governments. Admittedly, a real security risk would inevitably have been involved in their transfer, for German agents could have easily infiltrated the ranks of genuine refugees.

Finally, there was an effort of a Jew, Joel Brand, to avert the shipment of Hungarian Jews to Auschwitz and other death camps in return for the delivery of 10,000 heavy trucks to Nazi Germany by the Western Allies. Brand, and others, wanted the British and Americans to bomb the railway lines in the Carpathians as another way of halting shipments to those camps. The Western Allies decided it was impracticable.

Some of the critics of the Western Allies have imputed base motives to that policy of procrastination. Thus, the Irgun leader, Samuel Katz, maintained that Britain wanted to freeze the numbers of Jews in Palestine in order to avoid giving offense to the Arabs.[17] In reality, the motives of the Western Allies were simpler. They were truly afraid of the security risk involved in bringing large numbers of refugees into Allied-occupied territory in time of war. They begrudged any payment to the Germans, whether in kind or in cash through Swiss banks, on the ground that it could prolong the war. Finally, they were preoccupied with the task of winning the war and not disposed to deviate from it.

It remains sadly true that world Jewry has a legitimate grievance against the Western Allies for their failure to do all that they could, both before and during the war. And world Jewry has another legitimate grievance relating to the conduct of the war. This was the refusal of Britain to accept proffered Palestinian Jewish help, to profit from it, and to give an adequate tribute to it afterward.

A word should be said here about the Arab contribution to the war effort as contrasted to that of the Jews. Of course, one can argue that the Arabs of the Middle East had no incentive and no need to help the Western Allies. The moral iniquity of the Nazi regime meant nothing to them; they may even have regarded Nazi liquidation of the Jews as being to their advantage. In World War I they stood to gain something concrete from an Allied victory, the end of Turkish domination over the Fertile Crescent and much of Arabia. Not so in World War II. And this time there was no Lawrence of Arabia to inspire them with a belief in the Allied cause.

Yet it is well to remember who, in the course of history, has been one's friend and who has not. The Arab states of the Middle East, with the honorable exception of Jordan, declared war against Nazi Germany at the last possible moment, with the obvious purpose of securing seats in the United Nations. Egypt delayed doing so until February 1945 and its Prime Minister, Ahmed Maher Pasha, was assassinated on his way to the Senate to confirm the declaration of war.

During the war the Egyptian government leaked plans for the British defense of Egypt to Italian intelligence. In Syria, Hitler's Youth Leader, Baldur von Schirach, later sent to prison as a war criminal, was given a tumultuous welcome, while the only pro-British figure of importance, Dr. Shabander, was murdered. In Iraq a pro-Axis *coup d'état* was launched by Rashid Ali, and King Farouk of Egypt sent him a telegram of congratulations.

The Mufti, Haj Amin Husseini, openly espoused the Nazi cause. He ensconced himself in Bagdad for much of the war and paid frequent visits to Germany for talks with Hitler and his ministers. From 1943 onward he collaborated in raising Moslem units in Bosnia, the Caucasus, and the Crimea, and concocted plans together with the racist Minister for the Eastern Territories, Alfred Rosenberg (later executed as a war criminal), for creating a muftiate for the whole of Southern Russia.[18] The Mufti gave his blessing to the "Final Solution" and urged the liquidaiton of Jewish children upon Nazi officials, who themselves were not soft-hearted but who were beginning to fear the effects of their bestialities on neutral world opinion.

As against all this, about 9000 Arabs were drafted for the Allied war effort. Roughly half of them deserted, usually with their rifles. Only a very few saw active service.[19]

The Jewish community in Palestine was, naturally, ready and eager to join in the war against Hitler, against the persecutor of their people and, it became especially clear when Field-marshal Rommel's Afrika Korps advanced into Egypt, a threat to their own existence. It is not my purpose here to spell out in detail what the Palestinian-Jewish contribution to the Allied war effort amounted to, but here are the salient facts. Out of a total population of 650,000, about 85,000 men and 54,000 women registered for war service. The rest of the community settled down to contribute as well as it could to the war effort. Jewish scientific and medical centers were placed at the disposal of the British forces. According to one authority, Jewish Palestine supplied $132 million worth of material to the British forces during the course of the war, including every one of the mines used by the British Eighth Army to hold up Rommel's advance into Egypt along the El Alamein lines.[20]

At Mishmar Haemek hundreds of Jews were trained in underground resistance in case of a German occupation of Palestine. Approximately 250 Palestinian Jews volunteered for parachute drops into Nazi-occupied Europe, an unbelievably brave act, for they knew that they would have no chance of survival if they were caught. On one occasion 32 men were dropped, mainly for the purpose of organizing underground resistance and escape routes. Most of them were killed. The bulk of the men who enlisted in the British forces were used as support troops along lines of communication or in base areas until July 1944, when Churchill approved the formation of a Jewish brigade group for front line service. Its units fought with great courage and distinction in Italy.

When the war was over some of these Jewish units were able to help Jewish refugees who had found their way over the Brenner Pass and through the valleys of Carinthia into Northern Italy. Moshe Sharett, later Foreign Minister and for a short time Prime Minister of Israel, gave a touching description of this event:

> A car came from one of the Jewish units to fetch a group of refugees to work on a military project. As the machine with the Star of David appeared, it was immediately covered with a swarm of gleeful, shouting tots. The driver stood in his machine, bronzed, powerful, broad-shouldered, and with a beaming face. The children clambered upon the car and the driver, felt in his pocket for candy, climbed into his arms and on his shoulders, clung to him on all sides. He stood, braced and happy, in the midst of the mob of youngsters, all brimful of energy and life.
>
> I did not know him, nor did I ask who he was. He seemed at that moment like the unknown Jewish soldier, the hero of this

suffering and fighting age in Israel. The children seemed like symbols of all the wandering children of Israel, rescued from the slaughter in ghettoes, hiding in Polish forests, sheltered by kindly non-Jews all over Europe. . . . And it seemed to me that, at any moment, the Unknown Driver would take his place at the wheel of the car with the Star of David, and drive it over hill and dale, splitting the sea like a sword, and would bring the children of our people's future, the precious remnants of our hopes, safely into the gates of the Homeland.

As in the time of World War I, there was again bitter disappointment over British uncertainty on the issue of raising exclusively Jewish military units. But during World War II this issue gave precedence to the problem of emigration from Nazi-occupied Europe. The inevitable result of the British policy of rigorously restricting immigration, first in accordance with the White Paper of 1939 and then in conformity with security regulations, was illegal immigration, which swelled into an organized campaign. During the war years, in spite of immense practical difficulties, over 50,000 illegal immigrants reached the shores of Palestine, with another 65,000 coming in during the last chapter of the British Mandate, 1945–1948.

Here only a few landmarks in this campaign of illegal immigration, known by the Jews as Aliyah Bet, need be mentioned.

In March and April 1939, before the White Paper had come out, three small Danubian river boats arrived near the Palestinian coast and were turned back by the British authorities. The ostensible reason for it was the refugees' having no visas. Besides, the British administration was worried by the deterioration in the economic situation and increasing unemployment.

In September 1939 the ship "Tiger Hill" succeeded in landing on the beach at Tel Aviv. The British authorities had by this time instructed the police to fire on ships which refused to answer their challenge. This was done, and two refugees were shot. There was a confused melée on the beach, but most of the refugees managed to escape the clutches of the police and go into hiding.

On November 11, 1940, the ships "Pacific" and "Milos" were intercepted by the British Navy and escorted into Haifa Harbor. There the passengers were transferred to the "Patria" bound for Mauritius where they would have been interned. On November 24 the boat was blown up by the orders of the Haganah. Their aim had been to put the boat's engines out of order and leave it lying waterlogged in shallow water. Instead, 240 refugees and a dozen police were killed by the explosion or died by drowning.[21]

On February 24, 1942, the Bulgarian cattleship "Struma" sank in the Black Sea. At Britain's insistence it had been held for two months at

Istanbul with 769 refugees on board. The Turkish authorities finally grew impatient, for they regarded the grossly overcrowded and shockingly insanitary ship as a public nuisance. They sent it back out of the Bosphorus into the Black Sea, where all the refugees but one were drowned.

On more than one occasion refugees were allowed to land, but only when their boats were demonstrably unseaworthy. Winston Churchill referred to one such occasion in a letter to the Secretary of State for the Colonies of March 1, 1941. "General Wavell, like most British military officers, is strongly pro-Arab. At the time of the licenses to the shipwrecked illegal immigrants being permitted he sent a telegram . . . predicting widespread disaster in the Arab world, together with the loss of the Basra–Baghdad–Haifa route. The telegram should be looked up, and also my answer, in which I overruled the General. . . . All went well, and not a dog barked."

Churchill added: "It follows from the above that I am not in the least convinced by all this stuff. The Arabs, under the impression of recent victories, would not make any trouble now. However . . . I do not wish General Wavell to be worried now by lengthy arguments about matters of no military consequence to the immediate situation."[22]

Here was the rub. Churchill, Wavell, and others were preoccupied with the immense task of getting on with winning the war. And, at least until 1943, for Britain it was a war of survival. The Jewish tragedy in Europe was barely noticed, so long as bombs were falling on London, British ships were being sunk in scores in the Atlantic, and British armies were in retreat everywhere. After 1943 the extent of the Jewish tragedy was still not realized by the British public. Indeed, there was a tendency to imagine that Nazi rule in Europe was not so bad as had been supposed. It was widely known that the German atrocities of World War I had been exaggerated. It was known that German behavior in Western Europe from 1940 onward had at least preserved some veneer of correctness. British prisoners of war in Germany appeared to have suffered no more than minor privations and indignities. In any case, the idea of a Nazi program of genocide was too awful to be believable.

The British authorities in Palestine have been accused of being unnecessarily vindictive in their actions against illegal immigrants. Their instructions allowed the police to arrest a suspect without a warrant and hold him in jail without trial. The police could prosecute for harboring an "illegal," an offense punishable with up to eight years' imprisonment.

Yet vindictiveness was not the guiding motive of the British authorities. They themselves were in an impossible position, as Sir Harold Mac-Michael, the High Commissioner at that period, explained to me.* Their

---

* MacMichael has come to be conventionally regarded as the archvillain among British administrators in Palestine. Jewish extremist organizations like Irgun and the

orders came from Whitehall, where "policy statements were drafted which read nicely enough, but might be next to impossible to implement." What was more, "we poor mugs of administrators on the ground had to carry out policies which were liable to change from one Colonial Secretary to the next."[23] In Sir Harold's view, limiting Jewish immigration was only a feeble effort to implement the second part of the Balfour Declaration, which undertook to protect the rights and interests of the Arab inhabitants of Palestine. And without underrating the consequences of preventing illegal immigration for a moment, the High Commissioner believed that had it been unchecked, Britain would have incurred violent hostility of the Arab world at a time when the outcome of the war hung in the balance.

Yet the terrible truth remains that Britain's wartime policy sent thousands of Jews to their deaths. One cannot escape this conclusion. Rabbi Abba Hillel Silver put it succinctly in a statement made in 1943: "We cannot truly rescue the Jews of Europe unless we have free immigration into Palestine. We cannot have free immigration into Palestine unless our political rights are recognized there. Our political rights cannot be recognized there unless our historic connection with the country is acknowledged and our right to rebuild our national home is reaffirmed. These are inseparable links in the chain. The whole chain breaks if one of the links is missing."

In fact, the British policy of checking illegal immigration stemmed from British procrastination over the broader issue of Jewish statehood in Palestine.

In a man like Eshkol the question of illegal immigration could only arouse extreme bitterness. Like other Jewish leaders, Eshkol was appalled by the fate of the illegal immigrants who were turned back. Knowing the conditions in Nazi Germany at first hand as he did, the thought of whole Jewish communities being trapped like animals and slaughtered without mercy was horrible. "I suppose I had still hoped against hope that we

---

Stern Gang posted notices which read "MacMichael: Wanted for Murder," and there were a number of attempts on his life. The last attempt was made almost on the eve of his departure from Palestine. His account was:

> My wife and I were on our way to Jaffa, to a farewell party given for us by the Arab Mayor. We were being driven in a Princess car. In the car with us were the police-driver, an armed escort, and my ADC. Just outside Jerusalem there is a stretch of road with a lot of sharp bends and we came to a point where we were out of sight of the police cars driving ahead and behind us. Suddenly, there was a fizzle under the car and a bomb went off. We slowed down sharply, and as we did so, Jews hidden somewhere up on the hillside to the left of the road opened fire. The driver was hit in the neck and my ADC in the body. Actually, the bullet punctured a lung and cured his chronic asthma. I got a knock on the leg from a spent bullet, a ricochet I should guess, which did no damage. We climbed out of the car as decorously as we could, as our police escort debussed and pursued the escaping gunmen up the steep hillside.

could achieve our aims in Palestine with the cooperation of the British, and not in defiance of them," he told me. "What happened to the illegal immigrants settled that question. It was a betrayal of the principles of humanity. From then on, we had to go our own way."

Possibly, Britain's immigration policy after the war had ended was most incensing of all. Under the Labor Government there was no letup in the restriction of immigration, even though the full facts of the Nazi holocaust were now known and the excuse that immigration constituted a security risk and interrupted the war effort was no longer valid. Jewish survivors of the holocaust had a desperate desire to get out of the charnel house, but movement to western countries was still subject to the existing, unrevised quota restrictions. The Anglo-American Commission sent to the "Displaced Persons" camps in Germany and Austria after the war found that out of every hundred inmates 15 wanted to join relatives in the United States or the British Commonwealth, 15 would go anywhere, and 70 wanted to go to Palestine. None of them wished to rot slowly in the genteel destitution of the DP camps.

Continued restriction of immigration led to the internment of some 25,000 Jews in Cyprus. There they were held in camps surrounded by barbed wire, sometimes within sight of the sea but out of reach of it, lacking enough food, water, sanitation, and every sort of amenity. When Golda Meir visited one camp, its children presented her with the only flower they could contrive, made of colored paper.[24] The internees were shipped from Cyprus to Palestine at a rate of 750 a month, and the camps on the island were not cleared for over four years.

Continued restriction on immigration led to the incident of the ship "Exodus." On July 18, 1947, she reached Haifa, carrying 4500 refugees from DP camps in Germany. The British authorities refused to allow them to land, and in the pitched battle fought with the howling, praying, beseeching people, three of the refugees were killed and over one hundred injured. The British Foreign Secretary, Ernest Bevin, ordered the ship to be sent back to Marseilles, its port of departure, and to disembark its passengers there. Only 130 disembarked and the remainder were sent by ship to Hamburg and forcibly thrust back into DP camps. The Jewish community in Palestine declared a day of mourning for, as Golda Meir put it, "the vanished justice and morality of Great Britain."[25]

Finally, continued restriction on immigration led to the illegal underground railway from DP camps to Palestine. The main "junction" on this route was the American Zone of Occupation in Austria. The Jews reached it from Poland, Hungary, and Rumania as well as from Germany. They were passed on to ports on the Mediterranean and Adriatic, where they waited for boats to take them to Palestine. From Palestine men were sent to act as liaison officers on this underground railway route. The Jews serving in the American and British armies of occupation helped. Of course, there were all sorts of difficulties in moving the

Jews along this route, but it is significant that virtually all of the "Exodus" passengers were reputed to have reached Palestine by the end of the War of Independence.* The route was used by virtually all of the 65,000 illegal immigrants who succeeded in reaching Palestine between the end of the war and the end of the British Mandate.

The influx of illegal immigrants was, indeed, disturbing to the Arabs of Palestine. Only one of their comments need be reported. It came from Azzam Pasha, an Arab who testified before the Anglo-American Commission of Inquiry in 1947.

> Our brother has gone to Europe and to the West and came back something else. He has come back a Russified Jew, a Polish Jew, a German Jew, an English Jew. He has come back with a totally different conception of things, western and not eastern. . . . He is not the old cousin, and we do not extend to him a very good welcome. The Zionist, the new Jew, wants to dominate, and he pretends that he has got a particular civilizing mission with which he returns to a backward, degenerate race in order to put the elements of progress into an area which has no progress. Well, that has been the pretension of every power that wanted to colonize and aimed at domination.

This attitude, and it was fairly typical of the more educated Arabs, boded ill for the future of Jewish-Arab relations in Palestine.

---

* The author had a curious experience on this illegal underground railway. In the summer of 1947, motoring from Kassel to Munich, he found himself in the small town of Eichstaett where a British officers' POW camp had once been located. Wishing to see it again, he stopped at the gate and told the khaki-dressed sentry, who spoke only bad German and no English, that he was a correspondent of the *Manchester Guardian* and would like to take a look at the place. Thereupon the author was taken into the building that once had housed the German Headquarters and suddenly and deftly locked in a room from which he was released only after his German driver had kicked up a tremendous fuss.

---

1. Howard Sachar, *Aliyah: The People of Israel*, p. 291.
2. *Ibid.*, p. 309.
3. Douglas Reed, *Insanity Fair*, p. 155.
4. *Ibid.*, p. 156.
5. William Shirer, *The Rise and Fall of the Third Reich*, p. 234.
6. Arthur Ruppin, *Three Decades of Palestine*, p. 274.
7. *Ibid.*, p. 316.
8. Walter Preuss, *The Labour Movement in Israel*, p. 116.
9. Eshkol, in personal conversation with the author.
10. Ludwig Pinner, *In Zwei Welten*, p. 136.
11. *Ibid.*, p. 134.
12. *Ibid.*, p. 144.
13. *Ibid.*, p. 153.
14. Norman Bentwich, *Wanderer Between Two Worlds*, p. 292.

15. Chaim Weizmann, *Trial and Error*, p. 440.
16. Harry Sacher, *Israel: The Establishment of a State*, p. 20.
17. Samuel Katz, *Days of Fire*, p. 63.
18. Alexander Dallin, *German Rule in Russia*, p. 267.
19. Sacher, *op. cit.*, p. 25.
20. *Ibid.*, p. 25.
21. Christopher Sykes, *Cross Roads to Israel*, p. 269. Sykes rejects the story in Arthur Koestler's *Promise and Fulfillment,* that the passengers blew the ship up themselves in an act of mass suicide.
22. Winston Churchill, *The Second World War,* Vol. III, p. 658.
23. Sir Harold MacMichael, in personal conversation with the author.
24. Marie Syrkin, *Golda Meir: Woman with a Cause,* p. 164.
25. *Ibid.*, p. 161.

8.

It is not always easy to see events and capture a real sense of the atmosphere through the eyes of another. But one of Eshkol's four daughters, Dvora, is a person whose recollections have remained vividly alive and whose ability to explain and transmit them is considerable. Dvora was born in 1930; as a result, she grew up very much aware of the nagging irritations of the Mandatory period and of the growing desire of the Jewish community to bring it to an end.

She grew up in a happy home. Yet Eshkol was intensely busy and, in terms of actual hours spent with his children, had little time for them during the 1930s and 1940s. His wife had a full-time job as a leading member of the Histadrut. She, too, could not see as much of her children as she would have wished. When the family was living in Tel Aviv, as it did for most of that period, she could see the children off to school and welcome them back in the evening. Much of their time in the 1930s, the children spent in the kibbutz at Degania B, which they learned to love and which they were sorry to leave for good in 1944. After that, they returned only for brief visits, except for one or two periods of stress and danger before and during the War of Independence.

Their mother was dearly loved, competent as a housewife and intellectually able. Their home can never have been dull, for it was always full of talk and visitors. They were encouraged to listen, and their father was always a leader in the discussion. The problems of agriculture, water, finance, and the political future all were discussed endlessly and with great animation. Very soon Dvora became aware that her father was a man of ideas; he had something to say on every subject. And she was even more aware of his tremendous energy, "He never seemed to be tired." He was also very patient, "The only times he shouted at us to stop our own noise was when he wanted to listen to the news on the radio."

Eshkol, according to his daughter, was always calm. Even at a moment of real crisis he never became overly excited. But the conversations at home did occasionally become heated when they turned upon internal politics, and even more so when the cardinal issue of whether to seek freedom and independence at once or to wait for the most propitious moment was being discussed. Eshkol did occasionally find himself embroiled outside his home in disputes which went beyond sharp words. "I can remember him coming home one evening with a very black eye. Someone had thrown a small primus stove at him and scored a bull's-eye. Mind you, he had already started laughing about the whole business."[1]

Possibly, his biggest contribution to the life of the family from the children's point of view was his endless fund of Yiddish and Hebrew stories and jokes. They had been food and drink to the Jews in the Pale of Settlement for centuries, and were passed down from one generation to the next—although extemporaneous Yiddish wit flourished too. Eshkol was always a successful storyteller. He took a serious interest in his children as well. "I used to think," Dvora told me, "that he was not very much concerned with us. That was because he never made it obvious. But in reality, as I found out since, he was always fully informed about us and what we were doing, and keenly interested in all our problems. I can remember how he used to put questions, most discreetly, to us and how he never seemed to impose himself."

Dvora can remember very well what seemed to her to be big occasions for the family or for the Jewish community as a whole, and what they meant to everybody. There was the excitement about her father going off to Nazi Germany in the mid-1930s and the questions about what he would do there. There were flares of real trouble during the 1936–1939 period of Arab unrest. Jewish families were often forced to flee from their homes and came crowding in for shelter to the kibbutzim or to big cities. Adults began to make a habit of carrying firearms, for life could be dangerous even on the main roads. School trips to the sea or the mountains were cancelled, and Dvora and her sisters were no longer allowed to roam around the streets of Tel Aviv or go down to the beach to paddle or swim. Sometimes children could not go to school for a day or two at a time.

There was the occasion when her mother was carried off to jail by the British police. That was in 1939, just after the terms of the British White Paper, limiting immigration and land purchase by Jews, had been announced. The women of Tel Aviv, with the backing of political parties and trade unions, staged a demonstration in the middle of the city. Children came to watch and some of them were taken up to the flat roofs of the nearby buildings to get a good view. Early in the proceedings squads of British police and soldiers arrived. The order was given to disperse the demonstrators, probably not because the British authorities cared about the demonstration itself but because they feared Arab rioting and consequent bloodshed. The Jewish housewives refused to budge, but police cars drove up and batches of women were hustled into the vehicles. Mrs. Eshkol spent about a week in jail for committing a "breach of peace."

There was the Black Saturday of June 1946. Dvora was 16 years old now and had fully developed political ideas of her own. Like virtually all of her young contemporaries she fervently believed in Jewish independence and the foundation of a new Jewish state. As on so many other weekends, she was at Degania B on that day. British police arrived at the kibbutz, rounded up its leading members, and interrogated them at length. There was a search for arms other than the rifles to which the kibbutz, even in British eyes, was entitled for its own defense. None, as far as she could remember, were found. Eshkol happened to be away at the time. Otherwise he would certainly have been arrested and taken off to jail. A number of leading members of Haganah and even of the nonmilitary Jewish Agency were treated that way.

There was, finally, the red-letter day of November 29, 1947, when the General Assembly of the United Nations approved the creation of a Jewish state through the partition of Palestine. Dvora was at Degania. Work at the kibbutz ceased as everyone listened to the radio, waiting to hear what had happened. Dvora's recollection is that the result of the General Assembly's debate came through only shortly before midnight. All the members of the kibbutz gathered in the dining room, where they danced and sang. The bells rang and the celebration continued far into the early hours of the morning.

In retrospect so much rejoicing may seem strange. The United Nations partition scheme had been before the public for some time. Moreover, the scheme as finally accepted cut about 500 square miles off the previously proposed Jewish state and left it with strange boundaries, far more difficult to defend than those which the State of Israel eventually acquired. But there were two reasons for calling this a red-letter day. The principal one was that the dream of a Jewish state, which had looked so unreal so often in the past, really was coming true. "We knew there was going to be a very difficult period ahead of us," Dvora told me. "But what did that matter, compared with the fact that we were going to have a country of our own, where we could look after our own?"

The second reason was almost obscure by comparison. It was that the British were leaving, for the codicil to the United Nations resolution provided for the departure of the British Mandatory power by May 1948. The sad fact was that the British had long before become the chief enemy of the Jews of Palestine, when in the first place they had been their protector and friend. It is equally sad that the British had managed to achieve the same change of relationship with the Arabs as well. And to the world at large, the British had long ago ceased to be the referee between Jews and Arabs in the Middle East. A referee is someone who has control of the game, but in the free-for-all political contest between the Jews and Arabs Britain had been demoted to the status of the football. One should note in passing that in this role it was altogether natural for the British to dislike the Jews more than the Arabs. The Jews kicked them so much more accurately and so much harder.

"The Arabs," Dvora told me,

> were not thought of so much as enemies as troublemakers. We had to watch our step with them, to deal with them if we had to, but we supposed that we could get on all right with them, in time. Towards the British we felt resentment, anger, even real bitter hatred. After all, one could excuse the Arabs for their ignorance and inability to understand. But the British had all the knowledge and experience in the world. Their worst crime, in our eyes, was their preventing

those poor, pathetic remnants of European Jewry from finding a new home.

People like Dvora Eshkol forgave the British their sins, real or imaginary, long ago. That is some consolation, but nothing more.

What had been the source of the British failure? One must go back a bit in history to examine that question and look at some of the landmarks of Britain's policy in Palestine.

The first such landmark was Churchill's White Paper of 1922. It will be remembered that it reaffirmed the right of the Jews to be in Palestine and to create a national home there, and repudiated the suggestion that Palestine should "become as Jewish as England is English." Weizmann, in spite of some misgivings, approved the White Paper on behalf of the Zionist Organization. The Arabs rejected it and boycotted the proposed elections to a legislative council.

The second landmark was the Passfield White Paper of 1930. It recommended strict limitation of Jewish immigration, of land purchase by Jews, and of importation of Jewish capital and stressed Britain's obligation to the Arab population. Lord Passfield, however, lost his nerve, began negotiating with the Zionists before his bill was debated in the House of Commons, and then virtually scrapped it. The Prime Minister, Ramsay MacDonald, once again reaffirmed Britain's commitment to the Jews in a letter to Weizmann.

Churchill's White Paper had angered the Arabs more than the Jews. Passfield's White Paper angered the Jews and its scrapping maddened the Arabs. That pernicious politician managed to secure the worst of both worlds, and when the British government in December 1930 proposed a round-table conference on a Palestine legislative council and constitution, the Arabs once more applied their boycott.

Yet another set of legislative proposals was served up in December 1935. They were rather less favorable to the Arabs than before, but the Arabs hesitated this time. In April 1936 the government, having waited long enough for some sign of Arab or Jewish support, dropped the proposals. Ten days later the full-scale Arab rebellion began.

This resulted in a new British effort to secure a settlement. On November 11, 1936, a royal commission under Lord Peel was sent to Palestine with the purpose of examining the whole political and constitutional position. The commission was to produce its report in July 1937 after a lengthy examination of Jewish and Arab arguments, those of the Arabs being inserted only after an initial, two-month boycott had been ended.

The most important witness on the Jewish side was, inevitably, Weizmann. Sykes refers to his "masterly performance" and to how "the three hours which it occupied seemed to pass like a few minutes."[2] Weizmann argued that Zionism was the crystalization of a long historical process, of a continual Jewish movement of return to their native land,[3] and he was tactful enough to express gratitude towards Britain while criticizing the negative aspects of British administration. Forty other Jewish witnesses were heard, including Jabotinsky, who urged Britain to explain the Balfour Declaration to the Arabs, to tell them that the huge Arab world could afford to allow Palestine to become a small Jewish state, and to give up the Mandate if she, Britain, could not discharge it.[4]

For the Arabs the key witness was the Mufti, Haj Amin Hussein. He argued their case largely on tenable historical and ethnological grounds, but descended periodically into wild rhetoric. Thus, he claimed that the Jews intended to destroy the Moslem holy places in Jerusalem, the Dome of the Rock and the El Aksa Mosque, and to rebuild the Temple of Solomon on their ruins, and he claimed that the Palestinian Arabs had been happier under Turkish than under British rule.[5] The Mufti demanded total discontinuance of Jewish immigration and the creation of an Arab state in Palestine with the same status as Iraq.

The key member of the Peel Commission was Professor Reginald (later Sir Reginald) Coupland, of All Souls College, Oxford. Coupland was deeply impressed by the fundamental differences between the Jews and the Arabs and by the absolutely unyielding intransigence of the latter. While the Jews were open to discussion on Palestine's future, the Arabs demanded the whole of it for themselves. Coupland noted that even George Antonius in his *Arab Awakening* shared this intransigence. The book "while it states the Arab case in moderate language, arrives at the same immoderate 100 percent conclusion."[6]

Coupland quickly decided that the only possible solution was partition. He asked Weizmann for his views, and the latter saw that partition must mean the creation of a Jewish state. He approved the idea; the Arabs did not.

Coupland noted:

> The Palestine problem arises from a conflict of "right with right" and of promises with promises. A just solution, therefore, cannot be achieved without concessions on both sides. By acquiescing in Partition, Dr. Weizmann and his colleagues have shown a willingness to compromise; but the Mufti and his colleagues maintain their original demand for 100 percent, namely, the stoppage of Jewish immigration and the subjection of the National Home to an Arab majority in an independent Palestine.[7]

Coupland pressed his ideas on Anthony Eden (later Lord Avon), the Foreign Secretary at that time. "I took the liberty of passing on to him the need for our diplomatic agents to make every effort to convince the governments of the Arab states and Egypt that the territorial limitations imposed by Partition on the growth of the National Home was the only effective and lasting means of preventing an ultimate Jewish domination of all Palestine."[8] Once again, the professor showed perception and finesse and he had other concessions to offer the angry but puzzled Arabs. There should be a $20 million contribution by the Jewish to the Arab Palestinian state, for "Weizmann was quite prepared to be generous";[9] and Britain's obligations to Transjordan should be cancelled by a single lump-sum payment of $8 million. The frontiers of the new Jewish state should be guaranteed by Britain and confirmed by the United Nations which, Coupland argued, should be enough to satisfy the most alarmist Arab. Finally, if the Arabs wanted it, there could be a federation of Arab and Jewish areas for a transitional period, with Jewish immigration restricted to the Jewish area.

Coupland has since pointed out that the British government did nothing to confirm the proposed payment of a subvention by the Jewish to the Arab state. It did not confirm the proposal of an exchange of population, which would be subject to Jewish-Arab agreement. Nor did it accept the Peel Commission's recommendation that martial law should be imposed, if there were another armed uprising like the Arab rebellion which had begun in April 1936.[10] It had already become a habit of the British government to ignore the recommendations of its own advisers.

The Peel Commission suggested boundaries between the Jewish and Arab states. The proposed Jewish state would have been, in comparison with the present State of Israel, very small. It would have included most of what is today Israeli Galilee, the coastal plain from Haifa to Tel Aviv, and then only a small fragment of Jewish territory to the south, with the port of Jaffa and a connecting corridor of Arab land. It would have comprised about one-third of what became the State of Israel after the 1948 War of Independence. From that point of view alone, it would have been a wonderful bargain for the Arabs, compared with what was to happen when the Jews had won their War of Independence.

The Arabs, predictably, rejected the findings of the Peel Commission. At the 20th Zionist Congress in Zurich, Weizmann managed to secure a guarded and qualified Jewish acceptance. The British government was at first enthusiastic. But that was the age of appeasement, when very little got done. Sykes' view was that the Peel Report owed much to the literary skill of Coupland and to the sincerity of the members of the Commission, but that its "partition scheme belongs perhaps to that interesting category of unaccomplished things which often exert a great hold on the affection and the imagination."[11] This is doubtless so, but the Peel Report had a lasting significance, not because it preached partition but because it accepted the idea of a Jewish state as a fair and feasible solution of the Palestine problem. This was something which a great many Jews had not dared to hope for.

The last prewar landmark of British policy in Palestine was the White Paper of May 17, 1939. This time the Whitehall seesaw took the Arabs up and let the Jews down with the most violent jolt of all. Nazi persecution of the Jews of Germany and Austria was becoming truly frightful. The western world had failed to open its doors wide to Jewish refugees, but the Jewish community in Palestine was ready to receive them and make any sacrifices to enable them to find new homes and fresh hope in life. The White Paper restricted Jewish immigration into Palestine to 75,000 for the next five years, stringently limited land transfers, and rejected all idea of creating a Jewish state in Palestine, however small.

It was a bitter blow, perhaps the most bitter the Zionist cause had ever suffered. And there was a terrible sense of inevitability about it. Churchill's 1922 White Paper had offended the Arabs, but Passfield's futile and foolish White Paper of 1930 had offended the Jews much more. The Peel Commission had taken a vast unpremeditated step in recommending partition, while the White Paper of 1939 turned Britain into enemy No. 1 of the Jews. The pendulum of British policy was swinging on an ever-widening arc with a blind disregard for beliefs and loyalties that got in its way.

In one sense World War II gave Britain breathing space. With fighting, real fighting, in the offing the Arab armed insurrection died away. The Jews expected the White Paper policy to be dropped, in return for Jewish participation in the war on the Allied side. It did not happen. They expected to be allowed to form their own brigades. They were prevented from doing it. When Rommel's army was poised to swoop on Cairo, they imagined that British restrictions would end. They were maintained. It says much for Jewish common sense that extreme national opinion was held in check, more or less, for the duration of the war.

At the outbreak of war Weizmann wrote the British Prime Minister, Neville Chamberlain, a letter that was in itself a memorial to common sense:

> Dear Mr Prime Minister: In this hour of supreme crisis the consciousness that the Jews have a contribution to make to the defense of sacred values compels me to write this letter. I wish to confirm, in the most explicit manner, the declarations which I and my colleagues have made during the last months, and especially in the last week: that the Jews stand by Great Britain and will fight on the side of the democracies. Our urgent desire is to give effect to these declarations. We wish to do so in a way entirely consonant with the general scheme of British action, and therefore would place ourselves, in matters big and small, under the coordinating

direction of His Majesty's Government. The Jewish Agency is ready to enter into immediate arrangements for utilizing manpower, technical ability, resources.

The Jewish Agency has recently had differences in the political field with the Mandatory Power. We would like these differences to give way before the greater and more pressing necessities of the times.[12]

The differences of course were those caused by the White Paper. Ben-Gurion coined the phrase which summed up the attitude of the Jewish leaders best "We shall fight the war as if there were no White Paper and the White Paper as if there were no war." Eshkol's attitude towards the White Paper was perfectly straightforward. He regarded it as thoroughly retrograde and he fully supported Ben-Gurion's view that it should be opposed in every possible way. The conclusions that he drew were that planning would have to begin for founding the Jewish state in defiance of Britain, and that efforts to build up Haganah as the military arm of the Jewish community would have to be redoubled. Eshkol began to spend more time than before in work for the Haganah, and for the first time agreed, even if reluctantly, to start demonstrations against British rule. His words on that subject were: "I came to this country in order to build the land and the state, and not to be a casualty in street demonstrations against the British police. But there's no longer any choice in the matter; we cannot skip this stage in the struggle, the stage of struggle against a hostile British administration."

The Jewish contribution to the Allied war effort has already been dealt with here as well as that by-product of the White Paper, illegal immigration. Something should be said about three other consequences of the White Paper.

It caused violent disgust among the big and influential Jewish community in the United States. For very obvious reasons many of its members had been opposed in the past to Zionist political aims. They were happy in America and they felt that the political enlightenment of the twentieth century would eventually bring happiness to Jews in other parts of the world. An influential group, *Ichud* (union), headed by Judah Magnes and Henrietta Szold, was formed and it urged rapprochement with the Arabs in a binational Palestinian state. There were similar groups in Europe. But on May 11, 1942, a congress of 600 leading American Jews meeting at the Biltmore Hotel in New York called for unrestricted immigration into Palestine and for the creation of a Jewish commonwealth. Differences of opinion among American Jewry continued to exist; but it is safe to say that from 1942 onward an overwhelming majority of American Jews supported Zionist political aims in Palestine. This was bound to have an effect on American governmental policy. Significantly, the U.S. Palestine Committee, composed of 68 senators and 200 members of the House of Representatives, denounced the White Paper in November 1942.

The second indirect consequence of the White Paper was a split in the Jewish labor movement. The left wing of the Mapai party began to demand a more dogmatic approach to political problems, as well as a moral regeneration of Palestinian socialism. Anger over Britain's policies was supplemented by admiration for the Soviet Union's tremendous struggle against Nazi Germany. The dissidents first formed a "Fraction B" within the party, then in 1942 split away altogether and formed a new party with the old name of *Achdut Ha'avoda*. The labor movement was to be beset with internal schisms for the next 25 years.

Of more immediate significance was the growing rift in the Jewish defense movement. The Haganah leaders preached only passive resistance to the White Paper policies, coupled with the need to help the Allies win the war. Jabotinsky died in 1940 and a less radical leadership of his defense organization, Irgun Zvai Leumi, urged only moral pressure on Britain to secure Jewish objectives. An offshoot of Irgun, the so-called "Stern Gang" formed by the activist Abraham Stern, advocated the use of violence against all established authority.

Whole books have been written about the activities of Irgun and the Stern Gang. Here there is room only for a very short account of them.

Irgun had already been active before the publication of the May 1939 White Paper, exploding bombs in the marketplaces of a number of Arab towns in February. Later, in 1939, the organization began to pass "death sentences" on members of the British administration, several of whom were murdered. When Jabotinsky was succeeded as leader by David Raziel, Irgun came to an agreement with the Haganah to concentrate on winning the war. Raziel was killed, and in January 1944 the new Irgun leader, Menachem Beigin, ordered a revolt. He had perhaps a thousand sworn followers, but many thousands of sympathizers. From then on, Irgun instigated or joined in innumerable acts of terrorism, including the blowing up of British police and military posts, the ambushing of British officials and their assassination, raids on British arms dumps, and indiscriminate destruction of British property.

The Stern Gang, formed in 1940, was even more bloodthirsty. The gang was broken up by British police action in February 1942, but reorganized in the following year, when it rescued 20 imprisoned Sternists. The gang was responsible for the many attempts on the life of the High Commissioner, Sir Harold MacMichael, and succeeded in assassinating Lord Moyne, British Deputy Minister of State, in Cairo on November 6, 1944.*

---

* Many Englishmen believed that even highly respectable Jews carried their single-minded determination to get their way to an extreme. Sir Harold MacMichael, for instance, claims that he once said to Pinhas Rutenberg, the creator of the Palestine

After the war was over, both Irgun and the Stern Gang redoubled their terrorist activities, for they could be far more sure than before of a degree of popular support. Irgun blew up a wing of the King David Hotel in Jerusalem in 1946, killing 91 persons and wounding 45. The Sternists hung two captured British sergeants as a reprisal for the execution of two of their members who had been convicted of murder. Two horrible features of this crime were that the sergeants were garroted and that booby-traps were left attached to their bodies.

One Jewish historian has given this account of Jewish terrorism:

> During 1946 and 1947, as the British intercepted one refugee ship after another off Palestine's coast, the Sternists ran wild throughout the country. Typically, they concentrated on shooting down British soldiers. On September 17, 1948, during the last phase of Israel's War of Liberation, a Sternist gunman carried out the "execution" of Count Folke Bernadotte, the UN mediator. None of these acts of violence contributed by one iota to the rescue effort, to the moral and political struggle to evict the British, to the military campaign against the Arabs, nor, finally, to the diplomatic effort of securing Israel's territorial integrity. Indeed, from every point of view—psychological, military, diplomatic—they were a disaster for the Zionist cause.[13]

The terrorists, obviously, thought differently. The fullest account of their thoughts and doings has been given by Gerold Frank in his book *The Deed*. Their murders were coldly and scientifically planned, and their purpose was "to confuse and bedevil the British," so that "ultimately they gave the problem over to the United Nations, and thus opened the door to the partition of Palestine and the first Jewish state in two thousand years."[14] The Sternists, and Irgun too, thought along the same lines as Sinn Fein in Ireland in 1919. And like Sinn Fein, they revered heroic figures of the past, in their case, Bar Kochba, in Sinn Fein's, Brian Boru.

In view of the terrible suffering of the Jews it might be thought unbecoming for a non-Jew to pass judgment on Irgun and the Sternists. Perhaps the most appropriate reflection is that wrongs and sufferings provide the surest entitlement to take up arms in one's own cause, but that the way in which one uses those arms remains a matter of ethics and humanity. Irgun and the Sternists represented an explosion of pent-up feelings caused by terrible persecution. They represented something deeper too—a revulsion against centuries of oppression. Pierre

---

electricity combine, "If we gave you a Jewish Army, the Jews of Iraq would get their throats cut." Rutenberg, according to Sir Harold, answered: "That would be their contribution to our aims." Rutenberg was a Jew who personally got on with Sir Harold very well and used to compare him jokingly to Sardanapalus, the "trimmer."

von Paasen once wrote: "The Jews have never, since Bar Kochba's defeat, really been a self-reliant, self-judging people. They suffered from the disease called 'schielen'—looking sideways at the eyes of others for a sign of approval or disapproval, waiting for others to make up their minds for them, placing trust and confidence in other people's politics."[15] Irgun and the Sternists carried their reaction to this submissiveness to an extreme; they believed that they should wipe out past shame in blood.

Abraham Stern recruited many of his followers in Poland, before the outbreak of World War II, which ended his more grandiose plan for launching a Polish-Jewish invasion of Palestine from the ports of Bari and Brindisi in Southern Italy. Himself scholarly, elegant, with great charm and some poetic gifts, Stern picked out young men who were fierce idealists. He was prepared to use 16- and 17-year-olds and girls. Total dedication was what he required of them.

To them he offered, in addition to the chance of striking a blow for the cause of Jewish freedom and independence, much glamor, a Carbonari-like atmosphere of intrigue and secrecy, and a whole-hearted commitment which the young adore. It is a somewhat worrying thought that, perhaps as a result of living under continuous stress for over 20 years, present-day citizens of Israel seem to have more, not less, admiration for the Sternists and Irgunists as time goes by. They tend to forget that, before the British Mandate was over, Haganah found itself forced to declare war on both groups and to cooperate with the British authorities in rounding up their members.

Eshkol was lucky enough to keep himself for the most part clear of this bitter, fratricidal strife. The early war years were for him a period of relative quiet, to some extent a hiatus in the turmoil of the struggle, when he could build up, expand and emancipate the Jewish community in Palestine. In 1940 he went back to Degania B. That was in no sense retirement, only a temporary withdrawal. He was 45 years old, strong and healthy. He was too old to volunteer for military service with the British or with a Jewish brigade, something which he would have done quite readily. The Histadrut had less for him to do in wartime, although he was ready to take on any job they offered him. At Degania he could farm again, and now every ounce of food produced there would be doubly valuable, for the import of foodstuffs had to be cut down in view of the shortage of ships and other transport facilities. Degania was handy, too, for his duties as director of the Mekorot water board. The bulk of its work was still in northern Palestine.

He was also a member of the high command of Haganah, which meant that he had to pay frequent visits to Tel Aviv headquarters and to command posts all over the country. Eshkol concerned himself with two tasks for Haganah: he was its treasurer and he helped them to procure arms. His Haganah work created for him a double existence:

he was a farmer by day and a defense specialist at night. Very often he worked 15 or 16 hours a day, and his children became aware of the fact that they were seeing less of him than ever. His work in procuring arms reached its climax during the War of Independence, when he had already been appointed Director-General of the newly formed Ministry of Defense in Ben-Gurion's first Israeli government.

In 1944 Eshkol was appointed Secretary-General of the Tel Aviv Labor Council. The post may not sound interesting, but it was in reality a key political appointment. Mapai was alarmingly weak in Tel Aviv, where a predominantly liberal, antisocialist bourgeoisie had settled. Tel Aviv, moreover, was increasing in size at a formidable rate. From the small collection of shacks which Eshkol remembered in 1914, it had become the epitome of Jewish urban colonization, bustling, noisy, brash, a metropolis in the making. With Jerusalem divided between the Jews and the Arabs and lorded over by the British High Commissioner, Tel Aviv was the natural Jewish capital. It was also the chief center of Jewish politics, and the Tel Aviv Labor Council was the pace-setter in over-all trade union development, with the same central importance which the Paris Commune had in the French Revolution.

Nowhere and at no time were Eshkol's assets more badly needed. Mapai and Achdut Ha'avoda had split, and their supporters had divided in the Histadrut and in the municipal trade union bodies as well. The worst year of the war in a material sense was 1944. Food was in short supply, transport was hard to come by, there was no heating in winter; and Tel Aviv is a damp place in the rainy season. The bitter feeling against the British authorities was increasing (although they were, after all, only carrying out duties which were often distasteful to them) and so was the controversy over using force against them. To this tense atmosphere Eshkol brought patience, persistence, and shrewd, caustic, but basically kindly, wit.

One of his friends recalls that on his first day in his Tel Aviv office he was confronted by a gigantic pile of papers and documents on his outsize desk. He swept the whole lot off and remarked, "Anything which really requires my attention is going to come through that door."[16] He got down to work with a will. According to his secretary at that time,[17] he arrived at his office generally a little before the official hour of 7 A.M. He worked through until 2:30 in the afternoon without a break, then began his round of visits and meetings. He usually ate a frugal lunch while he worked but often did not eat until evening. The only times his secretary saw him somewhat annoyed were when petty interruptions interfered with his work. But he never regarded a chance visitor as an interruption if he had business to discuss with him. Eshkol, she remembers, had a peculiar ability to put down any work he was doing, embark on a totally new subject, then pick up his work again and resume exactly where he had left off.

His even temper and his wit were famous. Once when visiting the Church of the Nativity in Bethlehem he lit a candle of remembrance for Christ and was asked by a surprised Christian Arab guide, "But you're a Jew, aren't you? Do you want to do this honor for the founder of the Christian faith?" Eshkol answered without hesitation: "Why not? He was one of us, after all."[18]

Eshkol's first task was to establish good human relations with the workers. Working conditions were bad, with long hours, low pay, a sharp increase in unemployment immediately after the end of the war, and industrial as well as political uncertainty. The Tel Aviv workers liked Eshkol at once, because he spoke their language, gave himself no airs, was deeply interested in their problems, and offered advice only when asked for it. They enjoyed his endless fund of Yiddish stories, jokes, and Biblical quotations.

Probably they liked him most for his being not a desk man but the very opposite of a bureaucrat. Two incidents can illustrate this.

Eshkol used to pay frequent visits to factories and other enterprises to hear about grievances and difficulties on the spot. He put aside two full days for this, Thursday and Friday, which were known as "wasted days" by the office staff but which he regarded as his most worthwhile work during the week. He used the lunch break for a discussion with all workers who wanted to take part, and at one of these informal meetings a group of thoroughly disgruntled workers broke in and demanded to know what Eshkol "had ever done." His answer came fast: "I started to work with my hands in 1914 and I still work with my hands whenever I get the chance. I can plant, build, harvest, and shovel manure."[19]

The second incident occurred when Eshkol paid a visit to a basement where unemployed workers used to gather together, generally for aimless complaints. Eshkol decided to make changes in that depressing place. He raised money with the help of the Labor Council and turned the cellar into the Beit Brenner recreation center, where workers got something to eat, chairs to sit on, papers to read, light and warmth to make them feel at home. The center became one of his favorite ports of call on his rounds.[20]

"Eshkol's way of doing things," one of his friends and associates on the Labor Council, Gershon Sack, told me, "constituted practical democracy in operation. We had quite a few in Tel Aviv in those days whom you might call extremists. Eshkol's sympathy, interest, and sense of humor won most of them over. He encouraged them to air their views and never 'talked down' to them. He was clever; he knew how to get them onto his side." The result was that in less than a year he had a solid, middle-of-the-road, moderate trade union membership behind him. At a later date Eshkol emerged as the leading protagonist of working participation in industrial management. One of the first undertakings into which he introduced it was the Palestine Electricity Corporation. At its council meeting he appealed to the workers' leaders to "sit at the top of the table and not behave like men at the gate."

There was a political aspect to Eshkol's work too. The breach between the Mapai and Achdut Ha'avoda political parties could not be healed; nor was it as if Eshkol's job to try to do so. But supporters of the two parties in Tel Aviv had to be reconciled as far as possible with one another. One reason for the breach had been a difference of opinion as to what the independent state of Israel should comprise; Mapai was ready to accept any fair offer, whereas the followers of Achdut, especially in the kibbutzim, wanted to preserve the territorial integrity of the whole of Palestine. Another issue had been the composition of the Histadrut. Mapai came out for centralized elections, and got its way; Achdut wanted kibbutzim and moshavim to send their own, locally elected delegates. Eshkol's tact and delicacy in human relationships did, in the long run, bring a degree of reconciliation between the two groups in the trade unions.

A note here on the tremendous growth of the trade union movement in Israel. In less than ten years, to 1948, the Histadrut's membership rose from 80,000 to 130,000. Its funds went up from $5.5 million to $42.8 million. The business done by its Solel Boneh contracting company multiplied ten times. The Histadrut, more than ever before, had become a "state within the state."

Working and living in Tel Aviv brought Eshkol once again into the closest touch with the planning of land settlement. There was a very obvious need to settle some of the new immigrants on the land; many of the "illegals" were dispirited and listless, and needed some manual work, simple but satisfying, out in the open under the sun. There was a need, too, to maintain a balance between town and country. Eshkol "lent himself" to the settlement department of the Jewish Agency, and combined work for them with his exploration of water resources for Mekorot.

Some of the settlements established during the war had failed. These so-called "tower and stockade" settlements were often built in the course obvious need to settle some of the new immigrants on the land; many of them were badly planned, with insufficient water and ill-chosen sites. Late in 1946 Eshkol came forward with a crash program. Drilling for water, he had found a plentiful supply of it south of Ashkelon, close to what has since become known as the Gaza Strip. He was convinced that he would find more water to the south, and that colonization of the Negev desert would be the result.

The Jewish Agency owned some scattered plots of land to the south of Eshkol's new wells and springs. His proposal was to found 15 new settlements and pipe water to them from Ashkelon. One of his collaborators in this scheme, Raanan Weitz, told me that it was planned to be "a long pipeline, which looked like a big pipe dream." But the plan was a brilliant success. On the eve of the Day of Atonement (Yom Kippur) 11 groups of young pioneers worked around the clock and put up 11 new settlements. Some of these settlements and one in particular, Yad Mordechai, were to play a disproportionately large part in the 1948 War of Independence. They lay in the path of the advancing Egyptian Army and all but one of them held out against attackers who sometimes used tanks and medium artillery against them. Their gallant defense effectively defeated the Egyptian plan for an advance on Tel Aviv. Ironically, their water was pumped from Ashkelon through six-inch pipes, 200 miles of pipeline in all, bought in Egypt. In Raanan Weitz's view, "This little group of settlements might be said to have saved Israel. The Egyptians could not bypass them and leave their lines of communication exposed. They went on hammering away at them, until we had collected enough men to counterattack and drive them back into the Sinai Peninsula."

In all, 53 new settlements were established between the end of World War II and the beginning of Israel's own War of Independence. But the period of really large-scale land settlement lay ahead, after the British Mandate came to an end.

In the period immediately preceding the War of Independence, Eshkol was also closely concerned with building the Jewish community's self-defense capabilities. The Haganah high command had been reorganized and plans were afoot to establish a training college for officers. More important, arms were being brought into the country for the now unavoidable struggle which lay ahead. Ben-Gurion had taken the lead in the field of arms procurement. He paid a visit to the United States, taking with him two members of the Haganah high command, Yakov Dori and Chaim Slavin, leaving the latter there for 18 months. Slavin bought unused World War II equipment, available for sale as surplus stock. He spent $800,000 of the money raised mainly by the Jewish community in the United States, and obtained arms worth several million dollars. Other arms were being bought from France and Czechoslovakia, and stored.

Storage was a major problem, as the discovery made by a British officer showed. "Lieutenant-Colonel West, quite by a fortuitous accident, discovered a Haganah arsenal in a settlement at Mesheg Yagur. It was unbelievable the extent to which they had gone to conceal their arms and their armories. Many were hidden in panels in children's bedrooms and many were underground; in the farmyard an old piece of apparently useless farm machinery was in fact one of the air inlets to an underground magazine constructed of concrete and stocked with arms far in excess of the requirements of one settlement. Another air inlet was found to be concealed in the tubular steel frame of a children's swing."[21]

Such ingenuity was absolutely necessary. Haganah remained technically an illegal organization for the whole period of the British Mandate. As a result it had to be highly disciplined as well as immensely circumspect, perhaps more disciplined than a regular army. Its members generally had to find time to perform their service for Haganah after their working day was over. They had to be ready to risk prosecution as civil offenders. And those members who had few worldly goods had to make special sacrifices. Of the three men in one cell only two were able to attend meetings at their local headquarters since they owned only two pairs of shoes among the three of them. They had to trudge long miles to the weekly meetings and in any case go without a meal that day.[22]

Eshkol played his part in arms procurement. One of his achievements was to obtain a patrol boat, which was to become the "senior" craft in the future Israeli navy. It was an American vessel which was intended to be used as an icebreaker, and its top speed was eight knots. Eshkol's work for Haganah brought him into close contact with David Ben-Gurion. A firm friendship grew up between the two men which was to lead to Eshkol's becoming Ben-Gurion's right-hand man in Mapai and later in the Israeli government. Much later still, their friendship was to end under unfortunate circumstances.

1. Dvora Eshkol Rafaeli, in personal conversation with the author.
2. Christopher Sykes, *Cross Roads to Israel*, p. 197.
3. *Ibid.*, p. 194.
4. Arthur Hertzberg, *The Zionist Idea*. Jabotinsky allegedly said that Britain should not cling on, knowing she was not fulfilling her responsibilities: "No, sir, that cannot be done. That is not cricket!"
5. Sykes, *op. cit.*, p. 199.
6. Coupland Papers, Rhodes House, Oxford.
7. *Ibid.*
8. *Ibid.*
9. Letter of December 8, 1938, from Coupland to Lord Lothian.
10. Coupland, in *The Round Table,* Jan. 25, 1939.
11. Sykes, *op. cit.*, p. 216.
12. Barnet Litvinoff, *Gen-Gurion of Israel*, p. 132.
13. Howard Sachar, *Aliyah: The People of Israel*, p. 410.
14. Gerold Frank, *The Deed*, p. 10.
15. Meyer Weisgal, ed., *Chaim Weizmann*, p. 44.
16. Shimon Horn, in personal conversation with the author.
17. Dora Lisbona, in personal conversation with the author.
18. Dora Lisona, in personal conversation with the author.
19. Gershon Sack, in personal conversation with the author.
20. Gershon Sack, in personal conversation with the author.
21. Gen. Sir Richard Gale, *Call to Arms*, p. 169.
22. Alouf Avidar, a Haganah leader, told the author this story.

9. The end of the British Mandate in Palestine had been in sight for at least two years before that historic date, May 14, 1948, when the last British High Commissioner, Sir Alan Cunningham, embarked on a British warship in Haifa harbor. Every factor in the postwar situation had contributed to this. The White Paper policy had brought Palestinian Jewry to the boiling point. The Arab population was in a state of grave unrest and determined to accept no compromise. Law and order in the country were vanishing. And both the British public at home and the British forces in Palestine were heartily sick of being blamed by both sides and, in the case of the sorely tried soldiers, being shot at by both.*

It is sure that the Mandate could have been preserved only if Britain had possessed a strong and clear-sighted government at this stage. Clement Attlee (later Lord Attlee) was not, in a general sense, a bad Prime Minister, and his Labor government had come to power in July 1945 full of high hopes. One or two of these hopes were fulfilled, but the Labor government's policy in Palestine was unquestionably disastrous. To understand the strangeness as well as the fullness of its failure one must first look back. Ten years is far enough.

In 1935 on the eve of the general election, Attlee declared:

> The Labor Party recalls with pride that in the dark days of the Great War they associated themselves with the ideal of a national home in Palestine for the Jewish people, and that, ever since, the annual conferences of the Party have repeatedly reaffirmed their enthusiastic support of the effort towards its realization. They have never faltered, and will never falter, in their active and sympathetic cooperation with the work of political and economic reconstruction now going forward in Palestine.

The following was the statement made by Mr. Attlee's deputy in the House of Commons, Herbert Morrison, in the 1939 debate on the White paper:

> We regard the White Paper and the policy in it as a cynical breach of pledges given to the Jews and the world. . . . It comes at a time of tragedy and apprehension for the Jewish race throughout the world, and it ought not to be approved by the House today. . . . If we do this thing we shall have done a thing which is dishonorable to our good name, which is discreditable to our own capacity to govern, and which is dangerous to British security.

---

* One British officer stationed in Palestine during the war expressed the views of many when he said that he "developed a hearty dislike of both Jews and Arabs, and an additional profound contempt for the latter."

The White Paper was denounced, less histrionically but more cogently and with complete consistency, by Winston Churchill. Even at the height of the war, he made it clear that it would have to be "superseded." But Morrison, along with the Labor party and the Labor government, was to become executor of the policy which he had called "cynical," "dishonorable," and "discreditable."

At the 1944 Labor Party Conference, Attlee, acting for the national executive, secured the adoption of a resolution containing the following passage:

> There is surely neither hope nor meaning in a "Jewish National Home" unless we are prepared to let the Jews, if they wish, enter this tiny land in such numbers as to become a majority. There was a strong case for this before the war. There is an inevitable case now. . . . Let the Arabs be encouraged to move out as the Jews move in. Let them be compensated handsomely for their land and let their settlement elsewhere be carefully organized and generously financed. The Arabs have many wide territories of their own; they must not claim to exclude the Jews from this small area of Palestine, less than the size of Wales. Indeed we should reexamine also the possibility of extending the present Palestinian boundaries, by agreement with Egypt, Syria, and Transjordan.

Nothing could have been more explicit than this, and it would be interesting to speculate what territorial additions to Palestine Attlee had in mind. Sinai, perhaps? In that case, the 1967 war could have been averted, for Egypt would never have been in a position to blockade the Straits of Tiran and Gulf of Aqaba. Or perhaps the old territories of the tribes of Reuben, Gad, and half Manasseh, on the eastern bank of the Jordan? Then the State of Jordan would long ago have ceased to exist, as it would have been reduced to a strip of desert. Or was Attlee's statement mere verbiage?

In his *Palestine Mission*, Richard Crossman, himself a member of the Labor party, pointed out that, until 1945, his party had reaffirmed its support of Zionism on at least 11 occasions. The last such occasion was early in 1945 when Dr. Hugh Dalton (later Chancellor of the Exchequer) said that it was "morally wrong and politically indefensible to impose obstacles to the entry into Palestine now of any Jews who desire to go there."[1] There is no need to belabor the point further; the Labor party had committed itself time and again to Zionist aims, and in 1945 Palestinian Jewry had a right to expect the Labor government to fulfill its promises.

One of that government's first actions was to announce the formation of a joint Anglo-American Committee to examine the question of the Jews and Palestine. The announcement was made on November 13, 1945, by the new Foreign Secretary, Ernest Bevin, who coupled it with some unfortunate remarks about the Jews' exploiting "their racial position" or trying "to get too much to the head of the queue." But two months later Bevin gave a public assurance that if the Anglo-American Committee produced a unanimous report, he would do all in his power to have its recommendations put into effect.[2]

The committee went ahead and produced its report in April 1946. Its main points were that 100,000 Jewish immigrants should be allowed into Palestine at once, that all restrictions on Jewish land purchase should go, that the country should remain under trusteeship, and that the aim should be to turn it eventually into a binational Jewish-Arab state. The figure of 100,000 was not an arbitrary one; it had already been selected by President Harry Truman, and proposed by him to the Labor government in August 1945.

According to his biographer, Lord Francis-Williams, the report threw Bevin into "one of his blackest rages." Once again, he made some unfortunate statements, among them that the United States "did not want their Jews in New York," and that the admission of 100,000 refugees would cost the British taxpayer $800 million. According to Maurice Edelman, a Labor member of Parliament, Bevin threatened the aged and half-blind Weizmann with the words "If you want a fight, you can have it," and said to Edelman himself, "The trouble with the Zionists is that they are not educated."[3] This intemperate language suggested a truly frightening degree of insularity.

Bevin, admittedly, had done nothing original in rejecting the findings of the Committee. Indeed, if there were two things which were predictable in the sad story of the Mandate they were that the Arabs would boycott whatever mission was authorized by the Mandatory power, and that Britain herself would not act on its findings. Bevin came to be regarded as the archenemy largely because he was in charge during the last, most critical and most chaotic period of the Mandate. For the Jews, he must have been a maddening person to deal with, because of his ignorance of the Middle East and his total unreceptiveness to rational argument. His sole concern seems to have been to safeguard Britain's interests by keeping the United States out of the area and by consolidating it against possible Soviet pressure and infiltration. Improbable though it sounds, Bevin seems to have believed that "Arab democracy" could be built up, under British protection, thus adding his own private pipe dream to T. E. Lawrence's vision of a "brown-skinned" dominion of the British Empire.

The attitude of Bevin and his Labor government came as a terrible disappointment to leaders of the Jewish community in Palestine. Ever since the Mandate came into existence they had regarded British Labor as preceptor, friend, and prospective protector. Men like Eshkol had grown up with the belief that British socialism was the best of all political models to imitate and would, in due course, produce model government in its own country. Eshkol and his fellows presupposed an understanding and enlightened Labor outlook on the Palestine question and towards its Jewish community. One of their expectations was that the presence of a Labor government in Whitehall and Westminster would lead to greater enlightenment on the part of the British authorities in Palestine.

Nothing of the kind occurred. For the first time the British military authorities were instructed to inflict corporal punishment on arrested Jewish terrorists. Irgun retaliated savagely, by flogging captured British soldiers who had committed no crime. Such insensate reprisals were inexcusable and were indeed frowned upon by the official Haganah leadership. But the British Government also organized counterterrorist units, on the same lines as the Black and Tans during Ireland's War of Independence.[4] Bevin (since someone has to be held responsible) did this nearly 30 years after the shame and scandal of the earlier episode had been chronicled as one of the blackest moments in British history.

When passions run high, it is often some purely ludicrous incident which provides the most appropriate focus. One must, for a moment, go back in time. In July 1946, a wing of the King David Hotel in Jerusalem was blown up. The British officer who had to take suitable action was General Sir Evelyn Barker, a gallant officer but one who totally, one might even say deliberately, disinterested himself in political issues of every kind. His *Order of the Day* is a monument ot the carefully nurtured ignorance and prejudice of British army officers of Sir Evelyn's generation.

> The Jewish community of Palestine cannot be absolved from responsibility for the long series of outrages culminating in the blowing up of a large part of the Government offices in the King David Hotel causing grievous loss of life. Without the support, active or passive, of the general Jewish public the terrorist gangs who actually carried out these criminal acts would soon be unearthed, and in this measure the Jews in this country are accomplices and bear a share of the guilt.
>
> I am determined that they shall suffer punishment and be made aware of the contempt and loathing with which we regard their conduct. We must not allow ourselves to be deceived by the hypocritical sympathy shown by their leaders and representative bodies, or by their protests that they are in no way responsible for these acts. . . . I have decided that with effect on receipt of this letter you will put out of bounds to all ranks all Jewish establishments, restaurants, shops, and private dwellings. No British soldier is to have social intercourse with any Jew. . . . I appreciate that these measures will inflict some hardship on the troops, yet I am certain that if my reasons are fully explained to them they will

understand their propriety and will be punishing the Jews in a way the race dislikes as much as any, by striking at their pockets and showing our contempt of them.

Some valuable adjutant, one supposes, inserted those helpful words "as much as any" in the final sentence of this absurd *Order of the Day*. Otherwise, it was miserably mistaken, containing as it did obvious undertones of anti-Semitism, xenophobia, and class consciousness. General Barker, evidently, had learned nothing about Zionist aims and ideals, and nothing about the desperate worries of the great mass of the Jewish community. His reaction to the King David Hotel outrage was to strike at the innocent in order to hurt the guilty. That was precisely what the guilty wanted, in order to secure wider support for terrorism by the mass of the Jewish community.*

The General's insulting *Order of the Day* had the purely negative effect of diverting attention from the King David Hotel bomb outrage and focusing it on the inevitably unpleasant aspects of what British military rule had become. In January 1947 General Barker made himself once again the object of popular hatred when he confirmed the death sentence of a young terrorist, Dov Gruener, who had been implicated in the murder of a policeman. Irgun had kidnapped a British judge and another British civilian in Tel Aviv and held them as hostages for Gruener. Then they released their two prisoners. But Gruener was executed.

Whitehall was in a ferment over what to do about Palestine. Another Commission came and went, this time led by United States Ambassador Henry Grady. Grady conferred with the British government, then recommended a new partition plan which conferred local autonomy on Jewish and Arab provinces, kept Jerusalem under British rule, and allowed 100,000 Jewish immigrants to be admitted within a year after the adoption of the plan. Bevin toyed with his own emendation of this plan, partition under the Mandate, which would continue for five years, and the admission of 4000 refugees a month. But on February 14, 1947, the British government at last gave up: the Palestine question was turned over to the United Nations, and the General Assembly was convened at Britain's request on April 28, 1947. At the May 9, 1947 session a United Nations Special Committee on Palestine was appointed, with 11 states supplying its members.†

The Committee reported on September 1, 1947, in favor of the partition of Palestine. It was a majority report, supported by seven mem-

---

* To most of those who served with and under him, General Barker was merely an efficient and often endearing commander, utterly dedicated to looking after the men under his command, with a passion for physical fitness which verged on the eccentric, in appearance curiously like Low's "Colonel Blimp."

† The 11 states were: Australia, Canada, Czechoslovakia, Guatemala, India, Holland, Persia, Peru, Sweden, Uruguay, and Yugoslavia.

bers, with three opposing and one abstaining. The form of partition which it proposed was unrealistic. The Arab and Jewish states were both divided into three segments, with points of interaction between segments* "entwined in an inimical embrace like two fighting serpents."[5] This bizarre territorial arrangement was at first unacceptable to both Arabs and Jews, but the Zionist General Council decided on reflection to accept the plan in principle. The General Assembly of the United Nations debated the plan, and the result was the redefining of the boundaries of the southern segment of the Jewish state, which lost 500 square miles and the town of Beersheba. The Jewish negotiators, however, accepted this too. In November two world powers, the United States and the Soviet Union, approved the partition plan, and the United Nations General Assembly did so on November 29. The results were Arab riots in a half-dozen towns in Palestine, Arab attacks on Jewish communities elsewhere in the Middle East, the declaration in Cairo of a holy war against the Jews, and the proclamation of a three-day strike in Palestine, to begin on December 2, by the Mufti. Scattered fighting, all over Palestine, began almost at once.

The British Mandate was practically at an end, although its official demise was announced in Parliament only on December 11, 1947, and the withdrawal of all British forces was timed to be completed by May 15, 1948. The Jewish War of Independence had begun. Its first phase amounted to a civil war between the Jewish community and Palestinian Arabs who operated with considerable help from the Arab world outside Palestine's borders. Its second phase was to involve the regular armies of Arab states which invaded Palestine the moment the British High Commissioner had left and the State of Israel had been proclaimed. But before giving some account of the war, one must assess the reasons for Britain's failure to make the Mandate work, as well as the situation created by that failure. First, then, why did the Mandate finally break down?

Of course, the growing and eventually total incompatibility of the Jewish and Arab communities was a primary reason for the failure of the Mandate. Britain ceased to be the arbiter between the two communities and became caught between them. To maintain the Mandate would have required firm and consistent policies, backed by the ready use of force. Britain had no firm and consistent policies, deviating first in one direction and then in another in efforts to fulfill obligations to both Jewish and Arab communities. Force was used as a last resort.

Equally incompatible were the demands of the two communities. The Jews were demanding complete freedom of immigration, the right to settle wherever it was possible, and the development of their national home into an independent Jewish state. The Arabs insisted on stopping

---

* The actual points of intersection were the towns of Afula in the north, and Rehovoth in the south.

all immigration, the protection of Arab-owned lands, and independence for Palestine under the control of its Arab majority. Any compromise between these two sets of demands was denounced by both sides. Britain's way has always been one of compromise; a Mandate operating on this principle was doomed.

A kind of "prepartition," under a continuing Mandate, could probably have been peacefully introduced at the time of the Peel Report—indeed at any time before World War II broke out. But after the war the Arabs were convinced that partition of any kind was a plot, "a scheme for the liquidation of Arab Palestine and the establishment of a Jewish state in the greater and only viable part of the country."[6] Britain failed completely to set Arab fears at rest, or to explain to the Arabs that the strange little starfish of a Jewish state proposed by the United Nations would have had to come to terms with the Arab world all around it and, given some form of United Nations-backed political and military guarantee, would not have been allowed to expand into Arab Palestine.

Possibly the most basic reason of all for the British failure in Palestine lay in the nature of British colonial rule. Past experience had shown it to be successful only when operating in a political vacuum or near-vacuum. Where a genuine national movement had grown up, even with a very limited political content, British colonial rule was unwanted and had to be removed. That happened even in small, easily dominated countries like Cyprus and the South Arabian Federation. In Palestine there were two national movements. One of them, the Jewish, was intensely self-aware and politically sophisticated. The other, the Arab, was supported by the whole, politically burgeoning outside Arab world. The Mandate might have been further preserved for a year or two at the most. Bevin's subsequent assertions that his last-minute plans for maintaining the Mandate were foiled by a world Zionist conspiracy, backed by the United States, were beside the point.*

The situation left by the ending of the Mandate was chaotic in the extreme. The United Nations "entwined serpents" plan would have created a Jewish state with 500,000 Jewish inhabitants and 416,000 Arabs; the Arab state would have contained 715,000 Arabs and 8000 Jews. The city of Jerusalem and its surroundings which were to remain under British rule had roughly equal numbers of Jews and Arabs, 100,000 of each. A large peace-keeping force would have been needed to compel these two states to settle down in peace with one another; no such force was envisaged.

---

* Jewish dislike of Bevin was sometimes pleasantly relieved by Jewish wit. The story is told of an old lady who actually "blessed" Bevin. Asked why, she gave three reasons. He did not mince his words, so at least one knew where one stood with him. He was such a bungler that he played into the hands of the Jews. And by being thoroughly unpleasant, he managed to double the size of the State of Israel.

For their part, the Arabs were in a state of complete disunity over what should be done with Palestine, which they proposed to "liberate" from both the British and the Jews. Jordan wanted to annex Palestine, and had the support of the dynastically allied Hashemite state of Iraq. Egypt was chiefly concerned with keeping the holy city of Jerusalem out of Jordan's clutches. Syria and the Lebanon would probably have liked to carve Palestine up, while the Mufti wanted to gain control of an independent and united Arab state. Had the Arab states destroyed the infant Jewish state in 1948–1949, there would then have probably been an inter-Arab war over the spoils.

To have participated in creating a condition of chaos may have been more Britain's misfortune than her fault. To have abdicated all responsibility was far worse. Christopher Sykes' comment is altogether fair: "When one compares the British and French records in protectorate administration, the advantage to a fair-minded person is strongly in favor of the British, but there is nothing in the French record in next-door Syria comparable in mischievous incompetence to the British record in Palestine from November 1947 to May 1948."[7]

Certainly most Jews would agree with this judgment. One Jew wrote: "The average Englishman in Palestine doesn't like us and doesn't believe us. One reason is that we have plugged him with too much propaganda. Bring any Jew in touch with a Gentile and at once he becomes a high-powered salesman."[8] To the counterproductivity of some Zionist propaganda must be added the cumulative effects of nearly five years of Jewish terrorism and the cumulative frustrations of nearly 30 years of half-hearted effort to implement the promise made to the Jews in the Balfour Declaration.

Almost every Jew in Palestine was convinced of the anti-Jewish bias of the British government, British administrators, and soldiers. Their view was understandable. Britain appeared quite ready to leave them to their fate, out of what one historian has called an "abandonment of duty, from failing will."[9] To the Jews there was something criminal in the way in which Britain contemplated a state of total anarchy arising when the Mandate ended. But abandonment of the Jewish community which Britain had helped to install in Palestine was accompanied by an increased British preoccupation in maintaining some influence in the Arab world, with an eye to its oil resources, to the strategic requirements of the Empire, and to the Suez Canal.

A British military mission including 18 officers was sent to Iraq. Another military mission with 9 officers was established in Saudi Arabia. Supplies of arms to Egypt were stepped up. The Arab Legion in Jordan continued to be armed, trained, and officered by Britain with an annual subsidy of $10 million. When subsequently accused of supplying arms to a war area, Britain pleaded treaty commitments and Hector McNeill was able to tell the Commons on February 16, 1948,

"I have no evidence to suggest that arms supplied to Middle East Governments in virtue of these treaties . . . are being made available for warfare in Palestine." For pure casuistry this statement is hard to beat, and one detects a sad parallelism with the attitude towards the 1968 war between Nigeria and breakaway Biafra. On both occasions a Labor government's objective was to absolve itself from responsibility.

Later, when the State of Israel had been proclaimed and the War of Independence had moved into its second stage, Britain demanded the withdrawal of Israeli troops advancing on the town of El Arish in Sinai and sent Spitfires over the Jewish lines in the southern desert of the Negev. Britain continued to maintain a garrison at Jordan's port of Aqaba, denying it to the Israeli forces, which had advanced to the Gulf of Aqaba and which had established themselves on the Red Sea coast.

There is no room in this book to describe the War of Independence in full. The first phase of civil war in Palestine began in December 1947. On January 25, 1948 the guerilla leader Fawzi el Kawakji arrived from Syria to lead a mixed Syrian-Palestinian "army of liberation." A second such army was already operating around Jerusalem under the command of Abd el Kader Husseini. There was also the Arab Legion, led by Brigadier John Glubb, but hampered in its activity by its close connection with the British Mandatory authorities. The two irregular forces mounted an increasing number of attacks on Jewish settlements, while on the Jewish side Haganah organized convoys to relieve the settlements and keep lines of communication open. The fighting was sporadic but often fierce.

It grew steadily in intensity. In the first four months Jewish settlements showed that they were fully capable of looking after themselves. Arab attacks on key kibbutzim like Mishmar Haemek and Ramat Yohanan were beaten off. In towns the Jews turned to the offensive and gained control of four cities with mixed population, Tiberias, Haifa, Safed, and Jaffa. More important, Haganah had been able to buy 450 machine guns and 10,000 rifles from Czechoslovakia and divert for its own use a further large consignment of Czech arms which was destined for the Arab side. This more than offset the loss of 750 of Haganah's best men.

It was largely an "amateur" war, fought with small arms by men who for the most part had had no proper military training. In such a war, fighting spirit and leadership were the most important factors and Haganah had plenty of both. And while the Arabs were fighting to regain the land which they had bartered away and oust a people whom they regarded as alien, the Jews fought for survival.

The one big area in which Haganah was in grave difficulties was Jerusalem, for the large Jewish community in and around the city was completely isolated from the rest of Jewish Palestine. The roads leading to the coast and the Jewish strongholds of Tel Aviv and Petach Tikva ran through the wild Judean Hills, where ambushes were easy to set up. It became necessary for the Haganah not only to keep the main road to the west open, but also to capture the villages on either side of the hill that commanded the route. In several of these villages some of the most bitter fighting of the war took place.

To the south of Jerusalem the Haganah tried to maintain the four small and isolated settlements of the Etzion bloc. One by one they fell, and when the last was overrun the Jewish survivors were massacred. In April 1948 a convoy traveling to the Hadassah hospital outside Jerusalem was ambushed, and 77 Jewish doctors, nurses, and volunteer workers were slaughtered. There was a British military post only two hundred yards from the place of the ambush, but telephone calls to it were not answered from 10 A.M. until mid-afternoon. By then the massacre was over.

Four days earlier, on April 8, Irgun patrols had seized the Arab village of Deir Yassin, to the southwest of Jerusalem. Men, women, and children, 254 in all, were massacred. Irgun apologists claimed afterwards that although the villagers had put out white flags, they defended every house, and that they had failed to evacuate women and children when called upon to do so.[10] They also claim that eight Jews were killed and 57 wounded in the attack. Even so, there could be no possible justification for this hideous massacre. Men like Eshkol were horrified at what had happened and have expressed their disgust ever since. Unwisely, the Arabs inflated the story, which was terrible enough, and attributed it to a deliberate over-all plan of extermination. This undoubtedly contributed to the exodus of Arabs from their homes which had begun and was now impossible to stop. By the end of April most Arabs had fled from Jewish-controlled towns, more than 30 Arab villages were empty, and up to 150,000 Arabs were homeless refugees.

That voluminous exodus of refugees, comprising some 20 percent of the Arab population in areas under Jewish control, was the main feature of the first phase of the war. The second phase was the successful Jewish struggle in Jerusalem. Admittedly, this was the one area where the Jews had suffered conspicuous territorial losses. They included the four settlements of the Etzion bloc, two more on the northern and one on the eastern outskirts, and most of the Jewish Quarter of the Old City, and the Wailing Wall, the last remnant of Herod's Temple. But Haganah retained New, or Jewish, Jerusalem intact and reopened a land corridor running to the coast. On April 17 and 20, two big convoys forced their way through. Later the famous Burma Road across Jewish-held territory, out of range of rifle and machine-gun fire from Arab villages, was to be constructed.

On May 8, 1948, there was a cease fire in Jerusalem. And on May 9 the first provisional postage stamps for the new Jewish state were sold on its streets. They were Jewish National Fund stamps, showing the map of partitioned Palestine and stamped over with the word *Doar* (Post). One old man was heard saying a lengthy blessing over a stamp as he stuck it on an envelope: "Blessed art Thou, O Lord our God, King of the universe, who has kept us in life, and has preserved us, and has enabled us to reach this season."[11]

The first phase of the war ended with the proclamation of the State of Israel on May 14, 1948. It contains this key passage:

> We extend our hand in peace and neighborliness to all the neighboring States and their peoples, and invite them to cooperate with the independent Jewish nation for the common good of all. The State of Israel is prepared to make its contribution to the progress of the Middle East as a whole. Our call goes out to the Jewish people all over the world to rally to our side in the task of immigration and development, and to stand by us in the great struggle for the fulfillment of the dream of generations for the redemption of Israel. With trust in the Rock of Israel, we set our hand to this Declaration.

The proclamation was made from the home of the mayor, Meir Dizengoff, in Tel Aviv (the house is an art museum now). There were 37 signatories. It had been prepared two days earlier by the newly formed Jewish National Executive, which allegedly voted 6–4 in favor of this action.[12] The 600 chosen witnesses of the ceremony did not know that there was no text on the parchment which the 37 leaders signed. The text was added only a week later: after "a venerable Torah scribe" had "scratched it out with a goose quill, letter by letter, in the ancient script."[13] The opponents of this step had learned from Moshe Shertok, who had just been to America as Ben-Gurion's envoy, that the United States would oppose the declaration on the grounds that it could lead to a major war. Actually, President Truman accorded recognition to the State of Israel within 11 minutes after its being proclaimed. The day after the declaration a full-scale war broke out, and the regular armies of the neighboring Arab states invaded Israel.

Israel had a field army of about 35,000 men, mostly untrained, although among them there were some veterans of World War II who had fought under the British flag. Of these men 30,000 belonged to Haganah, 3000 to the *Palmach,* shock troops mainly recruited from the kibbutzim, and 2000 to Irgun. There were also a few hundred members of the Stern Gang.

These forces were reasonably well provided with rifles, machine guns, and Sten guns. They started with no artillery other than a half-dozen mortars. Later, the newly invented *Davidka* (little David) mortar, a home-made contraption with a range of less than a mile, went into action as well. They also improvised armored cars and various forms of grenades, from the Molotov Cocktail down to the smallest smoke bomb. The Israeli "airforce" consisted of a score of training Austers, bought from the

British army surplus stocks and refitted as bombers, with the copilot holding hundred-pound home-made bombs on his lap; and half a dozen other obsolete reconnaissance planes.[14]

The "navy" was at first the single small boat which Eshkol, who was now Director-General of the Ministry of Defense, had procured. This former United States patrol boat, which had been partially converted to an icebreaker, had the speed of only eight knots and there was considerable difficulty in fitting it with a gun. Three small corvettes were added later.

The Haganah high command was pessimistic. Prior to the building of the Burma Road they had considered either evacuating Jerusalem or asking the United Nations to declare it an open city—which would have meant its loss to the State of Israel. Jewish Jerusalem was to be held at all costs, but it was feared that Arab regular armies would all too easily drive wedges through the Jewish-occupied territory, west of the Sea of Galilee, down to the coast from the Judean Hills, and northward from Gaza into the plain of Sharon. Those indeed were the objectives of the Arab armies.

They appeared to have ample forces to achieve them. Egypt had about 40,000 regulars in its Army and could, in theory, call up another 150,000 conscripts (according to one source, 80 percent of them were disqualified as being physically unfit).[15] In addition, Egypt had over 150 planes in ten wings, eight of which were combat wings, and six small naval craft. Syria had an army of about 8000 and Lebanon of 3500. The Iraqi army was much more formidable, about 35,000, and Jordan's armed forces, 40,000 strong, included the much-vaunted British-officered Arab Legion. Saudi Arabia was also prepared to send troops belonging to its 12,000-strong militia, but contributed only a single battalion. To these 130,000 Arab troops should be added Kawakji's 20,000-odd guerillas. No Arab country except Egypt had an airforce worth the name.

What has never been established is the strength of Arab tank forces at that time. Egypt, Syria, and Iraq all had armored units. But a fair estimate is that not more than a score of Syrian and Iraqi tanks were used on the northern front in Galilee and about 60 Egyptian tanks in the south. One of the major Israeli worries was that antitank guns ordered from France and Czechoslovakia had not arrived when the Arab invasion began.

The war was divided into three phases, with two truces intervening before the final cease fire. The first phase lasted from May 15 to June 11. The Israelis were almost entirely on the defensive. They lost some territory in the south, the settlement of Mishmar Hayarden in Galilee, and their last strongholds in the Old City of Jerusalem. There, 290 Israeli prisoners were taken by the Arab Legion and over 1000 women and children were passed through the lines to Jewish Jerusalem. It was a militarily minor but psychologically bitter defeat, for the Jewish Quarter of the Old City was the jewel of Jewish settlement in Palestine and the Wailing Wall was by far its most treasured holy place. But elsewhere the Israeli defense had been successful. The Syrian drive south of the Sea of Galilee towards the port of Haifa was repulsed, and the Egyptians were stopped 25 miles south of Tel Aviv. Incredibly, six new Jewish agricultural settlements were established during the first four weeks of fighting.

The first truce, arranged by Count Bernadotte, as United Nations mediator, lasted from June 11 to July 6. Bernadotte tried to prolong it and his efforts, which might possibly have led to lasting peace in the Middle East, only narrowly failed. Israel, Jordan, Iraq, Lebanon, and Saudi Arabia were ready to accept his proposals; Egypt and Syria were not. The latter two countries believed that the small Israeli community could be bled to death. It had already lost nearly 1000 dead, and the Arabs were clearly not aware of the important arms consignments on their way from Europe to Jaffa and Haifa. Accordingly, Egypt and Syria attacked for the second time, with disastrous consequences for the Palestinian Arabs. In this second phase of the war, which lasted only from July 7 to July 21, the Israelis captured Nazareth and all of western Galilee in the north, Ramleh, Lydda (Lod), and a widened land corridor between Jerusalem and the Mediterranean. Israeli aircraft bombed Cairo and Damascus, and the Israeli corvettes managed to fire a few shells into the port of Tyre.

The United Nations Security Council ordered the second truce on July 18 and it began three days later. During the truce, on September 17, the mediator, Count Bernadotte, was murdered by members of the Stern Gang. The act was their response to his efforts to secure viable peace terms, including the internationalization of Jerusalem, and the surrender by Israel of the whole of the southern desert of the Negev, as a sop to Egyptian pride. The Israeli government has been accused of "laxity" in tracking down the murderers.[16] Yet scores of Sternists were arrested and Irgun was given 24 hours to disband. As a concession to Irgun's recalcitrant leader, Menahem Beigin, Palmach was also officially dissolved, although its units in the field remained intact.

The third phase of the war began on October 14, 1948. Once again, the Egyptians were responsible, since they began a new drive northward on Tel Aviv. The Israelis were well prepared, repelled the attack, and advanced on Beersheba. They captured this key town on October 21 and, with only a six-day truce intervening, proceeded to occupy the whole of the Negev, including the former Palestine police post of Um Rash, which later grew into Israel's Red Sea port of Eilat. In December, General Yigal Allon launched Operation Horeb, penning a large Egyptian force in the Gaza Strip and advancing deep into Sinai. The Israeli pursuit of the fleeing Egyptian army was called off only after Britain had tried unsuccessfully to invoke the Anglo-Egyptian Treaty of 1936 and the United States had, more effectively, advised the Israeli Government to order a withdrawal from the Sinai Peninsula.

Ben-Gurion wanted to carry out one military operation more to mop up the Jordanian forces deployed to the west of the river Jordan. He believed that a final thrust on both sides of Jerusalem would force the Jordanian forces out of Hebron, Nablus, and the whole of the west bank. The Israelis had a pretext for launching the attack—the blowing up of cisterns and water-pumping installations near Latrun, which depleted Jewish Jerusalem's water supply. But Ben-Gurion was overruled by the majority of his Cabinet.[17]

Armistices were eventually signed with Egypt on February 24, 1949, with Lebanon on March 23, with Jordan on April 3, and with Syria on July 29.* And on May 14, 1949, Israel became the 59th member of the United Nations.

The war had been costly. Israel lost 4000 combatants and 2000 civilians. These may seem small casualties in a War of Independence, but it was one percent of the population, roughly as much as Britain, for instance, lost in World War II. In addition, the Jewish Quarter of the Old City had been lost, as well as a few small settlements in what became the west bank of Jordan. As a result of Arab breaches of the truces, Israel increased her territory by one third as against the area awarded her by the United Nations partition plan; Jerusalem was linked with the coast by a wide land corridor; and the invaluable outlet to the Red Sea and Indian Ocean was secured at Eilat.

The Israelis won their first war because of their fighting spirit, native intelligence, and absolute determination to survive. The Arabs lost it because, as one observer puts it, "Arab armies reflected the social structure of their countries—poverty and subjection in the ranks, wealth and tyranny in the officers. Dr. Weizmann, when asked why the Egyptian Army fared so ill, replied: 'The men were too lean and the officers too fat.'"[18]

It was a ruthlessly fought war and it left a great residue of bitter humiliation among the Arabs. Not for the last time, the Israelis managed

---

* Most of the credit for the armistice arrangements with Egypt belongs to the United Nations mediator, Dr. Ralph Bunche, who succeeded Count Bernadotte in that capacity. He organized the armistice talks, which began on January 12, 1949 on the island of Rhodes. As a story would have it he had a number of plates inscribed "Rhodes Armistice Talks 1949" and showed them to both delegations. He used the same formula with each: "Have a good look at them! If you reach an agreement, each of you will get one to take home. If you don't, I'll break them over your heads!" (Walter Eytan, *The First Ten Years*, p. 33.)

The armistice talks with Jordan took place in King Abdullah's winter palace at Shuneh, in a long room at the end of which hung a painting of the Battle of Trafalgar, the gift of King George V. Certainly, a wonderfully inappropriate present for the head of an Arab state with a total seaboard of five miles! (*Ibid.*, p. 40.)

to win too convincingly to be forgiven. But it must be remembered that Israel had accepted a United Nations partition plan which the Arabs rejected, that Israel was attacked by seven Arab armies the very moment she proclaimed her statehood, and that Egypt and Syria broke truces which had some chance of leading to a lasting settlement. Israel made two attempts to reach peaceful agreement with Jordan, the Arab neighbor most implicated in the affairs of Palestine. In November 1947 and again in May 1948 Mrs. Golda Meir, who was to succeed Eshkol as Prime Minister, had secret meetings with King Abdullah. The King was amenable to the partition of Palestine, made it clear that Jordan would annex Arab Palestine, but was unable to give any pledge not to take part in a war.*

The hideous murders perpetrated by both sides were especially disgusting features of the war. But the immense majority of Israelis wanted to fight only fairly and cleanly, in their own self-defense. Typical of this majority view was the order issued to his troops by Colonel Moshe Carmel, before attacking Nazareth:

> Nazareth is a Christian sanctuary, a city holy to many millions. The eyes of Christians throughout the world are upon it. It holds churches, monasteries, and holy places. Our soldiers, when they enter, will fight with determination against the invaders, but will show the utmost forbearance from damaging any holy place. They will not enter any churches, fight from them or fortify them, unless under the most explicit orders from their leaders. No soldier shall lay his hand upon any property. . . . If any soldier offends, he will be tried immediately and without indulgence, and will be punished severely.

Eshkol did not take part in the fighting during the War of Independence in person. But his job of Director-General in the Ministry of Defense kept him extremely busy. Once again, his comings and goings were so frequent and so sudden that his family never knew when to expect to see him. His wife told the children "not to ask unnecessary questions"; that was the only wartime discipline imposed on them.[19] But they were dimly aware that their father, still in charge of the Mekorot water board, helping to organize new agricultural settlements and to solve the problems of the old ones, constantly in consultation with the Haganah high command about the distribution of available arms, was working himself to death. A disproportionate amount of time, which he could not afford to waste, was spent on the road. Eshkol somehow even found time to accompany convoys into beleaguered Jerusalem.

As usual, Eshkol showed himself to be eminently practical and personally concerned with practical detail. He made it his business to super-

---

* According to Eshkol, Golda Meir concluded the second meeting with the words, "Then it looks, Your Highness, as if we shall have to meet on the battlefield."

vise the assembly of materials for building the first armored cars, called "frogs" because they looked so incredibly clumsy. He organized the first workshops for their construction, mainly in and just outside Tel Aviv. It was the desire of seeing his own frogs in action that was chiefly responsible for his trips with the Jerusalem-bound convoys.

He was convinced that Israel should build up its own armaments industry, and it was on his initiative that the first armaments "factories" were set up just before and during the War of Independence. They were primitive little workshops, but they turned out mortars, grenades, and armor plate. Eshkol's view was that Israel should not be dependent solely on the arms industries of countries which might be friendly one day and hostile the next. Years later, he was to give the Israeli arms industry the maximum backing in moving into new fields of production.

Eshkol's gift of making fast decisions was particularly valuable in time of war. One of his friends, Raanan Weitz, recalls how Eshkol telephoned him in the middle of the night and asked him if he had taken chemistry for his University degree. He had. Eshkol greeted this information with the words, "Right! You are, as of now, in charge of chemical supplies for the duration of the war." During this conversation Weitz was lying in bed, exhausted. Eshkol, he said, sounded "quite fresh."

Another typical performance of Eshkol's occurred during the building of the Burma Road. Food supplies in Jerusalem had fallen to their lowest, and the Jews who went out foraging in the fields on the outskirts of the city were shot at by Arab snipers within sight of their homes. Eshkol mobilized a "ration party" of 200 volunteers in Tel Aviv and took them to the *moshav* (farming collective) of Bilu, where there was a large supply of flour. The 200 volunteers spent a day packing the flour into 20-pound bags, then they carted the precious supply of flour all the way to Jerusalem, along stretches of road where they had to carry the bags on their backs.

He found time to visit Degania B. His kibbutz was in the forefront of the fighting. By April 15, 1948, all British troops had left that part of Galilee. On May 15, 1948, the Syrians attacked on both sides of the Sea of Galilee. Syrian armor and infantry moved down from the escarpment of the Golan Mountains and thrust towards the Jordan and the bridges at Degania and Almagor. The two Degania kibbutzim bore the brunt of the fighting at the southern end of the lake. In Degania B there were only 40 people of fighting age—all the rest had left with the Haganah or Palmach for the fronts in the south or around Jerusalem. The settlers had rifles, a few machine guns, and a small cannon which was a historical relic of the French incursion into Mexico in the 1860s.

There was a three-day battle from May 15 to 18 before the Syrians drew back. The settlers counterattacked, with the young Moshe Dayan playing a prominent part. More than once the settlers sallied out at night, remembering the offensive and surprise tactics of Orde Wingate. Degania

B lost seven of its members. A number were wounded. But like every Israeli outpost it fought off an enemy immensely superior in numbers and weapons. A burned-out Syrian tank stands in a little grove of trees close to the main gate into Degania A to this day. It had been knocked out by dropping a grenade down its turret.

1. Richard Crossman, *Palestine Mission*, p. 61.
2. *Ibid.*, p. 66.
3. Maurice Edelman, *Ben-Gurion*, p. 134.
4. Christopher Sykes, *Cross Roads to Israel*, p. 367.
5. *Ibid.*, p. 384.
6. Edward Atiyah, *The Arabs*, p. 177.
7. Sykes, *op. cit.*, p. 399.
8. Harry Levin, *Jerusalem Embattled*, p. 25.
9. Harry Sacher, *Israel: The Establishment of a State*, p. 112.
10. Samuel Katz, *Days of Fire*, p. 215.
11. Levin, *op. cit.*, p. 134.
15. David Ben-Gurion in *Jewish Observer & Middle East Review*, April 9, 1965, p. 20.
13. Moshe Brillant, in *Israel Magazine*, Vol. I, No. 4, 1968.
14. Sacher, *op. cit.*, p. 210.
15. David Ben-Gurion in *Jewish Observer & Middle East Review*, April 9, 1965, p. 20.
16. Sykes, *op. cit.*, p. 436.
17. Ben-Gurion, in the paper *Maariv*, October 1968.
18. Sacher, *op. cit.*, p. 249.
19. Dvora Eshkol Rafaeli, in conversation with the author.

10.

The proclamation of the State of Israel had been carried out with due ceremony and with a certain amount of rejoicing. But there was nothing like the wave of emotion when the United Nations decided to accept partition of Palestine and creation of a Jewish state. Ben-Gurion, for one, told the ministers of his provisional government that he felt no gaiety, only a deep anxiety. Typical of the precarious situation of the new, infant state was the Haganah notice posted outside the hall where the proclamation was made. It read:

> The enemy threatens invasion. We must not ignore the danger. It may be near. The security forces are taking all necessary measures. The entire public must give its full help.
> Shelters must be dug in all residential areas and the orders of Air Raid Precaution officers must be obeyed.
> Mass gatherings in open areas and streets must be avoided.
> Every assistance must be given to the commanders of the security forces in erecting barriers and fortifications.
> No panic. No complacency. Be alert and disciplined.

That had been before the invasion of Jewish Palestine by seven Arab armies. Eight months later, after the war had been fought and won, the position of the new State of Israel was no less precarious than at the beginning of its existence. Casualties, just over 6000 dead, had been much lighter than might have been expected. But there had been a vast amount of material damage. There had been pitched battles in the streets of some towns. Dozens of settlements had been shelled by the Arab armies, and some had been overrun and completely destroyed. There had been extensive damage to power plants and irrigation installations. Communications were in a state of chaos. The 1948 harvest had been only partially gathered and there was a considerable shortage of food. But there was a shortage of everything—machinery for industry and farms, household goods, building materials, clothing, and even schoolbooks.

The Arabs had always maintained that there had been no room for Jewish colonists in Palestine. In reality, not only had the Jewish community quadrupled in 30 years to 650,000, but the number of Arabs in Palestine had roughly doubled to some 1,200,000. One commentator pointed out that "if all the Jews of Europe should settle in Palestine and its surroundings, and do what the original stone-breakers and builders of the soil have done, there would not be fewer and poorer Arabs but more and richer Arabs in the Near East."[1] The Jews, indeed, had cultivated the land which had been expressly designated by the Arab leaders and the British Mandatory authorities as totally useless—the sands of the plain of Sharon, the rocks of the Judaean highlands, the malarial swamps of the upper Jordan valley. After 30 years Palestine was providing better living conditions for almost three times as many people as had been living there at the beginning of the Mandate.

But now the Israelis had to face the major problem of mass immigration. The provisional government decided that any and every Jew who wished to come to Israel would be readily accepted and warmly welcomed. This basic precept has been maintained ever since. The days of illegal immigration were over. There was no longer any need for an underground railway; the Jews of Europe, Africa, and Asia could come openly and freely. The only question was how to deal with all those who wanted to come.

A few figures tell their story. Already in 1948, soon after the declaration of the State of Israel on May 14, 101,000 immigrants arrived. In 1949, 240,000 arrived, and in 1950, 170,000. The next year the number was 175,000, but from then on far fewer came. By the end of 1951 the great mass of Jews who needed urgently to leave their makeshift or unhappy homes in Europe had already reached Palestine, that is, with the exception of the Jews of the now "curtained" Communist bloc. In four years the Jewish population of Israel jumped from 657,000 to 1,404,000. And one has to remember that a great many of these immigrants were still suffering bitterly from the effects of Nazi persecution; most of them arrived with only the clothes on their backs and a few pitiful personal possessions. Some brought other problems with them, like the Moroccan Jew who arrived with eight wives.[2] Among the new immigrants there were 300,000 former inmates of Hitler's concentration camps and 250,000 Jews from Asia.

There is no space in this book for the details of this huge transplantation of largely destitute and suffering humanity. Whole Jewish communities were moved. Thus, 100,000 were brought by airlift from Iraq in the so-called "Operation Magic Carpet," and the great Jewish community which had grown up there in the days of the Babylonian Empire ceased to exist. All the Jews of the Yemen, 45,000 of them, were brought home after an exile of 26 centuries, carried, as they themselves described it, "on the wings of eagles." An Israeli Ministry report proudly announced that "a whole living community with their holy books was saved from peril and degradation." The small Jewish communities in China and Southern India were transported *en bloc,* and 30,000 out of 33,000 left Libya.[3]

Admittedly the Israelis "inherited" land and buildings from the Arabs who had fled from their homes. Much of the land was underfarmed; many of the villages were primitive in the extreme. At least there was to be no immediate lack of living space. But Israel was now left with an immensely serious political problem, that of the Arab refugees.

Roughly ten years later the spokesmen of Arab countries claimed that there were over a million Arab refugees. By 1968 this figure had grown to one and a half million. The Arab claims include all people found in refugee camps, and a great many besides who have been registered as Palestinian refugees along with their families. Even the official figures given by the United Nations Relief and Works Agency

(UNRWA), which undertook to feed and clothe the bulk of the refugees from 1950 onwards, have never been accurate. Its records have included thousands of holders of forged ration cards and the names of people long since dead. It quickly became standard Arab propaganda to exaggerate the numbers of refugees.

In *The Refugee in the World,* Joseph Schechtman notes that the refugees left their homes in three waves. The first consisted of 30,000 members of wealthy or at least well-to-do families. They left after the United Nations partition plan had been announced, believing that a civil war was inevitable and would result in an Arab victory, enabling them to return home. The second wave took place after the early Jewish victories against Kawakji's irregulars, with perhaps 60,000 leaving Haifa and 70,000 Jaffa. About 200,000 in all may have left during this second wave. After the invasion by five Arab armies the third wave began, eventually comprising another 300,000. The total number that fled may have been around 550,000.[4]

The *total* Arab population of those parts of Palestine which were incorporated into Israel was less than 700,000 in 1948. There were between 1,100,000 and 1,200,000 Arabs in the whole of Palestine, of which the West Bank was annexed by the Kingdom of Jordan and the Gaza Strip occupied by Egypt. About 150,000 Arabs either remained in Israel or were enabled to return to their homes there. This, too, suggests that something over half a million Arabs became refugees as a result of the war.[5]

There were a number of very different reasons for the Arabs' leaving their homes, as more than one unbiased writer has pointed out: "Some with greater prudence than patriotism had moved to safety betimes; some had allegedly been promised a speedy return in the wake of 'victorious' Arab armies; some had been quickened by Israeli psychological warfare or panicked by direct terrorism; no doubt many joined in the flight without knowing why."[6] There were obviously basic differences between the Jewish and the Arab community in Palestine. The members of the former were determined to stay where they were, put themselves in a state of readiness, and cooperate with their own defense forces in every possible way. The Arabs, on the other hand, were highly disorganized, had only a semideveloped civic or communal sense, and had to place their trust either in Kawakji's wild guerillas or on foreign Arab armies. The Jewish community was, in fact, an entity; the Palestinian Arab community was not and never had been.

The Jews could hardly have been expected to encourage the Arabs to stay where they were. Yet this did occasionally happen. Haifa's mayor, Shabetai Levy, implored the Arabs to stay in their homes and wept when they fled. On April 26, 1948 the British Police Headquarters at Haifa reported: "Every effort is being made by the Jews to persuade the Arab populace to stay and carry on with their normal lives, to get their shops and businesses open, and to be assured that their lives and interests will be safe." Two days later, "there is no change in the situation in Haifa. The Jews are still making every effort to persuade the Arab populace to remain and settle back into their normal lives in the town."[7] General Sir Hugh Stockwell, commanding British troops in Palestine, expressed his dismay at the decision of the Haifa Arabs to continue to leave. Yet the Arab National Committee of Haifa, a body of exiles, found a ready explanation of such solicitude in a memorandum presented to the Arab League in 1950. It was that the Jews tried to hinder the evacuation of Haifa "to prove to the world that the Arabs in Haifa live in peace and security in the shadow of Jewish rule."[8] The end of the matter was that only 5000 out of 62,000 Haifa Arabs stayed in their homes.

The British authorities made it plain that they could, or would, do nothing to help the Arabs. Arab radio and press outside Palestine made its own contribution by blowing up or inventing atrocity stories, while at the same time urging the utmost violence against the Jews. It was this vicious incitement which convinced many Arabs that the Jews would be sure to treat them in the same way. Thus, the Arab propaganda boomeranged. The massacres which did take place had their own impact. General Sir Hugh Stockwell's view was expressed in simple terms, "The Arabs' leaders left first, and no one did anything to stop the mass exodus, which became first a rush and then a panic."[9] That is as fair a summing up as one is likely to get. The consequence was a bitter, gnawing, nagging refugee problem which has lasted ever since. The Israeli offer, at the Lausanne Conference in 1949, to readmit 100,000 refugees, allow some reunion of families in addition, and pay compensation within the capacity of the State of Israel, was turned down flat.

More must be said about the problem of the Arab refugees. Psychologically, it was an additional burden for the young State of Israel. It was ringed with Arab enemies, and efforts to make progress towards a genuine peace with both Lebanon and Jordan ended in 1952, with a change of Lebanese government and the murder of King Abdullah of Jordan by an agent of the Mufti (as Sykes wrote pithily, "his offense being common sense"[10]). King Hussein of Jordan, who saw his grandfather shot down, has since written that he has "always felt that Egypt was largely responsible."[11] All thought of a peace between Israel and her two other Arab neighbors, Egypt and Syria, was out of the question. What became the consensus of Arab feeling has been described by one Arab writer, Edward Atiyah: "In Arab eyes the Israelis have perpetrated against the Arabs an evil as ugly as that perpetrated by the Nazis against the Jews. They are aggressors who have deprived a whole Arab people of its country.... To the Arabs, Israel is an alien, hateful, and dangerous intrusion into the Arab world—the expression of a militant and fanatical nationalism which is incompatible with the existence and healthy development of the Arab community."[12] Israel, in short, had in Arab eyes no right to exist.

The Israelis had to resign themselves to the reality of uncompromising and lasting Arab hatred. With an area of only 8000 square miles, they had nearly 600 miles of frontier to guard. This frontier was easily defended only along a short stretch of the river Jordan and an even shorter piece of Dead Sea coastline; elsewhere it meandered through stony uplands and sandy desert. Israel was back in the same position as in Biblical times, on a crossroads between hostile countries which coveted the soil of Palestine and distrusted one another. But in Biblical times the children of Israel could always retreat into the vastnesses of the Judaean and Samarian highlands. Now, the geographical situation had changed dramatically; the Israelis were largely confined to the plains that had once been the domicile of the Philistines and to the southern desert which had barely been colonized even in the reign of King Solomon.

In confronting the future, the Israelis used an appropriate phrase at this time, "Last year we were making history; this year we have to make a living." This represented Eshkol's own philosophy of life. He was desperately anxious to begin working productively again, and his first thought was how the new immigrants should be settled on the land. Immediately after the armistices with the Arab countries, he was appointed head of the Land Settlement Department of the Jewish Agency. This gave him his chance.

His first concern was to get enough immigrants on the land. "I was afraid that so many of them, like the Moroccans out of their mellahs, wouldn't face it, that it would take a bulldozer to drive them into the fields. I was afraid that these persecuted little men would head off for the kiosks in the towns, and start trying to sell something, anything."[13] "The soil was there, crying out to be used, and used properly. But the small drugstores of Tel Aviv could wait. And there was another thing about it; we of the Second Aliyah discovered that the soil had turned us into something more than we had been before. How much more these new immigrants needed the soil of Palestine to help them, whether they were survivors of the concentration camps, or ignored and underprivileged Jews of Africa and Asia!"[14] For the remnants of persecuted European Jewry, Eshkol never tired of saying, Palestine was really the last haven. It was the answer to their faith which had enabled them to survive, but which was no greater than the faith of the millions of Jews who had gone singing and praying over the threshold of the gas chamber.

On the land, Eshkol believed, one could achieve what was useful, rational, and healthy. Somehow, Israel had to be a balanced community. In the beginning of the state's existence, one observer wrote: "Will it be a corner of the West, Western thoughts and values projected into the East? Will it become corroded by the slick superficiality of the Levant? Will it express the old Hebrew social idealism? Maybe the new ways of life on the land are already a presage of what it may yield. . . . Whatever we evolve, it will, at least, be our own."[15] And the same observer wrote of what a Jew from Budapest had told him: "In the camps they taught me what labor is. I want to start life anew, like Israel, for myself now. I want to dig with my hands into the earth and know that it is mine and that I'll never have to leave it."[16] This was the sort of thinking which Eshkol understood, and the sort of men he wanted to help.

Some years later Eshkol explained the principles and ideas which had animated him when he began his work for the Jewish Agency after the War of Independence.[17] He had believed in the land, for the land's sake and for its associations with Biblical history. King David had been "a herdsman and a dresser of vines," and the dream of plenty had been that of "each man under his vine and under his fig tree." It was "the light of the vision of the prophets" which had inspired the settlers of the Second Aliyah, and many besides, in their fervent belief in social justice and equality before the face of God. This belief in social justice had in turn helped them to evolve the principles of collective farming. There were four that really mattered: land should be owned by the nation and for the nation, water and the products of the soil should be justly divided, settlers should be self-employed and men of the soil in their own right, and the working of the land should be based on mutual assistance and cooperation.

In this particular speech Eshkol made one additional valuable point. When Moses sent his scouts ahead into the land of Canaan, they brought back two reports, not one. The first one has since been much quoted: "We came into the land whither thou sentest us, and surely it floweth with milk and honey." The second report was down-to-earth: "The land through which we have passed to spy it out, is a land that eateth up the inhabitants thereof." In fact, part of the land of Canaan was rich, or potentially rich; but much of it was very poor. This was the case with the land of Israel in the twentieth century, and much or even most of it had been sadly neglected for centuries. Eshkol's message was that it would take much hard work to redeem it.

One of Eshkol's first tasks was to provide for the emergency needs of the existing settlements. War damage had been considerable, especially in the south.* One estimate of the damage was 4 million Israeli pounds, approximately $15 million at the rate of exchange of that time. This was a staggering sum. Eshkol was concerned mainly with such things as the reestablishment of an effective water supply, the financing of a program for supplying seed, livestock, and farm equipment, and grants in aid for uprooted agricultural settlers.

Much more important was the task of creating new settlements. At the end of the War of Independence there were well under 100,000

---

* There was, for instance, the small settlement of Negbah. It had only 300 inhabitants. The Egyptians fired 15,000 shells at and into it, and Egyptian planes bombed and strafed it 227 times. In two frontal assaults, the Egyptians lost 12 tanks. Negbah was little more than a few heaps of rubble when the war ended.

people living on the land. Eshkol evolved a crash program for creating over 100 new settlements with a population of 15,000. Raanan Weitz, who worked under him in the Jewish Agency, described their first conversation on the subject:

> Eshkol called his advisers in, including myself. He asked us, "How many villages can you build in a year?" The average since 1945 had been about 15, and someone said he thought that we might build 25. Eshkol's answer was that there were going to be thousands of newly arrived immigrants who needed a real home and a stake in the soil, who could not be left mouldering away in the tin huts of refugee camps. He told us, "I want you to help me build 125 new settlements in the next year." We thought this was just plain crazy. But we built 122, one new village every three days.
>
> That was the beginning of the big push. It meant that we were able to give thousands of families something really worthwhile to do. It was the first stage in a four-year program in which we settled 30,000 families on the land in all. Of course, we made a lot of mistakes in the course of it. But we managed to avoid the worst mistake of all, which would have been to do too little at a time when there was so much to be done.

The crash program, Weitz believed, brought out three qualities in Eshkol. Hard work and application were not among those he listed, for he was well known for both already. But a program of this size required daring, imagination, and the capacity to pick out a good team to work under him.

His daring lay in the sheer scope of the project. By the time it was completed, nearly 500 new settlements had been built, 120 of them collectives, either kibbutzim or moshavim. These new settlements were spread over the length and breadth of Israel, but two motives were plain in their location—to firm up the frontier areas, which needed a screen of settlers to safeguard them against Arab infiltration, and to spread land settlement southward toward and into the Negev desert. Eshkol's daring lay in turning refugees to whom the open country was completely foreign into pioneers, whether they came from the mellahs of Bagdad or the ghettos of Central Europe. It lay, too, in his invitation to destitute and physically wretched people who would gladly have lain down in the shadow of the meanest urban slum to accept the hardships of this completely new existence.

> We had to put them in tents while we built shacks, and then into the shacks while the houses went up. They, we, the lot of us were living close to the starvation line. So we had to feed them first, long before we could get them to grow the food that they needed. We fed them on lentils, eggplant, a bit of flour, and frozen fish, anything

we could collect for them. And we had to give them hope and keep them where they were. We knew that if they once got their noses into the towns we should never get them out again.[18]

Eshkol's daring was matched by his imagination. Raanan Weitz described graphically how the two of them would drive through the empty wasteland in the early postwar years, with the roads reverting into dusty tracks, telephone wires still strewn along the ground, land on both sides of the roads fallow and sprouting weeds. "When you drove late at night you could hear the emptiness speak." Then Eshkol would spot something, stop the car, and get out to look. It might be a site for a new settlement that had attracted his attention, or perhaps a path leading off the road to where there had once been an Arab village. Weitz remembers one such occasion when Eshkol jumped out of the car, marched along a path to where an empty Arab village stood, surveyed its solidly built stone houses, and then remarked: "We can patch the place up in a week and shove 50 families in. They can start growing stuff right away. We'll plan everything properly when they're in." The 50 families were installed a week later and began clearing the fields. In time they were given new houses. A score of settlements were founded in this way on the remains of Arab villages.

Some of the new settlements failed and had to be abandoned. But they had at least played their part in giving temporary shelter and work. There were frequent cases of families deserting the land and running for cover to the towns, particularly in 1950–1951 when most immigrants were arriving in Israel. Eshkol was never in the least deterred; he used to remark that if a single settlement failed, one should set out to build three in its place. He made a point of escorting the first group to every new settlement, a ceremony which he described as "kissing a bride through her veil." Another useful innovation was to send several old settlers along with the newcomers, to stay a year or two with them until they were able to stand on their own.

Typical of his imagination was his application of the principle of self-help for pioneer settlers. Years before, probably in 1927, he had been returning from Central Europe to Palestine and found himself for a day in Salonika, waiting for a boat. He spent his day looking at a new suburban agricultural settlement for the Greeks who had been ejected from their homes in the Smyrna area by Kemal Ataturk. He came back to the harbor area in the evening and sat at a water-front café reflecting on what he had seen. The Greek settlers were given a minimum of equipment to build their houses. Eshkol developed this principle for his crash campaign, giving settlers timber, cement, glass, and carpenter's tools. The system worked very well.

Eshkol was responsible for the first large-scale reforestation plan. It was worked out by a committee of six members formed under the auspices of the Jewish Agency. In their four centuries' occupation of Palestine the Turks denuded it of trees, especially during World War I. James Parkes has described the drive from Jerusalem to Nablus and farther on to Jenin in the early days of the British Mandate.[19] The road ran through desolate, rock-strewn countryside where Arab villagers grew minimum subsistence crops of olives and fruit. On the entire 50-mile journey there was only a single pine to be seen that was taller than the stunted olive and fruit trees. Eshkol's reforestation committee planted one billion trees within five years. Reforestation has moved steadily ahead since then. During Israel's first 20 years nearly a quarter of a million acres were planted over with trees.

Eshkol's third special attribute was his ability to pick a good team to work with him. As the servant of the Jewish Agency he worked largely with Raanan Weitz and an occasional other adviser. In 1951 he became Minister of Agriculture, which meant a great expansion of his activities. He set himself general objectives that provided for the nation's food supply, the diversion of one quarter of the new immigrants to the land for the purpose of social stability, the progressive settlement of the land's open spaces, the doubling of irrigated land in four to five years, and the steady addition of new settlements. He built teams to coordinate and guide all of these undertakings. Later, he evolved the idea of field working teams for each major new settlement project. The principles of these field working teams were described to me by one of his former assistants.

The team was first brought together under one roof, that of the Jewish Agency. A site for a major project in a development area was then chosen and the team was sent down to survey it. The different aspects of the plan—soil, water, communication, types of settlement to be established—were coordinated. The completed plan would be duly approved or amended by the Jewish Agency and the Ministry of Agriculture.

The second task of the team was to see the plan put in operation. This meant that the members of the team remained on location, making sure that the plan was implemented as intended and helping to iron out whatever difficulties arose. There were usually plenty of them. The team, needless to say, maintained close liaison with the Jewish Agency and the Ministry; one of the advantages of being a small country is that personal contact is generally a matter of a motor ride to Jerusalem and back.

The third and final task of the team was to assign people to new settlements. Once it had completed suvervising this, its job was done. Throughout all three stages. Eshkol himself remained in close contact with the team and paid frequent visits to the building sites.[20]

In one sense, he was a tough taskmaster. He worked very hard himself and expected those who worked under him to do so, too. "I need a man to work for me who is an orphan and a bachelor" was what he said to one of his assistants, Aryeh Eliav. His recipe for anyone coming to work for him was like Churchill's promise of blood, sweat, and tears to the British people during World War II. Eshkol told them that they might get no holidays, no free weekends, perhaps no time off for lunch. They would not even be well paid. Israeli salaries have remained incredibly low by western standards, and there was no question of extra pay for extra work. Their satisfaction lay in knowing that they were doing work for the poorest of their own people and for a man who treated them as comrades and was deeply appreciative of everything they did.

Eliav told of Eshkol's working methods at that time. He demanded reports which were short and to the point but which contained every important detail. Israel, he used to say, is in a hurry and has no time for mountains of paper. A favorite remark of his to anybody who sounded long-winded was, "Start from the end. Tell me what you want." His encyclopedic knowledge of Israel's geography enabled him to give flesh and sinew to every skeleton of a plan. He could visualize at once how water could best be piped to the area in question and from where, what crops could be grown in that particular region and where they could be marketed, how new roads could link new settlements.

On his frequent trips to see for himself he always took one of his assistants with him. They took turns driving; when Eshkol was at the wheel he thought aloud and when he was in the passenger's seat he took notes about the settlement which he had just visited or one he was about to see. He made a habit of stopping the car whenever it occurred to him that on that particular spot something could be done in due course. "Then the farmer in him came out at once and he would scratch up the soil with his boot and decide what should be planted there when the time came."[21]

Eshkol can truthfully be said to have created a "philosophy of settlement" in which love of the soil and love of the men who tilled it combined with exactness in planning and in implementation. Eshkol worked at a furious tempo, and one is reminded of the remark of a young American who came out to fight in the War of Independence: "I thought Palestine was full of Jews with long beards wanting to pray at the Wailing Wall, and I wasn't going to let any goddam Arab stop them. Now I find it plenty tough to keep up with these Jews."[22]

Eshkol's enthusiasm was infectious. He was still in charge of the Mekorot water board, an additional load which he bore cheerfully. His daughter Dvora tells of his excitement over the building of a new pumping station near Haifa. "It was the biggest and best so far. He insisted on having flowers planted around it, and I honestly believe he had every stone in the place cleaned for the opening ceremony. It was not far off the road from Haifa to Degania and we seemed to pass it pretty often during the year. He never missed an opportunity of looking in to see how things were going there."[23] Dvora believes that this could well have been the happiest period of her father's life, for he was not ambitious in the sense of craving promotion and high office. Being in charge of Israel's agriculture gave him a supreme sense of purpose and achievement.

There was one crisis in the field of agriculture, in the winter of 1950 and spring of 1951. This was over the draining of the Huleh marshes in the extreme northeastern corner of the country. The marshes lay on both sides of the river Jordan but for the most part to the west of it, on the Israeli side of the frontier. Under the 1949 armistice agreement part of this area was a demilitarized zone. The area had been included in the United Nations partition plan within Israel's borders. It was wild and largely uninhabited country and was overrun by the Syrians during the War of Independence. The Syrians agreed to withdraw from it after the war, but only on condition that Israeli armed forces should not enter the area (there were two other, similar demilitarized zones farther to the south).

Eshkol decided to drain the Huleh swamps. Their only asset was the wild duck which flocked to its excellent feeding grounds and provided much fun for sportsmen. Indeed, former officers of the British army who were stationed in Palestine consider it as a chief "offense" of the Israelis that they have so sadly reduced this wonderful wild-fowl area. The Syrians, looking down on the swamps from the steep escarpment of the Golan Mountains, decided that the cleaning of this stretch of the Jordan and the cultivation of the soil were, in some obscure way, contrary to the agreement on demilitarized zones. In particular, the cutting of canals changed the character of the area and altered the status quo. The Huleh swamps, as the Syrians saw it, should have been left to the wild ducks and mosquitoes.

In the winter of 1950–1951 the Syrians took to sniping at Israeli farmers and the men working on the drainage project. Then they attempted to ambush Israeli workers and escorting police, finally succeeding in doing so, killing seven Israelis. In April 1951, as a reprisal, Israeli aircraft bombed Syrian gun emplacements on the crest of the Golan plateau. The pattern had been established for the frontier incidents which continued in this area up to the June 1967 war. These incidents were invariably provoked by the Syrians on the pretext that the character of the frontier regions was being unilaterally changed. Unimpressed, the Israelis hit back whenever they felt they had to. The Huleh swamp project was successfully completed on time. Virtually the whole marshy area on the Israeli side of the frontier was converted into farmlands and fishponds.

In 1952 Eshkol moved from the Ministry of Agriculture to the Ministry of Finance, an immensely important promotion, since it made him in effect the second man in the Cabinet after the Prime Minister,

Ben-Gurion. But this move in no way diminished his interest in either agriculture or water. He remained a member of the board of the Jewish Agency and director-general of Mekorot. And he played a principal part in two major projects, the Lachish land settlement plan, and the construction of the Yarkon-Negev water conduit.

Lachish is an area of about 350 square miles midway between Tel Aviv and Beersheba. From the point of view of agricultural development, its strategic importance was obvious. Outside the plain of Sharon, stretching as far as the border of the Gaza Strip in the south, only a few oases of agricultural development had been established. Beersheba was the only town there; for the rest there were only small, isolated kibbutzim and moshavim doing little more than feeding and maintaining themselves, linked often only by a single road. A solid block of settlement in Lachish was a necessary first stage in the long-term plan to spread settlement far into the Negev and turn Beersheba, reduced to a mere 3000 inhabitants by 1948, into a desert metropolis of a quarter of a million.

The Lachish project came to fruition in 1955. It was a major attempt at regional development, with a single, central town of Kiriat Gat, three rural centers of Nehora, Segula, and Even Shmuel, and 15 villages grouped around them. The villages were mostly moshavim and were purely agricultural. The rural centers supplied them with essential services like schools, libraries, cultural centers, cooperative stores, clinics, banks, and repair shops for collectively used farm equipment, and village buses. Kiriat Gat (its "Gat" is the modernized version of the Gath of the Philistines) provided the amenities of a middle-sized town, including shopping centers, cinemas, sports grounds, secondary schools, and a civic center.*

The regional plan envisaged only 12,000 people settling in Lachish. But the need to find outlets for immigrants was such that the population of the region reached 35,000 in the first ten years, with 20,000 in Kiriat Gat alone, and was expected to treble itself again by 1980. In the first ten years 27, instead of 15, new villages were built, growing sugar beets, cotton, vegetables, peanuts, and wheat. In Kiriat Gat factories were opened for processing wool and plastics, ginning and weaving cotton, refining sugar, making furniture and electronic equipment, and cleaning and packing citrus fruits.

The regional plan inevitably had some teething troubles. For a time its educational services were insufficient, and there were one or two minor housing scandals, due to miscalculations of the planning authorities. But in general the regional plan was a success, and it offered an outstanding

---

* For a time it provided a single prostitute as well. Prostitution is frowned upon in Israel, and she was duly prosecuted for soliciting customers. With charming candor she explained that she thought that what she was doing was "all right" because it was "what was expected" in a town.

example of the integration of new immigrants from Africa and Asia, or Sephardic Jews, with those of European, or Ashkenazi, stock. Over 50 percent of its population is of African or Asian origin.

One writer has pointed out that the Jews of Africa and Asia, for the most part arriving in Israel later than their European cousins, see no special virtue in a Spartan way of life. "One quality that most of the Oriental groups share in common is a certain Mediterranean *aisance*. They are not inclined to the sort of spiritual rigor and puritanism that characterizes Northern Europeans."[24] Oriental Jews have shown no urge to take part in the kibbutz movement, for they value the independence of the family unit. Eshkol rightly believed that they would settle down well enough in moshavim, where they would be taking part in a farming cooperative but would have their own plots of land. He believed, too, that they retained a certain clannishness and would prefer to live with their own kind. So, in the settlements grouped around Nehora, Kurdish immigrants were installed at Noga, Moroccans at Sde David and Otzem, Tunisians at Zohar. In another group of settlements, Sharsheret became North African, Melilot and Givolim Persian, and Shebolim mixed Syrian and Iraqi. This system of grouping immigrants has worked well.

Lachish had to be provided with water. This meant launching a major water project, something after Eshkol's heart. He decided to get most of the water from the river Yarkon, which rises in the Samarian hills and flows into the Mediterranean just north of Tel Aviv. The Yarkon had an estimated annual flow of 350 million cubic yards, much of which was needed by Tel Aviv and urban centers close to it. A part of the Yarkon's flow could be diverted southward. So in 1955 the first of the two pipelines started three years earlier was completed, stretching almost as far as Beersheba. Work on the second Yarkon-Negev pipeline began in 1958 and was finished in 1961. The whole project cost about 60 million Israeli pounds, or $20 million. By the time it was completed, an even bigger project, that of harnessing the waters of the river Jordan, was in progress. Looking back at what was a sensational breakthrough in bringing water to the southern desert, Eshkol told me that he regarded water as "the spirit of our country and of its soil, the spirit which gives life to our flesh, nothing less than the secret of life."[25] In 1955, inaugurating the first Yarkon pipeline, he quoted the song of Israel (Num. 21:17–18). "Then Israel sang this song, Spring up O well, sing ye unto it: The princes digged the well, the nobles of the people digged it with the sceptre, and with their staves." Eshkol concluded his address with the words: "This is the opening of a new chapter, and now the Yarkon's big brother, the Jordan, is waiting for us. The ancient river, the Yarkon, has been held back, to take its water to the Negev and irrigate its thirsty fields. Let creation be renewed and changed; the Yarkon shall no longer carry its sweet waters into the futility of the Mediterranean. The dream of the years has become a reality."

As Minister of Agriculture Eshkol laid a firm foundation for the tremendous progress which has been made since then. As a member of the Board of the Jewish Agency he continued to exercise considerable influence on Israeli agriculture. When he became Prime Minister in 1903, it remained one of his special interests. The achievement of Israeli agriculture has been truly remarkable. In 20 years over-all output has multiplied almost six times, although the area under cultivation has been increased only one and a half times. This performance was made possible because of increased mechanization, careful selection of crops grown on different types of soil, and the increase of land under irrigation from 75,000 to 400,000 acres.

Although her population trebled in 20 years, Israel is now able to produce about 85 percent of the food she consumes, as well as handsome surpluses of citrus, vegetables, and flowers worth approximately $120 million a year and amounting to 20 percent of the country's exports. The picture will improve still further as the waters of the Jordan are being increasingly utilized in the southern part of the country, and the Golan plateau, captured from Syria in the June 1967 war, is reconverted into the wheat-growing area it used to be in Roman times. Eshkol's particular service to Israeli agriculture was to set a rapid rate for expansion, to improvise brilliantly during the difficult early postwar days, and to instil tremendous enthusiasm in all who worked with him.

He was an incurable optimist. In the early days of his searches for water, he discovered that the long-established principle of drilling mainly in valleys was wrong. There were often larger sources of water lying closer to a rocky surface. Near Afula, to the south of the Emek of Jezreel, he organized deep drilling on which he pinned high hopes. "My instinct told me that there was water there. There *had* to be! But the engineers drilled deeper and deeper, and still there was no water! At about 700 feet they told me that we might as well give up. But something told me that we were nearly there. I said: 'Give it just six more feet.' We struck water, lots of it, only three feet further down."

While Eshkol was Minister of Agriculture, Chaim Weizmann died. He had been President of Israel since the foundation of the State, but he was a sick man for the last few years of his life and slipped into the shadows while Ben-Gurion emerged as the great national leader. On Weizmann had fallen the mantle of Theodor Herzl, and for 40 years he had been both prophet and planner for the Jewish people, imbued with a sense of Messianic destiny. At the same time he was a polished and accomplished diplomat, who put his gifts of political vision and personal persuasiveness unreservedly at the disposal of his people. Sir Ronald Storrs, in *Orientations,* thought he combined "an almost feminine charm with a feline deadliness of attack." Weizmann had done most, if not almost all, toward convincing Lord Balfour that there should be a National Home. He continued to speak to the outside world, on behalf of Jewry, with the voice of reason. And he remained, for virtually the whole of his life, truly representative. As one critic put it, he "stood near the center of the consciousness of his people, and not on its periphery."[26]

It was Weizmann's tragedy that he might have even seen himself in his last years as a failure. Isaiah Berlin has explained some of the reasons why: Religious Jews regarded him as a secular Philistine, usurping the Messiah. Jews who had become acclimatized in western countries felt he was stirring up too much thought, and drawing attention on them. Social reformers feared he was deviating into a cul-de-sac of petty Jewish nationalism. There were Jews who regarded Zionism as a dream, and Jews who—they can hardly be blamed—wanted to be left alone. There were increasingly many Jews who could not comprehend Weizmann's undying attachment to English love of independence and freedom, sense of style and human dignity.

He may have become almost an object of suspicion, although, as Isaiah Berlin again suggests, he was probably the first totally free Jew in the modern world.[27] If this were true, he certainly suffered in the cause of his own emancipation. He was often filled with despair,[28] and he may, in his last years, have become increasingly aware of the terribly complex nature of the problems which still faced Israel, so much his child and the fulfillment of his dream. In 1923 Weizmann said: "Palestine is not an object that can be bought. It must be won by suffering. It must be paid for with the pangs of birth. Our relation to Palestine can only be the relation of a mother to her child. She bears her child with pain, she begets it with pain, and the first years of its life are years of pain and anxiety."[29]

Weizmann could well have added that a child's years, thereafter, are not necessarily free of pain and anxiety either. This has manifestly been true of the first 20 years in the life of Israel.

Eshkol knew Weizmann not intimately but reasonably well. Members of the Jewish community in Palestine made a habit of knowing one another; the tradition was carried on in the State of Israel. Eshkol first met Weizmann towards the end of World War I—Weizmann told a group of young settlers then that the Balfour Declaration had cost him a thousand private interviews and mass meetings.[30] A year or two later, Eshkol was one of a small delegation of soldiers serving in the Royal Fusiliers who asked Weizmann to help to get them drafted for active service. Eshkol met him many times after that, got to know him well enough for the Russian-style bear-hug and kiss on both cheeks to be automatic between them.

"His speeches," Eshkol told me,

> always brought me near tears. He had a fine sense of history and a human pathos. When someone is much bigger than yourself, it

brings your heart to your throat. There was a regal quality about him and in him. And he was so often looking far into the future, into a future in which an Israel, which was not like other nations, would take its place among them. He believed in every Jew; and I liked best his answer when Lord Balfour asked him if there were many Jews like himself. Weizmann replied: 'Enough to pave the streets.'

In Eshkol's view, Weizmann managed to absorb three different cultures. The first was Jewish and traditional. It gave him humor and compassion, an understanding of poverty and persecution, and an all-embracing knowledge of the Jewish world. The second was European and intellectual. It produced a dispassionate judgment and an emotional independence. The third was British and personal. He loved Britain and its way of life, even in the face of the disappointments of his declining years.

1. Dorothy Thomson, ed., *Jewish Frontier: An Anthology*, p. 129.
2. C. Gershater, *Thirty Days in Israel*, p. 39.
3. Owen Mecker, in *Israel Reborn*, gives the best account of this.
4. Joseph Schechtman, *The Refugee in the World*, pp. 184–190.
5. Terence Prittie, *Israel: Miracle in the Desert*, p. 120.
6. George Kirk, *A Short History of the Middle East*, p. 225.
7. Schechtman, *op. cit.*, p. 191.
8. *Ibid.*, p. 192.
9. General Sir Hugh Stockwell, in a letter to the author.
10. Christopher Sykes, *Cross Roads to Israel*, p. 444.
11. King Hussein, *Uneasy Lies the Head*, p. 3.
12. Edward Atiyah, *The Arabs*, p. 235.
13. Eshkol, in personal conversation with the author.
14. Eshkol, in personal conversation with the author.
15. Harry Levin, *Jerusalem Embattled*, p. 149.
16. *Ibid.*, p. 261.
17. In a speech to the Agricultural Convention in 1959, on "Achievements and Experiences in Israel."
18. Eshkol, in personal conversation with the author.
19. James Parkes, *The New Face of Israel*, p. 19.
20. Aryeh Eliav, his principal assistant in the Ministry of Agriculture over a number of years, in personal conversation with the author.
21. Aryeh Eliav, in personal conversation with the author.
22. Levin, *op. cit.*, p. 272.
23. Dvora Eshkol Rafaeli, in personal conversation with the author.
24. Ronald Sanders, *Israel: The View from Masada*, p. 200.
25. Eshkol, in personal conversation with the author.
26. Isaiah Berlin, *Chaim Weizmann*, p. 25.
27. *Ibid.*, p. 59.
28. Sykes, *op. cit.*, p. 89.
29. Meyer Weisgal, ed., *Chaim Weizmann*, p. 295.
30. Eshkol, in private conversation with the author.

11.

The Arabs, as has already been made clear, were totally and irreconcilably opposed to the creation of a State of Israel. This was the real basis of their quarrel with the Jews. They picked on Zionism as the ostensible enemy, because Zionism had supported the establishment first of a Jewish National Home and then of a Jewish National State. But the Arabs needed a pretext, too; the question of the Arab refugees offered a convenient one.

The mass exodus of Palestinian Arabs from their homes in 1948–1949 was due, it may be recalled, to the imminence of a "holy war" which was being proclaimed by the Arab states, and to the launching of that war by seven of them. Whether 750,000 Palestinian Arabs lost their homes or, as seems more probable, only 550,000, is immaterial. A huge human problem, involving considerable human suffering, had been created. It was the duty of everyone—of Israel, the Arab countries, and the outside world—to do everything possible to alleviate that suffering.

The Arab states insisted on the principle of repatriation of every single Palestinian Arab refugee. No other offer was acceptable to them or even worth contemplating. The Arabs have been consistent in this all-or-nothing attitude. But was it justified?

After World War II, eight million Germans were expelled from the territories east of the Oder-Neisse Line, and nearly five million more Germans from other parts of Central and Eastern Europe. All of them had to be resettled; none of them was repatriated. Two years later over eight million Hindus and Sikhs fled to India from Pakistan, and six and a half million Moslems moved in the opposite direction. There was no question of their repatriation, only of their resettlement. The same was true of the one and a half million French expelled from Algeria and the two and a half million Koreans who fled from the north to the south. Hong Kong has absorbed over a million Chinese refugees, and Italy took in half a million from Istria and her former colonial empire in Africa.

Case after case of mass resettlement of homeless and, generally speaking, blameless refugees can be cited.[1] When repatriation is impracticable, the obligation of the outside world is to help to give refugees a new start in life, in fact, to resettle them. But there has been not a single case of any organized repatriation of refugees since World War II.

There has been considerable difficulty in dealing with some of the postwar refugees who had to be resettled. Displaced Hindus and Moslems lived in abject misery for years without any prospect of gainful employment. Hong Kong had to grow upwards, skyscrapers sprouting like toadstools. The older pre-1946 generation of East German refugees has kept up an unceasing clamor for the right to return to their old homes—a clamor which has been frowned upon by the Western world and denounced as vicious irredentism by the Communist Bloc.

However sad their fate, there was ample room in the Arab world for the Palestinian refugees. Iraq was and still is in need of immigrants. Saudi Arabia and the oil-rich sheikdoms can use anyone who can read and write and the most unskilled labor as well. Syria has reserves of living space. Only Egypt, since the mid-1950s, has been confronted with the problem of its own population explosion. But the Arab world was always large enough to absorb the Palestinian refugees without the slightest physical difficulty.

Israel made three offers to the Conciliation Commission at Lausanne in April 1949. She was prepared to make the refugee question the first item on the agenda in negotiations for a peace settlement. She offered to repatriate 100,000 Palestinian Arabs as part of a peace settlement. And she was ready to give the indigenous inhabitants of the Gaza Strip Israeli nationality if the Strip were incorporated in Israel, and at the same time carry out the repatriation and resettlement of the Strip's 200,000 refugees. The Arabs flatly refused to consider these offers and Israel kept them open only until July 1950.

In August 1949 the Conciliation Commission undertook to send an economic survey mission to Arab states to estimate their capacity to absorb refugees. Gordon R. Clapp, an American and chairman of the board of the Tennessee Valley Authority, was appointed head of the mission. He reported on February 16, 1950, on the mission's failure:

> We were not well received in the Middle East. There was a fear in the minds of the Arab peoples that we were coming to their countries to impose upon them some preconceived plan . . . which would settle upon them these 750,000 refugees. . . . I shall not attempt to judge the basis of their fears and apprehensions. I just state it as a fact that for two weeks or so, the mission was more or less immobilized in the Near East because the governments were not quite sure whether they wanted to discuss with us any plans or ideas that they thought we might have. We found that resettlement was a subject that the Arab governments were not even willing to discuss, with the exception of King Abdullah.[2]

The Clapp mission found itself restricted to recommending four small-scale resettlement projects, one in Lebanon, one in Syria, and one on either bank of the river Jordan on Jordanian territory. But Clapp remained convinced that the refugee problem could be solved. In February 1950 he told the Congressional Foreign Relations Committee, "Some of the refugees, I am sure, when they begin to get some of the mobility that work gives them, will begin to think less about wanting to go home and more about where they want to live in the future. Some of them will want to settle where they are."[3]

The Conciliation Commission had a final shot at getting progress in the refugee question in the summer of 1951, when it invited Israel and her Arab neighbors to a conference in Paris in order to adopt the following declaration: "In accordance with the objections of States Members of the United Nations and of signatories to Armistice Agreements; the Governments of Egypt, Jordan, Lebanon, and Syria, and the Government of Israel solemnly affirm their intention and undertake to settle all differences, present and future, solely by resort to pacific procedures, refraining from any use of force or acts of hostility." This admittedly not very precisely worked resolution was probably left deliberately vague, as the Commission wanted only to provide a basis for negotiations. Israel agreed to sign; the Arab states refused.

The United Nations was already providing material aid for the unfortunate refugees. Three quarters of UNRWA aid for the refugees has come from the United States and Britain, the American share being by far the larger. In November 1951 the General Assembly of the United Nations began a pilot project for the rehabilitation and employment of refugees, and voted $250 million for a three-year period. The plan was to cover resettlement in new homes, as opposed to the wretched refugee camps in which they were living, and the launching of public works programs which could have been coordinated by the UN Relief and Works Agency in Beirut. Israel meanwhile released blocked accounts of refugees amounting to an estimated $16 million.

The UN plan envisaged resettling from 150,000 to 250,000 refugees, at a minimum rate of about 50,000 a year. About one third of the refugees would be put in urban areas, another third on irrigated land, and one third onto other lands. In this way it was hoped to move all the refugees in the overcrowded Gaza Strip and about two thirds of those in Jordan. The main receiving countries would be Syria and Iraq, and there was an additional project for settling about 50,000 refugees in Sinai, mainly in the area of El Arish, and providing them with water which would be pumped from the Nile under the Suez Canal.

The rehabilitation fund was never used. Syria, Iraq, and Egypt blocked resettlement. As far as those governments were concerned, the refugee problem was political, not humanitarian, and the refugees could be used as pawns in the Arab campaign to bring political pressure to bear on Israel. The most flagrant offender in this respect was Egypt, who refused to allow the inhabitants of the Gaza Strip either to become Egyptian citizens or to have the right to move to Egypt. They became, instead, prisoners in a glorified but exceptionally uncomfortable ghetto, kept close to the borders of Israel as a reproach and threat to Israel's government.* The only one of Israel's neighbors which genuinely did its best

---

* In September 1955 the Cairo Court of Administrative Jurisdiction ruled that Gaza was outside Egyptian territory, and that in the Strip Egypt was exercising "a kind of control over part of the territory of Palestine."[4] A year later it was estimated that only 15 percent of 50,000 families were self-supporting. Writing in 1961 Martha Gellhorn gave this description of the place:

The Gaza Strip is not a hell-hole, not a visible disaster. It is worse; it is a

for the refugees was the poorest, Jordan. There, they were given full citizenship and considerable efforts were made to resettle them.

One more major effort to assist towards mass resettlement of the refugees was made under United Nations auspices. In 1952 UNRWA entered the negotiations for what was called "Land and Water Agreements" with the governments of Jordan, Syria, and Lebanon. The hope was that agreements could be reached on the utilization of the waters of the Jordan, Yarmuk, and Litani rivers,* leading to irrigation of land in these three Arab countries and in Israel, with this leading in turn to refugee resettlement on a large scale. To assist in working out detailed plans, President Eisenhower sent a special representative, Eric Johnston, to the Middle East in 1953. Johnston spent two years at this task, consulted all the governments concerned, and reached an understanding with them on all technical aspects of the over-all plan which he drew up.[6] This plan envisaged utilizing about one billion 300 million cubic yards of water, mainly by Israel and Jordan. Of this amount, 625 million cubic yards would have gone to Jordan, 525 million to Israel, and the remaining 150 million would have been divided between Syria and Lebanon.

Both President Eisenhower and his representative were looking far beyond the scope of a single plan. They wanted to introduce the principle of Arab-Israeli economic cooperation; its adoption could have led, in time, to the organization of a Middle East Common Market. This would, if only in the long run, have insured some form of reconciliation between Israel and her Arab neighbors. It would have been a major contribution to maintaining peace in the Middle East, as well as restoring the kind of prosperity which the area had not enjoyed since Roman times.

The Johnston Plan would have resulted in the resettlement of at least 240,000 refugees, most of them on the land and some in ancillary employment. The plan was so obviously constructive and forward-looking that the Arab governments for a time toyed with adopting it. They might have done so but for Egyptian pressure and the growing political radicalism of Syria. Eric Johnston voiced his deep disappointment at their eventual refusal: "After two years of discussion, technical experts of Israel, Jordan, Lebanon, and Syria agreed upon every important detail

---

jail—with a magical long white sand beach, and a breeze, and devoted welfare workers to look after the prisoners.

The Egyptian Government is the jailer. For reasons of its own it does not allow the refugees to move from this narrow strip of land. The refugees might not want to leave at all, or they might not want to leave for good; but anyone would become claustrophobic if penned, for 13 years, inside 248 square kilometres.[5]

* The little-known Litani has a flow larger than that of the other two rivers combined. Its waters have not been exploited since it rises and flows through Lebanon, where there is no shortage of water.

of a unified Jordan plan. But in October 1955 it was rejected for political reasons at a meeting of the Arab League."7 Israel was to go ahead later with its own water plan, and the chief loser through Egyptian and Syrian intransigence was Jordan.

One has to mention only one more effort on the part of the United Nations to assist toward refugee resettlement. In June 1959 the Secretary General, Dag Hammarskjöld, reported to the Fourteenth Assembly of the United Nations on relief measures in the Middle East. He advised investing $1.7 billion, mainly for resettlement, and the rapid expansion of UNRWA program for agricultural and vocational training. His view was that the integration of the refugees into Arab communities was feasible and that the existing reservoir of unemployed refugees could become an asset.

The Hammarskjöld report was rejected by the Arab states. They declared that they would never accept a plan which involved refugee resettlement outside Israel's borders, and demanded repatriation instead. Two years earlier, the delegates of the same Arab states had stated at the Refugee Conference in the Syrian town of Homs that "any discussion aimed at a solution of the Palestine problem which will not be based on ensuring the refugees' right to annihilate Israel will be regarded as a desecration of the Arab people and an act of treason."8

The Arab countries have made it plain that they do not want to resolve their quarrel with Israel. On the contrary, at an earlier date they took a major step to deepen that quarrel. As early as January 1946 the Council of the Arab League decided to impose a boycott of Jewish goods, by withholding import licenses for all the products of Palestinian Jewish firms and organizations. In 1948 the League established a Central Boycott Office in Damascus to enforce these discriminatory trade practices.9 In February 1950 Egypt took a very important step by decreeing that oil was among those "strategic goods" which should not be transported to Israel, either through the Suez Canal or by way of the Gulf of Aqaba to the still embryonic port of Eilat. This decree, even though it was difficult to inforce, cost Israel an estimated $25 million during the next six years. At the end of that period, war with Egypt resulted in the reopening of the previously blockaded Gulf of Aqaba.

The Arab League decided to black-list all ships which called at Israeli ports and to confiscate all goods designated for delivery to those ports. It stated that no airlines bound for Israel could fly over Arab territory. Planes coming from farther east and bound for the main Israeli airport at Lod had to circle around Syria and Iraq, over Persia, Turkey, and the Mediterranean. By interfering with the passage of goods through the Suez Canal, Egypt flouted the 1888 Constantinople Convention, under which it was agreed that the Canal was an international waterway. By its restrictions on peaceful movement by air, the Arab League infringed on the Chicago Convention and the rules of the International Civil Aviation Organization.

In 1954 the countries of the Arab League gave an ultimatum to international airlines. The latter were informed that if a single plane flew to Israel, all planes of that company would be barred from all Arab airfields. After energetic protests backed by the governments concerned, the Arabs backed down. However, the maritime nations showed a lack of determination and unity in dealing with restrictions placed on their ocean shipping. By the end of 1956, over 100 ships, sailing under 15 different flags, had been black-listed by the Egyptian Government. They were not allowed to load or unload at Arab ports, were given no facilities there, were forced to undergo rigorous search when passing through the Canal, and were often delayed on their voyages. Arab discriminatory action was thus extended from Israel to the outside world in general if it dared to trade with Israel.

A single Israeli ship, the Bat Golim, tried to sail through the Suez Canal in September 1954. Bound from Eritrea to Haifa, it was stopped at Suez, searched, and impounded. The ship and its cargo were confiscated, and its crew was released only after 14 months' imprisonment. The United Nations Security Council voiced condemnation of the piracy, with no effect whatever.

When a reparation agreement was signed between Israel and West Germany in 1952, the Arab states threatened the Federal German Republic with a total trade boycott. It was not enforced, however, when the agreement was ratified in March 1953 by the Bonn Parliament, but it had an effect on West German political opinion. The ruling Christian Democratic Party was split down the middle by this threat to German trade, and almost all Free Democrats opposed ratification of the agreement with Israel. German concern was understandable; German trade with the member countries of the Arab League had multiplied four times between 1947 and 1953.

What amounted to an Arab blockade against Israel was based on the contention that the Arab states were still in a state of war with Israel. On September 1, 1951, and again on October 13, 1956, the Security Council called on Egypt, in particular, to lift restrictions on shipping and abandon the claim that a state of belligerency existed. A Security Council resolution in March 1954 on ending the blockade of the Gulf of Aqaba was vetoed by the Soviet Union.

By 1951 a new element had been added to the increasingly explosive Israeli-Egyptian relationship. Bands of Arab raiders began crossing Israel's southern borders and attacking settlements and single farmers in the fields. That year these raiders, the *fedayeen,* killed or wounded 137 Israelis. In 1952 the casualties were 147 and in 1953, 162. Fedayeen began to operate from Jordanian territory too, probably as offshoots of the Egyptian bands. In 1955, Israel's losses in the Egyptian sector alone were 48 killed and 144 wounded and during 1956 the situation worsened; there were 23 fedayeen attacks during one 48-hour period in April.

The murderous activities of the fedayeen were openly acclaimed by the Egyptians. On August 31, 1955, for instance, Radio Cairo broadcast: "The fedayeen reached Israel, within a few kilometers of your capital. . . . They kill and blast and put an end to every hope of Zionism. Israel tastes the taste of death."[10] A month later, an Egyptian Minister of State, Colonel Anwar Sadat, praised those fedayeen who had been killed while carrying out terrorist activities in Israel. "Those who fell at Gaza," the Colonel declared, "did so while fulfilling the Commandments of the Prophet Mohammed who also fought the Jews. . . . It is our duty to fight the Jews for the sake of Allah and our religion and it is our duty to bring to a conclusion the war which Mohammed commenced."

It is customary for the apologists of Arab terrorism to explain that it is not really terrorism at all, but military resistance against the illegal occupation of Arab territories. But Israel's creation was sponsored by the United Nations and the United Nations recognized Israeli sovereignty. There were differences between Arab terrorism and the French wartime Résistance, to which the Arabs compare their raids. The French attacked German military posts and military personnel; the Arabs usually attacked civilians. The difference between terrorism and military resistance is clear-cut.

The stepping up of this guerilla warfare against Israel owed much to political changes in Egypt. In 1952 King Farouk's corrupt regime fell and the king left the country. General Neguib, a man of probity and some political vision, took control of the government. But he was ejected from power, in turn, by a group of younger Army officers led by Colonel Abdel Gamal Nasser.* Nasser had already outlined his aims in a booklet called *The Philosophy of the Revolution*. In addition to preaching the need to install a "revolutionary socialist" new order in Egypt, Nasser proclaimed three principal aims: to gain power over all Arab countries, to become the head of all Moslem peoples, and to become the "leader" in Africa.

Under Nasser, the Egyptian Government for the first time openly supported fedayeen terrorism and stressed a new strategy: the fedayeen were instructed to strike deep into Israeli territory instead of operating on the frontier. On May 15, 1956, Radio Cairo announced: "The war now is not confined to the border but has reached the heart of Israel and places which were considered to be safe from danger."[11]

Colonel Meinertzhagen suggested that Nasserite policy was "based on

---

* According to Ben-Gurion, Neguib stated, after seizing power, that he and most of the officers of the Egyptian Army had been opposed to the invasion of Israel in 1948, and that King Farouk had been responsible for that disastrous military decision and debacle. Ben-Gurion at once declared that there was no cause for dispute between Israel and Egypt—"The two countries are separated by a broad and extensive desert, and there is therefore no room for border disputes; there was not, nor is there now, any reason for political, economic, or territorial antagonism between the two neighbors" (*Israel: Years of Challenge*, pp. 64–65).

five points—a pan-Arab Republic with him at the helm, immediate possession of the Suez Canal, elimination of Britain from the Middle East, inviting Russia to come on the scene with arms and money, and lastly the destruction of Israel."[12] Nasser was to fail to destroy Israel, and his efforts to organize a pan-Arab Republic came later in history. But he sought to achieve his three other objectives as quickly as possible.

Possession of the Suez Canal was directly linked to the elimination of British imperialism. Nasser understood that control of the Canal gave him a bargaining position between East and West which could be invaluable. In July 1954, Britain undertook to withdraw her troops within 20 months from the Suez Canal Zone. Under this Canal Agreement Egypt undertook to uphold the Constantinople Convention which guaranteed freedom of passage for international shipping using the Canal. The only reservation, not explicitly stated in the Agreement, was that Israeli shipping could not use the Canal, because Egypt was in a state of war with her. But Nasser was not satisfied with the British military withdrawal; on July 26, 1956, he nationalized the Canal, an act which that staunch Arabist, Sir John Glubb, called "not an heroic action by a small nation rightly struggling to be free, but rather a breach of a commercial agreement."[13]

Nasser, indeed, had both reasons and pretexts for his illegal action. He had become sharply aware of the need to increase Egypt's prestige when he had attended the Afro-Asian Conference at Bandung in April 1955. He regarded the organization of the Bagdad Pact of Turkey, Iran, and Pakistan, and Britain's accession to it in April 1955, as a threat to Egypt's aspirations in the Middle East, and he was angered by the mission to Amman in December 1955 of General Templer, who tried to bring Jordan into the Pact. Nasser was almost certainly the chief instigator of the riots which then took place in Jordan, the first of many attempts to dethrone King Hussein. The king's sympathies were well known and were confirmed by what he subsequently wrote: "I realized that, if Jordan joined, the free world would gain an enormous moral victory."[14]

Nasser had a more obvious reason for complaint in the wrangling with the two Western powers, the United States and Britain, over the Aswan Dam. They backed a proposal for some $270 million of aid for the building of the high dam. Of this sum, $200 million was to come from the World Bank, $56 million from the United States, and $14 million from Britain. World Bank aid would have been dependent on acceptance of American and British help. But that help was withdrawn, essentially as the result of a decision made by the American Secretary of State, John Foster Dulles. Nasser learned of the decision on July 19, 1956. He waited only one week before nationalizing the Suez Canal.

Nasser was undoubtedly glad to have a pretext for nationalization and was perfectly ready to turn to the Soviet Union as an alternative source of help; he had already turned to the Soviet Union for assistance over another, more pressing matter. This was the supply of arms to Egypt for the war against Israel, about which Nasser had probably already made up his mind.

One must, for a moment, go still farther back in time, to May 25, 1950. On that day the governments of France, Britain, and the United States signed a tripartite declaration on "Security in the Arab-Israeli Zone."[15] The three governments opposed an arms race in the Middle East but recognized that "the Arab states and Israel all need to maintain a certain level of armed forces for the purposes of assuring their internal security and their legitimate self-defense." Therefore, "all applications for arms or war material for these countries will be considered in the light of these principles." The three governments undertook, too, to "take action, both within and outside the United Nations" to prevent the violation of existing frontiers and armistice lines in the Middle East.

Israel welcomed the tripartite statement in principle, but urged the taking of all necessary steps to secure a lasting peace settlement in the Middle East. The Arab League, on behalf of the Arab states, expressed doubt over the clause of the tripartite statement concerning action by the three powers to prevent violation of frontiers, rejected any action which might curtail Arab sovereignty, and demanded the return of the Palestinian refugees to their homes.

The tripartite statement was well meant, but its effectiveness depended on arms' being supplied to the Middle East only by the three signatories, or by countries upon whom they exercised real influence. The statement did, for the time being, result in a curtailment of arms supplied to Middle East countries, essentially because these countries had been traditionally dependent on the West for their weapons. An uneasy arms balance was, indeed, maintained—a fact illustrated by the equally vociferous complaints of Israel on the one hand and the Arab states on the other that they were being starved of arms while their opponents were being unduly favored. But in September 1955 the situation was radically and dangerously altered; Egypt concluded a major arms deal with, ostensibly, Czechoslovakia. In reality, the Czech government concluded the deal only in order to screen the real source of the arms, the Soviet Union.

Under the agreement Egypt was believed to have received 150 MIG fighters, 40 Ilyushin bombers, 400 modern Soviet tanks, several submarines, and at least two small destroyers. According to General Moshe Dayan, Israeli Chief of Staff at that time, the arms deal gave Egypt a 4-to-1 advantage in combat weapons, tanks, and planes.[16] This may be an exaggeration, but there could be no question that the arrival of those arms gave Nasser confidence amounting to unforgivable rashness. He at once extended the blockade of the Gulf of Aqaba to include *all* ships bound for the Israeli port of Eilat, and not simply ships flying the Israeli flag. This blockade was effective, for the Straits of Tiran which connect the Gulf with the Red Sea were controlled by the shore batteries of the Egyptian fort of Sharm el Sheikh and by the islands of Tiran and Sinafir in the mouth of the straits which had been seized by Egypt in 1950.* Nasser followed this up by forbidding Israel's commercial planes to fly over the straits on their way to the Far East. Then, on October 20, 1955, Egypt signed a military agreement with Syria, and on October 27 a similar agreement with Saudi Arabia. Pressure was brought to bear on Jordan to complete the "ring of steel" around Israel which the Cairo press was gleefully proclaiming.

The Egyptian-Soviet arms deal ended the dream of peace in the Middle East. It is just possible that the United States, Britain, and France could have prevented war from breaking out. But there was no hope whatever of their being able to do so once the Soviet Union entered the arena as a ready supplier of arms to Arab states. Its reasons for doing this were purely selfish and mainly mischievous.

First, there was the Soviet interest in Middle East oil. In 1945 the Soviet Union controlled about 12 percent of the world's oil; the Middle East contained nearly 45 percent. The Soviet Union had enough oil for its own needs and for those of its satellites. But some measure of control over Middle East oil would have been of tremendous tactical importance in the Cold War. Virtually all of the Middle East's output went to Western countries. These countries could be denied the oil they needed so badly, or at least be bludgeoned with the threat of cutting off this supply. "If a giant, standing on the frosty Caucasus, were to look towards the warm-water ports of the Persian Gulf, it would be clear to him that if he advanced in that direction he could tread on an oil field at every step: North Iran, Iraq, South Iran, Saudi Arabia, Bahrein, Qatar. And it is important to keep in mind the difference between the holding of a concession and permanent command over the resources which it represents."[17]

Quite as important as the Middle East's oil was its control over communications between East and West, over the biggest trade route in the world. Both for military and economic reasons it was vastly important for the Soviet Union to end the Western democracies' dominance in the Middle East. This thought had inspired the Soviet Union's immediate recognition of the State of Israel; at that time the Soviet Union visualized the new state as a counterbalance to Arab countries which were under either British or French influence. There may even have been some confused idea that Israel, owing so much to its Russian-Jewish immigrants, would look to Russia as a natural protector and friend.

Behind this muddled Soviet reasoning was the old, powerful urge to reach the warm waters of the Mediterranean and the Indian Ocean. In

---

* Ownership of these islands was debatable. They were uninhabited, and Saudi Arabia had at least as good a claim to them as Egypt.

the eighteenth century Catherine the Great had proposed expelling the Turks from Constantinople and establishing a Byzantine satellite state there. In World War I the Tsarist regime extracted a promise from the other Allies to permit an actual Russian annexation of Constantinople and a free hand for Russia in Northern Persia. In 1918 the Bolshevik writer Troyanovsky was urging the conquest of Persia and called that country "the Suez Canal of the Revolution." Later, Soviet policy towards the countries of the Middle East became wildly confused. The Soviet Union was deeply suspicious of any form of pan-Islamism, because of the possible effects on its millions of Moslem subjects. In addition, Islam was both a religion and a way of life which made the conversion of Arab peoples to Communism extremely difficult.

The Soviet rulers were quite ready to encourage Arab opposition to British and French "imperialism." In the 1930s, however, they found that Fascist Germany and Italy were more skillful propagandists than they. Before the outbreak of World War II the Soviet Union became increasingly alarmed by the spread of Nazi influence in the Middle East. The Nazis enlisted the Grand Mufti as their agent, distributed their ideological literature, including Hitler's *Mein Kampf,* exploited internal quarrels in Arab countries, and organized pro-Axis groups, especially among Arab youth.[18]

The Hitler-Stalin Pact of August 1939 gave only a transient illusion of a community of Nazi and Communist interest in the Middle East. Thus, the Soviet Union was exultant over the pro-Axis coup of Rashid Ali in Iraq in April 1941. But two months later Hitler's armies swept into Russia, and Rashid Ali overnight became a "Fascist hireling."[19] Then the Soviet view of Iraq, which had been totally inaccurate and ill informed, was simply unexpressed for the duration of the war. The Soviet rulers were at least wise enough to realize that ignorance should be veiled in silence. This did not prevent them from continuing to misinform themselves about the Middle East. They developed a fixation that the German Jews who fled to Palestine were really German agents who were spreading sinister Nazi influences. For a time they thought that the kibbutzim were potential torchbearers for Soviet communism, and their views of Zionism were violently colored both by the fear of its becoming a disruptive force among Russian Jews and by the hope that it would help to form a world-wide alliance against Nazi Germany.[20]

It was quite in keeping with the Soviet Union's ignorance that Russian newspapers accused the United States and Britain of encouraging Arab armies to invade Israel in 1948 and branded the Arab League first a British creation and later, a tool of American oil imperialism. Soviet ignorance was equaled only by Soviet cynicism and opportunism. Nasser, looked upon in countries like Britain with mixed feelings as a potential reformer and an indubitable patriot, was being vigorously denounced by the Soviet press in 1954 and early 1955. Syria, with its increasingly unstable, leftist government, seemed to the Soviet rulers to be the only worthwhile place for their peaceful infiltration.

The Russian communists have often showed that when they seriously put their minds to a problem, they can change their views and policies overnight and learn by the simple process of studying facts. The Soviet rulers did this in 1955, and here is what they learned: first, that the Arab world was by no means dominated by the Western democracies. Arab nationalism suspected and disliked those countries. Second, Arab hatred of Israel was widespread and could be used as a tool of Soviet policy in the Middle East. Third, low living standards, lack of education, and the wide gap between the rich and the poor rendered the Arabs worthy of Soviet "sympathy," as well as of potential Soviet exploitation. Finally, internecine Arab feuds and astonishing Arab gullibility made the Arab masses easy prey for Soviet propaganda, especially when it would be directed unceasingly and unsparingly at "Western and Zionist imperialism."

It may well be that Soviet political involvement in the Middle East played an even greater role than deliveries of Soviet arms in turning Nasser's thoughts towards war with Israel, a war of annihilation which would help him to attain the objectives laid down in his *Philosophy of the Revolution.*

In retrospect it is hard to see what Israel could have done apart from preparing for war herself. She had already attempted to stem Arab aggression by sharp, tough retaliation. Thus in 1953 Israeli regular army units carried out a raid in Qibya in which 66 people were killed. At least one authority has condemned the attack as a "brutal reprisal."[21] But the Israelis had been pushed beyond passive endurance of Arab raid, murder, and sabotage. In 1955 Israel struck back again, at both Egypt and Syria, with retaliatory raids which raised howls of protest in the Arab world. These raids had two purposes: to induce her Arab neighbors to stop guerilla activities and to discourage them from attempting a larger-scale military action. A subsidiary reason was to placate opinion at home; for between the beginning of 1949 and October 1956 434 Israelis had been killed by the fedayeen and there had been 11,650 armed clashes. These casualties furnish an eloquent answer to those who would have it that Israel was the aggressor in the war with Egypt which broke out on October 29, 1956.

The situation on the eve of war was that Egypt was blocking both the Suez Canal and the Gulf of Aqaba to all shipping bound for Israeli ports. Egypt and the other Arab countries were conducting a total boycott of Israeli goods and were trying to put pressure on non-Arab countries to join in the boycott. Constant guerilla warfare was being waged against Israel, who for her part asked only to be left in peace. Heads of Arab governments and the whole Arab press were proclaiming that a state of war with Israel already existed and that its purpose was the annihilation of the State of Israel. Egypt was arming to the teeth and throughout October moved considerable parts of her army up into the Sinai peninsula where they were poised for attack. Military pacts had been signed with other Arab states and the diplomatic backing of the Soviet Union had been secured. The threat to Israel's very existence could scarcely have been more obvious.

It was under these circumstances that the Prime Minister, David Ben-Gurion, decided to seek the help of at least one Western power. He flew to Paris with two of his advisers, General Moshe Dayan and the head of Israeli military intelligence, Shimon Peres, for talks with the French government which began on October 22 at Sèvres. The French leaders who took part included Mollet and Pineau, and they were joined during the talks, which lasted for three days, by the British Foreign Secretary, Selwyn Lloyd. Although much has been written about the Sinai War and events leading up to it, there is still some doubt as to exactly what transpired at the Sèvres talks. But two things are clear: agreement on joint military action was reached between Ben-Gurion and the French leaders, and a similar agreement was reached between the French and the British. Fixing the date, October 29, for military action against Egypt probably took place on October 24. For on that day Egypt, Jordan, and Syria reached agreement on the integration of their armies under the command of an Egyptian. This exposed Israel's long and indefensible frontier with Jordan to possible attack by united Arab armies. Israel simply could not wait for Arab forces to advance across a border which was only 15 miles from Tel Aviv and which ran through the middle of Jerusalem.

The charge of collusion has ben leveled ever since against Israel, France, and Britain. The French government was possibly wiser than the British in dealing with the charge; it justified military action against Egypt on the valid grounds that Nasser had threatened Israel's existence, declared that his country was already at war with her, had piratically seized the Suez Canal and ridden rough-shod over international agreements. Britain tried to defend and excuse herself at the same time, and a disproportionate amount of blame was attached to her as a result. The upshot of the "collusion" was that France and Britain sent an ultimatum to both Israel and the Arab states on October 31, two days after the Israeli army had attacked in Sinai and at a moment when it was already halfway to the Canal. The ultimatum demanded that there should be no military movement by either side within ten miles of the Canal. This had a most inhibiting effect on the Israelis, but Egypt paid no attention to it whatever. Britain and France undertook joint action, landing troops at Port Said after a preliminary aerial bombardment and advancing into part of the old Canal Zone. Far from helping Israel, this slow and incomplete military action, coming only on November 5, robbed her of some of the fruits of victory.*

Nevertheless Nasser may have held troops and planes in reserve to deal with a possible Anglo-French landing. France sent about 60 planes, mostly fighters, to Israel, giving her something approaching parity with the Egyptian airforce. Flying their own planes, French pilots carried out supply drops in Sinai and French warships screened Israel's coast. Even so, there seems little doubt that Israel would have won her clear-cut military victory without any outside intervention. Her armed forces routed the Egyptian army in Sinai, advanced to within a few miles of the Canal, and captured Sharm el Sheikh, thus reopening the Gulf of Aqaba to Israeli shipping. The short, seven-day campaign was brilliantly planned and executed. General Dayan, who commanded the Israeli forces, subsequently made some sharp criticisms in his book *Diary of the Sinai Campaign*. He mentioned that mobilization was slow, that not enough civilian vehicles were requisitioned, that paratroopers dropped at the Mitla Pass disobeyed orders by pressing on too fast, and that the element of surprise was forfeited on the frontier by a premature armored attack. Dayan was a perfectionist. No Arab country raised a finger to help Egypt.

Colonel Meinertzhagen's estimate in advance of the Egyptian military fiasco was:

> Military equipment, unless overwhelming and of the most modern quality, is of little avail by itself. The man behind the gun is more important than the gun. . . . The Egyptian Army was utterly defeated in 1948, and so recent a disaster will be constantly in the minds of all Egyptians in a second campaign. Moreover, a morale based on fear, hatred, and revenge is unlikely to prevail over a morale based on patriotism, justice and self-preservation. I am aware of the fatal error of underestimating an enemy, but, in this case, I consider the Egyptian army to be a vastly inferior machine to that of Israel.[22]

Meinertzhagen was writing nearly a year before the Sinai campaign, but his predictions were absolutely accurate. Once again, Chaim Weizmann's observation that Egyptian officers were too fat and their men too lean was proved right. In some places, the Egyptian soldier fought well; but his officers usually deserted him, making off for the Canal to put it between them and the enemy. Nasser managed to restore his prestige after the débacle by making much of the dignity with which Egypt had faced three foes, including two great powers. The Soviet Union did what it

---

* Years afterwards an Israeli diplomat told Lord Boothby that on November 5 he had been "sitting quietly in the sunshine on a little hill above the town Ismailia, your ultimate military objective. And what did you do? You sent us an ultimatum ordering us to go back into the Sinai Desert!" (Lord Boothby, *My Yesterday, Your Tomorrow*.)

could to help in the diplomatic field; on November 5 Marshal Bulganin wrote to Ben-Gurion, describing Israel as "criminally and irresponsibly playing with the fate of the world."*

The United Nations pressure forced the Israeli forces to withdraw from the Sinai peninsula after four months. Israel had never intended a campaign to become a full-scale war but only to achieve three limited objectives. The first was to end fedayeen activity on both her Egyptian and Jordanian borders, for it was perfectly well known that all fedayeen raids were inspired by Egypt. The second was to open the Gulf of Aqaba to shipping and restore its status as an international waterway. The third was to reach the Suez Canal and sit on its banks until Egypt undertook to observe the Constantinople Convention and open the Canal to Israeli ships.

The first objective was attained. Nasser called off all fedayeen activity, and the Egyptian-Israeli border was peaceful for ten years. This effectively made a lie of Arab propaganda claims that the fedayeen were patriots who acted independently of any Arab government. The second objective was also attained; a United Nations Emergency Force was installed on the frontier with Egypt and took over the fort of Sharm el Sheikh. The Egyptian military presence was removed from the Straits of Tiran and the Israeli port of Eilat blossomed from that day on as an entry port for all of Israel's trade with Africa and the Far East, including virtually all of Israel's oil supplies.

The third objective was not attained, because of the ponderous and confused Anglo-French diplomatic and military action. The Anglo-French ultimatum resulted in Israeli forces, not "firming up" on the line of the Canal and staying there until the Constantinople Convention was re-enforced. The Anglo-French attack on Port Said came belatedly on November 5, the day when Israeli troops captured Sharm el Sheikh. It was difficult to justify morally and was militarily superfluous. The *Manchester Guardian,* the only British newspaper entirely consistent in its fierce criticism of the British government, called the Anglo-French ultimatum "flagrant aggression" and claimed that no military action could be justified unless Nasser closed the Canal to British and French shipping.[23] The same paper expressed the comforting thought that the reputation of the United States remained "unsullied."[24] If so, this was to do the United States little good. The Arabs have chosen to forget the violent condemnation of the Anglo-French action by the Secretary of State, John Foster Dulles, while remembering all too well that he withdrew financial aid for the Aswan high dam with a suddenness and brusqueness which infuriated Nasser and helped to drive him into the arms of the Soviet Union. Nor did Dulles' diplomatic reputation benefit from it.

* Ben-Gurion was in no way abashed by Soviet diplomatic pressure. He wrote back to Bulganin accusing Nasser of "a lust for power and the ambition to impose his rule on all the Islamic peoples."

One critic, Lord Boothby, blamed Suez on his "bullheaded brinkmanship" and pointed out that Dulles helped to sponsor the Bagdad Pact and the Suez Canal-Users' Association (to fight Nasser's nationalization decree), and then opted out of both.[25]

The long-term consequences of the Anglo-French action were serious. British and French credibility in the eyes of the Arab world was forfeited for at least a decade. Lebanon was torn by a civil war, fortunately not a bloody one, but it resulted in a shift of power from the Christian to the Moslem half of the community. King Hussein of Jordan felt forced to dismiss his last British advisors (he had already gotten rid of the British commander of the Arab Legion, Brigadier Sir John Glubb). Even so, King Hussein found himself labeled by many Arabs as a stooge of Britain, and he was nearly deposed in April 1957.

His cousin, King Feisal of Iraq, was murdered in July 1958, along with his Prime Minister, Nuri es Said, and a revolutionary regime took over. Iraq, ever since, has been politically unstable. The Syrians merely blew up the oil pipelines to the Israeli port of Haifa, but they were later to join with Nasser in a series of plots to murder King Hussein. Worst of all, the Soviet Union had been given an admirable chance to ingratiate itself with the Arab states. From 1956 on, Soviet influence in the Middle East grew steadily, especially in the so-called "socialist" states: Egypt, Syria, and, after 1958, Iraq. Soviet influence has been destructive, designed to disrupt normal Arab trade relations with the Western world, to develop an arms race in which Arab states would be forced to seek Soviet help, and to keep the Middle East in political ferment.

In 1956 the Middle East was drawn into the Cold War, even though the Cold War was officially entering a period of thaw. One American attempt was made to keep the Middle East out of the East-West struggle. Early in 1957 the so-called "Eisenhower Doctrine" was evolved and was approved by Congress. It set forth four principles: economic cooperation among the states of the Middle East; military assistance for them, in the event of their being attacked; their independence and territorial integrity to be guaranteed; and American aid to be readily granted to any Middle East state threatened by Soviet Communism.

The Israeli Parliament debated the Doctrine and approved it. The Arab states regarded it with mixed feelings; Jordan and Lebanon were to invoke American support under its terms in 1957 and 1958; the socialist Arab states would have nothing to do with it. In February 1957 the Soviet Union produced its own Middle East Charter which set forth the nonalignment of Middle East countries with "Great Power blocs," the liquidation of foreign bases, and "untied" economic assistance to the area. This Charter had far more appeal for the socialist states; they were in the future to look to the Soviet Union for protection rather than to a United States besmirched by its friendship and close association with "imperialist" Britain and France.

Eshkol had an important role to play before and during the Sinai campaign. He had become Minister of Finance in 1953 and he had to produce the funds first for equipping the Israeli armed forces and second for paying for the war. The campaign had been relatively cheap in both blood and money; even so it cost about $300 million, a large sum for a small and still not economically viable country. Money flowed in from Jewish communities abroad, particularly from the United States. There was a major drive to sell State of Israel bonds in friendly foreign countries. The reopening of the Straits of Tiran was to produce a substantial saving in Israel's bill for imported oil, which now came quickly and cheaply from Iran and the Persian Gulf sheikdoms.

"I had no intention," said Eshkol of the Sinai campaign, "of going down in history as the man who said 'no' and stopped something being done which had to be done. The first thought, Ben-Gurion's, as it happened, was that we needed 60 to 70 million dollars to mobilize and, maybe, fight if we had to. My answer was that, financially, we simply had to manage. There was no alternative."[26]

Eshkol recalled that the Sinai campaign convinced him that the time had come to develop the southern desert of the Negev, whose outlet to the Red Sea was now open again. In the next ten years the port of Eilat grew from a huddle of shacks to a town of 15,000. The nearby copper mines of Timna were reopened and extensive development of the Negev's other considerable mineral resources began. Two "new towns" were to be built at Dimona and Arad, and the first efforts made to restore agriculture to the valley of the Arava running between the Dead Sea and the Gulf of Aqaba. From 1956 Eshkol became wedded to the idea of developing the Negev as the next big stage in the building up of Israel.[27]

1. For these and other figures, see *Jewish Observer & Middle East Review*, Nov. 22, 1968.
2. Joseph Schechtman, *The Refugee in the World*, p. 214.
3. *Ibid.*, p. 216.
4. *Ibid.*, p. 240.
5. Martha Gellhorn, *The Atlantic Monthly*, October 1961.
6. Terence Prittie, *Israel: Miracle in the Desert*, pp. 58–60.
7. Schechtman, *op. cit.*, p. 222.
8. *Ibid.*, p. 227.
9. Walter Eytan, *The First Ten Years*, pp. 90–103.
10. Prittie, *op. cit.*, p. 156.
11. *Ibid.*, p. 184.
12. Col. Richard Meinertzhagen, *Middle East Diary*, p. 267.
13. Sir John Glubb, *Britain and the Arabs*, p. 334.
14. King Hussein, *Uneasy Lies the Head*, p. 87.
15. J. C. Hurewitz, *Diplomacy in the Middle East*, Vol. II, p. 308.
16. Moshe Dayan, *Diary of the Sinai Campaign*, p. 4.
17. Sir Reader Bullard, *Britain and the Middle East*, p. 165.
18. Walter Lacqueur, *The Soviet Union and the Middle East*, pp. 118–119.

19. *Ibid.*, p. 124.
20. *Ibid.*, p. 138.
21. George Kirk, *A Short History of the Middle East*, p. 278.
22. Meinertzhagen, *op. cit.*, p. 276.
23. *Manchester Guardian,* leading articles of Aug. 2, 1956, and Oct. 31, 1956.
24. *Manchester Guardian,* leading article of Nov. 1, 1956.
25. Lord Boothby, *My Yesterday, Your Tomorrow,* p. 56.
26. Eshkol, in personal conversation with the author.
27. Eshkol, in personal conversation with the author.

12.

In 1952 Eshkol was moved from the Ministry of Agriculture to the Ministry of Finance. His family was sad about the change; Eshkol himself was not altogether enthusiastic. His family knew that he had been entirely happy as Minister of Agriculture, that he had begun thinking far into the future and that he may have seen himself as exactly the right person to go on following the idealistic example of A. D. Gordon and other pioneers, preaching the virtues of toil on the land, redeeming the soil, building up a balanced community, giving the children of Israel a feeling of wholeness, wholesomeness, and health. Eshkol knew that the move was a promotion, but he loved land and he understood it. Being officially parted from it was a wrench; but it was not as bad as it might have been. He remained a member of the board of the Jewish Agency, which continued to exercise a major influence on the settlement of the land of Israel. And, as Minister of Finance, he oversaw the work of a number of junior ministries—Commerce, Communications, Housing, and Agriculture.

From 1948 onwards, the Prime Minister took on the additional burden of the Ministry of Defense. Ben-Gurion realized that, from 1948 onward, Israel's defense was so closely bound up with the existence of the State that the Prime Minister of such a small country had to shoulder an extra burden. The key consideration in every government decision was whether it would help Israel to survive. Defense needs played the operative part in that decision. With the Prime Minister in charge of defense, only two other Ministries stood out: Foreign Affairs and Finance.

The Ministry of Foreign Affairs was a very tough assignment. It involved the most careful probing of opinion abroad in order to build good relations with as many countries as possible while maintaining a firm front against the Arab world. Perhaps the most difficult part of this assignment was to state Israel's case in the United Nations, where Israel found herself confronting a half dozen deeply involved Arab states and a dozen other Moslem countries which sympathized with them. The Ministry of Foreign Affairs, initially, had to display a neutral attitude between East and West, in the vain hope of encouraging the great powers to leave the Middle East out of their wrangles. When this posture became impossible, Israel still had to cultivate good relations with the Soviet Union and Soviet bloc. For a small Middle Eastern state to throw down the gauntlet to the Soviet Union, now one of two world powers, or even to take sides, would have made peace more difficult to maintain.

Israel's foreign relations have always been, necessarily, inhibited by the policies and interests of the great powers. The Israelis have been sufficiently practical to accept this situation on almost all occasions, asserting their own interests only when they have been grievously threatened.

The Minister of Foreign Affairs had to do a balancing act. So had the Minister of Finance. His job was at least equally important and in the early years, at least, was probably more so, making him the second man in the government, a sort of unofficial deputy to the Prime Minister. Building up the State of Israel meant primarily the organizing of its economy. To survive Israel would have to pay her way. She faced tremendous, almost insuperable, problems in this respect.

The country's geographical position was one of almost total isolation. Not only were all her land frontiers closed, they were shooting frontiers, and Israelis straying too close to them were shot at without warning, even though on Israeli territory. Israel's outlet to the Red Sea, the port of Eilat, was useless as long as the Egyptians maintained their illegal blockade of the Gulf of Aqaba. The pipeline from the Iraqi oil fields to Haifa was cut. The only access was from the Mediterranean. Israel, from the point of view of communications, was a dead end.

Everything that the Israeli economy needed, food and other consumer goods, capital equipment for her agriculture and her infant industries, building materials for the huge influx of refugees, her oil, steel, and coal had to cross the Mediterranean. In the same way, her exports had to travel away from markets just across her borders. Inevitably, Israel's exports would become geared to the needs of economically sophisticated countries ready to pay for quality goods after the long haul across the sea. Inevitably, about 85 percent of her exports would go to Western Europe or America. Israel's trade was forced into this position by the unnatural circumstance of the Arab blockade and boycott.

The external geographical factors were enough to daunt any small, young country in the process of doubling its population in the course of five years, 1948 to 1953, by accepting hordes of penniless immigrants. The internal economic situation looked equally unpromising. The country suffered from an acute shortage of water and of raw materials; in particular, it had no coal, no iron ore and, initially, no oil. It lacked any of the sinews of a modern economy. The Bible had called this "a land of wheat and barley and vines and fig trees and pomegranates, a land of olive oil and honey." That was what it was; although those resources were geared to the needs of 12 tribes and not to a population that was doubling from 870,000 to 1,670,000.

In the two years before Eshkol became Minister of Finance, Israel's trade figures were alarming. They appeared to confirm, beyond all doubt, the gloomy prophecies of those who claimed that the country could never pay its way, even if its land frontiers were thrown open. In 1950 Israel's exports brought in $35 million, while her imports cost her $300 million. The trade deficit was $265 million. In 1951 the figures were $45 million and $382 million; the deficit had risen to $337 million. Some cutback of imports seemed unavoidable. Yet a growing population had to be fed, housed, and given the means of earning a livelihood, which cost the most money of all.

In spite of the tribulations which were endured in the early, pioneering years and subsequently when Israel faced the threat of Arab armed aggression, 1952 may have been the nadir in the history of the creation of the State of Israel. Much of the first flush of enthusiasm was vanishing. About a hundred thousand immigrants were still sitting in camps. At least double that number were housed in miserably inadequate shacks and huts. Eshkol, who was still treasurer of the Jewish Agency in addition to his other duties, was worrying about the country's becoming a kind of ramshackle army barracks.

The food situation was no better. Dr. Zvi Dinstein, working then under Eshkol in the Ministry of Finance and now, in 1969, 17 years later, Deputy Minister, associates that time with the ubiquitous fish fillet. Sometimes it was salted herring, which at least had a taste, but more often it was frozen coarse fish which tasted of nothing at all.[1] Frozen fish from Northern Europe was cheap and plentiful; indeed, it was about the only foodstuff of which Europe had a surplus.

Another memory of that time is of the only other foodstuff which was readily available in Israel. It was *aubergine,* or eggplant. Just why so much eggplant was available at the time is not clear; possibly the kibbutzim and moshavim were growing it in large quantities because it produced a good yield per acre and had good nutritive value. One settler can still remember that upon his arrival in Israel he was amazed at the perpetual presence of eggplant at mealtimes.[2] There were about 20 different ways of cooking it; it could, for instance, be used to make a sweet or a sour cream salad, a bitter "apple sauce," an ersatz "chopped liver," a soup, or a pudding. It could be fried, baked, boiled, sautéd, or scrambled. People became sick at the sight of it.

There was little, far too little, bread, some potatoes, vegetables mainly for those living in the country, olives and skimmed-milk cheese. There was a theoretical egg ration of three a month and no meat ration at all. "We considered ourselves lucky if we got a hundred grams of meat per person half a dozen times in the year."[3]

The Israelis were full of idealism about their new, very own state. But it requires a vast amount of idealism to go on accepting life in a tin hut and on an empty stomach. Grumbling, suspicion, nervousness about the future, and envy grew, especially perhaps of the *Yecke,* the German Jews who had brought a small amount of property and money into the country with them before 1939, and who had applied their thrift and energy to building up modest fortunes. National morale, which had been astoundingly high in the darkest days of the Mandate and the War of Independence, was beginning to droop.

Eshkol had to do the most awkward of all balancing acts—stimulate production while cutting back consumption. Strictly speaking, this is economically unrealistic, if not impossible. In 1952 the import bill was reduced from $382 million to $322 million. Both agricultural and industrial output faltered and exports dropped by over a million dollars to

$43.5 million. The trade deficit had been cut from $337 million to $278.5 million, but unemployment was up and at least as many people as before were living below subsistence.

1953 and 1954 were both austerity years. The import bill was still further reduced in 1953, to $280 million, and exports showed a significant increase, to $57 million. The deficit was thus cut to $223 million. In the next year a corner was turned in the long road to economic viability; imports were held almost steady at $287 million while exports climbed to $85 million. Exports had nearly doubled in two years, the biggest jump they were to make in the first 20 years of the State of Israel's existence. This success was due to two factors in particular—the export trade in citrus fruits was rationalized and thus immensely increased, and small but significant beginnings were made in the export of industrial goods.

By the end of 1954 the worst of the economic crisis was over. It had required considerable courage to impose tough austerity measures on people who had suffered so much already and whom Eshkol would have preferred to have given so much. During those times, one of his secretaries met him one day on the street when she was with her small son David. After staring at him fixedly for a time the boy asked, "Why do you look so pale and worried?" The smiling Eshkol replied, "Who wouldn't, if he's Minister of Finance?"[4] Talking of his long term of office as Minister of Finance, Eshkol, after becoming Prime Minister, was inclined to remark: "For over ten years I was the most cursed and most discussed man in Israel, sitting in my office in the Treasury. Now I'm lucky enough to be just a plain Prime Minister, and yesterday's enemies have become today's best friends."

There were, admittedly, some circumstances which worked in Eshkol's favor. In the first place, the Prime Minister, Ben-Gurion, gave him a completely free hand. Eshkol became, in effect, the "Prime Minister for Economic Affairs," a phrase used about him by government officials at the time.[5] Ben-Gurion not only trusted him implicitly; he refused to interest himself in economic matters and even boasted about his ignorance of them.

Eshkol was able to collect his own team of advisers and assistants. His own knowledge of economics was of a strictly practical nature; he needed trained economists and found them chiefly among the young men of the Hebrew University who had completed their military service and taken their economics degrees. He was neither ashamed nor embarrassed to take suggestions of people young enough to be his sons. He asked them to work very hard in the Treasury, starting at 8 o'clock in the morning and often finishing at 10 o'clock at night, with a snack in the office and a break of one hour in the heat of the afternoon.

His adjutant in the Finance Ministry was Pinhas Sapir, ten years younger than Eshkol and like him a member of Mapai. Sapir became Director-General of the Ministry in 1953 and was promoted at the end of

1955 to be Minister of Commerce and Industry, where he worked in close liaison with Eshkol. Eight years later, Sapir was to succeed him as Minister of Finance. He was a man after Eshkol's own heart, tough, very hard-working, essentially practical, with a similar if rather earthier Yiddish humor. Sapir was a man who got things done, a man in a hurry, and a man who never ignored a point of detail. Not the least of the reasons why Eshkol liked and trusted him was that he had held a post on the executive of Eshkol's favorite brainchild, Mekorot, the national water board.

His closest adviser did not belong to this group of enthusiastic young men. David Horowitz was only a few years younger than himself and a friend of more than 30 years. He and Eshkol had first met in the post-1918 pioneering days when both of them were working in the fields with hoe and shovel. After becoming Minister, Eshkol asked Horowitz to help him to establish the Bank of Israel. Together they prepared the law which set up the Bank, and in 1954 Horowitz became its first governor, a post which he still held 15 years later.

The Bank took over the management of the national debt, all governmental fiscal and banking arrangements, and control of the currency. It supervised the liquidity position of the commercial banks, accepted deposits from them, and made short-term advances to the government. Most important, its governor acted as the principal economic as well as financial adviser of the government. Eshkol was very much a team player; his ten-year partnership with Horowitz was to be brilliantly successful, and was maintained as a close personal association as long as Eshkol was Prime Minister. Horowitz has a razor-sharp mind and a gift for coming straight to the point. He is a strictly practical man, tied to no economic theories. He is also immensely courageous, a necessity for a man who has had to help steer a deficit economy. Not the least of Horowitz's qualities is his easy, engaging way of explaining complex financial problems to the layman.

Horowitz played a part in organizing the sale of State of Israel Bonds abroad, whose proceeds flowed into a special devolopment budget and were spent on building up agriculture and industry, improving communications, and developing water supply and mineral resources. The first series of bonds was issued in 1951 and produced $145 million by the middle of 1954, an immensely valuable injection of ready money for spending. Other issues since then have brought in upwards of $1 billion, but it was the first issue which produced the shot in the arm for the staggering economy.

Another source of external aid was the United Jewish Appeal, which raised its funds from Jewish communities in the United States. In 1954 the UJA paid over $73 million to the Israeli treasury, and although this figure was not reached again during the next ten years, the average annual increment from this source was about $40 million. The United

States Government began to service a "development loan," which averaged another $60 million a year. Money began to flow in from the Jewish communities in Great Britain and other countries. Israel's leaders have sometimes been reproached for the readiness with which they accept outside "charity." To Eshkol, there was nothing about it that was *schnorr*—a Yiddish word which suggests the perfunctoriness of charity from the giver's point of view and the meanness of its acceptance. The thought that aid from the Diaspora could be regarded as schnorr drove Ben-Gurion to castigating donors for providing "conscience money" as an alternative to emigrating to Israel. Eshkol took a more rational view: that the Jewish world itself recognized its duty to contribute whatever help it could to a Jewish state.[6] In 1953 he appealed to American Jewry to assume "collective responsibility" for providing economic aid for Israel and made a trip to New York to boost the idea.

Yet another source of financial aid was the German Federal Republic. In 1952 the West German Chancellor, Konrad Adenauer, and the Israeli Foreign Minister, Moshe Sharett, concluded a reparations agreement under which West Germany was to pay the State of Israel $822 million in goods and money over the next 12 years.[7] This meant an annual payment of about $70 million. The Israeli government set up its own office at Cologne to scrutinize the lists of goods offered by the West German government as payment in kind and to make selections from those lists. The West German economic miracle was already fully under way; German goods were of excellent quality and the Germans were scrupulous in their delivery. Perhaps the chief value of the reparations agreement was that it did not have any inflationary effect. Acting under the instructions of the Ministry of Finance, and advised by the Bank of Israel, the Israeli representatives in Cologne mainly bought capital goods needed by the economy and constituting capital investment in it.

The reparations agreement, however, caused desperate heart-searchings among the Israeli people. Could one accept material aid from Germany, only seven years after the end of the Nazi holocaust? Would acceptance not give fresh substance to that unpleasant and unjustified image of the Jew as a maker and manipulator of money, which has been so popular for so many centuries throughout the world? Was it either honorable or sensible to take German "charity"?

The debates on the reparations agreement, in both Jerusalem and Bonn, were protracted and sometimes violent. Ben-Gurion had readily entered into preliminary negotiations with the West German government. He has been quoted as saying that "Jewish history, which is replete with acts of slaughter against Jews, knows no parallel to the crimes of Nazi Germany. Deeds like hers can never be forgotten nor forgiven, certainly not by our generation."[8] But, equally, Ben-Gurion asserted, "I do not hold, as do some of my opponents, that Germany today is the Germany of the Kaiser or Hitler. I believe that she will never again command her former influence; her days of hegemony in Europe have gone."

Ben-Gurion's most operative thought was: "If Germany can be a source for the strengthening of Israel, then surely we must do what we can to keep that source open."[9] Here spoke the strictly practical man of politics, and Eshkol agreed implicitly with him. But it was not so easy to convince the parties in the Knesset. Opposition was particularly fierce on the extreme right and the extreme left, and members of the rightwing *Herut* and the leftwing *Mapam* combined to denounce the Government for traducing the memories of the millions of Jewish martyrs. It was fortunate that Herut, under Menachem Beigin, was at its postwar weakest at that time, and that Mapam was restricted temporarily by its alliance with Achdut Ha'avoda. Yet the Knesset debates led to rioting in the streets, the first sign of a lack of unity among a people committed to tackling its problems in the most practical and unemotional manner.

During the first 20 years of the life of the State of Israel the distinguishing features of the relations between the Jews of Israel and the Arab minority was a veiled distrust of the Arabs, a degree of submerged resentment on their part, the maintainance of a minimum of security regulations by the Israeli authorities, and the considerable material advancement of the Arab minority. The minority's standard of living became immensely higher than that in Arab states like Jordan and Egypt. Along with economic benefits, the Arab minority was given complete religious freedom, good law courts, its own schools, and greatly improved health and other welfare services. Its numbers increased in 20 years from 150,000 to 250,000, and the Israeli government was already becoming worried about the demographic effects of a soaring birth rate, before territories containing one million more Arabs were occupied during the Six-Day War.

In one sense the Arabs of Israel have been among the unhappiest Arabs of all; they have a sense of "not belonging" and at the same time of being despised by the rest of the Arab world. The Israelis were agreeably surprised when there was no sign of unrest among their Arab minority during the Six-Day War. But this minority is still not fully integrated in the Israeli community, or reconciled to its spiritual isolation. One observer (Walter Schwartz, *The Arabs in Israel,* p. 111) kept hearing phrases such as, "Nasser is the biggest, the biggest in the world. Bigger than Saladin, as great as Mohammed."

The debates in the West German Bundestag were less acrimonious but equally intense. The agreement was approved only on March 18, 1953, and the final vote produced a split in the government coalition. Most of the principal government party, the Christian Democratic Union, voted for the agreement. Some Christian Democrats voted against it, and so did most of the junior coalition party, the Free Democrats. The

Levi Shkolnik as a student at the Hebrew Gymnasia, Vilna, at the age of 16, 1911.

Theodore Herzl, 1860-1904.

First Zionist Congress, Basle, Switzerland, August 29, 1897.

Letter written by Theodore Herzl in which he proposes design for Zionist flag.

Herzl aboard ship sailing for Palestine, 1901.

Left, David Ben-Gurion, 1886-   , former Premier of Israel; right, Itzhak Ben-Zvi, 1884-1963, late President of Israel, as law student at the University of Istanbul, 1914.

Eliezer Ben-Yehuda, 1858-1922, the father of modern Hebrew.

Levi Eshkol at Petach Tikvah, 1917.

The Work Distribution Committee at Petach Tikvah. Seated, left to right: Abraham Hafet, Levi Eshkol, Jacob Path; standing, left to right; Chaim Puterman and Rivka Mahareshek.

The Government with President Itzhak Ben-Zvi, 1952.

Levi Eshkol standing second from left with the Work Distribution Committee of Petach Tikvah, 1916.

The beginnings of Degania B, 1920.

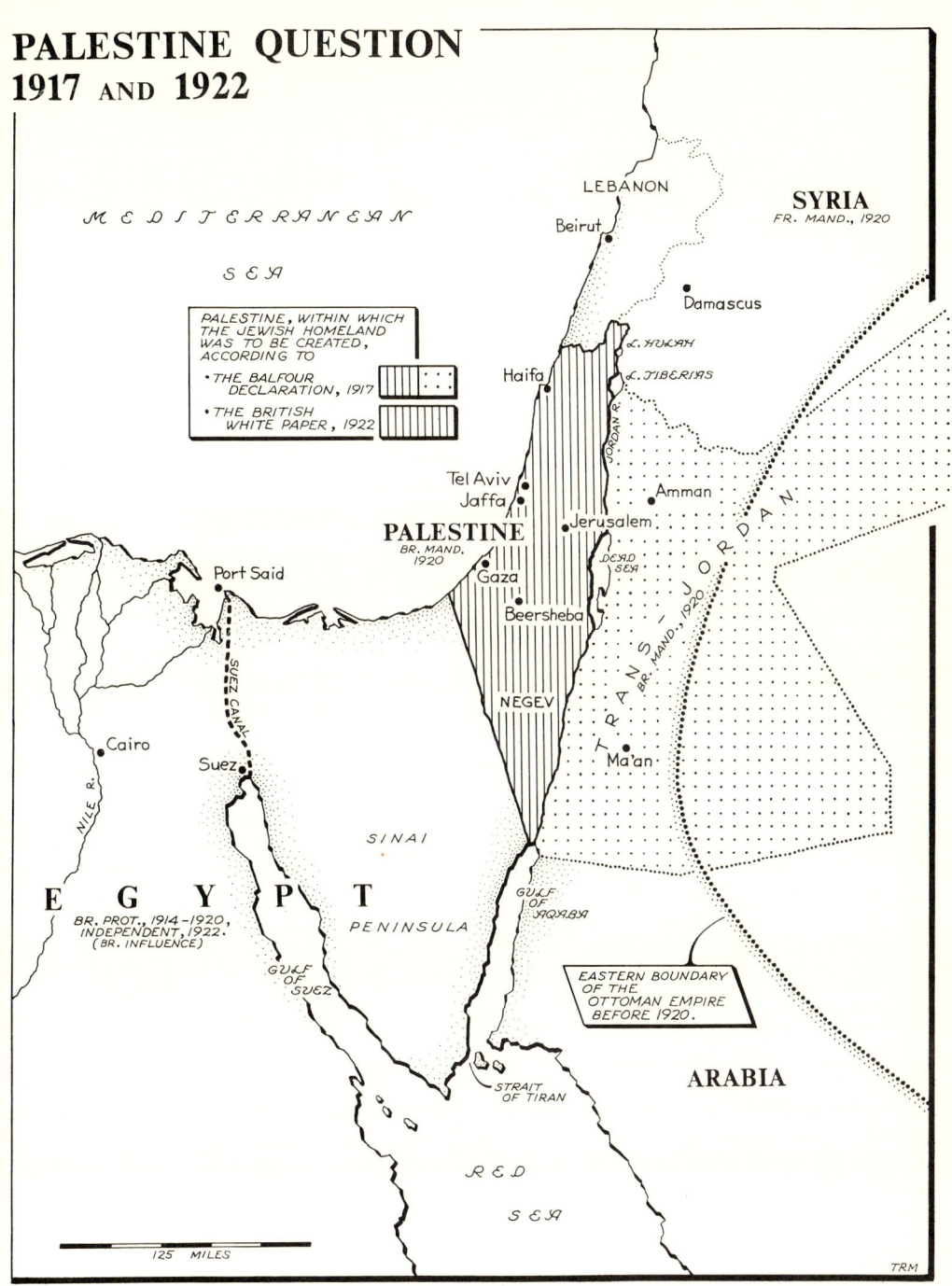

Eshkol with his wife Elisheva, and daughters, Dvora and Tema, 1941.

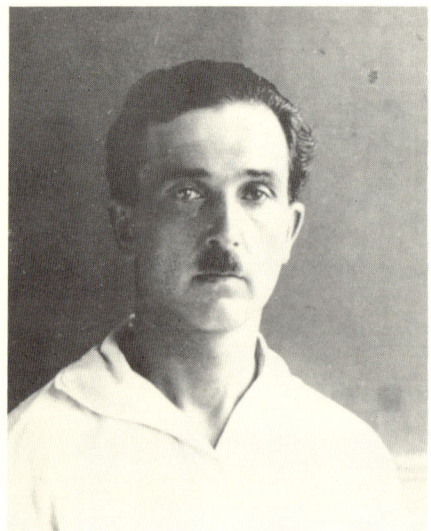

Levi Eshkol, 1919.

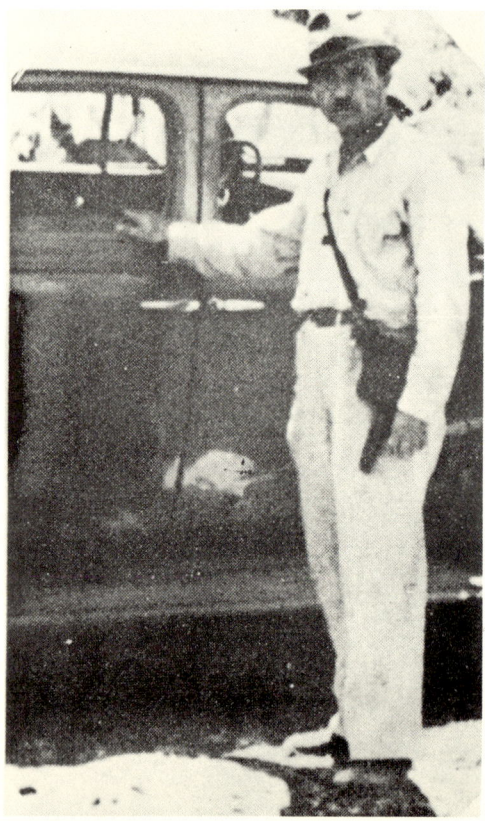

Levi Eshkol inspecting the water cisterns of Emek Jezreel, 1937.

Eshkol practicing for self-defense, 1937.

Levi Eshkol with his
second wife, Elisheva,
and his daughter, in
the 1940s.

Labor demonstration in Tel Aviv, May Day, 1947.

Eshkol with Chaim Weizmann, 1874–1952, first President of Israel, Jerusalem, 1948.

Vladimir Jabotinsky, 1880-1940, during World War I, 1914-1917.

David Ben-Gurion as a member of the Jewish Brigade during World War I.

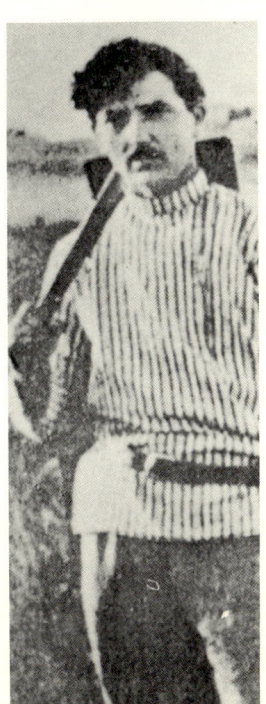

Levi Eshkol at Petach Tikvah, 1916.

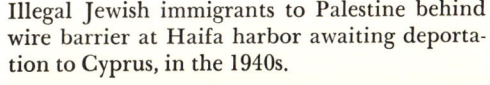

Illegal Jewish immigrants to Palestine behind wire barrier at Haifa harbor awaiting deportation to Cyprus, in the 1940s.

Eshkol drilling for water at Mekorot Water Works, 1936.

Levi Eshkol at Timna Copper Mines, 1953.

Levi Eshkol, 1950.

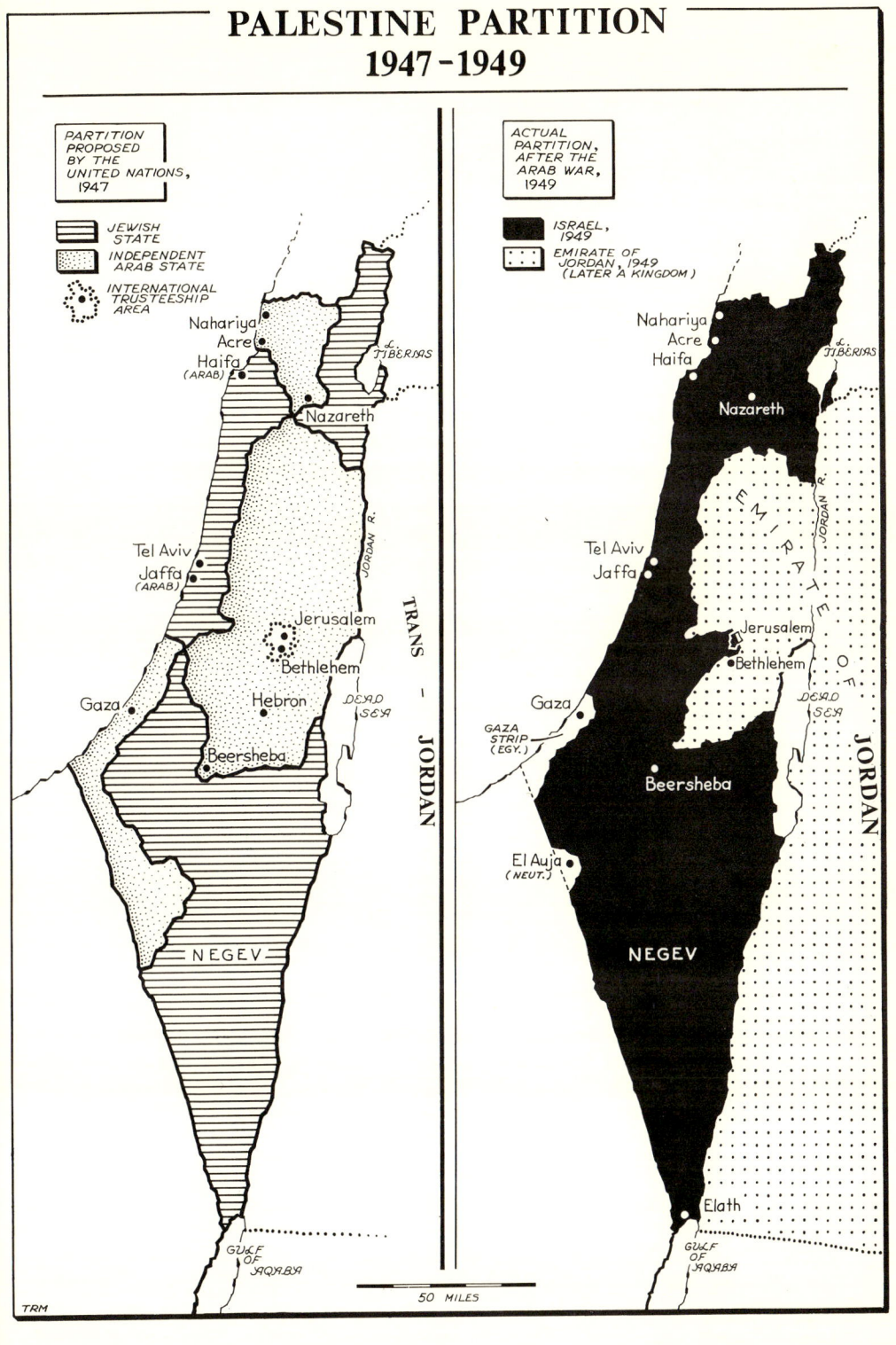

Eshkol, as Premier of Israel, inspecting his troops.

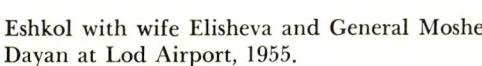

Eshkol with wife Elisheva and General Moshe Dayan at Lod Airport, 1955.

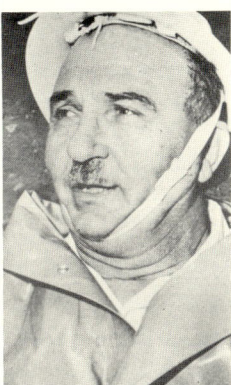

Eshkol, as Premier, visits an aqueduct project.

Levi Eshkol, 1965.

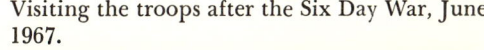

Visiting the troops after the Six Day War, June 1967.

Prime Minister Levi Eshkol, Oct. 24, 1895—Feb. 26, 1969.

Mrs. Miriam Eshkol.

Eshkol with his grandson, 1963.

agreement was approved thanks to the unanimous support of the main opposition Social Democratic Party.

Adenauer had taken a risk over the reparations agreement, and this was never forgotten by Ben-Gurion and Eshkol in later years when West Germany dragged its feet badly over opening diplomatic relations with Israel. The German Free Democrats argued that the payment of large-scale reparations would seriously antagonize the Arab countries, a far bigger market for German goods than Israel could ever be. Indeed, Arab leaders had explicitly stated that any payment of reparations to Israel would be regarded as an unfriendly step and had hinted darkly at damaging reprisals against West Germany.[10] To the Free Democrats trade with the Arab world was more important than the payment of a debt of honor, and they were strengthened in their argument by the fulminations of a part of the Israeli press, which kept pointing out that no payment, of any kind or size, would in any way recompense for the ghastly cruelties inflicted on the Jewish people by Hitler's Germany.

Yet another kind of financial help for Israel was to come from the new democratic West German state. This took the form of restitution to individual Israelis, for loss of property, money, personal freedom, and means of earning a livelihood, incurred as a result of Nazi brutalities. The terms for this type of restitution were codified in the *Bundesentschaedigungsgesetz,* or Federal Law of Compensation, which was passed in 1956. The Law envisaged total payments of $10 billion; much of this money would flow to former Jewish persecutees who had become citizens of Israel.

No time limit was set on the fulfillment of these payments, and they were still going on 13 years later. Indeed, total payments under the Law of Compensation passed the $10 billion figure in 1967. Even so, the Law could not be regarded as entirely satisfactory by world Jewry; many categories of Jewish claimants had been excluded, many others received derisory amounts for their shocking suffering, and there was a tendency for German courts of adjudication to regard themselves as representatives of the West German treasury and committed to finding every possible reason for refusing or postponing payment.

The payment of millions of dollars as compensation to individual Israeli citizens had an inflationary effect on the country's economy. In an era of extreme austerity, thousands of former Central European Jews found themselves with often sizable capital. This resulted in spending on consumer goods which the country, because of its trade deficit, could not afford to import. The trade deficit tended to be inflated while Israel's gold and hard-currency reserves improved. Eshkol, who never worried about his personal popularity, accepted the advice of the Bank of Israel and pursued a tough, very tough taxation policy in order to curb consumption. Income tax was increased, with tax-free allowances of only about $1000 for a family of four and a maximum tax rate of over 60 percent. The corporation tax moved up to between 40 and 50 percent. Heavy indirect taxes were imposed on anything which could be regarded as a luxury. This included, inevitably, automobiles and even such conventional household appliances as washing machines and refrigerators.

Israelis accepted these restraints on personal spending with some grumbling but virtually no organized opposition. Typical of their attitude was the whimsical remark made to me by a prominent newspaperman: "One of my brothers drives a Ford Cortina in the States, and another keeps a Rover in London. I drive my little Ford Anglia, when I can afford the petrol for it, but at least I can say that I own a car which cost a great deal more than either of theirs."

Austerity has imposed sacrifices on all but a very few Israelis, and it has required a great deal of idealism. Nowhere have sacrifices been greater than among government employees. Ever since the State of Israel was founded, a great many of them have risen as early as 5 A.M. and have worked hundreds of hours overtime a year without thinking of asking for a cent of extra pay. Government employees habitually take work home with them in the evening. Ministers have set an example by surrendering a part of their salaries at times of national emergency, and those salaries have remained very low. Even in 1969 junior Ministers were being paid only about $500 a month. Some of them were still living in three-room apartments in Jerusalem. Senior civil servants often rent a single room, leaving their families on a kibbutz or elsewhere and visiting them only at weekends. This modesty in personal spending is common to almost the whole population. The few luxury hotels in Israel are generally filled with foreign tourists. The country boasts only a single golf course, because it is a "rich man's game" and, perhaps more important, uses up potentially valuable land. A New England frugality, which has nothing to do with meanness, pervades the whole nation.

Eshkol never had any doubt about the need for frugality, and he did everything he could to foster this national mood. He lived extremely simply himself, drinking no alcohol, occupying a modest apartment in Jerusalem, owning no family car for much of his time as Minister of Finance. But in encouraging frugality, he deviated in one important respect from the usual pattern of spending curbs. In Western countries the first part of the economy to react to austerity is the building industry. Eshkol refused to regard home-building as nonproductive; in his view it had high priority, ranking close behind food and jobs. Providing homes would keep immigrants in Israel and would attract others in the future. In the first 20 years of Israel's existence, over 350,000 new homes were built, housing over two thirds of the population. More than half of them were built by the government.

In 1953, after he had been in office only a few months, Eshkol organized an economic conference, the second held in Israel. The first, in 1950, was designed to produce emergency measures to tide the economy over its first four years. Eshkol's conference produced a seven-year plan: its biggest item was the raising of $1,700,000,000 half of which would have to come from the Jewish community in the United States, for the equipping of industry and agriculture for an all-out export drive. Eshkol asked for an immediate $100 million from American Jewry; he got it.

As Eshkol saw it, the two central problems were industrialization and export. There were a host of other problems too, of course, but the need for industrialization was paramount. Agricultural output had to be forced up, but the old dream of a pastoral state based on the back-to-the-soil cult was dead. Israel would have to feed a steadily increasing population, and feed it steadily better; there would never be more than limited agricultural surpluses for export.

Fifteen years later, Eshkol told me:

No one had been keener than I was on getting back to the land. I loved the land, and it was central to my philosophy of life. But when I became Minister of Finance, it was at once clear to me that Israel's prosperity, security, and very existence depended on being given an industrial base. We had to produce goods which we could sell to the outside world. We had to make as much as we could of the equipment needed by our farms. We had to begin producing the weapons which we needed for our own defense, for we could not remain almost totally dependent on arms grudgingly allowed us by foreign governments.[11]

When his assistants asked him whether further investment in industry could really be afforded, Eshkol's answer was: "It took us 50 years or more to make our agriculture pay. We've got to make our industry pay a lot quicker than that. So, if we need money to do it, then the money must be found! We shall have to pay for our mistakes as we go along."

The problems of industrialization were gigantic. Half the population of Israel in 1953 consisted of postwar immigrants, and hundreds of thousands of these were peddlers, clerks, or small merchants. There was only one compensation; they were used to living in towns. Eshkol set as targets for his seven-year plan the doubling of the 90,000 men and women employed in industry, and at least the trebling of productivity. Exports had to be pushed ahead at maximum speed, and Eshkol decreed that they should be of two particular types: industrial exports based on locally available raw materials, and industrial exports involving the import of raw materials which were either lightweight (to reduce freight charges) or which made up a small proportion of the final value of the finished product.[12] The first category included, for example, canned or frozen foods and fertilizers; the second, industrial diamonds and clothing.

During his 11 years in office, Eshkol saw exports rise from $43 million to $338 million. Industrial exports, which were negligible in 1952, made up over two thirds of all exports by 1960 and over three quarters by 1963. In spite of excellent harvests, the proportion of industrial exports has since risen to well over four fifths. The economy of the country has, in fact, been revolutionized. Polished diamonds have played the biggest part in this revolution, but flourishing industries have been created in textiles, chemicals, mining products, light machinery, and canned and other foodstuffs. Whereas in 1953 Israel was paying for only 11 percent of her imports with exports, by 1963 she was paying for well over 50 percent.

One major sacrifice was needed in order to boost exports. In 1948 the value of the Israeli pound had been fixed at par with the British pound sterling and was worth four U.S. dollars. It soon became plain that this rate of exchange could not be maintained. In 1952, before Eshkol took over the Ministry of Finance, the exchange rate was adjusted downward to 1.8 Israeli pounds to the U.S. dollar. Eshkol had to devalue a second time, in 1962, when the rate became 3 Israeli pounds to the dollar. In 1967 the rate again changed to 3.5 Israeli pounds to the dollar, since Israel was obliged to devalue the moment Britain did.

Eshkol's 1962 devaluation was unpopular. It had been easy to explain that the original parity with sterling was unrealistic. But in 1962 devaluation meant that Israel would have to pay substantially more for her imports at a time when they were already costing more than twice as much as her exports brought in. The trade deficit was substantial, and Eshkol himself was inclined towards the view that devaluation could give Israeli exports a slight edge at a time when exporters were searching desperately for good markets for their products. Eshkol's closest assistant, Pinhas Sapir, opposed devaluation. Horowitz and the Bank of Israel favored it. Eshkol devalued on Horowitz's advice, who pointed out that steadily increasing imports had encouraged internal inflationary pressures and vice versa. This trend had to be checked, particularly since the country's reserves were being boosted by reparations and other payments from abroad, and the amount of currency in circulation actually rose 73 percent in three years.[13] Even more important, Israeli exports had to be kept competitive. The export drive could not be allowed to lose its momentum. Devaluation worked. It was another of Horowitz's perfectly calculated gambles, but Eshkol had to take the ministerial and parliamentary responsibility for it.

There were other problems confronting him which also needed courage. He had to hold government expenditure steady and produce balanced budgets, for the government had to set an example in saving and husbanding its resources. Financing the early deficit budgets had added to the national debt. Eshkol produced a series of budgets which were either balanced or produced small surpluses. The importance of the example set by government cannot be overrated; in this instance it gave credibility to Eshkol's policies of wage and price restraint, high taxation rates, and the restriction of credit. These policies could only work with the cooperation of the trade unions and the public; it was, therefore, the government's duty to secure that cooperation. Israel's example in this respect was something which European governments of the 1960s, especially Britain, could have studied with advantage.

Balancing Israel's budgets was a particularly difficult job because the country's defense needs have, ever since 1948, been totally out of proportion to its resources. In an actual war; Israel has depended on a citizen army. The great bulk of the male population between the ages of 18 and 40 has been kept either under arms or in a state of some military preparedness, entailing a long initial period of military service followed by periodic refresher courses. This has necessitated keeping a standing force under arms, with a steadily increasing number of reservists available for call-up within a period of 72 hours. By the 1960s the standing force totaled 60,000 men and the reservists more than 250,000. Defense costs have averaged almost a quarter of the total budget, a frightening amount, during a period when the population has trebled and the economy has had to be revolutionized. Defense costs have never stopped growing, and Eshkol never failed during his 11 years in charge of the nation's finances to appreciate the paramount need for military preparedness. Typical of his understanding that Israel could not economize on her defense was his appeal to the people in December 1956 to tighten their belts yet again. Egyptian rearmament after the disastrous Sinai campaign was under way, and the Israeli government had ordered a score of Sabre jet fighters, at $600,000 each.

It was during his long term as Finance Minister that the public became aware of Eshkol's exceptional human qualities. Curiously, there were many jokes about Eshkol after he became Prime Minister which suggested a lack of decisiveness. His slogan was said to be, "Don't postpone until the morrow what can be postponed until the day after tomorrow," and one of Israel's leading comedians said to the Minister: "You take most of my money away from me in taxes. I don't mind that too much. But I do object to people laughing more at you than they do at *me*." Another story tells how Eshkol was asked at some gathering whether he would have coffee or tea, and answered after some hesitation, "Half and half, please."* Yet Eshkol made his name as an administrator who despised bureaucratic procedure and was expert at cutting red tape. One Israeli journalist has told me how a representative of the kibbutzim, Abraham Harzfeld, was summoned by Eshkol for a discussion of government credits for the purchase of capital

---

* Eshkol told me that he invented this joke himself. It is a Jewish habit to make jokes about Jews.

equipment. Eshkol snapped, "How much do you want?" Harzfeld answered, "One and a half million pounds." *"Gemacht"* ("Done"), Eshkol said, in Yiddish. "But you haven't even heard all our arguments to support this figure," his visitor protested. "I don't need to," was all that Eshkol, smiling broadly, replied. He had gotten off more lightly than he had expected.

He gave short shrift to verbose bureaucrats, but was always ready to spend time convincing the ordinary citizen that he was doing his best for him and for the country. A porter at one of the government buildings buttonholed him one day and complained that he was being robbed by high taxation. Eshkol spent a good ten minutes explaining why people had to pay taxes and what was done with their money. And a small girl once wrote to Eshkol personally, telling him that she had been losing 2-and-a-half-agorot pieces because they were so small. Eshkol wrote her, enclosed a purse and some new agorot pieces with his letter, and expressed the hope that she would keep her money safe in the future.[15]

He had that invaluable and elusive quality, the common touch, a gift for understanding what was in a simple man's mind, talking about it with him as an equal, making him feel that he mattered. Politicians in large countries can very easily become remote, even pompous and affected. Israel has always been small enough to be a real community, where its people regard one another as neighbors. All men are not, of course, equal in all respects; but there is no country in the world with less insistence on privilege. Eshkol fitted well into this society.

His 11 years as Minister of Finance were hard, slogging years, during which every action had to be carefully and exhaustively discussed with his advisers. The country was no sooner over one hurdle than another loomed. The 1950–1952 crisis was overcome, but the 1956 Sinai campaign put a huge new burden on Israel's finances. Eshkol's last five years in office produced something like a real breakthrough for the country's export trade, with exports up by 150 percent to $338 million. But discreet efforts to bring Israel into the European Common Market came to nothing, and the country remained economically isolated and alone. During those years the economy appeared to be moving forward, only to run into a minor roadblock of wage demands and unofficial strikes, and then into a major one of impending war with the Arab world, which required ever larger allocations to defense. There was the new, nagging worry that the Middle East would in due course become a theater of war in which sophisticated, hugely expensive weapons would be used.

Defense costs played the largest part in record budgets, year after year. Eshkol had to look for help wherever he could hope to find it. In 1956 and 1957 he negotiated loans of $135 million and then of $75 million from the Import-Export Bank. In March 1957 he declared at a press conference in Paris: "The people of Israel are already bearing a burden that cannot be increased. I must confess, and this is something I would not dare to say in Israel, that I cannot see how I can raise taxes any higher, although that is exactly what I am going to do." After several meetings with Prime Minister Guy Mollet, Eshkol secured a $30 million loan from the French government.

But there was a serious setback in 1960, when a long drought cost Israeli agriculture an estimated $25 million. On January 6, 1961, Eshkol found himself forced to announce new tax increases, roughly three cents more on a bottle of beer, four cents on a pack of 20 cigarettes, nine cents on a bottle of brandy, six cents on a bottle of wine, and increases year as Minister of Finance, it was producing 130,000 tons, or about ten once in conflict with the Histadrut, which was calling for an across-the-board six percent wage increase for industrial workers.

During those 11 years of Eshkol's stewardship of his country's finances, oil was discovered in 1955 at Heletz-Bror, not far from Ashkelon. It was a comparatively small oil field, but by 1963, Eshkol's last year as Minister of Finance, it was producing 130,000 tons, or about ten percent of the country's requirements. Three years later 38 wells were yielding 200,000 tons a year, but proved reserves were slender; they could dry up by 1980. Still, an oil field near Ashkelon suggests that more oil may be found. In 1958, a field of natural gas was discovered at Rosh-Zahar, close to the Dead Sea. Its annual capacity was estimated at another 90,000 tons of oil equivalent; its life may be longer than that of the Heletz-Bror oil field.

In April 1957 the first flow of oil began through the new Eilat-Beersheba pipeline. This was a direct and quick consequence of the Sinai campaign of the year before and the freeing of the port of Eilat from Egyptian blockade. The Eilat pipeline became fully operational only in 1960, when oil from Iran was pumped all the way through to the Mediterranean and to all of Israel's main centers of population and industry. The importance of this cannot be exaggerated. Israel has come to look on Eilat as the key point on a lifeline, a lifeline to which Israel has every right. Ben-Gurion regarded the opening of the Gulf of Aqaba to normal traffic and the restoration to its role as an international waterway as the principal gain from the 1956 Sinai campaign. Eshkol would be forced to go to war with Egypt, 11 years later, because the Gulf had again been blocked and Eilat cut off from its natural and needed traffic.

In 1957 too the final stage of the draining of the Huleh swamps, in Israel's northeastern corner, was completed. That was a landmark in Israel's history. The drainage of the swamps was a test case in the development of a frontier area. Syria claimed that Israel was altering the character of the country by turning 15,000 acres of pestilential, malaria-breeding marshes into fertile farmland and fishponds. Eshkol never ceased to push this project ahead; it was self-evident to him that understanding between Israel and her Arab neighbors would not be promoted by reducing agricultural problems to nonsense. The completion of the drainage of the Huleh swamps was a reminder that Israel intended to build her economy sensibly and scientifically, and to give an example to the Arab world by doing so.

In April 1961 Eshkol launched the first five-year plan for the development of the rural areas inhabited by the Arab minority. Four out of five of the 200,000 Arabs living in Israel were either on the land or in small market towns. The five-year plan was intended to bring Arab living standards up to Israeli ones, or as near to them as possible. Farmers were to be given machinery, marketing facilities, and advice in the growing of crops. Arab villages were to receive all the basic amenities of a modern community—proper roads, electricity, running water, improved housing, and handicrafts to supplement an existence never much above subsistence. The five-year plan was a brilliant success. The living standards of the Arab minority in Israel were lifted far above those of communities in the rest of the Arab world. And the reorganization of Arab farming resulted in a useful reserve of labor being released for the needs of industry in Haifa and its environs.

In 1962 Eshkol attended the inauguration of the new town of Arad, in the northeastern Negev, when its first houses became officially habitable. This was a crucial step in the development of the southern half of the country. Arad is halfway from Beersheba to the Dead Sea and sits on a plateau 2700 feet above the Sea, with magnificent views across it to the mountains of Jordan. The intention is to make it an industrial center for the whole of the eastern Negev. It serves as the dormitory town for the Dead Sea Works, operating the potash fields of Sodom. Its climate is as good as Sodom's is oppressive, humid, and unbearably hot. In the immediate area of Arad are sizable deposits of phosphates, methane gas, gravel, and red marble. Within easy distance are phosphates at Oron and Ein Yahav and ball clay at Mitspe Ramon. Arad can become a center of tourism, too. The medium-term plan is to create a town of over 50,000, with a dozen hotels and more than two thousand beds for visitors.

While still Minister of Finance, Eshkol studied and approved three plans for regional settlement in addition to that of Lachish. The three areas marked out for planned development were Besor, close to the Gaza Strip, Korazim, to the north of the Sea of Galilee, and the Arava valley between the Dead Sea and the Gulf of Aqaba. These three plans will begin to take definite shape only about 1970, when regular settlements will begin taking the place of the establishments temporarily set up for pioneering pilot projects and surveying. A strikingly successful start has been made in the Arava, where salty, totally barren soil has been irrigated by storing water from winter rains, and is now producing forage grass for livestock and a wide range of vegetables. This pilot project, begun only in 1962, produced what one observer called "a miraculous transformation" in four years.[16] By then a settlement of 70 people had been established in what had been repellently bleak desert.*

Needless to say, Eshkol never lost sight of the problems of water supply while he was looking after the country's finances. He remained the head of the Mekorot water board. Eshkol strongly believed that Israel could not wait indefinitely for Arab countries to learn to see the virtues of Eric Johnston's plan for the joint Arab-Israeli utilization of the waters of the Jordan and Yarmuk. The Arab League's veto of the plan in 1955 meant that Israel and Jordan both decided in principle to go ahead with separate water projects. For Jordan this involved the damming of the Yarmuk a short way above its confluence with the Jordan, and the building of a canal running southward parallel to the river Jordan and just to the east of it. The Yarmuk's flow is 650 million cubic yards a year, as against the Jordan's 850 million cubic yards just to the north of the Sea of Galilee.†

Jordan went ahead with the utilization of the waters of the Yarmuk, without hindrance from Israel. But the Israeli planners had to give up their original project for building a dam and drawing water from the Jordan at Bnot Yakov, about 12 miles north of the Sea of Galilee. Bnot Yakov (Daughters of Jacob) is about 600 feet above the Sea and roughly at the level of the Mediterranean. There the Jordan's waters are sweeter than in the Sea itself, where there are underwater saline springs and where 190 million cubic yards of the Jordan's flow are lost by evaporation. But Bnot Yakov was on the fringe of a demilitarized zone. Syria protested against the building of a dam there, and the Israeli government decided to pump water directly from the Sea of Galilee at Eshed Kinrot on its northwest shore, and close to the place where Christ performed the miracle of the loaves and fishes.

The water conduit south was planned to extend to Eilabun in the Galileean hills, along the little rift valley of the Beit Netufa and then southwest to the outskirts of Tel Aviv. At Rosh Ha'ayin it was to be linked with the two Yarkon-Negev pipelines running on to the Negev. The main section of the conduit to Tel Aviv was in fact completed

* In the Arava, Israeli water conservationists experimented with piles of pebbles placed at regular intervals in straight lines, with no mud or sand between them. Pebbles heat up more quickly in the day and cool off more quickly at night than hard-packed soil. In the early morning the air close to the pebbles yields moisture, and dew trickles through into whatever catchment has been arranged. Desert nomads used this method more than 2000 years ago, and scientists estimate that a "dewfall" of 15 inches a year can be obtained in this way.[17]

† Jordan's use of the Yarmuk was also designed to produce local irrigation, some of it for Syrian use, and hydroelectric power from a plant built at the Maqarin Dam. By 1965 the first stage of the Ghor Canal was completed and 40,000 acres of land were being irrigated from it. This was one third of Jordan's total irrigated land.

by the middle of 1965, carrying 260 million cubic yards a year. The whole system, taking 410 million cubic yards a year from the Sea, was scheduled to be completed by the end of 1970. Sticking to the Johnston Plan estimates, Israel will otherwise take only 104 million cubic yards from the Jordan and Yarmuk for local use in Galilee.

Eshkol interested himself in every detail of the preliminary planning of the National Water Carrier, which he regarded as the future hub of Israel's water system. "My ambition, and indeed my intention, was to see a network of water pipes covering the whole country, like the veins of the human body."[18] As early as 1959 he boldly predicted that the Carrier could be completed in four years. He supervised the installation of the three electrically driven intake pumps at Eshed Kinrot, which lifted the water of Galilee 812 feet through a conduit 2350 yards long. At that point, high in the hills, the water enters a canal 11 and a half miles long and so flows into the Netufa storage reservoir from which it passes into the pipeline.[19] Eshkol was disappointed by the decision not to go ahead with the Bnot Yakov project. Another setback had been the discovery that there were saline springs under the Sea of Galilee, which it is hoped can be "caught" and diverted southwards towards the Dead Sea. "I looked on the National Water Carrier at first as a second-best," he told me.

> The ideal would have been a Middle East regional water plan taking in the Litani, the Euphrates, and the rivers of Syria as well as the Jordan and the Yarmuk. But we had to do our best on our own. At least we went further than the pioneers of water planning in the Middle East, like the American professor Walter Lowdermilk. They foresaw using water only locally for irrigation or drinking. We took it the length of our country, and we were justified in doing so. Our share of the Jordan's waters is ours to use as we see fit.[20]

This use of the waters of the Jordan by Israel was to lead to bitter controversy with neighboring Arab countries, Syria in particular. It was to be a contributory cause of the 1967 war, after Syria had encouraged plans to divert the Jordan's headwaters and starve Israel of the water which she needed.

Eshkol suffered a major personal loss during his term in the Finance Ministry. In 1959 his second wife died of cancer. It was typical of both Eshkol and his wife that they bore alone the burden of knowing that her disease was incurable. Her visits to the hospital were passed off as being of no particular importance, with mild jokes about the body's becoming rebellious when it grows old. To his daughter Dvora, working in the United States, Eshkol wrote, "If it's not too inconvenient for you, try to come home for a vacation, as your mother has been missing you and would like to see you soon." Dvora knew at once that her mother must be seriously ill and made arrangements for getting back to Jerusalem.[21]

Elisheva Eshkol's death was a great shock to her husband. She had borne him three daughters, and although he would have dearly loved to have had a son, he never spoke of the matter. Their marriage had been ideally happy, for they shared the same hopes and beliefs. Like her husband, Elisheva was the best kind of humanitarian socialist, with a deeply rooted determination to help the underdog. She was a good and efficient housewife and a much loved mother; she was especially at home at the Degania B kibbutz. Like her husband she was a compulsive worker, but that does not seem to have interfered with the easy gaiety of their private lives, even in the darkest days of the Mandate and the most desperate moments of the War of Independence. Eshkol, again typically, went back to work as soon as his wife was buried, as normally and practically as he could.

1. Zvi Dinstein, in personal conversation with the author.
2. Ben Avital, an official of the Foreign Ministry, in personal conversation with the author.
3. Ben Avital, in personal conversation with the author.
4. Mrs. Lisbona, in personal conversation with the author.
5. Zvi Dinstein, in personal conversation with the author.
6. Eshkol, in personal conversation with the author.
7. Richard Hiscocks, *Democracy in West Germany*, p. 52.
8. Moshe Pearlman, *Ben-Gurion Looks Back*, p. 162.
9. *Ibid*, p. 169.
10. Terence Prittie, *Israel: Miracle in the Desert*, p. 196.
11. Eshkol, in personal conversation with the author.
12. David Horowitz, *The Development of the Economy of Israel*. Pamphlet published 1965.
13. *Ibid*.
14. *Ibid*.
15. Shimon Horn, an Israeli businessman.
16. Ruth Halliday, *The Shells to make the Desert Bloom*. Pamphlet of Anglo-Israeli Association, 1966, p. 29.
17. Leonard Carter, *A World Geography of Irrigation*, p. 59.
18. Eshkol, in personal conversation with the author.
19. Carter, *op. cit.*, gives full details.
20. Eshkol, in personal conversation with the author.
21. Dvora Eshkol Rafaeli, in personal conversation with the author.

13.

When the new state of Israel was founded in 1948 there were, broadly speaking, three major political philosophies in it. The principal one, owing much to the Russian and Polish immigrants of the Second and Third Aliyahs, was socialist. The second was religious, taking the form of political parties that pressed for large, even dominant, religious content in Israel's political life. The third was secular, nonsocialist, and less distinctive than the other two.

When the first elections to an Israeli Parliament, the Knesset, took place in January 1949, there was nothing approaching unity within any one of these three political groups. The religious parties were most closely unified; the National Religious Party, *Agudat Israel,* and *Poalei Agudat Israel,* although they remained distinct from one another, were able to submit a joint list of candidates campaigning within a United Religious Front. The socialists were split between Mapai, the majority group to which Eshkol belonged, Mapam, and Achdut Ha'avoda. The two smaller parties submitted a joint list.

The most important elements of the third, nonsocialist grouping were the Herut, or Conservative, party and two liberal parties. There were a dozen smaller parties, none of which was ever to play a significant part in Israeli politics.

Eshkol had been a socialist from his earliest days in Palestine. He believed in secular, socialist government as the only answer for a people which had been persistently bullied and persecuted. It was natural that the Jews of Russia and Poland should have been unreservedly on the side of political progress, equally natural that they tended to see progress in terms of socialist ideals and democratic principles. Obviously, there were exceptions to this rule. Deeply religious Jews disliked all secular government, while the creation of a Jewish middle class in Palestine pushed towards private initiative and a capitalist form of society. Hitler's early persecution of the Jews in Germany and Austria resulted in a chiefly middle-class exodus, while the mass immigration after the war of the Jews from African and Asian countries brought an influx of people with no first-hand knowledge whatever of democratic government.

Jewish individualism resulted in a degree of political fragmentation. The socialist grouping is a case in point.

Mapai, Mapam, and Achdut Ha'avoda all believed in very much the same social ideals. They all supported the idea of a planned economy. They agreed on the principal national aims—the ingathering of the Jewish people, the reclamation of the land of Israel, the achievement of peace with the Arab world, the strengthening of the Jewish community in Israel by every possible means. In view of the huge tasks which confronted the young state and the threatening challenge of Arab hostility the need for socialist unity did exist.

Achdut Ha'avoda split from Mapai in 1944. Mapam was formed as an independent party in 1948. The two remained aligned for only the first two Parliamentary elections, in 1949 and 1951. At the third, in 1955, they campaigned separately. Both of them stood to the left of Mapai and preached "pure" Marxism, which had far less in common with Russian Communism than its supporters supposed. Both parties laid a heavy emphasis on working-class rights and interests and were not disposed, as the Mapai leaders were, to compromise with capitalism in evolving a national policy. Both parties were strong in the kibbutzim, whose members sometimes carried socialist dogma to extreme lengths. Both, particularly Mapam, believed in a neutral foreign policy between East and West; indeed, Mapam's leadership professed an affection for the Soviet Union based partly on ideology and partly on sentiment. Soviet Communism, after all, had liberated the masses of Russian, including millions of Jews, from Tsarist tyranny. This, at least, was a tenable theory. Attachment to the Soviet Union was further encouraged by that country's ready and immediate recognition of the new State of Israel. Both Mapam and Achdut Ha'avoda believed that the great powers would not extend their quarrels to the restless, potentially explosive Middle East. They were to be bitterly disappointed in this, as in others of their somewhat starry-eyed hopes.

Eshkol's own nature was such that he was always certain to remain a pillar of Mapai. He believed in giving every man his due and in political compromise as a means to that end. This meant that although he was a convinced and dedicated socialist, he was automatically opposed to some of the tenets of Marxist philosophy. Marx believed in a monolithic form of society; Eshkol believed that social diversity had to be accepted. Marx believed in class struggle and in total victory of the proletariat; Eshkol believed in the Jews, of every political persuasion, living free lives in a Jewish state. The idea of class warfare, directed against fellow Jews, was alien to him. In my conversations with Eshkol, I was struck most by his humanity, by his respect for the feelings and the opinions of the individual, even if they were not the same as his own. To Eshkol, what mattered most, in the internal political sense, was to help create a real community, a community not founded on class warfare and class hatred.

As a man of compromise, Eshkol was always on the side of socialist unity. He thought that it was attainable as well as desirable. He made no personal enemies in Mapam and Achdut Ha'avoda. To him this would have been merely foolish; the people of those parties were as much "his" people as the most fervent Mapai supporters. Their eventual return to the fold, he believed, would help to consolidate a socialist movement in which idealism and practical experience would be properly blended. He believed, at least in my opinion, that the best kind of socialism is one that regards every citizen as its charge.

The history of Israel's parties is enthralling only in a mathematical sense. Parties prospered and declined, moved into alignment with one another and out again, contributing to a complex and changing kaleidoscope. Thus, the National Religious bloc was maintained for the life of only one Parliament; the National Religious Party then split from its two junior partners. They put forth a joint list until 1959, then parted company. The two liberal parties, the General Zionists and the Progressives, produced a joint list until 1959, then merged to form a single Liberal Party. Mapam and Achdut Ha'avoda kept a joint list only until 1951, then separated. During the first 12 years of Israel's existence only Mapai and Herut kept their independence and identity unchanged.

During these 12 years, too, Mapai's vote remained almost constant, never below 32 percent of the poll and never above 39 percent. In the first five Knessets, Mapai, therefore, never held less than 40 seats and never more than 47. It was the leading party in every government coalition, giving continuity to Israeli politics. Mapai has given the country a modified welfare state, in which citizens have still been encouraged to develop private initiative and pioneering spirit. Mapai's strength has lain in the reasoning and enlightened socialism of a large section of the electorate, in its close connection with the Histadrut—in which there has been a Mapai majority for almost the whole of the last 20 years—and in ability to form and lead governments based on compromise.

Compromise, of course, had its cost. It affected social and especially social-religious matters. The Knesset has 120 members; Mapai generally needed about 30 supporters from other parties in order to govern with a convincing mandate. It turned first to other socialist parties; but all-socialist coalitions would never have had much more than 60 seats in parliament. Mapai mustered some support among the quarter of a million Arab minority, but the party had to find support among the religious groups, too, or get it from the liberals. Every Israeli government could be said, in some sense, to have been a government of national emergency. It was generally politic, therefore, to form as broadly based a coalition as possible and take in both religious and liberal groups.

The religious parties have gladly entered coalition governments, since they regarded themselves as responsible for maintaining religion in the life of the country and required some measure of political power in order to be able to do so. Perhaps it has been an advantage that the religious parties have had a share of political responsibility, averting even greater friction than has occurred between the deeply religious and the less, or even nonreligious members of the community. But friction there has been, sometimes of a violent nature, while efforts to obtain some religious reforms and bring religion more into line with the ethos of a modern state have been sidetracked. Governments which have depended on the support of religious parties have, perhaps unwillingly, left the relations between religious and secular authorities alone.

Religious extremists have been especially active in Jerusalem, which they regard as their capital and even as their own domain. The Mea Shearim quarter is a sanctuary of the Orthodox, and the Sabbath is kept by them as a totally holy day. The barriers which are set up on all roads leading into Mea Shearim on the eve of the Sabbath are evidence of this determination to maintain tradition, and the presence of one or more policemen at each barrier is a reminder that the inhabitants of Mea Shearim are very ready to use force to discourage a motorist or even a noisy or flamboyantly dressed pedestrian. The Orthodox have not always confined their rules to their own quarter; they have sallied out into other parts of the city, protesting against Sabbath motoring, sporting events, and the use of clubs and swimming pools by men and women together. There has been rioting and fighting on many occasions, and demonstrations in which the Orthodox lie down in rows on main streets to stop all traffic.*

The behavior of the Orthodox of Mea Shearim is, of course, an extreme example of religious intolerance. There has been no parallel to it in any city outside Jerusalem. Governments have tried to find some compromise, for instance banning public transport on the Sabbath, but allowing private motorists complete freedom to go where they will, maintaining the dietary laws of kosher in all public eating places but not forcing them on the individual citizen, and allowing the modification of the law of *Shemittah,* under which all land must lie fallow every seventh year. The attitude of successive governments has been determined by the desire not to cause or widen a rift between the different peoples of Israel.

But this attitude is being increasingly denounced by people who are neither Orthodox nor atheists, who feel that government has avoided the real issue, the careful reform of religious law in order to weld a more cohesive and, quite possibly, more rationally religious community. These moderate reformers believe that matters of personal status should be taken out of the hands of the rabbinate and entrusted to civil authorities, as they are elsewhere in the world. They ask why the rabbinate should have sole jurisdiction over marriage and divorce. Sometimes this leads to ridiculous, even tragic, situations. In 1968, for instance, a Yemenite Jew was serving a prison sentence, which could be indefinitely prolonged, for beating his wife. The rabbinate had decreed that he should be divorced for his crime. The man refused to

* In October 1963 members of the Neturei Karta sect (Guardians of the City) attacked the police with shouts of "Nazis!" and "Gestapo!," and in the next year tourists were mobbed and stoned on the outskirts of Mea Shearim.

be divorced or to accept the jurisdiction of the rabbinate. A civil court sent him to jail, giving him the option of accepting the divorce after each three month period. He still refused; by the end of 1968 he had been in jail five years.

Reformers point out that the rabbinate has refused to allow men and women to pray together at the Wailing Wall, which fell into Israeli hands during the Six-Day War of June 1967. Men and women are separated in the synagogue, and the Wailing Wall is the holiest of all Jewish holy places. The reformers did not dare to send men and women to pray together at the Wall; they realized that this would cause bloodshed. Instead, they petitioned the government, and were told that they could press their demand if they could secure sufficient political support. The Government, in fact, would not intervene in the field of religion, in conformity with what has become standard policy—to yield to the religious parties on religious matters, just as long as the religious parties give way on political issues. No government will quickly forget that it was a religious question, the religious education of immigrant children, which broke up the first Israeli government in 1951.

There are other examples of religious intolerance. For example, in the winter of 1967–1968 there was a snowfall in Jerusalem. The Ministry of Labor allowed emergency work on the Sabbath, to help freezing householders. There were angry demonstrations by the Orthodox, and the police were forced to intervene between them and a crowd of others who were defending the workmen.

Perhaps the Orthodox were trying to create trouble in order to give a reminder of their readiness to cause civil disturbance—just in case an all-socialist government comes to power at the end of 1969 and the religious parties, for the first time, are not part of a coalition. Equally, the Orthodox may believe that the force of religious example is the most important guarantor of Jewish survival. This could be true if the State of Israel were one day to be overwhelmed by its Arab neighbors, or even if it were a part of a Middle Eastern, predominantly Arab, confederation and began to lose its identity.

The break-up of the government coalition in 1951 was Israel's first internal political crisis. A second crisis seemed to be in the cards when Ben-Gurion decided to retire from active politics in 1953. Ben-Gurion had played so great a part in founding the State of Israel that his withdrawal came as a real shock to many Israelis. He announced that he was suffering from spiritual fatigue, resigned in November 1953, and retired to the newly founded kibbutz of Sde Boker in the Negev. He thought that the time had come to hand the government over to younger men. Moshe Sharett succeeded him, but invited him back as Minister of Defense early in 1955. Not only did Ben-Gurion agree to take this post, but he ran once more for the post of Prime Minister in the late summer of 1955 and returned to that office after the elections. It is significant that his retirement led to a reduction of Mapai's vote to its lowest figure of the whole post-1948 period, 32 percent.

In 1954, while Ben-Gurion was happily leading the life of a farm laborer in the Negev, Mapam and Achdut Ha'avoda split. They campaigned separately in the 1955 elections. An event took place in the same year which, while causing surprisingly little comment at the time, was destined in the long run to alter the whole face of Israeli politics. This was the opening move in the so–called "Lavon Affair," usually known more simply as "the Affair," a tortuous episode which could not be said to be finally closed even 15 years later. Eshkol became personally and deeply involved in "the Affair"; in fact, it was to be instrumental in shaping his political career.

In 1954 Pinhas Lavon was Minister of Defense. He was 50 years old, a man of great probity, a pillar of Mapai, lacking some flexibility of mind, perhaps even, as his critics would have it, opinionated. Lavon knew little about defense problems when he was appointed Minister. It is perfectly possible that he had been chosen as a good "party man," whose ignorance would insure that he carried out defense policies which the Prime Minister himself would formulate. In any event, Lavon quickly fell afoul of the Israeli Chief of Staff, General Moshe Dayan, to whom he must have appeared a most unsuitable choice as Minister of Defense. Dayan has native-born, Israeli pragmatism and is ready to look at every problem objectively; Lavon, to him, was a bureaucrat, a part of a political machine, and an awkward customer to deal with.

Early in 1954 Israeli military intelligence appears to have hatched an extraordinary plan which was never submitted to the government for approval, and certainly not to the operative Minister, Lavon. This plan was to explode bombs in Cairo which would at the very least indicate Egyptian internal instability and which might even lead the U.S. and Britain to suspect a growing Egyptian terrorism directed against them and their nationals. If that really were the plan of Israeli military intelligence, and this has still not been proven beyond a doubt, then it was a classic example of *agent provocateur* techniques.[1]

Implicated in the plot were Avraham Dar, an Israeli intelligence officer who had been sent to Egypt as early as 1951 to work as an undercover agent, and Colonel Benjamin Givli, Chief of Military Intelligence in 1954. Dar had organized a network of agents, some of them Egyptian, and had been joined by a second Israeli officer, Paul Frank, at the beginning of 1954. About May 1954 Colonel Givli gave Dar the signal to proceed with the planned bombing in Cairo.

The bombs were home-made incendiary concoctions with their chemicals stuffed into rubber condoms. Three were exploded on July

14, 1954. One caused a big bang on a bookshelf in the library of the United States Information Service. A second injured a schoolboy. The third, and most successful, just managed to set fire to a mailbox.

Whatever the plan was, it did not pay off. The Egyptian police acted with a precision which had never distinguished the Egyptian army. They quickly arrested 11 Jewish agents. Dar and Frank got away. There was no publicity, in either Egypt or Israel. Egypt did not want to endanger its own stability; Israel hardly wanted to publicize a plot which had miscarried.

On July 16 a conference took place at the Ministry of Defense in Tel Aviv. Lavon and Givli were present, and it appears that the latter sought Lavon's approval for an operation which had already taken place and had failed.[2] If this is what happened, Givli was guilty of an act of gross deception. He compounded this deception, first by informing General Dayan, three days later, on July 19, that Lavon had given him permission to go ahead, and then by telling Lavon on July 26 that the operation had failed. But Lavon claimed that he had never given his permission on July 16.

Dayan had been informed while in Washington. He returned early in August and instituted an immediate investigation of the affair. The Prime Minister, Moshe Sharett, had been informed of some of the circumstances but was not satisfied with the available evidence concerning the organization of the plot. He ordered an official inquiry, and appointed Chief Justice Olshan and the former Chief of Staff, Yakov Dori, to carry it out.

On November 12 the Egyptian Government published a detailed indictment of the 13 accused, including Dar and Frank, who had left the country. The Egyptian press linked the Israeli plot with an attempt made on October 26 by the Moslem Brotherhood to assassinate President Nasser. This attempt led to the trial of a number of Moslem Brotherhood leaders, and on December 9 six of them were sentenced to death and others to long terms of imprisonment. The trial of the 11 Jewish prisoners had already opened, on December 7. It ended on January 27, 1955. Two of the accused were sentenced to death and were executed four days later. The rest received prison sentences varying from two years to life.

Olshan and Dori had meanwhile failed to establish how the bomb plot had been planned and on whose authority. They reported only that they had not been convinced "beyond reasonable doubt"[3] that Lavon had authorized Givli to carry out the operation. Their failure probably owed much to the evasiveness of Colonel Givli, to the intractability of Defense Minister Lavon, and to the distrust of him in his own Ministry as well as in the army. Their failure certainly was crucial; it led to a crisis in the Ministry, where Lavon asked for the dismissal of his director-general, Shimon Peres, and to a severe shock to morale in the higher echelons of the Army. The immediate result was the restoration to the Ministry of Defense of Ben-Gurion, the one man who was felt to be capable of restoring confidence. He came back from the Sde Boker kibbutz unwillingly, and declined Sharett's offer of the post of Prime Minister. His first action was to transfer Colonel Givli from army intelligence to a field command. Lavon had already taken the course of resigning, although protesting his complete innocence of any part in the misguided and miscarried bomb plot.

The matter should have ended there. If the Ministry of Defense had wanted to get to the bottom of the affair, it could have instituted its own private inquiry. Lavon became Secretary-General of the Histadrut within a few months, and was apparently satisfied with what is one of the most influential positions in the country. But the Lavon Affair came to life again in 1959, when Paul Frank, one of the two agents who had escaped from Egypt, was brought back to Israel. Frank, it turned out, had been a double agent. He had almost certainly informed the Egyptian authorities about the other plotters in 1954, which explained the speed with which they had been rounded up. At his trial, Frank accused two officers of falsifying evidence in 1954 in order to place the blame on Lavon. At almost the same time Lavon was told by an Intelligence officer that secret files had been tampered with for this same purpose.

In April 1960 Lavon decided to reopen "the Affair." He wanted to rehabilitate himself completely and he believed that he now had enough material to do so. Accordingly, he sent a memorandum to Ben-Gurion, who was once more Prime Minister. The latter appointed a committee of investigation headed by Chief Justice Haim Cohen. This was not exactly what Lavon had expected; he had thought that the new evidence was quite sufficient to warrant his rehabilitation. Instead, all the circumstances of the Affair were to be sifted afresh, and he was likely to be left out in the cold.

This was, in effect, what happened. Ben-Gurion restricted the Cohen committee's terms of reference to the question of the reliability of the Army officers who had been involved in the Affair. The unreliability of at least a few of them was clearly proved, for the inquiry revealed that the July 1954 bomb plot had been in preparation since the end of May. Some of the operative facts of the Affair were established, and Ben-Gurion drew, doubtless, the appropriate conclusions. But he was concerned primarily with the Army and the efficiency of its intelligence service; he refused to rehabilitate Lavon on the grounds that his resignation, indicating his unfitness for the post of Minister of Defense, had been accepted by Sharett, not by himself.

Lavon, understandably, was furious. A judicial investigation had concentrated on internal Army matters and had made no attempt to clear his name. However, surprisingly, Lavon refused a government probe when Ben-Gurion suggested it in September 1960. Ben-Gurion was by now behaving erratically. On October 2, 1960, one of his Ministers, Barzilai, proposed the appointment of a Cabinet committee. Ben-Gurion flatly refused, declared there was nothing to investigate, and would not allow the Cabinet to vote on the proposal.

The Affair was now assuming menacing political proportions. Political and public opinion was split between Lavon and Ben-Gurion. The major contention in favor of Lavon was that, if innocent, he had a right to be rehabilitated. On behalf of Ben-Gurion, the more obscure argument was put forward that this was a security matter and that it was, therefore, not in the public interest to delve any further into it.

What was unknown at the time to the public, or to most politicians, was that the Attorney General, Gideon Hausner, had called on Ben-Gurion at his home and had pointed out that the politically paramount conclusion which could be drawn from the Cohen committee findings was that Lavon had been in no way responsible for the 1954 bomb plot.

The Affair now entered its strangest phase. Influenced by some of his friends. Lavon decided to forego his demand for complete public rehabilitation. This followed a public statement by Sharett that the new evidence showed Lavon had been falsely accused in the first place. Lavon decided that this was sufficient to soothe his pride and clear his name.

But Ben-Gurion's interest was suddenly reawakened. He advised Colonel Givli to demand a fresh investigation, and made it clear that he would support such a demand. This was an extraordinary about-face, which has never been fully explained. It seems inconceivable that he thought that more should be done to exonerate Lavon, and he could scarcely have thought that a new investigation would benefit Army intelligence. The Cabinet decided on October 30, 1960, to appoint a ministerial committee of seven, headed by the Minister of Justice, Pinhas Rosen. Ben-Gurion had already voiced his preference for an independent judicial committee, but at this Cabinet meeting he neither pressed for it nor opposed the creation of the ministerial committee. In fact, he abstained from voting, in order to retain the right to reservations about the procedure being adopted.

The ministerial committee spent two months on the Affair. It found that Lavon had not given the order to launch a bomb plot in Cairo. It found "reasonable grounds" for believing that a high-ranking officer had faked evidence in order to incriminate Lavon. The report was endorsed by the Cabinet, with four members abstaining. One of them was Ben-Gurion, who refused to have anything to do with the report. On January 19, 1961, he wrote to Pinhas Rosen: "After acceptance of the conclusions of the Committee of Seven, I firmly decided not to deal any further with this matter but to make my views public. And, having done this, I shall not deal with the matter any longer. The Government, as far as I am concerned, has a free hand to act or to refrain from acting in this matter, and I shall not intervene, for or against." His letter was read to the Cabinet by Rosen on January 22.

Nine days later Ben-Gurion resigned. His action, according to all accounts, came as a bolt from the blue. No one had thought about his resignation, let alone asked for it. His letter to Rosen suggested that he was at last prepared to let the Lavon Affair drop. According to one of Lavon's friends, Professor Arieli, he resigned "because he would not brook the opposition of his own Cabinet, because he would not accept the decision of the ministerial committee, and because he had formed a violent antipathy to Lavon and would not sit in the Knesset with him."[4]

Ben-Gurion revealed his objection to the very existence of the ministerial committee's investigation—it was that to which he objected rather than its findings. Pinhas Rosen remembers this very well. "I directed the committee in its work absolutely honestly and straightforwardly," he told me. "Its members set out to establish the truth about Lavon. We sifted the evidence thoroughly and we formed conclusions which we knew were right."[5]

The curious thing was that Ben-Gurion's main personal resentment was directed against Eshkol, his own trusted lieutenant. Eshkol had little to do with the Affair during its early stages. When Ben-Gurion demanded the appointment of a new investigating committee in October 1960, Eshkol was far from enthusiastic. His private opinion was that the Affair should be regarded as dead and buried, and that no more dirty linen should be washed in public. But Eshkol had always been a man of compromise. Rosen had been the first to propose a ministerial committee; Eshkol took the idea up and discussed it with party leaders. He found a broad degree of agreement among them, and so played a leading part at the Cabinet meeting of October 30, 1960, which approved the formation of the committee. On the next day he had a talk with Ben-Gurion on the purely technical question of whether five or seven should serve on the committee. Ben-Gurion was at first in favor of only five but withdrew his opposition. Eshkol maintained that Ben-Gurion subsequently wished him and the committee (Eshkol was one of its members) "good luck" on more than one occasion.[6]

Indeed, Ben-Gurion seems to have been at pains to conceal his furious resentment against Eshkol at this time. He had one good reason; he had decided to pursue his campaign against Lavon in another theater, that of Mapai, the principal socialist party. Ironically, he turned to Eshkol for support; even more ironically, he got it. On February 4 Eshkol spoke at the party conference in favor of party unity. The inference was plain; Lavon should be sacrificed in the interests of that unity. The party voted 159 to 96 for Lavon's dismissal from the post of Secretary-General of the Histadrut. Lavon accepted its verdict and went into retirement. His small group of followers, mainly intellectuals, were to leave political life too, but much later. Ben-Gurion, mollified, returned as Prime Minister, to serve with those same Ministers who had comprised the Committee of Seven and whose activities he had denounced—yet another extraordinary about-face.

Eshkol's main preoccupation had been party unity. He risked a total break with the Lavon group. But this was of minor importance compared to the danger of Ben-Gurion's splitting Mapai down the middle. Lavon had a small group of followers; Ben-Gurion was still the leader of the nation and its prophet. In the early stages of the Affair, which caused Israel's one and only major internal political crisis, it became clear that there was a growing dissatisfaction with the establishment, the caucus of Mapai and the Histadrut, and that this dissatisfaction could easily focus on the one great individualist with a national following. Men like Dayan and Peres were prepared to exploit the crisis in what they believed to be the national interest; that meant following Ben-Gurion against his party.

Eshkol was so keenly aware of this that he backed Ben-Gurion against Lavon within the Mapai party. He did not intend to be Machiavellian, only practical. It looked, initially, as if he had succeeded. The 1961 election campaign was fought on practical lines, and Mapai's concern was to instigate a withdrawal from the Affair. Ben-Gurion collaborated fully; as soon as the elections were over, he agreed to head a new coalition government. Early setbacks led him to give Eshkol the task of negotiating with the parties on his behalf, which could be interpreted as either a mark of complete confidence in his lieutenant or a somewhat shameless use of his talents as a negotiator. The new government was formed, and Ben-Gurion said nothing in his inaugural address to the Knesset about the Affair. Once again, it appeared to be buried.

Nothing of the sort. Ben-Gurion was still dissatisfied. He next asked a journalist on the staff of the newspaper *Davar,* Haggai Eshed, to carry out a complete survey of all available material on the Lavon Affair. At the same time he engaged two lawyers to look into the legal aspects of the case. It was a big task, and it took time. In October 1964 Ben-Gurion passed on a 500-page dossier to the Minister of Justice, Dov Joseph. His purpose was to obtain an opinion from the Attorney General, and this opinion was given to the Cabinet on December 6, 1964, and published on December 8. It amounted to a detailed criticism of almost every aspect of the handling of the Affair and, in particular, of the work of the Ministerial Committee of Seven, Ben-Gurion's archenemy. The Attorney General's summing-up was, of course, based on a compendium of evidence which had been amassed with a partisan aim. The dossier was Ben-Gurion's testament of personal vindication.

Long before it had been produced for analysis by the Attorney General, the seed sowed with the stormy winds of the Lavon Affair had reaped a political whirlwind. Ben-Gurion resigned, for the third and last time, on June 16, 1963, two days after receiving Haggai Eshed's report. He proposed Eshkol as his successor, and told him, curtly, to stop "being a compromiser."[8] The Grand Old Man of Israeli politics was to go, even though this was not his intention, into the political wilderness. Eshkol was jockeyed, almost against his will, into the Premiership. Israeli public confidence was given a terrible jolt, and the majority Mapai party was allowed a breathing space of only a few months to contemplate the prospect of a bitter feud between its long-established leader, Ben-Gurion, and the man whom he had thrust almost contemptuously into his place, presumably believing that he could be as easily cast out again.

Ben-Gurion's retirement had many consequences. Lavon's followers dropped out of politics during the next year and a half, not because of Ben-Gurion's deadly hostility but because it became clear that Eshkol was not going to restore Lavon to high office. Once again, Eshkol's reason was plain; Lavon had become the symbol of discord, and socialist unity could be held to matter more than the career of any individual. Eshkol's view was that there was nothing dishonorable in this position, just as there had been nothing dishonorable about asking Lavon to resign from his Histadrut post. To ask a sacrifice, Eshkol maintained, was very different from the "excommunication and boycott" threatened by a Ben-Gurion, who said he would not "sit under the same roof" with him.[8]

The second result of Ben-Gurion's resignation was that, believing that he now had a completely free hand, he made it plain at the end of 1964 that he wanted the whole, tortuous Affair reopened. As if Israeli politics in general, and Israeli socialism in particular, had not already suffered enough from it! It does appear that Ben-Gurion had developed what Oscar Wilde would have called "the enthusiasm of the short-sighted detective"; he was evidently determined to hunt down Lavon, although his apologists have since claimed that his real purpose was the high-minded one of vindicating the independence of the judiciary.

Eshkol considered that the issue had now been transposed into a matter of confidence in him personally. He therefore offered his resignation on December 14, 1964. Indeed, according to his own account, Ben-Gurion urged his resignation on the grounds that Eshkol no longer represented him, Ben-Gurion!

The Mapai Central Committee refused to let Eshkol go. Its members had to choose, then and there, between a man who had resigned in a mood of furious frustration, and a successor who resigned simply and straightforwardly on a question of confidence. A leader and prophet had become obsessed with a complex problem which he believed concerned him in the most personal way of all; it involved his historical image. Ben-Gurion was already a major part of the history of the amazingly gallant achievement of the State of Israel. He refused to accept a very minor reverse. Eshkol, who was nothing more than Ben-Gurion's lieutenant, resigned out of reasons of probity and common sense. The members of the Mapai Central Committee decided that they wanted good government to continue; Eshkol, even if he appeared to lack charisma, was the man to do it. He was reinstated as Prime Minister.

Ben-Gurion's resignation in June 1963 brought a third development, as it happened the most important one of all. This was his own withdrawal from Mapai in the summer of 1965 and his creation of a splinter socialist party called Rafi, or the Israel Labor List. He left Mapai, one has to suppose, very largely because he had failed to get his way over the Lavon Affair. The only obviously new plank in the new party's program was electoral reform; Ben-Gurion wanted something closer to the British system of direct vote and direct representation. There is something beautifully, Jewishly, paradoxical about his fervent sponsorship of a measure of electoral reform which would have swept his own splinter party out of existence. The full story of the Rafi break-away belongs to a later chapter, one in which Eshkol was in undisputed control of the nation's destinies.

It is almost in the nature of a footnote to remark that Pinhas Lavon, the man around whose prickly person the whole controversy had raged, simply disappeared from public life. Little sympathy was offered him, although his name had been besmirched every time a new inquiry was opened, and his immensely promising political career had been prematurely ended.*

One voice which was raised in Ben-Gurion's defense was that of the editor of the *Jewish Observer and Middle East Review,* Jon Kimche. In his weekly, published in London, Kimche argued that Ben-Gurion had two purposes in his efforts to reopen the Lavon Affair. One was to insure that "the supremacy of the law, untarnished by political considerations, should be made absolute."9 The other was "to have it publicly and incontrovertibly stated by Israel's highest judicial authority that neither Ben-Gurion, Dayan, nor Peres had any responsibility for any aspect of the mishap." Kimche was convinced that Ben-Gurion had no political motive, such as ousting Eshkol from office, but that he wished to prove that the ministerial committee had been in error and that it had been wrong to appoint such a committee at all.

In Eshkol's view, however,

* Lavon reappeared on television on December 10, 1968, when he urged unilateral Israeli military withdrawal from occupied territories, without waiting for any peace agreement with the Arabs.

The truth is that the principle of the separation of powers, about which one hears so much, does not apply at all in the present case. There is no room here for a resignation over the violation of a principle, because no principle has been violated. The rule calls for the separation of the administrative and investigatory bodies on the one hand, and the courts of law on the other. It is the courts of law alone which comprise an independent judiciary; and the State of Israel can be proud of them.

But an investigating committee appointed by the government is part of the *executive* branch. It has no judicial powers; it hands down no verdicts; it does not acquit or convict in the legal sense, and it is not empowered to sentence or punish.[10]

On balance, Eshkol's argument that a Cabinet committee was the appropriate body to look into the controversy over a Cabinet minister, Lavon, was probably more convincing than Ben-Gurion's demand for an independent judicial inquiry.

At the very least, differences of opinion over the composition of the committee should never have been allowed to provoke a major political crisis and split the Mapai party. Responsibility for this must rest primarily on Ben-Gurion.

Eshkol outlined his reasons for deciding, ultimately, that the Lavon Affair should not be reopened.[11] It had already been exhaustively examined. There had been a further time lag which would make fresh inquiry more difficult than before. None of the principals in the matter had any further interest in an investigation. Security matters had already been sufficiently discussed in public; this is not always in the public interest. Finally, although Eshkol did not mention this, political feelings had been severely shaken and a further inquiry could have only a disruptive effect on the majority Mapai socialist party.

Eshkol used to speak of the "unbearable heartache" which the Affair had caused him. It had been a stern test of his personal and political fortitude. It resulted in his becoming Prime Minister, a position which he had not sought. In addition, he had to take over the leadership of the country, not with the blessing of the man whom he had served and revered, but in face of his bitter personal opposition. It is never easy for a man of modest, if firm political stature, to take over from a political giant. Sympathy was lavished on Harry Truman when he succeeded Roosevelt, and on Anthony Eden when he succeeded Churchill. But the first took over when his predecessor died, and the second with his predecessor's full approval. Eshkol's position vis-à-vis Ben-Gurion was parallel to that of Ludwig Erhard's vis-à-vis Konrad Adenauer in West Germany. And Adenauer's personal rancor played a major part in Erhard's eventual political fall.

The Lavon Affair was a traumatic experience for Eshkol, but at the same time a highly formative one. His political staying power was put to an extreme test and he survived it. This is one reason why I have had to describe the State of Israel's biggest internal political crisis, a muddled and in part sordid affair, at such length. I have asked men of independent views how they feel Eshkol came through this crisis.

Gershon Sack, one of the elder statesmen of Mapai, felt that in the Lavon Affair Eshkol never ceased trying to secure a decent compromise in the interests of his political party. Sack saw the issue as being complicated by the fact that Ben-Gurion had never cared for Lavon and may even have regarded him as a potential rival; "there had been 40 years of friction between the two of them."

Yigal Allon, who was Eshkol's Deputy Prime Minister, did not commit himself over details of the Lavon Affair. But he felt that Eshkol's motive was always to find a consensus; this, to him, was the best way of serving the community. Allon saw Eshkol, too, as an essentially practical politician. Thus Ben-Gurion used to proclaim before the Sinai campaign that it "did not matter what a Gentile says, but what a Jew does." But Ben-Gurion waited for British and French military help and withdrew from Sinai without consolidating Israel's military victory. Ben-Gurion, again, talked for 30 years about socialist unity and succeeded only in splitting the socialist movement twice.

Pinhas Rosen, who led the Ministerial committee which excited Ben-Gurion's anger, is retrospectively certain that Eshkol never sought to influence the committee. He was "a loyal and valuable member of the committee, that was all."

Most important of all is the opinion of Professor Arieli, who might have been expected to be very critical of Eshkol, as he was a friend of Lavon. Arieli told me that Eshkol was utterly unbiased and interested only in getting at the essential facts; "he did not want the broad issues to be buried beneath a mass of detail." Eshkol's chief object, Arieli thought, was to heal the dangerous divisions in the party and the government. He operated pragmatically, remained strictly practical.

By any standards, the Lavon Affair was a wretchedly and barrenly unproductive episode in Israel's short history. Without his ever having worked to that end, it brought Levi Eshkol to power as Prime Minister in June 1963. His own hope, expressed openly and often, was that posterity would look at the Lavon Affair with an unjaundiced eye and would judge him, on the whole, to have done his best, with a clear conscience. His hope will be realized.

1. E. A. Bayne, "The Lavon Affair," in *Jewish Observer & Middle East Review*, Dec. 18, 1964.
2. *Ibid.*
3. *Ibid.*
4. Professor Arieli, in personal conversation with the author.

5. Pinhas Rosen, in personal conversation with the author.
6. Eshkol, in personal conversation with the author.
7. Eshkol, in personal conversation with the author.
8. Eshkol's words, in quotation marks, as transmitted to the author.
9. *Jewish Observer & Middle East Review*, Jan. 15, 1965.
10. Eshkol, in a letter to a friend, Schimel Dayan, dated August 10, 1966.
11. *Ibid.*

14.

Eshkol's first task in June 1963 was to form a new government. His experience fitted him admirably to govern his country. He knew every corner of it, and an astonishing number of its people. He had worked in three Ministries—Defense, Agriculture, and Finance—had been regarded as indispensable in the second and had become indispensable in the last. He had very wisely left the technicalities of financial and fiscal policy in the capable hands of Horowitz and the Bank of Israel; as a result he had remained in the closest touch with every important problem: immigration, housing, industrial expansion, settlement on the land, and development of water resources. As Ben-Gurion's deputy, he had had enough to do with foreign affairs to understand his country's problems and requirements perfectly.

His administrative abilities were probably greater than Ben-Gurion's. He had boundless patience, vigor, and great powers of application. His memory was very nearly as good as Ben-Gurion's, which was fantastic, and his grasp of detail probably greater. His abilities as a team player caused others to work very willingly for him. Perhaps even more than Ben-Gurion, he possessed that peculiar ability to improvise which has been the distinguishing feature of the 20 years of the State of Israel. He had worked with his hands, and worked intelligently with them, before he had needed to concentrate on working with his brains. He could, metaphorically, put his hand to any task, for he had a mind which was ready and eager to grasp new problems. And he had one particular advantage over Ben-Gurion: he liked people and got on with them. It is no bad thing for a Prime Minister to be able to relax, to have friends, and to be able to laugh with them.

Eshkol's qualities as a politician are less easy to assess. Of course, he knew the ins and outs of work in the Cabinet, in Parliament, and in the Party. He lacked two qualities which made Ben-Gurion preeminent. The first was a dominant personality; Israelis are wont to speak of Eshkol as "having had no charisma," and the phrase, although imprecise, says much. He did not appear to be a born leader because he did not stand out from other men in the way that a Churchill, an Adenauer, or a de Gaulle has done. In comparison with Ben-Gurion, he appeared an ordinary mortal. One must remember that the Jews of Palestine had looked for someone who was more than an ordinary man to lead them to sovereignty and independence through situations which had bristled with dangers. Ben-Gurion was a unique combination of politician and prophet. He was also a very fine public speaker, with a wonderful command of words and a gift for inspiring his audience.

Eshkol never became a good speaker, in spite of his ability always to talk good sense. The best that can be said of his speeches is that they were informative, sound, and down to earth. There was nothing in them which needed to be forgotten, but seldom much which was remembered.

Perhaps Eshkol could have made a much better speech in Yiddish than in Hebrew; he had a real command of the Yiddish idiom. Unfortunately for him, Yiddish simply does not translate into Hebrew, just as Welsh does not translate into English. Eshkol's lack of command of the Hebrew language, as an orator, cost him much on the public platform, even more when he spoke on the radio.

Eshkol, reputedly, lacked another of Ben-Gurion's characteristics, the ability to make quick, firm decisions. A good listener as well as mixer, Eshkol was thought to change his mind too often. Indeed, this was one of Ben-Gurion's chief complaints about him. But his lack of firmness may have been over stressed. It was always Eshkol's custom to ponder and talk problems over at some length. He understood his own method and made a habit of reaching the right decisions in the end. Yigal Allon, who became Eshkol's Deputy Prime Minister in 1968, said of Eshkol's deliberate way of examining problems, when comparing him with a contemporary rival: "When Dayan is hesitating, his admirers say that he is thinking; but when Eshkol is thinking, his critics say that he is hesitating."[1]

Politics is the art of the possible, an art which Eshkol understood very well. He had learned by observation and example; impervious to flattery, he never neglected good advice. His greatest strength may well have been the modesty which made him a man of the people. Allied to this modesty were realism, moderation, and human sensitivity. He convinced his supporters by solid argument and eternal patience, never by bulldozing them into submission in the manner of Ben-Gurion. One of the latter's Ministers told me how another member of the Cabinet had said to him, after a particularly heated meeting, "I'm dead against B.G. over this but I shall have to vote on his side for totally irrational reasons."[2]

In taking over from Ben-Gurion, Eshkol faced one minor but unpleasant problem. He told the staff of the Prime Minister's office that every one of them who wanted to stay at his post and work for him would be automatically welcome. The staff of the Prime Minister's office were civil servants. Different countries have different traditions in the matter of succession to posts of this kind. In Britain, for instance, only one or two senior officials in the Prime Minister's office would be changed. In Germany or in the United States there would be major changes of personnel only if a different party had come to power. Eshkol was bound to lead very much the same sort of coalition government as his predecessor. There was reason to believe that the staff of his personal office would have stayed on.

Two factors worked against this: the overpowering strength of Ben-Gurion's personality and his furious resentment of Eshkol. One by one, the members of the Prime Minister's office drifted away, but long before they had gone there were some purposeful leaks of information. "I didn't blame them for leaving, when they had a different center of gravity," was Eshkol's subsequent thought. Nor did he complain of their minor acts of disloyalty. "If I wasn't able to win them over, then I suppose I deserved a black eye," was his only comment.³

Eshkol faced, of course, a much more troublesome problem than the petty disloyalty of petty officials: the violent hostility of Ben-Gurion. Up to the late stages of the Lavon Affair, Eshkol had served him unquestioningly, diligently, and with some affection. He had obeyed Ben-Gurion's instructions and given Moshe Sharett loyal support when the latter took over from Ben-Gurion in January 1954. He had welcomed Ben-Gurion back in the following year. As long as it was possible, he had worked for a compromise between Ben-Gurion and the Mapai party over the Lavon Affair. In 1961 when Ben-Gurion once more decided to retire—subsequently changing his mind—Eshkol was the man who picked up the pieces. He held Mapai together, then organized the next coalition government on Ben-Gurion's behalf after over two months of patient negotiation, and simply handed it over when the latter announced that he was ready to return to the leadership of government and country.

Now, Eshkol found himself confronted by the dominant political personality in Israel, who blamed him for the course taken by the Lavon Affair, who had resigned in a huff but was by no means ready for final political retirement, and who lost no opportunity of denigrating his successor. It was a daunting prospect for a man who was popularly supposed, however wrongly, to be lacking in the power of decision and in personality. There is a story that at his first big military parade since becoming Prime Minister, Eshkol looked around for Ben-Gurion to take the salute. And there are photographs of party meetings at which Eshkol presided, unhappily looking over his shoulder at an outwardly passive but doubtlessly inwardly fulminating Ben-Gurion sitting on his right. To take over from Ben-Gurion, a born and acknowledged leader, would have been difficult enough in any event. To take over from him, when he was announcing to all and sundry that his successor was a flabby character who was not fit to govern, was the sternest possible test. History will judge whether Ben-Gurion should have put him to this test, and whether Eshkol satisfactorily surmounted it. Certainly, Eshkol required all of his resilience and fortitude.

The formation of a new Cabinet would have been a very difficult task had Ben-Gurion chosen to carry his personal hostility towards Eshkol immediately into the political field. Fortunately, the "Grand Old Man," thoroughly disgusted with politics for the moment, retired for most of the time to the kibbutz at Sde Boker. It took Eshkol only ten days, from June 16 to June 26, 1963, to form his new government. The main changes were his own assumption of the Defense portfolio in addition to being Prime Minister—in doing this he was following Ben-

Gurion's example—and the appointments of Abba Eban and Pinhas Sapir as Deputy Prime Minister and Minister of Finance. Sapir, who had worked under Eshkol in the Ministry of Finance, was a natural choice. So was Eban, like Eshkol and Sapir a middle-of-the-road pragmatist who had been Minister of Education, after eight years as Israel's representative at the United Nations. Eban's post went to Zalman Aranne, hitherto a staunch supporter of Ben-Gurion but from then on a most useful member of Eshkol's Cabinet.

Two key members of the Cabinet remained at their posts, Yigal Allon as Minister of Labor and Mrs. Golda Meir as Minister of Foreign Affairs. Moshe Dayan, rather surprisingly, stayed on as Minister of Agriculture; the general expectation was that he would follow Ben-Gurion into the political wilderness. Allon had risen to the rank of General in the War of Independence and, along with Dayan, was one of the outstanding younger political figures in Israel. Mrs. Meir had already been Minister of Foreign Affairs since 1956. Her experience and shrewdness were of the utmost value to Eshkol.

It was a strong team, mainly inherited from Ben-Gurion's government, and Eshkol had enough backing in the Knesset. His government was based on Mapai, with 42 seats in the Knesset, and was supported by Achdut Ha'avoda and the National Religious Party. This gave him only 62 seats out of 120. Criticism that he depended too much on the establishment and brought in too little new blood began almost at once to be leveled against Eshkol. But Eshkol took over from Ben-Gurion in mid-term, and nothing was more natural than to depend on very much the same people who had been serving under his predecessor. One must remember, too, that government by coalition entails accepting as Ministers the nominees of the smaller coalition parties. The possibilities for change were limited largely to the principal party, Mapai. Even there, a Mapai Prime Minister's scope for change was restricted by the need to reward long and valuable service to the party. Politicians, of course, tend to hang on in any country, and this tendency is probably greater in a small country like Israel than in, say, the United States or Britain. For former politicians there is an obvious dearth of interesting jobs outside politics.

Ben-Gurion was to make much of Eshkol's supposed dependence on an aging, even atrophying establishment. He himself grouped a number of younger men around him, including Dayan, Shimon Peres, Teddy Kollek, at that time in charge of the Government Tourist Office, and Chaim Herzog, a businessman with political affiliations. Ben-Gurion may have genuinely believed that new blood was needed in the political system. But his personal frustration over the Lavon Affair and irritation with the Mapai old guard played its part too. The idea of a group of young activists in Mapai was not, however, a bad one; it could have helped to keep the leadership in close touch with the rising generation.

Under Ben-Gurion, unfortunately, the activist group was to develop deviationist tendencies.

In his inaugural address to the Knesset Eshkol stressed three points in particular: the need for more immigrants, for steady material progress, and for peace in the Middle East.

Immigration had dropped drastically after 1957, when 71,000 immigrants came to Israel. Only 75,000 arrived in the next three years all together. There had been a better year in 1962, with 61,000, thanks partly to Rumania's relaxation of its restrictions on movement. But it was obvious that the reservoirs of emigration to Israel were drying up. A large proportion of the Jews of the Arab world had already reached Israel. Sharp disappointment had been caused by the fact that many Jews who left Algeria as a result of that country's war of independence went, not to Israel, but to France. These Algerian Jews felt themselves to be Frenchmen first and Jews second, a nasty eye-opener to the Israeli government, which had expected them to use France only as a port of call. The Jewish communities of Germany, Poland, and Austria were decimated. The 70,000 left in these three countries were mostly old people. Italy and the Low Countries held another 100,000, but these were essentially settled Jews, sufficiently integrated to be thoroughly at home.

From behind the Iron Curtain there were more Jews to come, and more did come, from Rumania and Hungary. The two and a half million Jews of the Soviet Union enjoyed no such freedom of movement. Eshkol, himself a Russian Jew, had to equate his country's desire to receive Russian Jews with his government's awareness of the Soviet Union's determination to deny the existence of any Jewish problem and to keep its Jewish population in Russia. Soviet governments regarded the desire of the Soviet Jews to maintain some sort of separate identity as a slur on the Soviet system. From this attitude it was only a short step to deny them the right to their own religion.

Otherwise, the only reserves left to world Jewry were in Britain and the New World. These Jewish communities had one thing in common; during the last century they had been discriminated against only socially. Their members were becoming increasingly integrated. They were losing the urge to move, even when the undreamed-of opportunity to return to Eretz Israel had, at long last, presented itself. Another thought may be apposite: to talk and dream of the return through the ages is one thing, but to grasp the chance to realize the dream is another.

Eshkol had no panacea for the immigration problem. His appeal to the Jews of the Diaspora had only a slight effect. The 1963 figure for immigration was 64,000, but it dropped in 1964 to 54,000, and to 30,000 in 1965 and only 16,000 in 1966.[4] The Prime Minister was to make a fresh effort to deal with this problem in 1968, in the knowledge that Israel's optimum population by the year 2000 should be about 5 million and that she was only halfway there with just over 30 years to go.

The second point in Eshkol's inaugural address, material progress, was something which he understood very well. As Minister of Finance, he had already helped Israel to make remarkable progress during the previous decade. The eightfold increase in exports was probably the most significant single achievement. In his inaugural speech, he indicated the guidelines of future policy: moderation in consumer spending, the building of a more efficient economy, price and wage discipline in order to combat inflation, and government economy in manpower and budgetary expenditures as an example to the whole community. In the year 1963, 15 years after Israel had won her independence, Eshkol could not easily appeal for a tightening of belts which had never been loosened. His task was to emphasize the need to raise productivity, to keep pace with rising consumption. It is much easier to be the apostle of abstinence during a pioneering era than to organize the distribution of the first fruits of that initial self-sacrifice.

Peace was more important than population or progress. Eshkol's first foreign policy statement came on July 12, 1963. He made a personal offer to President Nasser of Egypt, to talk to him "at any time and in any place." Eshkol explained: "If only we can meet face to face, the Arab leader would soon find that peace is in the best interests of all, and that differences can be ironed out by negotiation and discussion."[5]

The apologists of the Arab cause are ready to explain away Israeli offers of face-to-face talks as mere tactical maneuvers, with the sole purpose of "being seen to be doing something," in the curious phrase invented by Britain's Prime Minister, Harold Wilson. Eshkol's offer was not a maneuver. He was a man of peace, incapable of a Ben-Gurion's clarion call to arms. His offer was spurned by President Nasser, as every similar Israeli offer has been spurned, before that date and after. There is no reason to doubt that it was sincere. How easy, indeed, it would have been for Eshkol and Nasser to negotiate in 1963! Egypt and Israel had no territorial claims on one another. They had many material reasons for wishing to coexist peacefully, and no material reason for not doing so. Israel, certainly, wanted the Suez Canal reopened as an international waterway. Egypt insisted on the return of the Palestinian refugees to their homes. A compromise should not have been impossible; but the operative thought is that Egypt refused to discuss anything at all. Two months after making his offer to Nasser, Eshkol declared that Israel would give aid to the very maximum of her capacity in helping to resettle the Palestinian refugees. And in a speech to Arab *mukhtars,* or village headmen, in Jerusalem he declared, "Let us remember only those things that unite us, and forget those that divide us."[6] There can be no doubt that Eshkol would have wanted to apply this same principle in his relations with the Arab countries.

Eshkol was quickly confronted with difficulties inside his government coalition. Moshe Dayan had been a member of the Cabinet for four years.

He had served willingly under Ben-Gurion, a man whom he venerated for his dynamism and vision. Dayan was 47 years old, 20 years younger than Eshkol, with whom he had little in common. Eshkol had regarded the Ministry of Agriculture as a challenging and fascinating assignment; Dayan was less interested in details and in the human aspects of settlement on the land. The post may, too, have seemed mundane, after his long spell as Israeli Chief of Staff and his brilliantly successful leadership of the armed forces in the Sinai campaign. In August, Dayan was irritated over Eshkol's decision to entrust the new Galilee development project to Raanan Weitz and the Jewish Agency. In Dayan's view, control of agricultural development should not be shared between the Government and the Agency. He resigned on September 6, 1963.

The implications of this step have still not been fully realized. While Ben-Gurion had merely talked about giving the younger generation greater political responsibilities, Dayan implicitly believed that this was overdue. Eshkol, as he saw it, would retain the Mapai old guard in positions of authority for another ten years. He and the other "Young Turks" of Ben-Gurion's political bodyguard would be closer to 60 than 50 at the end of that time. Dayan and his friends argued that Israel was a young state and needed young men with political dynamism as well as political ballast at the helm. Yet Dayan, an astute politician, intended his resignation essentially as a gesture of independence. He withdrew it exactly one week later.

This, of course, was not the end of the story. Only a few weeks later, Dayan deliberately flouted his leader at the Mapai party conference. Eshkol had spoken in praise of the individual pioneer; Dayan chose to scoff at an older generation whose members were likely to lapse into sentimental reminiscing. Increasingly, Dayan became a lone wolf in the Cabinet, giving the impression of being a frustrated, unhappy man. Both his heart and intellect were with Ben-Gurion, but the break with Eshkol, when it did come, was over a political rather than a personal issue.

Eshkol had never ceased to be the apostle of socialist unity. Just as he had deplored the rivalry of Poalei Zion and Hapoel Hatzair 40 years earlier, so now he regarded the splintering of the socialist movement among Mapai, Achdut Ha'avoda, and Mapam as an unnecessary and grievous dissipation of constructive thought and effort. He was determined to promote socialist unity, and he decided that the first thing which could be done was to bring Mapai and Achdut Ha'avoda closer together. In this aim he was supported by Achdut's leader, Yigal Allon. A practical man, Allon thought that agreement between the two parties could be the starting point for an over-all rationalization of the party-political complex.

Eshkol and Allon decided to work for an Alignment of the two parties, rather than total merger. The two parties would be allies, in the coming election as well as in the then existing government. They would produce a joint list of candidates for the Knesset, and members would be returned to the Knesset on an equitable proportional basis (at the time, Mapai's strength in the Knesset was roughly five times that of the smaller party). A joint policy would be hammered out; indeed, differences were very slight between the two parties. The two components to this Alignment would bind themselves to remain united for the full four-year term of the next Knesset, which was due to be elected in the autumn of 1965.

Ben-Gurion was totally opposed to the Alignment. He regarded the inevitable interparty haggling as unsavory. He maintained, quite unrealistically, that it was absurd for Mapai to make concessions to a socialist group which was so much smaller than itself. In reality, Achdut Ha'avoda prided itself on being the purer socialist party of the two, something which should have appealed to a perfectionist like Ben-Gurion. Finally he accused Eshkol of plotting to subvert party policy, his argument being that Mapai would lose real freedom of action if it made too many compromises. This objection loses much of its force when it is remembered that Israel was a community of a mere two million inhabitants. So small a community could not afford the luxury of a plethora of political parties, including three which were all socialist. It required, far more, a consensus, wherever this could be found. A consensus, strictly socialist and progressive, was exactly what Eshkol and Allon were working for.

Ben-Gurion still had luster, as a cartoon in an issue of the *Jerusalem Post* of July 1964 illustrated. It showed Eshkol and Allon confronting a bottle labeled "Alignment" and both asking: "What seems to be the problem?" The cork of the bottle was the head of Ben-Gurion. The thought behind this cartoon was that Ben-Gurion, no longer a member of the Cabinet, was still so outstanding a political and national figure that the Alignment could not be formed against his wishes. Ben-Gurion began, at about this time, to insist that the Alignment was unwanted, because a full merger was far preferable. He did not explain how this could be achieved without making concessions to Achdut Ha'avoda.

On November 6, 1964, Dayan resigned his post as Minister of Agriculture for the second time. His reason was the Alignment and the way it was being organized. On November 20 Ben-Gurion resigned from the Mapai Central Committee, also over the Alignment. The explanation which he gave was somewhat elusive; that the Alignment would paper over the fundamental question of electoral reform, which he thought was badly needed in order to reduce the number of parties in the Knesset. There was a sort of logic to this argument; Ben-Gurion did indeed favor electoral reform and the institution of something like the British system of direct election in single member constituencies. The British system would have given Mapai an over-all majority in the Knesset, and this would have encouraged the nonsocialist parties to coalesce and form a right-of-center bloc.

Eshkol, rational and pragmatic, believed that electoral reform of such a sweeping kind was not attainable. His view was that no party but Mapai could afford to vote for a measure which was immediately disadvantageous to it and which could lead to its virtual extinction at the polls. Eshkol preferred to work step by step towards socialist unity, as one process which could be planned and controlled.

In November and December 1964 Ben-Gurion's attacks on Eshkol redoubled in frequency and violence. He was infuriated by Eshkol's friendly gestures towards the parties of the right, against whom he had battled since the days of Jabotinsky's leadership in the 1920s. He may, for that matter, have been angered by Eshkol's decision to have Jabotinsky's body brought from the United States for reburial with all honors in Israel on July 9, 1964, the twentieth anniversary of the death of the Revisionist leader. Ben-Gurion's sworn rival. Yet another source of irritation to Ben-Gurion was a conciliatory letter from Eshkol to the small group of Lavon supporters.

Ben-Gurion was still trying to reopen the Lavon Affair; he even proposed judicial action against the seven Ministers who had conducted the Cabinet inquiry into it four years earlier. Such was the ferocity of his onslaught that Eshkol offered his own resignation on December 18, 1964. He was, in fact, asking for a vote of confidence. He got it, in the shape of a wave of popular feeling which was utterly opposed to further investigation of the Lavon Affair and which resented Ben-Gurion's back-seat driving when the man whom he himself had groomed for the succession was Prime Minister. Eshkol took only one week to form a new Cabinet, and it entailed making only one minor change. He had the confidence of the leaders of Mapai and the parties which were allied with Mapai in the government coalition.

Eshkol had won a clearcut tactical victory. Typical of the reaction to his resignation was the comment of the *Jewish Chronicle* of London.[7] Its editor's view was that Eshkol's action showed "that he will stand no nonsense . . . that he was not prepared to allow Mr. Ben-Gurion to dictate policy, or to involve the Government in the ex-Premier's vendetta against Mr. Lavon." The *Jewish Chronicle* advised Ben-Gurion to "give up back-seat driving." Ben-Gurion had other ideas. In January 1965, he attacked Eshkol for allowing a "brain drain" of Israeli teachers and technical instructors to the outside world. Eshkol's case was that the so-called brain drain consisted largely of Israelis taking courses in the United States and elsewhere in the Diaspora, thus maintaining contact with world Jewry.

Ben-Gurion reserved his main assault for the Mapai Party Convention in February. There he demanded the reopening of the Lavon Affair and the dropping of the plans for the alignment with Achdut Ha'avoda. He was defeated on both issues. Sixty percent of the Convention voted against reopening the Lavon Affair, after former Premier Moshe Sharett, gravely ill at the time, was brought into the convention hall in a wheelchair to urge that it should be closed forever and that Ben-Gurion and Eshkol should, as a natural corollary, effect a reconciliation. Sixty-three percent of the representatives voted for this. Eshkol had won the second round, and if the margin of victory does not seem to have been substantial, it has to be remembered that his opponent was the man who had ruled Israel for the best part of 15 years and who had retained all his glamor as a captivating and commanding personality.

Ben-Gurion had no intention of giving up the struggle. The "Young Turks" were solidly behind him and the two convention votes had shown that he still commanded a great deal of popular support. In April he was sniping at Eshkol again, this time over the decision to hold the May Independence Day parade in Tel Aviv rather than Jerusalem, a tactful gesture which was directed at the great powers and the United Nations rather than at the unchangingly recalcitrant Arab neighbors. At the end of May, Ben-Gurion's active and ambitious lieutenants staged a mass demonstration in his favor. On May 27, 3000 Mapai followers met at Avihail and called upon Ben-Gurion to take over the leadership of the party once more. Ben-Gurion made no secret of his belief that Eshkol's tenure was no more than a short transition period before a younger generation took over from the Mapai establishment. It was not altogether clear, however, whether he himself intended to be king, king-maker, or regent after Eshkol's confidently predicted fall.

The third round of the struggle took place when the Central Committee of Mapai met in June 1965. Ben-Gurion held several cards up his sleeve. His first was the demand that the Party Convention, and not the Central Committee, should make the operative decision as to who should be Mapai's candidate for the premiership in the November elections. The battle over this point, which might appear to be diversionary or merely academic, was fierce. Ben-Gurion and his followers insisted that the Convention was the true democratic forum for this choice, ignoring the fact that the Central Committee had always made it in the past. They insisted that this was a vital matter since major policy decisions were involved: the Alignment, electoral reform, and a reshuffle of posts inside the party. Ben-Gurion's powerful oratory contrasted with Eshkol's plodding style. The Central Committee decided that it was competent to make the choice of candidate for the premiership and other important decisions, but only by 167 votes to 150.

Ben-Gurion now opposed Eshkol's candidacy. This time he was defeated by 179 votes to 103. His next move was to announce that his followers would place their names on a separate list of candidates at the November elections. On June 29 the Mapai Party split, but out of the entire Central Committee only 40 members joined Ben-Gurion in opposition to the party leadership. The urge to maintain party unity was much greater than the allure of Ben-Gurion's magnetic personality and his promise to push through electoral reform which could give Mapai a clear majority of seats in the Knesset. Surprisingly, Dayan did not at once follow Ben-Gurion. Always an individualist, he pressed for political and economic modernization. It was obvious, however, that he had no intention of supporting Eshkol.

On July 12, 1965, Ben-Gurion formally announced the name of his new group, which he called *Reshimat Poalei Israel,* The Israel Labor List, or *Rafi,* for short. The Mapai Central Committee countered by announcing that anyone who put his name on the Rafi list of electoral candidates would automatically be expelled from the party. Mapai refused to accept the fiction that Rafi candidates were really Mapai members who were simply campaigning on a separate list. This Mapai decision drew down on Eshkol's head the furious accusation of the Minister of Housing, Joseph Almogi, that Eshkol "will go down in history as the great splitter of Mapai." It is interesting that Almogi, who followed Ben-Gurion out of Mapai, returned to the fold three years later.

Eshkol's sense of humor did not desert him during this critical time; he later recalled with relish that it was at this precise moment that his government was defeated on a bill in the Knesset. It was on the earth-shaking question of what down payment there should be on the installation of telephones in private homes.[8]

Mapai district and local committees all over the country were split by the Eshkol-Ben-Gurion controversy and the formation of Rafi. On August 15 there was actual fighting on the docks at Ashdod. In spite of the massive support given to Eshkol by the Central Committee, confidence at first drained away within both Mapai and its junior partner in the Alignment. At the Histadrut elections in September, the joint vote of the two Alignment parties dropped from 74 percent to 51 percent. Rafi picked up 12 percent of the votes, although the new group had barely begun to organize. Mapai's vote alone fell from 55 percent to 32 percent. It was an ominous overture for the November elections to the Knesset.

Mapai was confronted by its biggest challenge since the State of Israel came into existence. It had shown its strength at the elections in 1949 because of its identification with the pioneering era and the struggle for independence. In 1951 the main issue had been the practical achievements of socialist-led government. In 1955 the need for unity in face of growing Arab pressure was paramount; the established political leadership won a vote of confidence. In 1959 the chief preoccupation had been with the absorption of Oriental Jews. In the 1961 elections the personalized issue of the Lavon Affair had first come to the fore, and Mapai had suffered as a result. Now, in 1965, Mapai seemed for the first time to be in serious danger of losing the leadership of the nation. The split in the party was its most serious problem. But the popular mood gave grounds for concern too; the old idealism had faded, an acquisitive society had succeeded a pioneering one, the younger generation was becoming restive. Perhaps, many Israelis began to think, Mapai had been too powerful and had been in power too long.

The *Jewish Chronicle* was to call the 1965 elections "the longest, the bitterest, the dirtiest, and the most expensive in the State's history." There had been tough elections in the past. The mantle of Jabotinsky fell on Menachem Beigin's Herut conservative party and the old Jabotinsky-Ben-Gurion controversy was never laid to rest. The religious parties did not mince their words either. The leftist deviation of Mapam had caused much bitterness in socialist ranks. But all this paled by comparison with the violent personal hostility towards Eshkol and the establishment which Ben-Gurion introduced into the election campaign of 1965.

Rafi certainly had a case. That I learned in a long talk with one of its leading members, Chaim Herzog, a man who fought with distinction in the 1948 and 1956 campaigns, who had become a highly successful businessman, and who was to play a valuable role in and after the Six-Day War of June 1967. Herzog believed that the Mapai establishment was stale and sterile. In his view, it had lost all impetus and had developed into a caucus of party hacks and position-seekers.[9] The Rafi leaders objected to the hierarchical make up of Mapai, with committees producing committee leaders who voted one another into posts in the party's administrative machine. The "Young Turks" of Rafi wanted a new look as well as new ideas; they asked for more style in government, more flair and less expertise, and greater contact between political leadership and the people. I wrote in 1967, "A party that had been in power as long as Mapai had was liable to regard government as essentially its private concern and primarily a matter of administrative technique and finesse. Rafi's leaders believed there should be more progress and change, greater social unity, and social justice. There was to be a new type of Israeli politician, not the dusty, conventional man-of-the-people, but a vital, vigorous individualist."[10]

What, then, did Rafi propose? Obviously, younger men should be given posts to responsibility. Obviously, there should be a shakeup within Mapai's internal administration and, maybe, within the internal administrations of other parties. But there could be no return to the pioneering days of total self-sacrifice and idealism; people had learned to ask for a little more and to grumble a little more. They had worked hard, and expected to see some personal return for that work. They had, in the first place, come to Israel for a great variety of reasons, not like the Jews of the Second and Third Aliyahs who came to Palestine with the inspiring vision of reclaiming a Promised Land which had been sadly, even shockingly neglected for hundreds of years. The post-1945 immigrants came to avoid persecution, to escape from the charnel house of Central Europe, to get to some place that they could call home. To them, Rafi's appeal seemed somewhat ingenuous and vague. They wanted security and sound administration.

The one new plank in Rafi's political platform was electoral reform. There was an extraordinary variety in the makeup of the population of Israel, and this was reflected by the large number of parties. The man in the street did not notice the flaws which resulted from this, the uneasy compromises within government coalitions, the lack of personal contact between electors and members of the Knesset who were nominated by party committees, the lack of an effective Parliamentary opposition. The man in the street could have come from any one of a hundred countries, could be deeply religious or antireligious, socialist or antisocialist, a former European, an Oriental Jew, a native-born sabra. On the whole, he liked the crazy-quilt pattern of Israeli politics. It would have required, it probably still does require, a breakdown of administration to convince him that electoral reform would benefit him as well as the country.

Municipal elections took place at the same time as the elections to the Knesset. In the former, the Alignment lost control of four cities, including Jerusalem, and 12 local councils. Voters were interested in personalities, like Teddy Kollek and Abba Hushi, both Rafi men, who became mayors of Jerusalem and Haifa. But in the national elections the Alignment just about managed to hold its own. It held 45 seats in the Knesset, against the 42 held previously by Mapai and eight by Achdut Ha'avoda. Rafi collected only ten seats. The struggle for supremacy within the socialist movement was over almost as soon as it had officially begun. Eshkol had won.

Ben-Gurion had, in effect, defeated himself, by a display of rancor which had little appeal to Israeli citizens who could not forget that their country was a small island in the sea of Arab states and that it needed to behave as a community based on mutual aid and mutual respect. The cartoonist Dosh saw in Ben-Gurion a nihilist who was ready to ruin his own reputation in order to get even with his opponents. He depicted a dwarfish Ben-Gurion, armed with a hammer, attacking a huge statue of himself, with the caption "De-Bengurionization." The phrase was originally Dayan's, but he had used it when accusing Eshkol and the establishment of taking all individuality, initiative, punch, and panache out of Israel's political life.

The socialist parties, including Mapam, collected 51 percent of the votes, against 49 percent in 1961. In six elections the average vote for the socialist parties had been 50 percent. The three religious parties collected 14 percent, against an average of 13 percent. For the first time, there was an effort to form an antisocialist front; Beigin's Herut combined with the bulk of the liberals to form the *Gahal* right-of-center bloc. It returned 26 members to the Knesset, against the Alignment's 45. This was the nearest that the antisocialist parties had come to being able to offer an alternative government. But it was clear that Beigin could not find nearly enough outside support to form a coalition. Once again, it fell to Eshkol to do this.

The drama of the conflict with Ben-Gurion had taken its toll of Eshkol. In December he was hospitalized, suffering from exhaustion. He was then in the middle of negotiations for forming a new government, and the statutory period of 28 days in which this had to be done expired on December 28. On December 17 Eshkol was discharged, but he became ill again on December 28, this time with influenza. He completed his government only on January 12, 1966. The new coalition consisted of the Alignment, Mapam, the National Religious Party and the smaller religious group of Paolei Agudat, and the Independent Liberals. It commanded 75 seats in the Knesset, and the new Cabinet was approved by 71 votes to 41. Ben-Gurion might well complain that it was "the mixture as before"; the only important change was the appointment of Abba Eban as Foreign Minister, while Mrs. Golda Meir withdrew from the government to become Secretary General of Mapai.

In his statement of government policy, Eshkol stressed two principal tasks which lay ahead, checking the arms race in the Middle East and economic retrenchment at home. The first belongs to a later chapter; the second requires some brief explanation.

The country's balance of payments had deteriorated seriously in 1964. Exports were pushed up with some difficulty from $338 million to $351 million. But imports leaped, sensationally, from $662 million to $813 million. The trade gap widened from $324 million to $462 million. Worse, the proportion of imports covered by exports dropped from 51 percent to 43 percent. This was only the third year since 1949 in which there had been a drop of this kind, and 1964's was much the largest.

Israel's foreign currency reserves continued to grow, for the country was receiving from $400 million to $500 million a year from German reparations, restitutions to private citizens who were victims of Nazi persecution, the sale of Israeli bonds abroad, and contributions by Jewish organizations in the Diaspora. The trouble was that much of this money had an internal inflationary effect. Thus, while reparations were used chiefly to buy capital equipment, private restitutions gave a part of the community money to spend on consumer goods. In 1965 there was a successful effort to check the imbalance of trade; exports were pushed up to $406 million and imports held steady at $811 million. More than $50 million was knocked off the trade deficit.

But in 1965 the danger to the economy came from a different quarter. Thanks to the cooperation of the Histadrut, wages had been held remarkably steady. In 1965 average monthly earnings were still only $300 for industrial workers, $160 in commerce and finance, and only

$100 in agriculture. Low wages combined with curbs on imports to cause growing industrial unrest. In particular, there was a rash of wildcat strikes during the second half of 1965 by municipal sanitation men and in the Histadrut's own milk-marketing cooperative, by hospital staffs and lecturers at the universities, by various groups of industrial workers. The response of management, including the Histadrut in its capacity as large-scale employer, was to grant substantial fringe benefits and cost-of-living allowances. Wage earners became proficient in the arithmetic of wage scales and the like. All sorts of groups of workers argued that their cases were special, like the workers at the Timna copper mines and the Dead Sea potash fields and the dockers at Eilat and Ashdod, and generally got their way. Even government ministries found themselves involved in collective bargaining.

Fortunately, all this did not mean that the economy was basically unsound. In ten years agricultural output had more than doubled and industrial output had multiplied three and a half times. In 1966 Eshkol was to launch a Five-Year Economic Plan which aimed at stepping up productivity, securing the more rational use of human resources, doubling exports, and reducing the trade gap by 1970 to $280 million. This was a tall order, and its fulfillment depended to some degree on the maintenance of peace in the Middle East. This was something which was not to be granted to Israel.

But Eshkol had already come a long way in the two and a half years in which he had been Prime Minister. Possibly his greatest accomplishment had been gaining the confidence of the people who worked for and with him. The most important among them were the Secretary General of Mapai, Mrs. Meir, the Achdut Ha'avoda leader, Yigal Allon, and his two most trusted lieutenants in the Cabinet, Pinhas Sapir at the Ministry of Finance and Abba Eban at the Ministry of Foreign Affairs. Eshkol now had a smoothly working team. In addition, he had built up a compact and dedicated staff in the Prime Minister's Office, probably the most overworked people in the whole administration. Eshkol was inclined to talk about them in somewhat Machiavellian terms. He told one friend, "I like having young men working for me who don't mind taking a header into a rough sea. If they survive, well and good; and if they drown, well, it can't be helped."[11] In reality, Eshkol's relations with his personal staff were excellent; if he asked them to work hard, he was always human, friendly, and appreciative.

Of considerable importance in Eshkol's life was his third marriage, on March 3, 1964, to Miriam Zelikovitz. Born in Rumania in 1927, she was a person of drive, imagination, and considerable intellectual ability, who had served in the War of Independence, had been a schoolteacher, and had then become librarian, first at the Hebrew University and later at the Knesset. She had also become a friend of the family, in fact, of Eshkol's daughters, who were her age. Eshkol had been a lonely man since his second wife's death; as a Prime Minister he was particularly in need of someone to help him with his problems and responsibilities. His third marriage was ideally happy.

In this chapter of Eshkol's story one must necessarily add a postscript on Ben-Gurion. In January 1966 he again took his seat in the Knesset, but his heart was no longer in politics. Rafi's relatively poor showing at the polls was a slap in the face. It was a tragedy that this last phase of his political life should have been so embittered by disputes with his former friends and helpers. How serious a strain was put on Eshkol by his enmity is easily forgotten and there is no purpose in emphasizing the point. Ben-Gurion will surely be remembered for his tremendous services to Israel rather than for troubles in the twilight of his career.

He talked to me in November 1965, only a few weeks after the elections. I kept him away from internal politics; indeed, I was much more interested in his views about the future of his country and his people. He was bursting with ideas, on the problem of peace in the Middle East, on the settlement of the Negev, on the need to obtain more immigrants and to make those who had already come from Oriental countries Israeli citizens in the fullest sense of the term, on the future of world Jewry. His mind ranged freely and lucidly over these and other problems. Apparent in all his thoughts was his sense of history, and his immense faith in the future of the people of Israel.

One can snatch at only a few phrases: "Our future lies in Asia, even if our way of life is modeled on Europe; for Asia contains two-thirds of the human race. Israel stands at the gateway to Asia." Or, "We shall build industries in the Negev, for our mineral resources are already there, the potash of the Dead Sea and the copper of King Solomon's mines. Why not a canal from the Red Sea to the Mediterranean, and another out of the Dead Sea?" Or, again, "Part of our treasure has been the will to survive and to maintain our identity. Never forget that there were four to five million Jews in the Roman Empire!" Finally, a fleeting thought on the selfishness of the Jews of Whitechapel, in London's East End, who dodged rationing regulations in World War II and were not overanxious to enlist for military service, contrasted with the sober, almost sullen pride of the sabra.[12]

1. Yigal Allon, in personal conversation with the author.
2. Pinhas Rosen, in personal conversation with the author.
3. Eshkol, in personal conversation with the author.
4. Figures from *Facts about Israel 1968,* Israeli Ministry of Foreign Affairs publication.
5. *Jerusalem Post,* July 13, 1963.
6. *Jerusalem Post,* August 16, 1963.
7. *Jewish Chronicle,* December 25, 1964.

8. Eshkol, in personal conversation with the author.
9. Chaim Herzog, in personal conversation with the author.
10. Terence Prittie, *Israel: Miracle in the Desert,* p. 145.
11. Raanan Weitz, in personal conversation with the author.
12. Ben-Gurion, in personal conversation with the author.

15.

In the field of foreign affairs the chief preoccupation of any Israeli Prime Minister has always had to be his country's relations with its Arab neighbors. In the long run, everything, prosperity, progress, and peace, for the whole Middle East as well as for Israel, will depend on them. But there were other international problems as well.

Israel's relations with the principal Western powers, the United States, Britain, and France, have been generally good, with the short intermission of American disapproval over Israel's military victory in Sinai. Something of a special relationship was built up with France, who became Israel's principal ally in the United Nations and her main supplier of arms. This special relationship was to last until the June 1967 war and President de Gaulle's declaration of neutrality, a declaration which owed much to France's desire to restore her old political influence in the Arab Middle East and to use it in order to expand her oil interests, especially in those areas of Northern Iraq, promised to her in the 1916 Sykes-Picot Agreement.

Elsewhere Israel developed good relations wherever she could, notably in Africa and in underdeveloped countries on other continents. Israel's chief means of developing friendly relations with such countries was by giving technical aid in the shape of small, compact, intensely hard-working teams that advised on agriculture and water conservation, town and country planning, labor relations, and communications. Giving this technical aid was costly to a country as small as Israel and so badly in need of its own labor resources. But it paid handsome dividends in the shape of friendship and support in the United Nations.

Two countries posed particular problems for Israel, the Federal German Republic and the Soviet Union. Relations with the former long remained overshadowed by Germany's Nazi past and with the latter by Soviet distrust of Zionism and of its own Russian Jewish minority, as well as by Soviet involvement in the Arab Middle East.

The West Germans began to pay reparations in kind to Israel in 1953, for the material damage caused to the Jewish communities of Central Europe and for resettling European Jewish survivors in Israel. By 1966 the Federal Republic had paid the full amount of $860 million prescribed by the Luxemburg Reparations Agreement of September 1952. The reparations in kind had included ships, railway equipment, machinery, steel, pig iron, oil, coal, and a wide range of other industrial and agricultural goods. By 1966, individual citizens of Israel had received nearly $1 billion in cash, as restitution for their suffering and their lost property. Long before this date, the stage seemed set for the resumption of normal relations between the two countries. Yet several factors combined to delay this step.

The first such factor can only be described as the legacy of the Nazi past. The understandable view of Israel's leaders was that the past could not simply be forgotten. There had to be expiation, most of all for the sake of the health of the German community. War criminals of every sort had to be brought to book; otherwise they would remain cankerous testimony that crime does pay. There is no place here to describe the uneven and sometimes lagging course of German war crimes trials. German legal procedures were often long-winded and German judges reluctant to sentence men who had acted under orders, especially in time of war. Evidence was not always easy to collect—the Germans were able to set up their own central tracing service only in 1958. The time lag made identification of the accused difficult. Yet a great deal was done. Between 1958 and 1965 German courts convicted and sentenced 6000 wrongdoers, and another 2000 cases had been listed as pending by the Laender authorities. Some major criminals admittedly slipped through the net, and in May 1960 one of the worst of them, Adolf Eichmann, was captured by Israeli secret service agents in Argentina and brought to Israel.

Eichmann's trial, which began in April 1961 and resulted in his execution on May 31, 1962, was a traumatic experience both for the Germans and for the Israelis and Jews of the Diaspora. Eichmann had been one of the key agents of the Nazi regime in dealing with the persecution of the Jews from 1935 on. He took part in the January 1942 Wannsee Conference at which the Nazi leaders mapped out their plans for the "Final Solution" of the Jewish question, involving the mass deportation and mass murder of the Jews of Europe. Eichmann had been fully aware of all the salient details of the extermination program; indeed he was quoted as having said that he would "leap laughing" into his grave for the knowledge of having destroyed the lives of millions.

There was a ghoulishness about the whole long trial—about its grisly details of testimony, about the way in which witnesses who had been tortured and almost broken in spirit gave their evidence, about the criminal himself, seemingly a meticulous, soulless bureaucrat sitting in a bullet-proof glass cage in the courtroom. The trial was indeed salutary, for it unrolled a story of unique savagery which needed to be told, and it provided what the *Manchester Guardian* called "a touch of Old Testament justice" for this "murder manager and carnage clerk." But while the trial lasted, it caused torments of mind both to the guilt-conscious Germans and to the Jews, who suffered all over again the outraged feelings of shame, indignity, and helplessness with which their fellow Jews had been herded to the slaughter houses. Possibly, there had to be a trial of this sort before at least some of the complexes about the past, those haunting specters of fear and hate, could be laid to rest. Possibly, the normalization of the German-Israeli relationship would have had in any case to wait for this event.

Eshkol himself never had any doubt that Israel had, as he put it, "both the right and the duty" to judge Eichmann and, having found him guilty, to execute him. It was right, too, that he should be tried in Jerusalem, the City of Justice.*

But in the early 1960s the German-Israeli relationship was bedeviled by another development. This was the curious affair of German scientists working in Egypt for President Nasser. Before the end of 1962 the Israeli government had become seriously concerned by Nasser's readiness to give asylum to former Nazis and had drawn the attention of the West German government to this. They included men like the former SS officer and propaganda official, Johannes von Leers, the Nazi security expert Leopold Gleim, the former SS General Dirlewanger, and a number of Gestapo officials, concentration camp doctors, and members of Josef Goebbels' Ministry of Propaganda. Nasser gave these men passports, employment, and his blessing to continue to pursue their anti-Semitic activities. By the end of 1962, however, the Israeli government had become aware of the fact that Nasser was bringing in Germans who were even more dangerous, though in a very different way.

These were rocket experts who included Professor Eugen Saenger, the head of the West German rocket research center at Stuttgart, Dr. Paul Goercke, the chief of the center's section for electronic steering apparatus, and Wolfgang Pilz, who had worked in the Peenemuende rocket station on the Baltic during the war. These men began to visit Egypt in 1960. In the course of the next three years they helped to develop two single-stage rockets, with a range of between 250 and 350 miles, and a two-stage rocket with a range of 600 miles. The rockets were adapted for use from launching pads which could be moved towards Israel's borders. The German rocket experts also advised Nasser on ways of producing so-called "radioactive rubbish bombs" that would have a limited fallout of radioactive material and could be used to poison food, water, and the atmosphere. Nasser even examined such unlikely propositions as the procuring of small nuclear bombs by his (presumably foreign) agents, the exploding of strontium 90 shells on Israeli territory (they could be fired at short range by light mortars or bazooka-type weapons mounted on MTB's), and the making of his own nuclear bombs by smuggling in enriched uranium.

Nasser plainly was considering the use of weapons of genocide, or at the very least weapons with a genocidal element in them. He was entirely prepared to enlist the help of former Nazi experts, who were equally ready to serve him. A whole German colony was established on the banks of the Nile, with their own "golden ghetto" of homes, social club, restaurant, and sports facilities. Wisely the Israeli government pressed the West Germans to introduce legislation discouraging their citizens from serving the warlike designs of other countries. In mid-1963

* Eshkol, in personal conversation with the author.

the West German government began somewhat laboriously to draft legislation to prevent this. The legislation never became effective, but the publicity had done the trick. The German scientists became uncomfortable and began to return home by the autumn of 1964. Nasser was left with three types of rockets which could in theory inflict considerable damage on Israel but which still lacked effective steering devices. In retrospect one must wonder whether the German experts had withheld these in order to prolong their stay under conditions of neocolonial comfort and prestige.

The question of establishing normal German-Israeli relations remained. The responsibility for settling this question rested squarely with the Germans. In March 1960, Ben-Gurion had gone out of his way to meet the West German Chancellor Konrad Adenauer at the Waldorf-Astoria in New York. It was Ben-Gurion's way of showing that he was prepared to let bygones be bygones. His assumption was that Adenauer would jump at the chance of establishing normal relations and so add to that aura of respectability that the people of West Germany craved. Indeed Ben-Gurion must have thought that he was taking a political risk as well as making a friendly gesture. Opinion in Israel had been sharply against establishing relations with the Germans. People wanted time to get over the shock of the Nazi holocaust.

But the wily Adenauer, who posed as the friend of Israel, did nothing to follow up the meeting in New York. Instead he allowed all sorts of reasons to be put forward for not taking the decisive step of establishing diplomatic relations with Israel. A minor one was that the main German obligation to Israel, the payment of reparations, was already being scrupulously fulfilled. Another was that Germany could not endanger her "special role" in the Arab world—that of the West's honest broker, since the United States was becoming increasingly unpopular and France and Britain had wrecked their "image" at Suez. Then there was the possibility of damaging Germany's trade with the Arab countries. One must remember that big steel and engineering firms like Krupp, Kloeckner, and Demag constituted a powerful lobby in Bonn.

The main argument was that the Arab countries would counter a West German step by recognizing the East German Republic. It was an article of faith with all West German parties that their country and government constituted the only legitimate representative of the whole German people. If the Arab states recognized the East German Republic, other countries might follow their example. The West German government held by the so-called "Doctrine" laid down by Professor Walter Hallstein, that it would feel bound to break off diplomatic relations with any country which recognized the East German regime. It now applied this Hallstein Doctrine in reverse, insisting that West Germany must not put herself into a position in which resulting Arab action would force application of the Doctrine. Responsible servants of the

West German government even stated to me (I was the *Manchester Guardian* correspondent in Germany at the time) the argument that the breaking off of relations between West Germany and the Arab states would lead to a wave of resentment against the Jews and outbursts of anti-Semitism in both Germany and the Middle East.

Adenauer, I believe, never had any intention of establishing relations with Israel. Keenly aware of the possibility of political repercussions, he was always able to find a politician's excuses. It was otherwise with his successor, Professor Ludwig Erhard. He was a man of great probity; indeed, his political opponents suggested that his simplicity of character and his honesty combined to make it impossible for him to be a real politician at all. Early in 1965 Erhard decided that the time had come to request normal diplomatic relations with Israel. It was a much bolder step than it may seem. He did not have the full backing of his Cabinet and he knew that a section of his own Christian Democratic Party as well as the Free Democrats would oppose him. Nor could he be sure of a sufficiently favorable response in Israel. When the Knesset debated the subject, Menachem Beigin produced the monstrous libel that Erhard had acted as professional adviser to a Nazi Gauleiter and had served as head of the Hitlerite Economic Research Institute. No such institute had ever existed nor had Erhard ever worked for the Nazis. He had in fact been forced out of lucrative employment and harassed by them continually, because he was a man who spoke his mind and who thoroughly disliked the Nazis for their arrogance and inhumanity.

Eshkol threw his weight on the side of an Israeli-German understanding. He did this without false sentimentality. In his view, the Nazi crimes against the Jewish race could never be forgotten. As he reminded me, hundreds of thousands of Jews still carried tattooed concentration camp numbers on their skins. He was not ready to follow the purely utilitarian approach of Ben-Gurion, who roundly declared that friendship with Germany should be sought because it would benefit Israel in a material sense. Ben-Gurion allegedly twice risked the unity of his government over Germany—in December 1957, by proposing to send General Dayan to Bonn to negotiate an arms deal, and in 1958 by pushing through an agreement under which Israeli submachine guns were sold to West Germany.[1] Eshkol took a simple, practical stand on the question of relations with Germany. He regarded them as the basis for an understanding which would take years to mature. Wisely he linked approval—given on March 14, 1965—with the application of German government pressure on the Nazi scientists to return home from Egypt. This pressure was discreetly and successfully applied.

In announcing his decision to reopen relations with Germany in the Knesset on March 16th, Eshkol said that the initiative had necessarily come from Bonn, for it involved a real struggle of conscience and emotion for the people of Israel. Germany had a moral duty to prove its desire to make a clean break with the Nazi past. Pungently Eshkol reminded the Germans that their government had yielded to President Nasser's "blackmail" by reneging on security undertakings and endlessly postponing the opening of diplomatic relations with Israel.

Eshkol, incidentally, was subsequently involved in a brush with Adenauer. This happened in May 1966, when the ex-Chancellor was visiting Israel. He dined at Eshkol's residence in Jerusalem and was scandalized by a phrase in Eshkol's after-dinner speech. Eshkol said that the Jewish people continued to look for testimony that Germany recognized the burden of the past and sought a new path for herself in the comity of nations. Adenauer chose to interpret this as a stricture on his government's good intentions and refused to raise his glass in answer to the toast to German-Israeli understanding.

In fact, Eshkol's admonitory warning was not necessary. German-Israeli relations have prospered since 1965. The Erhard government sent an excellent ambassador to Israel, Rolf Pauls, a man of modesty, charm, and much common sense. The Erhard government, again, replaced reparations with economic aid of about $45 million a year. In three years trade between the two countries doubled. There were valuable cultural contacts and, even more significantly, exchanges of students on an increasing scale. When the June 1967 war broke out, thousands of young Germans volunteered to go to Israel for whatever service they might be called upon to perform. Hundreds of others came during the years to work without pay on Israeli farms and in Israeli factories, as part of the so-called *Aktion Suehnezeichen* (Expiation), showing goodwill in the readiest and most useful way possible. West German feeling was overwhelmingly pro-Israeli in the 1967 war. It looks as if a happier chapter has opened in German-Israeli relations, even though there are bound to be occasional setbacks.

By contrast, Israel's relations with the Soviet Union have made no progress whatsoever since the mid-1950s. The Soviet Union has emerged as the big brother of the Arab states of the Middle East, supporting their claims on every occasion in the United Nations, munificent in economic and technical aid, and ready at all times to build up Arab armed strength. Behind all this activity has been the belief that a new "East-West balance," favorable to the Soviet Union, should be struck in the Middle East because it is an area of immense strategic importance and because the Soviet Union has no intention of allowing the Western powers to be arbiters in this area.

In the decade up to the 1967 war it had become plain that there were a host of reasons why the Soviet Union should aid and sponsor the Arab cause. The Middle East is a crossroad in the world's lines of communication. The two highroads which it controls are those leading from the Mediterranean to the Indian Ocean and from Asia to Africa.

The first is important chiefly because of conventional trade, the second may turn out to be important more for the passage of ideas. If the Soviet Union wishes to export Communism to the developing countries of Africa, a bridge across the Arab Middle East is of real value. Israel is only one small piece in the Middle East mosaic. The Soviet Union's best means of utilizing this bridge is through friendship with the Arab states.

The chief product of the Middle East, oil, may not have seemed in the past to have been of paramount importance to the Soviet Union.* But the Soviet leaders plan far ahead, and two factors make Middle East oil of increasing significance in the East-West confrontation. The first is the dependence upon it of the Western powers. According to one estimate, Western European oil consumption tripled in the decade after the Suez crisis of 1956 and should triple again by 1977.[2] This suggests that Western Europe will need eight billion tons of crude oil in the decade up to 1977, and at least two thirds of that amount will have to come from the Middle East. Dominant Soviet influence in the Arab world would pose the threat of the denial of these vital supplies.

The second factor making Middle East oil important to the Soviet Union is the near-certainty—it is not more definite than that—that it will be needed quite soon to supplement Soviet resources. The West's leading oil combines have estimated that the Soviet Union and its East European partners will become major importers of crude oil by the mid-1970s.[3] One can use only the expression "near-certainty" because of the lack of precise Soviet official data. Soviet oil production is still being raised year by year, but the informed view is that new resources are not being discovered at a rate which would allow oil production to keep pace with the Soviet Union's economic and demographic growth. And it is a tenet of Soviet ideology that demographic growth cannot be curbed. To the Soviet leaders population is power. The oil supplies that the increasing population will need have to be secured.

Soviet official data may be imprecise, but Soviet activity in the oil producing countries of the Middle East is an acknowledged fact. This activity does not register what might be called an orthodox trade interest. Soviet oil interests are not concerned with development for development's sake. Soviet oil interests mean, in exact terms, Soviet government agencies operating exclusively on behalf of the regime. The interest can be political as well as economic.

Thus, in Egypt, Soviet technicians have been actively helping Nasser's General Petroleum Authority for a long time. Egyptian oil production will be used primarily in Egypt's economic interest. But

* At the end of 1968, the United States and Soviet Union were roughly self-sufficient in oil. Western Europe produced 8 million tons a year and used 420 million tons. The Middle East and North Africa produced 600 million tons and used 60 million. Its remaining surplus went to Japan, South Africa, etc.

the Soviet political interest will be served at the same time. Egyptian dependence on the Soviet Union suits Moscow, not Cairo.

But of more importance has been Soviet negotiation of contractual agreements with oil producing countries to help in their exploration projects and in the marketing of their product. By 1969 Soviet advisers were active in Syria, Iraq, and Iran. Under Soviet direction other East European countries were concluding barter agreements for the purchase of Middle East oil. Soviet technical aid was being thrown out as bait, even to anticommunist countries like Kuwait. The Soviet Union is, in fact, engaged in getting in on the ground floor in the oil producing countries. Denial of oil resources needed by the West and exploitation of resources needed by the Soviet bloc would appear to be twin objectives.

Much has been made of Arab antipathy towards Communism as a limiting factor to Soviet influence in the Middle East. Certainly the Arab peoples of the Middle East have shown little interest in Communism as an ideology, and Arab governments have kept it politically in check. In April 1957 King Hussein of Jordan suppressed the local Communist Party at the same time as he deposed a government which was showing left-wing tendencies.[4] On October 3, 1960, he denounced international Communism before the UN General Assembly in New York. Even Nasser has not hesitated to act against Egypt's Communists. The Soviet Union has not bothered to shed even crocodile tears over the misfortunes of Arab Communism and by the mid-1950s had come to terms with the realization that Arab nationalism was a far more worthwhile ally. Deprived of Soviet backing, Arab Communist parties have withered, even in countries like Syria and Iraq where economic and social conditions might be held to be ideal for proletarian revolution. And as an internal compensation, the Soviet Union's friendship with Arab governments has resulted in a decline of Pan-Arab sentiment among the Moslems of the Soviet Union.

There has been another, inverse reason for Soviet support of the Arab cause in the Middle East. Since 1948 the Soviet government has striven to secure the total assimilation of the three million Jews of the Soviet Union. Stalin tried to do this by brutal repression, which culminated in the calumny of the ostensibly Jewish-organized "Doctor's Plot" against his life. Stalin died in time for the lives of innocent Jewish doctors charged with this fictitious crime to be saved. His successors adopted a different line towards the Jewish minority: it simply had no sort of separateness from the rest of the Soviet community. This meant that its Jewishness had to be discouraged by persistent pressure and restrictions, weapons more in keeping with the times than persecution. The Soviet leaders regarded the Jewish sense of separate identity as a slur on the social system of the Soviet Union and an insult to Soviet nationalism. But they insisted that this implied no anti-Semitism on their part, only anti-Zionism. The focus of Zionism was Israel and that was another reason for regarding Israel's Arab foes as the Soviet Union's friends.

It was also a reason for discrimination against the Jews of the Soviet Union. They were placed under constant surveillance, even in their places of worship, which have been reduced to a minimum, with only one synagogue in Moscow where there used to be dozens. The main reason for surveillance is to prevent contact with the outside world, which could foster Zionist thought and belief and increase the desire of Soviet Jews to emigrate to Israel. Emigration is forbidden, and the few Jews who have been allowed to leave the Soviet Union by special dispensation have for the most part been old people who wanted to rejoin families from whom they were torn by the German invasion in 1941.

Accounts of surveillance of Soviet Jews show that it is carried out partly by police spies and partly by the despised *Yevsektzia* Jews who try to ingratiate themselves with the authorities. One American Jew who visited the Soviet Union in 1967 found that the synagogues in three big cities were being constantly watched[5] and was able to identify the agents who carried out this surveillance. He had the greatest difficulty in meeting Jews privately. In one synagogue a note was passed surreptitiously to him. It read: "Dear Friend, My friends and I very want to see you. That is very hard. If you want, please come today at 7 PM to the Central Post Office. If I can come, I will come, or will come my friends. If I cannot come greet my friends. All we want very, very, is to come to Israel." The American Jew was eventually caught in the act of receiving another clandestine note (he managed to slip it under his vest). He was toughly interrogated by the police and expelled from the Soviet Union for "spying, subversive activity, speculating in synagogues, acting with Godliness, spreading religious and Zionist propaganda, bourgeois doctrine."

According to one British newspaper,

> One of the biggest grievances is that Russian Jews alone, out of some 150 national minorities and ethnic groups, are now denied facilities to enable them to preserve their national culture. Of the officially quoted figure of 2,260,000 Jews living in the 15 Soviet republics, 487,000 declared Yiddish as being their mother tongue at the last census. Yet there is not a single school in the whole of the Soviet Union where Yiddish is taught, although Article 121 of the Soviet constitution guarantees instruction in schools "in the native language."[6]

Speaking Yiddish has been discouraged in every way possible, and an average of only two books a year are published in Yiddish as against

437 published in a single prewar year, 1935. Under Lenin the Jewish minority had a wide measure of cultural freedom. Thus, from the same British newspaper report,

> Within a few years the Jews had established a network of schools; in 1932, in the Ukraine alone, they had nearly 800 with Yiddish as the language of instruction. They had their own colleges, theaters, newspapers, scientific academies. There were about a dozen Yiddish dailies, and some 60 weeklies and monthlies. There were more than 30 Jewish theatres, and a number of flourishing drama colleges. All were closed under Stalin.[7]

On November 10, 1967, the president of the World Jewish Congress, Dr. Nahum Goldmann, appealed to the Soviet Union to pursue a more liberal policy towards its Jewish minority. He asked for more synagogues to be allowed to remain open; in Kishinev only one remained open out of over 60, and in Odessa there was only one for a Jewish population of nearly 100,000. He asked for Jewish schools to be reopened and for toleration of the Yiddish language. He asked that kosher slaughtering and cooking be permitted, pointing out at the same time that the Soviet authorities had only recently allowed the baking of Passover matzoh. His most important requests were for the end of surveillance and the reestablishment of contact between the Jewish community in the Soviet Union and Jewish communities elsewhere in the world.

He could well have asked, too, for the ending of propaganda which the Soviet press maintains is merely anti-Zionist but which has anti-Semitic overtones. The absurd and perverted fairy tale of the *Protocols of the Elders of Zion,* the so-called Jewish "plot against world civilization," is still propagated in the Soviet Union (and in Arab countries too). Soviet cartoonists depict Dayan reading Hitler's *Mein Kampf* and make fun of his eye patch, forgetting that he lost an eye fighting against Nazi Germany. Propagandists like Yuri Ivanov, T. K. Kichko, and Yuri Konstantinov have poured out anti-Semitic writings, and the Soviet, like the Arab, press likes to depict Zionists as hook-nosed subhumans, in the style of the *Stuermer* cartoons of Julius Streicher, the Nazi Gauleiter of Nuremberg. Yevtushenko was bitterly criticized for his poem *Babi Yar,* a song of sympathy for the Russian-Jewish victims of the Nazis. So was Anatoly Kuznetsov, who wrote a book on the Babi Yar massacre. A reason why the writers Daniel and Sinyavsky were singled out for persecution may well have been that Daniel was a Jew and Sinyavsky was married to one.

Soviet suppression of the Jewish minority was slavishly copied by the Gomulka regime in Poland, which was becoming by the end of 1967 more violently and openly anti-Semitic. There were fears that the same thing might happen in Czechoslovakia, after the Soviet invasion of the country in September 1968. Israel's leaders have had to endure terrible frustration, for there has been so little they can do about the suffering of Jewish minorities in the Soviet bloc, apart from drawing attention to the facts.

Inevitably relations with the Soviet Union, the instigator of suppression, have been adversely affected. Eshkol had always made it plain that he would welcome more cordial relations with Moscow, on two grounds. It could lead to the modification of Soviet support of the Arabs and could bring some amelioration of the lot of the Jews of the Soviet Union. Within a few months of becoming Prime Minister in January 1964, Eshkol was exchanging letters with Nikita Khrushchev. The latter produced his package peace plan, calling for the ending of belligerency among all member states of the United Nations, guaranteeing nonaggression, and accepting existing frontiers. Such a plan, if implemented, could have brought peace closer between Israel and her Arab neighbors. Eshkol dearly wanted peace and had not the slightest desire to change Israel's existing frontiers. He gave his wholehearted approval to the Khrushchev package plan, hoping that it could be followed up by profitable Soviet-Israeli conversations. Nothing whatsoever happened.

In October 1964 Eshkol made another friendly gesture. He authorized an agreement under which Russian state property in Jerusalem was officially bought by the State of Israel. Israel paid $2 million for the property, which included buildings which are being used by the Israeli High Court, by the police, and by the government press office. These buildings had belonged to the Tsarist regime, and Israel was under no obligation to pay for them, having inherited them from the British Mandatory power. The Soviet government undertook to take up part of the sum in the form of Israeli goods. This has not yet been done.

The truth was that the Soviet Union had no interest in developing closer or friendlier relations with Israel; rather the reverse was true. Closer and friendlier relations would arouse Arab suspicion and involve making some concessions over the treatment of the Jewish minority in the Soviet Union, concessions to which the Soviet leaders were implacably opposed. It came as no surprise to find Eshkol, after the exercise of great patience, denouncing the Soviet Union, in May 1968, accusing it of a "criminal policy" of supporting "with every political means, by providing modern weapons of aggression, and by threats against Israel, those who aspire to war and murder."[8] Eshkol expressed the view that the Soviet Union had joined with the Arabs "in a bid to do to the Jews of Israel what the Nazis did to European Jewry." He linked Soviet policy with the activities of the Polish government of Gomulka, "an undemocratic, inhuman regime of persecution, which is exploiting the existence of a handful of Jews in their country in order to cover up the failure of a despicable, hateful policy of repression."

Repression of the Jewish minority and political support of the Arab states of the Middle East, then, were two principal Israeli complaints against the Soviet Union. The third principal complaint was caused by Soviet readiness to supply arms in very large quantities to Arab countries, especially Egypt. An article in the *Jerusalem Post* pointed out that the Soviet Union may have claimed to be maintaining a military balance in the Middle East, but was in reality always ready to give Egypt a lead over Israel in armaments.[9] Before the 1956 Sinai campaign the Soviet Union delivered T-34 tanks, S.U. self-propelled guns, Stalin-3 tanks, MIG-15 and -17 fighter aircraft, and Ilyushin-28 bombers The scale of the Soviet arms deliveries was undoubtedly one factor which caused the Israelis to go to France and Britain for arms and military help. In 1960 Egypt, with the help of Soviet as well as German technicians, began developing ground-to-ground long-range missiles. In 1961 the Soviet Union started delivery of the latest MIG-19 fighters, along with personnel to train Egyptian pilots. In 1961 deliveries began of MIG-21's, Tupolov-16 heavy bombers and Antonov-12 transport planes, as well as T-53 tanks. In 1964 Egypt began to receive supersonic MIG-21's and T-55 tanks. Israel, according to the *Jerusalem Post*, was always in search of defense. She bought new weapons only when she had to, when the Soviet Union had already given Egypt a clear advantage in quality as well as quantity.

The Soviet arms deliveries in 1964 hastened Eshkol's already projected visit to the United States for talks with President Lyndon B. Johnson in June. At and after the talks both men emphasized the need for a lasting peace in the Middle East. At the Overseas Press Club Eshkol said that war would be very costly to both sides and that there was an urgent need to halt the arms race. He told the President that he was deeply worried by Arab rearmament, which was directed against Israel and Israel alone. He used phrases that expressed the physical, almost visceral apprehension of the people of Israel: Israel was "not a state like other states, but a last refuge for her people," and Israel was "not afraid so much of losing a war as of losing a whole people."

From Washington Eshkol went to Paris, where he had completely satisfactory meetings with President de Gaulle, who spoke warmly of Israel as "our friend and ally." France promised to go on supplying arms, and France had already become Israel's main source of up-to-date aircraft. De Gaulle, evidently, had not yet begun to toy with the idea of a policy of neutrality between Israel and the Arabs.

What Eshkol had obtained from his visits to Washington and Paris was a firm assurance that Israel would be helped with arms supply, if it were shown that the balance of armed strength in the Middle East was being significantly changed by the influx of Soviet weapons. This was all that he needed to know, for in war Israel would not depend on a superiority of weapons but on rapid mobilization, good military intelligence, expert leadership, and a high fighting morale. Israel's qualities in all these respects had been proved in both 1948 and 1956, and Eshkol's view at this stage was that the Arab countries were not ready to risk another conflict.

But in the summer of 1964 there was a new worrying development that was destined to increase tension during the next three years to a point when war once again became probable. One of the reasons for the Sinai campaign of 1956 was the activity on Israel's borders of the Arab guerilla fedayeen. The fedayeen had been Egyptian-sponsored and one of the Israelis' justifications for the Sinai campaign was that it destroyed their bases and induced Egypt to call off this type of irregular warfare. Now a new menace appeared, this time on Israel's borders with Syria, Jordan, and Lebanon. A so-called Palestine Liberation Movement had been founded and its strike force, El Fatah, was now organized and based in Damascus. The Syrians were intent on showing that they were better Arabs than the Egyptians and readier to provoke Israel.

Israeli intelligence had advance information of El Fatah's organization and aims. On September 4, 1964, Eshkol warned King Hussein not to be drawn into any military or paramilitary adventure and called the Palestine Liberation Movement "the time bomb under Amman's throne." Eshkol was under heavy personal pressure at the time. Dayan was threatening to resign his post as Minister of Agriculture and did so a few weeks later. Ben-Gurion was openly risking splitting the Mapai party once again, over the Lavon Affair. The economic situation was causing concern, and at the end of September Eshkol had an operation for a cataract of his right eye. Early in 1965 El Fatah began active operations. During the course of the year they were to launch 38 raids into Israeli territory, penetrating up to distances of 12 miles, mining roads and trying, usually unsuccessfully, to blow up isolated buildings.

Almost equally worrying were Syrian threats to cut off part of the headwaters of the river Jordan. The Israelis had begun to take water from the Sea of Galilee in September 1964 when the Eshed-Kinrot pumping station was completed. The pipeline was intended to take up to about 260 million cubic yards a year at first, as against the almost 420 million allowed under the Johnston Plan. Israel's success in completing the pumping station and the water carrier to the south infuriated the Arabs. Once again, the Syrians took the lead. Of the Jordan's headwaters, the Banias springs were in Syria, the Wazzani tributary flowed from Lebanon through Syrian territory on its way to the Jordan, and only the Dan springs and river were inside Israel's frontier. The Syrian plan was to divert the waters of the Banias and Wazzani within a few hundred yards of the Israeli frontier into a canal which would take them to the east and deprive the river Jordan of about half its normal flow.

On January 22, 1965, Eshkol warned that any diversion of the Jordan's headwaters would be regarded as "an encroachment on our borders" amounting to an act of war. In dealing with such encroachment Israel, Eshkol hinted, believed that she would have the sympathy of the United States and other countries; but, he added, "in the final analysis, we must rely on our own deterrent power." Eshkol later had talks with Averell Harriman, President Johnson's special envoy, and reached an understanding with him that Israel would react only if the Arabs took more than their share of the Jordan's waters, as allocated by the Johnston Plan. Harriman gave him an assurance that the United States would continue to supply arms which Israel needed for her defense.

Eshkol's next port of call was London, in late March. He was worried by the fact that the Labor government, while preaching peace, continued to supply arms on a considerable scale to the Arab countries. This was of course part of the price that Britain paid to safeguard her oil interests, something which Eshkol understood very well. But he could hardly have been impressed by the argument put forward by Prime Minister Wilson, that Britain's sale of arms was designed to preserve the military and political balance in the Middle East. The sale of arms to Jordan certainly helped King Hussein to shore up his teetering throne, and Israel appreciated that Britain wanted to help the King and felt under an obligation to him. But the sale of arms to Egypt and Iraq was less easily defensible; they could be used against either Hussein or Israel. A balance between Jordan and Arab regimes plotting the King's downfall was being created at Israel's expense, for Israel had to arm herself to deal with the possible eventuality of a unified Arab front against her. Eshkol never ceased to underline this ultimate danger to his own ministers, even though many of them considered that his fears were without foundation.

Eshkol did not ask Wilson for British arms. He did manage to extract a statement from him, made to the House of Commons on April 1, that Britain would not sacrifice her ties with Israel in order to get better relations with Egypt. But Eshkol was rapped on the knuckles for implied criticism of the United Nations, something which British Labor politicians liked doing so long as Gibraltar and the Falkland Islands were not under discussion, and he was said to have been sorely tried by the academic arguments of Wilson and his ministers. According to one source, he cried out in anguish—and in Yiddish—after one meeting, *"Mee ret, mee ret, un mee shusket zich!"*—"One talks, and one talks, and nobody listens!"[10]

Wilson did at least make plain to Eshkol Britain's interest in peace in the Middle East. In early 1965 he was still talking more frankly and more to the point than he was a year or two later, when his phrase "seen to be doing" had become embedded in British governmental jargon. Britain's interest in peace in the area is so great that it is truly frightening to consider how little Britain has done in a strictly practical way to give it practical application. Eshkol mulled over his London conversations. He accepted the British arguments in favor of preserving peace. On May 17, 1965, he produced a statement in the Knesset on foreign relations which contained the germ of a peace plan.

In his speech, he told the Arab countries that "ambition to wipe a nation off the map cannot be realized in modern times. Quite simply, we will not allow it, nor the world tolerate it." He emphasized Israel's desire for peace, adding that "the foundation of it is full respect for the independence, sovereignty, and territorial integrity of all the States in the region." He quoted the United Nations Charter in support of this utterly justifiable wish. Eshkol suggested that the existing distribution of territory in the Middle East provided a fair basis for mutual coexistence and friendship—the Arab world covered an area of 4,500,000 square miles, while Israel occupied just 8000 square miles, less than one five-hundredth part of that total area. "In this situation," Eshkol said, "there is neither sense nor justice in territorial changes to Israel's disadvantage." Eshkol argued for the status quo and only that.

He went on to stress the historic claim to the Promised Land. This claim was based

> on the fundamental and natural historic rights of the Jewish people to its Land, to its own Homeland, from which it was expelled by brute force. To this Land it has lifted up its heart and its prayers during the years of Exile. In every generation, throughout the tribulations of epochs and regimes, its sons have come forward, braving hardship and suffering, to settle on its soil. . . . Never has the Jewish people abandoned its Land, never has that Land been devoid of a Jewish population. In recent generations the Jewish people dedicated itself to the task of safeguarding its rights to its Homeland under the law of nations. Through its toil and sacrifice, and with the support of humanity's finest sons, after the most appalling of history's tragedies, the State of Israel arose in a partitioned Land of Israel.

Eshkol called for "a mutual undertaking to refrain from aggression, so that our justified apprehensions and vain Arab fears may be dissipated at one and the same time." He then outlined the benefits of peace to the whole Middle East.

> The State of Israel stands at the crossroads of Asia and Africa. If the entire region becomes an open area, dedicated to cooperation and mutual aid, that will be a blessing to the peoples of both Continents, and, among them, to ourselves and the Arab States as well.
>
> Orderly land transport by road and rail; freedom of transit

through airports; radio, telephonic, and postal communications; access to our ports on the Mediterranean in the form of free areas in them, under suitable conditions, for the benefit of Jordan, which has no outlet to that sea; facilities for the sale of oil by reviving the oil pipeline or building larger ones; encouragement of tourism to all the lands of the area; free access to the Holy Places with amenities for pilgrimage to centers sacred to all religions—all these are only part of the picture that will take shape as the outcome of the liberation of the Middle East from the oppressive atmosphere that now prevails.

Eshkol urged the advantages of joint exploitation of raw materials, joint research in such fields as the desalination of water and the conquering of disease, joint measures to secure a realistic solution of the refugee problem, full economic and social cooperation in order to create a Middle East Common Market. He pointed out that a program for peace was "no fantasy"—"I do not imagine that the cooperation which exists today in Western Europe seemed less fantastic 20 years ago. We are approaching a score of years since the War of Independence. It can be done here too."

His summing up was: "The beginning of wisdom is the courage to free oneself from the self-hypnosis of hate propaganda, to sit down at the conference table without prior conditions and in full mutual respect." His speech writers, perhaps unwisely, placed his criticisms of Nasser's activities at the end of the speech, criticisms of the latter's brutal aggression in the Yemen, his intrigues in Aden, his plots against King Hussein of Jordan and King Idris of Libya. The speech lost, as a result, some of its force; but its meaning was plain. Israel wanted, and was prepared to talk, peace.

What sort of peace terms did Eshkol envisage at this juncture? Undoubtedly the principal point was recognition of the State of Israel, within its existing boundaries. A few days before his Knesset speech of May 17, 1965, Eshkol referred to the impossibility of reversing what had happened in 1948: "An egg broken 18 years ago cannot be put together again."

The second point was resettlement of the refugees, or at least the great bulk of them, in the ample Arab world. Not long after this speech I asked his Foreign Minister, Mrs. Golda Meir, whether Israel would at least accept back a token number of Palestinian Arab refugees. She said that Israel would do so if this were part of an over-all peace settlement. After some hesitation she agreed that 60,000 might be a fair and feasible number. But the reintegration of even that number in Israel's economy would be difficult, especially on the land. Agrarian Palestinian Arabs had practiced a simple, even primitive, husbandry. Any who returned would find themselves in the thick of a modern, highly competitive community. Both Eshkol and Mrs. Meir did not see the refugee question any longer as a matter of right and wrong; half a million Arabs had fled from their homes in 1948, and half a million Jews had left their homes in Arab countries and come to Israel. Two wrongs did not make a right, but they justified an equalization which took account of this involuntary exchange of population.

The third point in a peace settlement acceptable to Israel was restoration of normal freedom of movement in the Middle East. Israeli ships and goods had been denied passage through the Suez Canal, in defiance of international agreements and the resolutions of the United Nations. Israeli pilgrims had been denied access to their holiest shrine, the Wailing Wall in the Old City of Jerusalem. Israel's borders had been hermetically sealed by her Arab neighbors, who often shot to kill people who merely came close to them.

A fourth point would presumably have been a mutual security pact between Israel and her Arab neighbors, guaranteed by the United Nations and, possibly, by the great powers, the four permanent members of the UN Security Council, the United States, the Soviet Union, Britain, and France.

Eshkol's personal desire for peace was beyond doubt. But his proposals were rejected with contempt by the politicians and the press of the Arab world. The Arab answer indeed was to step up their anti-Israeli propaganda and the armed incursions of El Fatah. On May 27, 1965, Israeli patience snapped; Israeli infantry crossed the Jordanian border and blew up a flour mill and an ice factory at Jenin and 11 water pumps at Qalkilya. At a third point, Shuneh, houses which were known to be in constant use by El Fatah raiders were destroyed. The Israeli forces took great pains to avoid the loss of life, and there was not a single Arab casualty in the raids on the three places.

The Israeli government warned both Jordan and Lebanon that counteraction would be taken if the activities of El Fatah continued. Israel was aware that the Syrians were the prime movers in these activities and that Jordanian and Lebanese bases were used to shield Syria from retribution. But Israel believed too that effective action by the Jordanian and Lebanese authorities could prevent El Fatah operations. Until 1965 the Lebanese border had been relatively quiet. The Lebanese are a thrifty and unwarlike people, and there had even been some mild fraternization between their frontier farmers and police and their opposite numbers in Israel. Villagers on both sides made a habit of returning livestock which strayed across the frontier; police gave each other information about marauders or illegal frontier runners. But El Fatah raids out of the Lebanon provoked Israeli counteraction on the night of October 28–29. Israeli infantry crossed the frontier to blow up the dam of a small reservoir at Meiss el Jebel and houses at the village of Houlé. Unfortunately an old woman fast asleep in one of the houses was killed. There was a wave of sympathy abroad for Lebanon, the smallest and least hostile of Israel's neighbors (the same thing was to happen in December 1968 when Israeli commandos attacked Beirut international airport).

The year 1965 closed without any sign of an improvement in Israeli-Arab relations. Alone among Arab statesmen, President Bourguiba of Tunisia was urging the Arab world to forsake military force in favor of diplomatic action and demographic pressure against Israel. In what was in effect a New Year's message to the outside world, Eshkol appealed for an end of the arms race in the Middle East.[11] He asked the Soviet Union not to extend the Cold War into the area, but instead, to reach agreement with the Western powers on arms limitation for the Middle East, and to cease giving open support to Arab sabotage, terrorism, and violently aggressive propaganda against Israel, a fellow member of the United Nations. This appeal, too, fell on deaf ears. The Soviet Union was on the way to committing the ultimate folly of encouraging the Arab states to make war on Israel.

1. The *Times* (London), March 16, 1965.
2. *The Economist* (London), May 27, 1967.
3. *Ibid.*, August 10, 1968.
4. Walter Lacqueur, *The Soviet Union and the Middle East*, p. 275.
5. Hellel Levine, the American Jew in question, was expelled from the Soviet Union for making contact with Soviet Jews. He named the cities in question, but preferred that their names not be published.
6. Joel Cang in the *Times* (London), April 11, 1968.
7. *Ibid.*
8. *The Israel Digest,* May 3, 1968.
9. The *Jerusalem Post,* May 19, 1966.
10. The *Jewish Chronicle* (London), March 27, 1965.
11. Speech to the Knesset, January 11, 1966.

16.

The clouds of war continued to gather during 1966, even though Israel's leaders hesitated to believe that any Arab state would be ill advised enough to risk another Suez or another 1948. Men like the Chief of Staff, General Itzhak Rabin, or one of the foremost experts on Arab affairs, Brigadier Jehosophat Harkavi, felt that Israel's manifest military preparedness was a sufficient deterrent. Military preparedness was their creed. Both the Israeli military and political leadership had not the faintest illusion about the Arab desire to encompass and destroy Israel and the Arab determination to reject every overture of peace. As one of Eshkol's advisers on Arab affairs put it, "The Arabs will first be ready to talk to us when we are under the waters of the Mediterranean."[1]

Yet Egypt, it was felt, had learned its lesson in 1956. Jordan was too small to launch an attack on its own, and the instability of his throne discouraged King Hussein from military adventures. Most Israelis, moreover, believed that in his heart he was, like his grandfather, Abdullah, prepared to reach an understanding with Israel if only his fellow Arab rulers would allow him to do so. There was an undercurrent of friendly sentiment towards the "little King," dispelled only when Jordan entered the 1967 war of its own volition. Lebanon, plainly, did not want war. Its chief interests were trade and tourism, its eyes were turned to the West, and the Lebanese community was precariously balanced in roughly equal Moslem and Christian groupings. The Syrians were full of sound and fury but not a military force which Israel could fear, or even respect.

Nor did Israelis feel in 1966 that the Soviet Union would allow the Arabs to go to war before the odds were heavily in their favor. This was definitely not yet the case. Indeed the feeling was that Red China was more likely to emerge as the new danger element in the Middle East.[2] There were, early in 1966, large Chinese missions in Egypt and Syria. The Chinese Government was prepared to send arms to both countries and there was an unpleasant possibility that the Chinese would advise the Palestine Liberation Movement on ways of conducting irregular warfare and would try to turn the Middle East into a second Vietnam.

At the end of February 1966 the relatively moderate socialist (Baathist) government in Syria fell as a result of an army coup. The new head of state, President Nureddin el Attassi, called for the "liberation" of Palestine and the annihilation of Israeli Zionism. He declared on March 10 that Arab unity would be "forged in the flames of the liberation war" and urged a quick and decisive action. In May, Attassi called for a "people's war" of resistance, sabotage, and terror. "We want a policy of scorched earth and it is only through this policy that we can hope to build a new life for the Arab masses." Here was an uncomfortable hint of Viet Cong tactics and Chinese advice. Moreover, Syria was getting vociferous Soviet support. On May 7 the Soviet newspaper *Izvestia* accused Israel of armed provocation against Syria, and this accusation was repeated by the Soviet official news agency, Tass, on May 27 in the form of an open statement which was pompously delivered to the Israeli Government. The operative passage of this pseudodiplomatic communication read: "The Soviet Union cannot and will not remain indifferent to the attempts to violate peace in a region located in direct proximity to the borders of the Soviet Union." Any child's atlas could show that this assertion was geographically ridiculous.

Syrian governments had fallen in the past with monotonous regularity. Both Israel and the outside world were inclined therefore to predict a short life for the Attassi regime. Unfortunately it had come to stay, and Syria was henceforward to be the pacesetter on the Arab side in preaching the need for war and its inevitability. Attassi probably had two ulterior motives, to wrest the hitherto undisputed leadership of the Arab Middle East from President Nasser and to keep his own political opponents at home quiet. The comparative stability of his regime, and unreserved Soviet backing of it, were to be significant factors in provoking war in 1967.

The Soviet Union meanwhile was giving equally strong moral and much greater material backing to its favorite son in the Middle East, Nasser. In March, according to one well-informed source,[3] a secret defense agreement was signed between Egypt and the Soviet Union after talks between Nasser and the Soviet Deputy Defense Minister, Gretchko. It was believed that the Soviet Union was given naval facilities at the Mediterranean ports of Mersah Matruh and Sidi Barrani, at the Red Sea port of Quseir and at three Red Sea fishing villages, Berenice, Hurghada, and Jebel Zabara. At least three airstrips were put at the Soviet Union's disposal, and Soviet planes were given what amounted to blanket rights in landing and refueling wherever they wanted to in Egypt. In return, the Soviet Union undertook to increase its shipments of arms as well as the number of Soviet technicians working for the Egyptian government. On May 15 President Kosygin arrived in Cairo and pledged Soviet support for Egypt's "struggle against imperialism." In June, at the United Nations, Kosygin designated Israel as the chief imperialist power involved in the Middle East, a unique distinction for a country with a population less than half that of Moscow!

In April Eshkol was advising Nasser to wage war on illiteracy, poverty, hunger, and economic backwardness, instead of inciting his people to make war on Israel.[4] In May and June Eshkol answered the Soviet accusations of Israeli provocation of Syria. The boot was very much on the other foot: armed attacks on Israel were taking place with increasing frequency, some of them directly across the Syrian-Israeli frontier. Thus, on January 23, 1966, the reservoir at Kfar Yuval was attacked, on February 7 a bridge at Hagroshim, on April 18 field workers and their tractor at Maayan Barukh, on April 25 houses and water pumps at Beit Yosef, on April 30 houses at Kfar Giladi, on May 16 a tractor at Almagor. Early in July there were half a dozen attacks by raiders operating from bases in Syria. Eshkol ordered retaliatory action in the form of an air strike. On July 14 Israeli planes swept across the Sea of Galilee, bombed and machine-gunned Syrian batteries in the Golan Mountains, and destroyed tractors and excavators which were being used on the project for diverting the headwaters of the river Jordan. One Syrian MIG fighter was shot down.

Israel was, of course, assailed in the United Nations Security Council for this highly effective air strike. The Soviet chief delegate, Nikolai Fedorenko, used extravagant language. Israel, he said, had

> used means of extermination as radical as napalm bombs . . . had made international piracy into part and parcel of its normal actions towards Syria and other Arab states. Israel has shown an exaggeratedly militaristic attitude because it could count not only on its own forces but on the support of the Western powers as well. Israel's activities are an obvious echo of the imperialistic policies of these Western powers and of their clandestine reactionary intervention in the Middle East.[5]

The truth was that the Syrian-sponsored El Fatah had made over 50 murderous attacks on Israel since the beginning of the year. The great majority of these attacks were on civilians and their property, and the raiders mined and bombed even sheep pens and chicken coops. Only about a quarter of the attacks were made directly across the Syrian-Israeli frontier, but Syria was the prime mover in organizing and helping the El Fatah campaign. The Syrians indeed openly proclaimed this and regarded El Fatah headquarters in Damascus as a valuable "card" in their contest for leadership of the Arab world.

It cannot be repeated too often that the initiative for attacks across the frontier, including firing across it, almost invariably came from the Arab side. I wrote in 1966,

> In the outside world, it is often imagined that frontier incidents between Israel and her neighbors amount to "six of one and half-a-dozen of the other," that both sides have aggressive tendencies and that acts of provocation are roughly equally divided. This is very far from being the case. The Israelis want to use their land, if possible, right up to the frontier. They want to improve communications in the frontier zone—with, it has to be admitted, the subsidiary purpose of simplifying the patrolling of their side of the frontier.
>
> The approach of the Arab countries is in many cases diametrically opposed. Their basic idea is to prevent the Israelis from build-

ing up their economy and from utilizing all of their land. The chief method of doing this has been to create incidents by applying periodic pressure in the frontier area. A secondary method has been to infiltrate agents into Israel in order to organize acts of sabotage there.[6]

The pattern was one of Arab attack, repeated again and again until Israel felt bound to take strong counteraction. This pattern was described in forceful terms by Eshkol, when he addressed the Knesset on October 17, 1966. He accused Syria of arming, financing, and training El Fatah and its *corps d'élite* of skilled saboteurs, *El Assifa;* and he pointed out that Syria spoke with three separate and distinct voices on the subject of armed terrorism. In statements for consumption abroad Syria claimed that Israel was always the aggressor; in the United Nations Syria protested her innocence; but in Damascus the government and the government-controlled radio and press openly proclaimed their support of the guerillas. Eshkol concluded his speech by branding as a lie Syrian claims that Israel was concentrating her regular armed forces on Syria's frontier and was conspiring to overthrow Syria's so-called "progressive" regime. He offered Syria a nonaggression pact, an offer which was rebuffed at once by the Minister of the Interior, Ashawi, who added that "battle with Israel is coming, and we are ready for that battle at any time."[7]

It has often been supposed, quite wrongly, that Eshkol was inclined to be hesitant in an emergency. He showed no hesitancy at all as the situation continued to deteriorate in 1966. It was Eshkol and not the supposedly more hawkish members of the Cabinet who at Cabinet meetings continually warned against the danger of a united Arab attack on Israel. Ministers tended to discount this danger, visualizing, at the worst, an attack by Egypt alone, or perhaps prematurely by Syria. It was Eshkol, again, who overrode objections in the Cabinet to increased military expenditure. According to Yigal Allon, Minister of Labor at the time:

> Eshkol's first action when he took over Defense along with the Prime Minister's office was to order a thorough survey of all defense arrangements. From then on, he required periodic reappraisal of the military situation, and he was always insistent that Israel must be able to wage a real campaign, not just a war of one week. As a man who was cautious in the best sense of the word, he was ready to prepare for the worst. He believed in building up the reserves which would be needed—perhaps his experience as settler, farmer, and Minister of Finance helped.

In Allon's view Eshkol made two particular personal contributions to the country's defense. The first was to insist on the reequipment of the army's tank force. The second was to give his Chief of Staff as free a hand as possible. One could add a third contribution to military preparedness—it was to put a standard question to the Chief of Staff, "Why don't you ask for more?"

In November 1966 Eshkol raised the period of military service for men from 26 to 30 months. Women continued to serve 20 months. The Prime Minister justified this step by explaining that something like a permanent state of alert now existed. In October and early November there had been a further dozen incursions of Arab terrorists, culminating in a command car's being blown up just across the border from Hebron, with three soldiers killed and six wounded. Loss of life has always enraged the Israelis, for to them every member of the community is valuable, even precious. There had been a series of incidents in the Hebron area; Eshkol decided that the retaliatory strike should take place there too. Accordingly, an Israeli commando group crossed the frontier south of Hebron on November 14 and blew up about 50 houses in the villages of Samu, Khirbet Markaz, and Khirbet Jinawa. The inhabitants of the villages had been evacuated, but Jordanian police and frontier guards fought fiercely, killing one Israeli soldier and wounding ten others. At least 50 Jordanians lost their lives. The true number has never been disclosed. The Jordanians kept it secret because they did not want to depress the already shaky morale of their own people.

Once again Israel came in for sharp criticism from the world's press, both for the scale of the attack and because it was launched against Jordan. Once again, the popularity of King Hussein played a big part in eliciting sympathy. And, as usual, the Israeli government found itself in a quandary. If it did not strike back, then terrorist attacks would have multiplied. But when it did strike back, it found itself labeled an aggressor. There has never been a solution to this quandary. On balance, experience has shown that tough retaliatory action brings some respite, for the terrorists have realized that they can only make themselves unpopular by bringing retribution down on the heads of the local Arab population.

At the end of the year pressure for the broadening of the coalition in order to form a truly national government which would include the break-away socialists of Rafi and the conservative-liberal Gahal block was beginning to be felt. The pressure came initially from the National Religious and Independent Liberal parties. Their leaders argued that the Arab threat was growing, that Israel's economic position was deteriorating, that national confidence was ebbing away—in particular, emigration from the country was on the increase—and that Eshkol was not a decisive enough leader. Israel, certainly, seemed increasingly encircled and embattled. In the United Nations Soviet attacks were redoubled before Christmas, with Nikolai Fedorenko giving spurious details of a huge Israeli military build-up on the Syrian frontier. The head of the United Nations Truce Supervisory Organization, General Odd Bull, went up to Galilee to investigate this charge and found no sign whatever of a build-up. But Syria took the opportunity to proclaim that the war had really begun, and Radio Damascus began broadcasting El Fatah bulletins as war communiqués.

In January 1967 Egypt began bringing pressure to bear on King Hussein to allow "allied" Arab forces into Jordan. The King refused, and Nasser publicly denounced him as an "American puppet." Jordan withdrew her ambassador from Cairo, but the pressure on Hussein continued. In January, too, the Soviet Union promised to supply Nasser and his hungry subjects with 250,000 tons of grain. Fortified by this promise, Nasser threatened to default on all debts to the Western world, including $250 million of short-term loans from Western banks.

Divisions in the Arab camp and Nasser's gestures of defiance against the West caused Eshkol and his government no worry at all, but in the early months of 1967 there were other, much more sinister developments. First, the terrorist attacks of El Fatah, which had abated somewhat before Christmas, were stepped up all along Israel's eastern frontier. Then, the Jordanian press began to castigate Nasser for using big words but not backing them with action and for leaving Jordan and Syria to bear the brunt of Israeli "reprisals." The Jordanian taunts carried a real sting, for they were so plainly true. They probably did much to convince Nasser that his leadership of the Arab world would have to be asserted by a bolder and more aggressive policy towards Israel.

Then, on February 3, *Izvestia* published a circumstantial report of Israel's preparations for a war which was allegedly imminent. The Soviet newspaper claimed that the Israeli armed forces had been placed in a state of alert, that all furloughs for their members had been cancelled, that reservists were being called up en masse and, once again, that there were large troop concentrations on Syria's frontier. Each and every one of these assertions was demonstrably false. They could have been the inventions of either knaves or fools. Soviet diplomacy is sometimes obtuse and ill-informed, but on the subject of Israel's war preparations it is impossible to give it the benefit of any doubt. The fable that Israel was about to mount a full-scale war against Syria was concocted with the obvious purpose of reminding the Arabs of their dependence on Soviet tutelage.

Unfortunately, a lie, if repeated often enough, tends to be believed. This particular lie was given added credence when, on April 7, 1967, Israeli aircraft again attacked Syrian batteries on the Golan Mountains. This time the Syrian airforce was ready for them. But the MIG's and their pilots were no match for the Israeli Mirages, which shot down six without loss. The Syrian Prime Minister, Attassi, contented himself with claiming a victory "on land," in reference to the shelling of four Israeli settlements, the shelling which had actually provoked the Israeli air strike. The Soviet and Arab press treated the April 7 action as a harbinger of the full-scale military assault which they had been forecasting; and partly as a result of popular clamor, the Commander in Chief of the Egyptian Airforce, General Mohamed Sidky Mahmoud, was sent to Damascus on April 10 for a 12-day conference, being followed there, on April 17, by Egypt's Prime Minister, Mohamed Soliman. In order to give more backbone to the Arab discussions on joint military action, the Soviet Union assailed Israel on April 21 in a note which contained the remarkable assertion that the air strike of April 7 was carried out on behalf of "imperialist forces" because of the gallant Arab "struggle against the oil monopolies." What the Soviet Union was asking the world to believe was that the Western powers were deliberately endangering their so-called "oil monopolies" in order to appease warmongering, oilless Israel!

Soviet propaganda produced a chain reaction of the most dangerous kind. Totally untrue Soviet reports of Israeli troop concentrations had inflamed and incited the Arab press. Arab public opinion was thereupon brought to the boiling point. This forced Arab governments into warlike postures which they might otherwise not have assumed, and encouraged El Fatah to increase its raids into Israel. This compelled Israel to carry out retaliatory air strikes, which in turn increased popular support in the Arab countries for full-scale war against Israel. Add to all this the facts of a Middle East situation made permanently and highly combustible by the Arab-Israeli conflict, and the Arabs' extreme excitability. A war psychosis was being created, primarily by the Soviet Union.

Perhaps one should look back for a moment at some of the Arab statements made before the war of June 1967. Apologists for the Arabs insist that they do not really mean what they say, that the Arabic language lends itself to hyperbole and verbal fantasy, and that the speeches even of ostensibly responsible statesmen should be largely discounted. There is something in this. A classic example of hyperbole verging on sheer nonsense, for instance, was Nasser's Victory Day speech at Port Said on December 23, 1964. The speech, which was to celebrate the "triumphant" campaign of Suez and Port Said of 1956, contained passages like these:

> I want to say that we are getting wheat from the Americans. We must disclose the matter openly. We get wheat, meat, and chicken. By God, we do not get factories! They give us the equivalent of about 50 million [Egyptian] pounds a year. Our annual budget is 1100 million pounds. We spend some 400 or 500 million pounds on the Plan. If the need arises, we could spare this 50 million pounds, on our food, and it would not bother us a bit, by God! . . . I would like him [the American Ambassador] to know that whoever

does not like our behavior can go and drink up the sea. If the Mediterranean is not enough, there is the Red Sea too. . . . We are a quick-tempered people. We are born like that. We are a people with dignity. We are building our country and are absolutely not prepared to sell our dignity. We are building our country and continuously preserving this dignity more and more. . . . To anyone who says one word against us we retaliate with ten.

It would appear that the whole tenor of Nasser's speech on this occasion was to deny any obligation to feel grateful for American aid, which amounted to about 5 percent of Egypt's total budget. The way in which a benefactor was thanked was to invite him to "drink up the sea." And the ultimate purpose of the speech was to insist, somewhat pathetically, on Egyptian "dignity."

Arab statements before the June 1967 war were rather more precise than this one of Nasser's. Speaking on Radio Cairo as early as May 18, 1962, Nasser himself said: "We will launch a full-scale war when the right moment arrives." Two years later President Aref of Iraq reiterated this motif. On Radio Bagdad he declared on November 2, 1964, "We must put an end to Israel's existence." Aref and Nasser, in a joint communiqué issued in Cairo on May 25, 1965, reaffirmed that the twin objectives of their governments were the "liberation of Palestine" and the "eradication of Israel." Syria's Foreign Minister, Ibrahim Makhous, was more specific speaking on Radio Damascus on May 22, 1966. He said then: "We have nothing to lose by fighting the popular liberation war. The people must be ready, from now on, for all eventualities. We must fear nothing. The Arab nation can unite only through battle, and Israel can be eliminated only through battle."

Syria's president, Nureddin el Attassi, made two clear-cut statements at this time. On May 11, 1966, he said: "We desire the liberation of Palestine and we have planned the way to a popular war to achieve this end." And on May 22, 1966, he was equally precise: "We raise the slogan of the people's liberation war. We want total war with no limits, a war that will destroy the Zionist base." Exactly one year later, on May 22, 1967, Attassi made it clear that the time for war had come. On Radio Damascus he stated that "in the light of the many authenticated reports concerning the Israeli troop concentrations, it has been agreed between us and Egypt to take all the necessary measures, not only to thwart the plot and repel the aggression, but to launch the battle of liberation, and to take the first step." This statement may have helped to impel Nasser to issue, four days later, a clarion call to the Egyptian people to be ready to wage total war, with the certainty of victory.[8] The Arab leaders refused to be outdone by one another. But their threats could not be dismissed as Arab hyperbole, especially when they began to be backed by action.

Israel's leaders had done their best to remain calm and confident that Arab threats would not be implemented. Back in November, 1966, the Foreign Minister, Abba Eban, told the editor of the *Manchester Guardian*, "The two least likely things that can happen in the Middle East in the near future are war or peace. We are destined to live for some time in a sort of twilight zone between the two."[9] Eban repeated his opinion at a luncheon of the Foreign Press Association in Jerusalem on January 24, 1967, that Jordan, Egypt, and Syria did not want full-scale war. Eshkol echoed his Foreign Minister's view on April 17, 1967, when he gave an interview to *U.S. News & World Report*. He said then: "I do not think there will be full-scale war in the next few years—although we are, of course, preparing for such a possibility, and I say that openly to the world." Eshkol, too, agreed that there were no prospects of real peace. Of the Arab world he said only, "Some states are at different stages of hatred towards us." At the same time, he repeated, for perhaps the twentieth time, his warning to Syria not to provoke a war, either by intent or by pure foolishness.

Israel's leaders remained calm as long as they possibly could. But in the second week of May things began to happen which suggested at first that war was a real possibility after all, then that war was inevitable. The first move came from the Soviet Union, on May 13. President Nasser's account of this move was given on Radio Cairo nine days later. He said then:

> On May 13 we received accurate information that Israel was concentrating on the Syrian border huge armed forces of about 11 to 13 brigades. These forces were divided into two fronts, one south of Lake Tiberias and one north of the Lake. The decision made by Israel at the time was to carry out an attack against Syria starting on May 17. On May 14 we took action, discussed the matter, and contacted our Syrian brothers. The Syrians also had this information.

The information came from Soviet Intelligence. Possibly it was intended as mere mischief-making, or just to keep up the fable of an imminent, full-scale Israeli attack on Syria. The information was utterly false. To anyone who had stood on the ridge of the Golan Mountains and looked directly down on the parts of Galilee named by Nasser, the thought of a "huge" troop concentration which was invisible to the Syrian observation posts would be patently absurd. From that high ridge of the mountains one can pick out individual farmers in the open fields below. There is not enough cover in the whole area to hide a couple of brigades, let alone 11 to 13. The roads running into the area from the west are plainly visible to the naked eye for miles ahead.

As it happened, there were no unusual Israeli troop movements of any kind before May 17. Even then, no reinforcements were sent to the Syrian border, which had always been extremely lightly held. On May

17 a single brigade was moved up to the Egyptian border in Sinai. It was inconceivable that the Russians could have information of major troop movements in Galilee which were not plainly visible to the Syrians on the Golan heights. That both Syria and Egypt believed the Soviet intelligence fabrication suggests that Nasser and Attassi were either ready for war, or at the very least ready to force Israel to the very brink of war.

The Arab press, as was to be expected, went into action and war fever mounted. On May 14 the Egyptian Chief of Staff, Mohamed Fawzy, flew ostentatiously to Damascus for military consultations. On May 15 the Egyptian army began to move into the Sinai peninsula. According to one account, the Egyptian troop movements were carried out "in an obvious and spectacular fashion. Convoys converged on Cairo from camps farther south, passed through the city for hours, causing major traffic dislocations on their way, and headed out in the direction of Alexandria and Ismailia. Next day, May 16, a state of emergency was proclaimed for the Egyptian armed forces."[10]

It was this proclamation, accompanied by the violent saber rattling of the entire Arab press, that induced Eshkol to send the single brigade up to the Sinai frontier. On May 15 Eshkol instructed Israel's representative at the United Nations, Gideon Raphael, to ask Secretary General U Thant to convey a message to Nasser. The message was that Israel had no intention of initiating any military action. One looks in vain for any similar assurance by a single Arab leader. Instead, all Arab leaders were proclaiming the imminence and desirability of war.

Eshkol asked the United Nations observers in Jerusalem to report to U Thant on the alleged Israeli troop movements on the Syrian frontier. This they did on May 18. They found no sign of any troop movements whatever. Eshkol also invited the Soviet ambassador to inspect the areas where the 11 to 13 brigades were allegedly hidden. He refused to go there. Had he gone, he would have found the settlers of the frontier kibbutzim repairing their slit trenches and putting their children into underground shelters and he would have found in addition about a dozen platoons of regular soldiers, or around 400 men in all, strung out along the Syrian frontier.

One may recall that ten years earlier when Soviet intelligence "discovered" that Israel's Red Sea port of Eilat was in the process of being handed over to the United States Navy, the Israeli government invited a Tass correspondent to fly there to see that this was not so. He refused to do so on the ground that his wife was going to have a baby.[11] In May 1967 the Soviet ambassador produced no excuse at all.

The next Egyptian move toward war took place on May 16. On that day General Mohamed Fawzy sent a message to Major-General Indar Sit Rikhye, the Commander of the United Nations Emergency Force in Sinai and the Gaza Strip. This force had been installed after the Sinai campaign of 1956 and its main task, which had been discharged with success, was to patrol the Israeli-Egyptian border and prevent or discourage armed clashes. Fawzy told the United Nations Commander that the force would have to be withdrawn and the posts at El Sabha and Sharm el Sheikh evacuated immediately. Rikhye sent a message back that this was a grossly improper procedure and that he would inform the Secretary General of the United Nations at once. This he did. He received a further demand for the withdrawal of UNEF at midday on May 17. The demand was rejected and on May 18 the Egyptian commander delivered an ultimatum to the United Nations garrison of the strategically vital fort of Sharm el Sheikh at the southern end of the Gulf of Aqaba. He gave the garrison 15 minutes to leave; but the garrison stayed at its post. Only on the night of May 18 did General Rikhye receive instructions from U Thant to withdraw, instructions which he at once began to carry out. With the men of UNEF gone, Egyptian and Israeli troops confronted each other across the Sinai frontier for the first time since 1956.

Arab apologists have found an explanation for the Egyptian action. Nasser, they maintain, did not really "mean" to eject the United Nations troops and so open the way for war with Israel. He demanded their withdrawal but expected his demand to be rejected by U Thant. All that he wanted to do, so the explanation goes, was to give the Israelis a scare and boost his prestige by making a challenging gesture. This was just what one would expect Nasser to do; therefore, it was what he really did do.

The facts are very different. Egyptian troops, acting under Fawzy's orders, occupied the important post of El Sabha on the morning of May 17. The men of the Yugoslav contingent of UNEF at El Sabha were surrounded and held virtual prisoners. Egyptian troops forced the Yugoslavs out of the posts of Kuntilla and El Amr on the morning of May 18. It is simply not credible that Fawzy acted on his own initiative and had no instructions from Nasser; the latter, indeed, made no attempt to maintain this. The conclusion is inescapable that Nasser ordered his troops to occupy every UNEF post, before U Thant could reach a decision and before he could give instructions to General Rikhye. Arab rhetoric and hyperbole had nothing to do with the matter; Egyptian troops moved in and could have done so only on Nasser's orders.

Eshkol and his ministers regarded this Egyptian move to be of crucial importance. Egypt had flouted the United Nations and removed the UNEF "trip wire." Nasser, they argued, would only do this if he meant business. The Israelis are probably politically more alert than the people of any other country in the world, and every Israeli citizen is alive to the dangers which confront his country. Even if the Israeli government had pronounced Nasser's move to be a harmless publicity stunt, nobody would have believed it for a moment. Egyptian troops were pouring into Sinai, and some counteraction had to be taken. Eshkol ordered a partial mobilization of reserves and, as we have seen already, sent a single brigade to the Sinai frontier on May 17. He could scarcely have done less.

Much has been written on the question whether U Thant was right to order the withdrawal of UNEF, a question which seems to me to be largely academic. U Thant's understanding was that if Egypt formally requested a withdrawal, then UNEF had to leave. Almost certainly, U Thant could have delayed the withdrawal and given the Egyptians time, or forced them to reflect carefully before continuing to implement their plans for war. The understanding of Dag Hammarskjöld, UN Secretary General at the time that UNEF was brought into being, had been that the force would remain on the frontier until its task was done. Clearly its task was not done in May 1967. It should have stayed until there was a peace settlement between Israel and Egypt.

The force consisted of only 3400 men, occupying posts strung along a 295-mile-long frontier. It could not have interposed itself between combatants. The most that U Thant could have done was to induce Egypt to await a United Nations inquiry into the situation and, possibly, a debate in the General Assembly. U Thant did not try to secure this breathing space. In the United Nations Abba Eban complained on June 19 that the Secretary General's action in withdrawing UNEF had been "disastrously swift." Eban asked dramatically, "What is the use of a fire brigade which vanishes from the scene as soon as the first smoke and flames appear?"

At least the Yugoslav contingent did not finally leave Sharm el Sheikh until May 23. But the day before they left, Nasser announced the blockade of the Gulf of Aqaba while on a visit to his troops in Sinai. Nasser phrased the announcement as follows:

> The armed forces yesterday occupied Sharm el Sheikh. What does this mean? It is the affirmation of our rights and our sovereignty over the Gulf of Aqaba which constitutes territorial waters. Under no circumstances will we allow the Israeli flag to pass through the Gulf of Aqaba. The Jews threaten war. We tell them, you are welcome, we are ready for war, but under no circumstances will we abandon any of our rights. This water is ours.

Two days later, on May 24, the Cairo newspaper *Al Ahram* announced that the Straits of Tiran, which connect the Gulf of Aqaba with the Red Sea, had been closed by the guns of the fort at Sharm el Sheikh, by Egyptian naval craft patrolling the area, and by mines laid in the main channels of the Straits.

Once again, Nasser's defenders maintained that this step did not necessarily mean that he wanted to go to war. It was argued that he had the right to close the Gulf to Israeli shipping, that the Straits of Tiran were indeed Egyptian territorial waters, and that Israel could still have managed economically in spite of a blockade.

These arguments can be dealt with briefly. Nasser had no right to close the Gulf, which was indisputably an international waterway, to Israeli or any other shipping. He had no right to do this with the Suez Canal, but the Canal did at least run through Egyptian territory. The

Gulf of Aqaba was bounded by Israel, Jordan, and Saudi Arabia as well as Egypt. Despite the Straits of Tiran running between Egypt and Saudi Arabia, the islands in the Straits had been forcibly occupied by Egypt in defiance of the Saudi Arabian claim to them. (This claim seems to have been tacitly dropped subsequently.)

As for the Egyptian blockade's being "peaceful," one need only refer to Nasser's own words: "The Arab people want to fight. We have been waiting for the right time, when we would be completely ready. Lately we have felt that our strength is sufficient and that, if we do battle with Israel, we will be able, with the help of Allah, to be victorious. Sharm el Sheikh implies a confrontation with Israel. Taking this step makes it imperative that we be ready to undertake total war with Israel."[12] Radio Cairo produced the corollary to this statement by Nasser, on May 30, 1967: "Following the closure of the Gulf of Aqaba, there are now two courses open to Israel either of which is drenched in her own blood: she will die of strangulation under the Arab military and economic siege or else she will perish under the fire of the Arab forces encompassing her on the north, south, and east."

Early on the morning of May 23, Eshkol said to one of his advisers: "I am afraid the chips are down. I wish it could be otherwise!"[13] Until May 23 Eshkol had hoped that Nasser could be induced to defer irrevocable action at Sharm el Sheikh. His hope, too, was that the Western powers would, through normal diplomatic channels, make it crystal clear that they could not countenance a blockade of the Gulf of Aqaba and interference with their own shipping. The Western powers, as Eshkol saw it, had every right to insist on that. Their argument was a demonstrably sound one—that the Straits of Tiran had to be regarded as an international waterway until Egypt proved a case to the contrary. Geographically and historically, the Straits were an international waterway. If this were asserted with real conviction, war in the Middle East could still be averted. Eshkol wanted to avert war.

The Western powers failed, most lamentably, to assert or even properly present their case that the Straits were an international waterway. Pathetically feeble efforts were made by American and British statesmen to demand freedom of passage for shipping through the Straits. The British Foreign Secretary, George Brown, suddenly emerged as the protagonist of action by the maritime powers and just as suddenly drifted into the sort of diplomatic backwater in which British diplomacy so often floats. For a brief moment, there was talk of forcing a passage through the Straits; the talk died away, and nothing was done.

The Western powers may have hoped that divisions within the Arab camp might slow down the now manifestly dangerous drift towards war. In Jordan Radio Amman was ever ready to taunt Nasser. On May 21 it asked Egypt, pointedly, if she would really blockade the Gulf of Aqaba and, failing that, if she had any right to assert her leadership of the Arab world. The Syrian press was meanwhile active in attacking Jordan. On May 23 a Syrian bomb exploded in a Jordanian village, killing 14 people, and Jordan broke off relations with Syria. The Egyptian press, perhaps the most irresponsible in the whole world, was marking time making fun of King Hussein and rejecting the idea of any alliance with politically reactionary Jordan.

To the Israelis, Arab disunity was nothing new, but the blockade of the Gulf of Aqaba was a hard fact. What exactly did it mean to them? In 1956 the blockade of the Gulf had been a contributory factor to the war in Sinai. But in 1956 Eilat, Israel's only settlement on the Gulf, was no more than a collection of shacks chiefly inhabited by a small army detachment. Its port was in an embryonic stage, and it had no hinterland; the mineral resources of the southern Negev were as yet unexplored.

The picture in 1967 was very different. In the previous year Eilat's port had handled well over a million tons of cargo; the 1970 target was a million tons. This amount could be trebled when the Negev moved into full-scale industrial expansion in the mid-1980s. By 1967 Eilat's population had grown to about 15,000. Plans were under way to make it a major center of tourism. But that was secondary to its potential as a trade *entrepôt*. Eilat was already Israel's oil port, for the great bulk of the oil that she uses comes from the Persian Gulf. An oil pipeline was being built from Eilat to Ashdod on the Mediterranean. And Eilat was already handling over 30 percent of the minerals exported by Israel. The Timna copper mines are on its doorstep, and Japan had become Israel's biggest customer for copper. The minerals of the Dead Sea are only 60 miles away. They probably constitute Israel's biggest growth industry.

Eilat means Israel's connection with Asia and its developing countries. It means an outlet for the present mineral and future industrial production of the Negev. It means a line of direct communication with the budding markets of East Africa. It means a great part of Israel's future. Nasser's blockade of the Gulf of Aqaba on May 22, 1967, was a blow to that future. It was something which had to be resisted, not just because it was contrary to international law, but because to accept it would have been to accept a cruel, crippling loss.

Eshkol wasted no time in making his views known. He addressed the Knesset on May 23, and he did not mince his words. "Any interference with the freedom of shipping in the Gulf and in the Straits," he said, "is a coarse infringement on international law, adversely affects the sovereign rights of other nations, and constitutes an act of aggression against Israel. . . . Free passage through the Straits and the Gulf has taken root as an international reality, expressed by hundreds of sailings under dozens of flags, and has become a far-flung, developing complex of commerce and communications."

He warned Egypt against implementing the blockade which Nasser had proclaimed: "Should there be a criminal attempt to impose a maritime blockade against a member state of the United Nations, a dangerous precedent would be created, pregnant with serious results for international relations and for the freedom of shipping on the high seas. . . . I again call upon the great powers to act without delay to maintain the right of free access for shipping to our southern port."

Eshkol's speech was regarded in some Israeli quarters as too soft.[14] But on the morning of May 23 the United States government privately asked Eshkol to give the maritime powers 48 hours to contrive appropriate diplomatic action in order to get Nasser to hold his hand. Reluctantly, Eshkol agreed. He was temporarily encouraged by a statement by President Johnson, on May 23, that "the United States considers the Gulf to be an international waterway and feels that a blockade of Israeli shipping is illegal and potentially disastrous to the cause of peace. The right of free, innocent passage of the international waterway is a vital interest of the international community." On May 24 the British Prime Minister, Harold Wilson, declared that the Straits of Tiran were an international waterway and that Britain would assert "the right of passage" both "on behalf of British shipping" and in the international interest.

There was, at that moment, some stirring talk in British Government circles about "stepping in and stopping the rot." For a brief moment it looked as if the British lion really had been roused and was ready to pounce. Not so. The statement of May 24 was one of many examples of Wilson's desire to "be seen to be doing" something positive. There was never the slightest possibility of Britain taking or instigating positive action to keep the Straits of Tiran open. Instead, Wilson sent his Foreign Secretary, George Brown, off to Moscow. Although the times had changed and the situation was not exactly parallel, one is reminded of Chamberlain's disastrous dashes to Godesberg and Munich in order to keep the peace with Hitler.

A British Foreign Office brief, dated May 29, tells the story of vacillation which probably owed most to the Prime Minister's desire to make an effective gesture while doing nothing and intending nothing. The document explained that Britain should not be drawn into legal intricacies; but from then on, the brief dealt with nothing else. Its summing-up was that the International Court of Justice had ruled in the Corfu Channel case that passage through an international waterway could be forced. This might have sounded encouraging to Israeli ears, but the British government had long since abdicated any right of action over the Straits of Tiran. And May 29 was long after, lamentably long after, May 22. Much had happened in the seven-day interval, and Mr. Brown's announcement on May 31 in the House of Commons of British readiness to support a declaration by the maritime powers had the ring of a posthumous oration about it. The time for action by those powers had passed.

Eshkol's own view on the "action" of the maritime powers was commendably charitable. He was aware of British and American good intentions. He was aware that Britain was obsessed with the need to safeguard her huge Middle East oil interests, and that the United States was preoccupied with the Vietnam war. On the whole, he never expected the maritime powers to do much, and so he was not too sadly disappointed when they did nothing at all. The informed Israeli view was that the United States tried harder than Britain, but tried very hard at the same time not to "be seen" to be doing this (Harold Wilson's technique, applied exactly in reverse). The United States informed Eshkol that a fair measure of international support was needed if, for instance, a ship were to be sent through the Straits of Tiran, inviting and returning gunfire. Apart from Britain and the United States, only four maritime nations backed Brown's May 31 statement in the House of Commons. That, in the American view, was not enough.

But, as mentioned, so much had happened after May 23 that Eshkol was being presented with a situation which changed from day to day, requiring new decisions by his government. On May 24 the Israeli Cabinet held a vital session to hear the strictly military views of the General Staff. General Itzhak Rabin's situation report showed, in particular, how far the Egyptian military build-up had gone. That build-up could still have been discounted, but for two elements in it—the manning of the fort of Sharm el Sheikh in order to cut Israel's lifeline to Asia, and the ejection of the United Nations Emergency Force. Israel's position was plainly dangerous.

Eshkol was, at that moment, becoming unhappily aware of the fact that war could no longer be averted. Two Egyptian statements on May 26 may have convinced him. One was by Nasser, who told the Arab Trade Unions: "I said once that we could tell UNEF to leave within half an hour. Once we were fully prepared, we could ask UNEF to leave. And this is what has actually happened. . . . Taking over Sharm el Sheikh meant confrontation with Israel. Taking such action meant that we were ready to enter war with Israel. It was not a separate operation." And in the Cairo newspaper *Al Ahram,* Nasser's "pet editorial writer," Mohamed Hasanein Haykal, declared that war was inevitable. He discoursed at length on his theory of the first and second blow. Israel would be forced to strike first by the closure of the Gulf of Aqaba, Egypt would ward off the blow and would deliver a knock-out. These were statements too explicit for Eshkol to ignore.*

* The operative passage of Haykal's article read as follows:
This week the closure of the Gulf of Aqaba to Israel was an accomplished fact imposed, and now being protected, by the force of Arab arms. To Israel this is the most dangerous aspect of the current situation. . . . Hence I say that Israel must resort to arms. An armed clash between the U.A.R. and the Israeli enemy is inevitable. . . . This is because I am confident that for many reasons, chiefly the

On the night of May 26–27 there was a further development. Both in Egypt and in Israel, the Soviet ambassadors were instructed to call on the heads of state. Nasser's subsequent story was that the Soviet ambassador, Dmitri Pozhdaev, urged him "not to fire the first shot." For once, the Egyptian version can be believed, for this was precisely what the Soviet ambassador in Israel, Dmitri Chuvakhin, was telling Eshkol at 2:30 A.M. on May 27. Eshkol was extremely irritated by this nocturnal incursion. The Soviet ambassador brought him no assurance of the slightest value. An insistent demand for peace to be maintained, after the Gulf of Aqaba had been blockaded and Egyptian troops marched up to Israel's frontiers, could be regarded only as effrontery. Had the Soviet Union any real desire to restore the situation, its first action should have been to induce Nasser to call off the blockade. Eshkol, according to the account which he subsequently gave to the newspaper *Maariv,* was deliberately elusive.[15] He told Chuvakhin that the Egyptians were already mining roads in Israel and firing on peaceful settlements.

On the evening of May 27 the Israeli Cabinet was once more in session. This was its most vital meeting so far. It had to decide then and there on peace or war.

The meeting lasted throughout the night of May 27–28 and did not end until 5 A.M. when a rosy dawn was breaking over Mount Scopus and the hills of Moab. The issue was whether Israel should strike at once against her main adversary, Egypt, or whether she should continue to strive for peace, assuming that international action would secure the reopening of the Gulf of Aqaba. There were indeed some Cabinet members who believed that the time for war had already passed and that there was no alternative to peace. This view was being propagated by Ben Gurion, conventionally supposed to be a fire-eater, and his words, uttered from semiretirement at the Sde Boker kibbutz, still carried weight. But Eshkol was perfectly aware that Israel might have to fight, realizing that there was now little hope of international action over the Gulf. Perhaps the most important problems discussed during that long night by the Cabinet were the attitude of the United States and the strictly military implications of taking decisive military action or delaying it.

The Foreign Minister, Abba Eban, had just returned from a flying visit to Washington to sound out American thinking. The result of his visit was the dispatch of two warnings to Israel not to take unilateral military action from President Johnson and Secretary of State Dean Rusk. The President's message contained the information that the Soviet

---

psychological, Israel cannot accept or remain indifferent to what has taken place. In my opinion it simply cannot do so! The next move is up to Israel. Israel has to reply now. It has to deal a blow. We have to be ready for it and to minimize its effect as much as possible. Then it will be our turn to deal the second blow, which we will deliver with the utmost effectiveness. . . . Let Israel begin! Let our second blow then be ready! Let it be a knock-out! (*Al Ahram,* May 26, 1967.)

government had informed him of its determination not to let down its allies, Egypt and Syria. The diplomatic backing of the United States was vital to Israel; without it there could even be a danger of Soviet military intervention.* Could Israel afford to attack and risk the withdrawal of United States support? Convinced of the justice of Israel's case, Eshkol was on the whole of the opinion that the risk could be taken.

The military considerations had already been exhaustively discussed by the Cabinet on previous occasions. The General Staff was producing daily situation reports which kept ministers informed almost up to the hour. Since Eshkol had personally insisted ever since 1964 on plans for offensive defense to be continually revised and brought up to date, there was unanimity over the outcome of a possible war with Egypt. There was less confidence about dealing with a ring of Arab enemies, including Syria, Iraq, and Jordan. It was distinctly to Eshkol's credit that Israel was completely prepared for all eventualities. His had sometimes been a lone voice arguing that Israel might have to confront a unified Arab alliance.

There has been a mistaken notion that Eshkol's military advisers argued strongly in favor of instant action on May 27. This is a misreading of General Rabin's appreciation of the situation. He had to explain what the prospects for immediate action were, and for deferred action as well. Much hinged on the question of Israeli casualties. Rabin's view was that an immediate strike would take the Israeli army to the banks of the Suez Canal, with a minimum of casualties in the field, but that every day's delay would increase the number of casualties, perhaps substantially.

Even so, the Cabinet was equally divided on the main question before it, whether or not to go to war at once. Nine members were in favor of action, nine against. Contrary to what was popularly supposed at the time, Eshkol favored action. But as Prime Minister he had to bow to the fact that the Cabinet was split. In theory he could, in his dual capacity of Prime Minister and Minister of Defense, have given a tie-breaking vote. Instead, he sent a reply to President Johnson agreeing to a waiting period of an unspecified length of time.

Eshkol's critics have subsequently accused him of hesitancy and have created the picture of a weak man confronting the resolute Rabin. In reality, the latter, desperately overworked and terribly conscious of what

---

* There is a widely held view that Israel's readiness to go it alone tends to make her people impervious to outside criticism, and totally uninterested in it. This is not so; Israelis are well aware that their country needs friends. Walter Eytan tells a delightful story which is illustrative. Three young men broke into a house in Jerusalem, found a safe in it, opened the safe, and pocketed its contents. They were arrested by the police a day or two later, but had hidden the money in the meantime and refused to disclose its whereabouts. Then the police told them that the house they had burgled was the Dutch Legation, and that Holland was one of Israel's best friends. The miscreants were most upset and confessed at once where they had hidden the loot. (Walter Eytan, *The First Ten Years*, p. 215.)

war was about, was very close to exhaustion. Eshkol has also been accused of having contributed to Rabin's troubles by making him attend Cabinet meetings and state the case which should have been put by himself in his capacity of Minister of Defense. Both these accusations were unjustified; Eshkol used Rabin in order to keep the Cabinet exactly informed and he took account of Cabinet feelings.

The situation continued to worsen. The whole of Egypt's strategic reserve, the Fourth Division, began to move into Sinai on May 26.[16] On May 28 Nasser declared at a press conference that "Israel's existence is in itself an aggression," that war with Israel "has existed since 1948," that Israel had provoked the present crisis by planning to attack Syria, and that the Gulf of Aqaba would remain "irreversibly" closed to Israeli shipping. On May 29 he repeated the substance of this in a bellicose speech to the Egyptian National Assembly, and demanded a return to 1948, in fact the restoration of a unified Arab Palestine and the elimination of the State of Israel. On the same day, May 29, Iraq ordered an oil embargo directed against all states allegedly supporting Israel, in particular Britain and the United States.

On May 30 came the worst blow of all so far. King Hussein of Jordan flew to Cairo and signed a military pact with Nasser. A joint command was established under the Egyptian General, Fawzy, and plans were made to move Egyptian troops to Jordan. Iraq was to join the pact five days later and move troops into Jordan.

What this meant to Israel was explained by Eshkol: "The pact with Jordan was truly serious for us. It exposed the long, narrow waistline of Israel to an attack which could sever it. Until then we had supposed that Hussein would never consent to have Egyptian troops on Jordanian soil or put Jordanian troops under Egyptian command. We were left with only the bare hope that Hussein would somehow keep out of military action which was now looking inevitable."[17]

The near-certainty now was that Israel, if she did fight, would have to fight on three fronts—against Egypt in the south, Syria in the north, and Jordan along her rambling, indefensible eastern frontier all the way from the Sea of Galilee to the Gulf of Aqaba.

With Israel's military preparations completed, and seven Egyptian divisions now massed in offensive positions in Sinai, one must turn for a moment to the Israeli "home front." On May 28 Eshkol broadcast to the nation. According to one authority,

> The whole nation was listening, waiting for a lead: civilians at home and in cafés, the army in their messes or on transistor sets in their tents in the desert. The performance was a disaster. The Prime Minister was tired; he had a bad cold; he lost his place in the script; and he had nothing particular to say. Israel, he said, would try to resolve the crisis by diplomacy, but she would defend herself if necessary.

She would remain in a state of readiness, and the army could be relied on to do its duty. No trumpet could have been more uncertain. The worst suspicions of the government's indecisiveness seemed to be confirmed.[18]

The writer might have added that Eshkol had been up until 5 A.M. and, after a brief rest, had been in continuous sessions with his Cabinet ministers and military advisers. In addition he got the microphone just two minutes before his broadcast began, was confronted by a script which he had not yet read and had to broadcast live (on previous occasions his statements had always been recorded in advance). On top of all this, Eshkol had never been a good speaker and he could not have a decisive message to give. The only such message would have been the news that Israel was at war, since that was what the whole population now considered unavoidable. Popular feeling had moved faster and farther than that of the Cabinet.

Popular feeling was already strongly in favor of broadening the government, to give it a truly national character and to enable General Moshe Dayan, the hero of the 1956 campaign, to be included. The people of Israel needed reassurance, not simply because Eshkol had made an unconvincing speech on the radio, but because their country's existence was at stake. On June 1 Eshkol took the necessary step of bringing the Gahal and Rafi parties into the coalition, and giving Dayan the post of Minister of Defense. Insofar as he appointed Dayan, he yielded to the popular demand; he would have preferred to have Yigal Allon, who had fought with great distinction in the 1948 campaigns. Dayan of course inherited a ready-made military plan of action and, in Rabin, a Chief of Staff who would carry this plan out. Dayan's contribution was to be largely one of morale, although his talents would have been invaluable had the tide of war turned against Israel.

The next three days were no more than a period of waiting. No light appeared on the international horizon. Instead, the Soviet Union sent a threatening note on June 2, warning Israel not to try to break the blockade of the Gulf of Aqaba. This note could have been designed only to discourage a localized military action, not a full-scale war. It was not the least of the Soviet Union's disservices to the cause of peace. In the United Nations the Soviet Union produced a wild yarn about a projected American blockade of Cuba, presumably in order to distract international attention from the Middle East crisis and to discourage international action to prevent war from breaking out there.

Meanwhile, the Arab military build-up continued. The military assessment produced at the Israeli Cabinet meeting of June 3 was the gravest yet. On June 4 Iraq officially joined the Arab alliance. To wait any longer would have been the height of folly for Israel. War was inevitable: war accordingly broke out on June 5, 1967.

1. Ezra Danin, in personal conversation with the author.
2. Brig. Harkavi and Shimon Peres, in personal conversation with the author.
3. The *Jewish Observer and Middle East Review*, March 25, 1966.
4. Eshkol, speech of April 28, 1966.
5. Fedorenko's speech in the UN Security Council, July 26, 1966.
6. Terrence Prittie, *Israel: Miracle in the Desert*, pp. 155–156.
7. *Daily Telegraph* (London), October 21, 1966.
8. Nasser, Radio Cairo, May 26, 1967.
9. Abba Eban, talking to Alastair Hetherington, *Manchester Guardian*, November 18, 1966.
10. Michael Howard and Robert Hunter, *Israel and the Arab World: The Crisis of 1967*, p. 16.
11. Walter Eytan, *The First Ten Years*, p. 175.
12. Nasser, Radio Cairo, May 26, 1967.
13. Eshkol was speaking to Aviad Yafeh, the head of the Prime Minister's office in Jerusalem.
14. Howard and Hunter, *op. cit.*, p. 21.
15. Eshkol, in *Maariv*, October 4, 1967.
16. Theodore Draper, *Israel and World Politics*, p. 94.
17. Eshkol, in personal conversation with the author.
18. Howard and Hunter, *op cit.*, p. 26.

17.

One of the last Arab statements made before the Six-Day War of June 1967 broke out was by President Nasser. Speaking on Radio Cairo he declared to Israel, on June 4: "We are facing you in battle and are burning with desire for it to start in order to obtain revenge for the 1956 treachery. This will make the world realize what the Arabs are and what Israel is. It will also learn that the Arab soldier is a brave and tough fighting soldier and that the Arab people are a brave, self-sacrificing, and heroic people." The style of the statement was declamatory, but the sense of it was plain. The Egyptians had not brought a large army up through the wilderness of Sinai to the borders of Israel for nothing. Egypt wanted war and was ready for it to begin—either by a preemptive strike or by goading Israel, in the manner suggested by the Egyptian press, into making the first offensive move.

One should at this point briefly recapitulate the steps taken by the Arab countries which led directly up to the outbreak of war.[1]

In October 1966 the Syrian Prime Minister, Attassi, openly sponsored guerilla attacks on Israel, and on November 4, 1966, signed a defense pact with Egypt. Syria began, at this stage, to speed the installation of guided missile sites and the strengthening of already very powerful fortifications on the Israeli frontier. This was done with the help of large reinforcements of Soviet technicians.

In early May 1967 the all-out Arab propaganda campaign backed by the Soviet Union began against Israel on the grounds that she was about to launch a full-scale war against Syria.* On May 15 Egypt began to move considerable armed forces into the Sinai peninsula, and on May 16 proclaimed a state of national emergency.

On May 16 Egypt demanded the withdrawal of the United Nations Emergency Force from its positions along the Egyptian-Israeli frontier, and on May 17 Egyptian troops began to occupy these positions before the Secretary General of the United Nations had given his approval.

On May 22 Egypt announced the blockade of the Gulf of Aqaba and of Israel's only port on the Red Sea, Eilat. This blockade, in defiance of the fact that the Gulf was an international waterway, was to be carried out with the use of artillery at the southern end of the Gulf and the patrolling and mining of the Straits of Tiran.

---

* One more pleasant tidbit of Moslem propaganda which was being distributed in London in 1968 was a pamphlet entitled *A History of Jewish Crimes*, published by the Asian Book Center in Karachi. Acclaiming a book of this name as "a valuable and brilliant exposition" and "a splendid work of genuine scholarship," it listed, among other Jewish crimes, the killing of Christ, the reviling of God, the debauchery of the Prophets, the economic domination of the New World, the organization of international vice and crime, and the instigation of world war. The Jews were described in the pamphlet as "fiendish," "diabolical," and "moral cannibals," and the book was acclaimed as "the first of its kind which in spite of authentic research material would read as the raciest novel."

On May 30 Egypt signed the defense pact with Jordan, enabling Egyptian troops to be moved into Jordan and up to Israel's long and highly vulnerable frontier with that country. Algeria had declared her support of Egypt and had mobilized on May 27; Morocco followed suit on May 29.

On May 31 the first contingents of Iraqi troops arrived in Jordan, even before Iraq formally joined the Arab alliance against Israel. The first two battalions of Egyptian troops arrived in Jordan on June 4.

During this period of what Israel could only interpret as deliberate preparations for her destruction, Arab propaganda organs produced an unending stream of violent and threatening abuse. I have already cited statements by so-called responsible Arab statesmen. Two of the less responsible statements speak for themselves. The "Voice of the Arabs" promised two Tel Aviv girls for every Arab "conqueror," and Radio Damascus declaimed: "Fight, Arabs! Let them know that we shall hang the last imperialist soldier with the entrails of the last Zionist!"[2]

It was this sort of statement which prompted Eshkol to say, "If the Arabs had won, Hitler's six million victims of World War II would have been joined by another two and a half million victims of the Arab lust for destruction."[3] He added, "The people of Israel could not be left defenseless." Virtually every Israeli citizen thought exactly as Eshkol did. This was no ordinary war; it was a war to avert total annihilation of the State and people of Israel. As a completely outside observer, one shudders to think of what horrors would have been perpetrated by the Arabs in the hour of victory and thereafter. But whatever might have happened it would have been the responsibility not of the Egyptian, Syrian, or Iraqi citizen, but of leaders like Nasser, Attassi, and even Haykal, who had fostered feelings of fanatical hatred by playing on their human emotions.

During the crucial days of May and early June no great power, no friend of Israel, did one single constructive thing to avert war. The United States government did indeed give Eshkol private assurances that it would not allow Israel to be destroyed. Britain's Foreign Secretary, George Brown, did make efforts, however futile, to get the Egyptian blockade of the Gulf of Aqaba lifted. But in a practical sense nothing was done. Israel was left on her own, a small, encircled community of two and a half million people. For the Israelis worst of all was to have to sit and wait for a war that had become inevitable.[4] This period of waiting was agonizing in the extreme, as scores of Israelis have since told me. It requires moral courage to gird oneself for the battle; it requires vastly greater moral courage to remain resolute while the battle is being postponed, especially when every day's postponement weighs the balance more heavily against one's country.

Eshkol was blamed in some quarters for the postponement of combat. Nothing could have been further from the truth. It was Eshkol who had steadfastly maintained that Israel had to be ready to face a united Arab assault. It was Eshkol who had insisted that no expense should be spared in building up Israel's armed forces. It was Eshkol again who was ready to go to war on May 27, believing, quite rightly, that war was then unavoidable. The allegation of Eshkol's hesitancy was too readily accepted abroad; an epic example was the summing up of the situation by the London *Observer* on June 4. Its unsigned editorial was entitled "Israel's Choice: Sitzkrieg or Blitzkrieg." The article explained that Eshkol was the apostle of the first, Ben-Gurion of the second. The exact reverse was the case; ironically Ben-Gurion was actually using the phrase "sitting out" the crisis for the next six months. Eshkol made, as one member of his family pointed out, no pretense of being a hero type;[5] such types are popular in times of real stress. Eshkol was a shrewd, thoughtful statesman, seeking the right line of action in face of some confused opposition within his own Cabinet, a visceral sense of self-preservation among the citizens of Israel, and a complex and unpromising international situation. He never sought to be more than he really was. This was wise and completely in character.

Writing shortly after the 1967 war, I expressed the view that "it may never be proved beyond doubt who fired the first aimed shot in this war. It was probably the Israelis. Thus, Winston Churchill, Jr., in his excellent book *The Six-Day War:* 'Israel, like a cowboy of the old Wild West, did not wait for her enemy to draw; she had seen the glint in Nasser's eye.' The analogy is not, perhaps, quite correct—Nasser had already 'drawn,' but he was still spinning his gun around and playing fancy tricks with it before taking aim. He had, moreover, deliberately sought out his opponent and announced his firm intention of shooting him dead."[6] One need no longer qualify in any way the fact that the first aimed shots on June 5, 1967, came from the Israelis. They followed heavy but entirely indiscriminate Egyptian firing on Israeli kibbutzim close to the frontier, which began on June 2, doing some damage to buildings and setting crops on fire. The Israelis struck on land and in the air, at 7:45 A.M.

As they saw it, the preemptive strike which Nasser and Haykal had contemptuously invited was completely justified. There have been various estimates of the armed strength of Israel and her Arab assailants on June 5, 1967. The picture was roughly as follows:

Israel had between 250,000 and 275,000 men under arms, 80 percent of them reservists who had been called up in groups after the middle of May. She had a maximum of 800 tanks (Pattons, Centurions, AMX's and Shermans), and 250 self-propelled guns. She had about 300 combat planes, including 120 strike aircraft and about 100 interceptors. Finally, she had a small but attack-minded navy, of which the major units were two destroyers and four submarines.

Her immediate adversaries, Egypt, Syria, Jordan, and Iraq, had not less than 350,000 men under arms, about three quarters of them in the battle area. They had at least 1800 tanks, with Soviet T-34's, T-54's and

T-55's predominating, and around 300 self-propelled guns. They had at least 600 combat planes, but not more than 85 of them were strike aircraft. The Egyptian and Syrian navies (Jordan had none, and Iraq's was in the Persian Gulf) were about three times the strength of Israel's. In general, one could say that the Arab military potential immediately available was about twice as great as Israel's. In the matter of quality, Israel had the edge in aircraft, the Arabs in tanks. The Arab reserves of manpower were one cogent reason why Israel could not allow her enemies to strike first. Even more important, all of Israel's main centers of population were less than 15 minutes' flying time from Israel's borders, and one of them, Jewish Jerusalem, was already on the firing line.

The Israelis did not feel that they needed any justification for striking on June 5. The Arab states claimed that they were already in a state of war with Israel, that they had been at war with her since 1948. Denied any of the benefits of peace, Israel could at any stage take the Arabs at their word. This implied no Machiavellian concept; it was straight, sharp logic.

The Six-Day War can be divided into four main phases. The first phase was that of the Israeli air strike, which was also the first major military action of the war. At 7:45 A.M. the Israelis attacked ten Egyptian airfields; nine more were attacked later in the morning. The time chosen for the strike depended on three considerations.[7] The morning mist normally cleared by then. The dawn stand-by of the Egyptian air force would have ended and the men would have gone to their breakfast. And Egyptian commanders, even at the time of a crisis like this, would arrive at their offices only at 9 A.M. Israeli intelligence was precisely informed, and the air strike was carried out with even more startling precision.

Within three hours the Israeli airforce flew over 1000 sorties. Some pilots may have flown half a dozen sorties in all during the day. They used the so-called "dibber" bomb which carried an Israeli-made device for deceleration in the air and a booster for increased penetration on striking the target.[8] In those first three hours nearly 300 Egyptian planes were destroyed,* and afterwards the commander of the Israeli airforce, General Mordechai Hod, admitted that in "my wildest dreams I would never have thought this kind of record possible. I reckoned on at least half a day, maybe even a whole day or a day and a night."[9]

The Egyptian airforce was in ruins, but in the meantime Syria, Iraq, and, most important of all, Jordan, had entered the war.

Shortly after the Israeli air strike against Egypt began, Eshkol broad-

---

* The Egyptian planes destroyed included 30 Tupolev-16's, 27 Ilyushin-28 medium bombers, 12 Sukhoi-7 fighter-bombers, which Egypt had only just received, 90 MIG-21 interceptors, 20 MIG-19's, 75 MIG-17's, and 32 big transports and helicopters. This tally was compiled by the official Israeli history of the war, published by the Ministry of Defense. The vast majority of these kills were made on the ground. The initial Israeli attack caused such chaos on the Egyptian airfields that only a very few planes were able to get off the ground before the second wave of attacks began.

cast the message that Israel "will not attack any country which did not first launch an attack against us. But any aggressor can be sure of being met by the full might of Israeli arms."[10] Jordan ignored this warning and at 8:30 A.M. Jordanian artillery began shelling Jewish Jerusalem, an action which caused bitter resentment on the part of the Israelis, who would in any event have wished to treat the whole of Jerusalem as an open city. In the Jordanian shelling only a handful of civilians were killed, most of them because they went out into the streets to see what was going on. Relatively few buildings were destroyed, but about 600 were damaged and about $2 million worth of damage was caused.

In his efforts to localize the war Eshkol ignored the shelling and sent an urgent message to King Hussein through General Odd Bull, the head of the United Nations Truce Supervision Organization. The message was sent at 9:30 A.M. and General Bull immediately relayed it to King Hussein from his headquarters in East Jerusalem. The message read: "We shall not initiate any action whatever against Jordan. However, should Jordan open hostilities, we shall react with all our might and he [Hussein] will have to bear the full responsibility for all the consequences."

The Jordanian answer was to continue firing into Jewish Jerusalem, and to begin shelling the outskirts of Tel Aviv. Even then, Eshkol stayed his hand; he still hoped that Hussein was doing it to clear his conscience in this way but would in due course call the action off. Israeli troops on the ground made no move until 1:00 P.M. By then it was clear that Jordan was in the war. According to one authority,[11] an ambassador of a western country was present when Hussein decided to reject Eshkol's overture. Hussein told the ambassador that he would have to join in the war, because he had just received an assurance from Nasser that the Egyptian army was advancing on Tel Aviv and that the Egyptian airforce would be able to give Jordanian forces amply sufficient air cover. Nasser never attempted to explain or justify these lies he had told Hussein.

The Israeli airforce accordingly turned its attention to Jordan, attacking Amman and Mafraq airfields shortly after 2:00 P.M. All of Jordan's 20 Hunter interceptors were destroyed. Meanwhile, in just over one hour, two thirds of the Syrian airforce were destroyed and, rather more as a warning than anything else, Israeli aircraft attacked the Iraqi base of H-3 and put six MIG-21's and three Hunters out of action. All in all, on the first two days of the war the Arab airforces lost an estimated 416 aircraft and 100 pilots. Israeli losses were 26 aircraft and 17 pilots, two of them crucified by the Syrians after capture. The score in aerial dog-fights was 50-0 in Israel's favor, and during all these operations Israel kept a total strategic reserve of exactly 12 aircraft for repelling intruders.[12]

The second phase of the war was that of operations on land against the main enemy, Egypt. In Sinai, Egypt had massed two armored and five infantry divisions, with between 900 and 1000 tanks. That was a formidable assault force, whose orders were to push through to Tel Aviv and Jerusalem in under three days, after repelling whatever initial attack the Israelis could mount. In Sinai Israel could field only three full divisions, with a small support group covering the port of Eilat and the virtually roadless southern half of the Sinai front. Yet this much smaller Israeli army, of course with increasing support from the air, won signal victories in every action and reached the eastern bank of the Suez Canal on June 8, the fourth day of the war. The Egyptian army was totally destroyed; nothing more need be said save that the most important single objective of all, the fort of Sharm el Sheikh, was taken by a landing party from a detachment of torpedo boats on June 7. The plan had been to drop paratroopers around the fort, but the Egyptian garrison fled before anyone arrived. No single incident of the war was more revealing of the low state of Egyptian morale and of the senseless nature of prewar Arab boastfulness.*

The third phase of the war was directed against Jordan. That was, in one sense, a war of King Hussein's choosing. Israel offered him peace, even after his artillery had started shelling Jewish Jerusalem and Tel Aviv. But, in a different sense, the war was forced upon him by his own Arab allies. Hussein believed that if Jordan stayed out of the 1967 war, as it had stayed out of the 1956 war, his throne would be forfeit. If Egypt and Syria'won, they would combine to oust a king and dynasty they regarded as basically reactionary and far too pro-Western. If the Arabs lost the war, either Egypt or Syria would vent its spleen on him; with the support of the Palestinian section of the Jordan population, either Egypt or Syria, who had plotted against him so often before, would engineer his downfall. Both countries had organized attempts on his life in the past. They would have done so again, had Jordan stayed out of the war, and they would almost certainly have succeeded in having him murdered. Hussein, a remarkably brave man, was not in the least afraid of death, but he was very much afraid of what his death would mean to his country.

Seldom has a head of state been confronted with so terrible a choice. Seldom has a small country been in such a predicament. Even Belgium in 1914 had real friends and allies. Nasser and Attassi were neither friends nor allies to Hussein. They were interested only in involving him in a war which could never benefit Jordan, for, paradoxically, the greater threat to Hussein's throne was posed by a possible Arab victory. Israel, defeated

---

* British Brigadier Peter Young estimates (p. 89 of *The Israeli Campaign 1967*) that Egypt lost 700 tanks in the Sinai fighting. Israeli losses were 61 tanks, and the Israelis captured scores of completely undamaged Egyptian tanks, self-propelled guns and artillery weapons. The Israeli army showed a singular magnanimity in victory; Egyptian officers were taken and held prisoner, but their men were turned loose and in many cases helped on their way to the Canal with food and water. Arab propaganda tried at first to show that this was done so that the men should die in the desert.

and conquered, would have become an Egyptian satrapy, and Jordan would have secured for a neighbor a country and regime utterly alien to Hussein and utterly determined to achieve his downfall. Nasser would have turned Jordan into a second Yemen.

The Jordanian phase of the war has a deeper and much sadder significance than the others. For it constituted a war between two small states who need to live peacefully together and who have everything to gain by doing so. Between them, these two small states occupied the whole of Mandatory Palestine. Their future was bound up with that of the Palestinian Arabs. Coexistence between them could have been the cornerstone of peace in the Middle East.

At 1:00 P.M. on June 5 Jordanian forces carried out their sole offensive on the ground. It was hardly to their credit that it was directed against Government House in southeast Jerusalem, the United Nations headquarters. Early in the afternoon the Arab Legion started moving up tanks to the frontier, to the northwest of Jerusalem. Israeli counteraction was clearly required. First, Government House was captured, and the UN personnel who had sought shelter in the main building were evacuated to Jewish Jerusalem. Israeli forces pressed on to the east and south. In spite of some very tough fighting, the whole of Jerusalem was in Israeli hands by June 7. Not only Jerusalem, but the whole of Jordan west of the river Jordan was occupied. Unlike the Egyptians, the men of Jordan's Arab Legion fought bravely and were ready to counterattack. But they had no coherent defense plan, and the Israelis had complete command of the air.

The fourth phase of the war was on the Syrian front. It will be remembered that the entire Arab military build-up was based on the contention that Israel was about to invade Syria and had concentrated 11 to 13 brigades in Galilee, close to the Syrian frontier. Just how absurd this contention was, the events of June 5–8 made plain. This was a front on which Israel could not squander troops; all they had there was a thin defensive screen. As a matter of fact, she was not able to attack the immensely strong defensive Syrian positions on the ridges of the Golan Mountains until June 9. By then the first appeals were already coming in from the United Nations for an immediate cease-fire. But Israel regarded Syria as the original instigator of the crisis and the main agent in provoking the war. Eshkol had no intention of letting Syria off and leaving the Syrian batteries in a position still to shell Israeli settlements at will and open fire on Galilee fishermen going peacefully about their business at night.

The main Israeli objective was the Golan plateau, running the whole 40-mile length of the Israeli frontier, from its northeastern tip at the settlement of Dan to the southern end of the Sea of Galilee. The secondary objective was the small slice of Syrian territory to the north and northwest of Dan, which contained the springs of the Banias River and where the excavations had been made for diverting the headwaters of the river Jordan.

During the first four days of the war the Israeli forces on this front remained strictly on the defensive. In 1948 the Syrians had tried to break through south of the Sea of Galilee in a thrust designed to reach the Mediterranean at Haifa. In 1967 they did no more than probe half-heartedly down this same line and to the north of the Sea and shell the kibbutzim close to the border. Perhaps the Syrians partly or even wholly believed the Soviet fairy tale of a big concentration of Israeli troops in this area, and therefore made no plans for a general offensive. Equally possible was that the Syrians waited to see what would happen first on the Egyptian and Jordanian fronts.

The Golan Mountains represented a formidably difficult objective.

> The Syrian heights above the Upper Jordan Valley are a steep escarpment rising 1000 feet to the bare plateau which stretches eastwards to Damascus and beyond. The Syrian army had not only constructed positions from which they could dominate the valley but also fortified the plateau to a depth of some ten miles with a continuous zone of wire, minefields, trenches, gun emplacements, pillboxes, and tanks. Constructed under Russian direction, it was a masterpiece of defensive fortification, and suitably equipped with artillery, machine guns, antiaircraft batteries, and rocket launchers. Viewing the ground afterwards, it seemed impossible that any army in the world could have taken it, except by a campaign lasting for weeks.[13]

On June 9 and 10 the Israeli army scaled these bare and menacing heights, performing the most heroic deeds of the war, and thrust about 20 miles eastwards to a line running through the towns of Kuneitra and Boutmiye. From this line, they dominated the remainder of the Golan plateau and were within a day's march of Damascus. The Syrians resisted fiercely for the first few hours, then broke and fled. Their force of 10 to 12 brigades was utterly routed. Down in the valley of the Jordan the Israeli settlers were able to come out of their slit trenches and shelters, move about freely again, and begin the task of repairing their shattered homes, schools, and communal meeting places. They had been under the eyes and the guns of the Syrians for 20 years, pitilessly exposed. This threat to their existence had been removed at last, they believed forever.

In strictly military terms the Arab countries had suffered a shattering defeat. Their losses in men alone may have been as high as 30,000 (no official figures have ever been published). The Israelis retained only 5500 officers and NCO's as prisoners of war. The Arabs lost around 450 first-line aircraft and between 800 and 1000 tanks and assault guns, as well as a vast amount of supplementary military equipment. Nearly all of it was Russian. From 1955 onwards the Soviet Union had supplied the Arab states with 2000 tanks, 700 planes, 540 field guns, 200 heavy mortars, 175 rocket launchers, 650 antitank guns, 7 destroyers, 14 submarines, and 46 torpedo boats. Some of this equipment had become obsolete since 1955; of what remained, in all about half was destroyed, including at least two thirds of the Arab planes. According to one estimate, abandoned or destroyed Egyptian equipment in Sinai alone had a value of two billion dollars.[14] One of the military byproducts of the Egyptian fiasco was the suicide of Field-marshal Hakim Amer and the dismissal of 50 high-ranking officers.

Perhaps more important than the military losses of the Arab states was the new military geographical position which had been created, at least until a peace settlement could be reached. Before the war started, all Israeli centers of population were within a quarter of an hour's flying time from the frontier. Any Arab advance into Israel, save in the far south of the Negev desert, would have affected thickly populated areas and vital lines of communication. Part of Israel's long and narrow "waistline" to the north and south of Tel Aviv, as well as Galilee, was directly looked upon by Arab artillery positions. So was the main road to Jewish Jerusalem, as well as the city itself.

After the war ended, Israeli troops were within striking distance of the three capitals of the states against whom they had fought—Amman, Damascus, and Cairo. Jewish Jerusalem was no longer on the firing line, and the whole of Jerusalem had been united. Israel's conquests gave her, for the first time, defensible natural land frontiers, which were half the length of the old ones. The frontier with Syria now ran along the eastern ridge of the Golan plateau, instead of immediately below its precipitous western ridge. In the south the frontier of more than 200 miles between the Sinai and Negev deserts, with the threatening spike of the Gaza Strip into Israel, was gone and had been replaced by the 80-mile length of the Suez Canal. Even more striking was the change on the Israeli-Jordanian frontier. Israel had pushed east of the former long and rambling border to the straight, north-south line of the river Jordan and the Dead Sea.

What had the war cost Israel? Only 40 planes and 80 tanks were lost, while at least 200 Russian T-54's and -55's and Pattons were captured undamaged. Much more important in Israeli eyes were the losses in battle of 679 killed and 2563 wounded. Insignificant as these figures appear, compared with those of Arab losses, they still represented a real sacrifice for a state of only two and a half million people. Israel mourns her own bitterly. The civilian casualties caused by Syrian artillery fire were 29 women and children of the border kibbutzim, 16 of which suffered damage. The war cost Israel, in purely financial terms, about $500 million. This sum, which no Israeli citizen begrudged, was more than made good by the generous and ready contributions of world Jewry.

The war had cost Israel much besides. The strain on the nerves of the population had been terrible during the preliminary period of waiting.

> The world preferred talk to action. And when Israel mobilized her reserves and took up defensive positions in the Negev and formed a national unity government, the powers called on her "to wait," "to show restraint," "to seek a diplomatic solution." Israel, taut and ready, waited. Children dug slit trenches. Women blacked out the windows of their homes. The aged donated blood. The men in uniform sat it out in their forward positions, waiting for the "diplomatic solution" that no one believed in, or some hasty act by an enemy drunk with success that every one of them knew would come.[15]

Never before had the people of Israel been so much aware of their aloneness; with war imminent, the outside world had abdicated. It must be said, in parentheses, that the outside world had, two years afterwards, still not shown a suitable spirit of remorse for an inaction which was wholly shameful.

The Israelis reacted to this period of strain in the best possible way. Yael Dayan, General Dayan's daughter, described this in *A Soldier's Diary:* "The 'back home,' meanwhile, knew a wave of dedication and devotion. Everybody volunteered to do something, money was donated, people were gentler, kinder, more polite. They gave of their time and means; it was as though the country were one large livingroom populated by one large family." Such a national reaction was not unique; the same thing happened in Britain during Hitler's 1940–1941 blitz. It is, possibly, significant that Britain, too, was entirely alone at that time.

The patriotism of the Israeli as an individual was a reminder of the fact that Israel is probably the most closely knit and consciously organic community in the world. Among the very many acts of individual patriotism were, typically, the advance payment of income tax of $14,000 by a Tel Aviv lawyer, who at the same time lent the government $56,000 interest-free; the baking of 100 huge cakes by the officers' wives of a tank regiment for the reservists who had been called up and drafted to this unit; and the free shampoo for any girl in uniform by a Safed hairdressing salon.

Israel, in addition, had to stand up to a welter of criticism from the outside world. This was, admittedly, not so before the Six-Day War began; rather the reverse. Typical of opinion in the West was a Gallup Poll taken in Britain between May 29 and June 4. Exactly half of those who were asked who was in the right, took a neutral position. Who should blame them? The Middle East was a long way from home, and the rights and wrongs of countries which to them were only names on the map were beyond their comprehension. But, of the remainder, 46 percent favored Israel and only four percent Egypt. Public opinion in Germany and France was overwhelmingly pro-Israel. Israel was supported because she was small and alone and because the Arab moves to drive her to war were accompanied by such violent and blood curdling threats. But public opinion tended to move against Israel as soon as the war was over. As paradoxical as it may sound, her military victory had been *too* clear-cut and convincing. Public opinion is fickle. Although the principal facts of the Israeli-Arab confrontation remained the same as before, sympathy was now directed towards the temporarily abased as well as defeated Arabs. This was likely to remain the case, as long as Israel occupied the Arab territories conquered in the Six-Day War.

In the United Nations, opposition to Israel was mobilized without delay by the Soviet Union and its bloc. Many years before the Six-Day War, voting in the United Nations had become all too often an affair of lobbies, with votes being cast on a bloc or even interbloc system. The principle of "I'll take in your washing, if you take in mine" is perhaps not the best on which to run the only approximation to world government that exists today. Israel knew that two blocs would vote unanimously against her—the Soviet and the Arab. There would be a tendency to do so, too, in the Afro-Asian lobby. There was no single bloc on Israel's side, although there was a readiness on the part of most NATO countries to defend her as the small but sturdy bulwark against Soviet infiltration into the Middle East. But de Gaulle had, with one gesture, bulldozed away the hitherto well-cemented Franco-Israeli alliance. At the outset of the war he dramatically warned Israel against firing the first shot, and later denounced her for doing so. From then on, de Gaulle was to develop, in defiance of French public opinion, an increasing bias in favor of the Arab states.

In the battle of words which now began in that latter-day Tower of Babel, the United Nations headquarters in New York, Israel was at least able to strike the first blow. The Israeli Ambassador to the UN, Gideon Raphael, lost no time in getting in his word about the Egyptian aggression against Israel. As one writer put it: "Israel had perhaps scored a point, but in truth it is one of purely academic interest. Beyond question she had started the battle. But it is equally certain that Nasser had begun the campaign when he occupied Sharm el Sheikh. The war itself had started in 1948. An armistice is not a peace."[16] The Arab protest against Israeli aggression followed hard on the heels of Raphael's statement.

The Security Council held its first emergency meeting on June 6. All of its members agreed to appeal for an immediate cease-fire, but the Soviet Union, intent on winning some advantages for its Arab protégés at the conference table after having led them by the nose into war, made a cease-fire conditional on Israeli forces' retreating to their starting points. To responsibility for the outbreak of war the Soviet Union added responsibility for its continuation. On June 7 the Soviet Union realized that every hour was bringing fresh Israeli victories and dropped its demand for Israeli withdrawals. The Security Council accordingly voted unanimously for a cease-fire.

King Hussein accepted the cease-fire on the evening of June 7, and it became effective on the Israeli-Jordanian front at 10 P.M. But Nasser failed to react and on June 8 Radio Cairo announced that Egypt would "continue fighting until the last drop of blood." What was in Nasser's tortuous mind? One can think of only one possible line of thought: he must have hoped that the Soviet Union could be induced either to give him direct military aid or to threaten its use against Israel. This idea could well have been the origin of the weird conversation which Nasser had on the telephone with Hussein on June 7 (the date was confirmed by Nasser himself) and which the Israelis managed to monitor and record. Nasser was heard telling Hussein to join with him in claiming that Anglo-American armed intervention had begun, and that large numbers of British and American planes were actively engaged in the fighting. Some of the recording was indistinct, but Nasser's references to what he and Hussein should say had an unmistakably typical ring about them.

The purpose of this maneuver was plain. The Soviet Union was to be made to believe that Britain and the United States were taking part in the fighting and was then to throw its military strengh on the Arab side. Nasser indeed had not waited until June 7 to begin propagating this stab-in-the-back legend. On June 6 Radio Cairo announced "large-scale air intervention by the United States and Britain on behalf of the Israel enemy." It specified that "British Canberra bombers, bearing the official British insignia, took part in attacks against our positions in Sinai," and claimed that only the "strong air umbrella" of the Anglo-Americans had enabled the Israelis to make some military headway.

The Arab accusations were of course blatantly untrue and were at once denied by both the British and American governments. It remains anybody's guess whether the Soviet Union at any time believed them. On June 7 the Soviet government contented itself with sending a stern note to Israel. It castigated Israel for allegedly refusing to comply with the Security Council's demand for a cease-fire. The note would have been more appropriately directed to Egypt; only late at night on June 8 did the Egyptian government decide to comply with the Security Council's demand. By then, Israeli troops stood along the whole length of the Suez Canal. Soviet diplomacy had been of no more help to Nasser than Soviet arms.

Syria accepted the cease-fire on June 9 when the Israeli attack on the Golan Mountains was being launched. But the Syrian guns were at that moment still shelling the border kibbutzim, and Radio Damascus was continuing to call for the extermination of the people of Israel. Both sides, locked in combat, ignored the cease-fire appeal on this front; it came into force only at 6 P.M. on June 10.

In the United Nations the Soviet Union turned from the Security Council to the General Assembly, and in a few days collected enough support to convene an emergency session on June 17. An hour before the session began, President Johnson broadcast a foreign policy speech in which he asked for a fair and lasting peace in the Middle East. The Soviet Prime Minister, Alexei Kosygin, opened the General Assembly debate in a different vein; he demanded an immediate and unconditional withdrawal of all Israeli troops from the territories which they had occupied, the payment of astronomical damages for all war losses inflicted on the Arab nations, and the indictment of Israel as the only aggressor.

Kosygin was answered by Abba Eban. The Israeli Foreign Minister was brought up in Britain and may well be the most lucid debater ever produced by the Cambridge University "Union." He marshaled his arguments brilliantly.

The Arab nations, he pointed out, had begun preparing for war, and openly announcing the fact, as far back as 1962. He quoted extensively from the utterances of Egyptian and Syrian leaders to emphasize this point. A single one of those remarks sets the pattern for the rest. In February 1964 Nasser said: "The possibilities of the future will be war with Israel. It is we who will dictate the time. It is we who will dictate the place."

Eban went on to outline the steps taken by the Arab states from 1962 onward: the building up of their armed strength, the creation of a unified military command, the encouragement given to terrorists to attack Israel, the massing of troops on Israel's frontiers, the ejection of the United Nations Emergency Force in Sinai, the blockading of the Gulf of Aqaba, the conclusion of the Egyptian-Jordanian-Iraqi Defense Pact.

He outlined too the actions of the Soviet Union in arming the Arab states, encouraging them to dream of bloody military victory, and frightening them into the belief that Israel was about to strike at Syria. Eban pointed out that the Soviet Union had five times used its veto in the Security Council to prevent steps towards agreement in the Middle East. On January 22, 1954, the Soviet Union prevented the peaceful exploitation of the waters of the Jordan. On March 29, 1954, the Soviet Union blocked a resolution on the use of the Suez Canal as an international waterway. On August 19, 1963, the Soviet Union thwarted a resolution condemning Syrian bandits for murdering two Israeli settlers at Almagor. On December 21, 1964, it upheld the Syrian shelling of three peaceful settlements, Dan, Dafna, and Shear Yashuv. Once again the Soviet Union intervened on Syria's side when Japan, the Netherlands, Argentina, New Zealand, and Nigeria joined in expressing regret over the loss of life caused by Syrian raiders in October and November 1966. Eban pointed out that this was one of the few resolutions sponsored by states in five different continents.

Eban concluded by asking for free negotiation between Israel and each of her Arab neighbors with the purpose of arriving at a lasting and honorable peace. "The Arab states can no longer be permitted to recognize Israel's existence only for the purpose of plotting its elimination. They have come face to face with us in conflict, let them now come face to face with us in peace." Eban asked the General Assembly to appeal to "the recent combatants to negotiate the conditions of their future coexistence."

Free negotiation—here was the crux. It is just possible that the Arab states, after so signal a defeat in the field, and lacking, at least for the time being, confidence in the Soviet Union as an ally, could have been convinced that the path to an honorable peace lay through negotiation. They could surely have been convinced that they risked nothing and need lose nothing by embarking on negotiations, for they could withdraw from them at any time. The Arab leaders must have been aware of their subjects' readiness for peace and of their subjects' human interests, which required a settlement enabling the Arab world to begin to solve its urgent economic and social problems.

The Arab leaders, again, must have known that Eshkol was not a man of war; his own countrymen's prewar accusations that he was playing the role of a Neville Chamberlain were proof enough of that. Two days before the war began he had made a most constructive proposal in a letter to Soviet Prime Minister Kosygin. Eshkol had appealed in the letter to Kosygin to support three principles—the territorial integrity of all Middle East states, condemnation of hostile infiltration and acts of terrorism, and noninterference in the internal affairs of the countries of the Middle East. He got no answer to his proposal. Visiting troops in Sinai before the war was over, Eshkol said that Israel had not gone to war to secure territorial annexations but to preserve her existence. On June 12 he told the Knesset that "we look, not backward, but forward to peace," although he added that Israel, having fought alone, was "entitled to determine what are the true and vital interests of our country and how our future shall be secured." On June 26 Eshkol appealed for a "new deal" in the Middle East. Its aim should be the peaceful coexistence and mutual cooperation of its component states; and this aim should be realized through direct negotiations. Eban, even when he was being foolishly and destructively heckled in the United Nations, reiterated these thoughts of Eshkol's. Israel's attention was focused on the worthwhile objective of a peace which would be mutually advantageous to Israel and her neighbors.

The arguments of Eshkol and Eban fell on deaf ears, at least as far as the Arab and Soviet blocs in the United Nations were concerned. The Arabs understandably were gripped by feelings of inferiority. They had lost a war and did not want to lose the peace. But this natural inferiority complex fused with Arab prejudices of much longer standing. To the Arabs, the Israelis remained "Zionist intruders"; with them, no peace at all was desirable. To sit down at the same table with them meant betraying the Arab cause which had been defeated in 1948. It meant betraying the confused and ineffectual Arab efforts to prevent peaceful Jewish immigration into Palestine during the 30 years of the British Mandate. It meant, finally, forswearing—one must use spectacular words when describing Arab emotions—the logical objective of the largely stillborn Arab revolution, to rid the Arab world of outside imperialistic influences and to re-create Arab greatness in the Fertile Crescent.

Lebanon was not affected at all by the Six-Day War; it took no real part in the war, and the Lebanese government tactfully ignored the shooting down of a single Lebanese plane which infringed on Israeli air space.

Syria, perhaps surprisingly, was little affected. The left-wing Baathist regime successfully sold its story of being left alone on June 9, after the United Nations had called for a cease-fire, after Egypt and Jordan had been knocked out of the conflict, while Iraq had sat back without making any effective contribution. The Baathist regime was able to survive. Syria had lost only a part of the Golan plateau, which was a granary two thousand years ago under Roman rule, but which had been turned into a "Siegfried Line" in depth before June 1967, with an almost exclusively military population. Syria could afford to lick its wounds and waste no thought on the morrow.

Jordan had suffered grievous losses. Its territory was almost halved. It had lost possession of East Jerusalem, including the Old City, and three quarters of the holy places. With them went a tourist revenue estimated at not less than $12 million a year, a huge proportion of the total income of this small desert kingdom. Over 160,000 refugees flooded across the Jordan into the rump kingdom. Nearly two thirds of them were "old" refugees, who had been living mainly in camps since 1958 and whose existence was largely subsidized by UNRWA. The other one third were Arabs of the west bank who had fled from their homes because they feared Israeli retribution, probably wrongly. The first thought of impartial observers was that Jordan was literally ruined. This estimate was revised as outside aid flowed in, and Hussein, on behalf of his people, reaped the well-earned rewards of his innate decency and undisputed courage and patriotism.

Egypt's postwar position was more difficult to gauge. Nasser was the principal architect of Arab defeat. Ambition, vanity, deceit, and good will were all uniquely combined in this remarkable man; defeat made no difference to him. On June 9, 1967, Nasser resigned his post as President, exactly one day after the end of hostilities with Israel, with his armed forces in ruins and Israeli troops sitting along the Suez Canal. It was a "grand" gesture, made with great unconcern. His resignation was never meant to be accepted, nor was it. Mobs turned out once more in the streets of Cairo and Alexandria, chanting this time, not for the annihilation of Israeli citizens, but for the reinstalation of their leader. The mobs had no real alternative; they had no one else to whom they could turn. Nasser's type of personal dictatorship now gave them a choice between some army leader who had not been utterly disgraced by the Six-Day War, some minor official who had served him, or some unknown of the anti-Nasserite Moslem Brotherhood. Once again the mobs chose Nasser; Nasser had relied upon their judgment. He had relied, too, upon the fact that they were forlorn and adrift, and that they had nowhere to turn.

This shoddy little episode could not completely conceal Egypt's plight. The loss of the Sinai peninsula did not amount to very much, even though its oil resources were only just beginning to be exploited and could have satisfied perhaps a quarter of Egypt's own needs. But the Suez Canal was closed and was likely to remain closed until there could be a peace settlement. The Egyptians, reacting in the nihilistic manner approved by their leader, sank ships of every kind in the Canal and kept foreign craft, caught in the act of plying their trade at that moment, immured in the Great Bitter Lake, where they had huddled for safety's sake. The closure of the Canal cost Egypt, at the then estimates, over $30 million a month, or about $380 million a year. That was a huge slice out of Egypt's already inadequate national income.

Some of it would be made good by other Arab states. Nasser banked on this. After some deliberation, the oil-rich Arab states, which had been denounced by Nasser himself as reactionary, imperialistic pawns and lackeys, decided to subscribe an annual subsidy of $225 million for Egypt. One would like to think that this subsidy represented a degree of Arab patriotism; unfortunately, it was more representative of the readiness of the oil-rich sheikdoms to pay conscience money for staying out of the war, or tribute for Egyptian protection from potential Egyptian intervention in their affairs.

Nasser's Egypt escaped for the moment from its parlous predicament. Nasser's type of personal rule, the Middle East version of Gaullism, survived. The basis of this survival was refusal to contemplate a lasting peace settlement, with the corollary of increasing dependence on the diplomatic backing of the Soviet bloc. While Egypt, like Dr. Faustus, made what amounted in genteel, twentieth-century terms to its pact with the devil, only King Hussein threw out positive ideas for the future of the Middle East. He spoke, on Radio Amman and in London, on the need for Arab reappraisal, in order to consider a settlement which would restore the sense of purpose and self-respect to the Arabs. The so-called "revolutionary" leadership of the Arab world was not interested in realism like this. In early August an Arab Summit at Khartoum pronounced its three No's—no negotiations with Israel, no full diplomatic recognition of Israel, and no peace settlement with Israel. It is an alarming thought that Nasser needed only eight weeks from June 9, 1967, to recapture and consolidate his leadership of the Arab world.

The Six-Day War was a barren historical episode, except that it proved Israel's ability to defend herself in the face of ultimate pressure. Out of it emerged the sad truth that an area of the world which needs peace is not going to be helped to achieve that peace by great powers obsessed by their own rivalries. In particular, one great power, the Soviet Union, was shown to be concerned only with spreading its own influence and meddling mischievously in a gullible Arab world. Israel's victory confronted her with new dilemmas, perhaps even more insoluble than those of pre-June 1967. Once again, I would quote the view of an informed observer. "The sad truth was that the odds were very heavily against the third campaign of the Palestine war being its last. There was no likelihood that Russia would wish to see this running sore healed. Nor was there much reason to suppose that the Israelis would quit all, or some, of their territorial gains. The Arab leaders could not afford to sit around the table with their opponents, without the recovery of the lost territories, and the solution of the refugee problem. These were not circumstances that promised a settlement of any sort, far less a lasting one."[17]

This chapter can end with a footnote. After the Six-Day War ended, the Israelis asked for direct negotiations. The Arabs sought only diplomatic protection from the Soviet Union and Soviet bloc. President de Gaulle produced an aimless kind of neutrality, precluding constructive suggestions but setting a high premium on French self-righteousness. Britain, too, sought a kind of neutrality, leading nowhere.

American diplomacy is often criticized, sometimes with reason. But on June 19, 1967, President Johnson produced five basic principles for a settlement which do seem valid. They were:

Each Middle East nation's acceptance of the right to existence of all Middle East nations.

A just settlement of the Palestinian Arab refugee problem.

Respect for maritime rights in international waterways.

The limitation of the arms race in the Middle East.

The preservation of the territorial integrity of all Middle East states.

Had the Soviet Union wished to begin a serious dialogue over the Middle East, these proposals of President Johnson's did indeed offer an appropriate start. Had Britain, or some other power, wished to promote constructive discussion in the United Nations, these proposals could have been put forward there. They were simple and straightforward and, at least for the next two years, were not replaced by proposals which were in any way better. By June 19, 1967, the paradox had become self-evident—that an Israel that had won a resounding victory in the field was going to be denied the fruits of peace. This was the conundrum which confronted Eshkol and his government from June 1967 on.

1. These are excellently set out by Brig. Peter Young, in his book *The Israeli Campaign 1967*.
2. Ian McIntyre, *The Proud Doers*, p. 3.
3. Eshkol, in personal conversation with the author.
4. This period of waiting has been well described by Yael Dayan, in her book *A Soldier's Diary*, pp. 32–62.
5. Mrs. Eshkol, in personal conversation with the author.
6. Terence Prittie, *Israel: Miracle in the Desert*, p. 237.
7. Young, *op. cit.*, p. 87.
8. *Ibid.*
9. From the official Israeli history, *The Six-Days War* (Israeli Ministry of Defense), p. 32.
10. *Ibid.*, p. 85.
11. Theodore Draper, *Israel and World Politics*, p. 115.
12. Young, *op. cit.*, pp. 88–89.
13. Michael Howard and Robert Hunter, *Israel and the Arab World: The Crisis of 1967*, p. 38.
14. *The Six-Days War*, p. 150.
15. From *Bahamare*, Israeli Defense Forces weekly, June 12, 1967, p. 6.
16. Young, *op. cit.*, p. 141.
17. *Ibid.*, p. 183.

18.

On June 12, 1967, Eshkol made his first major government statement since the end of the Six-Day War. His speech, delivered in the Knesset, sounded a note of satisfaction and confidence mingled with sadness over the casualties and losses which had been suffered both by the armed forces and the civilian population.

First he outlined the gains made by Israel. An enemy overwhelmingly superior in numbers and military potential had been defeated; his military might had been smashed and his military bases close to Israel's frontiers destroyed. The standing threat to Jerusalem, to frontier settlements, and to Israel's coastline had been removed. The Gulf of Aqaba had been reopened to Israeli ships. Jerusalem was united. With deep emotion Eshkol declared: "This is the first time since the establishment of the State that Jews can pray at the Wailing Wall, the remnant of our Holy Shrine and of our historical past, and at Rachel's Tomb. This is the first time in our generation that Jews may pray at HaMachpela, the tomb of our patriarchs in Hebron, and fulfill the promise: 'Your deeds shall be rewarded and ye shall return into thy boundaries!'"

After a tribute to the national effort of Israel, Eshkol spoke of the reaction of world Jewry:

> In those days the fortress of the unity of our people was built. The people of the Diaspora hurried to identify themselves with our State, with the heart of the nation. Thousands of sons of our people came from near and far to our help. Hundreds of thousands, even millions, were ready to help us in our struggle with all their means. . . . Their hearts went out to our country during the campaign. The unity of the whole Jewish people was strengthened. Jerusalem was again united and by this reunion, as our forefathers prophesied, all Israel became brethren.

Eshkol gave a short account of the war, and then said about Jerusalem:

> Despite the shelling of Jerusalem by the Jordanians, which caused losses of life and many wounded, and much damage to property, we refrained from all shelling inside the city, on account of its holiness and in accordance with our policy of avoiding harming the civilian population.
>
> Immediately after the city was freed, and even before I visited the Wailing Wall, I assembled the heads of the Christian and Moslem communities and told them this: "You can live in safety and in the knowledge that no harm will be permitted to the places holy to your faiths. I have requested the Minister for Religious Affairs to get in touch with the religious leaders in Jerusalem, to ensure close contact between them and our forces, and the continuation of

their spiritual activities without disturbance. Arrangements were made at once to ensure that the holy places of the Christian faith were placed in the hands of the priests of that faith, and the holy places of Islam were placed in the hands of the priests of the Moslems."

Eshkol might have added that, for the past 20 years, Jews had been barred from visiting their own holy places in East Jerusalem, that at least 40 Jewish synagogues in the Old City had deen destroyed, that the big Jewish cemetery south of the Garden of Gethsemane had been aimlessly desecrated, and that a public latrine had been erected close to the Wailing Wall. Under Israeli control there was to be complete freedom of access to all the holy places of Jerusalem, irrespective of nationality or creed.

Perhaps the most important passage of his speech was the following:

Let this be said—there should be no illusion that Israel is prepared to return to the conditions that existed a week ago. The State of Israel was established and exists lawfully, and for this our people were forced to fight. We have fought alone for our existence and our security, and we are therefore justified in deciding for ourselves what are the genuine and indispensable interests of our State, and how to guarantee its future. We shall never return to the conditions prevailing before. No more will the Land of Israel be no-man's land, violated by acts of sabotage and murder. . . . We are not looking back, but forward, and to peace in particular. We shall observe the cease-fire faithfully, provided the other side does so.

Finally, Eshkol had this message for the Arabs.

To the Arab nations I want, at this hour, to say: We were not glad that we had to go to war. We acted in the absence of any other choice, to protect our lives and our rights. We have the same obligations to our country as you have to yours. As old as the days of this world, so old are the roots of the people in this land. Down the generations Israel preserved in the lands of the Diaspora her spiritual and material ties with this country; she was never severed from it, not even when she went into exile. And, in return, this country conserved its loyalty towards us, and never abandoned itself to any strange people. It waited and longed for the return of its sons and the ingathering of its exiles. Today the whole world bears witness that there is no power than can uproot us from this land.

Eshkol's speech should have made it plain that the mood of the people of Israel, in which relief and joy intermingled, was one of peace. He was to say this explicitly, times without number, in the course of the next two years. His Foreign Minister, Abba Eban, repeated his wish for peace in the less personal, more articulate terms of the professional diplomat. That the Israelis themselves wanted peace is beyond doubt. Victory in war could bring material gains of one kind and another; but peace could presage a golden era in the Middle East.

A word should be said here about the feelings of the Israelis in that hour of victory. The threat and fear of annihilation vanished in the first day or two of the war. Then came the fruits of victory, showering forth from their cornucopia. The conquest of Sinai meant little, except for reopening the Gulf of Aqaba and forcing the retreat of the Egyptian army from Israel's borders. The conquest of the Golan plateau had a localized importance; the settlers of Galilee could once again go freely about their business, knowing that the Syrian guns would never again open fire on them. The west bank of Jordan meant a great deal more, for it was the Biblical heartland of the children of Israel. It had contained Samaria and Shechem as well as Hebron and Jericho. It was to the hills to the north and south of Jerusalem that the children of Israel had retreated when Egyptian or Assyrian armies marched and countermarched northward and southward along the coastal plain of Sharon.

The reunification of Jerusalem meant more than all other territorial gains put together. The capture of the Old City was the supreme hour of glory. The following account by a reporter of the journal *Bahamane*, Yosef Bar-Yosef, speaks for itself:

> I for one had never seen the Western Wall. But this was true for almost all the others who were here with me today [June 7]. We dashed in through St. Stephen's Gate and began to run, no one said where, but we all knew—to the Temple Mount and the Wall. We didn't know the way, and we dashed around like blind people, I was suddenly terribly afraid I wouldn't find it. But then we did.
>
> Some of the soldiers simply caressed the stones. Some kneeled, some cried. They cried and then embraced and hugged each other. They were at a loss over what to do next. Strange sounds began to issue from one soldier's mouth; another began to stammer: "We're in the Old City, we! Do you understand? The Wall, the Wall!" He looked around and everyone understood. "Jerusalem is ours!" one soldier cried out, as if what we had before was not Jerusalem.[1]

The capture of the Wailing Wall had a symbolic and emotional significance which no Gentile can ever fully understand, although he may be able to guess at it. The Minister of Defense was the first member of the Cabinet to reach the Wall. Dayan said, "We have returned to all that is holy in our land. We have returned never to be parted from it again."[2] Eshkol arrived later in the day, accompanied by the two chief rabbis. In the course of a short speech, he said: "It is a great honor for me to stand here next to this symbol of our past glory. I see myself as a representative of the entire nation and of many past generations whose souls yearned for Jerusalem and its holiness."

What made tough, courageous Israeli paratroopers, many of them men who did not attend synagogue or consider themselves to be religious, stand weeping at the Wall? It was the last surviving fragment of the Temple, but the Temple had ceased to exist as an entity two thousand years ago. It was only a bare wall of weathered stones. But for days and weeks thereafter thousands upon thousands of Israelis flocked to the Wall; there has been steady stream of them ever since, even after the first great rush was over.

About three months after the war was over, a survey was made of the feelings of about 140 soldiers who had fought in the Six-Day War and who belonged to kibbutzim. The men of the kibbutzim (and the women too) were rightly regarded as something of an élite in the armed forces; the kibbutzim produced roughly four times more officers and senior NCO's, proportionate to their total manpower, than the rest of the population. The kibbutz type, highly disciplined and conscientious, used to the open spaces and adept in self-defense, was ideal material for military service. Two hundred kibbutznikim fell in the war, again a high proportion. The views of the people interviewed, most of them young, were published later.[3]

The war had stirred all of them deeply, much more than they would have expected. "We are not usually the kind of people who are given to soul-searching." They were unanimous that war had been inevitable, weeks before it broke out. "Suddenly everybody was speaking of Munich, of the holocaust, of the Jewish people which was on its own." And the immediate thought was "never again to be led to the slaughter!"

There was a universal urge to identify themselves with their Jewishness. Fighting in the war enabled them to equate their Zionism with the exact and efficient execution of their orders, particularly in the saving of Jewish lives, the hallmark of the totally comprehending citizen-soldier. These young people believed that the Arabs, if victorious, would have perpetrated a wholesale massacre of men, women, and children. But there was a tendency to regard the Arabs as dupes; far worse, as one young soldier saw it, was "the terrible treason of Soviet Russia, the faith of youth turned murderer."

Victory was wonderful but terrible too. Those young victors did not want to talk much about it. But they did not turn, instead, to religion as a panacea, regarding it rather as a valuable historical bond; and they were apt to shy away from politics, with their divisive, sectional tendencies. "We have, after all, taken part in something more important." There was an innate distaste at having had to take human life, an instinctive uneasiness over Israel's producing a conquering army, a new restlessness which is not a new concept for anyone who has fought with comrades at his side.

There was an uneasiness and restlessness among the population as a whole. Significantly, after the first bright visions of peace had begun to fade, one found more and more people talking of having perhaps to fight again. In the early weeks it was otherwise, and certain concepts formed then died only a lingering death and were not always dead years afterward.

There was the belief that Israel's victory had radically changed the balance of power in the Middle East. One prescient observer remarked, "There were those who thought that Israel's 1967 blitzkrieg had won her ten years' peace, but in fact her strategic position, never brilliant, was only marginally improved, since air power was the key to the situation."[4] This was a strictly military evaluation. There were other considerations. The Arab world had lost, at least for the time being, a limited amount of territory. But it remained a huge area in comparison with tiny Israel. Its economic and ultimately its military potentials were far greater than those of Israel, unless the latter with one great leap forward joined the "nuclear club." Soviet interest in the Middle East remained as intense as ever and Soviet influence continued to expand in an Arab world which had become even more receptive to it than before.

There was the belief that Israel's victory had substantially eased Israel's problems of defense. It had not. Once again for the time being Israel had secured buffer zones in Sinai, the Golan plateau, and the west bank of Jordan. But these buffer zones, or considerable parts of them, might have to be given up in order to obtain a peace settlement. In the interim period, between war and a peace settlement, effective defense of Israel plus the newly occupied territories had to be maintained. And this cost money, particularly in the south, where very expensive lines of communication, up to the line of the Suez Canal, had to be kept going. Once again, the attitude of the Soviet Union was all-important. The Soviet government continued to pour arms into the Arab countries. Israel had to arm at a pace commensurate to that of her Arab neighbors. But the Soviet Union believed in bulk issue of weapons exported to the Middle East, weapons increasingly more sophisticated but never as sophisticated as those the Soviet Union needed for itself. The Nazis did exactly the same thing in the Balkans before 1939; they created an export market for weapons which they did not need, thus broadening the scope of their own armaments industry.[5]

Soviet support of the Arab countries in the shape of cheap arms in bulk threw a heavy burden on Israel. The second lesson which Israel learned was that its victory in the Six-Day War did not mean a reduction of defense costs, but an immense increase. The defense burden grew from about 15 percent to well over 30 percent of the budget.

There was a third Israeli misconception. That was that the Six-Day War would convince the Arab leaders of the need for peace. Of those who had taken part in the war, only King Hussein decided that the need for peace was paramount. Egypt, Syria, and Iraq did not. In the rest of the Arab world President Bourguiba of Tunis continually lifted up his voice in favor of peace. President Boumédienne of Algeria did the opposite, while King Feisal of Saudi Arabia, obsessed with the need to counter Nasserite revolutionary Arab socialism, adopted a violently anti-Israel attitude. The Arab world remained fragmented, incapable of unified action and, to a large degree, of coherent reappraisal. It was manifestly utterly incapable of making peace.

A fourth Israeli misconception, in the early days after June 1967, related to the position of King Hussein of Jordan. There was no question that Hussein was ready to seek peace in the interests of his people. But he had never been strong enough to do so vis-à-vis Nasserite revolutionary socialism. And he was very soon to be confronted with a more deadly rival than Nasser in the shape of the various Palestine liberation movements which fastened, like a cancer, on his small kingdom. Hussein had to carry on his personal struggle for survival. Jordan could never be strong enough to go it alone in negotiating with Israel.

Finally Israel believed that victory on the battlefield had been a boon for the Western powers. Just after the Six-Day War one heard a lot of talk in diplomatic circles of Israel's having struck a decisive blow for the maritime powers, too uncertain of themselves to be able to stand up for their own rights. The Western powers may have benefited in one obvious sense: an Arab victory would have given the Soviet Union a lasting diplomatic and political predominance in the Middle East. Israel's victory at least restored something like a balance, an uneasy one certainly and one which the Western powers were painfully incapable of exploiting to their own advantage.

To the Israelis, the post-June 1967 Middle East policies of the Western powers must have seemed singularly immature. The United States struggled with the problem of deciding whether to back Israel and forfeit influence in the Arab Middle East, or to steer a middle course between Israel and the Arabs. Britain, under the volatile and ephemeral direction of that most unusual Foreign Secretary, George Brown, had a brief, futile fling at taking command in the diplomatic free-for-all. De Gaulle's France adopted a frankly cynical attitude of self-interest.* The Western powers had a unique chance of speaking with one voice in the summer of 1967. They never looked like doing so.

---

* France's feeling toward Israel has always followed the lines of national self-interest. France turned a blind eye to the movements of Jewish illegal immigrants, fully understanding how much this embarrassed Britain, her own rival in the Middle East. In the 1950s French friendliness toward Israel was the consequence, not of any love for Israel, but of Nasser's support of the Algerians in their war against France. The restoration of better French relations with Algeria brought the end of the illusory French honeymoon with Israel. In November 1967, de Gaulle described the Jews as "an élite people, sure of itself and domineering." That drew down on his head a 15-page letter of reproach from Ben-Gurion—to which de Gaulle countered

Visiting Israel in October 1967, I was able to gauge something of the changing mood of the people. Resentment, resignation, and disappointment were beginning to struggle for mastery. The worst feature of the situation was that peace was as far off as ever. New frontiers, certainly, had been gained but were being held only on a day-to-day basis. Lack of confidence in the Western powers had further developed the latent Israeli instinct to go it alone. Total disillusionment with the United Nations had precisely the same effect. Long-term problems looked more insoluble than ever, as the Middle East became increasingly involved in the East-West confrontation of the great powers. Moreover, every short-term Israeli gain implied a long-term loss. Holding Arab territory increased Arab hatred. Closing the Suez Canal made Nasser more dependent on the Soviet Union. Winning the arms race, when it meant buying the newest, most sophisticated aircraft from abroad, saddled the economy with fresh indebtedness. Other victor nations before Israel have found victory to be vain.

The problems which Israel inherited directly from the war were considerable, indeed almost overpowering for so small a country. She found herself in possession of territories roughly three times as large as herself; the Sinai peninsula alone was double Israel's size. In these territories was an Arab population of over one million, another 300,000 having either been evacuated before the fighting or having fled during it and afterwards. This meant that, in all territories under Israeli control, there were 1.4 million non-Jews against 2.3 million Jewish Israelis.*

Here was the kernel of the first problem that Israel's leaders had to consider. Israeli troops could continue to sit on the cease-fire lines indefinitely if the Arab countries refused to grant a peace settlement. Israel could also indefinitely postpone an internal settlement for the occupied Arab territories. But if there were a settlement which left all of these Arabs in the State of Israel, even under some federal arrangement, what were the demographic implications? Arab Palestinian families produce, on the average, seven or eight children. Jewish Israeli families produce three. Jewish immigration into Israel has dwindled; a reason-

---

by saying his description of the Jews was intended as a compliment. The strength of the Jewish community in France has been largely instrumental in organizing a number of popular demonstrations in favor of Israel. Eshkol's commentary on the Jewish community, made in Paris, was, "There are half a million Jews in this country, but you would have to search the beautiful streets of Paris with a lantern to discover any Jew ready to leave in an aliyah to help to construct the homeland."

* According to the census carried out by the Israeli authorities in the occupied territories during the late summer of 1967, fewer than 150,000 west bank Arabs had fled across the Jordan. The census also established that there were 354,000 persons living in the Gaza Strip, as against a pre-1967 Arab estimate of 454,000. After the Six-Day War, only 3,000 left the Strip in the first three months, but this number swelled to 20,000 in the first year of Israeli occupation (*Israeli Digest* [London], October 20, 1967).

able deduction would be that there would be more Arabs than Jews in an enlarged State of Israel by 1985.

The demographic problem colored all Israeli thought on the subject of a peace settlement. The second problem left by the war, an even more immediate one, was that of the administration of the occupied territories. More must be said about this in due course. Here it need only be noted that Sinai produced no administrative problem; its total population, partly nomadic, was about 50,000. Nor did the Golan plateau, from which Syria evacuated about 90,000 inhabitants before the 1967 war. That left only 8000 Druses, who quickly settled down under Israeli rule and probably preferred it to Syrian. The two administrative problems had to do with the west bank, with a population of 700,000, and the Gaza Strip, with half that number. Their administration required understanding, tact, firmness, imagination, and economy. Economically they had to be made self-supporting as far as possible. Socially they had to be encouraged to become more progressive. Politically they had to be kept quiet.

Israel was confronted with the now much more pressing problem of Arab terrorism. It became more pressing because the Arab armies suffered such a disastrous defeat. Encouraged by the example of Algeria, the Arab countries fell back on the concept of guerilla warfare as the most effective means of harrassing Israel. Boumédienne gladly tendered advice. The gist of it was that terrorism against women and children is a more paying proposition than an honorable and essentially military resistance to enemy occupation. El Fatah and other Arab guerilla organizations accepted the Algerian model rather than that of the Résistance in wartime France, or even the IRA in post-1918 Ireland. The chief weapons of the Arabs became the mine laid on the busy highway, the bomb planted in the theater or bus station, the hand grenade in the marketplace, even the submachine gun used indiscriminately on the passengers of a civilian airplane. These were the tactics of terror. Two years after the war, the Israelis were finding them ever more difficult to deal with.

Behind these immediate problems of the occupation were the more endemic ones of the arms race in the Middle East, the rivalry of the great powers there, the frenetic mobilization of support in the United Nations by the Arabs, and the maintainance of the political and economic fabric of the State of Israel in the face of all these pressures. All of these problems would dwindle, if only there could be peace. But Ben-Gurion may well have been right when he told a BBC correspondent in the late summer of 1967, "Only Russia can help to bring peace between Jews and Arabs. I don't see any prospect of peace in the next ten years without their help."[6]

The future of the occupied territories was naturally bound up with the frontiers Israel needed for reasons of security. Views on this question differed widely. There were those who believed that Israel should hold on to every square mile of territory conquered in a war which she had not sought. There were those who wanted certain relatively minor annexations of conquered territory, returning the rest to its original owners. And there was a smaller, fluctuating group which wanted to set up a new Palestinian entity, after taking only what was strictly necessary for Israel's minimum security. All three groups agreed on one point: there could be no question of parting with East Jerusalem. A fourth, but very small group, was in favor of handing back all territory won in battle, but only on the condition that Israel would get a lasting peace settlement in return.

The annexationists were not very vocal immediately after the Six-Day War. During the late summer they organized themselves into the Land of Israel Movement and published their first manifesto in September 1967. The principal point which it made was that no Israeli government had the right to hand back any of the land won in battle. The government was only the trustee for the people of Israel in the land of Israel. As a trustee, it had a responsibility to every generation in the last two thousand years and to every generation to come. Israel's inherent claim was to its whole land, including Mount Sinai in the south, Mount Hermon in the north, Jericho, Bethlehem, and the Judean and Samarian hills.[7] By implication, Israel laid claim to nearly all the habitable part of the Kingdom of Jordan, for this comprised the lands of the tribes of Reuben and Gad, and half the tribe of Manasseh.

The Land of Israel Movement wanted development of the conquered territories to begin at once. Just as Jewish New Nazareth had been built next door to Arab Nazareth, so new twin cities should be built beside Nablus, Hebron, Jericho, and other Arab centers on the west bank. Wasteland in Sinai and the Golan Mountains should be brought under cultivation again, as it had been in the days of King Solomon. The leaders of the Movement argued that a Greater Israel would attract considerably increased immigration and would cease to be a vulnerable objective of Arab aggression. Its survival could be ensured by its own strength and dynamism. The leaders of the Movement were of the opinion that little trust could be placed in outside powers and that the Arabs could not be trusted at all.

This argument, with the corollary that peace depended on the strength of the Israeli community and not on peace treaties which the Arabs would observe only under duress, was explained in detail by Eliezer Livneh, one of the many intellectuals who joined the Movement.[8] He took the view that Egypt and Syria had torn up treaties without number and that King Hussein's state of Jordan was a fictional entity which had had its true independence ground away to nothing between the millstones of Nasserism and the terrorists of the Palestinian guerilla organizations. After a long talk with Professor Harold Fisch, later rector of Bar-Ilan University, I came to the conclusion that he and his colleagues were not dreamers but hard-headed *Real-Politiker,* in the Bismarckian mold. In concrete terms Professor Fisch talked of raising immigration to an annual 40,000, of stimulating the birth rate, and of paying due attention to geopolitical considerations—like keeping the Red Sea an international waterway from bases in Sinai, and reactivating the Haifa oil pipeline.[9]

Two more things must be said about the annexationist Land of Israel Movement. The first is that, as the years go by and Israel is denied a peace settlement, the Movement's strength will tend to grow rather than diminish. The philosophy of "What I have, I hold" is not alien to any sovereign nation. Continuing possession breeds its own kind of familiarity. The second point is that the influence of the Movement will remain very difficult to gauge. For it has its supporters in almost every political party, although they are strongest in the liberal-conservative Gahal blocked by Menachem Beigin. These supporters are of the most varied types: intellectuals imbued with a sense of history, religious people who see prophecies being fulfilled, hard-headed businessmen who want Israel to have a substantial hinterland to exploit, small tradesmen who crave security, soldiers who regard the return of land won through the sacrifice of their comrades' blood as a kind of treason.*

The Movement's influence will probably be all the greater because it has not campaigned as a political party on its own. After June 1967, in the press of Western countries there was much loose talk of Israeli doves and hawks, with the Cabinet allegedly fairly equally divided between the two. The real hawks, where peace terms were concerned, were the men of the Land of Israel Movement. The Cabinet, by contrast, went on operating on a basis of consensus, and remained restricted to the inevitably wayward deviations of a purely pragmatic pursuit of acceptable peace terms. They were wayward, one should add, not because Israeli thinking encouraged this, but because Arab governments alternated between moods of hope and despair and between protestations of a desire for peace and assertions that another war was inevitable.

So far, even two years after the war of June 1967, one can safely say that the Movement enjoyed the steady support of only a minority of the population of Israel. A very definite majority was prepared, if given

---

* One such soldier who made his views crystal-clear was Lt.-Colonel Zvi, who commanded a battalion in the attack on Gaza. In a discussion published by *Israel Magazine* (Vol. 1, No. 4, 1968), Zvi said that the cease-fire lines gave Israel ideal borders, for security reasons and also because they correspond to the boundaries "of the traditional Eretz Israel." Two of the others taking part in the discussion agreed with him and felt that a return to the west bank, in particular, was a "return home." The three others in the group disagreed; they regarded the occupied territories as "unfamiliar" and their retention as unnecessary, save as a means of securing peace negotiations and a peace settlement.

a written and guaranteed peace settlement, to return most of the conquered territories, either to the Kingdom of Jordan or to a newly created Palestinian entity. What did this majority want to retain for Israel? East Jerusalem, as I have already indicated, was a "must." More will have to be said about the problem of Jerusalem later, but only regarding the details of its incorporation into Greater Jerusalem.

Apart from East Jerusalem, the question really was just what territories were wanted by Israel for security requirements.

From north to south: The first ridges of the Golan Mountains had to be annexed from the security point of view. The settlements of Galilee could not ever again be under the guns of Syrian artillery. The Syrians had converted this region into an armed camp. They totally neglected its economic potential (it has a reasonable amount of rainfall and, five miles from the Israeli border, a reasonable soil which does not grow stones). Two years after the war, it looked as if Israel would annex the whole of this area, which they will certainly develop into a valuable granary (something which the Syrians never did). Late in 1969 the position was that about 25 Israeli settlements were either established or in the process of being established on the Golan plateau. It is worth recording that the Syrians continued to regard this area as military terrain; they had no thought of exploiting its economic potential.[10]

There was a strong case for annexing the first ridges of the Samarian hills, running from north to south, opposite the plain of Sharon. Israeli thought, at least until 1969, remained flexible on this subject. The outskirts of Tel Aviv had been bombarded from gun emplacements just inside the Jordanian border during the Six-Day War. Israeli public opinion was not seriously worried by this sector. Minor frontier rectifications would have been acceptable to a great many Israelis.

Perhaps, partly for sentimental reasons, there was a stronger case for widening the so-called "corridor" to Jerusalem, especially where an Arab salient cut the old Jerusalem-to-the-coast road close to the Trappist Monastery of Latrun. The self-imposed silence of the Trappist monks contrasted oddly with the fury of Arab artillery fire from the heights above Latrun, in both 1948 and 1967. A minor rectification of the frontier would put the old main road and enough of the heights above it inside Israel.

Farther south, the reunification of Jerusalem satisfied Israel's overriding requirement. South of Jerusalem, just off the main road from Bethlehem to Hebron, was the site of the old Jewish settlement of Etzion. There had, in fact, been four different small Jewish settlements there. In the 1948 war their inhabitants had fought a gallant battle in almost total isolation. Some of the survivors were still alive 20 years later. Etzion was reestablished, sitting on a hill amid wasteland which the latest generation of pioneers would cultivate in the pride of their remembrance. Resettlement at Etzion meant once again a minor frontier rectification. The place was near the pre-1967 Israeli frontier; early in 1968 a new road from Etzion to Israel proper was begun.

On the shores of the Mediterranean, the Gaza Strip posed a much more awkward problem. It had a population of 350,000, two thirds of them still registered as refugees and receiving UNRWA help. In 1968 I wrote:

> Nasser maintained the Gaza Strip as a huge refugee squatting ground at best, and a kind of concentration camp at worst. Unable to leave, without capital investment to build up industries, with no Egyptian attempt to integrate them, the Palestinians there lived as second-class Arabs. Unemployment was widespread. Very often there was a curfew. Nasser never even carried out a census, in order to be able to claim that there were more than half a million people there. Inhabitants of the Strip were taught to hate Israel, and were not taught very much else. Israeli soldiers who occupied the area in the June war were horrified to find to what lengths propaganda had been carried. Eight-year-old children had been taught to draw anti-Semitic pictures that would have gladdened Hitler's heart. The local press depicted Jews of hideous appearance being knifed, decapitated, or garroted. Only the gas chamber was missing from their revolting cartoons.[11]

This refugee pressure cooker was, so to speak, Nasser's secret weapon against Israel. For in 1967 Israel was saddled with the problems of Gaza which Nasser had never even pretended to try to solve. The view of the Israeli government was that, whatever else happened, the Gaza population should be given freedom of movement and not kept in a Nasserite ghetto, should be helped by vocational training which would enable them to find worthwhile employment elsewhere in the Arab world, should be equipped to develop light industries and build up a decent, self-sufficient economy. But whether to annex Gaza or not remained an open question. Annexed, the Strip loaded Israel with an acute social and political burden. But there was no plan for returning Gaza to Nasser, the man who had betrayed and neglected it. Could Gaza become a United Nations area? Here was a possible solution, but not one which the Israelis could formally propose until a peace settlement was in sight.

There remained Sinai. The majority of Israelis did not covet its bleak landscape. Its historical associations with the children of Israel were tenuous. But it contained the fort of Sharm el Sheikh, at the southern end of the Gulf of Aqaba. For purely military reasons, most Israelis did not relish the idea of returning Sinai to unfettered Egyptian sovereignty. They would have preferred to turn it into a demilitarized zone, with Israel retaining Sharm el Sheikh in order to guarantee the free movement of shipping through the Straits of Tiran. The demilitarization of Sinai, which would be best supervised by a joint Egyptian-Israeli commission, would not prevent Egypt from utilizing its oil resources or from implementing earlier plans for making the El Arish area a center of agriculture and fishing.

The essential thought behind these frontier changes, and others which were debated from the end of the 1967 war onward, was that Israel had the right to ensure her own security. Most Israelis considered that the west bank and the Gaza Strip, if returned to Arab rule, should, like Sinai, be demilitarized. This, they considered, should be done irrespective of whether the west bank were handed back to Jordan, or whether it and Gaza were linked together in some independent Palestinian entity. The demand for security led to demolitions being carried out in a number of places. These included Kalkilya, from whose outskirts Tel Aviv had been shelled, three small villages sitting above the Latrun-Jerusalem road which had been liberally used by guerillas, and Banias in the Golan Mountains, another guerilla base. The destruction of several hundred homes caused great hardship to their former Arab occupants, and some of the demolitions were carried out weeks after the war ended. Talking to Eshkol about it, I had the impression that he personally regretted what had been justified to him as a military necessity.

The question of turning the west bank into a separate Palestinian entity was debated with great animation but less conviction after the war ended. Such an entity could have been linked with both Israel and Jordan and could have contained the germ of a Middle East federation. Economically it could hardly be viable, at least at first. Understandably King Hussein had launched his industrial and other development projects on the east bank of the Jordan and as far from the Israeli frontier as possible. This had led to an unnatural drift of population away from the good soil and climate of the Judaean and Samarian hills to the arid semidesert of Transjordan. In 1948 there had been 800,000 inhabitants of the west bank and only 400,000 east of the Jordan. By 1967 about 350,000 people had crossed the river from west to east, but natural population increase kept the figure of the west bankers at 800,000. The population of Transjordan, on the other hand, had grown to 1,100,000. Another 100,000 to 180,000 were to cross from the west bank in 1967, giving Transjordan an actual majority of Palestinian inhabitants. The west bank had remained almost purely agrarian, with industry virtually restricted to the soap factories of Nablus.

To create an independent west bank entity would require Arab support. That the Israelis hesitated to put forward a plan was due to their desire not to commit themselves until peace negotiations were in sight. Preliminary probes revealed that there was not much more than toleration of Hussein's rule on the west bank. But they revealed, too, that Arab leaders were not anxious to commit themselves. With the exception of the mayor of Jericho, who fled across the Jordan, mayors of Arab towns stayed at their posts. The mayors of Ramallah, Jenin, and Jericho remained discreetly silent on their views about a Palestinian entity. Bethlehem, dependent on its tourist trade, was unaffectedly in favor of merging with Greater Jerusalem, created on June 27, 1967, when laws passed by the Knesset gave Jerusalem a unified administration. The two most important Arab leaders on the west bank, however, were the mayors of Hebron and Nablus.

Sheik Mohamed Jabari of Hebron was a former minister of Hussein's and a man of wisdom and moderation. He was reported in the early months after the war as saying that the "Palestinians have had enough to put up with" and of favoring an independent entity on the west bank. Jabari had managed to get the Israelis to treat Hebron in effect as an open city when it was captured, had discouraged guerila activity in his area, and had had difficulty with the occupiers only over the case of Machpela Tomb, which was taken over for a time by Israeli squatters from extremist religious groups. When I talked to him, I found Jabari reserved on the subject of a Palestinian entity, but he thought that a United Nations trusteeship of the whole west bank including East Jerusalem was a possibility. Jabari was a realist; one good point that he made was that the Arabs had made a sad mistake in driving Jews from their homes in Arab countries. These Jews had mostly come to Israel and made it a stronger state.[12]

In Nablus, Sheik Hamdi Kaanan was strongly in favor of the west bank's being returned to Jordan. He believed that an independent Palestinian entity would not be either politically or economically viable and that it would therefore eventually be annexed by Israel. He preferred continuing military occupation to creeping annexation. Kaanan had some complaints against the Israelis: they had put about 500 people who were suspected of aiding the guerillas in prison, had beaten up some of them, had not allowed citizens of Nablus who fled across the Jordan to return to their homes, and had imposed a curfew. He agreed, with great good humor, that there had often been a curfew when Nablus was in Jordan and that the people of Nablus had the reputation of being "the Irish of the Middle East" and chronically "agin the government."[13] A courteous and impressive man, his feelings illustrated the fact that a military occupation could never be easy.

The future of the west bank, of course, is intimately linked with the question of Israel's security. In the two-year interval since the war this was indicated by two proposals, suggested as ideas only, for militarily neutralizing the West Bank. One came from Yigal Allon, Minister of Labor at the time and about to become Deputy Prime Minister; the other from General Moshe Dayan who, as Minister of Defense, took on special responsibilities for the administration of the west bank.

Allon suggested that Israel, for security reasons, should go on holding the line of the river Jordan, irrespectively of the political future decided upon for the west bank. There would be only a thin screen of Israeli settlements and military posts along the right bank of the Jordan. Corridors would be left open through this screen, leading to the bridges across the river and to the Kingdom of Jordan beyond.

Dayan proposed establishing Israeli strongpoints of settlement on the west bank. These would be established at strategic places, commanding lines of communication. Purely military strongpoints would be held on the hills. The Israeli new towns would be given industries which would make them economically complementary to the Arab agricultural areas. Not an acre of farmland would need to be taken from the Arabs.

Eshkol was at first understandably reticent when I asked him about Israel's frontiers in general and the west bank in particular. Dayan and Allon are popular representatives of a generation younger than his; even so, they have both been sharply criticized for implying that most of the occupied territories could be evacuated by Israel. As Prime Minister, Eshkol could not launch a trial balloon. Prime ministers, clearly, must be especially careful if their words are not going to be seized upon and interpreted as constituting a definite offer of terms. But later he committed himself fairly definitely in personal conversation with me. He said, "I see Allon's plan as practicable. And if I were in Hussein's place, I would accept the plan with both hands. As far as the actual carrying-out of such a plan goes, we are in a position to do it—that's all that matters."

Eshkol's general thought on the subject of frontiers was: "Since the June 1967 war I've had letters from fellow Jews all over the world. Almost every writer has told me not to give up an inch of the territory won in battle. They tell me: this was an act of God."[14]

As Eshkol saw it, there was one overriding priority where frontiers were concerned. "What we seek is a real and lasting peace. The two necessities for such a peace are a binding and fair treaty and frontiers which give us the requisite measure of security." He went on: "The Suez Canal, and free passage through it, and the assurance that the fort of Sharm el Sheikh will not be used to blockade the Gulf of Aqaba, are matters of vital importance to us. Of course, given a real peace, we should not need to keep a foothold in either area. But I have to admit that securing such a peace is a dubious prospect."

In his view, "The river Jordan must be a 'security border' for us. If the people of the west bank wanted to belong to Jordan, and their wish could be granted, we would give them free passage across the Jordan bridges." Here was a clear hint that the Prime Minister regarded the Allon plan as a workable proposition. Eshkol was guarded on the subject of an independent Palestinian entity, "It can come about only if the Palestinians want it. The signs on the whole are that they are not yet ready for it. Those who favor it are hanging back, until there is wider support. We must simply wait and watch developments." Finally, there seemed little doubt in Eshkol's mind that some rectifications of the old, pre-1967 frontier were inevitable. He preferred not to specify what they should be until negotiations on peace terms, as opposed to pompous proclamations of peace principles, were in clear sight.

On one frontier question, action, as I have already indicated, was taken very soon after the 1967 war. This was the question of Jerusalem. The laws passed by the Knesset on June 27, 1967, enlarged the capital by including all of Arab Jerusalem, the former Israeli exclave of Mount Scopus, and an area to the north which included suburbs and the airport at Kalandia. The old Berlin-type wall through the middle of the city was torn down, along with its barbed-wire entanglements and machine gun posts. The Mandelbaum Gate, a temporary structure through which the only traffic between the two parts of Jerusalem used to pass, was swept away. "A new chapter had been opened in the history of the city. Not only had Israeli sovereignty been confirmed but also the shadow of guns, barbed wire, and death had been lifted from the city for the first time in 19 years."[15] This was indeed plain speaking; when the Knesset passed its laws, all that was said was that Jerusalem was being put under a "unified administration." Nothing was said about full Israeli sovereignty's being asserted, although this was what actually happened.

On the whole, the outside world disapproved of the Israeli measure. On July 4 the General Assembly of the United Nations voted on three different resolutions on the Middle East situation. A Yugoslav resolution demanding the unconditional withdrawal of Israeli forces from occupied territories received 53 votes against 46, with 20 abstentions. A Latin American resolution, linking the withdrawal of Israeli troops with the termination of a state of belligerency, received 57 votes against 43, again with 20 abstentions. In neither case did the resolution get a simple majority. But the third resolution stated that the Israeli measures to change the status of Jerusalem were invalid and called for a United Nations report on the situation; it was carried by 99 votes to none, with 20 abstentions. Israel refused to participate in the vote, on the ground that the resolution was outside the legal competence of the United Nations.

United Nations thinking was colored by the confused feeling that Jerusalem was an international city, and should not come under the exclusive rule of one power. This thinking had swung the United Nations in favor of the internationalization of the city 20 years earlier. There had been nothing international about it since the 1948 War of Independence, but ingrained ideas die hard. Israel's policy, in answer, was to say little about Jerusalem but to go straight ahead implementing the measures uniting the city. This became the particular business of the go-getting mayor, Teddy Kollek.

Kollek found himself in charge of a city covering about 25,000 acres of ground, two and a half times the size of Jewish Jerusalem. To the 196,000 inhabitants of Jewish Jerusalem were added 66,000 from East Jerusalem, four fifths of them Moslems and the remainder mostly Christians. For the first time, Israelis undertook to absorb a big Arab minority in a predominantly Jewish municipality. East Jerusalem was a rich prize. The Old City contains the Church of Christ's Holy Sepulchre and the Mosque of the Dome of the Rock, Islam's third holiest and perhaps most magnificent shrine. The Old City, along with other holy places like the Mount of Olives and Church of the Nativity in Bethlehem, produced 80 percent of Jordan's tourist income. Pilgrims who used to reach East Jerusalem by way of Lebanon and Syria are now coming through Israeli territory, spending money in Galilee and Nazareth and in the coastal towns as well.

Kalandia airport is being given a new runway long enough for transatlantic planes. Mount Scopus will blossom with university and hospital buildings and with the planned Harry S. Truman Peace Center. Around Kalandia an industrial area will be built, stretching as far as the outskirts of the Arab township of Ramallah. And between Mount Scopus and the eastern fringe of Arab Jerusalem a large tract of empty ground will be gradually built up into a new Jewish quarter. Jewish Jerusalem will, in fact, grow around Arab Jerusalem.

For two thousand years Jews have prayed three times for the restoration of Jerusalem-Zion: "And to Jerusalem, thy city, return in mercy and dwell therein; as thou hast spoken, rebuild it soon in our days as an everlasting building." And again, "May it be thy will, O Lord our God and God of our fathers, that the Temple be speedily rebuilt in our days . . . and there we will serve thee with awe, as in the days of old, and as in the ancient years."[16] Jerusalem was the tenth and final degree of sanctity in the Holy Land, and the apex of its sanctity was the Temple, on whose site Abraham bound his son Isaac as a sacrifice to Jehovah. In the Psalms is that well-worn phrase: "If I forget thee, Jerusalem, let my right hand lose its cunning," and again in the Psalms, the blessing: "Have mercy, O Lord our God, upon Israel thy people, upon Jerusalem thy city."*

The Jews were forced out of their "Quarter" of the Old City in

---

* There were very few complaints about the behavior of Israeli troops who conquered East Jerusalem. One story, which may or may not be typical, is told by the proprietor of the American Colony Hotel. The Israeli troops billeted on him behaved with scrupulous correctness and asked only for a few cans of food to supplement their hard rations. When leaving, the young Israeli Lieutenant in charge saluted and said, "Thank you, Sir, for the 'guesting.'"

1948. One of Kollek's first acts when the city was reunified was to restore Hebrew street names, alongside the names in Arabic. Only two Arab names were changed, of Port Said and Jehad (Holy War) streets. Work began on the excavation and reconstruction of a dozen of the destroyed synagogues. About 80 Arab families living in their semi-converted remnants were quickly evacuated and alternative accommodation found for them. Another 70 Arab families were moved from in front of the Wailing Wall, where a broad space of open ground has taken the place of a network of alleys behind the narrow lane which used to run along the Wall.

Kollek unified the municipal services, bringing considerable improvement to East Jerusalem in the way of better water supplies and garbage collection, better postal and telephone services. He employed Arab labor wherever it was available and wherever Arabs were ready to work. Arab schools were reopened as soon as possible, and Arab teachers, out on strike because of the withdrawal of some textbooks which contained offensive references to Israel and Jewry, were coaxed back to work. Better medical services were installed. The budget for East Jerusalem was increased to about three times what it had been under Jordanian rule.*

Israelis see great virtue in material progress. They find it harder to appreciate spiritual unhappiness—perhaps surprisingly, when it is remembered how much Jews have suffered in the past. The mood of the Jerusalem Arabs since the war has been one of mingled sadness, uncertainty, resignation, and resentment. In a material sense, they were very soon at least as well off as before the war, in spite of price increases for rice and other basic foodstuffs. Rates of pay rose, the pilgrims and other tourists returned, and visiting Israelis spent fairly freely. But the Arabs had lost status and "face," along with the Arab rule under which they felt at home. Hussein's best Palestinian citizens had been in Jerusalem, probably because they were the most privileged. Now they were powerless and frustrated. Only the common-sense attitude of the Israelis has kept incipient ill feeling within bounds. Kollek can look ahead to great achievements to come, to a Jerusalem which may have half a million inhabitants in twenty years. Among them, the Arabs

---

* There were wild stories, after the Israeli occupation of East Jerusalem, of a sensational increase in prostitution and in the sale of drugs. Impartial observers, among them the British Anglican Archbishop, were unable to confirm this. There was, however, an understandable slump in Arab morale which led to begging and the systematic pestering of visitors by Arab children. There was also an epidemic of pick-pocketing in the narrow alleyways of the Old City. The genuine Arab grievances in Jerusalem related to some compulsory purchase of land at low compensation rates, the demolition of houses close to the Wailing Wall, the restoration of Jewish synagogues, and the occasional pieces of high-spirited buffoonery, such as the landing without warning of a helicopter in the children's playing fields belonging to the Anglican St. George's Church.

will, at best, be a resigned minority. The problem of re-creating a healthy Arab-Jewish symbiosis is not going to be solved in Jerusalem in a mere decade or two.

1. From *Bahamane,* Israeli Defense Forces weekly, June 12, 1967, p. 42.
2. *Ibid.*
3. Avraham Shapiro, ed., *Soldiers Talk.*
4. Brig. Peter Young, *The Israeli Campaign 1967,* p. 185.
5. The Nazi arms export drive has been exactly analyzed in Paul Einziy's book *Bloodless Invasion,* pp. 30–33.
6. Ian McIntyre, *The Proud Doers,* p. 22.
7. Professor Harold Fisch explained these claims in *Congress BiWeekly,* New York, February 5, 1968.
8. Eliezer Livneh in the *Jerusalem Post,* June 25, 1968.
9. Professor Harold Fisch, in personal conversation with the author.
10. Israeli Foreign Office spokesman, in personal conversation with the author.
11. Terence Prittie, *Israel: Miracle in the Desert,* p. 242.
12. Sheik Jabari, in personal conversation with the author.
13. Sheik Kaanan, in personal conversation with the author.
14. Eshkol, in personal conversation with the author.
15. *The Six-Days War,* the official Israeli history, p. 188.
16. Translations of Jewish prayers before meals and on other occasions.

19.

The thought that military victories solve nothing is not new. For Eshkol, the victory of June 1967 brought no solution of Israel's basic problems; indeed, for him personally, the only gain was a temporary increase of prestige. He had led the nation through its biggest crisis since the War of Independence, had organized a national government and, in the hour of victory, had shown a welcome toughness of character in refusing to withdraw Israel's armed forces from the territories which they had occupied and, by so doing, bow to the renewed threats of the Soviet Union and the Arab world.

But Eshkol was faced with a mass of problems. There was the nationwide psychological reaction which was bound to come after a period of tremendous strain. Eshkol himself was desperately weary, mentally as much as physically, after shouldering responsibilities on behalf of the nation which forced him to take life and death decisions. His ministers were seriously overworked and, according to a report in the *Jerusalem Post* in August 1967, one of them was alleged to have complained that he had been able to sit down to a midday meal with his wife only twice in ten weeks.

There were some troubles inside the Cabinet. Beigin and the Gahal Bloc were making plain their desire that Israel should annex all the conquered territories. Dayan, who had emerged as a popular hero, announced publicly that the Gaza Strip should be annexed, that Israel should be ready to go it alone in defiance of the advice of her friends in the outside world, and that preparations should be made to resist Soviet armed intervention if necessary. A few weeks after the war was over, Eshkol had to administer a discreet reproof to Dayan; in an interview given to the evening newspaper *Yediot Ahronot,* he said that it was not dignified for one minister to thrust himself to the forefront at the expense of others.

Meanwhile, the preliminary talks due to be held on a possible merger between Mapai and Achdut Ha'avoda were held up. The idea of a merger was dear to Eshkol's heart, for it would constitute a decisive first step in the restoration of the unity of the Labor movement. There was no time to debate the state of the economy in the Knesset, although unemployment was up to 40,000 (over 4 percent of the labor force). Ben-Gurion was once again sniping at Eshkol and demanding that younger men should be put at the helm. All this was highly distracting to a Prime Minister who had two very much more important problems on his mind, the problem of securing peace with the Arab countries and the problem of administering territories taken from them in the meanwhile.

Eshkol was to say much later, "We received a beautiful dowry, but unfortunately we also got the bride." He meant a dowry of strategically valuable territory, but a bride in the shape of about one million Arab inhabitants. By the time the Arab Summit at Khartoum was over on September 8, 1967, it was obvious that Israel would have to look after these one million Arabs for a long time to come. The Arab refusal to consider a lasting peace settlement with Israel led Eshkol to declare that Israel would stand firm on the cease-fire lines and would not accept a return to the uneasy and unreal pre-June 1967 truce. "Where neighbors are unable to negotiate on boundaries, there is no alternative to a natural border. The Suez Canal is one such natural border."[1]

A military government had at once been established after the 1967 war for the administration of the occupied territories. It came under the control of Dayan, as Minister of Defense. He demonstrated his immediate interest in a typically personal way, going down to the military checkpoints established between Israel and the occupied territories, talking long and earnestly to the local population in fluent Arabic, listening to their views and complaints. Israeli military command posts were next installed under his direction in every Arab town of any size, contact was established with the Arab municipal authorities, and essential services like water, electricity, food supply, mail, and telegraphs were restored to working order. Arab municipal authorities were generally cooperative. The danger of a catastrophic failure of essential services was quickly averted.

Yet Israeli military government had a supremely difficult task on its hands. Public services were bound to be disorganized for some time to come. The banking system was paralyzed; the banks had transferred their deposits to Amman and for the most part put up their shutters when the Israeli armed forces arrived. The population was cut off from the centers from which it had been ruled for the past 19 years. It had lost sources of income arising from services for the armed forces of Jordan and Egypt. It lost too the remittances sent home by west bankers and others working in the oil sheikdoms or elsewhere in the Arab world. Agriculture and industry were cut off from their usual markets and tourism fell off badly during the early months after the 1967 war. In addition, the Israeli military authorities were to be plagued by the infiltration of terrorists from Syria, Jordan, and Lebanon. They had a major security problem on their hands in dealing with terrorists and their sympathizers in the occupied territories, and a troublesome humanitarian problem in deciding what should be done about those of the estimated 180,000 new refugees who had fled from the west bank across the river Jordan.

Israeli military government was brilliantly successful in solving the material problems of the occupied territories. It authorized the export of agricultural produce to the Kingdom of Jordan, the principal market. The bridges across the river Jordan were restored and traffic across them resumed as soon as the Jordanian authorities permitted it. For the first time since 1948 there was a normal, or at least partly normal, flow of goods between the Israeli-held and Jordanian territory. In the first year after the war, $16 million worth of west bank agricultural produce was exported to Jordan. Agricultural production was actually increased on the west bank, while in the Gaza Strip the Israeli authorities bought up the main crop of citrus fruits and marketed it for the Gazaians in Europe and Jordan. In this way, the chief problem —of disposing of agricultural produce for which Israel herself had no need—was overcome.

The Israelis expanded Arab tobacco production, developed reforestation, and introduced up-to-date methods of breeding and utilizing livestock. Work began on the construction of citrus-packing plants in the Gaza Strip and on the west bank, and plans were approved for joint Israeli-Arab growing and marketing of vegetables and flowers. Similar success was achieved in dealing with the industrial sector, and by the end of the first year of occupation about 90 percent of the industrial enterprises functioning before June 1967 were again in full operation. Surplus labor was partly employed on a project for modernizing roads, and was partly taken on by Israeli industrial enterprises. Gazaians appeared in the docks of Ashdod, and west bank construction workers in Jewish Jerusalem. By 1969 the occupied territories were becoming a useful market for Israeli exports. Within six months they were buying more from Israel than they were selling to her. Their export trade to outside countries was being stimulated by the same export incentives granted to Israelis. Where trade was concerned, the general trend was towards increasing integration of the occupied territories with Israel. This can have long-term effects which the Arab parent countries of these territories will not be able to ignore.

The Israelis dealt with other material problems with similar success. Banking activity was revived and remittances once again began to flow in from abroad. UNRWA became once again fully operational in dealing with the welfare needs of the refugees, but the Israeli military government thinking tended to be against encouraging indigence among the refugees. A Food for Work project was introduced in the Gaza Strip and north Sinai, and 50,000 Arabs were induced to work for additional food rations under the program. A budgetary deficit of about $17 million was allowed for all the occupied territories for the first year after the war and was financed by the Israeli government. For the second year the planned deficit was more than doubled, to $37 million.[2] There was increased government expenditure on public health and education in particular, although there was still a partial boycott being carried out by Gaza Strip schoolteachers 18 months after the occupation began.

It was shown in the occupied territories that Israelis and Arabs could live together and work together in solving material problems. Israeli military occupation was in some respects most self-effacing; soldiers were seldom seen in Arab towns, and military government headquarters were discreetly located away from main thoroughfares. Occupation forces were left mainly in uninhabited areas along the lines of the Suez Canal and the river Jordan. "The first year has seen the healing of the scars of war and a full normalization of life in the Israel-administered areas. Firm foundations for economic development have been laid, and the general well-being and improved prospects of the population have created an understanding that being at peace and in cooperation with one's neighbors is not only possible but even beneficial. This realization is slowly creating a situation in which the attainment of peace becomes a practical possibility."[3]

So much for the material side of occupation. It had, however, more awkward aspects. Almost everywhere the local population was quiescent; the obvious exceptions were Gaza and Nablus, where demonstrations led to periodic imposition of a curfew. The difficulties over school textbooks containing anti-Israel propaganda were resolved by calling them in, cutting out the pages with offensive passages, and inserting photostatted pages in replacement. Arab law courts continued to function, and the only Arab law which had to be repealed was the anti-Israel trade boycott law. But the activities of El Fatah guerillas led to numerous arrests and later Israeli armed counteraction. As before the 1967 war, the El Fatah guerillas were at first organized mainly from Syria, but raided across the Jordanian and Lebanese frontiers. In the first four months after the war over 300 members of El Fatah and the Palestine Liberation Movement were caught on the west bank alone. At the end of 1968 1400 terrorists and suspected terrorists were in jail. The scope of their activities had actually increased, and in Jordan in particular they had become a state within the state, with their own armed camps and military training grounds and with bases along the whole length of the Jordanian-Israeli frontier.

Terrorist activity affected the population of the occupied territories in two ways. It forced the Israeli authorities into carrying out frequent spot checks and searches, and rounding up and interrogating anyone suspected of giving any help to the terrorists. The local population had a difficult choice, between helping their fellow Arabs and risking punishment at the hands of the Israelis, or refusing to give help and being denounced as Quislings. Generally speaking, they gave as little help as surreptitiously as possible and refrained from any participation in acts of terrorism themselves. Even so, they had to put up with much unpleasantness. After an Israeli child at Ometz and a settler at the Hamadiya kibbutz had been killed, Israeli interrogation methods became fairly tough and there were some cases of Arabs who were suspected of having harbored terrorists being roughed up. Those who had definitely done so had their homes demolished, and that was still happening in 1969. Yet the Israeli military authorities were usually as humane as possible. The occupation produced few cases of brutality and not a single one of rape.

Terrorist activity had another adverse effect on the population of the occupied territories. Very soon after the war considerable pressure was put on Israel by other countries to allow the new refugees to return to the occupied territories. The view was forcibly expressed that the old refugee problem arising from the 1948 War of Independence was one of the main factors causing Arab-Israeli hostility, and that a new refugee problem would doom all hope of an understanding. The Israeli government, somewhat unwillingly, agreed to the repatriation of a proportion of the new refugees; its hesitation was at least partly due to the fear that terrorist organizations would recruit refugees for sabotage operations in Israel and that a proportion of these recruits would return to the occupied territories.

The Israeli authorities therefore made it a general rule that the first group of returnees would comprise only children under 16 and persons over 60. They estimated that about 40,000 new refugees would be eligible to return immediately. But the sheer ineptitude of the Jordanian authorities resulted in only 21,000 applications' being forwarded to the Israeli military government. These applications were approved, but even then the Jordanians procrastinated on the grounds that official Israeli stamps were being put onto the permits for this group of refugees. In the end only about 14,000 returned home, and the Israelis, exasperated by the endless delays, temporarily suspended the whole operation.*

The problem of terrorist infiltration continued to be a major one for the Israeli military government. In August and September 1967, the terrorists tried to set up bases in the occupied territories. There were a series of clashes between Israeli soldiers and infiltrators who tried to establish themselves in caves and woods on the west bank. The Arab infiltrators were invariably routed or captured; but the Israelis suffered many casualties. Their success became assured when they found that they could use west bank Arabs to guide them to El Fatah hideouts and were no longer dependent on police dogs. This phase of the anti-terrorist campaign ended in October 1967. From then on, the terrorists operated exclusively from bases outside Israeli-held territory.

* Israel and Jordan agreed that the 21,000 "approved persons" would be repatriated at a rate of 3000 a day up to August 31, 1967. In fact, the Jordanian authorities never presented more than half that number at the cease-fire line on any one day. Israel offered to repatriate 7000 west bankers who had received approval, but not presented themselves, after August 31. But the Jordanians did not bring them to the Allenby Bridge crossing point. A further Israeli offer, to consider applications by west bankers on behalf of members of their families who had fled east of the river Jordan, was ignored. On her part, Israel allowed any west banker to move east of Jordan who wanted to. From July 1967 to December 1968, 77,000 west bankers took advantage of this, including 20,000 from the Gaza Strip.

In the next phase clashes took place close to the river Jordan, with Israeli security forces often intercepting the raiders as they were actually crossing the river. Along stretches of the river bank the Israelis erected an electrified wire fence. They also countered Arab raids by attacking terrorist training centers which were well inside Jordanian territory. One such attack at Es-Salt was a complete success. It was conducted while the terrorists were having their midday meal and inflicted heavy casualties. Unfortunately, a number of Jordanian civilians who got mixed up in the fighting were killed. The second major Israeli counterattack on March 21, 1968, at Karameh, ran into difficulties.* Regular Jordanian troops arrived on the scene and inflicted some casualties. The Israelis were believed to have lost about 30 dead, but no figures were given. Karameh brought a wave of popularity for the El Fatah in the Arab world, but it also had the effect of forcing the terrorists to move their bases further away from the frontier. This was one of the objects of the Israeli strike.

The Karameh raid had another important result. From March 1968 onward the terrorists concentrated on two kinds of operation. The first was shelling Israeli patrols, military vehicles, and civilians in the fields and in their settlements. This always resulted in an instant Israeli response. Very often Jordanian or Iraqi artillery would join in, and a significant artillery duel would result. The second kind of operation was mining public places and roads. Increasingly, this became the work of agents, normally residents on the west bank recruited and armed by the terrorists while paying apparently innocent visits to friends and relatives in Jordan.

This second form of operation worried the Israelis. In September 1968 the terrorists planted a bomb in a Tel Aviv bus station. In October, a hand grenade was hurled into the midst of a crowd of Israeli sightseers at the Machpelah Tomb at Hebron. In November a car loaded with dynamite exploded in Machaneh Yehuda marketplace in Jerusalem. In all three outrages there were dead and wounded; in Jerusalem the casualties were by far the highest, with 11 people killed and 55 injured, 18 of them seriously.[4] Eshkol, who was convalescing at the time after a bout of influenza, flew to Jerusalem by helicopter and told the people in the Machaneh Yehuda marketplace that such acts of terrorism, which should be laid at the doors of the rulers of Arab states, did not count

---

* The Karemeh raid followed 37 cases in a month of El Fatah raids into Israel, most of them made from these three bases. In a letter to the London *Times* on March 28, 1968, the Israeli Ambassador, Aharon Remez, pointed out that there were four reasons why Israel's "regrettable but unavoidable self-defense action" had to be taken: the Jordanian government was doing nothing to control the El Fatah; Jordanian army units were increasingly aiding and abetting the terrorists; El Fatah's main bases had been shifted from Syria into Jordan; and Israel knew of plans for the substantial increase of El Fatah attacks mounted from Jordanian territory.

at all in the battle for Jewish independence and survival. On each occasion the Israelis took drastic counteraction, bombing terrorist bases in Jordan and making it plain that no Arab outrage would go unpunished.

There have, indeed, been even more spectacular cases of Arab terrorist action and Israeli counteraction. The first occurred on October 21, 1967, when Egyptian batteries in or near Port Said sank the Israeli destroyer "Eilat" off the coast of the Sinai peninsula. Fifty-one Israeli seamen were killed and 48 wounded after two Comar-type missiles with homing devices struck the vessel and put her engines out of action and another two missiles were fired at her as she lay helpless, burning and listing heavily. That three out of four missiles hit their target, with the fourth landing close to the "Eilat," suggested a standard of gunnery far beyond Egyptian capabilities. The strong suspicion remains that the missiles were fired by Soviet advisers to the Egyptian forces.

The Egyptian attack took place the day after a special British envoy had left Cairo. He was Sir Harold Beeley, who had been having talks with President Nasser on a resumption of diplomatic relations between the two countries, which had been broken off by Egypt during the Six-Day War. In spite of the sinking of the "Eilat," diplomatic relations were reestablished, the ways of the British Foreign Office often being inscrutable. The sinking was a blatant contravention of the terms of the Israeli-Arab cease-fire, and because of the casualties involved it caused the most bitter resentment in Israel. There was bound to be a response. It came on October 24, when Israeli artillery destroyed two Egyptian refineries at Suez which had an annual capacity of 5.5 million tons. That left Egypt with 1.5 million tons of refinery capacity at Alexandria.

The second spectacular case of Arab action and Israeli counteraction occurred in December 1968. On December 28 an Israeli commando unit, using helicopters, raided Beirut international airport in Lebanon. A dozen civil aircraft were either destroyed or so badly damaged as to render them unserviceable. The Israeli attack lasted 45 minutes and there was not a single casualty on either side. For the Israeli purpose had been to inflict severe material loss as a reprisal for an Arab terrorist attack on an Israeli El Al airplane at Athens on December 26. In this attack one passenger was killed and a stewardess was badly injured. The two Arab guerillas who carried it out sprayed the plane with machine gun fire and hurled five incendiary grenades at it. That was terrorism of the worst possible kind; on the other hand, the Israelis mounted a military operation in which loss of life was carefully avoided.

The rights and wrongs of carrying out reprisals are impossible to evaluate. In countries far removed from any particular conflict there is never a lack of protagonists of the Christian precept of turning the other cheek to an aggressor who would not hesitate to gouge out the surviving eye. The most relevant comment in advance of the Israeli raid on Beirut appeared on the morning of December 28, 1968 in the *Manchester Guardian*. An editorial contained the following passage, referring to the Arab attack in Athens:

"Confronted by such slippery fish, the Israelis seem to have no net small enough to catch them. Yet they cannot sit back and let the guerillas go unpunished. Those that argue that the Israelis may have overreacted so far must face the possibility that for them to do less would only encourage the guerillas to do more."[5]

After the Beirut raid, however, the press of almost the whole free world condemned the Israeli action, on the ground that it was too rigorous, that it should not have been directed against relatively inoffensive Lebanon, and that it "added a new dimension" to the conflict with the Arab world. Israel was utterly unrepentant; her government's view was that retribution was justified. The Arab terrorists who attacked the El Al plane at Athens had been trained and equipped in Lebanon and had set out from Beirut on their mission.*

The question of whether or not the answer to Arab terrorism should be massive Israeli reprisal cannot be convincingly answered. The opponents of reprisals have argued that they merely increase popular support of El Fatah and kindred organizations and also weaken the position of Arab moderates like King Hussein. The contrary view is that reprisals have nearly always resulted in a diminution of acts of terrorism in both scale and number, because terrorists did not want to make themselves too unpopular in their own Arab world. It is noteworthy that the Israeli shelling of the Egyptian refineries at Suez was not followed by any Egyptian action as spectacular as the sinking of the "Eilat."

The outside world may have been oversensitive to Arab, as opposed to Israeli, reactions to the interchange of Arab thrust and Israeli counterthrust in the Middle East cold war. It may well be that Israeli reactions will turn out to be the more important in the long run. One type of Israeli reaction in particular should be mentioned. This is, in the face of a situation in which peace has come no nearer after two years, simply to dig in in the occupied territories.

Towards the end of 1968 the Israeli Chief of Staff, Chaim Bar-Lev,

---

* One British writer who at once leaped to the defense of Israel was Winston Churchill, Jr., grandson of the late Prime Minister. In an article in the London *Evening News*, he contrasted the "calculated risk" taken by Israel, which "was meticulously planned and executed to avoid any loss of life or injury to civilians," with the deliberate Arab attempt at Athens to destroy the Israeli airliner with 51 people aboard. He added, pertinently: "Surely, even in our materialistic present-day society, human life—even one individual—is worth more than a handful of aircraft." Churchill's view was that the Israeli policy of "striking back with several times the punch for every blow they receive" was right in the short term, but might backfire by uniting Arab opinion more solidly behind the terrorists.

said in an interview, "During the coming year we shall continue settlement in all the territories. This is very important from the viewpoint of our current security, and of our security along the borders, inasmuch as such settlement controls a certain region, and the settlers take active part in everyday security."[6] What Bar-Lev was reiterating was the well-founded Israeli notion that frontiers are much better defended by settlers and soldiers than by soldiers alone. Collective settlements like the kibbutzim "firm up" a frontier. They provide a population which knows the ground and is alert and highly sensitive to what is happening on the enemy's side of the frontier. In addition, they provide a reserve of men trained in the use of their eyes and their rifles.

In the middle of 1968 a map was handed to delegates to the Zionist Congress in Jerusalem which showed 35 new or planned settlements in Israel and the occupied territories. Of these, three were in the Sinai peninsula, four on the west bank, and no fewer than nine in the Golan Mountains.[7] The implication seemed clear that Israel intends to hold on to the occupied territories, or at least to those portions of them which contain the new settlements.

Perhaps too much should not as yet be read into this map. Two of the Sinai projects were implemented in 1968, at El Arish and Bardawil. Two of the west bank projects were also implemented, both at Etzion. Other projects in Sinai and on the west bank were, in 1969, still in the drawing-board stage. One difference is that the Etzion settlements are definitely of a permanent nature, whereas El Arish and Bardawil are colonies of *Nachal,* an organization of pioneering youth groups attached to the army. Nachal colonists generally live in tents and can move at a moment's notice.

Most of the nine settlements established or in process of being established in the Golan Mountains by the end of 1968 were also organized by Nachal. But details had been leaked of a master plan to establish at least 25 settlements in this area, each to begin with a population of about 500.[8] They would be spread over the whole area captured from Syria in the 1967 war. A large part of this area had, by 1969, been planted with wheat, and several thousand head of livestock had been brought in for the upland grazing. The first Israeli baby was born in the Golan Mountains on March 20, 1968, while a settlement founded just afterwards was named after the Israeli civil airline El Al. The El Hamma colony of Nachal established itself in the long-deserted station buildings of the defunct Hejaz railway line, which they shared with cat-size rats and black-and-yellow scorpions. The overriding impression of the Israeli settlements in the Golan Mountains is that they are intended to be permanent, safeguarding frontiers which are theoretically temporary but which may have to be protected semipermanently.

The lack of a peace treaty is an even more pressing concern for the Israeli government than is the administration of the occupied territories. Some of the efforts made by Eshkol to bring a peace treaty a little nearer effectively give the lie to Arab and Communist propaganda depicting Israel as arrogant and interested only in preserving the fruits of her military victory. In October 1967 Eshkol sent a message to the Soviet Prime Minister, Kosygin, proposing a meeting in Moscow. Kosygin rejected this proposal on October 27.

On November 1, 1967, Eshkol offered to go to Amman to have talks with King Hussein. At the same time he invited the King to come to Israel as his guest at any time he chose. King Hussein ignored this proposal. A few days later he was in London and was interviewed on the David Frost Television Program. He refused to be pinned down by any question about how peace talks could be conducted, but he rejected Eshkol's offer. The difficulties of King Hussein's position need no emphasizing. It is sufficient to repeat that he might lose his throne or his head if he did anything which did not have the approval of Nasser, the Syrians, and the embattled extremists of the Palestinian terrorist organizations.

On December 1, 1967, Eshkol produced a five-point plan for peace at a press luncheon in Jerusalem.

1. Peace between Israel and her neighbors must be permanent.

2. It should be achieved through negotiations and a peace charter.

3. Israeli ships should have free passage through the Suez Canal and the Straits of Tiran.

4. Frontiers should be determined by peace treaties.

5. The refugee problem should be settled within the framework of peace and regional cooperation in the Middle East.

On January 11, 1968, Eshkol made an earnest appeal for peace when speaking at the Waldorf-Astoria Hotel in New York. He concluded his speech with these words: "There can be no going back to belligerence. History must be moved forward. It must move forward from cease-fire to peace. It must move forward from hostility to recognition. It must move forward from enmity to cooperation. If there is any desire at all to move forward honestly in this way, there is only one method of doing it—it is the method of direct meeting, of direct negotiations leading to an unequivocal, unambiguous peace treaty."

On February 29, 1968, Eshkol told Israeli troops in Sinai, "We do not want to think in terms of victors and vanquished. But there is no way of avoiding the necessity for the two sides to meet in order to settle their relations for the benefit of the peoples of the area. Logic requires that wisdom shall ultimately prevail among our neighbors."

In April 1968, Eshkol appealed to the Arabs to "dare to make peace." The operative passage of his speech was: "Our hands are stretched out for peace. We are ready to sit down with you to discuss all problems, and we are confident that we can arrive at an honorable peace. You have seen that hostility and barren hatred can solve nothing.

If you are really concerned with the welfare of your people, dare to make peace."

Again, on November 11, 1968, Eshkol appealed for peace, this time in a personal message to President Nasser. It would, he said, have to be a signed peace rather than some declamatory undertaking which could be unilaterally evolved and it would have to include free movement of all shipping on the international waterways of the Suez Canal and the Straits of Tiran. His message concluded, "Mr. President, if you really want peace, you will find us ready to agree to it with all our hearts and at any time." In the Knesset, Dayan revealed that in the previous 16 months the Egyptians had violated the cease-fire 119 times and that resulting Israeli casualties had been 101 killed and 300 wounded.

At the very end of 1968 Eshkol outlined his views about peace in a magazine article.[9] Peace, he wrote, had "now entered the realms of practical politics," for a situation had been created "in which Egypt and Jordan could no longer conceal from themselves a long-standing truth, namely, that they need peace with us no less than we need peace with them." But "The Arab leaders," Eshkol went on,

> and also others, including a Western elder statesman who was wont to call Israel his friend and ally [de Gaulle], have tried to pin upon us the label of an aggressor. If they are not prompted by sheer malice, then they are woefully ignorant. The millennial Jewish history is one of perpetual yearning for peace, a yearning which has become second nature to us. . . . Through all ordeals, the Jews placed their trust in the biblical promise that they would return to Israel and there at last find peace.

Eshkol urged the Arab world to recognize Israel's right to a small place in the Middle East. "The Arabs are not short of territory from the Atlantic to the Persian Gulf. When Palestine fell into their domains, they never regarded it as a promise, let alone as a country worthy of attention in its own right. The hills became denuded, the valleys turned into malarial swamps, the coastal plain was reduced to sand dunes. The land stood all but empty. In the mid-nineteenth century, the whole of historic Palestine embracing, prior to British mandatory partition, both sides of the Jordan had a population of less than half a million. It was the arrival of the Jews that attracted Arab immigrants."

The Arabs and the Jews, Eshkol stressed, could live together:

> I should think the most significant discovery made for a long time . . . is the feasibility of decent and useful cooperation between Arabs and Jews, as demonstrated since last June on the west bank of the Jordan and in the Gaza Strip. Outsiders had warned us that the Arabs in these areas hated us. Well, it is simply not true. . . . On the

contrary, there is between them and us a deep sense of kinship, of our belonging to the same Semitic family. This is no idle phrase. It is a fact. What is valid for the 1,300,000 Arabs with whom we now live under one roof applies to the scores of millions of other Arabs who surround us.

More than once did Eshkol return in the article to his principal point, the need for a lasting peace. That meant there could be no regression to the uneasy and unsatisfactory pre-1967 truce which left Israel living within insecure armistice lines under boycott and blockade imposed by the Arabs, denied access to international waterways, and threatened every second day of the week with genocide. A lasting peace, finally, could be achieved only by means of direct negotiations. "To sit down together is a lesser thing than to make peace. If the Arabs reject the lesser enterprise, then obviously they do not mean to go on to an enduring settlement with us."

Eshkol's thesis, then, could be summed up in three short sentences: There should be a lasting peace signed between Israel and her Arab neighbors. It should follow direct negotiations, which alone can resolve the very complex issues which are involved. The purpose of peace should be to guarantee Arab-Israeli coexistence, cooperation, and, eventually, friendship.

Yet one more account of Israel's efforts to secure peace was given by Foreign Minister Abba Eban while in London on December 13, 1968. Israel had offered direct or indirect negotiations—the latter through the Jarring mission—and the Arabs had rejected these offers. Israel had next suggested the drawing up of "peace memoranda" by both sides, which could be conveyed from one to the other by Jarring. Egypt turned this suggestion down, while Jordan did not commit herself. Eban had, therefore, put forward his own nine-point peace plan in the United Nations on October 8, 1968. The Arabs had ignored it. In mid-October, Israel offered Jarring clear-cut "formulations" on a half-dozen issues, including security, coexistence, the termination of belligerency, and free navigation of international waterways. Eban proposed that Egypt should put forward "counterformulations," but Egypt was not interested. Eban next met Jarring in Cyprus, hoping that he could still act as go-between in an exchange of ideas; but no Arab state sent a representative to meet Jarring in Cyprus. Eban, finally, told Jarring he would remain available for further meetings and for further efforts to make progress towards peace.

These is no space in this book to wade through the mass of conflicting Arab statements, news leaks, and inspired rumors on the subject of peace. Israel has always recognized that the key to peace lies in Cairo. Syria, the most recalcitrant of her Arab neighbors, would never be able to wage war against Israel on her own, that is, with the slightest chance of success. Jordan, Israel's Arab neighbor with the greatest interest in securing peace, would almost certainly accept a lasting settlement if President Nasser allowed it. Egyptian thinking on the subject of peace has been and still is decisive. It may, therefore, be useful to take a brief look at Egyptian statements, and statements inspired by Egypt, since the war of June 1967.

On September 30, 1967, a London Sunday newspaper, the *Observer,* reported that Nasser was "ready for serious negotiations to settle the Arab-Israeli conflict." The writer, Robert Stephens, the paper's diplomatic correspondent, had met Nasser several times and enjoyed excellent relations with the Egyptian government. He explained that Egypt would not negotiate with Israel directly, but through a third party, that Egypt would allow the Sinai peninsula to be demilitarized and Israeli cargoes to be carried through the Suez Canal, would guarantee free passage for Israeli ships through the Straits of Tiran, would agree to minor frontier changes, and might even be prepared to cede possession of the Gaza Strip.

Robert Stephens is a highly competent and reliable journalist, and there can be little doubt that the Egyptian government primed him with this most encouraging information. But there was no follow-up. Instead, Nasser's spokesman, Mohammed Haykal, wrote in *Al Ahram* on November 10, 1967, that another war with Israel was inevitable.[10] On November 23, 1967, Nasser himself said explicitly that Egypt wanted "no peace with Israel and no recognition of Israel."[11] Israel, he said, must withdraw from all territory occupied in the June war and would not be allowed to use the Suez Canal.

Undeterred, Robert Stephens paid another visit to Cairo and was able to report on December 31, 1967, in the *Observer,* that Egypt was ready to "coexist" with Israel. But the terms of such coexistence were imprecise. An "influential" Egyptian had told him: "If Israel is really concerned about recognition and security, what is she now worrying about? The Arabs have already *more or less* [my italics] recognized her existence as a State and her right to security within her pre-June frontiers. They have offered demilitarization, the presence of a United Nations force, and great power guarantees. What more does [Israel] want?" Stephens had learned in Cairo of a two-stage Egyptian peace plan. The first stage would entail Israeli troop withdrawals and steps to guarantee Israel's security within her pre-June frontiers. The second stage would involve the settling of "recognized" frontiers, a settlement of the Palestine problems left by the 1948 war, and arrangements for Israeli ships to use the Suez Canal.

Once again there was no trace of a diplomatic follow-up. On January 19, 1968, in *Al Ahram,* Haykal reiterated his belief that it was Egypt's destiny and duty to prepare for the next war with Israel.[12] Egypt had, he wrote, to take the lead in planning a military confrontation "on a scientific basis," for a political settlement was clearly impossible. Haykal concluded with a typical piece of bombast: "Even if Egypt left Israel alone,

Israel would not leave Egypt alone. Israel can only feel secure with Egypt impotent, wounded under its feet, bleeding and near to death."

Was this really the language of peace?

Nasser's address to the Egyptian armed forces at the beginning of May 1968, requires special mention. He assured them that "the course of events shows emphatically that the battle will inevitably come." Nasser claimed that the Jarring mission had failed, and promised that he would never "sit down to negotiate" with Israel. After urging the Egyptian armed forces to realize that the Israelis were not invincible, and were not "an extraordinary enemy, but a wicked, cunning, and evil one," he concluded with the scarcely encouraging words, "Every officer and soldier going into battle must know that there is a 90 percent chance that he will die and a 10 percent chance that he will return alive." Nasser's figures, presumably, were based on the standards of Egyptian generalship.

On July 5, 1968, the Egyptian Foreign Minister, Mahmoud Riad, said that "Egypt accepts realities, and one of these is Israel."[13] Great importance was attached to that statement, for Riad was on his way to Moscow to join President Nasser in discussions with Soviet leaders. This time there was some kind of follow-up. The *Times* of London reported that Egypt was about to offer Israel a termination of the state of belligerency, the next best thing to a peace treaty, as well as undefined concessions regarding the use of the Suez Canal, the internationalization of the Gaza Strip, and the demilitarization of the Sinai peninsula.[14] It took only a week for the Egyptian press to publish flat official denials of that report.[15]

On November 9, 1968, the London *Observer* was once again predicting, through its New York correspondent, that peace was about to break out in the Middle East, but its report lacked conviction. Ironically a message from the paper's Cairo correspondent was tacked onto this report; it began: "The Egyptian press, led by the authoritative *Al Ahram*, has written off the mediation mission of Mr. Jarring, the United Nations envoy, as hopeless." In January 1969 Haykal was once again ramming home his view that war was the only way out of the Middle East impasse. He accompanied his Cassandra-like prophecy with a sharp sideswipe at the Soviet Union. The great powers, he wrote, were showing themselves incapable of forcing Israel to accept a compromise. The result could be a dangerous growth of the power of the Arab guerillas, leading to chaos in the Arab world. His Master's Voice was, for once, out of tune. A few days later, on January 20, Nasser praised the Arab guerillas and promised that Egypt would not give up one inch of the territory, nor even consent to sit down to talk to the Israelis. "The Arabs will fight for every branch of a bush in every valley and on every mountain," he said.[16]

There has been a certain predictability about Arab war and peace propaganda. Encouraging ideas have been passed on to selected foreign newspapers. They have then been knocked down like ninepins by Nasser and Haykal. Egypt has spoken with two voices throughout, one for listeners at home, the other for listeners abroad. Dire threats against Israel have alternated with specious promises of moves in the direction of peace. The net result has been a total lack of a clear, firm, and coherent Egyptian policy. This has led, in turn, to a total lack of progress towards peace over the last two years.

One must return, at this stage, to the United Nations and its efforts to promote a settlement in the Middle East. In September 1967 the British government began to take the lead in efforts to work out a peace formula. The Foreign Secretary, George Brown, had quickly convinced himself that there was no point in urging the Arabs, and especially Egypt, to sit down to discussions with Israel. Brown was convinced, too, that a move to secure a peace formula in the United Nations should come from the West. He wanted Britain to head off France in this initiative. On November 22, 1967, a British resolution was presented in the Security Council by Brown's representative, Lord Caradon, and received the unanimous support of the Council's members. This was in the nature of a triumph for the British government, although the resolution needed of course to be implemented. During the next two years implementation did not seem likely.

The resolution laid down five principles for a Middle East settlement:

1. The withdrawal of Israeli armed forces from "territories occupied in the recent conflict."

2. The termination of all states of belligerency, and acknowledgement of the sovereignty, territorial integrity, and political independence of every state in the area.

3. The guarantee of freedom of navigation through international waterways.

4. The achievement of a just settlement of the refugee problem.

5. The guarantee of the territorial inviolability and political independence of every state in the area, through measures including the establishment of demilitarized zones.

Finally, the resolution requested the UN Secretary General, U Thant, to designate a special representative to go to the Middle East and help towards achieving a peaceful settlement. The special representative chosen was Gunnar Jarring, a Swede, and he began his work forthwith.

Since the resolution was the work of the British government, it might be as well to consider what it had in mind. In the first place, the loose wording of the five principles was not fortuitous. Thus, the British government did not visualize the withdrawal of Israeli forces from *all* territories occupied in the June 1967 war. The word "all" was left out deliberately, for Britain realized that Israel would insist on some frontier changes, in the interests of her security requirements. Then, the resolution did not expressly call for a peace treaty, but, at least according to Foreign Office spokesmen, the underlying purpose was that a peace treaty would be the logical result of the implementation of the resolution. The guarantee of freedom of navigation through international waterways sounded more definite, but it was Egypt's contention that both the Suez Canal and the Straits of Tiran were her territorial waters and were not international waterways at all. Finally, no indication was given as to how the refugee problem could be solved, or what demilitarized zones should be established.

All details would have to be worked out between Gunnar Jarring's mediation mission and the belligerent powers of the Middle East. The British hope was that the strong UN backing of the principles contained in the resolution would encourage the Arabs and Israelis to look for a compromise. Everything, in fact, depended on the Jarring mission; the UN resolution by itself meant very little.

Three different attitudes were taken up by the belligerent powers. Syria refused to have anything to do with the Jarring mission and took no official cognizance of the resolution. Egypt, Jordan, and Lebanon loudly proclaimed their support of the resolution, but stuck to the three No's of the Khartoum Conference—no negotiations with Israel, no recognition of Israel, and no peace settlement with Israel. Clearly, the second and third of these no's were incompatible with the five principles of the resolution and with the purpose of the British government which framed it. Moreover, the Arab countries maintained that the principles should be implemented in the order in which they appeared in the resolution. The withdrawal of Israeli forces became the prior condition for the implementation of the remainder of the resolution. That too had not been the British government's intention, which was that a package peace plan should be worked out and then implemented as a whole.*

The Israeli attitude was that the five principles contained in the resolution provided a basis for the peace negotiations which still had to take place. As for the negotiations, they would be best conducted face to face; but the Israelis indicated earlier that Jarring, or someone else acceptable to both sides, could act as intermediary. Negotiations could, in fact, be carried out from adjoining rooms, with the UN mediator acting as a go-between. This practical Israeli attitude was repeatedly denounced by the Arabs on the grounds that it did not constitute an unreserved acceptance of the UN resolution. Arab acceptance was of course largely illusory, for it did not entail acceptance of the basic aims of the resolution.

Jarring began talks in Middle East capitals in November 1967. His first round of talks took six weeks. Jarring quickly won himself the

* As explained to me, the British view was that such a package could, if necessary, be implemented in stages. But the whole package had first to be accepted without reservation by both sides.

reputation of having "an unlimited capacity for silence."[17] During his first three or four talks in Jerusalem, for instance, he scarcely uttered a word. These talks could hardly have been very productive, for the Israelis were most anxious not to commit themselves. Their position was that they would talk when there was a good purpose in doing so, with the Arabs and about peace terms. Jarring certainly gave an impression of sympathizing with this point of view; unofficially he let it be known that he could not propose solutions but only bring disputants together.

Jarring had made his headquarters in Cyprus. It appears that in the beginning he made discreet soundings to see if he could bring representatives of Israel and the Arab states together in Cyprus. A few months later he was examining the possibility, suggested by Jordan, of getting bilateral Israeli-Arab talks going in New York, where all the countries concerned had delegations at the United Nations. Half a year later, towards the end of 1968, Jarring reverted to the "next-door rooms" formula, with Israeli and Arab delegations collaborating with him in Cyprus. On none of these occasions was Jarring able to secure the assent of Egypt, let alone that of Syria, who continued to boycott his peace mission, for the talks to start.

During the long, fruitless months of discussions which Jarring conducted with the Israelis and the Arabs, various ideas for breaking the deadlock were considered and discarded. Israel, for instance, let it be known that she would allow the reopening of the Suez Canal if this were agreed upon in face-to-face talks with Egypt. Nasser rejected the proposal. Israel, on the other hand, refused to allow the unilateral Egyptian dredging of the Canal, blocked by ships which the Egyptians had themselves sunk in it during the Six-Day War. But Israel was ready to cooperate in the raising of the sunken ships in the southern part of the Canal since that would allow more than a dozen neutral ships stranded in the Great Bitter Lake to sail out into the Red Sea. Nasser hesitated between doing something which might ingratiate him with the neutral countries concerned and using the stranded ships as a diplomatic lever to force Israel to allow the dredging of the whole Canal. He decided on the second of these alternatives.

There was intermittent pressure on Israel to produce proposals to break the deadlock or to carry out unilateral actions for the same purpose. One suggestion, late in 1967, was that Israel should offer a global solution of the refugee problem, mainly in order to break the ice and get the Arab countries talking. Another was that Israel should carry out a partial withdrawal from the occupied territories. Yet another was for Israel to produce the bones of an over-all peace settlement acceptable to her. This proposal became fashionable in the United States State Department and may have caused Eshkol some misgivings when he went to America in January 1968 to meet President Johnson.

He need not have worried, for he found the President in excellent spirits and extremely friendly. Eshkol, allegedly, showed the utmost reserve when discussing possible peace terms and was quoted as saying, "We may have to live for 20 years or more behind the present cease-fire line." Johnson was believed to have given an assurance that 48 Skyhawks would be delivered according to the terms of an agreement discussed in 1966, and that the United States would never allow the balance of weapons in the Middle East to go against Israel. The two men got on excellently. They were both farmers, and they spent two days together at President Johnson's San Antonio ranch in Texas. As one of Eshkol's advisers put it, "They were the only two members of the house party who understood exactly what was happening when the whole party watched a calf being born."

On his way home from the United States, Eshkol stopped off briefly in London, on January 17, 1968, for talks with Britain's Prime Minister and Foreign Secretary, Harold Wilson and George Brown. This meeting was less satisfactory. Eshkol was worried by the impending British withdrawal from the Persian Gulf, which he felt would leave a vacuum in the area, and by Britain's readiness to supply arms to Arab countries. He pointed out that the Soviet Union had already replaced more than three quarters of the Arab military equipment lost during the Six-Day War. On the British side, Brown was believed to have urged the need for the Israelis to produce peace proposals, and to have argued that time was on the side of the Arabs.

In June 1968 Eshkol told a Mapai Central Committee meeting that Israel's readiness for peace could be likened to a hammer without an anvil. He repeated his conviction that Israel could not state peace terms in advance: "To declare a concession during such a process of bargaining is only an invitation to demands for fresh concessions." On September 10 President Johnson gave heartening support to this viewpoint in a speech at the Shoreham Hotel in Washington. He said: "One fact is sure. The process of peacemaking will not begin until the leaders of the Middle East begin exchanging views on the hard issues, through some agreed procedure which can permit discussions to be pursued. . . . How the talking is done at the outset is not important."

Nevertheless, Eshkol perfectly understood the argument put forward by the American State Department and the British Foreign Office that Israel should take a lead in breaking the ice. Israel could think rationally, the Arabs could not. Israel was not inhibited and embittered by having lost a war. Israel, again, genuinely wanted peace. He instructed his Foreign Minister to give an outline of Israeli thinking to the United Nations. Abba Eban duly did this in a speech to the General Assembly on October 8, 1968. In his speech he laid down nine principles for a lasting peace in the Middle East.

1. The establishment of a lasting peace, contractually expressed, in place of mere cease-fires and truces.

2. The recognition of permanent and secure boundaries for Middle East states.

3. Mutual security agreements between Israel and her Arab neighbors.

4. Open frontiers and free movement across them.

5. Freedom of navigation founded on equality of rights.

6. Short- and long-term proposals for a solution of the refugee question.

7. The determination of a status for Jerusalem which would give effect to the "universal character of the city."

8. Acknowledgement of national sovereignty and integrity in the Middle East.

9. Regional cooperation among the states of the Middle East, in order to lay the foundations of a new, cohesive community.

These nine principles give an idea of Israeli thinking. Both Eshkol and Eban had, in the past, spelled out just what regional cooperation could mean to the Middle East. It would mean free ports for Jordan on the Mediterranean and the full exploitation of Jordan's considerable potash resources at the southern end of the Dead Sea. It would mean the proper utilization of the waters of the Jordan, and Israel would certainly be prepared to put her growing knowledge in the field of water desalination at the disposal of peaceful neighbors. It would mean, too, improvement of means of communication for the whole area. Peace in the Middle East would bring a tremendous upsurge of trade. It is noteworthy too that Eban plainly hinted at arrangements for Jerusalem which could at least help to assuage the hurt pride of the Arabs. The latter, however, took not the slightest interest in his nine principles.

Eban continued to press Jarring for information about Egypt's willingness to accept the principle of a signed peace treaty. Jarring continued to send discreet inquiries about this to the Egyptian government. But in the absence of any Egyptian response the Israeli government did not feel able to reveal details of a proposed peace settlement. Its fear remained that Nasser would treat such details as maximal demands and would then whittle away whatever guarantees of her security Israel wanted. Eshkol was unable to do more than give a broad hint in the Knesset, on November 11, 1968, that Israel was ready to withdraw her troops from the bank of the Suez Canal if Israeli shipping were allowed to use it.

A week earlier Eshkol conveyed a memorandum to the Egyptian government, through Jarring.[18] The memorandum contained five main questions: Was Egypt prepared to sign a lasting peace agreement? Did Egypt accept the Israeli view that new, secure, and recognized boundaries should be established? Would Egypt join with Israel in working out details of a mutual security pact which would prevent a repetition of the Six-Day War and the events leading up to it? What was Egypt's policy on reopening the Canal to Israeli shipping? What was the Egyptian reaction to Israel's proposal for an internationally backed five-year plan to solve the refugee problem? There was no reply to any of these questions.

Arab intransigence was indeed beginning to have some effect on Israeli public opinion. A poll conducted at the end of November 1968 showed that 45 percent of Israelis believed a peace settlement to be possible, against over 60 percent in July 1967. Another Gallup Poll showed that 67 percent of Israelis regarded defense as the most important issue for their country and 59 percent believed that Israel would have to retain the whole of the west bank. Israeli public opinion was not only becoming more pessimistic, it was beginning to harden, and visitors to Israel found more and more Israelis convincing themselves that the only thing to do was to sit tight on all the cease-fire lines and consolidate behind them by producing semipermanent solutions for the settlement of the occupied territories. Arab intransigence, in fact, was making Israelis believe that they would have to hold on to everything they had whether they liked it or not. Peace, real peace, was becoming a progressively more remote concept.

Remote it certainly was. Early in 1969 the French government began talking openly of the need for a conference of the great powers to "enforce"[19] the Security Council's resolution of November 22, 1967. French Foreign Minister Debré hastened to add that "enforcement" was only possible with Israeli and Arab "participation." France, at almost the same time, decided to suspend all deliveries of spare parts for the Mirage aircraft which were the main component of Israel's strike force in the air. France had already declared 18 months earlier that she would not deliver 48 Mirages ordered by Israel and already paid for, a unilateral disclaimer of a straightforward commercial transaction which may cost the French aircraft industry dear in the long run. On January 14, 1969, Eshkol denounced the French action on grounds of commercial morality: agreements had been unilaterally and arbitrarily violated and France had even frozen the money paid by Israel for the planes.

Early in 1969, too, the Soviet government began its own Middle East peace offensive. This took the form of calls by Soviet ambassadors on the governments of the United States, Britain, and France, each of them bearing what was termed as a "summary of Soviet views." The Soviet Union expressed support for the Jarring mission, urged the implementation of the November 1967 UN resolution, and proposed a step-by-step procedure which was designed in the Arab interest. The Soviet formula was a diplomatic secret, but it was significant that very soon there were unconfirmed reports that the United States had rejected the idea of a complete Israeli withdrawal from all occupied territories. As I have already suggested, this had always been regarded by the Arabs, especially Egypt, as the necessary first step toward implementation of the UN resolution. It may have been significant too that government spokesmen in Washington and London admitted that the Soviet formula looked very like Nasser's peace manifestoes. The Russians were still trying to recoup their losses in the June 1967 war by achieving a diplomatic victory on behalf of Arab states whom they affected to befriend and whom they intended, in due course, to dominate.

A final word should be said about Israel feelings at what is yet another crossroads in Israeli history, for the two decisions on how to seek peace and what to do with the occupied territories were absolutely crucial. A British defense expert, Leonard Beaton, writing in the London *Times,* argued that the whole future of the Middle East had hinged on Nasser's decision to blockade the Gulf of Aqaba on May 22, 1967, and on the reactions of the Western powers to that decision.[20] President Johnson had called Nasser's action illegal. Britain's Foreign Secretary, George Brown, had begun organizing the maritime powers in order to oppose the unilateral Egyptian blockade. But in this case the Western or maritime powers did nothing although, like Nasser, they were committed to upholding the 1957 agreement which laid down that Israeli ships should use the waters of the Gulf.

Eshkol had pointed out that the concept of international law and security itself was at stake. President Johnson had responded by indicating that the United States was not in a position to uphold international law and security and had warned Israel against taking unilateral action. As Beaton put it: "The international order had been challenged and abdicated. The Israeli soldiers took over. Even then they went on assuming that there was an international order of a kind. They believed they had to get very fast results before any great power could act. The instinct that there is a great power system, built up over the years, faded away only gradually."

Eshkol "had said that if the major powers did not implement their 1957 commitments, a regime of international security and law would no longer exist. . . . Eshkol has since acted on that assumption. He is being denounced for public and savage violence in the name of an international order and standards of international conduct. But he and the men around him do not believe in this order. It proclaimed its retreat into exhortation in May, 1967."

The lack of security, order, and peace in the Middle East is, indeed, only a microcosm of the situation in the world as a whole. That in no way diminishes the need to secure peace in the Middle East, something which Eshkol always understood. In his own words, "Peace means most of all to us. It has to be a real peace, which gives us the possibility of a decent, orderly existence, useful to our neighbors as well as to ourselves."[21]

1. Eshkol, in a speech to the Knesset, September 8, 1967.
2. For these and other figures, the source is the Annual Survey of the Ministry of Defense.
3. Annual Survey of the Ministry of Defense 1967/68, p. 15.
4. The *Times* (London), November 22, 1968.
5. The *Manchester Guardian*, December 28, 1968.
6. As reported by the *Jerusalem Post*, September 20, 1968.
7. The *Times* (London), June 20, 1968.
8. The *Manchester Guardian*, December 2, 1968.
9. "The Struggle for Peace," *Israel Magazine*, Vol. I, No. 4, 1968.
10. From the *Times* (London), November 11, 1967.
11. *Ibid.*, November 24, 1967.
12. *Ibid.*, January 20, 1968.
13. *Ibid.*, July 6, 1968.
14. *Ibid.*, August 15, 1968.
15. From *Al Gomhouria* and other Egyptian newspapers, August 21, 1968.
16. From the *Times* (London), January 21, 1969.
17. From *The Jewish Observer and Middle East Review*, February 9, 1968.
18. *Ibid.*, December 6, 1968.
19. From the *Times* (London), January 4, 1969.
20. *Ibid.*, January 2, 1969.
21. Eshkol, in personal conversation with the author.

20.

At the end of September 1968 the Israeli government turned down a request by the Secretary General of the United Nations, U Thant, that a special UN representative should be admitted into the territories occupied by Israel during the 1967 war "in order to investigate alleged mistreatment of Arab civilians."[1] The Israeli government pointed out, politely but firmly, that a special UN representative, Nils Gussing, had already been allowed to visit the occupied territories in July and August, 1967. He had submitted a report to U Thant on August 18, 1967. Its findings were made public. Among the most important were that there was no evidence that Palestinian Arabs were being forced by the Israelis to leave their homes, that transport had been placed at the disposal of those who wanted to go, that some arrests had been made of suspected terrorists, and that several villages had been demolished, allegedly for security reasons. The Israeli view, a year after the Gussing mission, was that a second UN probe into the administration of the occupied territories was not justified. Foreign journalists and diplomats could go anywhere they pleased without hindrance in these territories and could report freely and without fear on what they found there.

The Israeli government pointed out that Arab governments had, since May 1968, been rejecting requests by U Thant for a UN probe into the condition of the Jewish communities in the Arab world. This would have been no more than a quid pro quo for the Gussing mission. But the Israeli Government was not fussily standing on its rights in this instance; it was deeply concerned over the conditions of Jewish communities which were isolated and persecuted. A great deal has been written about the post-1948 Arab refugee problem, very little about the post-1948 problem of Jewish refugees from Arab countries. Here are some relevant facts.

Between 1948 and 1968, roughly 900,000 Jews left their homes in Arab countries, where their communities had lived for centuries, even millennia. Many of them left because they were persecuted and the vast majority left because of fear and uncertainty. Well over a half million of these Jewish refugees came to Israel, for the most part penniless, bringing little with them but the clothes on their backs. At the time of the 1967 war there were about 80,000 to 100,000 Jews left in Arab countries. Their communities were small, scattered, poor, helpless, and deeply frightened. They had reason to be.

According to a survey,[2] little more than 1000 Jews were left in Egypt at the end of 1968 out of a community of over 75,000 20 years earlier. Of the 1000, about one fourth were imprisoned in the Thora (or Tourah) concentration camp near Cairo. During the previous 12 months 1500 Jews had been expelled from Egypt, but the Egyptians, like the Nazis, decided belatedly to keep the Jews where they were. One must assume that they were being held as hostages. There were reports of beatings, torture, and forced sodomy. A number of these helpless and innocent Jews committed suicide. None of them had committed any offence, or had been charged with any.

In Syria there remained about 3500 Jews out of what had been a flourishing community of over 40,000 in 1948. Since 1967 there has been a total ban on the emigration of Syrian Jews. The number in jail fluctuated, since it was the Syrian habit to round up groups of Jews on any pretext, imprison them for a time, and release them again at whim. Jews who have been released normally have to report to the police three times a day. In most parts of the country, their identity cards have been stamped "Jew"—this is yet another reminder of Nazi Germany—and they have been forbidden to travel more than three miles from their places of residence.

In Iraq mass arrests of Jews began soon after the 1967 war. A boycott of all Jewish tradesmen was proclaimed and about 100 leading members of the Jewish community were arrested and detained for varying periods of time. In Iraq, perhaps even more than in other Arab Middle East countries, Jews have been subjected to purely incidental molestation, a result of flagrantly anti-Jewish propaganda and the total inaction of the police when Jews are attacked. By 1969 only 3000 remained there out of the 1948 Jewish community of at least 730,000.

The Jews of Libya suffered the greatest violence and brutality after the 1967 war. Between ten and twenty were killed—lynched by mobs in the first ten days after the outbreak of war. Almost every shop belonging to members of the Jewish community of 4000 strong was burned to the ground. The Libyan government reversed its ban on emigration, with the result that virtually all Jews left the country. They were allowed to take along a maximum of $20 each. Italy and Spain were particularly helpful in accepting some of these emigrants.

Persecution of the helpless and innocent is a horrible thing at any time, but the worst is when the persecuted are held hostage, as in Egypt, Syria, and Iraq. A letter from a Jew in Bagdad in August 1967 described what it felt like:

> We can neither eat nor sleep. Day and night the fear has been constant of their coming to arrest us or search the house. . . . Some of us have been tied with chains, beaten at random with sticks, and slapped. . . . Each day we hear something different: first they are going to deport us, then they are going to kill us, and then again we are to be deported. . . . Those whom they fetch by car are told they will be burnt alive, shot one by one, or thrown into the desert. The Red Cross is not allowed to investigate, and even if they should come, nobody will dare to talk.

The persecution of the Jews of Iraq resulted in an act of singular barbarity. On January 27, 1969, 9 Jews were among 14 hanged as spies in Bagdad's Liberation Square.[3] They had been sentenced to death two weeks earlier after being tried in secret session by the Revolutionary Court at the beginning of January. Allegedly, they were sentenced to death for spying, but in all probability this was an act of legalized terrorism designed to distract public attention from the government's failure to put Iraq's economy in order and to bring the long war against the rebelling Kurdish community to an end. Ten more Jews were arrested early in January and hundreds of Iraqi citizens, including the former Prime Minister, Dr. Al-Bazzaz, were charged with complicity in "Israeli plots."

The public execution of Jews who were almost certainly innocent of any crime caused a wave of anger in Israel and disgust in the outside world. It was coarse, medieval, barbaric. Mobs, estimated at 200,000 people, marched past the dangling garroted corpses. Among these bloodthirsty sightseers, who were regaled by a running commentary on the radio, were enthusiastic detachments of the schoolboy section of El Fatah Palestinian terrorists. Eshkol, deeply moved, declared: "We know, and I solemnly say here that the Iraqi government knew as well, that all the charges brought against these nine Jews were totally unfounded. Their one and only 'crime' was to be Jews." Eshkol sharply criticized the great powers for their failure to bring pressure to bear on the Arabs to stop racial persecution and promised that "God will take vengeance for this crime." He pointed out, too, that not a single Arab spy or saboteur had been executed in Israel, although literally hundreds had been captured since the Six-Day War.

Israel has readily accepted every single new refugee from the Arab countries. Indeed, there is a fundamental difference in the Israeli and Arab attitude towards refugees. The Israelis regard every refugee as someone needing and deserving succor; the Arabs treat him as an unwanted burden. The Israelis are proud to look after their own; the Arabs do not recognize them as such and expect the outside world to feed, clothe, and house them. This is the principal reason why a Jewish refugee arriving in Israel realizes that he is coming home; an Arab refugee to, say, Syria is merely cast adrift.

The Israelis regard each new refugee as a potential asset. Israel needs immigrants very badly, wherever they may come from. One estimate of Israel's population growth[4] showed that the increase between the end of 1966 and the end of 1968 was only 116,000, from 2,657,000 to 2,773,000, and that 77,800 of this increase was in the Arab minority. The Jewish population increased only 40,000 in two years. The Jewish and Arab birth rates in Israel are 22 and 48 per 1000 respectively. This disparity inevitably causes concern.

Eshkol believed that Israel ought to have and needs to have a Jewish population of at least five million by the end of the century. As he put it,

> In principle, Israel is a haven for all the Jews in the world. In practice, of course, all Jews will not come here. But there will be surprises; who would have guessed, for instance, that Polish Jewry would be harassed from their homes, when they are such a small community? They have been leaving Poland at the rate of 100 a week, with 60 or more of them arriving in Israel. The Diaspora and Israel are a part of one another. What we ask of the Diaspora is to give us 50,000 immigrants a year, out of an annual natural increase of 100,000. We need them badly.[5]

Eshkol believed that Israel must be one of two magnets for world Jewry, with the United States the other. The movement towards concentration of the Jewish community uprooted from most of its traditional footholds in Europe, North Africa, and the Arab world cannot be halted or reversed. Nor is it desirable that it should be; the two foci of a national state and a nucleus in the greatest democratic community in the world comprise an altogether healthy development for world Jewry. Israel's own minimum target is 30,000 to 40,000 immigrants a year, with at least one tenth of them coming initially from the US and Britain in a progressively greater proportion as the years go by. "Immigration," according to one authority, "is not only Israel's life blood—the guarantee of her security and future, as Ben-Gurion has said. It is her very essence, her soul. The sin against immigration is the one sin she cannot forgive."[6]

Besides the overriding problem of war and peace, immigration and the fate of the Jews in the Arab world were merely two of very many questions which Eshkol had to resolve as Prime Minister. One of the most important was that of economic viability, not of course a new problem, but one which became even more pressing after the Six-Day War. Israel, cheated of the fruits of military victory and of the peace which she desired so earnestly, found herself engaged in an arms race with her Arab neighbors which looked likely to be far costlier than before and to continue permanently, or at least until the next Arab-Israeli war took place.

This was all the more frustrating since Israel had been making excellent progress in dealing with her standard economic problems—the combating of inflationary pressures, the balancing of her trade, the expansion of industry, and the boosting of exports. In 1966–1967 there had been a slowdown in overall economic growth, which may have been partly due to poor planning. There was a falling off in savings, a reduction in capital investment, periodic petty but irritating strikes due in some degree to the continuing wage freeze, and a stagnation in a government income which owed something to the fact that anything which could be remotely regarded as luxury goods was already taxed up to the hilt.

But the turning point had already been reached in April 1967, and the war proved an unexpected stimulus to the economy. As the special correspondent of a British newspaper pointed out,[7] unemployment was mopped up overnight, the defense industries went into top-gear production, patriotic fervor brought wage restraint, imports boomed, and foreign exchange reserves "increased by the staggering amount of 75 percent" to a total of $840 million. This was because the Jews of the Diaspora, rallying to Israel's help in an unprecedented manner, poured money into the country, money that came from the pockets of the humblest Jewish families as well as from the coffers of the richest Jewish companies. So great were these contributions and so intense was the desire of world Jewry to "buy Israeli," that, according to one spokesman of the Ministry of Finance, "we could be entirely self-supporting, if it were not for our defense expenditure."[8]

One or two figures suggest that this was not a wild exaggeration. The trade deficit dropped in 1967 from $321 million to $195 million. Per capita productivity rose by 8 percent in the year. Labor discipline meant that monthly wages rose by only half of one percent, against 18 percent in each of the two previous years, 1965 and 1966. Unemployment fell by 50 percent to about 8000, or well under one percent of the work force. The picture was one of a small but highly geared economy, having shed most of its nonproductive capacity during the mildly recessionary years of 1965 and 1966, now functioning with greater efficiency than ever before. This picture, moreover, did not change in many important respects during 1968. Over-all production and per capita productivity rose by over 10 percent, exports by about 17 percent, and capital investments by 25 percent. Prices increased almost 3 percent; wage restraint, in fact, was surviving the war largely because of a continuing state of national emergency. Imports, admittedly, were almost 30 percent higher, but this was the result of deliberate policy and calculated risk. The high rate of imports was intended to encourage an even more hectic rate of economic expansion.

A useful weapon in promoting industrial growth was the Law for the Encouragement of Capital Investment, which was revised and added to in 1967. Three types of enterprise now stood to benefit from tax revision and grants for site development and the purchase of machinery: those earning foreign currency, those producing import-saving goods, and those assisting in the industrialization of development areas.

David Horowitz, the governor of the Bank of Israel, said at the end of 1968,

We are in a period of unprecedented economic growth, but we are successfully combating inflation. Indeed, savings are going up, wages and prices are being held remarkably steady, the labor force is working more productively and more scientifically, and there is a mood of national confidence. Consumption is not going up fast, and our object will be to channel our increased imports into capital investment. We do have one major problem; that is the burden of defense, which is now almost one fifth of the Gross National Product. But Israel must have the weapons which she needs for her own defense, and she is going to be able to pay for them. One answer will be to expand our own arms production.[9]

The cost of defense, indeed, was phenomenal for a small country. Arms imports reduced foreign currency reserves to $600 million by early 1969. The 1969 budget, according to the Minister of Finance, Zeev Sharef, was to exceed $2350 million, or $185 million more than in 1968. The defense burden would be far heavier in 1969 than the $630 million spent on defense in 1968. And 1968 expenditure on defense had already caused a sensational increase in Israel's adverse trade balance. In 1968 it was expected to be up by $400 million to a record figure of $600 million. In 1969 it was bound to be at least as high. This meant cutting back the special development budget (roughly speaking, covering the government's capital investment program), increasing over-all taxation, and raising a defense loan by asking taxpayers to contribute 50 percent of one month's earnings payable in ten monthly installments.

Israel, obviously, is still some way off from paying her own way, particularly when it is remembered that she habitually receives about $500 million a year in foreign exchange from the sale of Israeli bonds abroad and from all other sources of aid from the Diaspora. As a further illustration of the fact that the trade gap cannot be closed in a hurry, one should remember that the Government's four-year export plan provides for an increase of only $775 million over the 1967 figure of $521 million in the value of exports by 1971.

The troublesome imponderable in economic planning is defense. There can be no question of Israel's cutting her defense budget at a time when the Arab countries have been clamoring for military revenge, and when the Soviet Union has been rearming them. It is sufficient to say here that, by mid-1969, Israel's Arab neighbors were better armed than they had been in June 1967. In particular, Egypt had secured new rocket weapons from the Soviet Union and had massed a huge concentration of artillery along the Suez Canal, while Iraq, which had suffered minimal losses in the 1967 war, had steadily built up armed forces which may be used against either Israel or her own Kurdish minority or the oil sheikdoms of the Persian Gulf.

On July 14, 1968, Eshkol said in Jerusalem that "Israel badly needs the Phantom supersonic jets, and must get them. . . . We would be asking for 100 Phantoms if we could afford them. When I visited President Johnson at his ranch in January, he promised to give me an answer on the Phantoms during this year."[10]

Eshkol was referring to the proposed sale to Israel of 50 American Phantoms, which had become doubly needed when France first refused to deliver the 48 Mirage aircraft for which Israel had already paid, and then suspended delivery of Mirage spare parts. There were long months of negotiations before the Johnson administration confirmed, on December 27, 1968, that the Phantoms would be delivered. The announcement came an hour after the three Apollo astronauts safely reached an aircraft carrier in the Pacific after their historical flight around the moon. More appositely, it came a day after the two Arab gunmen had attacked the El Al aircraft and its passengers at Athens airport.

The announcement, made by State Department spokesman, Robert McCloskey, said that delivery of the jets would begin before the end of 1969 and continue through 1970. The planes would cost Israel just over $200 million, and a small portion of the purchase price was being advanced to Israel in the form of a loan. Paradoxically, the Phantoms deal was politically highly desirable for Israel but from the financial point of view instrumental in imposing the heaviest burden that the taxpayer has yet had to bear. It was hardly surprising to hear the Finance Minister, Zeev Sharef, repeating a previous statement that Israel must begin building her own supersonic aircraft by the end of 1969.[11]

One other special economic problem was Israel's water supply. As the years go by, its solution becomes increasingly pressing. By 1980 Israel will be using every drop of water available to her from natural sources. These include the waters of the Jordan and other streams and springs, maximum use of rainfall, and treated water from sewage installations. The only major source of water left is desalinated salt or brackish water.

For the past decade Israeli scientists have been examining the possibilities of desalting water economically. On more than one occasion Eshkol discussed the subject with the United States government. The Prime Minister was confident that there would be a breakthrough in the production of desalted water. "I expect this to happen in the 1970s. Already our scientists at the Haifa Technion are planning for the start of a production program in 1971. We have an understanding with the United States government on this matter and I have had talks with President Johnson about it."[12] American scientists have also been active in this field and have cooperated with the Israelis in establishing two small pilot plants in Israel. American and Israeli research has been based chiefly on the consideration that desalted water can be most economically produced as part of a dual-purpose project. The other purpose would be to produce nuclear power.

In June 1967 a French Jewish financier, Baron Edmond de Rothschild, proposed the setting up of three large desalting plants to serve both Israel and Jordan.[13] He assessed the cost of each plant at about $200 million and estimated that each would produce 260 million cubic yards of pure water a year. The three plants would thus produce more than half the combined flow of the Jordan and Yarmuk rivers. The water problems of Israel and Jordan would be solved up to the year 2000.

The 260 million cubic yards a year are equal to over 100 million gallons a day. Baron de Rothschild did not estimate what the life of a desalting plant might be, nor, therefore, what the actual cost of the pure water which it produced would be. His view was that the expenditure of $600 million would be amply justified by solving the water problems of Israel and Jordan for the next 30 years and by launching a unique experiment in international cooperation in the Middle East.

In December 1967 the Haifa Technion (to which Eshkol had referred) announced that it had made significant progress toward reducing the cost of producing desalted water.[14] The head of the institute's aeronautical engineering department, Professor Abraham Kogan, claimed that his new desalting plant showed that desalted water could be produced 25 percent more cheaply than before. Professor Kogan began working on the construction of a pilot plant which will apply his process. In its initial stage the project is financed with $200,000 contributed by a New York businessman, David Rose. The plant will cost about $800,000 in all and should be in operation by the end of 1970. Professor Kogan claims that he has modified flash-distillation processes by cascading a stream of hot brine through a series of vapor-flashing stages. Vapor flashed off the brine is condensed by contact with a countercurrent of pure water. Kogan has called his process Direct Contact Distillation and has proposed a dual-purpose plant, with a nuclear boiler producing both electricity and desalted water.

Desalination was one of the principal subjects discussed in April 1968 when about 500 Jewish industrialists and financiers from all over the world assembled in Jerusalem for Israel's first international Economic Conference. The idea of such a conference came in the first instance from the Ministry of Finance. Eshkol gave it his unreserved backing. Opening the Conference, he promised that his government would give its utmost help to all productive initiatives emanating in either Israel or the Diaspora; in particular, Israel would give ready and grateful help to everyone who was ready to invest or work in Israel.

The Economic Conference had immediate results. The delegates to it submitted 16 recommendations to the government of Israel. They emphasized the need to build up the country's export trade, to reduce economic regulation, to encourage free enterprise, to reduce tariffs and other protectionist weapons, to raise productivity, and to modernize industry. The delegates also suggested a series of ten principal undertakings, including cooperation in the export field, development of know-how and patent agreements with Israel, assistance in the marketing of Israeli products, and the study of possibilities of investment in Israel. They also undertook to join in the formation of a company with capital of $100 million in its initial phase. A group headed by the Israeli government would take 20 percent of the shares in the company, each of $100,000, while the remaining 80 percent would be taken up by Jewish investors in the Diaspora. The company's principal purpose would be to channel investment funds into Israel and to scrutinize development projects there.

Fifty projects, 20 of them science-based, were recommended as being viable by the industrial committee set up by the Conference. One of the first to be considered was for the construction of an oil pipeline from Eilat on the Red Sea to Ashkelon on the Mediterranean, with an annual capacity of 60 million tons. This was about one third of the amount of oil which had passed through the Suez Canal prior to the 1967 war. The Eilat-Ashdod pipeline will be the alternative to the giant tankers' route around the Cape of Good Hope. Its installation will be a factor in the planned increase of Israel's export of chemicals and fuels by $60 million by 1971, and in the development of a completely new petrochemical industry. The pipeline should be operating by the end of 1969.

The Economic Conference was an unqualified success. According to Dr. Yakov Arnon, Director General of the Ministry of Finance, its principal, long-term effect will be to make Israeli industry more efficient.[15] Close cooperation with the many brilliantly successful Jewish firms of the Diaspora will mean substantial improvements in Israeli production methods, management techniques, and selection of goods for export markets. Showing Israeli industry to the Diaspora brought a flow of orders from abroad for Israeli goods. Delivery of Israeli goods remains, of course, a major problem and one which is essentially for Israeli firms to solve.

Eshkol always remained deeply interested in Israel's economic development and closely in touch with day-to-day economic problems. But his activity in economic matters was inevitably less, as well as less noticeable, than in political affairs, the usual experience of a Prime Minister in a democratic state. Eshkol could leave his Minister of Finance largely in control of economic problems. But on the political side there were a number of decisions which only the Prime Minister could make.

There had been the issue of peace or war in June 1967. There had been the formation of the national government in the same month. There had been the decision to preserve that government after the war was over. In all these decisions Eshkol sought a consensus of opinion, and secured it. But for one major problem he had to work out his own policy, and implement it by sheer persistence in the face of opposition, doubt, and procrastination. This was the problem of reunifying the Labor party, something in which Eshkol fervently believed. His success in carrying this through was a true measure of his real, underlying strength of character, for it was a masterstroke in the field of party politics, and it is perfectly possible that it will, in the long run, transform the Israeli political scene.

Although Eshkol had been given credit for his leadership of the country up to and during the Six-Day War, he was perfectly aware of the opposition to him in the coalition and even within the ranks of Mapai. On July 30, 1967, the restrained and reasonable London newspaper, the *Jewish Chronicle*, actually suggested quite bluntly that Eshkol was on the way out. The *Chronicle* assumed that the proposed merger of Mapai and Achdut Ha'avoda would go through, and that the leader of the latter, Yigal Allon, would become the obvious candidate for the premiership. On the other hand, as the *Chronicle* pointed out, the proposal had also been made for a tripartite reunion which would include Rafi. That would make Moshe Dayan, Rafi's favorite son, an even more popular candidate than Allon.

The *Chronicle's* thoughts were spelled out at greater length by the London *Times* a few weeks later.[16] As the paper's Jerusalem correspondent saw it, the move to restore the unity of the Labor party was essentially bound up with the transfer of power to younger men, and its success would depend on the approval of a younger generation which was bored with the maneuvering of parties and factions and with seniors who had been brought up in the Diaspora and were inhibited by Diaspora attitudes. As it happened, the *Times* correspondent was mistaken; the reunification of the Labor party was just as dear to the hearts of some of those inhibited seniors and dearest of all to Eshkol himself.

What was taking place behind the scenes was, in reality, a series of conferences between Mapai, Achdut Ha'avoda, and Rafi leaders, some of them bilateral and some of them internal party affairs. In these conferences a pattern was beginning to take shape. Achdut Ha'avoda was ready for reunion with Mapai. Its leader, Allon, was ready for this union to take place under Eshkol's leadership. Rafi was divided. Its Grand Old Man of the Israeli labor movement, Ben-Gurion, was opposed to reunion, especially under Eshkol. So, initially, was Dayan. Rafi had split from Mapai two and a half years earlier because the latter's leadership was allegedly tired, dull, and establishment-minded. That leadership was the same; Rafi continued to hesitate, and its leaders strove to secure special terms from Mapai before definitely making up their minds.

Had Eshkol been weak, he would no doubt have made concessions to Rafi. Dayan, after all, was a popular hero. If Rafi remained independent, it might get a greatly increased vote in the elections in November 1969. This could mean taking votes from Mapai, and the latter's losing the dominant Parliamentary position which it had held ever since 1948. Eshkol's nerve did not fail him. He reckoned that Rafi was not well enough organized to do any better in 1969 than it had done in the 1965 elections. He was perfectly right. In 1965 Rafi had expected to win

20 seats in the Knesset and was sadly disappointed with just half that number. It would have had a job to hold its ten seats in 1969.

Rafi continued to hold out for one particular concession. This was that a reunified Labor party should call a convention after holding internal party elections. The convention would elect a new leadership. Ben-Gurion had made it clear that he would not join Mapai if Eshkol remained head of it. Ben-Gurion was still, nominally, Rafi's leader. This Rafi demand was clearly aimed at ousting Eshkol. Once again, Eshkol might have given way. He did not, and in refusing to allow the junior member in the proposed merger to dictate to the senior he had the support of his own Mapai followers.

Rafi met in December 1967 to decide on its future. Over a thousand delegates attended the meeting in Jerusalem. Dayan and the party's Secretary General, Shimon Peres, supported the merger. Ben-Gurion opposed it and suggested going to the electorate in November 1969 with a list of independent, nonparty candidates. The vote on December 13 was 523 to 364 in favor of the merger. About 300 delegates either abstained or absented themselves. Rafi formally dissolved itself and the three-cornered merger was complete. On January 12, 1968 the *Jewish Chronicle* gave an appreciative account of Eshkol's assets: he had held the national coalition together, shown himself to be a man of peace and an astute political manager, instituted sound economic policies, and maintained his supremacy within Mapai. Certainly, it was Eshkol's hour of triumph.

He had always preached the need for a common language among Israel's political parties. "I tried to lower the internal tensions between the different parties. The last year or two of Ben-Gurion's rule was marked by very high tensions, especially between Ben-Gurion and Cherut [the Conservatives]. I tried to reduce tension and create a more relaxed climate."[17]

Eshkol had worked from 1963 onward for Labor unity, first by personal soundings, later by straightforward proposals backed by Mapai. He had hoped to bring the left-wing Mapam as well as Achdut Ha'avoda and Rafi back into the fold. Indeed, his next political move was to secure Mapam's alignment for the 1969 elections with the reunified Labor party. Eshkol had never been doctrinaire, or an individualist; he always regarded the divisions within the Labor movement as unnatural and absurd. In his view, every section of the Labor movement was based on principles connected with the building, development, and defense of Israel. Those principles should not be pursued in opposition, but implemented through cooperation in action, by participation in government. Another precept of Eshkol's was that no party should, as Mapam in particular did in the past, build a kind of Chinese wall around itself.

Eshkol was not rashly optimistic about the reunification of the Labor party. He described it as "only the beginning of the gradual, but essential process of union, which is representative of the will of the great mass of workers in Israel . . . representative, too, of the general realization that no party split can be a success."[18] He realized that there would be troubles ahead and he was concerned in particular about the possibility that Rafi and Achdut would remain distinct, cohesive factions in the Labor front, and that Mapai would gradually lose its identity. Eshkol realized, too, that there could be internal bickering which would strain the newly founded and somewhat fragile Labor unity. Lastly, he still dearly wanted the final and unconditional return of Mapam to the fold. It was partly because of his sentimental feelings for Mapam that he approached its leaders as soon as he became Prime Minister in 1963. About this approach Eshkol said: "What did I have to lose? Mapam in its heart belonged with us, in the kibbutz movement most of all, but also in the trade unions and in the Labor movement. Mapam produced ideals and spirit when so many Jews were lost in the holocaust. Mapam did so much in helping to absorb the post-1945 immigrants. I have talked to Mapam because I wanted to do so."[19] Admittedly, his early efforts were frustrated, "The Mapam leaders would not join us. They loved their ideological hobby-horses; that made them stick together and not want our company. And they made tremendous speeches at me—some of them went on for three or four hours at a time. My children always tell *me* to cut it short; I think they're right!"

Eshkol regarded the original break between Mapai and its Rafi offshoot as a "mere puncture," and he believed that Rafi's return to the fold, particularly when Ben-Gurion, in a huff, retired into the exclusiveness of a one-man party, was something which would last. Yet Eshkol's chief difficulties within the coalition were with Rafi, and there were at least three occasions in 1968 when the somewhat tenuous unity of the Labor movement was threatened, if only temporarily.

The first was in June, 1968, when Eshkol appointed Allon as his Deputy Prime Minister, with the special duty of dealing with the absorption of new immigrants. Eshkol was of an age when he could well feel that he needed a deputy; and more attention would have to be paid to immigrants' needs if Israel was ever to secure the influx of settlers from the United States which she wanted so badly. Eshkol, again, had an excellent understanding with Allon, a man of loyalty and tact. (When asked in London in February 1968 about possible successors to Eshkol, he quoted Weizmann, "It is impossible in modern Israel to be a prophet, the competition is too fierce.") But there was an inevitable suspicion that Eshkol and his closest ally in the Labor movement, Mrs. Golda Meir, had engineered Allon's appointment in order to promote him over Dayan. Mrs. Meir was popularly supposed to have done all that she could to prevent Dayan's becoming Minister of Defense and to have urged Eshkol's retention of that post, even when she was sounded on the possibility of her taking over the premiership herself.

Dayan chose to ignore what was generally regarded as a move directed against him, but he caused a second, more serious crisis in the same month of June 1968, by embarking on an unauthorized foreign policy statement. The occasion was a nominally private talk which he was giving to Knesset members and Labor party officials, but details were leaked to the press. Dayan interpreted the UN Security Council resolution of November 22, 1967, as meaning that Israel should withdraw from all occupied territories, and expressed the view that it was a mistake for Israel to accept the resolution in any way. This statement ran counter to Israeli foreign policy. Abroad it earned Dayan the reputation of being pure hawk where peace terms were concerned and drew down on his head a reproof from Eshkol. Speaking on the radio, Eshkol said that only he or his Foreign Minister, Abba Eban, could make foreign policy statements.

Once again it was Dayan who was involved in the third internal crisis which Eshkol had to deal with in 1968. This was over the controversy whether internal Labor party elections should be held in 1969, before the Knesset elections, or in 1970. The former Rafi members, still behaving like a party within the Party, wanted elections in 1969. They argued that the public wanted to see their leaders before the Knesset elections took place and that internal elections were democratic. The Mapai old guard maintained that the unified Labor party should be given time to settle down before being exposed to the possibility of internal controversy over the leadership. In the Labor Party Central Committee the old guard, including Eshkol and Mrs. Meir, won the day by 252 votes to 164. This meant that the component parts of Labor, as well as Mapam, would be given a representation on the Labor list of candidates for the Knesset proportionate to their parliamentary strength.

The formation of the new alignment between Labor and Mapam, which meant sharing an electoral list in November 1969, could well have stirred up more trouble than did, in fact, occur. In securing this alignment Eshkol was well aware of the fact that he was laying the ground for a revolutionary change in the makeup of Israeli politics.

The new alignment is virtually certain to gain an absolute majority of seats in the Knesset. A Labor leader will be in a position to form a purely Labor administration for the first time since the state of Israel came into existence. Ben-Gurion urged electoral reform in order to encourage a two-party system based on direct election to constituencies on the British system. Eshkol shelved the question of electoral reform but pursued his own gradual approach to it. The parties of the right have been put in a position which makes some kind of electoral unity necessary, or at least highly advisable, for their survival as a real opposition to Labor. Labor unity postulates the need for a more unified opposition.

In 1970 there is to be an electoral conference for the parties to discuss electoral reform. A Labor party select committee had already in 1968 proposed a measure of reform, allowing for 90 members of the Knesset to be returned by direct election and the remaining 30 from party lists through proportional representation. Such a reform would strengthen Labor's position in future Knesset elections. Although it would be unpopular among the smaller parties, its general effect would be to encourage an improvement of the political scene.

As the architect of the national government, Eshkol wanted to preserve it at least up to the 1969 elections. But he was aware that Gahal could break away beforehand in order to assert its independence and proclaim its desire that Israel should hold on to all the territories gained in the Six-Day War. Eshkol's view was that the national government of 1967–1969 proved its usefulness, indeed its indispensability. As he put it: "When I formed it, war was imminent. For a small nation of two and a half million people, that really does mean something. There was great administrative talent, especially among Rafi, which was in the political wilderness at the time. Israel needed that talent."[21]

Israel faces a difficult time during the 1969 elections. The national government is likely to be weaker then than at any time since it was formed. Party differences may be unwelcome when Israel is still ringed about with hostile Arab neighbors, and when pressure to force her to evacuate the occupied territories will have started up again in the United Nations. Internal differences of opinion will, perhaps, have again come to the fore within the Labor movement. Finally, there is the problem of who is to be Prime Minister after the 1969 elections are over. This, when it comes, can well turn out to be a major issue.

There is a widely held view in Israel that the time has come for a change in the upper echelons of the Labor movement. For the first 20 years of Israel's existence as a state, the pioneers of the Second and Third Aliyahs, the men who arrived before and shortly after World War I, have looked after the country. These men are now mostly in their seventies. In every country there is periodically a demand for administration to pass into the hands of a younger generation—one recalls the campaigns in Britain and West Germany against the octogenarians Churchill and Adenauer. In Israel there is the additional argument that a youthful state, under insistent and everlasting pressure, requires a relatively youthful leadership. There is a feeling, too, that the younger generation of men like Dayan and Allon is already passing into advanced middle age. Staleness may set in, and that could be fatal to a country permanently threatened by armed attack by its neighbors.

The question of a change in the upper echelons of the Labor movement becomes the more important when it is remembered that a Labor or Labor-led government is sure to be returned to power in the 1969 elections. Labor, in the shape of Mapai, has led every government in

Israel's short history. In a democratic country anything approximating one-party rule is likely to militate against good government sooner or later. Christian Democratic dominance in Italy led, by 1968, to a crisis of confidence in all government, not only in one particular type of government. The same thing happened in West Germany and in Ireland after two decades of CDU and Fianna Fail dominance. Power does not by any means always corrupt, but it very often debilitates.

It has become a convention in Israel, especially among the young, to declaim against the "establishment." The term is held to mean the leadership circles of Mapai, the Histadrut, and all governmental agencies and related organizations. Among the complaints against the men of the establishment is a claim that they settle important decisions among themselves and do not consult public opinion; share important posts among themselves and do not allow a sufficient infusion of new blood; discourage positive and purposeful discussion and dish out well-worn clichés. A similar antiestablishment feeling has been increasingly evident in a great many democratic (and even some authoritarian) states since the late 1960s.

For Israel, the weight of antiestablishment feeling, and its possible consequences, can be more far-reaching than for other countries. An infant state, more than any other, must turn to men of wisdom and experience in order to ensure both stability and progress. In twenty years Israel has had only three Prime Ministers, and one of them, Moshe Sharett, was only a caretaker while Ben-Gurion went into temporary retirement. The Israeli electorate tacitly accepted the need to rely on an old guard, and on the old guard of Mapai in particular. To most Israelis, it was axiomatic that their country was in a lasting state of national emergency which justified the retention of leaders who had worked hard and on the whole successfully for the community.

The two chief political characteristics of present-day Israelis are an ingrained conservatism and a burgeoning desire for change, paradoxical as this may sound. But the desire for change is largely limited to style rather than content, and to personalities rather than policies. Above all, there is the question of youth versus age. It is no coincidence that the first Israel-born Israeli citizens have just reached the age of 21. A coming of age implies a careful reassessment of what one is and what one wants.

Levi Eshkol died very suddenly on February 26, 1969, at 8:15 in the morning. He had been ill for over three weeks after suffering a heart attack on February 3. But his recovery was regarded as no more than a matter of time. He was his usual cheerful, alert self almost up to the moment of his death, and on the day before presided over a Cabinet meeting which was held at his bedside in his official residence in the Rehavia quarter of Jerusalem. Only two days previously the Deputy

Prime Minister, Yigal Allon, said in a television interview that Eshkol's strength was unimpaired and that his illness was not at all serious.

His wife and daughters were at his bedside when he died. As was to be expected of him, he was utterly uncomplaining during his last illness, intent only on getting down to work again. One of his last wishes was that Allon should take over the leadership of a caretaker administration, which was to carry on until the November elections. The El Fatah terrorist organization supplied a note of gruesome comedy by claiming that Eshkol died as a result of a rocket attack a few days earlier on the kibbutz of Degania B. No such rocket attack had ever taken place, and Eshkol had not been in Degania for months past. The whole nation was saddened by the loss of one of its dearest sons.

Eshkol had intended to run again, believing that he had the physical and mental vigor to continue his duties. However, with his death, Israelis will probably choose among four candidates: two Israeli-born sabras—Minister of Defense Dayan and Deputy Prime Minister Allon—and two, either of whom might have received Eshkol's blessing—the Secretary General of the Labor Party, Pinhas Sapir, and Foreign Minister Eban.

Dayan is a man of immense talent. He has many of the qualities of Machiavelli's Prince, a degree of ruthlessness, personal charisma, a dashing but not reckless physical courage, a calculating objectivity. He was a remarkably successful Chief of Staff and was acclaimed as the architect of victory in the 1956 Sinai campaign. He was less visible in other government posts, but returned to the limelight as Minister of Defense just before the 1967 war. He was, perhaps, given more credit than he deserved for the subsequent Israeli victory but less credit than he deserved for his administration of the occupied territories.

Dayan likes to work on his own, with a free hand and without interference from above. A total individualist, he would, had he been an Englishman or American in World War II, have collected himself a private army. He has been called, often enough, a law unto himself or a lone wolf. It is typical of the man that he has relished these epithets and has never sought to change his ways in the slightest degree. Perhaps the chief objection to him is that he does not care about people as individual human beings. His unconcern for human feelings is matched by his contempt for the views of others. There have, of course, been many prime ministers in history who have had all of Dayan's defects and little of his daring, panache, and quickness of intuition. Dayan is the only man who could become Prime Minister in the teeth of the opposition of the establishment.

Yigal Allon could be a compromise candidate. Like Dayan in his early 50s, Allon is vastly more tactful and vastly more of a team player. This has made him a particularly valued member of the Cabinet, and Eshkol undoubtedly took this into account when he appointed him

Deputy Prime Minister and Minister for refugee absorption.* Allon has all of Dayan's hardihood—he had an outstanding military record in the 1948 war and a more rounded and mature if less dominant personality.

Highly specialized circumstances could favor the candidacy of Abba Eban. He has been a successful Foreign Minister. Earlier, he argued Israel's case before the United Nations with an unmatchable lucidity and cogency. Eban's gifts have so far been employed only in foreign affairs. He has never had time to build up a personal following at home, which has hardly been his fault. Allon, after all, is the favorite son of the palpably still existent Achdut Ha'avoda faction in the Labor party, while Dayan has the backing of the former members of Rafi.

Pinhas Sapir could still emerge as the strongest contender. He is older than Dayan, Allon, and Eban—he was born in 1909. As Secretary General, he is in a dominant position in the reunified Labor party, and he has been relieved of the unpopular post of Minister of Finance, the government's tax-collector, which he inherited from Eshkol in 1963. Sapir is an old guard man par excellence; he knows all there is to know about Labor party organization, about the interacting responsibilities of party and trade unions, about the organization of Cabinet and Knesset business. He is a man of compromise, hard-working, human.

In the question of finding a successor for Eshkol, Mrs. Golda Meir, although she had been in retirement since early in 1968, emerged as a major behind-the-scenes force immediately after the Prime Minister's death. Mrs. Meir had already said in a newspaper interview that she would favor Eshkol's remaining Prime Minister after the 1969 elections. When he died she first supported the maintenance of a caretaker administration under Deputy Prime Minister Yigal Allon, then accepted this task herself when pressed to do so by both the Cabinet and the Labor party. She made no secret of her intention of carrying on only until the elections in the autumn. Her candidate for the premiership after that was Allon, but she would campaign if she had to.

Golda Meir brought to the post of Prime Minister a reputation for strength of character, long experience, and intimate knowledge of all the workings of the Labor party. She had served long years as Minister of Labor and Minister of Foreign Affairs, and had earlier been the first Israeli Minister in Moscow. A formidable matriarch to look

---

* Allon had already shown himself keenly interested in the question of absorption of immigrants. His view was that there should be heightened cooperation between Israel and the Diaspora in securing increased immigration, and he did not subscribe to Ben-Gurion's thesis that one should go on insisting that the State of Israel was exclusively the achievement of the Jews who settled there. But Allon maintains that Israel must have her own image, which should never be that of "Little America in Asia," and that everything possible should be done to secure more immigrants from Western countries—the figure of 7400 in 1967 was considered nowhere near good enough, and was one reason for Allon's appointment.

at, she had been called, jokingly, "the only man in Ben-Gurion's Cabinet" some years earlier. Her dedication was expressed in her thought that the worst moment of her life was when she had to buy herself a new hat, out of her country's money, when presenting her credentials in the Kremlin. Behind her formidable exterior there were wit, charm, and an abiding love of humanity. She was 70 years old when she took office in March 1969, making no Cabinet changes and maintaining the existing government of "national unity."

1. *Jerusalem Post,* September 30, 1968.
2. *Jewish Chronicle* (London), October 8, 1968.
3. The *Guardian* (London), January 28, 1969.
4. *The Jewish Observer and Middle East Review,* October 25, 1968.
5. Eshkol, in personal conversation with the author.
6. Walter Eytan, *The First Ten Years,* p. 204.
7. Harold Jackson, in the *Guardian,* June 15, 1968.
8. *Ibid.*
9. David Horowitz, in personal conversation with the author.
10. In a speech to the United Israel Appeal Mission, from Montreal.
11. In a speech made at a dinner in New York, September 8, 1968.
12. Eshkol, in personal conversation with the author.
13. In a letter to the *Times* (London), June 27, 1967.
14. *Israel Digest,* December 15, 1967.
15. Arnon, in personal conversation with the author.
16. The *Times* (London), September 15, 1967.
17. Eshkol, in personal conversation with the author.
18. Eshkol, in personal conversation with the author.
19. Eshkol, in personal conversation with the author.
20. Eshkol, in personal conversation with the author.
21. Eshkol, in personal conversation with the author.

21.

On January 24, 1969, when Eshkol announced that he would stand again for the post of Prime Minister,[1] he utilized the occasion for a statement on foreign policy. Israel's goal remained lasting peace, which could only be secured after face-to-face talks with the Arabs. Israel did not want territorial aggrandizement: "My formula is that I do not want to rule over areas heavily populated by Arabs." Israel would continue to strike back, to discourage terrorist activity, and Eshkol justified the Beirut raid on the ground that it had done just that: "It has resulted in quiet along parts of the lines." He expected the United States to continue to give sympathy and help to Israel, and he did not believe that another war in the Middle East was imminent. Israel would remain ready for peace, but determined to defend herself if the need should arise.

Eshkol, on an earlier occasion, had a word to add on the longer-term aims of his government and his country.[2]

> We want to go on building up our democratic state, founded on a do-it-yourself philosophy. We shall give our state good and stable government, and we shall use it to express our identity, channel our talents, and make our contribution to Jewry and to humanity. We shall preserve the best and most positive traditions of Jewish history, Jewish belief—in fact, of Jewishness.
>
> On the soil of Israel we are developing an independent Israeli way of life, which has blossomed with the growth of the State and community. This way of life is founded on the Bible and its culture, the revival of the Hebrew language, the transition to a life of labor in a complete society, on the ingathering of the exiles, their emotional consciousness of a return to Zion as a special source of inspiration, finally on the epic of the return to the land and its defense against all adversaries.

Israel's principal long-term internal problem, Eshkol told me, was to equate religious tradition with present-day social existence. The basis of compromise should be mutual toleration of the religious and the less religious elements of the population. Israel's principal long-term external problem was to find a modus vivendi with her Arab neighbors. Eshkol added: "Nasser is certainly the biggest obstacle to peace, because of Egypt's considerable influence in the area and because he has obstructed King Hussein's peace feelers." The next biggest obstacle was expansionist Soviet pressure in the Middle East. Israel, as Eshkol saw it, would have to go on developing her international relations in order to offset this Soviet pressure; otherwise it would seriously upset the balance of power in the Middle East—something which Israel could regard only with the gravest concern.

Eshkol was one of the most fundamentally optimistic men whom

I have ever met—by which I do not mean that he fondly supposed that everything would automatically go right for him and his country, but rather that there was no problem which could not be solved by understanding and forethought. He would have readily admitted that the deadly crescent of her Arab neighbors fences Israel in with more external problems than any small nation in history has had to face. To mention the most obvious, there are the violent hostility of the Arab world, its chaotic instability, the rising tide of Palestinian terrorism, the sinister influence of Soviet penetration, and the ever-escalating arms race. Israel, after 20 years of successful struggle, still presents the picture of a small, encircled community, under constant pressure while it tries to create social justice and humanitarian rule, evolve its own identity, link itself with world Jewry, and find a meeting place for modern Israel with Jewish eternity. Israel is trying to create a kind of embryonic "great society" on a small, beleaguered base which has necessarily to be used as a military launching pad.

Take a closer look, then, at the most pressing of Israel's external problems. First, the hostility of the Arab world is as great as ever, if not greater. The Arabs still regard Israel as an alien intrusion, still demand the reversal of what happened, not just in 1967, but in 1948 as well. They still preach and believe in the total annihilation of the State of Israel, and regard the 1967 war—admittedly a dreadful blow to their dignity and pride—as just another "round" in a war to the death. This continuity of belief in revenge has been well described by one spokesman for the Arab cause.

> What, after all, is irretrievably lost? An army, some reputations, perhaps a few scraps of territory—a minuscule Alsace-Lorraine. And what remains? A physical presence in all the Arab lands that surround Israel, a rapidly growing population unversed in, but no longer ignorant of, modern techniques and practices; tremendous economic resources in the shape of three quarters of the world's oil reserves; the backing of the whole Eastern bloc . . . and, most potent and incalculable of all, the terrible frustration of a people that feels itself victimized, humiliated, ground down. The Jews, indeed, should understand.[3]

More than a year later, the same writer reported from Beirut: "The talk is all of 'biding our time' until Israel goes the same way as the Crusader kingdom. . . . If I were an Israeli, I should be disturbed at the thought of this implacable and unhurried hostility."[4]

Arab hostility is epitomized in the person and policies of Nasser —a man of great patriotism, personality and drive, but a genius *manqué*. He has had a huge problem on his hands in the shape of the population explosion in Egypt. He has needed international good will to help solve this problem. Instead of seeking it, he has operated in the field of foreign affairs on a basis of guile, brutality, and threat, with the copious use of the begging bowl, proffered unashamedly to both East and West. While continually preaching the virtues of "national dignity," he has been an abject example of failure to understand what the first elements of human dignity are. Nasser has no rival in the Arab Middle East, but that has not induced him to show any love of his fellow Arabs. He plotted King Hussein's assassination, vilified traditionalist Arab rulers, made unsuccessful grabs at Syria and the Sudan, and launched a cruel war against the Arabs of Yemen.

Eshkol was doubtless right to see in Nasser the chief obstacle to peace. But a whole generation of Arabs is equally opposed to it. Lebanon is regarded as the most peaceful and "moderate" of the Arab states. Yet the Lebanese Foreign Minister said on a visit to London "Our generation considers that there will never be peace negotiations with Israel, or a peace treaty with Israel. By 'our generation,' I mean people like myself, the present leaders in the Middle East."[5]

Arab hostility is doubtless the most worrying of Israel's external problems; but the chaotic instability of the Arab world does not rank far behind. Internal chaos does not mean only inability to wage war; it means inability to make peace. The specter of revolution stands beside every Arab ruler in the Middle East. And revolution may not necessarily come from empty bellies or the lack of democratic liberties; it is just as likely to come if any Arab ruler makes any concession to the Israeli enemy. So far, only President Bourguiba of Tunisia has felt himself strong enough to make what is primarily a concession to common sense, in the admission that Israel almost certainly cannot be beaten by force of arms. But Bourguiba's contention still is that Israel has to be beaten, by the slower and less dramatic process of step-by-step economic absorption into the Arab world.

By 1969 Iraq had probably taken over from Syria as the archexample of chronic and chaotic internal instability. Only a few years before, an Iraqi prime minister had defined Arab aims in high-minded terms—the search for intellectual independence; the creation of a coherent historical tradition; the reliance on the "real" Islam, based on the Book of God and the revelations of His Prophet; the betterment of the life of the Arab peoples.[6] By 1968 this patriotic Iraqi was in jail, accused of the altogether improbable crime of plotting with the Israelis. In July 1968 Iraq's worst dictator came to power, Abu Baqr, a man who can be described only as a bloodthirsty bandit. No Iraqi parliament has met since 1958.

Syria was in little better shape, with a stagnant economy and a nihilist left-wing Baath government and a recurring struggle for power among its leaders. Its most enlightened socialist, Michel Aflaq, was living in exile in Brazil. Lebanon teetered unsteadily between Christian and Moslem factions but, left to itself, could still look after its own affairs. Jordan, on the other hand, knew that it would not be left alone. With Egyptian and Syrian backing, the Palestinian terrorists, who had now fastened like leeches onto Jordan, had begun to bid for control of the state. There were, indeed, two regimes, one royal and one guerilla. The subjects of the latter lived in their armed camps, outside the law of the land. They mounted their own military operations, and their leaders made no secret of their contempt for the Jordanian monarchy. One of them, Ahmed Shukheiry, stated openly that it was necessary to destroy the regime in Amman before destroying the regime in Tel Aviv.

The threat of guerilla revolt probably had much to do with Hussein's decision to go to war with Israel in June 1967, a criminally foolish decision if it is remembered that he had an "air fleet" of exactly 23 Hawker Hunters and an entirely unprepared army. It probably had much to do, too, with his statement of readiness to renounce sovereignty over the west bank of Jordan, if this would help towards a peace settlement.[7] Hussein subsequently denied having made this offer, but his disclaimer lacked conviction. The threat of guerilla revolt certainly prompted his later statement to the London *Sunday Times*.[8] In it he said that he "did not want to control or suppress" the guerillas, because they were "the fighting arm of the Palestinian people"; and he added that "the Jordanians will throw in their lot with the freedom fighters if there is no alternative in the form of a peace settlement." Only two months previously. Hussein had suppressed the extremist guerila organization *Kataeb-al-Nasr* (Phalanxes of Victory) in bloody fighting in the streets of Amman, and his troops had broken up demonstrations in which 10,000 people took part.

It is doubtful whether Hussein could risk a second showdown of this kind. One million of Jordan's 1,700,000 inhabitants are Palestinians. There is a strong Palestinian element in both government and army, and Palestinians comprise 65 percent of the population of Amman. The Palestinians set up at the end of 1968 a political body of their own, called the National Coalition[9] headed by the Nasserite former Prime Minister of Jordan, Suleiman Nabulsi. He was alleged to have demanded a switch to a pro-Nasser, pro-Soviet foreign policy and the purchase of arms from the Soviet Union. Often in the past, Hussein's regime has looked in danger but has survived; one can only say that it was, by 1969, in greater danger than ever before, with the Palestinian guerillas constituting a "state within the state" and 20,000 Iraqi troops still encamped on Jordanian soil.

There remains Egypt. In May 1968 Nasser held a referendum on his promised political reforms. They were approved by a vote of 99.989 percent. This result, combined with those of two previous referendums, marks Nasser as an even more efficient mobilizer of votes than Adolf Hitler or East Germany's Walter Ulbricht. The vote gave only an illusion of strength. Nasser was a sick man; he had been to the Soviet Union for medical treatment a few months earlier, without any details' being published about his complaint. Foreign visitors to Cairo in 1968 and 1969 found him tired and dispirited. The Six-Day War was not merely a shattering blow to Egyptian prestige and morale; it brought higher taxation, a slowing-down of industrial production, the blocking of the Suez Canal, and an end, at least for the time being, of the struggle to keep national growth ahead of the soaring birth rate.

The blocking of the Canal will have long-term results. At a rough estimate, Egypt is losing $340 million a year in Canal dues but is receiving an equalization subsidy from the oil-rich states of $230 million. In each of the two years since the 1967 war Egypt has lost at least $100 million. In theory these losses would cease once the Canal is reopened; in practice, this is not so. Since the Canal was blocked, by Nasser's own orders, maritime nations have ordered 150 jumbo-sized tankers, which are too large to pass through the Canal and will therefore use the Cape route. Charterers of tankers have been able to increase freight rates sevenfold. In the long run, the supertankers will be cheaper than small tankers using the Canal route. Moreover, the closing of the Canal has constricted activity in the Red Sea by both Egypt and her ally, the Soviet Union. The extra penny-halfpenny on a gallon of gasoline was a reasonable price for Britain to pay, as long as Nasser was prevented from some new adventure, like trying to seize power in Aden or to close the mouth of the Red Sea to international shipping.

After the Six-Day War, Nasser was able at first to conceal the extent of the disaster from the Egyptian people. From claiming sensational victories during the war itself,* the Egyptian propaganda machine turned to whipping up hatred against Israel and the Western powers. There was never any serious attempt to tell the truth to the Egyptian people, for one of the basic factors in Nasserite rule is their perpetual and blatant deception; but the trials and purges of army officers gave the public some idea of how badly things had gone. By the spring of 1968 there were signs of popular unrest and in November there were serious riots, with students taking the leading part but with the Moslem Brotherhood and extreme left wing groups also involved. Among the students' demands were freedom of the press, the banning of the use of force against the civil population, and the release from jail of all prisoners who had merely expressed their political views. For the first time, there were signs of active opposition to Nasser's authoritarian regime.

It is typical of Nasser's refusal to allow Egyptians to face facts

* "The first day's commmuniqués were greeted with shouts, arm-waving and bear-hugs by the crowds around the loud speakers. These reported air victory after air victory by Egyptians, Jordanians, and Syrians—and by nightfall, with 150 Israeli planes having been shot down, the battle was as good as won." Michael Wall, from Cairo, in the *Manchester Guardian,* June 14, 1967. He was not allowed to send his report from Cairo, and sent it from Athens, after leaving for Rome.

that his thoughts turned very soon after the Six-Day War to plans for massive rearmament. Dayan very rightly remarked that "while we spend our time wondering how to achieve peace, the Arabs are spending their time considering how to go to war again."[10] Fifteen months after the war, the Institute of Strategic Studies in London estimated that the Egyptian armed forces had grown from 170,000, before the 1967 war, to 211,000.[11] Egypt's tank strength had been brought up from 250 to 570 in a year, and the airforce had received 400 new planes from the Soviet Union since the Six-Day War. Syria's armed forces actually had far more tanks and aircraft at the end of 1968 than at the time of the Six-Day War, 350 tanks against 200 and 150 strike aircraft against 95. Jordan had more men under arms than ever before, and her airforce was in the process of being brought up to 40 strike aircraft, against 23 in 1967. Iraq's air strength was up from 100 to 215, and 20,000 of her troops now sit permanently within a short march of the Israeli frontier.

Egypt remained the principal threat to Israel's security and at the end of 1968 it was estimated that nearly 600 heavy guns had been massed by Egypt along the Suez Canal—the biggest concentration of fire power in the Middle East since the British victory at El Alamein over Rommel's Afrika Korps in October 1942.[12] Israel has not been able to relax her vigilance for a moment. Indeed, the French ban on arms shipments to her, and the long delay before the United States government authorized the delivery of the 50 Phantoms, convinced the Israeli government that Israel's own arms production must be stepped up. Israel was, by the end of 1968, building two new types of transport planes and had set up a factory at Beth-Shemesh for making engine parts for her French Mirages. The production of a prototype Israeli tank was under discussion, and big strides had been made in the production of artillery weapons.

There were rumors, too, that Israel might produce her own nuclear bombs. Experts believe that Israel now has a supply of unseparated plutonium sufficient to make two nuclear bombs a year and that Israel may have some small-scale separation facility. Nasser has stated that he would seek nuclear weapons if Israel ever obtained them. Eshkol said on several occasions that Israel will not be the first to enter the field of nuclear weaponry. Why should she, when she understands so well how to use conventional weapons? On the whole, it is reasonable to hope that Israel's 24-megawatt reactor at Dimora will continue to be used for purely peaceful purposes. Nuclear warfare in the Middle East would mean virtual genocide, for both Israel and Egypt.

It is reasonable to hope, too, that the Soviet Union will actively discourage the extension of Middle East warfare into the nuclear field, however mischievous Soviet policy has been in respect to encouraging an arms race in conventional weapons. Within a year of the Six-Day

War the Soviet Union had replaced $1.2 billion of military hardware lost by the Arabs, poured an army of 25,000 technicians into Middle East countries, and established a naval task force in the eastern Mediterranean. This task force, based mainly at Alexandria and Port Said, consisted initially of two large cruisers, nine destroyers, and twenty-four submarines. The strength of the force has fluctuated considerably since July 1967, but has never been equivalent to the 60 ships of the American Sixth Fleet, with its two large aircraft carriers and 200 strike aircraft. Late in 1968 the Soviet government was reported to be negotiating for the use of a base at Tartus in Syria, and of bases in Algeria. One particular Israeli fear was that the Soviet Union would assist Algerian-backed revolutionaries to overthrow the monarchy in Morocco, and that Soviet naval bases would be set up on the Atlantic and Mediterranean sides of the Straits of Gibraltar.

One may note, in passing, that the situation along the coasts of the Mediterranean has been transformed since 1945. Until then, they were under exclusive European control. Today, the entire southern and eastern coasts of the Mediterranean, from the Straits of Gibraltar to the Turkish-Syrian frontier, apart from Israel's short stretch of coastline, are controlled by "emergent" Arab nations. The Mediterranean has ceased to be a European lake, and a by-product of the changed situation has been the new Soviet naval presence there. The new vulnerability of the West is illustrated by the fact that three NATO powers, Italy, Turkey, and Greece, are almost totally dependent on supply by sea. The West's sole surviving strategic advantage is the control of two of the three outlets from the Mediterranean, the Straits of Gibraltar and the Dardanelles.

Arab hostility, Arab instability, Palestinian intransigence and Soviet infiltration are four of the principal negative factors in the Middle East situation. Taken in conjunction with one another, they comprise a formidable barrier to any Middle East peace settlement. They furnish a commentary, not only on the desperate nature of Israel's quest for peace, but also on the hopelessness of the situation of the Palestinians. It may be apposite to remark here that no Arab ruler has ever lifted a finger to help them—in legalistic terms, "without prejudice." Jordan sought to incorporate as many Palestinians as possible within her boundaries. Syria cast a selfish and covetous eye on Palestine. Nasser regarded the Palestinians as a pawn in his quest for power. The Palestinians have, in truth, never been regarded by the rest of the Arab world as a potentially viable entity. They have never been regarded as other than a potential appendage to Greater Egypt, Greater Syria, or Greater Jordan.

The season has now begun in which a little thought is at last being spared for the Palestinians. One observer has proposed a Jordanian-Palestinian federation, stating, "I believe there is no possibility of peace unless the conditions are created whereby the Palestinians—the original occupants of the territory through several millennia—are brought into the task of creating peace."[13] Israeli leaders have thrown out their own ideas on an independent Palestinian entity, even though it would comprise no more than the west bank and the Gaza Strip. Behind these ideas is the concept, still a misty one, of some kind of federal link between Israel, Jordan, and an independent Palestine. There are Israelis who see this sort of arrangement as offering a solution to the problem of Jerusalem; it could become the capital of the new "confederation." Here is an idea for future Israeli governments, for it would necessarily be left to Israelis to develop it constructively; Arab thinking is still too confused. A "confederation" would, at least, dispose of the problem of what to do with the occupied territories, whose population has remained passive and desirous of peace.

It would be a consoling thought that a solution to this and other Middle East problems could be assisted by the United Nations. So far, this has not seemed likely. The United Nations partition plan was the prelude to the 1948 War of Independence, which the United Nations were powerless to stop. Nor did the United Nations feel able to intervene when Egypt blockaded the Gulf of Aqaba in 1956, thus provoking an Israeli military response. The withdrawal of the United Nations Emergency Force was an important factor contributing to the renewal of war in June 1967. Thereafter, the Jarring mission struggled unavailingly to promote peace.

Israel has developed a suspicion of the United Nations. This is understandable but could become obsessive. It is understandable because Israeli delegates to the United Nations have had to fight an everlastingly uphill battle. Israel is a small country, and the United Nations put aside little time to consider Israel's interests. The hostile Arab lobby is not always effectual, but it is numerous. Israel's case can be stated, but at least eight Arab countries will rise to state the countercase; while in the Security Council Israel's case is prejudged by both the Arab and Soviet bloc lobbies. In the Security Council Israel's interests were further prejudiced in 1969 by the departure in rotation of Canada, Denmark, and Ethiopia, and by the election of Spain and Zambia. The Israeli battle for understanding in the United Nations has become even more uphill than before. It was typical of United Nations lobbying methods that Israel was sharply condemned for the December 1968 raid on Beirut, but got no sympathy for the whole series of Arab terrorist attacks. In a letter to the London *Times*,[14] Lord Donaldson referred to the famous cartoon by Low which showed a Japanese invader of Manchuria complaining that the Chinese had "hit me in the fist with his face." Arab complaints against Israel sometimes have the same flavor.

Writing in the *Israel Year Book, 1968,* Eshkol expressed the view that the Six-Day War had a tremendously positive result, in that "the consciousness of the age-old unity of the Jewish people the world over was reawakened." That consciousness is never totally dormant, but there has never been a time when it has needed to be more wary, more active, and more imaginative. For the crucial problems which concern Israel and an Israeli Prime Minister are not restricted to the country's security and place in the Middle East, let alone to such mundane matters as expanding industry and boosting exports. In *A History of the Jewish People,* Parkes raised a few questions of a more general nature which concern Israel as the young, hard kernel of world Jewry.

For instance, how will Israel maintain and develop her links with the Diaspora? What will happen to Soviet Jewry? Will British and French Jewry and, in time, American Jewry, too, become assimilated and ultimately un-Jewish? Will ghetto orthodoxy be converted, both inside and outside Israel, into evolutionary religion? There is, in fact, a "Jewish Commonwealth," and every one of its problems is Israel's problem too.

The maintenance of her links with the Diaspora will be Israel's second most important task in the future, next to the safeguarding and consolidation of her own statehood. Eshkol was a Prime Minister well suited for discharging this task. He never, like Ben-Gurion, spoke disparagingly of the Jews of the Diaspora; he remained keenly aware of their hopes and dreams, their doubts and inhibitions. The Jews of the Diaspora felt deeply for Israel in her hour of need and contributed much. Millions gave time and money, thousands went to Israel to help in the war effort. But few stayed on to settle there. Through the years, Ben-Gurion has tried to goad the Jews of the Diaspora into immigrating to Israel. This was not the way to secure increased immigration. Eshkol, had he lived a little longer, would have used more persuasive, more subtle methods.

Eshkol's preoccupation with Soviet Jewry was intense, but to help the Jews of the Soviet Union to preserve their identity is next to impossible. Judging from this account, Soviet Jewry is doomed:

> I received a detailed account of Jewish life in Kiev. Anyone who teaches his children Torah takes a dreadful risk. One who talks to a guest from abroad is reprimanded. They no longer imprison new offenders, but those incarcerated two years ago for the crime of "Jewish nationalism" have yet to be released. Jews are haunted by a relentless insecurity, afraid to speak Yiddish in the street, afraid to approach the government or even their own leaders with religious requests. Anti-Semitism is common among the general populace; Jews are made to suffer from it, but it is forbidden to talk, forbidden to complain.

Who knows what the day will bring? The Jewish spirit is deteriorating rapidly; it cannot hold out much longer.[15]

The plight of Soviet Jewry is, indeed, grim. Their survival depends now on the strength of their traditions and their spiritual staying power. Soviet policy is to wear down both.*

Soviet Jewry is being forced to assimilate; American, British, and French Jewry is merely free to do so if it wishes. One can kill as effectively by kindness as by violence or stealth. Plenty of Jews do assimilate in the Western democracies. But the Jewish communities there are being given one lease on life by the "malaise" which is sweeping the Western world, a compound of ebbing self-confidence, inability to tackle root problems, apathy, and a diminishing zest for life. The values which Jewry has treasured, partly because they have been so hard to preserve, should stand the Jewish communities of the West in good stead. And they can be given another lease on life if Israel becomes the model state which it seeks to be.

The problem of ghetto orthodoxy versus evolutionary religion will probably have to be solved in Israel herself. It may turn out to be one of the hardest nuts of all to crack. When I asked Eshkol his views, he was somewhat inconclusive in his answers.[16] Religion was embedded and entwined in Jewish history. It went beyond, far beyond, attendance at the synagogue or participation in religious festivals. Its essence was a sense of the eternal. But Eshkol had a certain distaste for latter-day "scribes and Pharisees." His feeling was that religious "die-hards" could not see the wood for the trees; they often opposed the concept of Israel, and in the United States such "ultras" even refused to visit the country. This sort of thinking was foreign and inimical to Eshkol, with his rooted belief in compromise. But it has to be admitted that Eshkol barely made a start during six years as Prime Minister on the reappraisal of religion's role in Israeli life which may have to come some day. Rather, he appeared to accept the status quo, believing that Israel's religious life must look after itself until her survival as a state has been assured. He may well have been right.

He had, after all, spent 55 years of his life in what was first Palestine, then Israel. He saw Turkish rule swept away after five centuries. He saw the brave beginning and miserable end of the experiment of the British Mandate, spanning nearly 30 years. He was involved in no fewer than five wars; two of them world wars, then the War of Inde-

---

* At the "Martyrs and Heroes Remembrance Day" celebrations in April 1968 Eshkol said that the Soviet Union was working for the "spiritual extinction" of Soviet Jewry, and that Poland's undemocratic, inhuman persecution of the Jews was designed to cover up the failures of the Gomulka regime. It is noteworthy that, as in Rumania and Czechoslovakia, there was a wave of popular admiration in Poland for Israel's military achievement in June 1967. The joke was current in Warsaw that "Polish Jews" had defeated "Russian Arabs."

pendence in 1948, the Sinai campaign in 1956, the Six-Day War in 1967. In the 1920s and 1930s there was, in addition, intermittent civil war. Fifty-five years, packed with so much experience, entitled a statesman to approach his problems with measured circumspection.

The Jews, and the Israelis, are perfectionists. They recognized in Ben-Gurion a great man, but impatiently dismissed his eccentricities in old age. They saw in Eshkol an ordinary Jew, and they will surely come to recognize something symbolic in his achievement—which proved that to an ordinary Jew, all things are possible. At the same time they have been very human in criticizing this "ordinary" man. Eshkol was taken to task for being lackluster, too fond of compromise, a poor public speaker, unable to make up his mind in a crisis, without imagination, a mere symbol of the Labor establishment. His good qualities were recognized too, so criticism has not been automatic but, rather, held tenaciously in reserve.

He took the big plunge of emigrating from one continent to another, while still in his teens. He stood up to real hardship to get to Palestine, and even more to stay there; the gravestones of Rishon and Hadera are mute testimony to the fate of so many of his contemporaries. He fought in two wars and helped to plan victory in three more.

Eshkol played an epic role in the settlement of the land and in the supplying of the whole country with water. He helped to organize his nation's means of defense, its trade union machinery, and its principal political party. He planned the nation's economy over 12 of its first 15 crucial and formative years. A man who had never sought power, he became Prime Minister, and he led his country through its greatest crisis of all. Almost without intermission, he planned for the reunification of the Labor party, which had been the mainspring of Israel's political, social and economic development.

Eshkol's true achievement is that he utilized in the fullest measure every talent that he possessed—always in the interest first of the Jewish, and then the Israeli community which he loved. Truly, he deserved well of his country and his people.

1. In an interview given to the newspaper, *Dvar Hashavua*.
2. Eshkol, in personal conversation with the author.
3. Michael Adams, in the *Manchester Guardian*, June 15, 1967.
4. Michael Adams, *Chaos and Rebirth*, 1968, p. 10.
5. Fuad Butros, May 28, 1968.
6. Al-Bazzaz, in a pamphlet entitled *On Arab Nationalism*, 1965.
7. Gavin Young, in the *Observer* (London), December 14, 1968.
8. Frank Giles, deputy editor, in the *Sunday Times* (London), January 19, 1969.
9. *The Jewish Observer and Middle East Review*, November 8, 1968.
10. Dayan, in an interview given to Geula Cohen, *Ma'ariv*, September 22, 1968.
11. Institute of Strategic Studies, *The Miltary Balance 1968/9*, published September 14, 1968.

12. *Jewish Chronicle* (London), December 9, 1968.
13. Tom Little, in the *Times* (London), December 30, 1968.
14. The *Times* (London), January 5, 1969.
15. Elie Wiesel, "Jews of Silence," from the *Jewish Chronicle,* January 3, 1969.
16. Eshkol, in personal conversation with the author.

Bibliography

Adams, Michael, *Chaos and Rebirth,* London: BBC Publications, 1968.
———, *Suez and After,* Boston: Beacon Press, 1958.
Aldington, Richard, *Lawrence of Arabia,* London: Collins, 1955.
Antonius, George, *The Arab Awakening,* London: Hamish Hamilton, 1938.
Atiyah, Edward, *The Arabs,* London: Pelican Books (revised ed.), 1955.
Avneri, Uri, *Israel Without Zionists,* New York: Crowell-Collier-Macmillan, 1968.
Baratz, Joseph, *Village by the Jordan,* London: Harvill Press, 1954.
Ben-Gurion, David, *Israel: Years of Challenge,* London: Blond; 1966.
Ben-Zvi, Rachel, *Coming Home,* Tel Aviv: Massadah Press, 1963.
Bentwich, Norman, *Israel Resurgent,* London, Benn, 1952.
———, *Wanderer Between Two Worlds,* London: Kegan Paul, 1941.
Berlin, Isaiah, *Chaim Weizmann,* London: Weidenfeld and Nicolson, 195 .
Boothby, Lord, *My Yesterday, Your Tomorrow,* London: Hutchinson, 1962.
Bullard, Sir Reader, *Britain and the Middle East,* New York: Hutchinson, 1951.
Campbell, J. C., *The Defense of the Middle East,* New York: Harper & Row, 1958.
Cantor, Leonard, *A World Geography of Irrigation,* Edinburg: Oliver & Boyd, 1967.
Carmichael, Joel, *The Shaping of the Arabs,* New York: Macmillan, 1967.
Childers, Erskine, *The Road to Suez,* London: MacGibbon & Kee, 1952.
Chouraqui, André, *L'Etat D'Israel,* Paris: Presses Universitaires, 1955.
Churchill, Winston, *The Second World War,* Vol. 3, London: Cassell, 1951.
Churchill, Winston and Churchill, Randolph, *The Six Day War,* London: Heinemann, 1967.
Cohen, I., *A Short History of Zionism,* London: Muller, 1954.
Cook, Stanley, *An Introduction to the Bible,* London: Cambridge, 1945.
Cremeans, Charles, *The Arabs and the World,* New York: Praeger, 1963.
Crossman, Richard, *Palestine Mission,* London: Hamish Hamilton, 1947.
Dallin, Alexander, *German Rule in Russia,* New York: St. Martin's, 1957.
Dayan, Moshe, *Diary of the Sinai Campaign,* New York: Schocken, 1967.
Dayan, Yael, *A Soldier's Diary,* London: Weidenfell & Nicholson, 1967.
Douglas-Home, Charles, *The Arabs and Israel,* London: Bodley Head, 1968.
Drabkin, H. D., *The Other Society,* New York: Harcourt, Brace, & World, 1962.
Draper, Theodore, *Israel and World Politics,* London: Becker & Warburg, 1968.
Edelman, Maurice, *Ben-Gurion,* London: Hodder & Stoughton, 1964.
Eden, Anthony, *Full Circle,* London: Cassell, 1960.
Einzig, Paul, *Bloodless Invasion,* London, Duckworth, 1938.
Eisenstadt, S., *The Absorption of Immigrants,* London: Routledge, 1954.
Epstein, Elias, *Jerusalem Correspondent,* Jerusalem: Jerusalem Post Press, 1964.
Eytan, Walter, *The First Ten Years,* New York: Simon and Schuster, 1958.
Forbes-Adam, Colin, *Life of Lord Lloyd,* London: Macmillan, 1948.
Frank, Gerold, *The Deed,* New York: Avon, 1964.
Gale, Sir Richard, *Call to Arms,* London: Hutchinson, 1968.
Gershater, C., *Thirty Days in Israel,* Johannesburg: Jewish Book Center, 1949.

Glubb, Sir John, *Britain and the Arabs,* London: Hodder & Stoughton, 1959.
———, *A Soldier with the Arabs,* London: Hodder & Stoughton, 1956.
———, *Syria, Lebanon, Jordan,* London: Thames & Hudson, 1967.
Graves, Robert, *Lawrence and the Arabs,* London: Jonathan Cape, 1927.
Gruen, George, *Israel, the United States and the United Nations,* New York: American-Jewish Committee, 1969.
Hertzberg, Arthur, *The Zionist Idea,* New York: Harper & Row, 1959.
———, ed., *Jewish Frontier,* New York: Jewish Frontier Association, 1945.
Hiscocks, Richard, *Democracy in West Germany,* London: Oxford, 1957.
Hollingworth, Clare, *The Arabs and the West,* London: Methuen, 1952.
Hurewitz, J. C., *Diplomacy in the Middle East,* New Jersey: Van Nostrand, 1956.
———, *The Struggle for Palestine,* New York: Norton, 1950.
Huxley, Julian, *From an Antique Land,* New York: Crown, 1954.
Kallen, Horace M., *Utopians at Bay,* New York: Stratford, 1958.
Katz, Samuel, *Days of Fire,* London: W. H. Allen, 1968.
Kedourie, Elie, *England and the Middle East,* London: Bowes, 1956.
Kerr, Malcolm, *The Arab Cold War,* London: Oxford, 1964.
Kimche, Jon, *Seven Fallen Pillars,* London: Secker & Warburg, 1950.
———, *Both Sides of the Hill,* London: Secker & Warburg, 1960.
———, *The Unromantics,* London: Weidenfeld & Nicolson, 1968.
Kirk, George, *The Middle East in the War 1939/45,* London: Oxford, 1952.
———, *A Short History of the Middle East* (revised ed.), New York: Praeger, 1964.
Koestler, Arthur, *Promise and Fulfillment,* London: Macmillan, 1949.
Lacqueur, Walter, *The Road to War,* London: Weidenfeld & Nicolson, 1968.
———, *The Middle East in Transition,* London: Routledge, 1958.
———, *Communism and Nationalism in the Middle East,* London: Routledge, 1956.
Landau, Jacob, *The Arabs in Israel,* London: Oxford, 1969.
Lawrence, A. W., *T. E. Lawrence by His Friends,* New York: McGraw-Hill, 1937.
Levin, Harry, *Jerusalem Embattled,* London: Gollancz, 1950.
Lewis, Bernard, *The Middle East and the West,* London: Weidenfeld & Nicolson, 1963.
Lie, Trigve, *Memoirs,* London: Macmillan, 1954.
Litvinoff, Barnet, *Ben-Gurion of Israel,* London: Weidenfeld & Nicolson, 1954.
Litvinoff, Emanuel, *Israel in the Soviet Mirror,* London quarterly, 1965.
Lofhbar, Chazi, *Eshkol,* Tel Aviv: Am Oved, 1965.
Lowenthall, Marvin, *Diaries of Theodor Herzl,* London: Gollancz, 1958.
McDonald, J. G., *My Mission in Israel,* New York: Simon and Schuster, 1951.
McIntyre, Ian, *The Proud Doers,* London: BBC Publications, 1968.
Malamud, Bernard, *The Fixer,* London: Eyre & Spottiswoode, 1967.
Malkosh, Noah, *Histadrut in Israel,* Tel Aviv: Haaretz, 1954.
Mansfield, Peter, *Nasser's Egypt,* London: Penguin, 1966.
Mecker, Owen, *Israel Reborn,* New York: Scribner, 1965.
Meinertzhagen, Richard, *Middle East Diary,* London: Cresset, 1959.
Mikes, George, *Milk and Honey,* New York: Allen & Wingate, 1957.

Miller, William, *The Ottoman Empire and its Successors,* London: Cambridge, 1923.
Monroe, Elizabeth, *Britain's Moments in the Middle East,* London: Chatton and Windus, 1963.
Mosley, Leonard, *Gideon Goes to War,* New York: Scribner, 1955.
Oliphant, Laurence, *Haifa, or Life in Modern Palestine,* London: William Blackwood, 1887.
Parkes, James, *Arabs and Jews in the Middle East,* London: Gollancz, 1967.
_____, *A History of Palestine,* London: Gollancz, 1949.
_____, *A History of the Jewish People,* London: Penguin, 1964.
_____, *The New Face of Israel,* Leeds: University Press, 1964.
_____, *Five Roots of Israel,* London: Valentine Mitchell, 1954.
Pearlman, Moshe, *Ben-Gurion Looks Back,* London: Weidenfeld & Nicolson, 1965.
Plessner, M., *Ist der Zionismus gescheitert,* London: Wiener, 1952.
Poliakov, Leon, *Harvest of Hate,* London: Elek, 1965.
Powell, Ivor, *Disillusion by the Nile,* London: Solstice, 1967.
Preuss, Walter, *The Labour Movement in Israel,* Jerusalem: Reuben, 1965.
Prittie, Terence, *Israel: Miracle in the Desert,* New York: Praeger, 1967.
_____, *Germany Divided,* Boston: Little, Brown, 1960.
Reed, Douglas, *Insanity Fair,* London: Jonathan Cape, 1938.
Robertson, Terence, *Crisis,* London: Hutchinson, 1965.
Robson, Jeremy, *Letters to Israel,* London: Valentine Mitchell, 1968.
Ruppin, Arthur, *Three Decades of Palestine,* Tel Aviv: Haaretz, 1936.
Lord Russell of Liverpool, *The Scourge of the Swastika,* London: Cassell, 1954.
Sacher, Harry, *Israel: The Establishment of a State,* London: Weidenfeld & Nicolson, 1952.
Sachar, Howard, *Aliyah,* Cleveland: World Publishing, 1961.
St. John, Robert, *Israel,* New York: Life Magazine World Library edition, 1962.
Samuel, Horace, *Unholy Memories of the Holy Land,* London: Hogarth, 1930.
Samuel, Maurice, *Blood Accusation,* London: Weidenfeld & Nicolson, 1967.
Sanders, Ronald, *Israel: The View from Masada,* New York: Harper & Row, 1966.
Schechtman, Joseph, *The Refugee in the World,* New York: Barnes, 1964.
Schwarz, Walter, *The Arabs in Israel,* London: Faber, 1959.
Sharef, Zeev, *Three Days,* London: W. H. Allen, 1962.
Shirer, William L., *The Rise and Fall of the Third Reich,* New York: Simon and Schuster, 1960.
Spiro, Melford, *Kibbutz: Venture in Utopia,* New York: Schocken, 1963.
Stein, Leonard, *The Balfour Declaration,* London: Valentine Mitchell, 1961.
_____, *Ben-Gurion,* New York: Doubleday, 1959.
Storrs, Ronald, *Orientations,* London: Nicholson & Watson, 1937.
Sykes, Christopher, *Cross Roads to Israel,* London: Collins, 1965.
_____, *Orde Wingate,* London: Collins, 1959.
Syrkin, Marie, *Golda Meir: Woman with a Cause,* New York: Putnam, 1964.
Taylor, Alan, *Prelude to Israel,* London: Darton, Longman, & Todd, 1959.
Thayer, I. W., *Tensions in the Middle East,* London: Oxford, 1958.

Ullmann, Arno, *Israel: Abenteuer einer neuen Heimat,* Duesseldorf: Droste Verlag, 1961.
Vester Spafford, Bertha, *Our Jerusalem,* Beirut: Middle East Export, 1950.
Weiner, H., *The Wild Goats of Ein Gedi,* New York: Doubleday, 1961.
Weisgal, Meyer, ed., *Chaim Weizmann,* New York: Dial Press, 1944.
Weitz, Raanan, *Agricultural and Rural Development in Israel,* Jerusalem: Jewish Agency, 1963.
Weizmann, Chaim, *Trial and Error,* London: Hamish Hamilton, 1949.
Wheelock, K., *Nasser's New Egypt,* New York: Stephens & Sons, 1960.
Wiesel, Elie, *The Jews of Silence,* London: Valentine Mitchell, 1969.
Young, Peter, *The Israeli Campaign 1967,* London: William Kimber, 1967.

Other Publications:

Sir Reginald Coupland's Papers, Oxford: Rhodes Library, 1939.
Europe Publications, The Middle East and North Africa, London, 1964.
Israel, from The Middle East and North Africa, London: Chatham House.
Israel, Government Year Books.
Israel, Ministry of Defence, *The Six-Days War,* Tel Aviv, 1967.
The Middle East, Royal Institute of International Affairs, London, 1961.
St. Anthony's Papers, Oxford: St. Anthony's College.
C. P. Scott Memorial Volume, Manchester Guardian, 1946.
Chaim Weizmann: Biography by Several Hands, London: Weidenfeld & Nicolson, 1962.

Index

Abdullah, 62, 69, 70, 134, 135, 141, 155, 241
Abraham, 19, 41, 296
Achdut Ha'avoda, 52, 86, 113, 116, 118, 178, 190–192, 195, 209, 212, 213, 215, 218, 220, 299, 330–332, 337
Acre, 63, 77, 80
Aden, 36, 60, 238
Adenauer, Konrad, 177, 203, 206, 226–228, 334
Aegean Sea, xi, 14
Aflaq, Michel, 341
Africa, x, 68, 139, 142, 150, 160, 168, 190, 223, 228, 229, 237
Afrika Korps, 98, 344
Afro-Asian Conference, 161
Afula, 81, 126, 151
Agudat Israel, 52, 53, 190
"Aktion Suehnezeichen," 228
Al Ahram, 252, 256, 311, 312
Al-Bazzaz, 323
Aldington, Richard, 59, 60
Alexander I, 6
Alexander II, 6, 7
Alexandria, 5, 31, 39, 250, 277, 305, 345
Al Fatat, 59
Algeria, 154, 210, 263, 285, 287, 345
Alignment, 212, 213, 219
Aliyah Bet, 99
Aliyah Hanoar, 91
Allenby, General Lord, 38, 53
Alliance Israélite Universelle, 12, 17
Allon, Yigal, 133, 204, 207, 209, 212, 220, 244, 260, 293, 294, 330, 332, 334, 336, 337
Almagor, 243, 274
Almog, Yehudah, 50
Almogi, Joseph, 216
Amer, Field-marshal Hakim, 270
America, 31, 37, 94, 96, 102, 112, 120, 147, 155, 156, 161, 164, 169, 173, 177, 181, 231, 247, 248, 253, 256, 260, 273, 327, 336, 347, 348
American Import-Export Bank, 184

American Zone of Occupation, 102
Amman, 69, 161, 266, 270, 300, 308
Andrews, L. Y., 82
Anglo-American Commission, 1945, 102, 103, 122, 123
Anglo-Egyptian Treaty, 1936, 134
Anglo-Jewish Association, 12
Anschluss, 93
Antonius, George, 58, 59, 63, 64, 109
Aqaba, Gulf of, 59, 70, 122, 129, 158, 159, 162, 163, 165, 167, 168, 170, 173, 185, 186, 251–257, 259–263, 274, 280, 282, 291, 294, 319, 346
Arab Higher Committee, 82
Arabia, 5, 16, 60, 62, 69, 97
Arabian peninsula, 60–62
Arab League, 141, 158, 159, 162, 164, 187
Arab Legion, 128, 129, 132, 169, 268
Arab National Committee, 141
Arab Summit Conference, 1967, ix, 278, 300, 314
Arab Trade Unions, 256
Arad, 170, 186
Aranne, Zalman, 209
Arava, 170, 186, 187
Aref, President, 248
Argentina, 224, 274
Arieli, Professor Y., 199, 204
Arlosoroff, Chaim, 88
Armenia, 8, 29, 64
Arnon, Yakov, 329
Ashawi, Minister, 244
Ashdod, 216, 220, 254, 301, 329
Ashkelon, 118, 119, 185, 329
Ashkenazi, 6, 150
Asia, x, 34, 51, 139, 142, 150, 190, 221, 228, 237, 254, 256, 337
Asiphat Nivarim, 68
Aswan Dam, 161
Atarot, 26, 27, 45
Ataturk, Mustafa Kemal, 145
Athens, 305, 306, 327
Atiyah, Edward, 64, 141
Attassi, President Noreddin, 241, 242, 246, 248, 250, 262, 263, 267

Attlee, Clement, 121, 122
Auschwitz, 96
Australia, 39, 125
Austria, 7, 93, 94, 96, 102, 111, 190, 210
Avidar, Alouf, 83
Avon, Lord, *see* Eden, Anthony

Baathist party, 241, 276, 341
Babi Yar, 232
Babylon, 5, 139
Bagdad, 61, 97, 100, 144, 322, 323
  pact of, 161
Bahrein, xii, 163
Balfour, Lord, 33, 36–38, 69, 71, 151, 153
Balfour Declaration, xiii, 16, 33, 37–39, 42, 53, 64–66, 69, 70, 73, 101, 109, 128
Balkans, 61, 95, 284
Ballin, Albert, 88
Banias, 235, 268, 292
Bank of Israel, 10, 176, 179, 182, 206, 325
Baqr, President Abu, 341
Baratz, Joseph, 14, 22, 44
Bardawil, 307
Barker, General Sir Evelyn, 124, 125
Bar-Kochba, 5, 16, 114, 115
Bar-Lev, Haim, 306, 307
Barksy, A., 14
Baruch, Chaim, 24
Bar-Yosef, Yosef, 282
Barzilai, I., 198
Basle, 10, 12, 35
Basra, 61, 100
Bat Golim, 159
Beaton, Leonard, 319
Beck, Col. Joseph, 90
Bedouin, xiii, 14, 19, 47, 64, 66, 67, 69
Beeley, Sir Harold, 305
Beersheba, 16, 78, 126, 133, 149, 150, 185, 186
Beigin, Menahem, 113, 133, 178, 217–219, 227, 289, 299
Beiliss, Mendel, 9
Beirut, 58, 76, 156, 240, 305, 306, 339, 340
Beit Netufa, 187, 188
Beit Zera, 45, 56

Belgium, 35, 267
Ben-Gurion, David, 20, 21, 30, 31, 42, 76, 83, 86, 112, 116, 119, 120, 131, 134, 138, 149, 151, 160, 166, 168, 170, 172, 175, 177–179, 185, 194, 195, 197–210, 212–221, 226, 227, 235, 257, 264, 285, 287, 299, 324, 330–338, 347, 349
Bentwich, Norman, 23, 54
Ben Yehuda, Eliezer, 25
Ben-Zvi, President, 31
Ben-Zvi, Rachel, 26, 30
Berlin, ii, 36, 92, 295
Berlin, Isaiah, 36, 152
Bernadotte, Count Folke, 114, 133, 134
Besor, 186
Bethlehem, 117, 288, 290, 293, 296
Beth-Shemesh, 344
Bevin, Ernest, 102, 122–127
Bialystock, 19
Bible, 3, 69, 117, 142, 143
Bierenson, 13
Birobidjan, 90
Black Hundreds, 7, 8
Black Sea, 6, 14, 99, 100
Blas, Simha, 80, 81
Bnot, Yakov, 187, 188
Bobruisk, 45
Bolshevik Revolution, xi, 12, 31, 56
Bonn, 159, 177, 226, 227
Boothby, Lord, 167, 169
Boumedienne, President, 285, 287
Bourguiba, President, 240, 285, 341
Brand, Joel, 96
Brenner Pass, 98
British Mandate, 54, 55, 63–69, 71, 75–77, 88, 95, 99, 103, 105, 108–112, 115, 119–129, 138, 146, 174, 189, 233, 268, 276, 309, 348
Brown, George, 253, 255, 256, 263, 285, 313, 316, 319
Bulganin, Marshal, 168
Bull, General Odd, 246, 266
Bunche, Ralph, 134 n.
Bund, Jewish, in Russia, 12, 13
Bundesentschaedigungsgesetz (Law of Compensation), 179
Bundestag, 178
"Burma Road," 130, 132, 136

Byelorussia, 6
Byzantine, 164

Cairo, 61, 64, 111, 113, 126, 133, 156, 163, 195, 198, 230, 242, 246, 248, 250, 252, 253, 256, 259, 270, 277, 305, 310–312, 321
Canaan, land of, 143
Canada, 125, 346
Cape of Good Hope, xi, 329
Caradon, Lord, 313
Carlsbad, 53
Carmel, 16, 18, 19, 23, 78
Carmel, Col. Moshe, 135
Casimir III, 5
Catherine the Great, 6, 164
Caucasus, 8, 28, 97, 163
Cecil, Lord Robert, 63
Central Europe, xiii, 6, 55, 61, 144, 145, 154, 179, 218, 223
Central Powers, World War I, 59
Chamberlain, Houston Stewart, 6
Chamberlain, Joseph, 34, 35
Chamberlain, Neville, iii, 255, 275
Charlemagne, 5
China, Republic of, x, 4, 8, 9, 16, 79, 117, 139, 154, 187, 241, 262, 346
Christ, 8, 9, 16, 79, 117, 187, 262
Christian Democratic Party (CDU), 159, 178, 227, 335
Christianity, xiii, 5, 7, 9, 33, 40, 58, 64, 65, 77, 84, 90, 94, 117, 135, 169, 241, 280, 281, 296, 305, 341
Churchill, Sir Winston, 36, 62, 69–73, 98, 100, 108, 111, 122, 147, 203, 206, 334
Churchill, Jr., Winston, 264, 306
Chuvakhim, Dmitri, 257
Clapp, Gordon R., 155
Cohen, Chief Justice Haim, 197, 198
Cold War, 163, 169, 240
Committee of Seven, 198–200, 204, 214
Communist party, in Israel, 53
in Jordan, 230
Conciliation Commission, 155
Constantinople, xi, 30, 36, 164
Constantinople Convention, 1888, 34, 158, 161, 168
Corfux Channel Case, 255

Council of the Arab League, 158
Coupland, Sir Reginald, 109, 110
Cromer, Lord, 35
Cromwell, Oliver, 5, 84
Crossman, Richard, 122
Crystal Night, 1938, 90
Crusades, xiii, 16, 94, 340
Cunningham, General Sir Alan, 121
Curzon, Lord, 63, 69
Cyprus, 34, 41, 95, 102, 127, 310, 315
Czechoslovakia, viii, x, 94, 119, 125, 129, 132, 162, 232, 348

Dafna, 274
Dalton, Hugh, 122
Damascus, 17, 61, 133, 158, 235, 243, 244, 247, 250, 269, 270
Dan, 268, 274
Dar, Avraham, 196
Dayan, Moshe, 22, 86, 136, 162, 166, 167, 195, 196, 200, 202, 207, 209–213, 216, 218, 227, 232, 235, 260, 271, 282, 293, 294, 299, 300, 309, 330–337, 344
Dayan, Yael, 271
Dead Sea, 16, 42, 142, 170, 185, 186, 188, 220, 221, 254, 270, 317
Debré, Michel, 318
Degania, A, 14, 22, 23, 44–46, 137
B, 45–52, 55, 56, 75, 79–81, 105–107, 115, 136, 137, 147, 189, 336
De Gaulle, General Charles, 206, 223, 234, 272, 278, 285, 309
Deir Yassin, 130
Denmark, 346
Diaspora, 23, 68, 91, 210, 214, 219, 224, 280, 281, 324–331, 347
Dimona, 170, 344
Dinstein, Zvi, 174
Dirlewanger, General Oskar, 225
Displaced persons, 102, 103
Disraeli, Benjamin, 33
Dizengoff, Meir, 131
Djemal Pasha, Ahmed, 29
"Doctors Plot," 230
Dome of the Rock, 109, 296
Donaldson, Lord, 346
Dori, Yakov, 85, 119, 196
Dosh, 218

Dreyfus Affair, 7
Druses, 33, 64, 287
Dulles, John Foster, 161, 168, 169

East Africa, 254
Eastern Europe, 6, 154, 229, 230
Eastern Mediterranean, xi, 14
East German Republic, 154, 226
Eban, Abba, 209, 219, 220, 249, 252, 257, 274, 275, 281, 310, 316, 317, 333, 336, 337
Economic Conference, 1968, 328, 329
Edelman, Maurice, 20, 123
Eden, Anthony, 109, 203
Egypt, viii, xi, xii, 17, 28–30, 33–36, 40, 54, 59, 60, 79, 97, 98, 109, 119, 122, 128, 132–135, 140–143, 155–168, 173, 178, 183, 185, 195–197, 211, 225, 227, 230, 234–236, 241, 242, 246–259, 262–277, 282, 285, 288, 291, 292, 300, 305, 306, 309–321, 326, 339, 340, 344–346
Eichmann, Adolf, 224, 225
Eilat, 133, 134, 158, 162, 168, 170, 173, 185, 220, 250, 254, 262, 267, 329
Eilat, 305, 306
Ein Harod, 85, 86
Eisenhower, President Dwight D., 157
"Eisenhower Doctrine," 169
El Aksa Mosque, 109
El Al airlines, 76, 305–307, 327
El Alamein, 98, 344
El Amr, 251
El Arish, 35, 40, 129, 156, 292, 307
El Assifa, 244
El Fatah, 235, 239, 243–247, 287, 302–306, 323, 336
Eliav, Aryeh, 146, 147
El Sabha, 251
Emek, 77, 80, 151
England, 5, 6, 12, 28, 36, 39–41, 60, 68, 108, 207
Enver Pasha, 30
Erhard, Ludwig, 203, 227, 228
Eshed, Haggai, 200, 201
Eshed Kinrot, 187, 188, 235
Eshkol, Dvora, *see* Rafaeli, Dvora Eshkol
Eshkol, Elisheva Kaplan, 189

Eshkol, Miriam Zelikovitz, 220, 221
Eshkol, Noa, 27, 87
Es Salt, 304
Ethiopia, 346
Etzion bloc, 130, 290, 291, 307
Euphrates, 79, 188
Europe, vii, x, 5, 12, 17, 20, 28, 33, 34, 51, 57, 94, 95, 100, 101, 108, 112, 138, 139, 142, 150, 173, 174, 178, 183, 223, 224, 301, 324, 345
European Common Market, 184
Evening News, 306
Even Shmuel, 149
Evian Conference, 1938, 96
Eytan, Walter, 258
Exodus, 102, 103
"Exportfoerderungsabgabe" (Export Incentive Contribution), 93

Fabian movement, 73
Faisal, King, 59, 62, 65, 66, 70
Faisal-Weizmann Agreement, 66
Falkland Islands, 236
Farouk, King, 97, 160
Fawzy, Mohamed, 250, 259
Fedayeen, 159, 160, 168, 235
Federal German Republic, 159, 223
Federenko, Nikolai, 243, 245
Fianna Fail party, 335
First Crusade, 5
First Jewish Battalion, 32
First World War, *see* World War I
First Zionist Congress, 10, 12, 13, 35
Fisch, Professor Harold, 288, 289
Five Year Economic Plan, 1966, 220
Foreign Press Association, 249
Fraction B of Mapai party, 113
France, 5, 6, 12, 28, 33, 34, 36, 41, 59–65, 70, 96, 119, 128, 132, 136, 154, 160, 162–169, 185, 204, 210, 223, 226, 234, 239, 272, 285, 287, 313, 318, 329, 344, 347, 348
Franconian, 6
Frank, Gerold, 114
Frank, Paul, 195–197
Frankfurter, Felix, 66
Free Democratic Party, 159, 178, 179, 227
Freier, Recha, 91

French Revolution, 116
Freud, Sigmund, 90

Gabbari camp, 31
Gad, 69, 122, 288
Gahal, 218, 245, 260, 289, 299, 334
Galilee, viii, 16, 17, 21, 22, 26, 29, 47, 78–82, 110, 132, 133, 136, 187, 188, 212, 246, 249, 250, 268, 270, 282, 290, 296
Galilee, Sea of, 22, 44, 45, 52, 132, 133, 136, 186–188, 235, 243, 259, 269
Gallipoli, 28, 41
Gallipoli Mule Corps, 31
Garden of Gethsemane, 281
Gaza, 16, 17, 40, 78, 132, 140, 156, 160, 289, 291, 292, 301, 302
Gaza Strip, 118, 133, 149, 155, 156, 186, 250, 270, 286, 287, 291, 292, 299, 301, 303, 309, 311, 312, 346
Gellhorn, Martha, 156
General Assembly of the United Nations, *see* United Nations
General Petroleum Authority, 229
General Zionist Party, 192
George V, King, 134
Georges-Picot, Charles Francois, 62, 63
Germany, 5, 6, 34, 37, 55, 80, 81, 88–103, 111, 154, 160, 164, 174, 177–179, 190, 207, 210, 219, 224–228, 231, 234, 272
Gestapo, 225
Ghor Canal, 187
Gibraltar, 236, 345
Gilboan Hills, 85
Ginzberg, Asher, 12
Givli, Col. Benjamin, 195–198
Gleim, Leopold, 225
Glubb, General Sir John, 69, 78, 129, 161, 169
Gobineau, Comte de, 6
Goebbels, Josef, 90, 225
Goercke, Paul, 225
Golan Mountains, viii, ix, 148, 151, 243, 246, 249, 250, 268–270, 273, 276, 282, 284, 287, 288, 290, 292, 307
Goldberg, Arthur, 40
Goldmann, Nahum, 232

Golomb, Eliahu, 55
Gomulka, Vladimir, 232, 233, 348
Gordon, Aaron David, 14, 44, 172
Government House, 67, 268
Grady, Henry, 125
Grand Mufti, *see* Hal Amin
Graves, Robert, 62
Great Bitter Lake, 277, 315
Great Britain, ix, xii, xiii, 16, 23, 30, 32–41, 46, 53, 54, 59–71, 77, 78, 82, 84, 94–103, 107–116, 123–131, 133, 140, 147, 153, 156, 161–164, 166–169, 177, 182, 183, 195, 204, 207, 209, 211, 213, 223, 226, 232, 234, 236, 239, 253, 255, 256, 259, 263, 271, 273, 274, 278, 285, 305, 313–319, 324, 333, 347, 348
  army of, 7, 31, 38–44, 75, 114, 124, 130, 132, 141, 148
  Consulate of, Odessa, 7, 8
  Consul-General of, Beirut, 58
  Eighth Army of, 98
  Empire of, 68, 128
  High Commissioner of, in Egypt, 60, 61
  High Commissioner of, in Palestine, 67, 71, 84, 100, 113, 116, 121, 126
  See also British Mandate
Great War, *see* World War I
Greece, 28, 95, 145, 345
Greek Orthodox Church, 7
Greenberg, Hayim, 58
Gretchko, Marshal Andrei, 242
Grey, Sir Edward, 37
Gruener, Dov, 125
Gussing, Nils, 321

Ha'am, Ahad, 12
Haavara, 92
Hacohen, David, 55
Hadassah Hospital, 130
Hadera, 26, 349
Haganah, 82–86, 99, 107, 112, 113, 115, 119, 120, 124, 129–132, 136, 138
Hagroshim, 242
Haifa, 63, 73, 77, 78, 80, 81, 85, 89, 99, 100, 102, 110, 121, 129, 133,

Haifa (*Continued*)
  140, 141, 147, 159, 169, 173, 186, 218, 269, 289
Haifa Technion, 327, 328
Haj Amin el Husseini, 67, 72, 82, 84, 97, 109, 126, 128, 141, 164
Halevy, Jacob, 40
Hallstein, Walter, 226
"Hallstein Doctrine," 226
Hamashbir Hamorkazi, 76
Hamburg, 88, 92, 102
Hamid, Sultan Abdul, 34
Hammarskjoeld, Dag, 158, 252
Hapoel Hatzair, 13, 15, 23, 24, 33, 39, 52, 86, 212
Harkavi, Brigadier Jehosophat, 241
Harriman, Averell, 236
Harzfeld, Abraham, 183, 184
Hashemite family, 61, 62, 128
Hashomer, 23
Hausner, Gideon, 198
Havlagah, 82
Haykal, Mohamed Hassanein, 256, 263, 264, 311, 312
Hebrew, vii, 3, 6, 12, 25, 41, 52, 56, 70, 82, 89, 90, 105, 142, 207, 297, 339
Hebrew University, 41, 220
Hebron, xiv, 16, 17, 26, 72, 83, 134, 245, 280, 282, 288, 290, 293, 304
Hejaz, 29, 59, 60, 62
Hejaz railway, 59, 60, 307
Heletz Bror, 185
Heluan, 14
Hermon, Mount, 22, 52, 288
Herod's Temple, 72, 130, 282
Herut, 178, 190, 192, 217, 218, 331
Herzl, Theodor, 4, 12, 13, 34–36, 151
Herzog, Chaim, 209, 217
Hess, Moses, 11
Hevrat Ovdim, 81
Hibbat Zion, 13
Histadrut, 54, 75–77, 81, 83, 86, 87, 105, 115, 116, 118, 185, 192, 197, 200, 201, 216, 220, 335
Hitler, Adolf, xiii, 7, 82, 90, 97, 98, 139, 164, 177, 179, 190, 227, 232, 255, 263, 271, 291
Hod, General Mordechai, 265

Hogarth, Commander D. G., 64
Holland, 94, 96, 125, 258
Hope-Simpson, Sir John, 77, 78
Horeb, Operation, 133
Horowitz, David, 10, 176, 182, 206, 325
Houlé, 239
House of Commons, 108, 121, 128, 236, 255, 256
Hovevei Zion, 13
Huleh swamps, 148, 185, 186
Hungary, 18, 94, 96, 102, 210
Hushi, Abba, 218
Hussein, King, xi, 141, 161, 169, 230, 235, 236, 238, 241, 245, 246, 254, 258, 266–268, 273, 276, 277, 284, 285, 288, 292, 294, 297, 306, 308, 339, 341
Hussein, Sherif, 59–65, 69
Husseini, Abd el Kader, 129

Ibn Saud, King, 61, 62
Ichud movement, 112
Idris, King, 238
Illustrated Sunday Herald, 69
Independent Liberal party, 245
India, 59, 68, 125, 139, 154
Indian Ocean, x, xi, 134, 163, 228
Institute of Strategic Studies, 344
International Civil Air Organization, 158
International Court of Justice, 255
Iran, xi, xii, 161, 163, 185, 230
Iraq, vii, xi, xii, 60, 62, 64, 97, 109, 114, 128, 132, 133, 139, 150, 155, 156, 158, 163, 164, 169, 173, 223, 230, 236, 248, 258, 259, 260, 263–266, 274, 276, 285, 304, 322, 323, 326, 341, 344
Ireland, 114, 124, 287, 293, 335
Irgun Zvai Leumi, 83, 86, 87, 96, 113–115, 124, 125, 130, 131, 133
Islam, 5, 57, 164, 168, 281, 296, 341
Ismailia, 167, 250
Italian-Abyssinian War, 1935, 93
Italy, 28, 35, 60, 93, 98, 99, 154, 164, 210, 322, 335, 345
Ivanov, Yuri, 232
Izvestia, 242, 246

Jabari, Sheik Mohamed, 293
Jabotinsky, Vladimir, 31–33, 72, 76, 83, 86–88, 92, 109, 113, 214, 217
Jaffa, xiii, 14, 16–20, 23–25, 67, 73, 82, 83, 101, 110, 129, 133, 140
Jaffa road, 72
Japan, 229, 254, 274, 346
Jarring, Gunnar, 310, 312–318, 346
Jenin, 82, 146, 239, 293
Jericho, 16, 282, 288, 293
Jerusalem, viii, xiii, xiv, 5, 16–19, 23, 25, 26, 30, 36, 40, 53, 61, 63, 64, 67, 68, 71, 72, 83, 101, 109, 116, 124–136, 166, 177, 180, 189, 193, 194, 215, 218, 225, 228, 233, 249, 250, 258, 265–270, 276, 280–283, 288, 290, 292–298, 301, 304, 307, 308, 315, 317, 326, 328, 330, 331, 335, 346
Jerusalem Post, 213, 234, 299
Jewish Agency, 27, 53, 54, 71, 78, 80, 81, 95, 107, 112, 118, 142–144, 146, 149, 151, 172, 174, 212
Jewish Bund, 12
Jewish Chronicle, 214, 217, 330, 331
Jewish Legion, 83
Jewish National Fund, 23, 29, 50, 53, 130
    See also Keren Kaymet
Jewish Observer and Middle East Review, 202
Jewish Palestine Legion Committee, 31
Jewish Quarter, 130, 134
Jewish Settlement Police, 84
Jezreel, valley of, see Emek
Johnson, President Lyndon B., 234, 236, 255, 257, 258, 274, 278, 315, 316, 319, 327
Johnston, Eric, 157, 187
Johnston Plan, 157, 188, 235
Jordan, viii, xi, 16, 60, 62, 64, 79, 122, 128, 129, 132–135, 140, 141, 156–158, 161, 163, 166, 168, 169, 178, 186, 187, 230, 235, 236, 238, 239, 241, 245, 246, 249, 253, 254, 258, 259, 263–268, 273, 274, 276, 282, 284, 285, 288, 290, 292–297, 300–305, 309, 310, 314, 315, 317, 328, 344–346
Jordan, river of, ix, 16, 17, 22, 42, 45–47, 69, 80, 122, 134, 138, 142, 148, 150, 151, 155, 157, 158, 187, 188, 235, 236, 243, 268–270, 286, 293, 294, 300–304, 317, 327, 328
Joseph, Dov, 200
Judaea, 16, 32
Judaean Hills, 79, 82, 130, 132, 138, 142, 288, 292
Judaean Regiment, 83

Kaanan, Sheik Hamdi, 293
Kalandia airport, 27, 295, 296
Kaplan, Elisheva, see Eshkol, Elisheva Kaplan
Karameh, 304
Katz, Samuel, 96
Katznelson, Berl, 75
Kemal Ataturk, see Ataturk
Keren Hayesod, 53
Keren Kayemet, 12, 45
Kfar Giladi, 243
Kfar Hassidim, 81
Kfar Yuval, 242
Khartoum Summit Conference, see Arab Summit Conference
Khedive of Egypt, 34
Khirbet Jinawa, 245
Khirbet Markaz, 245
Khorazim, 186
Khrushchev, Nikita, 233
Kichko, T. K., 232
Kiev, 3, 8, 9, 347
Kimche, Jon, 36, 37, 202
King David Hotel, 114, 124, 125
King Solomon's Mines, 221
Kiriat Gat, 149, 150
Kishinev, 7, 232
Kitchener, Field-Marshal Lord, 60
Kloeckner, 226
Knesset, 13, 178, 190, 192, 200, 209, 210, 213, 214, 216, 218–220, 227, 237, 238, 244, 254, 275, 280, 293, 295, 299, 309, 317, 331, 333, 334, 337
Kogan, Abraham, 328
Kollek, Teddy, 209, 218, 296, 297

Konstantinov, Yuri, 232
Koppelmann, Abraham, 19
Koreans, 154
Kosygin, Alexei, 242, 274, 275, 308
Krupp, 226
Kulturbund, 91
Kuntilla, 251
Kupat Cholim, 76
Kurdistan, 64, 150, 323, 326
Kuweit, xii, 230
Kuznetsov, Anatoly, 232
Kvutzat Avodah, 45

Labor Government of Britain, 102, 121, 123, 124, 129
Labor Party, of Britain, 122, 124, 236 of Israel, 329–334, 337
Lachish, 149, 150, 186
Laharanne, Ernest, 34
Land of Israel movement, 288, 289
Land Settlement Department, 142
Lanz, Adolf "von Liebenstein," 7
Latin American resolution, 295
Latrun, 82, 134, 290, 292
Lausanne Conference, 1949, 141, 155
Lavon, Pinhas, 195–204, 214
Lavon Affair, 195–204, 208, 209, 214–216, 235
Lawrence, Col. T. E., 57, 59, 61, 62, 70, 97, 123
League of Nations, 53, 68, 71
Lebanon, viii, 64, 128, 132–134, 141, 155–157, 169, 235, 239–241, 276, 296, 300, 302, 305, 306, 314, 341
Leers, Johannes von, 225
Levant, 58, 142
Levy, Shabetai, 140
Liberal Party, 192
Liberation Square, 323
Libya, 28, 35, 139, 238, 322
Lilienblum, Moshe, 4
Lisbona, David, 175
Litani river, 157, 188
Lithuania, 11, 12, 55, 56
Livneh, Eliezer, 288
Lloyd, Selwyn, 166
Lloyd George, David, 36, 64, 71
Lod, 133, 158
London, vii, 32, 36, 40, 53, 87, 100, 214, 221, 236, 237, 264, 277, 304, 308, 310–312, 316, 319, 330, 332, 344
Lovers of Zion movement, 13
Low, David, 125, 346
Low Countries, 210
Lowdermilk, Walter, 188
Lueger, Karl, 7
Luxemburg Reparations Agreement, 223
Luz, Kadish, 47
Lydda, see Lod

Maariv, 257
Maayan Baruch, 243
Macdonald, Ramsay, 108
MacMichael, Sir Harold, 71, 100, 101, 113, 114
Mafraq, 266
Magnes, Judah, 112
Maher Pasha, Ahmed, 97
Mahmoud, General Mohamed Sidky, 247
Makhous, Ibrahim, 248
Makphela's Tomb, 280, 293, 304
Malamud, Bernard, 8, 11
Manasseh, 69, 122, 288
Manchester, 32, 36, 69
Manchester Guardian, 36, 38, 95, 103, 168, 224, 227, 249, 306
Mandelbaum Gate, 295
Mapai, 53, 86, 88, 113, 116, 118, 175, 190–192, 195, 199–204, 208, 209, 212–220, 299, 330–335
  Central Committee of, 201, 202, 213, 215, 216, 316
  Party Convention of, 214, 215
Mapam, 178, 190–192, 195, 212, 217–219, 331–333
Maqarin Dam, 187
Maronites, 33
Marshak, Rivka, see Eshkol, Rivka Marshak
Marseilles, 102
Marx, Karl, 191
Marxism, 12, 191
Mashbir, 29
Mauritius, 99
McCloskey, Robert, 327

McMahon, Sir Henry, 60, 61, 66
McMahon-Hussein correspondence, 60–63, 66, 70
McNeill, Hector, 128
Mea Shearim religious quarter, 193
Mediterranean Sea, x, xi, 5, 6, 102, 133, 150, 158, 163, 173, 185, 187, 221, 228, 238, 241, 242, 248, 254, 269, 291, 317, 329, 345
Meinertzhagen, Colonel Richard, 7, 8, 38, 40, 160, 167
Meir, Golda, 9, 102, 134, 135, 209, 219, 220, 238, 332, 333, 337, 338
Meiss el Jebel, 239
Mekorot, 76, 81, 115, 118, 147, 149, 176, 187
Mensheviks, 12
Mersah Matruh, 242
Mersina, 61
Mesheg Yagur, 119
Mesopotamia, 17, 28, 61–63
Metullah, 30
Middle East, viii, x–xii, 33, 34, 36, 37, 40, 57–66, 69, 79, 87, 93, 97, 107, 123, 126, 131, 133, 155, 157, 158, 161–165, 169, 172, 184, 188, 191, 194, 210, 219–223, 228–230, 234, 236–243, 249, 253, 256, 260, 268, 271, 272, 274–278, 282, 284–287, 292, 293, 295, 306, 308, 309, 312–319, 322, 328, 339, 341, 344–347
Mikveh Yisrael, 17
Milos, ship, 99
Mir, 81
Mishmar Haemek, 98, 129
Mishmar Hayarden, 132
Moab, 42, 257
Mollet, Guy, 166, 185
Montefiore, Sir Moses, 17, 19
Morocco, vii, 139, 142, 150, 263, 345
Morrison, Herbert, 121, 122
Morse, Arthur, 96
Moscow, xi, 7, 56, 230, 231, 233, 242, 255, 308, 312, 337
Moses, 81, 143
Moslem, xiii, 18, 57–59, 65, 97, 109, 154, 160, 164, 169, 230, 241, 262, 280, 281, 296, 341

Moslem Brotherhood, 196, 277
Mosul, 63
Motza, 18
Mount Carmel, *see* Carmel, Mount
Mount of Olives, 296
Mount Scopus, *see* Scopus, Mount
Moyne, Lord, 113
Mozambique, 35
Mufti, *see* Haj Amin
Munich, 255, 283
  University of, 89

Naaman river, 80, 81
Nablus, 16, 17, 82, 134, 146, 288, 292, 293, 302
Nachal, 307
Namier, Sir Lewis, 62
Napoleon III, Emperor, 33, 34
Nasser, President Abdul Gamal, 160–169, 178, 196, 211, 225–230, 238, 242, 246–259, 262–268, 272–278, 285, 286, 288, 291, 305, 308–313, 315, 317, 319, 339–341, 344, 345
National Labor Organization, 86
National Religious Party, 190, 192, 209, 219, 245
National Water Carrier, 188
NATO, 272, 345
Nazareth, 85, 133, 135, 288, 296
Nazi Germany, vii, 88–101, 106, 113, 139, 141, 164, 177, 179, 219, 223–228, 232, 233, 284, 321, 322
Negev desert, 79, 129, 133, 144, 149, 150, 170, 186, 194, 195, 221, 254, 270, 271
Neguib, General, 160
Nehora, 149, 150
Nejd, 61, 62
Neturei Karta, 193
New York, vii, 10, 31, 112, 123, 177, 226, 230, 272, 308, 312, 315
Nicholas I, Tsar, 6
Nicholas II, Tsar, 7
Nile river, 35, 79, 156, 225
Noga, 150
Nordau, Max, 10
North Africa, 57–59, 150, 229, 324
Nuremberg, 89, 232
Nuri es Said, 169

363

Observer, 264, 311, 312
Oder-Neisse Line, 154
Odessa, 7, 8, 11, 13, 24, 31, 232
Old City of Jerusalem, 64, 72, 83, 130, 132–134, 239, 276, 281, 282, 296, 297
Oliphant, Laurence, 17–19
Olshan, Chief Justice, 196
Oman, xii
Omar, Mosque of, 64
Operation Magic Carpet, 139
Oratowo, xiv, 3–5, 9, 11, 15, 23, 56
Ottoman Empire, xii, xiii, 15, 31, 34, 36, 38, 58, 77
Otzem, 150
Overseas Press Club, 234

Paasen, Pierre van, 115
Pacific, 99
Pakistan, 154, 161
Pale of Settlement, Jewish, xiv, 6–9, 35, 49, 90, 105
Palestine, vii, xii–xiv, 4, 5, 11–40, 42, 45, 48, 50, 52–57, 60–87, 89, 91–103, 107–115, 118, 121–129, 131, 133, 135, 138–142, 145–148, 152, 154, 155, 162, 190, 206, 211, 217, 238, 248, 259, 268, 278, 286, 288, 290–295, 297, 308, 321, 323, 340, 345, 346, 348, 349
Palestine Electricity Corporation, 118
Palestine Liberation Movement, 235, 241, 302
Palestine Settlement Office, 46
Palestine Workers Fund, 29
Paltreu, 92
Palmach, 131, 133, 136
Palmerston, Lord, 33
Paris, 17, 36, 65, 66, 116, 155, 166, 185, 234
Parkes, James, xiii, 6, 16, 57, 58, 65, 146, 347
Parliament, Israeli, *see* Knesset
Passfield, Lady (Beatrice Webb), 73
Passfield, Lord (Sidney Webb), 73, 78, 108, 111
Passfield White Paper, 1930, 73, 78, 108, 111
Patria, 99

Patterson, Colonel J. H., 32, 40
Pauls, Rolf, 228
Peace Conference, 1919, 65
Peel, Lord, 108, 109
Peel Commission Report, 108–111, 127
Peres, Shimon, 167, 196, 200, 202, 209, 331
Persia, 125, 150, 158, 164
Persian Gulf, xi, xii, 34, 36, 163, 254, 265, 309, 316, 326
Petach Tikva, 18–20, 24–26, 30, 39, 45, 52, 67, 130
Philistines, 85, 142, 149, 152
Pilz, Wolfgang, 225
Pineau, Christian, 166
Plehve, Wenceslas von, 7, 12
Plumer, Field-Marshal Lord, 71, 72
Poalei Agudat, 53, 190, 219
Poalei Zion, 15, 23, 33, 39, 52, 67, 212
Pobyedonostzev, Constantine, 7
Poland, Polish, xiv, 5, 6, 10, 12, 19, 45, 86, 90, 94, 95, 99, 102, 103, 115, 190, 210, 232, 233, 324, 348
Port Said, 166, 168, 247, 297, 305, 345
Portugal, 5, 35
Posner, Rabbi Zalman, 11
Poyachevsky, Abraham, 21
Pozdhaev, Dmitri, 257
Progressive Party, 192
Protocols of the Elders of Zion, 7, 89, 232

Qalkilya, 239, 292
Qibya, 165
Quseir, 242

Rabbinate, 70, 193, 194
Rabbinical Council, 70
Rabin, General Itzhak, 241, 256, 258–260
Rachel's Tomb, 280
Radio Amman, 253, 277
Radio Bagdad, 248
Radio Cairo, 160, 248, 249, 253, 262, 273
Radio Damascus, 246, 248, 249, 263, 274
Rafaeli, Dvora Eshkol, 87, 105–108, 147, 188

Rafi party, 202, 216–218, 221, 245, 260, 330–334, 337
Ramallah, 26, 293, 296
Ramat Yohanan, 129
Ramleh, 133
Raphael, Gideon, 250, 272
Rashid Ali, 97, 164
Rathenau, Walter, 90
Raziel, David, 113
Red Sea, xi, 60, 129, 133, 134, 163, 170, 173, 221, 242, 248, 250, 252, 262, 289, 315, 329
Reed, Douglas, 89
Reich Ministry of Economics, 93
Reichsfluchtsteuer, 93
Reichsvertretung der deutschen Juden, 91
Remez, Aharon, 304
Reuben, tribe of, 69, 122, 288
Revisionist Party, 88, 92, 214
Rhodes, 134 n.
Riad, Mahmoud, 312
Riegner Plan, 96
Rikhye, General Indar Sit, 250, 251
Rishon-le-Zion, 19, 27–29, 30, 38, 39, 45, 349
Rohling, August, 7
Rome, Romans, xiv, 5, 16, 18, 151, 157, 221, 276
Rommel, Field-Marshal Erwin, 98, 111, 344
Roosevelt, President Franklin D., 96, 203
Rose, David, 328
Rosen, Pinhas, 198, 199, 204
Rosenberg, Alfred, 97
Rosh Zahar, 185
Rothberg, Mayer, 26
Rothschild, Baron Edmonde, 19, 21, 27
Rothschild, Jr., Baron Edmonde de, 327, 328
Rothschild, Baron Walter Lionel de, 37
Royal Fusiliers, 32, 40, 71, 75, 152
  38th Bn, 32, 33
  39th Bn, 40, 41, 44
  40th Bn, 41
Rumania, 18, 96, 102, 210, 220, 348
Ruppin, Arthur, 21, 90, 91

Rusk, Dean, 257
Russia, viii, xi, xiv, 3–15, 20, 22, 24, 27, 31, 34, 41, 60, 64, 87, 90, 95, 103, 152, 161, 163–165, 190, 191, 210, 223, 232, 233, 250, 251, 269, 270, 278, 287, 319, 348
Russo-Japanese War, 1905, 31
Rutenberg, Pinhas, 113, 114

Sachar, Howard, 50, 89
Sacher, Harry, 95
Sack, Gershon, 117, 204
Sadat, Colonel Anwar, 160
Saenger, Eugen, 225
Safed, xiii, xiv, 16, 73, 129
Salomon, Yoel Moshe, 18
Salonika, 95, 145
Samaria, 282, 290
Samarian Hills, 79, 82, 142, 150, 288, 292
Samu, 245
Samuel, Horace, 39, 40, 67
Samuel, Sir Herbert, 67
Sapir, Pinhas, 175, 182, 209, 220, 336, 337
Saudi Arabia, xii, 132, 133, 155, 163, 253, 285
Scandinavia, 13, 96
Schechtmann, Joseph, 140
Schirach, Baldur von, 97
Schreiber, Zvi, 92, 93
Schwarz, Walter, 178
Scopus, Mount, 41, 257, 295, 296
Scott, C. P., 36, 38
Sde Boker, 194, 197, 208, 257
Second Aliyah, vii, 26, 45, 75, 77, 142, 143, 190, 217, 334
Second World War, see World War II
Segula, 149
Sejera, 21
Sephardi, 6, 17, 150
Sevres, 166
Shabander, Dr., 97
Shah, of Iran, xi
Sharef, Zvi, 326, 327
Sharett, Moshe, 98, 131, 177, 194, 196–198, 208, 215, 335
Sharm-el-Sheik, 163, 167, 168, 251, 252, 256, 267, 272, 291, 294

365

Sharon, plain of, 23, 24, 67, 78, 138, 290
Shear Yashuv, 274
Shechem, 282
Shertok, Moshe, *see* Sharett, Moshe
Shkolnik, Benjamin, 56
Shkolnik, Deborah, 3, 25
Shkolnik, Joseph, 3–5, 56
Shkolnik, Levi, 3, 39, 40
Shuneh, 134, 238
Sidi Barrani, 242
Silver, Rabbi Abba Hillel, 101
Sinai Campaign, 166, 167, 170, 183, 185, 234, 235, 349
Sinai Peninsula, 35, 40, 119, 122, 129, 133, 134, 166–168, 204, 223, 250, 251, 254, 259, 262, 266, 267, 270, 273–277, 282, 284, 286–292, 301, 305, 307, 308, 311, 312, 315
Sinn Fein, 114
Six-Day War, 178, 194, 262, 265, 271, 272, 276–280, 283–290, 305, 316, 318, 323, 324, 330, 334, 344, 345, 347, 349
Sixth Zionist Congress, 35
Slavin, Chaim, 119
Social Democratic Party, 179
Socialist League of Jewish Workers, *see* Bund
Solel Boneh, 76, 118
Soliman, Mohamed, 247
Solomon, King, 142, 288
South Arabian Federation, xi, 127
South Yemen Federation, *see* South Arabian Federation
Soviet Union, ix–xii, 6, 49, 90, 94, 113, 126, 161–169, 172, 191, 210, 223, 228–234, 239–250, 257–261, 269, 272–278, 283–286, 299, 305, 308, 312, 316, 318, 319, 326, 340, 344–348
Spain, 5, 57, 322, 346
Spiro, Melford, 48, 49
Sprinzak, Joseph, 13, 24, 52
S. S., Nazi, 225
Stalin, Josef, 164, 230, 232
Star of David, 32, 98, 99
Stavsky, Abraham, 88
Stephens, Robert, 311

Stern, Abraham, 113, 115
Stern Gang, 101, 113–115, 133
Stockwell, General Sir Hugh, 141
Stolypin, 7
Storrs, Sir Ronald, 68, 151
Streicher, Julius, 7, 90, 232
Struma, 99
Stuermer, Der, 7, 90, 232
Sudan, xi, 28, 36, 59, 341
Suez, 169, 226, 229, 241, 247, 306
Suez, Canal, viii, ix, xi, 28, 34, 35, 128, 156, 158, 159, 161, 164–169, 211, 239, 252, 258, 267, 270, 274, 277, 284, 286, 294, 300, 302, 308–318, 326, 329, 344
Suez Canal Zone, 161, 166
Sykes, Christopher, 66, 72, 108, 128, 141
Sykes, Sir, Mark, 62, 63
Sykes-Picot Agreement, 62–64, 66, 223
Syria, viii, ix, xi, xii, 17, 22, 29, 52, 60–65, 70, 97, 122, 128, 129, 132–137, 141, 148, 150, 151, 155–158, 163, 165, 166, 169, 187, 188, 230, 235, 241–250, 254, 258, 259, 262–270, 273–276, 282, 285, 287, 288, 290, 296, 300, 302, 304, 307–310, 314, 315, 322, 323, 341, 344, 345
Szold, Henrietta, 112

Tartus, 345
Tass, 242, 250
Tel Aviv, viii, 16, 24, 26, 30, 71, 73, 81, 83, 88, 89, 99, 105, 106, 110, 115–119, 125, 130, 131, 133, 136, 142, 149, 150, 166, 187, 196, 215, 263, 266, 267, 270, 271, 290, 292, 304
Tel Aviv Labor Council, 116, 117
Tel el Kebir, 40
Templer, General Sir Gerald, 161
Third Aliyah, 45, 190, 217, 334
Thora (Tourah) camp, 321
Tiberias, xiii, xiv, 16, 45, 129
Tiger Hill, 99
Times (London), 37, 61, 304, 312, 319, 330, 346
Timna, 170, 220, 254

Tiran, straits of, 122, 162, 168, 170, 252–256, 262, 291, 308, 309, 311, 314
T'nuva, 76
Torah, 52, 131, 347
Trafalgar, battle of, 134
Transjordan, 22, 69, 70, 110, 122, 292
Treitschke, Heinrich von, 6
Trieste, 14, 15, 45
Troyanovsky, 164
Truman, President Harry, 123, 131, 203
Trumpeldor, Joseph, 31
Tsar, 3, 5–7, 31, 64, 90, 164, 191, 233
Tunisia, 28, 150, 240, 285, 341
Turkey, 17, 23, 24, 28, 29, 31, 33–35, 39, 44, 46, 53, 54, 57–60, 64, 65, 77, 95–97, 100, 109, 158, 161, 164, 345, 348
Twelfth Zionist Congress, 53
Twentieth Zionist Congress, 110
Tyre, 133

Uganda, 35, 69
Ukraine, 3, 4, 6, 56, 81, 232
Um Rash, 133
    See also Eilat
Union of the Russian People movement, 7
United Jewish Appeal, 176
United Nations, 107, 110, 114, 125, 127, 132–140, 148, 156–158, 160, 162, 168, 172, 215, 223, 233, 236, 237, 239, 240, 242–245, 250–252, 255, 260, 262, 263, 272, 274–278, 287, 291, 293, 295, 310–319, 321, 334, 346
  Charter, 237
  Emergency Force (UNEF), 168, 250–252, 262, 274, 346
  General Assembly, 107, 125, 126, 156, 230, 274, 275, 295, 316
  Relief and Works Agency (UNRWA), 139, 140, 156–158, 276, 291
  Security Council, 133, 159, 239, 243, 272–274, 313, 318, 333, 346
  Special Committee on Palestine, 125
  Truce Supervisory Organization, 246, 266

United Religious Front, 190, 192
United States, ix, xi, 9, 23, 31, 33, 78, 87, 96, 112, 119, 123, 125–127, 131, 132, 134, 156, 161, 162, 164, 168, 170, 176, 180–182, 188, 195, 196, 207, 209, 214, 223, 226, 228, 234, 236, 239, 255–259, 263, 273, 285, 316, 319, 324, 327, 332, 339, 344, 348
  Congress of, 169
  Congressional Foreign Relations Committee of, 155
  House of Representatives of, 113
  Navy, 250
  State Department, 315, 327
United States-Palestine Committee, 112
Ussishkin, Menahem, 68
U Thant, 250–252, 313, 321

Vaad Leumi, 68
Victor Emmanuel, King, 35
Vienna, 7, 12, 14, 34–36, 55, 94
Vietnam War, 241, 256
Vilna, 11–14, 24, 94
Vitkin, Josef, 20
Vladimir, Archbishop, 7

Wadi Fijas, 47
Wailing Wall, 40, 72, 130, 133, 147, 194, 239, 280–282, 297
Wannsee Conference, 1942, 224
War of Independence, 1948–1949, xiii, 51, 83, 85, 103, 105, 110, 114, 116, 119, 126, 129, 134, 136, 143, 147, 148, 189, 220, 238, 295, 299, 303, 346, 348, 349
War of Liberation, *see* War of Independence
Warsaw, x, 11, 94, 348
Washington, 196, 234, 257, 316, 319
Wassermann, 92
Water board, *see* Mekerot
Wauchope, Sir Arthur, 84
Wavell, General Sir Archibald, 84, 85, 100
Wazzani river, 235
Webb, *see* Passfield
Weimar Republic, 88

Weitz, Raanan, 118, 119, 136, 144, 145, 146, 212
Weitz, Yosef, 79
Weizmann, Chaim, 35–37, 53, 62, 65, 66, 71, 73, 78, 88, 94, 108–111, 123, 134, 151–153, 167, 332
West, Lt. Colonel Michael Alston Roberts, 119
Western Europe, x, xi, 100, 229, 238
West Germany, 159, 177–179, 203, 223, 225–228, 334, 335
Whitechapel, 101, 111, 124, 125
White Paper, British Government's, 1922, 70, 71, 108, 111
1939, 99, 106, 111–113, 121, 122
Wilhelm II, Kaiser, 34, 88, 177
Willstaetter, Professor, 89
Wilson, Harold, 211, 236, 255, 256, 316
Wingate, Captain Charles, 84–86, 136
Workers Agricultural Council, 25
World Bank, 161
World Jewish Congress, 232
World Zionist Organization, 53, 54, 66, 108
World War I, xi, 15, 21, 26, 29, 31, 37, 50, 58, 59, 62, 88, 97, 99, 100, 121, 146, 152, 164, 334
World War II, 50, 53, 71, 94, 97, 99, 111, 115, 119, 127, 131, 134, 147, 154, 164, 221, 263, 336

Yad Mordechai, 119
Yarkon river, 150
Yarkon-Negev water conduit, 149, 150
Yarmuk river, 157, 187, 188, 328
Yediot Ahronot, 299
Yemen, Yemenite, vii, xi, 40, 58, 139, 193, 238, 268, 341
Yiddish, vii, 6, 10–12, 18, 26, 105, 106, 117, 176, 177, 207, 231, 232, 347
Young, Brigadier Peter, 267
Young Turk movement, Turkey, 30
Yugoslav contingent, 251, 252
Yugoslavia, 95, 125, 295
Yushinsky, Andrei, 9

Zambia, 346
Zeire Zion, 13
Zelikovitz, Miriam Eshkol, *see* Eshkol, Miriam Zelikovitz
Zichron, 19
Zion, xiii, xiv, 4, 8, 11–13, 19–21, 23, 29, 32, 33, 35–38, 40, 52–56, 62–66, 69, 84, 86, 88–91, 103, 108, 112, 114, 122, 123, 125, 127, 152, 154, 160, 164, 165, 223, 231, 232, 241, 248, 263, 276, 283, 296, 307, 339
Zionist Council, 30, 126
Zionist Federation, 37
Zion Mule Corps, 41
Zohar, 150
Zvi, Lt. Colonel, 289
Zweig, Arnold, 90
Zweig, Stefan, 90